Criminal Litigation Handbook

putyourknowledgeintopractice

LPC GUIDES

Business Law
J. Scott Slorach and Jason G. Ellis

Foundations for the LPC
George Miles *et al.*

Lawyers' Skills
Julian Webb *et al.*

Solicitors' Accounts
Dale Kay and Janet Baker

Commercial Law
Robert Bradgate and Fidelma White

Employment Law
James Holland and Stuart Burnett

Family Law
Tina Bond, Dame Jill M. Black QC and Jane Bridge QC

Corporate Finance, Mergers and Acquisitions
J. Scott Slorach and Paul Rylance

LPC HANDBOOKS

Criminal Litigation Handbook
Martin Hannibal and Lisa Mountford

Civil Litigation Handbook
Susan Cunningham-Hill and Karen Elder

Property Law Handbook
Robert Abbey and Mark Richards

A PRACTICAL APPROACH SERIES

A Practical Approach to Civil Procedure
Stuart Sime

A Practical Approach to Conveyancing
Robert Abbey and Mark Richards

Criminal Litigation Handbook

MARTIN HANNIBAL

LISA MOUNTFORD

OXFORD

UNIVERSITY PRESS

OXFORD

UNIVERSITY PRESS

Great Clarendon Street, Oxford OX2 6DP

Oxford University Press is a department of the University of Oxford.
It furthers the University's objective of excellence in research, scholarship,
and education by publishing worldwide in

Oxford New York

Auckland Cape Town Dar es Salaam Hong Kong Karachi
Kuala Lumpur Madrid Melbourne Mexico City Nairobi
New Delhi Shanghai Taipei Toronto

With offices in

Argentina Austria Brazil Chile Czech Republic France Greece
Guatemala Hungary Italy Japan Poland Portugal Singapore
South Korea Switzerland Thailand Turkey Ukraine Vietnam

Oxford is a registered trade mark of Oxford University Press
in the UK and in certain other countries

Published in the United States
by Oxford University Press Inc., New York

British Library Cataloguing in Publication Data
Data available

Library of Congress Cataloging in Publication Data
Data available

Typeset by Laserwords Private Ltd, Chennai, India
Printed in Italy
on acid-free paper by Rotolito Lombarda SpA

ISBN 978-0-19-954232-1

10 9 8 7 6 5 4 3 2 1

CONTENTS

PREFACE

Our aim when writing the four editions of the *Criminal Litigation Handbook* has been to deliver a comprehensive text on all areas of criminal practice whilst at the same time providing a highly practical, innovative and contextual learning resource for students studying the compulsory Criminal Litigation element on the Legal Practice Course and/or an elective in Advanced Criminal Litigation. The extremely positive feedback we have received from students, lecturers and practitioners about the earlier editions of the *Handbook* have been very encouraging. We are not complacent however and welcome any constructive comments from all our readers about how the text or the extensive learning resources can be improved. Please contact us or direct your comments to OUP.

An important part of the innovative approach the *Handbook* adopts as a learning resource is the extensive Online Resource Centre which includes video clips of selected portions of the case studies that form the basis of ongoing exercises throughout the text. To accompany the third edition we refilmed the sentencing hearing in the William Hardy case study which takes place in the Crown Court. The revised scenario was introduced to take account of the more stringent sentencing regime under the Sexual Offences Act 2003. To give you a further insight into the practical application of the law, we also filmed a free-standing bad character application in the Crown Court. We hope that you find all the video clips a useful tool in adding to your knowledge and understanding of criminal litigation.

The *Handbook* is divided into six sections:

Part I is an introduction to criminal litigation.

Part II considers the process of investigation up to the decision to charge, including relevant rules of criminal evidence.

Part III considers post-charge procedures up to and including trial.

Part IV considers the remaining rules of criminal evidence.

Part V considers the post-conviction matters of sentencing and appeals against conviction and/or sentence.

Part VI considers youth justice issues.

The pace of legislative change affecting the criminal justice system has been relentless in recent years. For practitioners, students and lecturers keeping up to date and in some instances ahead of the changes has been difficult! A key number of important provisions contained in the Criminal Justice Act 2003 have still to be implemented. The delay has been caused in part by the extensively publicised problem of prison overcrowding. At the time of going to press it is anticipated that the new allocation procedure for deciding place of trial for either-way offences (Sch. 3 CJA 2003) will be implemented at some stage during 2008/09. This significant step is also likely to result in an increase in the sentencing powers available to magistates when passing a custodial sentence from a maximum of six months to 51 weeks. The recently enacted Criminal Justice and Immigration Bill introduces measures relating to youth justice and appeals. Whilst the rules of criminal litigation and evidence are always at the forefront of political controversy, public concern and legislative reform, a great advantage of our Online Resource Centre is that we will bring you any significant developments in the update section of the site.

The writing of the *Handbook* and the production of the video case studies and Online Resource Centre could not have been achieved without the co-operation and assistance of many friends and colleagues.

In relation to the video case studies of Lenny Whyte/William Hardy and Roger Martin we say a special thank you to the following:

His Honour Paul Glenn
Milena Srdanovic (CPS lawyer)
Simon Leech (Defence lawyer)
Celia Laing (Defence lawyer)
Peter Goold (Trainee solicitor and former Staffordshire LPC student)
Alison Bailey (Legal adviser)
Vicky Priestly (Legal adviser)
John Peel (CPS designated caseworker)
Jason Jamil (Staffordshire LPC student 2003–4)
Carol Hawthorne (Magistrate)
Dr Mike Carter (Magistrate)
Rev Christopher Dalton (Magistrate)

In relation to the Peter West Police Station Scenario, we would sincerely like to thank the following:

DC Keith Pagett (Staffordshire Police)
DS Angus Parker (Staffordshire Police)
Sgt Ian Cantrill (Staffordshire Police)
Lisa O'Shea (Accredited Police Station Representative with the Public Defender Service)
Peter Goold (Staffordshire LPC student 2004–5) who gave an outstanding and entirely convincing performance as Peter West, the suspect!

Each of these individuals very kindly gave up their time and volunteered their services for free thereby allowing us to bring our case studies to life.

Special thanks go to the camera crews involved in the filming of our various videos:

Ray Johnson (Professor of Film Heritage and Documentary, Staffordshire University)
Darren Teale (Final year media student 2004)
Richard Edwards (Final year media student 2004)
Gary Robinson (Final year media student 2004)
Peter Robinson (Senior Technician Staffordshire Law School)

We are indebted to Ray Johnson for his tremendous help in directing the early films and undertaking the voice-over analysis. Special thanks also go to Darren Teale who undertook the filming and editing of *R v Lenny Whyte* and *R v Roger Martin*. We are grateful to our dear friend and colleague Peter Robinson (Staffordshire Law School's Senior IT Technician) for helping us to film our Police Station Scenario and for his very patient editing of the material. Peter has also directed and edited the revised William Hardy scenario and the Nick Jones bad character application.

Thanks are also due to the Chief Constable's Office of Staffordshire Police for allowing us to take over Uttoxeter Police Station in rural Staffordshire for a day in November 2005 and for allowing us to use real police offices!

We would like to thank Dr N. J. F. Smalldridge BA (Oxon), BM, MRC Psych for the time and effort he undertook in devising and writing a psychiatric report on behalf of our fictional defendant Lenny Whyte.

We would like to single out Michael Benson for his immensely valuable comments and observations! Thanks also to Robin Lichfield, partner and defence solicitor with Lichfield Reynolds Solicitors, North Staffordshire and Andrew Keogh, partner and defence solicitor with Tuckers Solicitors in Manchester and creator of CrimeLine (www.crimeline.info/) for answering all our questions!

We thank the entire team at OUP (particularly Lucy Read, Helen Davis and Gareth Malna), our copy-editor, Jan Miles-Kingston, and our proofreader, Francesco Ingrao. Special thanks to Julia Whippy and her predecessor Kate Hilton (OUP's IT specialists) for their fantastic work in building and maintaining the Online Resource Centre. We also acknowledge the tremendous hard work of our former assistant commissioning editor Rebecca Webb on the first edition.

Most of all we thank our families (Merryn, Matt, Nick and Charlie Hannibal, Nick and Alexandra Mason) for their enduring patience!

The fourth edition is dedicated to all those extremely committed and hard-working criminal defence practitioners who continue to uphold access to justice in the face of adversity. Acknowledgement is also due to our enthusiastic and hard working students and colleagues on the Staffordshire Law School Legal Practice Course.

Any errors or omissions are entirely ours.

The law is stated at 1st April 2008.

Lisa Mountford
Martin Hannibal
Staffordshire Law School

GUIDED TOUR OF THE BOOK

The *Criminal Litigation Handbook* by Hannibal and Mountford is a pedagogically rich text which has been designed to facilitate your learning and understanding of criminal litigation. This 'Guided Tour of the Book' will explain how to make the most of your text by illustrating each of the features used by the authors to explain the practical aspects of the criminal litigation process.

WITHIN EACH CHAPTER

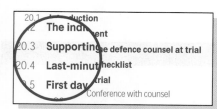

CHAPTER CONTENTS

A detailed contents list at the start of each chapter enables you to anticipate what will be covered and identify what the main topics of the chapter will be. Use this feature to also gain an understanding of how the topics fit together in the wider subject area.

EXAMPLES

Look for the example icon to find relevant, practical examples of how the law has been or could be applied in common situations. These examples bring the subject to life and allow you to examine how principles, rules and statutes work in practice.

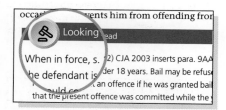

'LOOKING AHEAD' BOXES

These boxes are used to highlight areas where the law may change. Potential reforms are considered ensuring that once you go into practice, you're already aware of the changes on the horizon.

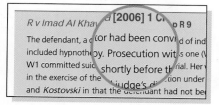

CASE OUTLINES

These case outlines give you an awareness of relevant case law in the subject area. Use these explanations to point you towards the most relevant case reports in your law library or to better inform your knowledge of how the law has been applied in court.

CASE STUDIES

Throughout the book, the authors refer to fictional case studies, which provide a practical focus to the law and procedures described in the text. The documentation for these case studies appears on the Online Resource Centre. See the 'Guided Tour of the Online Resource Centre' at p. xviii for more information.

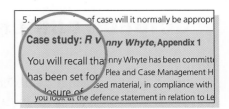

ONLINE RESOURCE CENTRE ICON

Wherever this icon appears in the margin, more information is available on the Online Resource Centre which accompanies this text. This may be video footage, case study documentation, or links to other useful websites or guidance. See the 'Guided Tour of the Online Resource Centre' at p. xviii for more information.

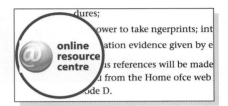

END OF CHAPTER FEATURES

KEY POINTS SUMMARY

The key points covered are summarised in a user-friendly list at the end of each chapter. Look to these summaries to help you consolidate your learning or to check your knowledge at revision time.

SELF-TEST QUESTIONS

These questions allow you to test yourself on particular areas of the law in preparation for your exams or to assess your learning throughout the duration of the course. Use these questions to highlight areas where you might need to improve your understanding by re-reading the text or asking your lecturer.

FIGURES

Flowcharts, shaded boxes, or example forms provide a visual representation of what has been described within the chapter.

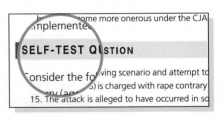

GUIDED TOUR OF THE ONLINE RESOURCE CENTRE

Online Resource Centres are developed to provide students and lecturers with ready-to-use teaching and learning resources. They are free of charge, designed to complement the text and offer additional materials which are well-suited to electronic delivery.

All these resources can be downloaded and are fully customisable allowing them to be incorporated into your institution's existing virtual learning environment.

STUDENT RESOURCES

All the resources in this area of the site are freely accessible to all, with no password required. Simply visit the site at: www.oxfordtextbooks.co.uk/orc/lpccrimhandbook08_09

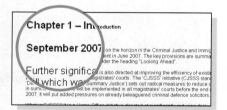

UPDATES

Updates are posted on the website when the law changes or when an important case passes through the courts, allowing you to keep fully informed of developments. The updates are freely accessible to all and offer an easy way to keep abreast of changes in this rapidly changing subject area.

CASE STUDY DOCUMENTATION

The fictional case studies in the book are accompanied by all of the documentation you would expect to see in reality. This allows you to see what a solicitor's file might typically contain and prepares you for what to expect when you go into practice.

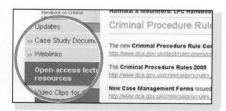

LINKS TO LEGISLATION, RULES, AND OTHER DOCUMENTATION

This part of the website provides links to useful information which is freely accessible elsewhere on the internet. Use this resource to find relevant guidelines, statutes, codes of practice and other documentation quickly and easily.

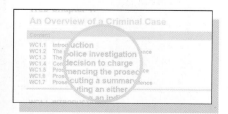

CHAPTER GIVING AN OVERVIEW OF A CRIMINAL CASE

For students needing to know more about the background procedures involved in a criminal case. This chapter covers the police investigation through to prosecution.

CHAPTERS ON REGULATORY CRIME AND FRAUD

For students whose course has a City focus, corporate crime will be an important topic. Written by two leading barristers in this area, Nicholas Yeo and Sarah Le Fevre, two online chapters on regulatory crime and fraud enable you to get to grips with aspects of criminal law which are key for City lawyers.

LECTURER RESOURCES

These resources are available solely to lecturers and are accessed with use of a free password. To obtain a password, follow the links on the main site at: www.oxfordtextbooks.co.uk/orc/lpccrimhandbook08_09; our web team will contact you with a password within 3 working days. All of the resources on this part of the site can be downloaded into your institution's virtual learning environment.

VIDEO CLIPS

High resolution video footage showing fictional criminal proceedings allows you to emphasise the practical application of what you describe in your teaching. Included on the site is video footage of:

- the case studies featured in the book;
- our 'free-standing' police station video scenario.
- our 'free-standing' bad character applications

(Selected, low resolution video clips of the *R v Lenny Whyte* case study are available to lecturers without a password.)

TEST BANK OF QUESTIONS

A bank of questions covering all aspects of the book is available to download into your virtual learning environment (VLE). Also available in Word format, the multiple choice questions give you the ability to provide a resource which your students can use to test themselves, or which you can use to assess their learning. Once included in your VLE, the questions are entirely customisable, enabling you to remove questions which are less relevant to your course, or to change the order of the questions to match the order in which topics are taught at your institution.

Each question is accompanied by feedback which shows why the selected answer is correct or incorrect and then points the student towards the relevant page of the textbook if they need to re-read.

LINKS TO GUIDELINES AND CODES OF PRACTICE

Use this resource to easily find documents important for criminal litigators. Collected together in one place, this resource provides you with all the important documents to which you may want to refer your students.

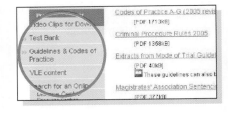

GLOSSARY

Listed below are some of the terms and abbreviations that you will encounter in the *Criminal Litigation Handbook* and later as part of training in criminal practice.

Access to Justice Act 1999	AJA 1999.
Accused/defendant	The natural or legal person against whom a criminal case is brought. In practice, the terms 'the accused' and 'the defendant' are used interchangeably.
Appeal	A request to a higher court to reconsider the defendant's conviction and/or sentence.
Appellant	The natural or legal person who is appealing against the conviction and/or the sentence.
Attorney-General	A-G—Appoints the DPP, initiates some prosecutions and issues guidelines.
Bail	The release of a person from custody by the police or the court with a duty to surrender to custody at a specified time, date and location.
Bail Act 1976	BA 1976.
Co-accused/co-defendant	The natural or legal person who is jointly charged with a criminal offence.
Criminal Defence Service	CDS.
Criminal Prosecution Service	CPS.
Crime and Disorder Act 1998	CDA 1998.
Criminal Evidence Act 1898	CEA 1898.
Criminal Justice Act 1967	CJA 1967.
Criminal Justice Act 1988	CJA 1988.
Criminal Justice Act 2003	CJA 2003.
Criminal Justice and Public Order Act 1994	CJPOA 1994.
Criminal Procedure and Investigations Act 1996	CPIA 1996.
Criminal Procedure Rules	Crim PR.
Crown Court Rules	CCR.
Detainee/suspect	A person arrested and detained by the police when investigating a criminal offence. 'Detainee' is used interchangeably with the word 'suspect'.
Director of Public Prosecutions	DPP—head of the CPS.
District Judge	Professional lawyer who tries cases in the magistrates' court.
Either-way offence	An offence that can be tried either in the Crown Court or in the magistrates' court.
European Convention on Human Rights 1950	ECHR 1950.

European Court of Human Rights	ECtHR.
Human Rights Act 1998	HRA 1998.
Indictable offence	Refers to both indictable-only and either-way offences.
Indictable-only offence	An offence that can only be tried in the Crown Court.
Indictment	The document detailing the charge the defendant pleads to at a Crown Court trial.
Indictment Act 1915	IA 1915.
Information	The document containing the charge that the defendant pleads to in summary cases.
Justices of the Peace Act 1997	JoPA 1997.
Legal Services Commission	LSC.
Magistrates' Courts Act 1980	MCA 1980.
Magistrates' Court Rules	MCR.
Oaths Act 1980	OA 1980.
Plea and Case Management Hearing	PCMH.
Police and Criminal Evidence Act 1984	PACE 1984.
Powers of Criminal Courts (Sentencing) Act 2000	PCC(S)A 2000.
Prosecution of Offences Act 1985	POA 1985.
Road Traffic Act 1988	RTA 1988.
Road Traffic Act 1991	RTA 1991.
Road Traffic Offenders Act 1988	RTOA 1988.
Summary-only offence	An offence that can only be tried in the magistrates' court.
Summons	A court order which requires the defendant or witness to attend court at a specified time and date.
Volunteer	A person who is helping the police with inquiries but who has not been arrested.
Warrant of arrest	A document issued by the court ordering the person specified should be arrested.
Youth Justice and Criminal Evidence Act 1999	YJCEA 1999.

TABLE OF CASES

TABLE OF CODES OF PRACTICE AND PROFESSIONAL CONDUCT RULES

TABLE OF STATUTES

TABLE OF STATUTORY INSTRUMENTS

Part I
INTRODUCTION TO CRIMINAL LITIGATION

Part I equips the reader with important background information that will inform the substantive areas covered in later chapters.

Chapter 1 explains the aims of the *Criminal Litigation Handbook* and its pedagogical features. It introduces the reader to the key personnel and organisations involved in the criminal justice system and explains the importance of the classification of a criminal offence. It also addresses human rights and rules of professional conduct in the context of criminal cases.

Chapter 2 provides an introduction to criminal evidence and advocacy.

1.1   INTRODUCTION

This introductory chapter serves several purposes. Our aims are to:

* explain the basic philosophy of the *Handbook* and its pedagogical features;
* introduce you to the key personnel and organisations within the criminal justice system and the Criminal Procedure Rules;
* explain the classification of offences according to their venue for trial;
* provide you with a summary of the jurisdiction of the criminal courts;
* stress the importance of the pervasive issue of human rights; and
* highlight professional conduct considerations in the context of criminal litigation.

1.2   PHILOSOPHY OF THE *CRIMINAL LITIGATION HANDBOOK*

The *Criminal Litigation Handbook* provides a new and innovative approach to criminal litiga-tion for those studying both the compulsory litigation element of the Legal Practice Course (LPC) and an elective in Advanced Criminal Practice.

In preparing the *Handbook*, our intention has been to provide an integrated and practical approach to the study of Criminal Litigation. As experienced Criminal Litigation teachers, we are aware of the need for a textbook that gives students an accessible and comprehensive explanation of the key substantive, procedural and evidential issues whilst also providing a learning resource that illustrates, through practice-based examples, diagrams, self-test exer-cises and case studies, the operation of the law in a very practical context.

Our experience has shown that utilising a wide range of interrelated learning resources is the most effective way to reinforce student understanding of the key legal issues. It also assists students to prepare for their written assessments (and where appropriate, their skills assess-ment in Criminal Litigation) as well as preparing them for the realities of legal practice.

1.2.1   WHAT DO WE MEAN BY TAKING AN INTEGRATED AND PRACTICAL APPROACH?

The integrated approach is reflected in our belief that LPC students should be aware that the constituent parts of criminal procedure, the rules of criminal evidence, professional conduct and legal skills are not discrete elements, but are part of the integrated picture that is involved in representing a client in a criminal case.

Our treatment of the rules of criminal evidence highlights this integrated approach. An understanding of the key evidential issues is relevant at all stages of the case, even during the solicitor's earliest representation of his client at the police station or during the first inter-view in the office. Chapter 2 entitled: 'An Introduction to the Law of Criminal Evidence and Advocacy', provides an overview of criminal evidence and is designed to encourage you to think about evidence at the very outset, before aspects of criminal procedure and the sub-stantive rules of evidence are covered in more detail later in the *Handbook*.

The practical approach is achieved in different ways. We have attempted to explain the law and procedure in an accessible and reader-friendly style. The substantive content of each chapter is supplemented by practical examples and diagrams as well as self-test questions and answers. The *Handbook* integrates three case studies throughout the book which are an essential part of our practical approach. The integrated case studies are:

Case study 1:   (*R v Lenny Whyte*)

Case study 2:   (*R v Roger Martin*)

Case study 3:   (*R v William Hardy*)

A selection of documentation supporting case study 1 is included in Appendix 1. The complete documentation to *R v Lenny Whyte* and the other two case studies can be found in the case study section of the Online Resource Centre. The case studies form the basis of ongoing exercises throughout the *Handbook*. The exercises are designed to give the reader, the opportunity to apply your knowledge of criminal procedure and evidence in the context of a 'real' case. You will be asked to consider some of the documentation in support of the three integrated case studies at the conclusion of this introductory chapter. We ask you to keep the case studies in mind as you work through the various stages of the criminal litigation process. Treat these fictional creations as your clients.

Key areas of practice and procedure in relation to all our case studies have been filmed. The 'cases' were heard before a bench of serving lay magistrates (and in the matter of *R v William Hardy* before a Crown Court judge). All the participants in the video clips kindly agreed to give up their valuable time in order to assist us in making the films. The clips (all of which are held on the Online Resource Centre) should be viewed as learning aids in that they seek to illustrate, in a practical way, aspects of criminal practice. The videos are not necessarily a depiction of how cases always proceed and they should not be regarded as definitive examples of how advocacy might be conducted before a criminal court. Commentary is included on the clips. Transcripts (based for the most part on the principal submissions made by the advocates) are included in the documentation that support the case studies.

1.3 ONLINE RESOURCE CENTRE

Our Online Resource Centre can be accessed at www.oxfordtextbooks.co.uk/orc/lpccrim-hand book08_09/.

Features included on the website are fully explained in the 'Guided tour of the Online Resource Centre' at page xviii but it will be useful to introduce the resource here also. The website is divided into useful sections to help the individual reader and includes the following resources:

Section 1: Password protected lecturer resources   A test bank of multiple choice questions to test students' knowledge and understanding. High-quality video clips bring to life the key procedural stages of the *Handbook*'s case studies and are formatted for download through broadband, suitable for viewing on a computer or intranet. Alternatively this resource is available as a higher resolution file on CD in order to project the clips on to a large screen in lectures. The clips include accompanying selective transcripts broadly based on the principal submissions made by the advocates. Also available in the lecturer resource section are two further role-play scenarios:

Case study 4:   (*Peter West: Police Station Scenario*).

Case study 5:   (*R v Nicholas Jones: Bad Character applications before a Crown Court judge*).

Case study 4 was filmed at an operational police station.

Full instructions on the use that you might make of these two learning resources are included.

A selection of Codes of Practice and Guidelines, including the Magistrates' Court Sentencing Guidelines are also included in this section.

Section 2: Open access lecturer resources   The video clips of the case scenarios are available for online browsing intended for lecturers to review the material available.

Section 3: Student resources   These are freely available resources and include updates to cover recent developments in criminal litigation and criminal evidence, accompanied by useful web-links. Here you will also find the complete documentation supporting case studies 1, 2 and 3.

Wherever you see this symbol there is a link to our Online Resource Centre.

In order to derive maximum benefit from this *Handbook*, we recommend you make full use of the learning and information resources on our Online Resource Centre.

1.4   LOOKING AHEAD—REFORM

These are challenging times for those who specialise in criminal practice. In recent years there has been considerable legislation affecting all aspects of criminal justice. This includes substantive law reform in the enactment of the Criminal Justice Act 2003; the Serious Organised Crime and Police Act 2005; Criminal Defence Act 2006; Police and Justice Act 2006; Road Safety Act 2006; and the Violent Crime Reduction Act 2006 and the Criminal Justice and Immigration Act 2008, to name but a few! We should not forget that case law continues to develop on all aspects of these reforms and new sentencing guidelines continue to be issued on a regular basis. Criminal justice is always high on the political agenda so we can expect further announcements and initiatives in 2008–2009. A number of provisions under the Criminal Justice Act 2003 are not yet in force and we can expect new legislation to be implemented on a piecemeal basis. The update section of our Online Resource Centre will provide an account of any significant changes during 2008–2009. Any reforms likely to be brought into force in the next 12 months are highlighted in the text by the heading 'Looking Ahead'.

As a matter of good practice, an LPC student should be aware of these changes, not only for learning and assessment purposes, but also because knowledge of recent legal developments is a common question at job interviews!

1.5   RESEARCH SOURCES

Legal research is an important part of your studies on the LPC. It is also an increasingly important skill that you will be required to apply in practice. While our Online Resource Centre provides invaluable links to related websites from which you can access further useful information, we include here a summary of useful practitioner texts and practitioner journals.

1.5.1   PRACTITIONER WORKS

Blackstone's Criminal Practice
Also published by Oxford University Press, *Blackstone's Criminal Practice* is an established leading research source for criminal practitioners. Annually updated and written in an accessible and user-friendly way, *Blackstone's* provides a detailed explanation of the main substantive criminal offences, the key stages of criminal procedure and the rules of criminal evidence. *Blackstone's* is also available on CD-ROM.

Archbold Criminal Pleading and Practice
This very well-established authoritative practitioner text is specifically directed to the practice and procedure of trials on indictment. *Archbold* now publishes a companion volume for proceedings in the magistrates' court.

Stone's Justices Manual
This is the most authoritative text for proceedings in the magistrates' court. Stone's is an indispensable source of reference for all criminal practitioners.

1.5.2 TEXTS

Defending Suspects at the Police Station (Ed Cape; published by the Legal Action Group)
This book offers a clear explanation covering all aspects of representing a client at the police station, including a detailed exposition of police powers and invaluable advice about the strategies to be adopted by the legal adviser.

Active Defence (Ede and Shepherd; Law Society Publications)
This is an excellent, informative guide to representing a client at the police station.

The Golden Rules of Advocacy (Keith Evans; Oxford University Press)
An informative, short and entertaining book!

1.5.3 JOURNALS

Journal articles provide an invaluable source of information on current issues and recent developments in criminal procedure and evidence.

Criminal Law Review
You will have encountered this authoritative journal during your academic studies. Published monthly, the *Criminal Law Review* contains articles on recent developments in substantive criminal law, procedure and evidence as well as informed analysis of recent cases.

Justice of the Peace
Published weekly, *Justice of the Peace* contains articles of interest and case analyses on issues of particular relevance to proceedings in the magistrates' court.

Legal Action Group Magazine
This is a monthly publication from the Legal Action Group which contains articles of topical interest for the criminal practitioner and summaries of important cases.

General legal journals such as the *Solicitor's Journal, Counsel, Legal Executive and the Law Society Gazette* will also contain articles of interest on criminal litigation and evidence and summaries of important cases.

1.5.4 ELECTRONIC RESEARCH SOURCES

Electronic research sources from the key criminal justice organisations and a comprehensive set of web-links can be accessed via the web-links section from our Online Resource Centre.

1.6 A MATTER OF STYLE

The use of the masculine he/his should be taken to include she/her. In using the masculine we do not want to give the impression that all advocates within the criminal justice system and those who stand accused of committing criminal offence are male—far from it!

1.7 THE CLASSIFICATION OF CRIMINAL OFFENCES

The most important classification is that which determines which court (magistrates' court or Crown Court) will deal with the offence. All criminal offences fall within one of three classifications which determine the trial venue of the offence. An offence will either be:

- summary-only;
- triable either way; or
- indictable-only.

You should always check the classification of an offence whether in an examination or in practice. You will soon remember the classification of the more common offences. The classification of all criminal offences can be researched in a practitioner work, such as *Blackstone's Criminal Practice*. The correct identification of the classification of an offence helps you to accurately explain to a client or an examiner the typical procedural course for the case you are concerned with.

1.7.1 SUMMARY-ONLY OFFENCES

The least serious offences are known as summary-only offences and are dealt with summarily in the magistrates' court, whether or not the defendant pleads guilty or not guilty. Summary-only offences begin and end in the magistrates' court. The offence of common assault, contrary to s. 39 Criminal Justice Act 1988 is a summary-only offence. Under s. 127 Magistrates' Courts Act 1980, the prosecution of a summary-only offence must normally be commenced within six months of its commission.

1.7.2 OFFENCES TRIABLE EITHER WAY

Either-way offences are middle-ranking offences in terms of their seriousness and can be tried either summarily before a magistrates' court or on indictment before a judge and jury in the Crown Court. An example of an either-way offence is theft, contrary to s. 1 Theft Act 1968. It is the defendant's indication of plea which determines where an either-way offence will be tried. If the defendant indicates that he will plead guilty, the case will remain in the magistrates' court and the court will proceed to sentence. The magistrates' court has the power to commit the defendant to be sentenced before the Crown Court upon conviction for an either-way offence where it considers its limited powers of sentence are insufficient.

If an adult defendant indicates a not guilty plea to an either-way offence the magistrates' court will conduct a mode of trial enquiry. At the mode of trial enquiry the magistrates' court must decide whether to keep jurisdiction of the either-way case (i.e. try the case summarily) or decline jurisdiction and commit the case to the Crown Court where the offence will be tried on indictment. Jurisdiction will be declined where the magistrates' court concludes its powers of sentence in the event of conviction will be insufficient or the case involves complex issues of fact or law. If the magistrates' court declines jurisdiction, the accused has no choice and his case will be committed to the Crown Court by a committal hearing which is held some weeks later. If the magistrates' court accept jurisdiction to try the either-way offence summarily, the accused has a choice: he can consent to summary trial, or he can elect trial by jury on indictment before the Crown Court.

1.7.3 INDICTABLE-ONLY OFFENCES

The most serious crimes are known as indictable-only offences, which will be tried at the Crown Court before a judge and jury. The common law offence of murder and the statutory offence of robbery, contrary to s. 8 Theft Act 1968 are indictable-only offences. Whilst the defendant's case will be disposed of at the Crown Court, the prosecution of an indictable-only offence will commence in the magistrates' court. Following the defendant's initial appearance before a magistrates' court, his case is sent to the Crown Court for trial under s. 51 Crime and Disorder Act 1998.

Where your client is charged with more than one offence with different venue classifications the general rule is that the most serious offence will dictate the procedural course of events. If your client is charged with two either-way offences, his indication of plea on each offence will be the determining factor.

Figures 1.1, 1.2 and 1.3 illustrate the stages of a summary-only, either-way and indictable-only offence. Figures 1.4 provides an overview of the criminal litigation process. In the student resource section of the Online Resource Centre you will find a free-standing chapter entitled: An Overview of a Criminal Case which explains in more detail the various stages illustrated by Figures 1.1, 1.2 and 1.3.

online resource centre

1.8 PERSONNEL AND ORGANISATIONS WITHIN THE CRIMINAL JUSTICE SYSTEM

1.8.1 INVESTIGATING AND PROSECUTING ORGANISATIONS

The responsibility for investigating and prosecuting a criminal offence is shared between several organisations.

The investigation of most criminal offences is undertaken by the police. At the completion of the investigation, the matter is passed to the Crown Prosecution Service (CPS) which decides whether there is sufficient evidence to charge the suspect. The CPS is divided into 42 areas, which are aligned to the number of police forces in England and Wales.

The conduct of most day-to-day prosecutions in the magistrates' court or the Crown Court will be dealt with either by a Senior Crown Prosecutor; Crown Prosecutor or a Designated Case Worker (DCW). The former are legally qualified solicitors or barristers; the latter are not. DCWs currently have restricted rights of audience before a magistrates' court. These rights are to be extended in the future although a DCW will not be entitled to conduct a trial involving a contested imprisonable offence.

The CPS employs a number of administrative staff known as caseworkers. A caseworker will assist CPS lawyers by preparing cases, attending court with counsel, liaising with witnesses and other criminal justice agencies as well as post-trial administration. Whilst the CPS clearly plays a dominant role in the prosecution of criminal offences, other state agencies also investigate and prosecute criminal offences in specific areas of responsibility:

- the Department of Trade and Industry investigates and prosecutes offences involving companies and company officers, including directors;
- the Serious Fraud Office investigates and prosecutes serious or complex fraud;
- HM Customs and Excise prosecutes offences relating to evasion of tax and customs duties;
- the Serious Organised Crime Agency, created by the Serious Organised Crime and Police Act 2005, has responsibility for the investigation and conduct of cases previously dealt with by the National Criminal Intelligence Service, the Home Office Immigration Crime Unit and HM Customs and Excise;
- the Health and Safety Executive (HSE) investigates and prosecutes criminal offences arising out of accidents in the workplace under the Health and Safety at Work Act 1974;
- local authorities investigate and prosecute offences under the Trade Descriptions Act 1968, Education Act 1996, environmental law cases and prosecutions relating to food and hygiene;
- the Environmental Agency investigates and prosecutes environmental crime;
- the RSPCA brings private prosecutions for offences relating to the welfare of animals.

1.8.2 **THE LEGAL SERVICES COMMISSION AND THE CRIMINAL DEFENCE SERVICE**

A detailed examination of public funding of criminal defence services is considered in Chapter 11. The provision of public funding for legal services in England and Wales is supervised by the Legal Services Commission. The day-to-day administration of the provision of public funding for criminal defence services is undertaken by the Criminal Defence Service (CDS). There are approximately 2,600 solicitors' firms having contracts with the Legal Services Commission to provide public funded criminal defence services. Public spending on criminal legal aid regularly exceeds £1 billion every year.

1.8.3 **THE PUBLIC DEFENDER SERVICE**

The Public Defender Service (PDS) provides an established alternative to a criminal client seeking advice and representation from a solicitor in private practice. Through the LSC, the PDS employs criminal defence solicitors to provide advice, assistance and representation to clients. Currently there are four PDS offices located in Darlington, Swansea, Pontypridd and Cheltenham.

1.9 **THE CRIMINAL COURTS AND PERSONNEL**

It is likely that you will have studied the hierarchy of the criminal courts during your academic studies. This section is intended to briefly remind you of the jurisdiction of each criminal court.

1.9.1 **MAGISTRATES' COURT**

Criminal defence solicitors spend the vast majority of their time preparing for and appearing in cases listed in the magistrates' court. It is the workhorse of the criminal justice system. Virtually all criminal prosecutions commence in the magistrates' court. Ninety-eight per cent of all criminal cases are dealt with in the magistrates' court, with the remaining two per cent of cases heard in the Crown Court. The practice and procedure in the magistrates' court is governed by the Magistrates' Courts Act 1980 and the Criminal Procedure Rules.

The magistrates' court has the following jurisdictions:

* tries and sentences offenders for summary-only offences;
* tries and sentences offenders charged with an either-way offence which is considered to be suitable for summary trial;
* deals with preliminary matters during the early stages of all prosecutions including:

    — the defendant's application for an adjournment;
    — the defendant's bail application;

* hears mode of trial proceedings under ss. 17–21 Magistrates' Courts Act 1980 to decide where either-way offences should be tried;
* commits a defendant under ss. 3 and 4 Powers of Criminal Courts (Sentencing) Act 2000 to the Crown Court for sentence where he has pleaded guilty or has been found guilty of an either-way offence and the magistrates' court consider its sentencing powers to be insufficient;
* hears committal proceedings under s. 6(1) or 6(2) Magistrates' Courts Act 1980 in respect of an either-way offence which the magistrates' court has determined should be tried at the Crown Court or because the defendant has elected trial at the Crown Court;
* sends indictable-only offences to the Crown Court for trial under s. 51 Crime and Disorder Act 1998.

1.9.2 MAGISTRATES

A magistrate is either a justice of the peace or a District Judge. Lay magistrates are unpaid, and whilst they are not required to hold any formal legal qualifications all magistrates undergo a period of induction and training. They are required to 'sit' for a prescribed number of days each year. There are approximately 30,000 active lay magistrates in England and Wales who normally try cases sitting as part of a Bench of three.

District Judges are appointed from solicitors and barristers who have been qualified for at least seven years and are paid a salary. A District Judge hears a case sitting alone and can exercise all the powers of a Bench of lay magistrates. Section 65 of the Courts Act 2003 now enables District Judges to exercise some of the powers of recorders who sit as judges in the Crown Court in certain cases.

1.9.3 THE JUSTICES' CLERK OR LEGAL ADVISER

When conducting a summary trial, lay magistrates will be assisted by an adviser who will usually be a solicitor or a barrister. The law maintains a strict division of responsibilities between the magistrates and their adviser. The magistrates are the sole arbiters of law and fact. The *Practice Direction (Criminal Proceedings: Consolidation)* [2000] 1 WLR 2870 provides that the adviser will sit with lay magistrates to advise the Bench on matters of law, evidence, human rights points and procedure. The adviser will also put the charge to the accused, take a note of the evidence in the case and help an unrepresented accused present his case.

When the justices retire to consider their verdict the adviser must only advise them on points of law and evidence (*Stafford Justices, ex p. Ross* [1962] 1 WLR 456).

1.9.4 YOUTH COURT

As a general rule, where the defendant is under 18, he should be dealt with in the Youth Court. All magistrates' courts have a youth court panel of specially trained magistrates who have been appointed because of their suitability for dealing with youth cases. The practice and procedure is more informal and less intimidating than in the adult court. A District Judge (who has undertaken the required training) may also sit alone in the Youth Court. The Youth Court is regarded as a specialist jurisdiction. You may not cover youth justice as part of the core Criminal Litigation Course. For this reason, youth justice is separately considered in Chapters 30 and 31.

1.9.5 THE CROWN COURT

The Crown Court deals with cases to be tried on indictment before a judge and jury. The practice and procedure in the Crown Court is now governed by the Supreme Court Act 1981 and the Criminal Procedure Rules. The Crown Court exercises the following jurisdiction:

- tries either-way offences committed for trial at the Crown Court;

- tries indictable-only offences and any related offences;

- sentences offenders convicted before it and those who are committed for sentence by the magistrates' courts (ss. 3 and 4 Powers of Criminal Courts (Sentencing) Act 2000);

- determines an appeal against conviction and/or sentence arising out of a decision made by a magistrates' court or youth court.

Section 66 Courts Act 2003, enables a Crown Court judge to exercise the powers of a District Judge (magistrates' court).

The following types of judge preside over sittings of the Crown Court:

- High Court judges;
- circuit judges; and
- recorders and assistant recorders who are part-time judicial officers.

1.9.6 THE HIGH COURT AND DIVISIONAL COURT OF THE QUEEN'S BENCH DIVISION

The Queen's Bench Division of the High Court has a limited jurisdiction in criminal matters. An action in judicial review can be commenced in the Queen's Bench Division against a public body such as a court or the CPS for exceeding or misusing its legal powers or for not following the correct procedure or for exercising its legal powers in an 'irrational' way.

The Divisional Court of the Queen's Bench Division hears appeals by way of case stated under s. 111 MCA 1980 arising from decisions taken in a magistrates' court. Both the prosecution and defence can appeal by way of case stated to the Divisional Court. This method of appeal is appropriate where it is submitted that the magistrates' court or its legal adviser has misinterpreted a point of law or evidence.

1.9.7 THE COURT OF APPEAL (CRIMINAL DIVISION)

The Court of Appeal (Criminal Division) hears appeals against conviction and/or sentence from those cases tried in the Crown Court. It also hears appeals or 'points of reference' from the Attorney-General (A-G) on points of law and sentences that are considered to be too lenient. The work of the Court of Appeal is presided over by the Lord Chief Justice. Cases are normally heard by the Lord Chief Justice sitting with two puisne judges or a Lord Justice of Appeal sitting with two ordinary judges.

The Court of Appeal additionally gives guidance on the procedures and practices of the criminal courts by issuing sentencing guidelines and practice directions.

1.9.8 THE HOUSE OF LORDS

The judicial work of the House of Lords is presided over by the Lord Chancellor. It is the highest court in the criminal jurisdiction and hears appeals from the Court of Appeal (and occasionally the Divisional Court) on points of law of public importance. Leave to appeal is required.

1.10 THE EUROPEAN CONVENTION ON HUMAN RIGHTS 1950 (ECHR)

The Human Rights Act 1998 (HRA) provides the legal framework for using the ECHR in UK domestic law. Section 1 HRA 1998 formally implements ECHR law into UK domestic law. This means that points of ECHR law can be cited in the criminal courts in support of your client's case.

As a pervasive subject on the LPC, an ECHR point may arise in any of the core subjects, or in the elective phase or as part of a skills assessment. However, since its implementation in domestic law, the ECHR has had a greater influence on criminal procedure and evidence than in any other area of legal practice.

1.10.1 HOW ARE THE RIGHTS GUARANTEED UNDER THE CONVENTION ENFORCED IN DOMESTIC LAW?

Section 3 HRA 1998 places an obligation on the criminal courts to interpret all legislation 'as far as possible' to comply with ECHR law. This is known as the interpretive obligation. In discharging the interpretive obligation to ensure compliance between Convention law and domestic law, s. 2 HRA 1998 requires courts not only have regard to the Convention itself but also to the jurisprudence of the European Court Human Rights (ECtHR). Therefore when citing a relevant ECHR point in support of your legal argument you should research relevant ECtHR's decisions on the point and any domestic case law that has considered the issue.

.10.2 WHAT IS THE POSITION WHERE IT IS NOT POSSIBLE TO GIVE EFFECT TO ECHR LAW?

The HRA 1998 does not give the courts the power to strike down legislation which is incompatible with Convention rights. Where it is not possible to give effect to the ECHR law in a case under the interpretive obligation, s. 4 HRA 1998 requires the superior courts (Court of Appeal and the House of Lords) to make a declaration of incompatibility. It is then a matter for parliament whether or not to amend the offending legislation.

.10.3 DOES THE HRA 1998 OFFER ADDITIONAL PROTECTIONS TO THE DEFENDANT'S LEGAL RIGHTS?

The most significant additional protection is provided by s. 6 HRA 1998, which places a duty on a public authority such as the police, the Crown Prosecution Service and the courts, to discharge its legal duties in compliance with the ECHR. Section 6(1) provides:

'It is unlawful for a public authority to act in a way which is incompatible with Convention rights.'

A range of remedies in the civil courts apply where a public authority acts in breach of its duties under s. 6 HRA 1998, including actions in tort and/or judicial review. Section 8 HRA 1998 requires that where a court finds that a public authority has acted unlawfully, it must grant a remedy that is 'just and appropriate'. In *R (on the application of TB) v The Combined Court at Stafford* [2006] EWHC 1645 Admin, the High Court held that the Crown Court had violated the rights to privacy of the alleged victim of sexual abuse in its procedural handling of a request by the defendant to have disclosure of the victim's psychiatric record. She was accordingly entitled to judicial review of the decision to disclose her records in accordance with s. 6 HRA 1998.

.10.4 ARTICLES OF RELEVANCE FOR THE CRIMINAL LITIGATOR

Article 3 – the prohibition of torture

'No one shall be subjected to torture or inhuman or degrading treatment or punishment.'

Thankfully this provision is unlikely to be invoked on a frequent basis although it might be relevant when seeking to challenge the admissibility of a defendant's confession on the ground that it had been obtained by 'oppression' under s. 76(2)(a) PACE 1984. Article 3 will be relevant when arguing that the manner in which the police interrogated your client (for example by shouting or making threats to the suspect), breached Convention law.

Article 3 is an absolute right from which no derogation is permitted.

Article 5 – the right to liberty and security

'1. Everyone has the right to liberty and security of person. No one shall be deprivsed of liberty save in the following cases and in accordance with a procedure prescribed by law:

   (a) the lawful detention of a person after conviction by a competent court;

   (b) the lawful arrest or detention of a person for non-compliance of a lawful order of a court . . . ;

   (c) the lawful arrest and detention of a person except for the purpose of bringing him before a court of competent legal authority on reasonable suspicion of having committed an offence or fleeing after having done so; . . .

2. Everyone who is arrested shall be informed promptly, in a language which he understands, of the reasons for his arrest and of any charge against him.

3. Everyone arrested or detained in accordance with paragraph 1c shall be entitled to trial within a reasonable time or to release pending trial. Release may be conditioned by guarantees to appear for trial.

4. Everyone who is deprived of his liberty by arrest or detention shall be entitled to take proceedings by which the lawfulness of his detention shall be decided speedily by a court.

5. Everyone who has been the victim of arrest or detention in contravention of the provisions of this article shall have an enforceable right to compensation.'

Article 5 is a qualified right allowing the state to derogate from it in defined circumstances.

Article 5 may be invoked where your client has been unlawfully arrested or otherwise detained by the police. As such, Article 5 may well be relevant when challenging the decision of the police or the court to refuse your client bail.

Article 6–the right to a fair trial

'1. In the determination of his civil rights and obligations, or of any criminal charge against him everyone is entitled to a fair and public hearing within a reasonable time by an independent and impartial tribunal established by law. Judgment shall be pronounced publicly but the press or public may be excluded in the interests of morals, public order or national security in a democratic society, where the interests of juveniles or the protection of private life of the parties so require, or to the extent strictly necessary in the opinion of the court in special circumstances where publicity would prejudice the interests of justice.

2. Everyone charged with a criminal offence shall be presumed innocent until proved guilty according to the law.

3. Everyone charged with a criminal offence has the following minimum rights:

(a) to be informed promptly, in a language which he understands and in detail of the nature and cause of the accusation against him;

(b) to have adequate time and facilities for the preparation of his defence;

(c) to defend himself in person or through legal assistance of his own choosing or, if he has not sufficient means to pay for legal assistance, to be given it free when the interests of justice so require;

(d) to examine or have examined witnesses against him and to obtain the attendance and examination of witnesses on his behalf under the same conditions as witnesses against him;

(e) to have the free assistance of an interpreter if he cannot understand or speak the language used in court.'

Article 6 is the most significant Convention right for criminal litigators and is relevant at all stages of a criminal case including:

• the defendant's right to have legal representation at the police station and at trial;

• the procedural and evidential rules adopted by the court at trial; and

• the principles applied when passing sentence.

The right to a fair trial in Article 6(1) is drafted in absolute terms. What constitutes a fair trial however is not defined. The presumption of innocence in Article 6(2) and the provisions of Article 6(3) are specified minimum general components of a fair trial. The jurisprudence of the European Court of Human Rights has implied a number of rights into Article 6, including the privilege against self-incrimination. In deciding the fair trial provisions under Article 6, it should be stressed that the ECtHR is not concerned with the actual guilt or innocence of the accused but rather whether the whole trial process was in accordance with Article 6.

It is always open to a defence advocate to argue that the admissibility of a particular piece of evidence in a case will violate the defendant's right to a fair trial in accordance with Article 6. Sometimes evidence is obtained by the police in violation of Article 8 which guarantees an individual's right to privacy. Article 8 is a qualified right. A defence advocate could nonetheless argue that his client's right to a fair trial has been compromised because the evidence has been obtained in violation of a Convention right.

.10.5 THE GENERAL PRINCIPLES OF JURISPRUDENCE UNDER THE ECHR

In addition to the substantive rights of the Convention itself, regard must also be had to the general principles of law that have been developed as a result of decisions by the ECtHR. These are briefly discussed below.

The rule of law

Some of the rights guaranteed under the convention are absolute rights; others are qualified rights. Qualified rights permit a member state to derogate from it. However, it is a fundamental principle of Convention law that any derogation in domestic law of a person's right under the Convention must be prescribed by a readily accessible law or regulation and not as the result of an arbitrary decision. Therefore, whilst arresting a person during a criminal investigation is *prima facie* in breach of that person's rights to liberty under Article 5, provided the arrest was made under the authority of a recognised legal power such as s. 24 PACE 1984, the rule of law principle will not be breached.

Legitimacy of aim

Where domestic law is permitted to derogate from a legal right of the ECHR, any interference with the right must be directed towards an identifiable, legitimate aim such as the prevention of disorder or crime. Once again, the interference with a person's right to liberty under Article 5 is permitted as it is directed toward the legitimate aim of investigating or preventing crime.

Proportionality

Any interference in domestic law with a legal right under the ECHR must be a proportionate response when measured against the objective the interference is intended to address. In colloquial terms, this means that the state 'cannot use a sledgehammer to crack a nut'.

When applying the principle of proportionality, the Court considers whether the interference with a Convention right is 'necessary in a democratic society' or is based on 'a pressing social need'. In determining the components of a fair trial under Article 6, the principle of proportionality is evident both in the application of domestic law and in decisions of the European Court of Human Rights.

1.10.6 THE ECHR AND THE RULES OF CRIMINAL PROCEDURE AND EVIDENCE

Whilst generally the practice and procedure of the English criminal trial satisfies the obligations laid down by the Convention, since the implementation of the HRA 1998, a number of important decisions have been made by the courts where Article 5 or Article 6 have been directly invoked. These decisions include:

- R *(on the application of the DPP) v Havering Magistrates' Court* [2001] 2 Cr App R 2 confirmed that proceedings under the Bail Act 1976 were governed by Article 5;
- *T and V v United Kingdom* (2000) 30 EHRR 121 decided that the boys tried for the killing of Jamie Bulger had not had a fair trial in the Crown Court under Article 6 because of their young age and the formality of the Crown Court procedures had prevented them from effective participation in the trial process;
- *R (Anderson) v Secretary of State for the Home Department* [2003] 1 Cr App R 32, the House of Lords decided that to comply with Article 6, where a prisoner was sentenced to life imprisonment, the decision as to how long the prisoner should serve in prison (known as the tariff) should be taken by a judge and not by the Home Secretary;

• *Murray v United Kingdom* [1996] 22 EHHR 29, the European Court of Human Rights held that adverse inferences could not be drawn from a suspect's silence at the police station where he had not been offered legal advice. United Kingdom domestic law was found to be in breach of Article 6(3) of the Convention. Section 34 Criminal Justice and Public Order Act 1994 had to be amended as a consequence.

These and other important decisions influenced by the ECHR are considered in more detail at appropriate places in the text. The recognition of a defendant's rights under Article 6 is specifically identified in Part 1 of the Criminal Procedure Rules as a component of the over-riding objective of dealing with criminal cases justly.

1.11 CRIMINAL PROCEDURE RULES (CRIM PR)

online
resource
centre

The Criminal Procedure Rules (Crim PR) came into effect on the 4 April 2005. The aim of the Rules is to provide a comprehensive Criminal Procedure Code that will govern the conduct of all criminal cases in the future. This has been achieved in that a myriad of pre-existing procedural rules have been brought together in one text. The Rules and all subsequent amendments can be accessed on the Criminal Procedure Rule Committee's website. The web-links section of our Online Resource Centre (Guidelines section) will take you there.

The overriding objective of the Crim PR is stated in Part 1 as being that all criminal cases must be dealt with justly. Part 1.1 defines this to include:

(a) acquitting the innocent and convicting the guilty;

(b) dealing with the prosecution and the defence fairly;

(c) recognising the rights of a defendant, particularly those under Article 6 of the European Convention on Human Rights;

(d) respecting the interest of witnesses, victims and jurors and keeping them informed of the progress of the case;

(e) dealing with the case efficiently and expeditiously;

(f) ensuring that appropriate information is available to the court when bail and sentence are considered; and

(g) dealing with the case in ways that take into account:

(i) the gravity of the offence alleged,

(ii) the complexity of what is in issue,

(iii) the severity of the consequences for the defendant and others affected, and

(iv) the needs of other cases.

Everyone involved in the criminal justice process must prepare and conduct cases in accordance with the overriding objective in Part 1.

To ensure that the overriding objective is achieved, courts are required to engage in robust and active management of cases (Part 3). Active case management is defined in Part 3.2 to include:

(a) the early identification of the real issues;

(b) the early identification of the needs of witnesses;

(c) achieving certainty as to what must be done, by whom, and when, in particular by the early setting of a timetable for the progress of the case;

(d) monitoring the progress of the case and compliance with directions;

(e) ensuring that evidence, whether disputed or not, is presented in the shortest and clearest way;

(f) discouraging delay, dealing with as many aspects of the case as possible on the same occasion and avoiding unnecessary hearings;

(g) encouraging the participants to co-operate in the progression of the case; and

(h) making use of technology

Active case management involves courts giving directions to the parties that are appropriate to the needs of the case and are consistent with the overriding objective.

Crim PR, Part 3.3 imposes a duty on all parties to actively assist the court in fulfilling its duty under Part 3.2. The extent to which the defence solicitor's duties under Part 3 conflict with duties owed to a client in the conduct of a criminal case are considered at para. 1.12.7.

The Criminal Procedure Rules are likely to be revised from time to time and occasionally rewritten. Any significant developments in this regard will be brought to you via the updating section of our Online Resource Centre. It should be noted that with effect from 7 April 2008, the Rules were amended to allow for the imposition of sanctions on parties for failing to comply with a rule or direction of the court (Part 3.5 (6)).

online
resource
centre

1.12 PROFESSIONAL CONDUCT

Another very important pervasive area of practice are the professional conduct rules which govern the solicitor's profession. The rules are set out in the Solicitors' Code of Conduct 2007. The code of conduct can be accessed online at www.sra.org.uk/code-of-conduct.page. The 2007 Code replaced the Guide to the Professional Conduct of Solicitors (1999). A failure to abide by the Solicitors' Code of Conduct may result in disciplinary proceedings being brought against you. If you are found to have broken the Code you could be disciplined or even struck off the Roll.

Criminal cases are conducted in an adversarial system of inquiry where the aim of each side is to win. Rule 1.04 of the code of conduct defines one of the core duties of a solicitor as being to act in the best interests of his client. In an effort to win, you will need to be a partisan advocate for and on behalf of your client. However, as an officer of the court, a solicitor also serves the wider public interest in upholding the highest standards in relation to the administration of justice (Rule 1.01). Serving the best interests of your client can sometimes bring you into conflict with your duty to the proper administration of justice.

The purpose of this final section is to provide an overview of your professional conduct duties, with specific emphasis on criminal practice. You will be reminded of some of the areas about to be addressed at appropriate intervals in the *Handbook*.

Professional conduct issues in relation to criminal clients are most likely to arise in the following contexts:

- duties to your client;
- duties to the court;
- confidentiality;
- conflict of interest;
- interviewing witnesses;
- specific duties on advocates.

1.12.1 DUTY TO YOUR CLIENT

Rule 1.04 imposes a duty on you to act in the best interests of your client. Detailed aspects of client care are covered in Rule 2 which includes giving your client full information as to likely costs. Rule 2.03 specifically imposes an obligation on a solicitor to discuss the availability of public funding for legal services. This is particularly apt in the context of criminal defence work.

1.12.2 DUTY TO THE COURT

Whilst you have a basic duty to act in the best interest of your client, Rule 1.01 requires you to uphold the proper administration of justice. You also have an overriding duty not to mislead the court. Rule 11.01 could not be more emphatic. It states:

> 'You must never deceive or knowingly or recklessly mislead the court.'

You will soon discover that some criminal clients will lie or be economical with the truth. What should you do if you become aware that your client intends to lie to the police or to the court?

The obligation not to knowingly deceive the court is further defined in paras. 11–14 of the Guidance to Rule 11. Your duty not to deceive the court will arise where, for example, you are satisfied that your client is adopting false particulars (name or address or date of birth) with the intention of deceiving a court by failing to disclose previous convictions to achieve a more favourable sentence or bail outcome. In such circumstances you would need to explain to your client that you cannot allow such a course to be pursued and that unless your client is willing to correct the details or is willing to change his mind, you will have to withdraw from the case (Rule 11.01, Guidance Notes 11 and 15).

Guidance Note 12 of Rule 11 lists the other (non-exhaustive) ways in which you might deceive or mislead a court. You might do so by:

(a) submitting inaccurate information or allowing another person to do so;

(b) indicating agreement with information that another person puts forward which you know to be false;

(c) calling a witness whose evidence you know is untrue;

(d) not immediately disclosing a document you have become aware of during the case which should have been, but was not, disclosed;

(e) attempting to influence a witness when taking a statement from that witness, with regard to the contents of their statement; and

(f) tampering with evidence or seeking to persuade a witness to change their evidence.

Rule 11 acknowledges that you may inadvertently mislead the court. If you become aware of this during the course of the proceedings, you must, with your client's consent, immediately inform the court. If your client does not consent, you must cease to act. You may believe that your client is being untruthful. However, suspicion is not the same as knowledge. If your client was to admit to you, during ongoing proceedings, that he misled the court or committed perjury, you must not act further unless your client agrees to disclose the truth (Rule 11.01 Guidance Note 15).

Are you under a duty to correct an omission or mistake by the prosecution?

What if the prosecution gives information to the court which you know to be incorrect? For example, if on checking your client's list of previous convictions you note that it is incomplete in that it fails to show your client's most recent conviction. When your client's record is submitted to the court upon sentence, are you under a duty to enlighten the court? Guidance Note 14 to Rule 11 provides you are not under an obligation to correct information given to the court by the prosecution or any other party which you know may allow the court to make an incorrect assumption provided you do not indicate agreement with that information.

The observation made above should be contrasted with the positive duty to assist the court as outlined by Rule 11 Note 17 where advocates on both sides must advise the court of relevant cases and statutory provisions. If one side omits to refer a court to a relevant statutory provision or case, it is the duty of the other to draw it to the attention of the court even if it assists the opponent. The obligation does not extend to the disclosure of facts or witnesses that may be of assistance to an adversary (Rule 11.01 Guidance Note 17 (b)) although it would extend to the disclosure of a document which had been filed in the proceedings and which is therefore notionally within the provenance of the court.

The prosecutor has a duty to act as a minister of justice and must never attempt to secure a conviction at all costs. The role of the Crown Prosecution Service is considered in Chapter 10. The onerous nature of the prosecutor's duty to make pre-trial disclosure of relevant material that undermines the case for the prosecution or assists the defence, is considered in Chapter 14. It is fundamental in ensuring the accused enjoys a fair trial in accordance with Article 6.

What action should you take where your client changes his version of events?

A commonly encountered professional conduct issue occurs where your client keeps changing his version of the facts in the case. There is no general duty upon a solicitor to inquire in every case as to whether your client is telling the truth. If your client makes inconsistent statements, this is not a ground for refusing to act. However, you need to be wary and you must cease to act where it is clear that your client is attempting to put forward false evidence as this will conflict with your duty as an officer of the court (Rule 11 Guidance Note 16). You should never suggest a defence to your client to fit the facts nor must you fabricate a defence. This extends to taking witness statements (Rule 11.01). You must never put words into a witness's mouth.

What is the position where your client admits his guilt to you but wants to plead not guilty?

The scenario expressed above could of course occur at the police station as well as at court. Can you continue to act? The previous version of the Code of Conduct contained the following statement:

> "A solicitor who appears in court for the defence in a criminal case is under a duty to say on behalf of the client what the client should properly say for himself or herself if the client possessed the requisite skill and knowledge. The solicitor has a concurrent duty to ensure that the prosecution discharges the onus placed upon it to prove the guilt of the accused."

The statement is not reproduced in the 2007 Code. In answer to the question posed above, you can continue to represent your client on a not guilty plea, as it is your professional duty to require the prosecution to prove its case beyond reasonable doubt. However, you must not do anything to positively assert your client's innocence. If at the close of the prosecution's case, your client sought to give evidence on oath or to call witnesses with a view to making a positive assertion of innocence (i.e. which expressly or by implication suggests someone other than your client committed the crime) you would be knowingly misleading the court. In these circumstances, if your client persisted in such a course, you would be required to withdraw from the case (Rule 11.01 Note 9).

In those cases where you cease to act for a client, do not forget that your duty of confidentiality to your client precludes you from informing the court of the reason for your decision.

What is the position if your client has a defence but wishes to plead guilty?

Your client may not wish to stand trial even though he has a defence to the allegation. It is your duty to point out such a defence. If your client insists on pleading guilty because it is more convenient for him to do so you can continue to act for him but you must warn him that when delivering your plea in mitigation on his behalf you will not be able to rely on any facts that would constitute a defence. You should keep a file note of your advice and get your client to sign a written statement confirming his wishes notwithstanding your advice.

1.12.3 CONFIDENTIALITY

In accordance with Rule 4, a solicitor is under a strict duty to keep confidential the affairs of his client. This may be of particular importance to a client under suspicion of a criminal offence. This duty continues for all time unless your client agrees to waive confidentiality. There are certain exceptional instances when the duty of confidentiality can be overridden. These are set out in the Guidance to Rule 4, paras. 10–20 and include money-laundering and child protection considerations.

Communications between a solicitor and his client are additionally protected from disclosure even to the court by legal professional privilege. The privilege extends in criminal cases to communications passing between a solicitor and a third party, such as a barrister or expert witness, provided the communication was made in connection with actual or contemplated litigation. Legal professional privilege does not extend to a situation in which the solicitor has been used in furtherance of a crime. In such a case the police would be entitled to seize documents relevant to such investigation. The rules of evidence relating to legal professional privilege are considered further in Chapter 24.

Issues of confidentiality are likely to arise in criminal cases where professional embarrassment (see your overriding duty to the court above) forces you to withdraw from a case. You cannot in these circumstances explain to a court the reason why you are no longer acting.

The issue of confidentiality may also arise at the police station. When advising a client to exercise his right to remain silent, the legal adviser may be called upon to explain the reasons for his advice if s. 34 Criminal Justice and Public Order Act 1994 is invoked at trial. He can only do this if his client consents to waive his privilege. The matter is considered further in Chapter 5.

The confidentiality rule often overlaps with the rules regarding conflict of interest.

1.12.4 CONFLICT OF INTEREST

Rule 3.01 provides that a solicitor should not accept instructions to act for two or more clients where there is a conflict or significant risk of a conflict between the interests of those clients. Rule 3.03 states that a solicitor must not continue to act for A and B where a conflict of interest arises between those clients. Can the solicitor continue to act for A but not B? Rule 3.03 stipulates that this is only possible where the solicitor's duty of confidentiality to B is not put at risk.

When considering instructions from more than one client the solicitor needs to ask himself: is there a conflict of interest between them and might a conflict arise at some point in the future? A conflict of interest can commonly arise when the solicitor is called upon to represent two or more suspects at the police station who are being investigated for the same offence. A conflict may subsequently arise in a case where both clients plead not guilty but one of them later pleads guilty. You need to be aware that even when two clients indicate that they will plead guilty, a conflict of interest could still arise when you come to mitigate on their individual behalf.

In the Guidance to Rule 3, paras. 24–36 make specific and extensive provision in relation to acting for co-defendants. For reasons of space we do not include a full text but *strongly* recommend you read the guidance notes. From a public funding point of view it is cheaper for the same solicitor to represent two clients than for separate firms of solicitors to represent each. However, the guidance notes make it clear that you should resist such pressure from whatever source it may come if it would be unprofessional for you to act or to continue to act for both.

.12.5 INTERVIEWING AN OPPONENT'S WITNESS

You will frequently encounter the phrase 'there is no property in a witness'. In a criminal case, this means that the defence solicitor may interview a prosecution witness and the prosecution may interview a defence witness. The Guidance to Rule 11, para. 18 provides:

'You are permitted, even when acting as an advocate, to interview and take statements from any witness at any stage in the proceedings, whether or not that witness has been interviewed or called as a witness by another party.'

This paragraph is subject to 12(e) and (f) which stipulates that you will be in breach of Rule 11.01 (deceiving a court) if you attempt to influence a witness or you persuade a witness to change their evidence. Guidance note 12(f) provides:

'To avoid such allegations it would be wise, when seeking to interview a witness for the other side, to offer to interview them in the presence of the other side's representative.'

If a defence solicitor wishes to interview a prosecution witness, it is sound professional practice to contact the prosecution, in order to ascertain whether a member of the prosecution team wishes to be present at the interview.

1.12.6 SPECIFIC PROFESSIONAL OBLIGATIONS ON ADVOCATES

There are further professional conduct rules which apply specifically to the solicitor acting as an advocate. They are detailed in Rule 11.07 and Guidance Notes 21–33. They cover the situation where an advocate or a member of the advocate's firm could be called as a witness at trial. They also govern the way in which an advocate should treat a witness whilst giving evidence.

Rule 11.07 states quite simply that you must not make, or offer to make, payments to a witness dependent upon the outcome of the case or the nature of the evidence the witness should give. It is however permissible to pay reasonable witness expenses (Guidance Note 29).

1.12.7 PROFESSIONAL CONDUCT AND THE CRIMINAL PROCEDURE RULES

A defence solicitor must always act in the best interests of his client (Rule 1.04). In a case where a solicitor is instructed by his client to plead not guilty, it is the duty of the defence solicitor to put the prosecution to proof of its case. In an attempt to frustrate the prosecution, the defence solicitor may feel his client's best interests are served by playing a tactical game perhaps by withholding certain information from the prosecution and the court. Such a tactical game could frustrate the obligation of the court to actively manage cases in accordance with Crim PR, Parts 1 and 3. The effect of the case management powers given to the court under Part 3 has significantly increased the pressures on all those involved in the conduct of criminal cases as they are now much more accountable to the court for a failure to actively progress a case. In a situation where a solicitor perceives a conflict between his duty to act in the best interests of his client and his duty to promote the administration of justice by actively assisting the court's management of cases, which wins out?

In R v Gleeson [2004] 1 Cr App R 29, defence advocates were reminded that:

'A criminal trial is not a game under which a guilty defendant should be provided with a sporting chance. It is a search for truth in accordance with twin principles that the prosecution must prove its case and that a defendant is not obliged to inculpate himself, the object being to convict the guilty and acquit the innocent. Requiring a defendant to indicate in advance what he disputes about the prosecution case offends neither of those principles.'

In response to the challenges posed by Crim PR, Part 3, the Law Society has issued an important Practice Note (March 2008), entitled *Criminal Procedure Rules: impact on solicitors' duties to the client*. It can be accessed at: http://www.lawsociety.org.uk/documents/downloads/practicenote_criminalprocedurerules.pdf

The Practice Note makes it clear that defence solicitors must assist a court to conduct cases justly and expeditiously and be aware of the consequences of failing to do so. However, a court cannot, in the exercise of its case management powers, compel a defence solicitor to breach a professional conduct obligation owed to a client. Thus, for example, a court cannot compel a defence solicitor to represent two clients where the solicitor concludes there is a significant risk of conflict between them, even though single representation might be more expeditious. Neither can a court require the defence solicitor to disclose privileged communications with his client (*R (on the application of Kelly) v Warley Magistrates Court (the Law Society intervening)* [2008] 1 Cr App R 14).

KEY POINT SUMMARY

- Understand that all criminal offences are classified as either summary-only, either-way or indictable-only and that the classification enables you to chart the procedural course of the case from the outset.
- Always research the classifications of the offence/s you are dealing with: never guess.
- Know the jurisdiction of the main criminal courts.
- Arguments based on Article 6 ECHR can arise in relation to many aspects of criminal litigation, including procedure and evidence.
- The right to a fair trial in Article 6 comprises many rights, some of which are specifically defined in Article 6, some of which are implied.
- Domestic courts must as far as possible, interpret domestic law in accordance with Convention rights.
- In determining rights under the Convention, regard must be had to the jurisprudence of the European Court of Human Rights.
- Human rights issues and professional conduct are pervasive—they can arise at any time. As a Legal Practice Course student always look for potential human rights arguments and issues of ethical conduct.
- Have a thorough working knowledge of the rules of professional conduct and know the typical instances where professional conduct dilemmas are likely to arise in the context of criminal litigation.
- You may not be asked specifically about a professional conduct point—nevertheless if, in your view, a professional conduct issue arises, deal with it.
- A solicitor is an officer of the court and should always conduct himself appropriately.
- If in doubt about your professional conduct obligations, always ask.

SELF-TEST QUESTIONS

online resource centre

1. We would like you to begin to familiarise yourself with our fictional clients, Lenny Whyte, Roger Martin and William Hardy and the nature of the accusations that have been made against each of them. Documentation pertaining to the first case study can be found in Appendix 1 of your *Handbook*. The complete version of the documentation supporting *R v Lenny Whyte* and the entire documentation supporting *R v Roger Martin* and *R v William Hardy* can be accessed from the student resource section of the Online Resource Centre. Analysis of all self-test questions can be found in Appendix 4.

(a) Case study 1. *R v Lenny Whyte*

Read document 1 (Lenny Whyte's initial statement given to his solicitor) and documents 18(A)–(P) which comprise the nature of the prosecution's evidence against Lenny. What offence is Lenny Whyte charged with having committed? What is the classification of this offence?

(b) Case study 2. *R v Roger Martin*

Read document 1 (Roger Martin's initial statement given to his solicitor) and documents 10 (A)–(F) which comprise the nature of the prosecution's evidence against Roger. What offences is Roger Martin charged with having committed? What is the classification of the offences he faces?

(c) Case study 3. *R v William Hardy*

Read document 1 (William Hardy's initial statement given to his solicitor) and documents 10(A)–(E) which comprise the nature of the prosecution's evidence against William. What offence is William Hardy charged with having committed? What is the classification of the offence William is charged with?

2. How are the following offences classified according to place of trial? (You may have to do some legal research to discover the answer to some of the questions. A good place to start is *Blackstone's Criminal Practice*.)

   (i)   Criminal damage where the value of the damaged property is less than £5,000, s. 1 Criminal Damage Act 1971.

   (ii) Criminal damage where the value of the damaged property is more than £5,000.

   (iii) Possession of a controlled drug, s. 5 Misuse of Drugs Act 1971.

   (iv) Careless driving, s. 3 Road Traffic Act 1988.

   (v)   Burglary, contrary to s. 9 Theft Act 1986.

   (vi) Affray, contrary to s. 3 Public Order Act 1986.

3. Explain what is meant by a summary-only offence.
4. Explain what is meant by an indictable-only offence.
5. In what circumstances would a mode of trial enquiry be held?
6. Identify the overriding objective of the Criminal Procedure Rules.
7. Explain how Convention rights are incorporated into domestic law and how a defence solicitor might make use of such Convention rights.
8. What are the potential consequences of failing to spot and deal with an aspect of the Solicitors' Code of Conduct?

FIGURE 1.1 SUMMARY OFFENCE

FIGURE 1.2 EITHER-WAY OFFENCE

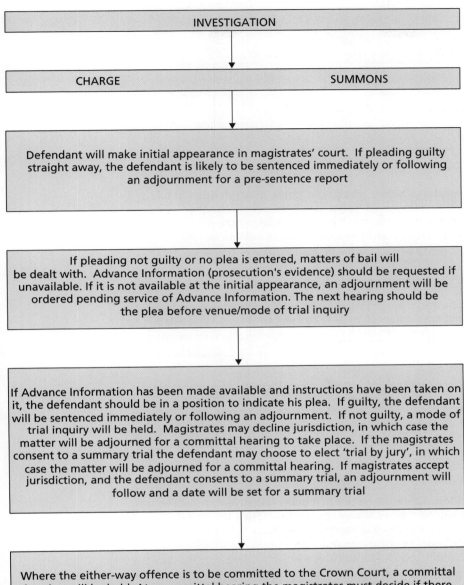

INVESTIGATION

CHARGE   SUMMONS

Defendant will make initial appearance in magistrates' court. If pleading guilty straight away, the defendant is likely to be sentenced immediately or following an adjournment for a pre-sentence report

If pleading not guilty or no plea is entered, matters of bail will be dealt with. Advance Information (prosecution's evidence) should be requested if unavailable. If it is not available at the initial appearance, an adjournment will be ordered pending service of Advance Information. The next hearing should be the plea before venue/mode of trial inquiry

If Advance Information has been made available and instructions have been taken on it, the defendant should be in a position to indicate his plea. If guilty, the defendant will be sentenced immediately or following an adjournment. If not guilty, a mode of trial inquiry will be held. Magistrates may decline jurisdiction, in which case the matter will be adjourned for a committal hearing to take place. If the magistrates consent to a summary trial the defendant may choose to elect 'trial by jury', in which case the matter will be adjourned for a committal hearing. If magistrates accept jurisdiction, and the defendant consents to a summary trial, an adjournment will follow and a date will be set for a summary trial

Where the either-way offence is to be committed to the Crown Court, a committal hearing will be held. At a committal hearing the magistrates must decide if there is a case for the defendant to answer. If there is, the matter will be committed to the Crown Court where a date will be set for a Plea and Case Management Hearing (PCMH)

At the PCMH before the Crown Court, the defendant will enter his plea. If guilty he may be sentenced there and then or following an adjournment. If not guilty an adjournment will follow and a date will be set for a Crown Court trial

FIGURE 1.3 INDICTABLE-ONLY OFFENCE

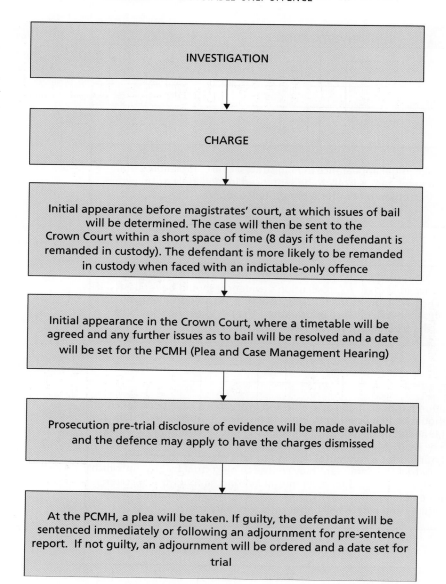

FIGURE 1.4 A FLOW CHART OF CRIMINAL PROCEDURE

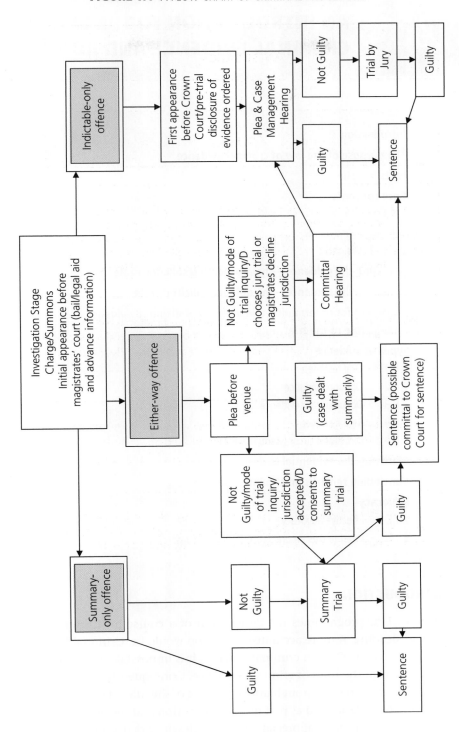

2 | AN INTRODUCTION TO THE LAW OF CRIMINAL EVIDENCE AND ADVOCACY

2.1 INTRODUCTION

On most LPC programmes the designation of a course in 'Criminal Litigation' is potentially misleading. A more accurate description would be 'Criminal Litigation and Evidence' because on the LPC, as in criminal practice, it is impossible to divorce the rules of criminal litigation from the rules of criminal evidence. Consequently every LPC student (and criminal lawyer) requires a thorough understanding of the rules of evidence and the way in which the principles are applied as part of the prosecution and the defence case.

It is also important to appreciate that the rules of evidence are relevant not only when preparing for trial and during the trial but are pervasive and significant throughout the whole case. One of the aims of this book is to try to reflect the integration of the rules of criminal evidence with procedure. For example, the way in which the police gather evidence against an accused during the investigation may have important evidential consequences at trial if the substantive provisions of PACE and the Codes of Practice are not complied with. The legal adviser at the police station needs to understand the rules of evidence in order to evaluate the strength of the evidence the police claim to have and to be able to advise his client accordingly: this might include advising him to exercise his right to remain silent.

Some of you will have encountered the rules of evidence at the academic stage of your studies, and your understanding of the rules is therefore assumed. Your challenge will be to recognise and apply the rules of evidence in the more practical context of the LPC. For those studying evidence for the first time, a steep learning curve is about to be encountered. You must simultaneously learn the rules and be able to recognise and apply them in the particular factual context. This chapter provides an introductory foundation for the main evidential rules which are considered in later chapters. In particular, it addresses the following:

* the purpose of the law of evidence;
* the core concepts of relevance, admissibility and weight;
* the different types of evidence.

Later chapters will explain the rules of evidence in more detail.

2.2 THE PURPOSE OF THE LAW OF CRIMINAL EVIDENCE

The law of evidence is the body of rules which prescribe the ways in which evidence is presented in a criminal trial. The rules regulate how the prosecution proves its case to the court and, in exceptional situations, how the defendant might prove his innocence. The law of evidence also seeks to ensure that the accused receives a fair trial and operates in close conjunction with the right to a fair trial under Article 6 ECHR.

2.3 FACTS IN ISSUE

Where the defendant pleads not guilty, the facts in issue identify what has to be proven by the prosecution for the defendant to be found guilty, or exceptionally what the defendant has to prove in order to establish his innocence. The facts in issue are determined by reference to the *actus reus* and the *mens rea* of the offence with which the defendant is charged. Your knowledge of substantive criminal law is assumed. The burden of proving your client's guilt beyond reasonable doubt rests, for the most part, on the prosecution. You should always research the required elements of the offence/s with which your client is charged so that you know the elements of the offence the prosecution must prove. In a charge of theft under s. 1 Theft Act 1968 the facts in issue are:

Actus reus	*Mens rea*
Appropriates	Dishonestly
Property	Intention to permanently deprive
Belonging to another	

The prosecution has to prove each element of the *actus reus* and the *mens rea* of the offence for the defendant to be found guilty. This is known as discharging the legal burden of proof. The prosecution will discharge the legal burden of proof by putting evidence before the court in support of each fact in issue. This is known as discharging the evidential burden. Legal and evidential burdens of proof are considered in greater detail in Chapter 18.

2.4 CORE CONCEPTS

There are three core concepts relating to evidence. They are relevance, admissibility and weight.

2.4.1 RELEVANCE

For evidence to be put before the court, it must be relevant or probative of a fact in issue. There are no special rules to decide the question of relevance—it is a matter of common sense. For example, on a charge of the theft of a bottle of wine from a supermarket, it is not relevant for the prosecution to put forward evidence that the defendant rode to the supermarket on a bike with defective lights, or that he has recently been divorced. It is relevant, however, for a prosecution witness to tell the court that she saw the accused put a bottle of wine under his coat and walk out of the defendant's supermarket without paying.

The relevance of evidence sometimes arises in the context of the admission of a defendant's past bad character. For example, X is on trial for sexual assault alleged to have been perpetrated on an 11-year-old boy. He denies the offence. How relevant would it be to make it known to the jury or to magistrates that two years ago X pleaded guilty to an offence of downloading indecent images of children from an internet site? Where an argument arises as to the relevance of a particular piece of evidence, the decision whether or not to admit the evidence is ultimately taken by the judge in the Crown Court and by the magistrates or a district judge in the magistrates' court.

2.4.2 ADMISSIBILITY

For the court to receive evidence it not only has to be relevant to a fact in issue but must also be admissible. Admissible evidence means evidence which as a matter of law can be received by the court. Evidence will be admissible unless it is excluded either under a mandatory rule of exclusion or in the exercise of the court's discretion to ensure the defendant enjoys a fair trial. Mandatory rules of exclusion apply to the opinion evidence of a lay witness and include the general rule that hearsay evidence is inadmissible unless the hearsay evidence falls within a recognised common law or statutory exception.

Every defendant enjoys the right to a fair trial. Such a right has many facets. Sometimes the right will require the exclusion of evidence which the prosecution seeks to have admitted. This may be because of the manner in which the evidence has been obtained (this could apply to a confession or identification evidence, or other evidence discovered by the investigating authorities in the exercise of their statutory powers of stop, search and seizure). Evidence may also have to be excluded if its admission would prejudice a fair trial. By prejudice we mean the damaging effect the admission of a particular piece of evidence might have on the minds of the jury or magistrates. Relevance and admissibility are closely entwined. Would a jury or magistrates attach too much significance to a particular piece of evidence to the neglect of other evidence in a case which might raise a reasonable doubt? Consider the prejudice that could be engendered by the admission of the previous conviction for downloading child pornography at the trial of X for sexual assault in the earlier example. The power to exclude evidence is contained in s. 78 PACE 1984 (unfairness) and/or s. 82(3) PACE 1984 (probative value outweighed by prejudicial effect).

Where the admissibility of evidence is disputed, the decision to admit or exclude evidence rests with the judge in the Crown Court and with the magistrates in the magistrates' court. A decision to admit disputed evidence which results in a conviction may provide grounds for an appeal against conviction. Equally, a decision to exclude a particular piece of evidence may have profound implications for the prosecution's ability to discharge its legal burden of proof beyond reasonable doubt.

2.4.3 WEIGHT

Even where a piece of evidence is relevant and admissible, this does not mean that the jury or magistrates will find the evidence convincing or persuasive. For example, a witness may state in court that she only caught a fleeting glimpse in poor light of a person accused of a crime as he ran down the street at night. Unless supported by other independent evidence, the court might attach little weight to this evidence. However, where the witness recognised the defendant as an old acquaintance, and saw the defendant in broad daylight from a short distance, then the court might give considerable weight to the identification. The statistical odds that are attached to modern-day DNA evidence often give such evidence huge probative value in the eyes of the jury or magistrates. The weight to be attached to a particular piece of evidence is a matter for the jury in the Crown Court and magistrates in the magistrates' court. Advocates on either side will wish to make representations about the degree of weight to be attached to particular evidence in the case.

In some instances (particularly in relation to identification evidence), the defendant's right to a fair trial requires the judge (in the Crown Court) to warn the jury about the dangers of relying on certain types of evidence. In other instances (relying on the evidence of certain types of witnesses) the requirement to give a warning lies in the discretion of the judge. Where a conviction results in part from a failure to give an appropriate warning, the defendant may have grounds for an appeal against conviction.

2.5 ASSESSING THE EVIDENCE—THE PROSECUTING SOLICITOR'S ROLE

In deciding whether a prosecution should be pursued, the Code for Crown Prosecutors requires the CPS lawyer to determine whether there is sufficient evidence to secure a conviction. In making this assessment, the CPS lawyer will be mindful of the rules of evidence. The CPS lawyer has no active investigative role and therefore must assess the evidence gathered by the police. This will include consideration of witness statements and items of real evidence which may have been subject to forensic analysis. Currently, the CPS lawyer has no direct access to witnesses. Based on the assessment of the evidence, the CPS lawyer might suggest to the police that further investigation is needed.

2.6 ASSESSING THE EVIDENCE—THE DEFENCE SOLICITOR'S ROLE

Irrespective of whether your client is to be tried summarily or on indictment, the rules relating to pre-trial disclosure of evidence mean the defence solicitor will know the nature of the evidence against his client before trial. In assessing the strength of evidence as disclosed by the prosecution witness statements and other material, you need to have in mind the core concepts of relevance, admissibility and weight of evidence. There is one important advantage to a defendant pleading guilty at an early stage in the proceedings, in that he is entitled to a sentencing discount of up to one third. Where a defendant pleads guilty, the evidence against him is never tested in open court. A defence solicitor should not of course advise his client to plead guilty unless the evidence against him is particularly strong and admissible.

2.7 PROCEDURE FOR DETERMINING ADMISSIBILITY OF DISPUTED EVIDENCE AND THE ROLE OF THE TRIAL JUDGE

The primary role of the trial judge is to ensure the defendant enjoys a fair trial. On occasions this will require the judge to exclude evidence from the jury's consideration. In the Crown Court, a strict separation of function exists between judge and jury. The judge determines all issues of law (including disputed evidence) in the absence of the jury. The jury determines issues of fact. In the magistrates' court, the magistrates are the ultimate arbiters of both fact and law. Legal advice on the law is provided by the magistrates' legal adviser. A *voir dire* (or trial within a trial) may be held to resolve a dispute about the admissibility of evidence. Such a procedure would involve the judge/magistrates hearing evidence about the manner in which the disputed evidence was obtained before applying the law and either excluding or admitting the evidence. The *voir dire* procedure works more effectively in the Crown Court given the separation of function between judge and jury. If, after hearing evidence and argument, the trial judge decides that the disputed evidence must be excluded, the jury will be immune from the knowledge that it ever existed. A further and very important function of the trial judge is to sum up the evidence for the jury at the conclusion of the trial and to direct the jury in accordance with the law. Judges are greatly assisted in this respect by the Judicial Studies Board specimen directions (www.jsboard.co.uk) which contain precedents on directing a jury on all aspects of criminal law and evidence.

2.8 TYPES OF EVIDENCE

Where evidence is relevant and admissible, it will be presented to the court in one of the following forms.

2.8.1 ORAL TESTIMONY

This is the evidence of a witness given orally in court and presented by the party calling the witness on factual matters within the witness's personal knowledge and experience. An example of a witness giving factual evidence would include the witness stating that: 'I saw the defendant break the car window and drive the car away at speed.' In the criminal trial, direct oral testimony is the preferred way for evidence to be put before the court and is likely to be the type of evidence that the court will find the most persuasive.

2.8.2 OPINION EVIDENCE

A witness is called at a trial to give evidence of fact based on the witness's personal knowledge and experience. The witness is not called to the witness box to offer an opinion on what he or she saw or heard. The general rule is that where a witness gives opinion evidence, it will be inadmissible. It would not be possible for a witness to state: 'It's obvious that the defendant killed him.'

There are two exceptions to this general rule:

1. An expert may give opinion evidence on a matter that goes beyond the ordinary competence of the court. In criminal cases it is very common for the prosecution to rely on the evidence of a forensic scientist. Expert evidence is considered in more detail in Chapter 21.

2. A lay person may state his opinion on a matter not requiring expertise as a way of conveying facts that he has personally perceived. A witness will be allowed to say that when she saw the accused 'he appeared to be drunk', or 'the car was speeding immediately before the car hit the pedestrian'.

2.8.3 DOCUMENTARY EVIDENCE

Relevant and admissible evidence may be contained in a document. A witness statement is an example of documentary evidence. Other types of documentary evidence include:

• photographs;
• maps;
• plans;
• computer print-outs;

- business documents;
- expert report.

2.8.4 REAL EVIDENCE

Real evidence comprises objects produced in court so the court may draw inferences from the condition and existence of the object. In a murder trial, a knife produced as the murder weapon, or the defendant's bloodstained clothing, would be examples of real evidence. In a public order offence, CCTV footage of the incident would constitute real evidence.

2.8.5 DIRECT AND CIRCUMSTANTIAL EVIDENCE

In whatever form evidence is admitted, it will have either direct or circumstantial relevance. Direct evidence requires nothing more of the jury or magistrates than an acceptance or rejection of the evidence that has been given. If X testifies that he saw Y walk up to Z, take out a knife and stab Z, this is direct evidence of the *actus reus* of murder. At his trial for murder, however, Y calls a witness who states she was with Y at the time of the alleged murder some 30 miles away. If accepted, this constitutes direct evidence of alibi. Circumstantial evidence requires the court not only to accept the witness's account but to draw an inference from the evidence. If X testifies that he saw Y running away from Z and that he observed Y had bloodstains on his clothing, this would constitute circumstantial evidence linking Y to the murder of Z. Expert forensic evidence may suggest that the blood on Y's clothing matches that of the victim Z. Again, if the evidence is accepted by the court, it provides circumstantial evidence that Y was in close contact with the victim of the crime at the relevant time. A criminal case may be based entirely on circumstantial evidence. The trial of Ian Huntley (2003) for the murders of Holly Wells and Jessica Chapman and the trial of Steve Wright (2008) for the murders of five prostitutes in Ipswich are examples of two high profile convictions based on circumstantial evidence.

2.9 CLARIFYING THE EVIDENTIAL ISSUES

In any contested criminal case there is bound to be a multiplicity of evidential issues. It is important, however, not to lose sight of the 'big picture'. Advocates need to make sense of the evidence and to develop a theory of the case which is supported by the evidence. In this way a coherent and focused case can be put before the jury or magistrates. The core issues in a case need to be distilled from the mass of detail and if the case is to be contested, a defence theory needs to be developed.

The defence theory is a clear and concise explanation of why the case should be resolved in the defendant's favour. In devising a plausible defence theory, the evidence that needs to be challenged and marshalled will become clear. On a charge of theft, for example, it may be that the defendant denies a dishonest intent. If this is the case, you should be marshalling your evidence and argument with this central issue in mind. Perhaps the defendant will challenge the prosecution's suggestion that he was responsible for the crime, on the basis that the case is one of mistaken identification. If this is the defence theory of the case, you should be concentrating on challenging the prosecution's evidence of identification and presenting any evidence which tends to support the theory advanced by the defendant such as evidence of alibi. The development of a defence theory will determine the nature of your cross-examination of each witness. This is why it is important to crystallise the facts in issue.

2.10 CONCLUDING REMARKS ON CRIMINAL EVIDENCE

This chapter has introduced you to some of the core concepts that apply in the context of criminal evidence. Later chapters will examine the evidential considerations that arise in the context of:

- a confession being made to the police;
- obtaining and relying on eye-witness identification;
- a defendant exercising his right to silence at the police station who subsequently advances a defence at trial;
- applying to admit hearsay evidence;
- applying to admit evidence of a defendant's bad character;
- applying to admit opinion evidence;
- reliance upon the uncorroborated evidence of a witness with a purpose of his own to serve in giving false evidence;
- the evidence of a child or mentally handicapped witness;
- prosecution evidence that has been obtained in a dubious or unlawful manner;
- the desire of the prosecution to withhold certain evidence from the defence.

The rules are significant at all stages of a criminal case and a good understanding of the law and the ability to apply the principles in a practical way to the facts of the case is important for the successful criminal litigation student. The rules of criminal evidence cannot be ignored—so in a determined and purposeful way, after carefully reading this introductory chapter, move on to the other chapters which deal with evidential rules in practice.

2.11 ADVOCACY

Advocacy is the legal skill most often associated with criminal litigation. Put simply, advocacy is the art of communication. Having come this far you will hopefully have begun to develop your oral communication skills and an ability to put forward structured and coherent arguments. Those skills now need to be harnessed and applied in a different context.

The most readily identifiable areas where a criminal advocate's oral presentation skills come to the fore are at contested bail hearings, pleas in mitigation of sentence and, of course, in conducting trials. It will be some time before you undertake any of these independently, although trainee solicitors do have rights of audience before Crown Court judges in chambers and may therefore represent a defendant on a bail application following a magistrates' court refusal to grant bail. In this short section on advocacy we identify some of the key components of the art of persuasion.

2.11.1 EFFECTIVE ADVOCACY

Effective advocacy depends on:

- good preparation; and
- persuasive oral communication skills.

Good preparation presupposes a thorough knowledge of both the facts in the case and the relevant law. For example, when making a bail application, you would be expected to have a good working knowledge of the Bail Act 1976 and to apply the facts of your client's case to the law. The submission of a plea in mitigation presupposes a thorough knowledge of sentencing principles and practice.

Similarly, if you were to make an application to have evidence excluded at trial, your preparation would have alerted you to the relevant legal basis of your submission and the facts that you would need to prove in order to substantiate your submission.

Whilst knowledge and understanding of the relevant law and facts are important, you must also be able to present your legal argument in a structured, coherent and persuasive way.

11.2 WHAT MAKES AN ORAL PRESENTATION PERSUASIVE?

The following checklist is based on our experience of developing and assessing advocacy skills on the LPC. Whatever the context of your presentation, awareness of what may be termed 'credibility factors' may help.

Eye contact

Eye contact greatly enhances an oral presentation. It shows you are confident enough to move away from a prepared script and enables you to assess and gauge the reaction your submission is having on your listener. If you want to get your message across you must engage your listener. Maintaining eye contact is an obvious way of helping to achieve this.

Posture

Do not slouch. Stand up straight with your head slightly elevated. Posture affects the resonance of your voice. Your posture should make you appear relaxed and confident.

Voice

Accents are not a problem, providing you are clear in your enunciation of words. The acoustics vary from courtroom to courtroom so you may need to explore your voice audibility levels. Avoid being too loud and aggressive, or too softly spoken. The latter does not inspire confidence. Deep breathing (from the diaphragm) can help your voice to resonate more, thereby making you more audible. If you think you have a monotone delivery, try to get some vocal variety into your voice. Try reading a children's story to a young relative: you will soon find out ways to make your delivery more interesting.

Pace

It is very important to correctly pace your submission. True advocacy is not about reading from a prepared script, as this will make it more likely that you will read too quickly and consequently your audience will be unable to follow your argument. Too slow a delivery can have a stultifying effect upon your audience. Experiment, and choose a pace that is suitable.

Pause

The pause is a simple but very effective persuasive device. Use it for dramatic effect. If you have a particularly telling point to advance, make the point and then . . . pause momentarily. Allow the point to be considered by your listener. Used in combination with voice inflection, the effect should resonate with your audience.

Distracting mannerisms

We all have them. You will be the best judge of what distracting mannerisms you have. If you have the opportunity, why not record yourself making an oral submission? When you review your performance, ask yourself: does my body language detract from the message I am putting across? Are you fiddling with the loose change in your pocket or juggling a pen in your hands? Do you sway from side to side? Are you constantly touching your face or your hair? Look at the expression on your face. Is it the face of someone who feels relaxed and confident in the submission they are making? Do you look up and smile occasionally or are you frowning/perplexed/refusing to make eye contact? All of these mannerisms distract from the message you are trying to put across.

Structure

A persuasive argument will be delivered in a structured fashion. Devising a structure should help you to avoid unnecessary repetition. The simplest and most effective structure for any submission is for it to have a beginning, middle and end. Break up your submission into listener-friendly portions, e.g.:

> 'Ma'am, I have three points I would like to make this morning: My first point is this ....
> my second point is this .... my third and final points is this. .... In summary,
> Ma'am................'

Sometimes the nature of your submission will determine its structure. When devising and delivering a submission on bail, for example, the Bail Act 1976 provides a logical structure within which to work.

Keep your submission concise. Cut down on the verbiage. Try to avoid reading out sections from statute and case law. Copy and highlight the relevant sections/passages and then hand them in for the bench/judge to read.

Brevity

You will soon come to realise that a court's time is very precious. With this in mind, always try to make your submission succinct. Developing a logical structure to your submission will assist. Try to avoid unnecessary repetition.

Persona

It is important when appearing as an advocate that you should look confident—even if you do not feel confident. Dressing suitably and smartly helps an advocate to step into the role. It also helps to inspire confidence in you and conveys the correct impression to the court and your client. First impressions really do count. Without being dramatic, your opening address needs to capture the attention of the court. What sort of individual engages you? The more open and the more interesting the personality is, the more likely the audience will listen. Behavioural psychology has much to teach the aspiring advocate!

Be prepared to make appropriate concessions. Avoid being arrogant or patronising. Organise yourself and your notes so that your composure and professionalism comes across.

Etiquette

You must familiarise yourself with the etiquette of the court you are appearing before. This includes knowing how to dress appropriately and the correct way to address other members of the court.

As a trainee solicitor you will not have a right of audience before a magistrates' court or indeed the Crown Court. You do however enjoy a right of audience before a Crown Court judge in chambers, for the purposes of making an application for bail as this is a closed hearing.

Solicitors have a right of audience before a magistrates' court and have a limited right of audience before the Crown Court on an appeal against conviction and/or sentence where the solicitor represented the defendant in the magistrates' court. Some solicitors have a Higher Right of Audience qualification which enables them to exercise full rights of audience before the Crown Court. When appearing as a solicitor-advocate before a Crown Court, a solicitor must appear duly robed (black stuffed gown and winged collar).

The correct form of address before a judge of the Crown Court (which would include a circuit judge or recorder) is 'Your Honour . . .' You should always defer to the court and be extremely courteous. With this in mind you will often hear the phrase: 'May it please Your Honour, I appear on behalf of the defendant in this matter.' 'Has Your Honour had the time to consider the pre-sentence report that has been prepared in connection with this matter? I am grateful for that indication.'

The correct form of address before a district or deputy district judge sitting in a magistrates' court is Sir or Madam.

When addressing a Bench of lay magistrates, the correct term of address is 'Your worships, or Sir/Madam and your colleagues . . . '.

Solicitors refer to a fellow solicitor as 'my friend for the prosecution' or 'my friend for the defence'. A barrister or counsel is referred to as being 'my learned friend'. It is customary to refer to the court's legal adviser as 'your learned legal adviser . . .'.

As an officer of the court, a solicitor should always be appropriately attired when appearing before a court. Where this does not require the solicitor to be duly robed, suitable attire will normally be a sombre-coloured suit.

Language

Persuasion is as much about your choice of language as anything else. Words can be very powerful tools with which to convey a message. Think carefully about your choice of words. Can you find a more powerful adjective to advance the point you are making? Try to use language which includes your audience. For example, you might say: 'Let's examine together the circumstances in which the defendant's confession was obtained. . . .' Personalise the situation: 'Ma'am, I invite you to consider what you would have done in the same situation as my client. . . .'

Some individuals are natural advocates. They have charm and exude confidence. If they combine their natural ability with knowledge and application of the law, they are capable of making a persuasive submission even in the most hopeless of cases. Other individuals might initially be less comfortable in the spotlight which the art of advocacy demands. Advocacy skills can be developed with practice and reflection.

If you are accessing our Online Resource Centre you will be able to see some examples of advocacy in our filmed case studies. *R v Lenny Whyte* contains a fully contested application for bail. *R v Hardy* and *R v Martin* both comprise pleas in mitigation. The specifics of each of these submissions are considered in the chapter on bail and the chapters on sentencing.

 online resource centre

KEY POINT SUMMARY

- For the most part the prosecution bears the legal burden of proving a defendant's guilt beyond reasonable doubt. The elements of the offence charged determine what the prosecution needs to prove if it is to secure a conviction.

- To be admissible, evidence must be relevant to the facts in issue but not all relevant evidence is admissible.

- Evidence can be excluded by the application of mandatory rules and through the exercise of judicial discretion in the interests of ensuring a fair trial.

- In the Crown Court, matters of relevance and admissibility of evidence are determined by the judge in the absence of the jury. Matters of fact are determined by the jury. There is no separation of function in the magistrates' court and so magistrates determine matters of fact and law.

- An accused person is entitled to pre-trial disclosure of the evidence to be used against him enabling his advocate to evaluate the strengths and weaknesses of the case against him.

- Where an accused person chooses to plead guilty, the evidence against him is not tested in open court.

SELF-TEST QUESTIONS

Case study 1: *R v Lenny Whyte*

Consider documents 1 and 18 (A)–(P) in Appendix 1. Given that we have yet to cover the rules of criminal evidence in detail, simply list the nature of the evidence that is said to link Lenny Whyte to the burglary allegation. In doing so, can you identify any issues of evidence this scenario is likely to give rise to? In simplistic terms at this stage, consider how Lenny will challenge the nature of the evidence against him and in doing so, start to formulate a theory of the defence case.

FIGURE 2.1 AN OVERVIEW OF CRIMINAL EVIDENCE

PURPOSES OF THE LAW OF EVIDENCE

- The law of evidence regulates how the prosecution or the defence proves its case to the court.

- The rules determine what evidence may be received and what evidential use can be made of that evidence, and in so doing they seek to ensure the defendant receives a fair trial.

- In the Crown Court, the judge determines the admissibility of disputed evidence in the absence of the jury.

- In a summary trial, issues relating to the admissibility of disputed evidence are resolved by the magistrates with legal advice provided by their legal adviser.

FACTS IN ISSUE

- The facts in issue are the *actus reus* and the *mens rea* of the offence charged.

- It is for the prosecution (or exceptionally the defence) to prove the facts that are in issue at a trial.

- The facts in issue can also include secondary facts which are relevant to the facts in issue such as the admissibility of a piece of evidence.

BASIC EVIDENTIAL RULES

- To be heard at trial, evidence must be:
- **relevant** to a fact in issue; and be
- **admissible** (i.e. as a matter of law, the evidence can be put before the court).
- The **weight** to be afforded to a particular piece of evidence is a question of fact for the jury/magistrates.

TYPES OF ADMISSIBLE EVIDENCE

- Relevant and admissible evidence will be presented at trial as one of the following types:
- oral testimony;
- documentary evidence;
- real evidence.

Part II

INVESTIGATION
AND CHARGE

Part II examines the process of investigation of criminal offences and the decision to charge.

In this Part we consider the general and specific powers of the police to investigate criminal offences (Chapter 3) and the process of detention and questioning (Chapter 4).

We also consider rules of evidence relating to a decision by a suspect to remain silent (Chapter 5) and the rules of evidence relating to unlawfully obtained evidence (Chapter 6), the admissibility of confession evidence (Chapter 7) and the admissibility of evidence of identification (Chapter 8).

Chapter 9 seeks to bring Part II together by considering the practical steps legal advisers might take at the police station. Finally, the decision to charge a suspect or to offer an alternative course is considered in Chapter 10, which also looks at the role of the Crown Prosecution Service (CPS).

3

THE POWERS TO STOP, SEARCH AND ARREST

3.1 INTRODUCTION

The police have extensive statutory powers to stop and search and to arrest a person in connection with the investigation of a criminal offence. Under the Police and Criminal Evidence Act 1984 (PACE), the power to stop and search and arrest are general powers, which can be used in a wide range of situations. The police may also use a vast array of specific powers to stop, search and arrest granted to them under various statutes, including the Terrorism Act 2000, the Misuse of Drugs Act 1971 and the Serious Organised Crime and Police Act 2005.

In this chapter we examine:

• the common law and statutory powers of stop and search before arrest;

• the statutory power of arrest under PACE 1984;

• the statutory powers to search a person and his property after arrest;

• the power to grant street bail; and

• the pervasive influence of the European Convention on Human Rights 1950 and the right to liberty under Article 5.

online resource centre

Reference will be made throughout this chapter to Code A issued under PACE 1984. Code A can be freely accessed online from the Home Office. Our Online Resource Centre includes a link taking you to the PACE Codes of Practice. You are alerted to the fact that the Codes of Practice are currently subject to an extensive and wide-ranging review and are expected to be revised at some future date.

3.2 STOP AND SEARCH BEFORE ARREST

The primary purpose of stop and search is to enable an officer to allay or confirm his suspicion about a person being in possession of stolen or prohibited articles or drugs without arresting him. Stop and search has long been one of the most controversial aspects of police powers and consequently the law provides detailed guidance as to what action the officer may take when questioning or searching a person in the street before arrest.

3.3 STOP AND SEARCH AT COMMON LAW

At common law, an officer does not have the right to stop or detain a person unless the person freely volunteers to co-operate with the officer (*Rice v Connelly* [1966] 2 All ER 64). Code A, Notes for Guidance, para. 1, recognises that an officer may speak to a member of the public in the normal course of his duties without detaining the person or exercising any compulsion over him. The person being questioned has a civic but not a legal duty to assist the officer to prevent crime and to discover offenders.

In the absence of the officer exercising a statutory power to stop and search or arrest, the person cannot be compelled to remain with the officer.

3.4 STATUTORY POWERS TO STOP AND SEARCH IN THE STREET BEFORE ARREST

The police have wide statutory powers to stop and search a suspect's person and/or his motor vehicle. Code A, para. 1.5 stipulates that an officer may only stop and search a person in the lawful exercise of a statutory power to do so even where the person consents to being stopped and searched.

Statutory stop and search can be exercised either under a general or a specific legal power.

3.4.1 THE GENERAL POWER TO STOP AND SEARCH—S. 1 PACE 1984

Section 1 PACE 1984 (as supplemented by Code A) gives the police the general power to stop and search a person before arrest in a public place or a place to which the public have access, where the officer has reasonable grounds for suspecting the person is in possession of stolen or prohibited articles. The power of search under s. 1 PACE 1984 extends to a vehicle.

Paragraph 1.1 Code A, requires that stop and search must be used 'fairly, responsibly, with respect for those being searched and without unlawful discrimination'.

To be a lawful stop and search under s. 1 PACE 1984, the following factors must be present:

(1) The stop and search must be in connection with stolen or prohibited articles
Stop and search under s. 1 PACE 1984 may be exercised in respect to:

- stolen articles; or
- prohibited articles; or
- an article relevant to the commission of an offence under s. 139 Criminal Justice Act 1988 (possession of a bladed instrument); or
- a prohibited firework.

What are stolen articles?
'Stolen' articles are given the same meaning as in the Theft Act 1968 and include items arising out of the offence of theft, burglary, robbery or criminal deception.
What are prohibited articles?
'Prohibited' articles include offensive weapons or articles made or adapted for use or intended use in an offence under the Theft Act 1968 and under s. 1 Criminal Damage Act 1971. The Theft Act 1968 offences include theft (s. 1), burglary (s. 9), taking a motor vehicle without consent (s. 12) or obtaining property by deception (s. 15) and will cover diverse items such as a crow-bar, car keys, a credit card or any relevant item provided the user has the necessary intent to commit an offence under the 1968 Act.

An offensive weapon is based on a definition similar to that under s. 1 Prevention of Crime Act 1953 as an article made or adapted for use for causing injury to a person or intended for such use. It includes articles that are offensive weapons in themselves such as knives and guns and everyday articles that have been made or adapted for use as an offensive weapon including, for example, a bottle that has been deliberately broken to give it a jagged edge or the end of a screwdriver sharpened to a point.

(2) The requirement for reasonable suspicion
Under s. 1 PACE 1984, reasonable suspicion will be present where:

- the officer has actual suspicion that the person is in possession of stolen or prohibited articles (the subjective test); and
- there are reasonable grounds for that suspicion (the objective test).

Detailed guidance on the meaning of reasonable suspicion is found in Code A, paras. 2.2–2.11. Code A stipulates that:

- reasonable suspicion will be determined on the facts of each case, including the time and the place the power was exercised and the suspect's behaviour, for example, where the suspect is seen by the officer on the street late at night and appears to be hiding something;
- reasonable suspicion can never be determined on the basis of the suspect's personal factors alone such as his race, ethnic background, religion, appearance or that the suspect is known to have previous convictions;
- reasonable suspicion should normally be based on good, reliable and recent police intelligence.

For judicial guidance on the reasonable suspicion test, see *O'Hara v Chief Constable, RUC* [1997] AC 286, at para. 3.7.6 below.

(3) Where can the stop and search take place?
The officer may only stop and search in a 'public place or a place to which the public has access', s. 1(1) PACE 1984. This wide definition includes the street or in a park or in a cinema,

which is a place to which the public has access. The power cannot generally be exercised in the suspect's home or in any other dwelling without the occupier's consent.

While the police do not enjoy a general right to search in a person's house under s. 1 PACE 1984, the power may be exercised in a garden or yard attached to a house where the officer reasonably believes that the suspect does not live at that address and is not on the land with the express or implied permission of the occupier.

(4) Additional rights under s. 1 PACE 1984 and Code A:

- The suspect is entitled to a written record of the officer's reasons for the stop and search, Code A, para. 3.10; recording requirements are detailed in para. 4. Recording requirements are likely to be substantially reduced in the future as the government seeks to minimise 'red tape' associated with operational policing.
- The officer must tell the suspect his name and police station, the purpose of the search and the reason for it.
- Section 1 PACE 1984 not only applies to stopping a suspect on foot but also covers an officer stopping a suspect's vehicle in order to check on who is travelling in the vehicle.
- The search must be conducted at or near the place where the suspect was first detained.
- Generally, only the suspect's outer clothing should be searched—where the search requires the removal of more than the outer clothing it should be conducted in private.

Consider the following example of a search conducted under s. 1 PACE 1984.

PC Atherton is on night patrol when he sees Danny walking through the town centre carrying a tool bag. There have been several burglaries in the locality in recent months. When the officer stops and questions Danny, he is exercising his powers under s. 1 PACE 1984. He will be acting lawfully if the following conditions are present:

- Danny has been stopped in a public place or a place to which the public has access;
- the officer had reasonable suspicion based on the recognised tests;
- the purpose of the stop and search was to discover whether Danny was in possession of stolen or prohibited articles or articles to be used in connection with an offence of criminal damage;
- the procedural requirements of Code A were complied with.

3.5 SPECIFIC POWERS TO STOP AND SEARCH BEFORE ARREST

There are additional stop and search powers available to the police to use in specific situations granted under various statutes. A summary of the main stop and search powers are contained in Annex A of Code A and include the power to search for drugs (Misuse of Drugs Act 1971).

3.6 THE CONSEQUENCES OF AN UNLAWFUL STOP AND SEARCH

If a suspect has been unlawfully stopped and searched, where, for example, the police officer cannot prove the 'reasonable suspicion test', the admissibility of any resulting evidence may be challenged at trial by the defence under s. 78 PACE 1984 on the basis that the admission of the evidence would have 'an adverse effect on the fairness of the proceedings'. This provision is considered more fully in Chapter 6. It might also afford a defence to a person accused of obstructing/resisting or assaulting a police constable in the execution of his duty. In *R v Bristol* [2007] EWCA Crim 3214, B's conviction for obstructing a police constable in the exercise of his duty was quashed as the officer, who was exercising a power to stop and search under the Misuse of Drugs Act 1971, had failed to give his name and police station when applying force to B's jaw in an attempt to get him to spit out a suspected ingestion of drugs. As a public body, the actions of the police are subject to potential judicial review.

3.7   POWERS OF ARREST

An arrest will occur during a criminal investigation where the police have the legal and factual grounds to justify depriving the suspect of his liberty. The usual reason for arresting a suspect is to question him about his possible involvement in or knowledge of a criminal offence.

3.7.1   WHAT IS AN ARREST?

While there is no legal definition of 'arrest', in *Christie v Leachinsky* [1947] AC 573, it was suggested that an arrest was 'the beginning of imprisonment'. On a factual basis, a person will be under arrest where he is deprived of his liberty, usually, though not exclusively, by physical restraint, so that he is not free to go where he pleases.

Common law and statutory powers of arrest exist in the following situations:

- at common law an officer can arrest the suspect for a breach of the peace;
- the execution of an arrest warrant obtained from a magistrate, s. 1 Magistrates' Courts Act 1980;
- arrest without a warrant by a police constable in connection with a criminal offence where the legal grounds under s. 24(1), (2) or (3) and s. 24(4) PACE 1984 apply;
- arrest without a warrant by a citizen in connection with an indictable offence where the legal grounds under s. 24A PACE 1984 apply;
- preserved powers of arrest continue to apply to a limited range of offences listed in Sch. 2 PACE 1984.

3.7.2   ARREST AT COMMON LAW

The common law power of arrest applies in connection with an anticipated or an actual breach of the peace. The arrest may be made by a police officer or a member of the public.

3.7.3   ARREST WITH A WARRANT—S. 1 MAGISTRATES' COURTS ACT 1980

Arrest under an arrest warrant is now a less common method of detaining a suspect. Section 1 Magistrates' Courts Act 1980 states that a justice of the peace may issue a warrant for arrest provided that:

- the accused has attained the age of 17;
- the offence alleged is indictable or punishable with imprisonment; or
- the suspect's address cannot be sufficiently established for the service of a summons.

3.7.4   STATUTORY POWER OF ARREST—S. 24 PACE 1984 AS AMENDED BY SOCPA 2005

Important changes to the power of arrest were made by ss. 110–111 of the Serious Organised Crime and Police Act (SOCPA) 2005 which took effect on 1 January 2006. The changes were supplemented with a new Code G which covers the 'new' statutory power of arrest. Code G can be accessed via the web-links section of our Online Resource Centre. There is now a single, generic power of arrest for all offences contained in s. 24 PACE 1984, as amended.

online
resource
centre

3.7.5   **ARREST WITHOUT A WARRANT BY A CONSTABLE**

The main power of arrest without a warrant under s. 24(1)–(3) PACE 1984 is exercisable by a police officer in connection with any criminal offence on the following grounds:

'24 (1) A constable may arrest without a warrant—

(a) anyone who is about to commit an offence; or

(b) anyone who is in the act of committing an offence; or

(c) anyone whom he has reasonable grounds for suspecting to be about to commit an offence; or

(d) anyone whom he has reasonable grounds for suspecting to be committing an offence.

(2) If a constable has reasonable grounds for suspecting that an offence has been committed, he may arrest without a warrant anyone whom he has reasonable grounds to suspect being guilty of it.

(3) If an offence has been committed a constable may arrest without a warrant—

(a) anyone who is guilty of the offence;

(b) anyone whom he has reasonable grounds for suspecting to be guilty of it.'

For the arrest to be lawful not only must one of the grounds in s. 24 (1)–(3) PACE 1984 be made out, the officer must additionally prove that he had reasonable grounds for believing that an arrest was *necessary* (s. 24(4)) for one or more of the reasons listed in s 24(5) PACE 1984.

The reasons include (s. 24(5) PACE 1984):

(a) to enable the person's name to be ascertained where the constable does not know and cannot readily ascertain the person's name or has reasonable grounds for doubting the name given by the person is his real name;

(b) to enable the person's address to be ascertained;

(c) to prevent the person in question:

(i) causing physical injury to himself or another;

(ii) suffering physical injury;

(iii) causing loss or damage to property;

(iv) committing an offence against public decency;

(v) causing unlawful obstruction of the highway;

(d) to protect a child or vulnerable person from the person; or

(e) to allow the prompt and effective investigation of the offence or, of the conduct of the person;

(f) to prevent the prosecution for the offence being hindered by the disappearance of the person in question.

The Government has suggested that the revised legal framework provides a 'straightforward, universal framework' that relates to all offences. Whilst the amended s. 24 PACE 1984 has simplified the law on arrest, defence lawyers have expressed concerns about the practical application of s. 24. First, the revised provisions have radically extended the range of offences for which arrest without a warrant is permitted without any reference to the nature or seriousness of the offence in question. Having said this, operational discretion is given to individual police officers to determine whether an arrest is necessary. Paragraph 2.6 Code G provides:

'Extending the power of arrest to all offences provides a constable with the ability to use that power to deal with any situation. However, applying the necessity criteria requires the constable to examine and justify the reason or reasons why a person needs to be taken to the police station for the custody officer to decide whether the person should be placed in police detention.'

Relevant circumstances will include such factors as the situation of the victim; the nature of the offence; the circumstances of the offender and the needs of the investigation (Code G 2.8). Instead of arresting an individual, a police officer could decide to report the person for summons, grant street bail (see below) or issue a fixed penalty notice.

A further concern is that a number of ancillary powers for example, searching the suspect's house, are exercised over a broader range of offences. Finally, there has been criticism of the very broad terms in which the 'necessity' grounds under s. 24(5) PACE 1984 are drafted. The test to decide whether the officer acted lawfully will include whether he had reasonable grounds for believing that one of the criterion in s. 24(5) applied at the time the arrest was made. Some of those grounds, especially where an arrest is necessary 'to allow the prompt and effective investigation of the offence', are almost unchallengeable from a defence perspective and therefore reduces further the opportunity for the defence to effectively challenge this aspect of the police investigation.

 Example

The application of the single power of arrest under s. 24 PACE has yet to be tested on appeal. Consider the following scenario. Do you feel PC Taylor's arrest was justified?

Miles is 26 but looks considerably younger. He drives an expensive sports car. On the 5 November at 1830 hours, his car is pulled over by road traffic police who pull up alongside him. Miles asks the police officer why he has been pulled over. The officer, PC Taylor, informs him that he wishes to check whether Miles is insured to drive such a powerful car. Miles assures PC Taylor that he is insured and that he does not wish to be delayed any further. Miles waits whilst the officer conducts a mobile check on his insurance details. The officer confirms there is no problem with the insurance. PC Taylor then asks Miles to get out of the car. When Miles asks why, PC Taylor replies that his colleague says he saw Miles using his mobile telephone whilst driving. Miles is incredulous and offers to show PC Taylor that his mobile telephone is in his jacket which is in the boot of his car. Miles informs PC Taylor that he is not prepared to be detained any longer and asks for PC Taylor's collar number. At this point, PC Taylor informs Miles that he is under arrest for driving whilst using a mobile telephone contrary to Road Traffic Act 1988. In reply to being cautioned, Miles is recorded as having said: 'I have nothing to say. This has to be some kind of wind-up right?' Miles is granted police bail to attend the police station in seven days time.

The arrest by PC Taylor is questionable on two grounds. The evidence suggests that Miles was pulled over because there were doubts about whether he was an insured driver. It is only when this is resolved in Miles's favour that it is suggested that Miles was driving whilst using a mobile telephone. This is denied by Miles. No attempt was made by PC Taylor to ascertain whether Miles was telling the truth about his mobile telephone being in his jacket pocket in the boot of his car. In the circumstances it is difficult to see how PC Taylor could have had reasonable grounds for suspecting that Miles has committed an offence. Even if PC Taylor had reasonable grounds, in what sense could PC Taylor form the view that it was necessary to arrest Miles having regard to the offence and the needs of the investigation (Code G, 2.8)? PC Taylor had Miles's name and address and, in the light of Miles's comments, upon being cautioned, there was no necessity to obtain evidence by questioning. Having regard to Code G and para. 1.3, in particular, the actions of the police on this occasion appear to be wholly disproportionate. Miles might seek a judicial review of the actions of the police in this situation.

3.7.6   **THE REQUIREMENTS OF A LAWFUL ARREST UNDER S. 24 PACE 1984**

In order to justify an arrest, a constable must have 'reasonable grounds' for suspecting that a person has committed or is committing or is about to commit a criminal offence and have reasonable grounds for believing that any one of the arrest conditions in s. 24(5) is made out.

While the test of 'reasonable grounds' for suspicion is not defined, it implies both an objective and a subjective element. The subjective element will be satisfied where on the facts known to the officer and in the circumstances existing at the time of the arrest, the officer actually believed the suspect was at some stage of committing an offence or had committed an offence and objectively, the reasonable person would also have formed the necessary reasonable grounds for suspicion.

In *O'Hara v Chief Constable, RUC* [1997] AC 286, the House of Lords confirmed that the test was in two parts:

- first, there must be actual suspicion on the part of the officer (or member of the public) that an offence was at some stage of commission; and
- second, there must be reasonable grounds for that suspicion.

The House of Lords decision in *O'Hara* was cited with approval by the European Court of Human Rights in *O'Hara v United Kingdom* [2002] 34 EHHR 32.

A lawful arrest also requires the application of s. 28 PACE 1984. On arrest the suspect must be told at the time or as soon as practical thereafter:

- the identity of the arresting officer(s);
- the police station at which the officer(s) is based;
- the fact that the suspect is under arrest;
- the grounds for the arrest; and
- the suspect must be cautioned.

What the suspect should be told on arrest is articulated in G para. 2.2 and in Note 3 of Code G and requires that on arrest, a person must be cautioned (see Code G paras. 3.1–3.7) in the following terms:

> 'You do not have to say anything. But it may harm your defence if you do not mention when questioned something which you later rely on in court. Anything you do say may be given in evidence.'

The suspect must then be taken to a designated police station as soon as is reasonably practicable (s. 30 PACE 1984), unless he is granted street bail (see below).

3.7.7 THE USE OF REASONABLE FORCE

Section 3(1) Criminal Law Act 1967 allows reasonable force to be used when making an arrest or when preventing a criminal offence. The 'reasonable force' test is decided by the magistrates or by the judge on the specific facts of each case.

3.7.8 CITIZEN'S POWER OF ARREST—S. 24A PACE 1984

Section 24A PACE 1984 now regulates a citizen's power of arrest, which may be made in the following circumstances. The reference in s. 24 A to indictable offences includes either-way offences.

Section 24A(1) PACE 1984 provides:

> 'A person other than a constable may arrest without a warrant—
>
> (a) anyone who is in the act of committing an indictable offence; or
>
> (b) anyone whom he has reasonable grounds for suspecting to be committing an indictable offence.'

Section 24A(2) PACE 1984 further provides that:

> 'Where an indictable offence has been committed a person other than a constable may arrest without a warrant—
>
> (a) anyone who is guilty of the offence or
>
> (b) anyone whom he has reasonable grounds for suspecting him to be guilty of it.'

Section 24A(3)(a) PACE 1984 requires that *in addition* to satisfying one of the grounds above in s. 24A(1)–(2) PACE 1984, the arrest will only be lawful if the citizen has reasonable grounds for believing that an arrest is necessary for one or more of the reasons listed in s. 24A(4) PACE 1984 below *and* it appears to the person making the arrest that it is not reasonably practicable for a constable to make the arrest instead.

Section 24A(4) PACE 1984 defines the grounds to include:

(a) causing injury to himself or any other person;

(b) suffering physical injury;

(c) causing loss or damage to property;

(d) making off before a constable can assume responsibility for him.

3.7.9 PRESERVED POWERS OF ARREST

The following statutory powers of arrest are preserved by the amendments to PACE 1984:

• arrest in connection with the taking of fingerprints at a police station, s. 27 PACE 1984;

• arrest for the taking of samples in certain circumstances, s. 63A PACE 1984;

• arrest for a failure to surrender to police bail, s. 46A PACE 1984;

• arrest of a person who has broken or is likely to break a condition of bail, s. 7 Bail Act 1976.

3.7.10 WHAT IS THE POSITION WHERE THE POLICE NEED TO ARREST A SUSPECT IN A PRIVATE PLACE?

Section 17 PACE 1984 provides that a police officer may enter and search premises without a warrant to *inter alia*:

(1) execute a warrant of arrest or a warrant of committal to prison;

(2) arrest a person for an indictable offence (this includes an either-way offence);

(3) arrest in respect of certain public order offences (e.g. possession of offensive weapons at public meetings and processions);

(4) where the officer is in uniform, for any offence under the Criminal Law Act 1977 ss. 6, 7, 8 or 10 (these relate to entering and unlawfully remaining on property);

(5) recapture a person unlawfully at large and whom he is pursuing; or

(6) save life or limb or prevent serious damage to property.

Except in relation to s. 17(6) above, a police constable must have reasonable grounds for believing that the person he is seeking is on the premises.

3.7.11 TAKING ACTION AGAINST AN 'UNLAWFUL' ARREST

A failure to comply with the correct procedure renders the arrest unlawful—although an unlawful arrest can be remedied after the proper formalities have been complied with (*Lewis v Chief Constable of South Wales* [1991] 1 All ER 206). Where the police have made an unlawful arrest, the defence may challenge the admissibility of prosecution evidence obtained as a result of it. The defence could submit that admitting the prosecution evidence would have an 'adverse effect on the fairness of the proceeding' s. 78 PACE (see Chapter 6 for consideration of the principles that apply to the exclusion of unlawfully obtained evidence).

Where a suspect has not been properly cautioned, an application can be made by the defence at trial to have any resulting evidence excluded. An unlawful arrest may be subject to judicial review.

3.8   **THE POWER TO GRANT STREET BAIL**

The traditional position has been that PACE 1984 has required an arrested person to be taken to the police station as soon as possible. It was then a matter for the custody officer to decide whether to charge the suspect or to detain him without charge or to release him on police bail.

Section 4 Criminal Justice Act 2003 created a new s. 30A PACE 1984 which provides that where a suspect is arrested at the scene of the offence, he may be given 'street bail' without being taken to the police station to be processed. The suspect will be obliged to attend the police station at a later date unless he is informed to the contrary. The suspect must be given a written notice stating the offence for which he was arrested and the time and date of the police station at which he is required to attend. There is a power of arrest for non-compliance.

Section 10 Police and Justice Act 2006 permits an officer to attach certain conditions to the grant of street bail for reasons set out in the section. Application may be made to the same or another custody officer serving at the same station or a magistrates' court to vary conditions of bail imposed as part of 'street bail'.

Police bail is considered further in Chapter 4.

3.9   **POLICE POWERS TO SEARCH THE SUSPECT'S PERSON AND/OR PROPERTY**

Where the suspect has been arrested, the police have a wide range of legal powers to search any property or premises owned or occupied by him for evidence relating to the offence(s) under investigation. The power of the custody officer under s. 53 PACE 1984, to search the suspect on arrival at the police station and to seize and retain property is addressed in Chapter 4 where the process of detention and questioning of suspects is considered.

3.9.1   **SEARCHING WITH THE SUSPECT'S PERMISSION**

The detained person may agree to his home or business premises being searched. Where consent is not given, however, the police have a wide range of legal powers to carry out a lawful search.

3.9.2   **SEARCH OF AN ARRESTED PERSON AWAY FROM THE POLICE STATION: S. 32(1) PACE 1984**

Where the suspect has been arrested away from the police station, s. 32(1) PACE 1984 permits a constable to search an arrested person if he has reasonable grounds for believing that:

- the arrested person may present a danger to himself or others; or
- may have concealed on him anything which he might use to assist him in escape from lawful custody; or
- may have concealed on him anything which might be evidence relating to an offence.

Section 32(1) gives the police wide discretion in the way in which the power to search is exercised. It means that a police officer may search an arrested person for 'anything' on him. In practice this means that the officer can search an arrested person for items which might be wholly unrelated to the reason why the initial arrest was made as the words 'relating to an offence' do not necessarily relate to the offence for which the arrest is made. These wide powers are limited to some extent as the officer must have reasonable grounds for believing that a search is necessary. Simply making a search at the time of arrest would be unlawful unless the officer could prove the necessary 'reasonable grounds' for his belief.

A police officer may not require a person to remove any of his clothing in public other than an outer coat, jacket or gloves, although it can include the search of a person's mouth (s. 32(4) PACE 1984).

3.9.3   SEARCH AT PREMISES WHERE THE SUSPECT HAS BEEN ARRESTED: S. 32 PACE 1984

Section 32 PACE 1984 confers on a police officer the power to enter and search any premises where the suspect was at the time of his arrest or immediately before his arrest, for evidence relating to the offence for which he is being arrested. The power of search is restricted unless the officer has reasonable grounds for believing that there is such evidence on the premises and applies only to an indictable offence (which includes all offences triable either way).

In every case it is a question of fact where entry is made under s. 32 PACE 1984, whether the officer considered that reasonable grounds existed for his belief that evidence might be found as a result of the search.

Where the reasonableness of the officer's belief and/or the admissibility of any evidence discovered as a result of the search is disputed by the defence, the issue will be decided prior to trial or in a *voir dire* (trial within a trial). Evidence obtained as a result of an unlawful search remains admissible subject to the court's discretion to exclude under ss. 78 PACE 1984 (see Chapter 6).

3.9.4   THE POWER TO ENTER AND SEARCH: S. 17 PACE 1984

Section 17 PACE 1984 allows a police officer to enter and search any premises for the purposes of:

(a) executing a warrant of arrest;

(b) arresting a person for an indictable offence;

(c) arresting a person for a specified non-indictable offence;

(d) recapturing any person who is unlawfully at large; or

(e) saving life or limb or preventing serious damage to property.

The power under s. 17 PACE 1984 can only be exercised if the police officer has reasonable grounds for believing that the person he is seeking is on the premises.

3.9.5   SEARCH OF AN ARRESTED PERSON'S PREMISES: S. 18 PACE 1984

Section 18 PACE 1984 deals with the search of premises occupied or controlled by a person who is under arrest for an indictable offence (which includes all offences triable either way). A search is permitted if there are reasonable grounds for suspecting that there is evidence on the premises (other than items subject to legal privilege) that relate either to the indictable offence or some other connected or similar indictable offence and usually (but not always required) the written authority of an inspector is obtained. Section 18(2) confers the power to seize and prior retain any item for which he is authorised to search.

3.9.6   THE POWER OF SEIZURE: S. 19 PACE 1984

Section 19 provides that a constable who is lawfully on any premises has power to seize anything which is on the premises if he has reasonable grounds to believe that it has been obtained in consequence of the commission of an offence, or that it is evidence in relation to an offence, and that it is necessary to seize it in order to prevent it from being concealed, lost, altered or destroyed.

The power of seizure does not extend to items the constable has reasonable grounds to suspect are subject to legal privilege (see para. 3.9.9 below). An additional power of seizure has been granted to the police under ss. 50 and 51 Criminal Justice and Police Act 2001. These new powers enable the police to remove material which cannot be practically examined on the premises with a view to determining whether it contains evidence capable of being seized or whether the material may be subject to excluded categories of material (see para. 3.9.9 below). The most obvious example of this would be a personal computer containing material that might disclose evidence of the commission of an offence or contain evidence relevant to an offence.

 Example

Police powers to search an arrested person and / or property under ss. 18 and 32 PACE 1984 can be confusing. Depending on the facts of the case in some situations either s. 18 or s. 32 can be used. In other situations only one of the provisions applies. Consider the following examples which illustrate the position.

James, who is a managing director of a small double-glazing firm, is arrested at work on suspicion of having committed fraud.

As James has been arrested, the police may search James's office under s. 32 PACE 1984 because he has been arrested in connection with an indictable offence provided the officers have reasonable grounds for believing that there is evidence in James's office connecting him to the fraud offences.

The appropriate power of search is s. 32 PACE which permits the police to search premises where the arrested person was immediately before or at the time of his arrest.

The term 'where the suspect was at the time of arrest or immediately before arrest' is given a restrictive meaning as s. 32 could not be used if the police searched James's office six hours after his arrest. To be lawful under s. 32 PACE 1984, the search must be almost contemporaneous with the arrest.

James may also be the subject of a personal search under s. 32 PACE if the officer reasonably believes that James has concealed on his person anything which may present a danger to himself or others; or anything which he might use to assist him to escape or anything which might be evidence relating to an offence.

The police would have entered James's office under s. 17(1)(b) PACE 1984 to arrest him for an indictable offence.

The police may PACE 1984 to search James's home and a lock-up garage that he rents close to home. Section 18 applies in this situation provided the police have reasonable grounds for believing there is evidence on the properties which relate to an indictable offence or to other similar or connected offences and the search is authorised by an officer of at least the rank of inspector. The house and lock-up garage satisfy the requirement that the properties are occupied or controlled by James. Section 32 PACE does not apply here because James was not at home or in the garage at or immediately before the time of his arrest.

If James had been arrested at home, the police could have searched under s. 18 or s. 32 PACE 1984.

3.9.7 PRESERVED POWERS OF ENTRY

A number of statutes provide police officers with a power to search a suspect's premises to obtain evidence in relation to the investigation of a specific offence. Section 23(3) Misuse of Drugs Act 1971 allows the police to enter and search premises in connection with an investigation under the 1971 Act. A warrant to enter the premises must be obtained from a magistrate.

3.9.8 SEARCH WARRANTS: S. 8 PACE 1984

The powers of search discussed so far give the police the power to search premises owned by the arrested person or to search the premises where the person was arrested. What can the police do where it is not possible or practicable to contact the person who could allow the police to enter premises to search for evidence in connection with an offence? In these circumstances, an officer of the rank of inspector or above can make a written application to a magistrate under s. 8 PACE 1984 for a warrant authorising the officer to enter and search the premises specified in the application.

To be granted a search warrant, the officer must satisfy the magistrate that there are reasonable grounds for believing that:

- an indictable offence has been committed; and
- there is material on the premises which is likely to be of substantial value to the investigation of the offence; and
- the material is likely to be relevant evidence; and
- the evidence does not include items subject to legal professional privilege, excluded material, or special procedure material; and
- *inter alia*, it is not practicable to communicate with any person entitled to grant entry, or if it was, it is likely that the purpose of the search will be frustrated or seriously prejudiced.

Two types of warrant may be issued. First, the traditional specific premises warrant may be issued authorising the police to search the address specified on the warrant. Alternatively, s. 8 (2)–(4) SOCPA 2005 has introduced an all-premises warrant which covers all premises owned or occupied by the person named in the application but where it is not reasonably practicable to specify all such premises at the time of the application. The application for an all premises warrant will specify that:

- because of the offence(s) specified in the application there are reasonable grounds for believing that it is necessary to search the premises owned or controlled by the person which are not specified in the application to find material which is likely to be of substantial value to the investigation; and
- it is not reasonably practicable to specify in the application all the premises which the person owns or controls which might need to be searched.

The warrant will allow access to all premises occupied or controlled by the person whether they are specified on the application or not. The warrant can authorise the police to make multiple visits on multiple occasions to the list of premises specified in the warrant—subject to the requirement that any second and subsequent visits must be authorised by an officer of at least the rank of inspector.

The entry and search under the warrant must be completed within three months of issue. From a defence perspective, it is likely that the exercise of power under an all premises warrant could be challenged under Article 8 ECHR 1950 as infringing the owner's right to privacy.

3.9.9 **MATERIAL THAT MAY NOT BE SEIZED**

It is important to note that certain categories of 'material' cannot be seized by the police. These items are subject to legal professional privilege; 'excluded material' and 'special procedure material'.

(1) Items subject to legal professional privilege

These are defined by s. 10(1)(a) PACE 1984 and include any communication containing legal advice. The doctrine of legal professional privilege requires that any written and/or oral legal advice passing between a lawyer and his client in connection with a case is privileged and cannot be divulged to a third party without the client's consent.

(2) 'Excluded' material

'Excluded material' is defined by s. 11 PACE 1984 and consists of personal records held in confidence by the person who created them. Personal records are defined as medical records, records of spiritual healing and files kept by social workers and probation officers about their clients.

(3) 'Special procedure material'

Section 14 PACE 1984 defines 'special procedure material' as material which has been acquired by a person in the course of his trade, business or profession or other occupation or office and who holds it subject to an express or implied undertaking to keep it confidential. It also extends to journalistic material unless it had been acquired in confidence, in which case it will be regarded as excluded material under s. 11 PACE 1984.

3.9.10 SAFEGUARDS

Sections 15 and 16 of PACE 1984 provide certain safeguards against potential misuse of the warrant by the police under s. 8 PACE 1984 (above), and any non-compliance with the sections renders a search and entry of premises unlawful. At trial the defence advocate could apply to have prosecution evidence obtained as a result of the unlawful search excluded under s. 78 PACE 1984 on the grounds that to admit the evidence 'would have an adverse effect on the fairness of the proceedings'.

3.10 THE PERVASIVE INFLUENCE OF THE EUROPEAN CONVENTION ON HUMAN RIGHTS (ECHR) 1950

Powers of arrest and stop and search are subject to the protections afforded by Article 5 ECHR 1950 (the right to liberty and security of the person including the right not to be detained by the police without lawful authority) and Article 8 ECHR 1950 (the right to privacy).

When exercising stop and search powers, the police will be required to show that:

• the power to stop and search was prescribed by law; and
• the power was exercised in pursuance of a legitimate aim; and
• the exercise of the power was proportionate to the aim to be achieved.

An arrest will satisfy the requirements of Article 5 ECHR 1950 where the person is brought before a competent legal authority such as a court either on reasonable suspicion of having committed an offence or to prevent him from committing an offence or from escaping after having committed an offence (*Fox, Campbell and Hartley v UK* [1990] 13 EHHR 157).

The lawfulness of an arrest may also be judged according to whether:

• the legal authority for the arrest is precise and accessible; and
• is procedurally fair and not arbitrary; and
• proportionate to the aim of depriving a person of his liberty.

The test of reasonable suspicion will satisfy Article 5 provided that an objective observer would be satisfied that the suspect may have committed an offence (*Fox, Campbell and Hartley v UK* [1990] 13 EHHR 157).

KEY POINT SUMMARY

• Know the legal grounds that permit a person to be stopped and searched before arrest (s.1 PACE 1984).
• Where appropriate, be prepared to challenge the legality of stop and search and any evidence obtained as a result of the unlawful exercise of power. The challenge may be made to the police or the Crown Prosecution Service or to the court at the defendant's trial.
• Know the legal grounds under which a person can be arrested (ss. 24 and 24A PACE 1984).
• Where appropriate, be prepared to challenge the legality of an arrest and any evidence obtained as a result of an unlawful arrest. The challenge may be made to the police or the Crown Prosecution Service or to the court at the defendant's trial.

- Have a good working knowledge of the law governing the powers to search the suspect and/or his property after arrest.
- Where appropriate, be prepared to challenge the legality of the power of search and any evidence obtained as a result of an unlawful search.
- Be aware of the pervasive influence of the ECHR 1950 in relation to stop and search and arrest and cite ECHR case law to support your submissions.

SELF-TEST QUESTIONS

1. Where can you find guidance on the reasonable suspicion or belief test?
2. Which caution should be given to the suspect on arrest?
3. Where are the police powers to search a person and his property after arrest contained?
4. In what circumstances will the police apply to a magistrate for a warrant to be issued under s. 8 PACE 1984?
5. Police are called to a public order disturbance in town. By the time they arrive, the incident appears to be over. CCTV operators have provided a description of a male individual wearing a football top who appears to have been the instigator of the trouble and who appeared to be waving some kind of bottle or weapon in his hand. One of the police officers notices a male wearing such a top walking towards a taxi-rank. On approaching the male (Trevor), he runs off. He is apprehended within a matter of minutes. What powers do the police have in relation to Trevor?
6. A short, factual scenario based on the exercise of police powers appears at the end of Chapter 6 (scenario 1); although the focus of the question is based on the admissibility of unlawfully obtained evidence, you may wish to consider what aspects of police procedure relating to stop and search and arrest might be considered unlawful.

FIGURE 3.1 POLICE POWERS OF STOP/SEARCH/SEIZURE AND ARREST

STOP AND SEARCH BEFORE ARREST
Section 1 PACE and Code A
- A person may be stopped and/or searched in a public place or in a place to which the public has access where:
  - the officer reasonably suspects the person is in possession of
    - stolen articles; or
    - prohibited articles.

SEARCHING THE SUSPECT AFTER ARREST
- with the suspect's consent; or
- under s. 32 PACE where the officer:
  - has reasonable grounds for believing the suspect may present a danger to himself or others; or
  - has concealed anything on him he might use to escape from custody; or
  - has concealed on him evidence which might be related to an offence.

SEARCH OF PREMISES AFTER ARREST
- search with the suspect's consent;
- search with a warrant in connection with an indictable offence, s. 8 PACE 1984;
- search the premises at which the suspect is arrested, s. 32 PACE 1984;
- search premises owned/controlled by the suspect, s. 18 PACE 1984;
- preserved powers of entry, e.g. s. 23 Misuse of Drugs Act 1971.

POLICE OFFICER ARREST WITHOUT A WARRANT
- s. 24 PACE 1984 where a police officer has reasonable grounds for suspecting that the person:
  - is about to commit an offence; or
  - is committing an offence; or
  - has committed an offence AND
  - it is necessary to arrest the individual for any of the following reasons (s. 24(5)):
    - to enable the person's name to be ascertained where the constable does not know and cannot readily ascertain the person's name or has reasonable grounds for doubting the name given by the person is his real name; or
    - to enable the person's address to be ascertained;
    - to prevent the person in question:
      - causing physical injury to himself or another;
      - suffering physical injury;
      - causing loss or damage to property;
      - committing an offence against public decency; or
      - causing unlawful obstruction of the highway;
  - to protect a child or vulnerable person from the person; or
  - to allow the prompt and effective investigation of the offence or of the conduct of the person;
  - to prevent the prosecution for the offence from being hindered by the disappearance of the person in question.

CHECKLIST FOR A LAWFUL ARREST—S. 28 PACE 1984
- There must be a legal ground for the arrest, e.g. s. 24 PACE 1984.
- There must be the factual grounds for the arrest, e.g. reasonable grounds for believing that an offence has been committed.
- The person must be cautioned as follows:
  - 'You do not have to say anything. But it may harm your defence if you do not mention when questioned something which you later rely on in court. Anything you do say may be given in evidence.'
- The person must be informed of the reason for his arrest.
- The person should be taken to a designated police station as soon as is reasonably practicable.

4 DETENTION AND INTERROGATION

4.1   INTRODUCTION

Following his arrest (unless granted street bail), the suspect should be brought to a designated police station as soon as is reasonably practicable. At this point, the suspect becomes the centre of the police investigation. It is likely that the police will want to question the suspect and undertake certain investigatory procedures, including -

- fingerprinting the suspect;
- taking a non-intimate sample from the suspect;
- taking an intimate sample from the suspect;
- photographing the suspect;
- requesting the suspect to participate in a formal identification procedure.

In this chapter, we consider the process of detention, questioning and charge. The procedures associated with obtaining identification of a suspect are considered in Chapter 8.

A detailed legal framework for the treatment of suspects at the police station is provided by the substantive provisions of PACE 1984 and the Codes of Practice, particularly Code C. The provisions define the power(s) the police may exercise over a suspect but also provide a number of safeguards. A copy of Code C is freely accessible from the Home Office website—our Online Resource Centre includes a link taking you to the Codes of Practice. You are reminded that the Codes of Practice are currently subject to a review and are expected to be revised in the future.

The safeguards contained in PACE 1984 and its accompanying Codes of Practice exist to ensure the suspect enjoys fair treatment while in detention but also to promote investigative integrity on the part of the police, thereby ensuring the quality and reliability of evidence obtained at the police station. Evidence obtained at the police station in breach of PACE 1984 and Code C is vulnerable to challenge, and a defence lawyer might seek to exclude any resulting evidence under s. 78 PACE 1984 (see Chapter 6) and under s. 76 PACE 1984, in the case of a confession (see Chapter 7). Section 67(11) PACE 1984 allows the Codes of Practice to be admissible in evidence if relevant to a matter to be decided by a court.

It is the legal adviser's duty at the police station to advance and protect his client's rights. To do this, the legal adviser needs a detailed knowledge of PACE 1984 and the Codes of Practice to challenge the police if they breach the letter and/or the spirit of the suspect's legal rights.

Be aware that there are more extensive powers governing the detention and interrogation of persons suspected of involvement in terrorist activities. These provisions are found in the Codes of Practice and the Terrorism Act 2000, and are outside the scope of this work. More details can be found in *Blackstone's Criminal Practice*.

In the password protected lecturer resources section on our Online Resource Centre, we are pleased to offer a 'stand alone' video case study/role-play, entitled the Peter West Police Station Scenario, with supporting documentation. The video is divided into a number of different sections covering the investigation of an offence of rape. It explores all aspects of a suspect's detention at the police station, including the role of the legal adviser and illustrates many of the points covered in this chapter and Chapter 9.

In this chapter, we explain the process of detention and charge including the following:

- the custody officer's role;
- the importance of the custody record;

- the circumstances in which a suspect can be detained without charge;
- the length of time a suspect can be kept in custody;
- the obligation to review the suspect's detention;
- the suspect's right to have someone informed of his arrest;
- the suspect's rights to legal advice ;
- the suspect's basic rights in custody;
- specific safeguards in relation to vulnerable suspects;
- the conduct of an interview; and
- the decision to charge and withhold bail.

We begin, however, by mentioning those who voluntarily attend at the police station.

4.2 THE RIGHTS OF A VOLUNTEER AT THE POLICE STATION

It is often reported in the media that a person is 'helping the police with their enquiries'. You may recall that during the murder investigation into the deaths of Holly Wells and Jessica Chapman, Ian Huntley and Maxine Carr 'assisted the police with their enquiries' before their arrests. This expression means that a member of the public is voluntarily assisting the police in the criminal investigation without having been arrested. A volunteer is entitled to leave police custody at any time (Code C para. 3.21).

If the police wish to detain the volunteer, he must be arrested, at which point his legal status changes to a suspect.

4.2.1 QUESTIONING A VOLUNTEER

If the police wish to question a volunteer to obtain evidence which may be put before a court, the volunteer must be:

- cautioned before replying;
- told that he is not under arrest;
- told that he is free to leave if he wishes; and
- told that he may obtain free and independent legal advice (Code C para. 3.21).

4.3 ARREST AND ARRIVAL AT THE POLICE STATION

Section 30 PACE 1984 requires an arrested person to be taken to a designated police station as soon as practicable after arrest. A designated police station is equipped with the appropriate facilities for dealing with a suspect in detention.

Once the suspect arrives at the police station he will be taken to the custody suite for 'booking-in'. This will be carried out by the custody officer on duty.

4.4 THE ROLE OF THE CUSTODY OFFICER

The custody officer plays an essential role in ensuring that the suspect's legal rights at the police station are complied with (s. 39 PACE 1984). The officer should always remain independent and impartial of the criminal investigation. He should not question the suspect about his involvement in the alleged offence. The custody officer is responsible for taking some important decisions in relation to the suspect, including whether he should be detained or released and, in conjunction with the CPS, whether he should be charged.

4.4.1 THE CUSTODY RECORD

The custody officer is also responsible for compiling the suspect's custody record. A custody record must be opened as soon as is reasonably practicable for each person brought to a police station (Code C para. 2.1). The suspect's legal adviser and/or appropriate adult have a right of access to the custody record 'at any time while the person is detained' (Code C para. 2.4). When a detained person leaves the police station, they are entitled to a copy of the custody record upon request (Code C para. 2.4A).

online resource centre

The custody record has very important evidential value to both the prosecution and defence by providing a detailed record of all aspects of the suspect's detention. (We have included extracts from the custody record in relation to our case study *R v Lenny Whyte* in Appendix 1. The complete documentation, including the full custody record can be accessed on our Online Resource Centre.)

The custody record will include details of the suspect's arrest, the reason for his detention, authorisation of search procedures or continued detention, requests for legal advice/medical advice, reviews of the suspect's detention, details of meals and refreshments given to the suspect and any complaints made by the suspect. The custody record should be carefully considered to ensure the suspect's rights have been respected.

Where questions about the admissibility of evidence obtained during the investigation arise, the custody record may be put in evidence at trial. For this reason, the solicitor or legal adviser should ensure that any representations he makes regarding his client's detention are recorded in the custody record.

4.4.2 WHAT RIGHTS MUST THE CUSTODY OFFICER INFORM THE SUSPECT OF ON HIS ARRIVAL AT THE POLICE STATION?

On arrival at the police station and in accordance with Code C para. 3.1, the custody officer should explain to the suspect that he has the following rights which may be exercised at any stage:

1. the right to have someone informed of his arrest;
2. the right to consult in private with a solicitor, such advice being free and independent;
3. the right to consult the Codes of Practice.

The custody officer is also required, under Code C paras. 3.5–3.10, to undertake a risk assessment to consider the specific needs of each detainee. This will include asking the suspect on his arrival at the police station whether he:

• wants legal advice;
• wants to inform someone of his arrest;
• might be in need of medical treatment;
• requires the presence of an appropriate adult;
• requires an interpreter.

4.4.3 SEARCH ON ARRIVAL AT THE POLICE STATION

The custody officer is obliged to check a suspect's property when brought into custody (s. 54 PACE 1984). Property and clothing may be seized and retained if it could cause physical injury, damage to persons or property or could be used to assist an escape from lawful custody. Strip searches and intimate searches require special justification (see Code C, Annex A).

4.4.4 IS THERE SUFFICIENT EVIDENCE TO CHARGE?

Following the arrested person's arrival at the police station and having completed the formalities, the custody officer, in conjunction with a CPS lawyer on rota at the police station, has a duty to determine whether there is sufficient evidence to charge the suspect with the offence for which he has been arrested.

The CJA 2003 has made some significant changes to the charging procedure at the police station, considered further in Chapter 10. For the most part, the decision to charge a suspect rests with the CPS (s. 28 and Sch. 2 CJA 2003, amending s. 37 of PACE 1984). As an alternative to charging the suspect the police/CPS have discretion to offer a simple caution or conditional caution.

If there is sufficient evidence to charge, s. 37(7) PACE 1984 requires that the suspect shall either be:

- released without charge and on bail or kept in police detention for the purpose of enabling the Director of Public Prosecutions to make a decision under section 37B (s. 37(7)(a);
- released without charge and on bail but not for that purpose (i.e. to allow for enquiries to continue s. 37(7)(b));
- released without charge and without bail (s. 37(7)(c); or
- charged (s. 37(7)(d).

Where the decision to charge is not taken immediately and the file is passed to the CPS for review (s. 37B), a suspect can be released on bail under s. 37(7)(a), pending a decision to charge. Bail granted for this purpose and for s. 37(7)(b) can be conditional (s. 37(D)). Any breach of bail granted in these circumstances carries a power of arrest (s. 37(C)). The provision gives a measure of public protection where the police have released a suspect on bail pending a charging decision by the CPS. However, it also means that some suspects will have to comply with onerous pre-charge bail conditions for a considerable time, which can amount to a significant restriction on a suspect's liberty. Police station legal advisers should be aware of this and be prepared to negotiate reasonable bail conditions. An application to vary conditions of bail imposed under s. 37(7)(a) may be made to the same or another custody officer serving at the same police station or a magistrates' court (s. 47(1E).

A failure to surrender or a failure without reasonable cause to abide by any conditions imposed under s. 37(7)(a) can result in the suspect being charged for the original offence for which he was arrested (s. 37(C)), and will be relevant to any subsequent bail hearing before a court.

If charged, the suspect may be kept in police custody (s. 38 PACE 1984) pending his first appearance before a magistrates' court, or released on unconditional or conditional bail (s. 47(1A) PACE 1984). The defendant's charge sheet will contain the date of the defendant's first appearance before a magistrates' court. A failure to answer police bail granted in these circumstances entitles the police to arrest without warrant (s. 46(A) PACE 1984).

4.5 DETENTION WITHOUT CHARGE

The continued detention of a person arrested, but not charged, is allowed under s. 37(2) PACE 1984 where the custody officer has reasonable grounds for believing that his detention without charge is necessary:

- to secure or preserve evidence relating to an offence for which he is under arrest; or
- to obtain such evidence by questioning him.

Where the custody officer decides that continued detention without charge is necessary, the justification for doing so must be noted in the custody record. The grounds are easily made out in a case where the investigating officer needs to interview witnesses or the suspect, or to undertake personal searches. Where the custody officer becomes aware at any time that the detention grounds have ceased to exist, there is an obligation on the custody officer to release the suspect immediately) without bail (s. 34(2) PACE 1984), unless it appears that there is a need for further investigation (s. 34(5) PACE 1984).

4.5.1 HOW LONG CAN A SUSPECT BE DETAINED WITHOUT CHARGE?

There are strict time limits on how long a suspect can be detained at a police station without charge. Unauthorised detention beyond the requisite time is unlawful.

4.5.2 INITIAL DETENTION PERIOD OF 24 HOURS

The general position is that the suspect can be detained at the police station without charge for 24 hours (s. 41 PACE 1984). The 24-hour period begins to run, from the time of the suspect's arrival at the police station, which must be noted in the custody record.

At the end of the 24-hour period the suspect must either be charged or released unconditionally or on bail.

4.5.3 DETENTION WITHOUT CHARGE BEYOND 24 HOURS?

The basic 24 hours of detention without charge can be extended up to 36 hours for an indictable offence (which includes either-way offences) where the provisions of s. 42(1) PACE 1984 apply. These are that:

- a senior officer of at least the rank of superintendent authorises the suspect's continued detention; and
- the officer has reasonable grounds for believing that it is necessary to detain the suspect without charge to secure or preserve evidence or to obtain evidence by questioning him; and
- the investigation is being conducted diligently and expeditiously.

Where these conditions apply, the suspect can be detained for an additional period of up to 12 hours making a total of 36 hours from the time of arrival at the police station. The reasons for extending the suspect's basic period of detention must be noted on the custody record. Continued detention is easily justified where investigating officers wish to interview or reinterview a suspect or to undertake an intimate search or to arrange an identification procedure.

4.5.4 DETENTION BEYOND 36 HOURS—WARRANT OF FURTHER DETENTION

Where the police wish to detain the suspect without charge beyond 36 hours, an application under s. 43 PACE 1984 must be made to the magistrates' court for a warrant of further detention. An application for continued detention beyond 36 hours can only be made in relation to an indictable offence (which includes either-way offences).

The suspect has the right to be present at the hearing and to be legally represented. The defence solicitor may make a submission to the magistrates about the suspect's continued detention. In practice, the application for a warrant of further detention is invariably granted by the magistrates.

Where the police persuade the court that the suspect should be detained for a further period without charge, the court may authorise detention for a further period of up to 36 hours making a total 72 hours from his arrival at the designated police station.

At the end of 72 hours, where the police wish to continue holding the suspect without charge, a further application can be made to the magistrates requesting that the suspect should be detained for a further period of up to 24 hours, making a total of 96 hours from the time of the suspect's arrival at the police station.

At the end of 96 hours, the suspect must either be charged, or released unconditionally, or on police bail (s. 44 PACE 1984).

In making an application for a warrant of further detention before a magistrates' court, the police must set out their reasons. In so doing, the police will need to explain the circumstances of the suspect's arrest, what investigatory steps have been undertaken so far and what further enquiries are needed. They will need to establish why the suspect's detention is necessary each time an application is made to have the detention period extended up to the maximum of 96 hours.

Where a suspect has not been charged but has been released on police bail, the custody time limit clock is suspended at this point. The clock resumes once the suspect answers his police bail.

4.6 OBLIGATION TO REVIEW A SUSPECT'S DETENTION

Section 40 PACE 1984 requires the police to carry out periodic reviews of the suspect's detention, the details of which must be recorded in the custody record. The purpose of the review is to ensure the suspect's continued detention is lawful.

Where the suspect has not been charged, the review of his detention must be carried out by an officer of at least the rank of inspector who has not been directly involved in the investigation. This officer is known as the 'review officer'. Provision is made under s. 40 PACE 1984 and Code C paras. 15.9–15.11, for reviews to be conducted over the telephone or via video-link. The suspect always has a right to make representations about his continued detention.

Where the suspect has been arrested and charged, the review can be carried out by the custody officer.

4.6.1 WHEN MUST THE REVIEWS BE CONDUCTED?

The first review of detention must be made no later than six hours after the detention was first authorised by the custody officer and thereafter every nine hours to ensure that the reasons for detaining the suspect's detention continue to apply.

The legal adviser should ensure the suspect's detention is lawful at all times. The custody record should help to determine this. If the detention ground under s. 37(2) PACE 1984 no longer exists or never existed or if a detention review was not carried out, the suspect's continued detention is unlawful.

4.7 WHAT RIGHTS DOES A SUSPECT IN CUSTODY ENJOY?

The importance of a suspect's rights at the police station cannot be overstated. Where incriminating admissions or inferences from silence have been obtained in breach of these rights, exclusion of such evidence can be sought under ss. 76/78 PACE 1984 (see Chapters 6 and 7).

4.7.1 THE SUSPECT'S RIGHT TO INFORM SOMEONE OF HIS ARREST: S. 56 PACE 1984

Section 56(1) PACE 1984 provides that where a person has been arrested and held in custody, he shall be entitled as soon as is reasonably practicable to inform a friend, relative or some other person of his arrest who is likely to be interested in his welfare . For some suspects, especially those who might be termed 'vulnerable', the right of intimation under s. 56 PACE 1984 is important.

Guidance on the right is contained in Code C para. 5 (supplemented by Annex B).

Contact can extend to the suspect speaking on the telephone to a specified individual (although this is unlikely to be a private call) and writing to the person concerned (although this correspondence is likely to be read). At the custody officer's discretion, the suspect can be visited at the police station by the specified individual.

4.7.2 WHEN CAN THE RIGHT TO HAVE SOMEONE INFORMED OF THE ARREST BE DELAYED?

The suspect's general right to inform someone of his arrest may be delayed where the grounds in s. 56(2)–(5) PACE 1984 Code C Annex B are made out.
Section 56 provides that:

- the suspect must have been arrested in connection with an indictable offence; and
- an officer of at least the rank of inspector authorises the delay on the basis that the officer has reasonable grounds for believing that telling the suspect's relative, friend or other person likely to take an interest in his welfare of the arrest will:
  — lead to interference with or harm to evidence connected with an indictable offence; or
  — lead to interference with or physical injury to other persons; or
  — lead to the alerting of other persons suspected of having committed such an offence but not yet arrested for it; or
  — hinder the recovery of any property obtained as a result of such an offence.

The authorisation for the delay may be given to the suspect orally or in writing. The reason for the delay must be noted in the custody record and if justified, may not exceed 36 hours from the time the suspect arrives at the designated police station.

4.7.3 THE SUSPECT'S RIGHT TO LEGAL ADVICE: S. 58 PACE 1984

The general right to legal advice under s. 58 PACE 1984 (supplemented by Code C para. 6 (Annex B)) is one of the most important protections against the abuse of the suspect's civil liberties by the police. The importance of ensuring a suspect has access to legal advice while being detained has been emphasised many times by the European Court of Human Rights: *Murray v UK* (1996) 22 EHRR 29 and *Condron v UK* (2001) 31 EHRR 1.

4.7.4 WHO PAYS FOR LEGAL ADVICE GIVEN AT THE POLICE STATION?

The Police Station Advice and Assistance Scheme administered by the Legal Services Commission enables a suspect to have free legal advice The suspect may request the services of a solicitor of his choice if he intends to pay privately for such services. Otherwise publicly funded legal advice is accessed by telephoning the Defence Solicitor Call Centre which determines whether legal advice should be limited to telephone advice or whether a solicitor should attend in person. Legal advice will be restricted to telephone advice if the detained person is:

- detained for a non-imprisonable offence;
- arrested on a bench warrant for failing to appear in court and is being held for production before a court;
- arrested on suspicion of driving with excess alcohol; failure to provide a specimen; driving while unfit;
- detained in relation to breach of police or bail conditions.

Attendance in connection with these cases may be justified if an interview or identification procedure is going to take place; the client requires an appropriate adult or interpreter; is unable to communicate over the telephone or is complaining of serious maltreatment.

4.7.5 THE OBLIGATION ON THE POLICE TO FACILITATE ACCESS TO LEGAL ADVICE

Code C places strict obligations on the police to ensure access to legal advice. The obligations include the following:

- All detainees must be informed that they have the right to consult and communicate with a solicitor in private and at any time, free of charge (Code C para. 6.1).
- Nothing must be said or done by the police with the intention of dissuading a detainee from obtaining legal advice (Code C para. 6.4).
- Any request for legal advice must be noted in the custody record.
- If the detainee declines to speak to a solicitor in person, it should be explained to him that he has a right to speak with that person on the telephone and if the detainee continues to waive his right, the custody officer should ask the detainee why and the reasons should be recorded on to the custody record (Code C para. 6.5).
- When a solicitor arrives at the police station to see the suspect, the suspect must be informed of the solicitor's arrival and asked if he would like to see him. This is so even if he has earlier declined legal advice (Code C para. 6.15).
- A detainee who wants legal advice may not be interviewed until they receive such advice unless the circumstances listed in Code C para. 6.6 apply.
- Where the suspect has access to legal advice, he must be allowed to have his solicitor present for the interview.
- If the solicitor requested is on his way to the station or about to set off, an interview should not normally be started until he arrives (note 6A).
- Where the suspect requests legal advice during an interview, there should be no further questioning until the suspect has spoken to his legal adviser (Code C para. 6.6).

The police are also required to remind the suspect about his right to legal advice at the following stages of his detention:

- immediately before the commencement or recommencement of any interview at the police station (Code C para. 11.2);
- before a review of detention takes place (Code C para. 15.4);
- after the suspect has been charged, if a police officer wishes to draw the suspect's attention to any written or oral statements made by any other person (Code C para. 16.4);
- after the suspect has been charged, if further questions are to be put to the suspect about the offence (Code C para. 16.5);
- prior to an identification parade, group identification or video identification is held (Code D para. 3.17);
- prior to the taking of an intimate body sample (Code D para. 6.3).

4.7.6 IN WHAT CIRCUMSTANCES CAN A SUSPECT'S RIGHT TO LEGAL ADVICE UNDER S. 58(8) PACE 1984 BE DELAYED?

The decision by the police to delay a suspect's access to legal advice is a serious step and must be justified, as it can have significant implications for evidence obtained from a suspect, (see Chapter 7). On numerous occasions, the European Court of Human Rights has stressed the fundamental importance of the right to legal advice at the police station (*Murray v UK* (1996) 22 EHRR 29; *Averill v UK* (2001) 31 EHRR 36 and *Condron v UK* (2001) 31 EHRR 1).

The right to delay access to a solicitor can only be exercised in accordance with the conditions laid down in s. 58(8) (Annex B Code C) i.e. when:

- the suspect has been arrested in connection with an indictable offence; and
- an officer of at least the rank of superintendent authorises the delay on the ground that he has reasonable grounds for believing that if the suspect was permitted to exercise his right to receive legal advice it will:
  - lead to interference with or harm to evidence connected with an indictable offence or interference with or physical injury to other persons; or
  - lead to the alerting of other persons suspected of having committed such an offence but not yet arrested for it; or
  - will hinder the recovery of any property obtained as a result of such an offence.

The reason for the delay must be noted in the custody record and, if justified, may not exceed 36 hours from the time the suspect arrived at the designated police station. The suspect must be informed of the reason for the denial of legal advice, s. 58(9) PACE 1984. If the grounds for delaying access to legal advice cease to apply, the suspect must be asked whether he wants to see his legal adviser (Code C Annex B, A.6).

The police may not delay access to a particular solicitor on the grounds that he may advise the suspect not to answer questions or that the solicitor was initially asked to attend the station by someone else (Code C Annex B, A.4).

If the authorising officer concludes that any of the risks identified above apply to the particular solicitor requested, the detainee must be allowed to choose another solicitor (Code C Annex B, A.3).

4.8 WHAT ARE A SUSPECT'S BASIC RIGHTS WHILE IN POLICE DETENTION?

Code C paras. 8–9 and 12 recognise that a detainee is entitled to certain fundamental rights while detained at the police station. They include:

- A right to an adequately heated, cleaned and ventilated cell; access to toilet facilities.
- At least two light meals and one main meal in any 24-hour period, taking account of special dietary requirements, and regular refreshments.
- A requirement that a detainee receives appropriate clinical attention as soon as reasonably practicable if the person appears to be suffering from physical illness, is injured, appears to need clinical attention or appears to be suffering from a mental disorder.
  If a detainee requests medical attention, a health care professional must be called. If a detainee needs to take prescribed medication, an appropriate health care professional must be called, and in some instances, may be the only person who can administer the medication.
- The requirement that in any 24-hour period, the suspect must be allowed at least eight hours' continuous rest, preferably at night and free from questioning (Code C para. 12.2).
- Breaks during the interview should occur at normal meal times, and short breaks should be held approximately every two hours (Code C para. 12.8).

4.9 THE TREATMENT OF VULNERABLE SUSPECTS

Code C makes specific provision for the identification and treatment of vulnerable suspects. Annex E provides a detailed summary of the important provisions in relation to detainees under 17, the mentally disordered or mentally vulnerable suspect. The risk assessment which the custody officer is required to undertake at the outset of the detention process in relation to all detainees should identify those detainees who might be described as 'vulnerable'. Aspects of criminal procedure specifically relevant to juveniles (those under the age of 18) are considered in Chapters 30 and 31.

A key right in protecting the vulnerable suspect is access to an appropriate adult. The custody officer must inform an appropriate adult as soon as possible about the detention and request the appropriate adult to attend the police station as soon as practicable (Code C para. 3.15).The appropriate adult is likely to be the vulnerable person's parent or guardian, a social worker, or another responsible adult. The role of the appropriate adult is to protect the vulnerable person's interests and to ensure that his legal rights are respected by the police. The right of access to an appropriate adult is additional to the right to legal advice. Code C para. 11.5 stipulates that in the case of a juvenile or mentally vulnerable person, no interview should be undertaken in the absence of the appropriate adult.

4.10   INTERVIEWING THE SUSPECT

The police investigation will involve questioning the suspect and interviewing other witnesses with a view to gathering sufficient evidence to charge the suspect or to exclude him from their investigations. Interviewing a person suspected of committing the crime is the centrepiece of many police investigations. Even for those people who are experienced at dealing with the police, being interviewed can be a very intimidating and unsettling experience. Vulnerability may lead some suspects to admitting to crimes they have not committed, or being susceptible to a particular line of police questioning, bullying or inducements. For these reasons, the substantive provisions of PACE 1984 and Codes C and E closely regulate the conduct of police interviews with the suspect. The duties of the police and the custody officer and the corresponding rights of the suspect in custody, exist to try and ensure the reliability and fairness of evidence resulting from the detention process. The admissibility of evidence, particularly confession evidence, is vulnerable to challenge under s. 76(2)(a) or (b) and s. 78 PACE where it has been obtained in breach (accidental or otherwise) of PACE 1984 and the Codes of Practice. The Codes of Practice are admissible in evidence for this purpose under s. 67(11) PACE 1984.

4.10.1   WHAT CONSTITUTES AN INTERVIEW?

Code C para. 11.1A defines an interview as:

'the questioning of a person regarding his involvement in a criminal offence where there are grounds to suspect him of such an offence or offences which, by virtue of paragraph 10.1 of Code C must be carried out under caution.'

All interviews must be carried out at a police station. The only exception to this is in the circumstances narrowly defined in Code C para. 11.1 where delay in conducting an interview would lead to interference with or harm to evidence connected with an offence, interference with or physical harm to other persons, or serious loss of or damage to property. In such a case, contemporaneous written notes must be kept.

The effect of Code C para. 11.1A is to permit an informal conversation between an investigating officer and a suspect, providing it does not relate to the circumstances of an offence which the police are investigating. This would cover such matters as verifying someone's identity, but would certainly not cover a prolonged conversation with a view to securing admissions capable of being used in evidence.

4.10.2 **WHEN MUST AN INTERVIEW CEASE?**

Code C para. 11.6 provides that an interview should cease when the officer in charge of the investigation:

- is satisfied all the questions considered relevant to obtaining accurate and reliable information about the offence have been put to the suspect, including allowing the suspect an opportunity to give an innocent explanation and asking questions to test this;
- has taken account of any other available evidence; and
- the officer in charge of the investigation, or in the case of a detained person, the custody officer, reasonably believes that there is sufficient evidence to provide a realistic prospect of conviction.

4.11 **THE REQUIREMENT TO CAUTION**

At the beginning of the interview the suspect must be cautioned. Where the interview recommences after a break, the investigating officer must remind the suspect that he remains under caution and, where he considers it to be appropriate, the caution should be read to the suspect again.

There are two ways in which the suspect may be cautioned, depending whether or not an adverse inference from the suspect's silence may be drawn under ss. 34, 36 and 37 Criminal Justice and Public Order Act 1994 (see Chapter 5).

Where an adverse inference may be drawn at trial from the suspect's silence at the police station, the caution should be given as follows:

'You do not have to say anything. But it may harm your defence if you do not mention when questioned something which you later rely on in court. Anything you do say may be given in evidence.'

This caution will be appropriate where the suspect has been offered and/or received legal advice.

Under Code C the police are required to administer an alternative caution where:

- a person has been denied a solicitor under s. 58(8) PACE 1984; or
- a superintendent authorises an interview to proceed under Code C para. 6.6(b) before the suspect has been given an opportunity to receive legal advice; or
- the suspect is to be interviewed after charge.

The revised caution reads:

'You do not have to say anything. But anything you do say may be given in evidence.'

The revised caution was introduced to comply with the European Court of Human Rights decision in *Murray v UK* (1996) 22 EHHR 29 and is given statutory effect in s. 58 Youth Justice and Criminal Evidence Act 1999.

4.12 **WHAT CONSTITUTES A FAIR INTERVIEW?**

4.12.1 **OPPRESSIVE INTERVIEWS**

It is an essential requirement of fairness that when interviewing a suspect about his involvement in an offence, the police do not abuse their position of trust by conducting the interview in an 'oppressive' manner. This requirement is recognised by Code C para. 11.3, which provides:

'No police officer may try to obtain answers to questions or to elicit a statement by the use of oppression.'

'Oppression' is not defined in Code C, but is partially defined by s. 76(8) PACE 1984, to mean torture, inhuman or degrading treatment and the use or threat of violence. Section 76(2)(a) PACE requires the court to exclude a confession that has been obtained through oppression and is considered further in Chapter 7.

Code C para. 11.4 requires the interviewing officer, at the beginning of the interview, to put to the suspect any significant statement or silence which occurred in the presence or hearing of a police officer before the start of the interview. A significant statement is one which appears capable of being used in evidence against the suspect.

.12.2 INDUCEMENTS TO CONFESS

Code C para. 11.5 makes it clear that no interviewer shall indicate, except to answer a direct question, what action will be taken by the police if the person being questioned answers questions, makes a statement or refuses to do either.

.12.3 FITNESS TO BE INTERVIEWED

Before any detainee is interviewed the custody officer must assess whether the detainee is fit to be interviewed (Code C para. 12.3). This would be particularly appropriate to a detainee who is drunk or under the influence of an illicit substance. In some instances, the custody officer will need to consult an appropriate health care professional to determine the suspect's fitness to be interviewed. As previously indicated, vulnerable suspects have the right to have an appropriate adult present during the interview (Code C para. 11.15).

4.12.4 PHYSICAL CONDITIONS OF THE INTERVIEW

An interview should take place in a room which is properly heated, lighted and ventilated (Code C para. 12.4). There are no limits on the number of officers who may be present during the interview, but the officer in charge must identify them to the suspect and he should be aware of the possibility that the presence of too many officers might be seen as oppressive.

4.12.5 THE ROLE OF THE LEGAL ADVISER DURING INTERVIEW

Code C Notes for guidance para. 6D acknowledges the nature of the legal adviser's role in the interview:

'A detained person has a right to free legal advice and to be represented by a solicitor. The solicitor's only role in the police station is to protect and advance the legal rights of his client. On occasions this may require the solicitor to give advice which has the effect of his client avoiding giving evidence which strengthens a prosecution case. The solicitor may intervene in order to seek clarification or to challenge an improper question to his client or the manner in which it is put, or to advise his client not to reply to particular questions or if he wishes to give his client further legal advice.'

We consider in some detail the practical aspects of the role of the legal adviser at the police station in Chapter 9.

Apart from a restricted number of exceptions, a suspect who has requested legal advice may not be interviewed or continue to be interviewed until they have met with their legal adviser (Code C para. 6.6).

4.13 HOW SHOULD AN INTERVIEW BE RECORDED?

4.13.1 THE REQUIREMENT TO TAPE RECORD POLICE INTERVIEWS

An interview in the investigation of indictable and either-way offences must be tape recorded (Code E para. 3.1). It is also common practice to tape record interviews in connection with the majority of summary offences. The practice and procedure of tape recorded interviews are governed by Code E of the Codes of Practice and the *Practice Direction (Crime Tape Recording Police Interviews)* [1989] 1 WLR 631. Interviews should be recorded with the full knowledge of the person being interviewed and will be recorded on two tapes. One is a working copy, with the other being sealed at the completion of the interview. A transcript of the interview is produced from the working tape and is required to be a 'balanced' version of the interview. The tape and the transcript must record where the interview took place, the identity of the people present, the time the interview commenced, the time of any breaks and the time the interview finished. The transcripts of interviews in our case studies (*R v Lenny Whyte; R v Roger Martin and R v William Hardy*) can be located in the case studies section of our Online Resource Centre. Appendix 1 includes the transcript of interview in relation to *R v Lenny Whyte.*

online resource centre

A written summary of the tape-recorded interview will be sent to the defence as part of the Advance Information requirements under Crim PR, Part 21. The defence has the right to have access to a copy of the tape to check the accuracy of the summary prepared by the prosecution. If the defence agrees that the summary served by the prosecution is accurate (subject to any legal arguments about the admissibility of the evidence at trial) the written summary will be part of the evidence in the case. If the defence does not agree with the summary, the tape will be transcribed in full for use at the trial. If necessary, the tape will be played in full at the trial.

A new Code F provides for the video recording of interviews with the suspect. The practice is the subject to pilot projects in a number of police force areas prior to expected national implementation.

4.13.2 HOW SHOULD AN INTERVIEW OUTSIDE THE POLICE STATION BE RECORDED?

Where an interview takes place outside a police station (in the limited circumstances set out in Code C para. 11.1), or where the interview is not tape recorded, the police are required to make an accurate written record of the interview which the suspect must be given the opportunity of reading and signing as correct (Code C paras. 11.7–11.14). Code C para. 11.13 requires an officer to make a note of any comments made by a suspect, including unsolicited comments, which are made outside the formal interview but are relevant to the offence. The note should be dated and timed and the suspect should be invited to sign the documented record and to make any amendments to it as he deems necessary.

The failure to accurately record an interview with a suspect as required by Code C and E has been consistently used for excluding evidence of the interview at trial (*R v Keenan* [1990] 2 QB 54) (see Chapter 7).

4.14 CHARGING A SUSPECT

As we have already seen, as soon as there is sufficient evidence to charge a suspect, s. 37(7) PACE 1984 requires the custody officer to charge or release the suspect. The decision to charge will, for the most part, be made by the CPS, in accordance with the statutory charging regime under the CJA 2003.

A new method of charging suspects has been created by s. 29 CJA 2003. The provision has been brought into force in some but not all areas. Under s. 29 CJA 2003, the formal commencement of all public prosecutions begins with the issue of a 'written charge' setting out particulars of the alleged offence coupled with a 'requisition' which requires the accused to appear before a magistrates' court to answer the written charge. In circumstances where s. 29 CJA 2003 is not currently operational, the formal commencement of proceedings begins with the accused either being charged at the police station or having a summons issued against him by a magistrates' court following an 'information' being laid by the prosecuting authority.

As an alternative to charging, you might seek to persuade the custody officer to offer your client a caution instead. A caution is an alternative to a prosecution and Code C Notes for Guidance 16A requires the custody officer to take account of alternatives to prosecution. The use of a caution and the conditional caution under the CJA 2003 as an alternative to prosecution are considered in Chapter 10.

14.1 QUESTIONING AFTER CHARGE

On charging or informing the suspect that he might be prosecuted for an offence, no further questions may be asked of him except in the circumstances provided for in Code C para. 16.5. They include where an interview is necessary:

- to prevent harm or loss to some other person, or the public; or
- to clear up an ambiguity in a previous answer or statement; or
- in the interests of justice for the officer to ask the question(s) and for the suspect to comment on, information concerning the offence which has come to light since he was charged, or informed that he might be prosecuted.

Before the interview starts, the detainee must be cautioned that he does not have to say anything, but that anything he does say may be given in evidence. The adverse inference provision under s. 34 CJPOA 1994 has no application in this situation.

14.2 POLICE BAIL AFTER CHARGE

Once the defendant has been charged the decision whether to remand or release him pending his first appearance before a magistrates' court is made by the custody officer. Section 38 PACE 1984 requires the custody officer to have regard to the same considerations as those which a court is required to consider when taking a decision under the Bail Act 1976. Bail as a substantive topic in its own right is considered in detail in Chapter 12. A custody officer can refuse bail if one or more of the grounds under s. 38(1) PACE 1984 apply. They include:

- The suspect's name or address cannot be ascertained, or the custody officer has reasonable grounds for doubting whether a name or address furnished by him is his real name or address.
- The custody officer has reasonable grounds for believing that the person arrested will fail to attend court to answer bail.
- In the case of a person arrested for an imprisonable offence, the custody officer has reasonable grounds for believing that the detention of the person arrested is necessary to prevent him from committing an offence.
- In the case of a person arrested for a non-imprisonable offence, the custody officer has reasonable grounds for believing that the detention of the person arrested is necessary to prevent physical injury to any other person or causing loss or damage to property.
- The custody officer has reasonable grounds for believing that the detention of the person arrested is necessary to prevent him from interfering with the administration of justice or with the investigation of offences or a particular offence.

- The custody officer has reasonable grounds for believing that the detention of the person arrested is necessary for his own protection.

These grounds are virtually the same as those applied by a court under Sch. 1 Part 1 para. 2 Bail Act 1976. In determining whether the accused is likely to abscond, commit further offences or interfere with the course of justice, the custody officer will have regard to the factors set out in s. 9 Bail Act 1976, including:

- the defendant's bail record;
- the nature of the offence;
- the defendant's community ties;
- the defendant's criminal record.

Instead of remanding a defendant into custody pending his first appearance before a court, the custody officer may impose conditions on the grant of police bail post-charge in accordance with s. 47(1A) PACE 1984 in much the same way as a court. This includes conditions of residence, reporting at intervals to a police station, the imposition of a curfew, prohibiting contact with a particular individual or access to a particular place. A custody officer may not, however, impose a condition requiring the defendant to reside in a bail hostel. Conditions may only be imposed where the custody officer considers them to be necessary to ensure the defendant surrenders to custody, does not commit an offence while on bail, or interfere with witnesses or obstruct the course of justice. Conditions may also be imposed for the defendant's own protection or welfare. A failure by an accused to abide by the conditions of post-charge police bail will result in the accused being arrested and brought before a magistrates' court (s. 7(3) Bail Act 1976). A proven failure to abide by such conditions would be a significant factor in determining whether the accused should be remanded into custody throughout the currency of the proceedings. The accused has the right to apply to the same or another custody officer serving at the same police station or a magistrates' court to vary post-charge bail conditions.

As a consequence of the statutory charging regime under the CJA 2003 (briefly outlined in para. 4.4.4 above), conditions can now be attached to the grant of bail pre-charge where the matter under investigation has been referred to the CPS for a charging decision (s. 37(7)(a) PACE 1984). If a defendant has been released on conditional bail during this time and has not breached any of the conditions, there is no reason why the custody officer should not then grant the defendant bail subject to the same conditions if the defendant is subsequently charged.

The legal adviser at the police station may well be required to make representations to the custody officer where it is proposed to remand the defendant in custody pending his first appearance before a magistrates' court or as to the appropriateness of bail conditions.

4.14.3 DRUG TESTING AT THE POLICE STATION

Section 63B PACE 1984, as amended by s. 7 Drugs Act 2005, gives the police the power to demand a urine sample from suspects upon arrest or after charge in order to test for the presence of a Class A drug. The power to take a sample arises in relation to certain 'trigger offences'. In addition, s. 9 Drugs Act 2005 gives the police the power to require a person who has tested positive to undergo an initial assessment to see if the person has a propensity to misuse Class A drugs and would be suitable for treatment. Where the test shows the presence of a Class A drug, the information will be passed onto a court which must take it in to account when making a bail decision under the Bail Act 1976 (Chapter 12, para. 12.4.2). A failure to give a sample or to consent to undergo an initial assessment or follow-up treatment results in the commission of an offence. The testing procedure is currently being piloted in several police force areas.

KEY POINT SUMMARY

- Be aware of the custody officer's extensive duties and responsibilities.
- Understand the suspect's right to legal advice and to have someone informed of their arrest at the police station and the circumstances in which the exercise of these rights can justifiably be delayed.
- Understand that the safeguards contained in PACE 1984 and in Code C not only seek to protect the suspect while in custody but that they also seek to promote the integrity of the investigative process so as to ensure the reliability of evidence obtained in consequence.
- Understand the importance of the custody record containing everything relevant to your client's detention at the police station, including the justifications for the decisions taken.
- Be aware of detention time limits and the obligation to charge or release when there is sufficient evidence etc.
- Know the definition of a vulnerable suspect and the additional rights that such a suspect enjoys.
- Know which caution should be administered in which situation.
- Understand that evidence obtained as part of the investigation into a criminal offence in breach of PACE/Code C is vulnerable to challenge under s. 78 PACE 1984 and/or s. 76 PACE 1984. Under s. 78 PACE 1984 such evidence can be excluded in the exercise of the court's discretion to ensure the defendant enjoys a right to a fair trial.
- Know the circumstances in which conditions can be imposed on the granting of police bail, both pre-charge and post-charge.
- Know the grounds upon which a custody officer can refuse police bail post-charge (s. 38 PACE).

SELF-TEST QUESTIONS

The self-test questions that support this chapter are located at the conclusion of Chapter 7, which considers the admissibility of confession evidence. Chapter 7 also includes analysis of the admissibility of the confession in our case study, *R v Lenny Whyte*.

FIGURE 4.1 MAXIMUM PERIODS OF DETENTION WITHOUT CHARGE AT THE POLICE STATION

Non-indictable offence: 24 hours maximum, after which defendant must be released (unconditionally or on police bail) or charged, s. 41 PACE 1984.

Indictable offence (which includes an either-way offence): 24 hours unless a superintendent or above authorises detention for further 12 hours (24 + 12 = 36 hours) where the officer has reasonable grounds for believing that:

* the detention is necessary to secure or preserve evidence; or
* to obtain such evidence by questioning the suspect; and
* the investigation is being conducted diligently and expeditiously, s. 42 PACE 1984.

Detention beyond 36 hours

* Section 43 PACE 1984 permits detention without charge beyond 36 hours.
* Police must apply to a magistrates' court for a warrant of further detention where:
  - the detention is necessary to secure or preserve evidence; or to obtain such evidence by questioning the suspect; and
* the offence is an indictable offence; and
* the investigation is being conducted diligently and expeditiously.

The warrant authorises detention for a further 36 hours (24 + 12 + 36 = 72 hours).
The police may apply for a further warrant of detention for 24 hours (24 + 12 + 36 + 24 = 96 hours).
At the end of 96 hours, the suspect must either be released on police bail or unconditionally, or charged (s. 44).

SUMMARY OF RIGHTS WHILE IN CUSTODY

* right to legal advice in private (s. 58 PACE 1984);
* right to have someone informed of your arrest (s. 56 PACE 1984);
* continual review of detention (s. 40 PACE 1984);
* right to an appropriate adult if you are vulnerable (Code C);
* right to medical advice (Code C);
* right to basic human rights (food/sleep/refreshments) (Code C).

5.1   INTRODUCTION

As we saw in the preceding chapter, the formal interview provides a significant opportunity for obtaining evidence against the suspect and remains the centrepiece of most criminal investigations. In some cases, the answers a suspect gives in the interview will lead to him being eliminated from the investigation. In other cases, the suspect's answers may provide evidence in support of the prosecution's case. Interrogation is a cheap and effective resource. Tactically, the police might reason that by engaging the suspect in answering their questions, he may well talk himself into trouble.

A suspect has a number of options open to him so far as the formal interview is concerned. He may:

- admit his guilt;
- answer questions and perhaps advance a defence to the allegations made against him;
- exercise his right to remain silent (which may include putting forward a prepared statement);
- choose to be selectively silent (answer some questions but not others).

The last option is never to be recommended, as it creates a very poor impression of the defendant in court.

In Chapter 9 we explore in detail the practical considerations a legal adviser will have regard to when advising a client which course to take and how to prepare for the interview.

In preparing a client for interview, the legal adviser may well consider that silence is the best strategy to adopt. However, silence is not without evidential consequences and a legal adviser must fully understand the law relating to the right to silence, if silence is to be advised.

5.2 WHAT ARE THE RISKS ASSOCIATED WITH REMAINING SILENT?

A suspect enjoys the right to silence at the police station. He cannot be compelled to answer police questions or otherwise respond to the allegations that have been made against him. However, if a suspect remains silent and is subsequently charged and then advances a defence at trial, there is a danger that the court may draw adverse inferences against his silence under s. 34 Criminal Justice and Public Order Act 1994 (CJPOA). Adverse inferences may also be drawn where a suspect fails to account for objects etc. found on his person (s. 36 CJPOA 1994) and/or from his failure to account for his presence at a particular place (s. 37 CJPOA). It should be noted however that an important safeguard is provided by s. 38 CJPOA 1994 which does not permit a conviction to be based solely on an adverse inference under ss. 34, 36 and 37 CJPOA 1994.

The purpose of this chapter is to explain the substantive law under the 'silence' provisions of the CJPOA 1994.

5.3 WHAT DOES S. 34 CJPOA 1994 STATE?

Section 34 provides:

'(1) Where, in any proceedings against a person for an offence, evidence is given that the accused—

    (a) at any time before he was charged with the offence, on being questioned under caution by a constable trying to discover whether or by whom the offence had been committed, failed to mention any fact relied on in his defence in those proceedings; or

    (b) on being charged with the offence or officially informed that he might be prosecuted for it, failed to mention any such fact, being a fact which in the circumstances existing at the time the accused could reasonably have been expected to mention when so questioned, charged or informed, as the case may be . . .

    (c) the court, in determining whether there is a case to answer; and

    (d) the court or jury, in determining whether the accused is guilty of the offence charged, may draw such inferences from the failure as appear proper.'

5.3.1 WHAT IS THE EFFECT OF S. 34?

Section 34 does not abolish a suspect's common law right to silence. Its effect is much more restrictive. It will apply where:

- on being questioned about an offence or being informed that he is to be charged for an offence or on being charged;
- the defendant fails to mention a fact which he later relies on at trial in his defence;
- in circumstances where a court (jury/magistrates) conclude it was reasonable in the circumstances which existed at the relevant time for the defendant to have mentioned the fact.

Section 34 is based on the simple rationale that if a suspect has an explanation to put forward in answer to an allegation made against him, he ought to put it forward at the first opportunity, namely in interview. If he does not, but later chooses to rely on facts in his defence which he could reasonably have mentioned at the police station, an adverse inference may be drawn. The evidential effect of s. 34 is to undermine the accused's defence at trial.

Section 34 is not limited solely to the suspect being questioned. An adverse inference can arise at the charging stage (s. 34(1)(b) (see *R v Dervish* (2002) 2 Cr App R 105)).

5.4 WHAT ARE THE CONDITIONS FOR DRAWING ADVERSE INFERENCES UNDER S. 34 CJPOA 1994?

There are a number of conditions that need to be satisfied before the court may draw adverse inferences under s. 34. The leading case of *R v Argent* [1997] 2 Cr App R 27 provides that the following conditions must be met.

1. There must proceedings against a person for an offence.
2. The alleged failure to answer questions must occur before the defendant was charged or on being charged with the offence or officially informed that he might be prosecuted for it.
3. The failure must occur during questioning under caution by a constable (i.e. 'You do not have to say anything. But it may harm your defence if you do not mention when questioned something you later rely on in court. Anything you do say may be given in evidence.')
4. The questioning must be directed towards trying to discover whether, or by whom, the alleged offence has been committed.
5. The alleged failure by the defendant must be to mention any fact relied on in his defence in the proceedings. This raises two questions of fact: first is there some fact the defendant has relied on in his defence; and secondly, did the defendant fail to mention it to the constable when questioned in accordance with the section?
6. The fact that the defendant failed to mention must be a fact which, in the circumstances existing at the time, he could reasonably have been expected to mention when questioned.

Section 34 has generated a considerable amount of case law in its relatively short history. Some of the cases further develop the prerequisites for drawing an adverse inference established in *R v Argent* (1997).

Under s. 34(2A) CJPOA an adverse inference cannot be drawn in circumstances where access to a solicitor has been delayed in accordance with s. 58 PACE 1984 (see Chapter 4, para. 4.7.6). In these circumstances, the suspect must be cautioned as follows: 'You do not have to say anything, but anything you do say may be given in evidence.' (Code C Annex C.)

What follows is intended to provide you with a simplified and succinct précis of what has become a complex and technical area of evidence law. Paragraphs 5.4.1 to 5.4.5 below seek to summarise the relevant case law.

5.4.1 '. . . IF YOU DO NOT MENTION WHEN QUESTIONED *SOMETHING YOU LATER RELY ON IN COURT . . .*'

Adverse inferences may only be drawn against a fact which the defendant fails to mention at the police station but which he 'later relies on' in his defence. What is meant by 'something you later rely on?'

A defendant does not need to remain completely silent in interview for s. 34 to be triggered. It is the defendant's failure to mention *any fact* which he subsequently relies on in his defence. If a defendant puts forward facts or an explanation at the police station but then departs from that version at trial or advances new facts, he is still at risk of an adverse inference.

Neither does a defendant have to give evidence on oath in order to trigger s. 34. There are a number of ways in which a defendant can be said to rely on facts in his defence. This includes facts elicited through cross-examination of prosecution witnesses (*R v Bowers* [1998] Crim LR 817) and by the defendant calling witnesses in his defence. If, through either or both of these means, the defendant is relying on facts not previously mentioned, he is at risk of an adverse inference.

Some further useful guidance on what constitutes 'a fact relied on' for the purposes of s. 34 is provided by the decision of the House of Lords in *R v Webber* [2004] 1 All ER 770. The House of Lords concluded that the word 'fact' should not be given a narrow or pedantic meaning. If a defendant advances at trial an exculpatory explanation or account which, if it were true, he could reasonably have been expected to advance earlier, then s. 34 is potentially operational. This applies when an advocate, acting on his client's instructions, puts a specific and positive case to a prosecution witness, as opposed to asking questions intended to probe or test the prosecution case. It is immaterial whether or not the prosecution witness accepts the assertions made.

Where a defendant does no more at trial than put the prosecution to proof of its case, s. 34 has no application (*R v Moshaid* [1998] Crim LR 420).

5.4.2 *FAILS TO MENTION A FACT* THAT HE LATER RELIES ON FOR HIS DEFENCE

A second important element to be considered is that the defendant must fail to mention a fact which he later relies on for his defence. For adverse inferences to be drawn, the failure to mention must relate to a fact, and not, for example, a theory or a hypothesis.

R v Nickolson [1999] Crim LR 61

The defendant had been arrested on suspicion of having raped his stepdaughter. In interview he denied the offence. He did say in interview that he was in the habit of masturbating in the bathroom. The girl's nightdress had been seized as part of the investigation. It was not appreciated at the time of the interview that traces of seminal fluid would subsequently be found on it. Asked at his trial to account for the seminal staining on the girl's nightdress, the defendant stated he had masturbated in the toilet on the evening of the alleged rape and that shortly after, the girl had gone to the toilet. Any semen on the toilet seat could have innocently found its way onto the girl's nightdress. The prosecution maintained the defendant was offering this explanation as a fact which he had not previously advanced. The trial judge agreed and directed the jury in accordance with the requirements of s. 34. The Court of Appeal held the defendant's statement had been offered as a theory or a possible explanation, and was therefore speculative in its nature.

If facts are not known at the time of the interview and the defendant subsequently offers an explanation for them at trial, s. 34 has no application.

R v B (MT) [2000] Crim LR 181

The defendant was on trial for raping his stepdaughter. He had failed to mention in interview that his stepdaughter might have been motivated by jealousy, which would explain why she had falsely accused him of raping her. In fact, whilst the defendant may have had suspicions as to his stepdaughter's motives, he did not know this as a fact. He actually learned it was a fact when the victim herself gave evidence. The defendant pursued the victim's jealousy further in his evidence. The Court of Appeal concluded this was not a fact the defendant could reasonably have been expected to mention at the police station. He may have had his suspicions as to his stepdaughter's motives, but this was not the same as knowing it as a fact.

In the Crown Court, the trial judge is required to identify to the jury the facts that can properly be said to have been relied on which were not mentioned in interview (*R v B* (2003) unreported).

5.4.3 ANY QUESTIONING MUST BE DIRECTED TO TRYING TO DISCOVER WHETHER OR BY WHOM THE ALLEGED OFFENCE WAS COMMITTED (S. 34(1)(a))

Suppose the police have already made up their minds to charge your client before commencing an interview? Your client remains silent but subsequently relies on facts at his trial. Is an inference permitted in these circumstances? In what sense would questioning during such an interview be directed at trying to discover whether or by whom the alleged offence was committed?

Code C para. 11.6 provides that an interview should cease when the officer in charge of the investigation:

- is satisfied all the questions they consider relevant to obtaining accurate and reliable information about the offence have been put to the suspect, including allowing the suspect an opportunity to give an innocent explanation and asking questions to test this;
- has taken account of any other available evidence; and
- the officer in charge of the investigation, or in the case of a detained person, the custody officer, reasonably believes that there is sufficient evidence to provide a realistic prospect of conviction.

This provision clearly gives the police greater leverage on the need to hold an interview before taking a decision as to whether there is in fact sufficient evidence to charge. Solicitors who choose to advise silence on the basis that there is sufficient evidence to charge without the need for an interview must therefore act with care.

5.4.4 WHAT INFERENCE MAY A COURT DRAW UNDER S. 34 CJPOA 1994?

The answer is, 'such inferences as appear proper' (s. 34(2) CJPOA 1994). The jury or magistrates do not have to draw an adverse inference. If they choose to draw an adverse inference, they may conclude that the defendant remained silent because he had no answer to the allegations being made against him, or none that he was prepared to put forward and have subjected to critical questioning by investigating officers. They may conclude that he has since made up his defence to fit the facts as disclosed by the prosecution.

5.4.5 'ADVERSE INFERENCES WILL ONLY BE DRAWN WHERE, IN THE CIRCUMSTANCES EXISTING AT THE TIME THE ACCUSED *COULD REASONABLY HAVE BEEN EXPECTED TO MENTION . . .* '

What is meant by the expression 'could reasonably have been expected to mention'?

The all-important question of reasonableness is a question of fact for the jury or magistrates (*R v Condron* [1997] 1 WLR 827; *R v Argent* [1997] 2 Cr App R 27). If a defendant wishes to persuade the court not to draw an adverse inference, tactically he needs to adduce evidence (perhaps by offering his explanation in the witness box or calling the legal adviser who gave him the advice at the police station) to explain his reasons for remaining silent at the relevant time. This will almost certainly require your client to waive his legal professional privilege (see below, para. 5.5.1). It will then be a matter for the jury or magistrates to decide whether it was reasonable in the circumstances for the defendant to have remained silent and if not, whether to draw an adverse inference.

What amounts to 'reasonable' will depend on the particular circumstances of each case.

In *R v Argent* [1997] 2 Cr App R 27, the Court of Appeal identified the following non-exhaustive list of factors on the issue of reasonableness:

- the time of day;
- the defendant's age;
- the defendant's experience at dealing with the police;
- the defendant's mental capacity;
- the defendant's state of health;
- the defendant's sobriety;
- the defendant's tiredness;
- the defendant's personality;
- whether the defendant remained silent on the basis of legal advice;
- the extent of the disclosure of the police case against the defendant.

The court or jury must consider these factors from the subjective perspective of the defendant at the time of his detention at the police station, not from the position of the reasonable man. If the court or jury concludes that it was reasonable for the defendant to have remained silent for the reason(s) given, an adverse inference should not be drawn.

5.5 DO ANY SPECIAL CONSIDERATIONS APPLY WHERE THE DECISION TO REMAIN SILENT IS BASED ON LEGAL ADVICE?

The reasonableness of a defendant's decision to remain silent is a question of fact for a jury or magistrates to decide. Consequently, a defendant is not insulated from having an adverse inference drawn against him, where he gives as his reason for remaining silent the fact that he relied on the advice of his solicitor.

In *R v Hoare and Pierce* [2005] 1 Cr App R 22, Lord Justice Auld made the following observations as regards s. 34:

'It is not the purpose of section 34 to exclude a jury from drawing an adverse inference against a defendant because he genuinely or reasonably believes that, regardless of his guilt or innocence, he is entitled to take advantage of that advice to impede the prosecution case against him. In such a case the advice is not truly the reason for not mentioning the facts. The section 34 inference is concerned with flushing out innocence at an early stage or supporting other evidence of guilt at a later stage, not simply with whether a guilty defendant is entitled, or genuinely or reasonably believes that he is entitled, to rely on legal rights of which his solicitor has advised him. Legal entitlement is one thing. An accused's reason for exercising it is another. His belief in his entitlement may be genuine, but it does not follow that his reason for exercising it is . . . '

How is a court to assess the reasonableness of the defendant's decision to remain silent unless it is told of the reason(s) for the advice? This has clear implications for legal professional privilege.

5.5.1 ADVISING SILENCE AND LEGAL PROFESSIONAL PRIVILEGE

Communications between solicitor and client are of course protected from disclosure in evidence by legal professional privilege. The privilege belongs to the client and, as such, only the client may choose to waive it. In *R v Condron* [1997] 1 WLR 827, the Court of Appeal observed that for the defendant to simply assert in the witness box, 'I choose not to answer questions on the advice of my solicitor', would be unlikely to impress the jury. If sufficient weight is to be given to the defendant's reasons for not mentioning relevant facts, more explanation would almost certainly have to be given. In order to achieve this, the defendant would need to waive legal professional privilege in order to explain the basis on which his solicitor's advice had been given. Having waived privilege, the defendant could expect to be subjected to cross-examination on precisely how much he told his solicitor at the relevant time. The Court of Appeal explained the position as follows:

> 'Communications between an accused person and his solicitor prior to interviews by the police are subject to legal professional privilege. But the privilege can be waived by the client, though not the solicitor. If an accused person gives as a reason for not answering questions, that he has been advised by his solicitor not to do so, that advice, in our judgment, does not amount to a waiver of privilege. But, equally, for reasons which we have already given, that bare assertion is unlikely by itself to be regarded as a sufficient reason for not mentioning matters relevant to the defence. So it will be necessary, if the accused wishes to invite the court not to draw an adverse inference, to go further and state the basis or reason for the advice. Although the matter was not fully argued, it seems to us that once this is done that it may well amount to a waiver of privilege so that the accused, or if his solicitor is also called, the solicitor, can be asked whether there were any other reasons for the advice, and the nature of the advice given, so as to explore whether the advice may also have been given for tactical reasons.'

The implication for legal professional privilege are considered further in Chapter 9 which examines the practical steps a legal adviser might take in advising a suspect at the police station.

In *R v Bresa* [2005] EWCA Crim 1414, the Court of Appeal observed in a case where no reason is put forward as to the basis for the legal advice given, the jury should be reminded that the defendant is under no obligation to reveal what transpired between himself and his legal adviser; however, he has a choice as to whether to make such revelation. The overriding question which always has to be answered is: could the defendant have reasonably been expected to mention the facts he is now relying on?

5.5.2 DIRECTING THE JURY ON THE EFFECT OF SILENCE CONSEQUENT UPON LEGAL ADVICE

The relationship between silence and legal advice has been influenced by decisions of the European Court of Human Rights (*Condron v UK* (2001) 31 EHRR 1 and *Beckles v UK* (2002) 36 EHRR 162). An important decision of the Court of Appeal in this regard is *R v Betts and Hall* [2001] 2 Cr App R 16, in which Lord Justice Kay, delivering the judgment of the Court of Appeal, held it is not the correctness of the legal advice with which the court is concerned but the genuineness of the suspect's reliance on it, and that if the jury concluded that the defendant's reason for silence was his genuine reliance upon legal advice, an adverse inference must not be drawn. However, *R v Betts and Hall* must be reconsidered in the light of the decision of the Court of Appeal in *R v Howell* which provides that the defendant's decision to remain silent must be both genuine and reasonable.

> ### *R v Howell* [2005] 1 Cr App R 1
>
> Howell was suspected of involvement in a serious assault on his flatmate. He told his solicitor, as he would later tell the jury, that he had acted in self-defence when he stabbed his flatmate. His solicitor asked the investigating officers if the victim of the attack had made a written statement. He had not. He had however given the investigating officers a detailed verbal account, including the specific allegation that the defendant had attacked him with a knife. The defendant had indicated to his solicitor that the victim might withdraw his allegation. Consequently the solicitor advised him to make no comment in interview. No evidence was forthcoming from the solicitor as to the reasons for his advice. The defendant was asked in cross-examination, why, if he was an innocent man, had he not taken the opportunity of putting forward his version of events. The defendant gave as his reason for not answering questions, the fact that he had simply followed the advice of his solicitor. In his summing-up the trial judge instructed the jury to consider whether the defendant had been right to act upon the advice of his solicitor.
>
> On the facts of *Howell*, the Court of Appeal concluded that the solicitor had been wrong to advise silence on the basis of the absence of a written complaint from the victim, especially as adequate oral disclosure had been given. This was not a case where it would have been difficult for the defendant to recall events. The defendant had been there in the flat. He must have known whether he acted in self-defence or not. In the circumstances it had been permissible for the jury to draw an adverse inference on the basis that it had been reasonable to have expected the defendant to mention such facts, notwithstanding the advice of his solicitor.

5.5.3   REMAINING SILENT ON LEGAL ADVICE AFTER R V HOWELL

In *Howell*, the Court of Appeal talked of the important responsibility defence solicitors have when giving advice at police stations:

> 'there must always be soundly based objective reasons for silence, sufficiently cogent and telling to weigh in the balance against the clear public interest in an account being given to the suspect by the police. Solicitors bearing the important responsibility of giving advice to suspects at police stations must always bear that in mind.'

As examples of the type of instance in which a solicitor could justifiably advise silence, the Court of Appeal cited such matters as the suspect's mental condition and his ability to recollect events without reference to documents or some other source.

The all-important question is what does not amount to a sound objective reason for remaining silent. Suppose your client genuinely relies on your advice but it later transpires that your advice was wrong or ill-conceived? How fair is it for an adverse inference to be drawn against your client in these circumstances? A suspect, particularly one who is inexperienced in police station procedure, is hardly going to question your professional judgement in this respect. We will further consider the issues raised by this case in Chapter 9 when we explore the practical steps a legal adviser might take when advising at the police station, with particular emphasis on the circumstances in which the advice to remain silent might safely be given.

In the later cases of *R v Hoare and Pierce* [2005] 1 Cr App R 22 and *R v Beckles* [2005] 1 All ER 705, the Court of Appeal gave a ringing endorsement of its earlier decision in *R v Howell*, and could in fact see no conflict between the decision in *R v Howell* and *R v Betts and Hall*. The critical test under s. 34 remains: was the fact which the defendant failed to mention one that the defendant could reasonably have been expected to mention notwithstanding genuine reliance on legal advice? You are reminded of the quotation taken from Lord Justice Auld's judgement in *R v Hoare and Pierce* that appears in para. 5.5.

5.6 THE RIGHT TO SILENCE AND PROTECTING THE DEFENDANT'S RIGHT TO A FAIR TRIAL

Although not specifically guaranteed under Article 6, the right to silence is an implied right. The fundamental importance of the right was stated in *Murray v United Kingdom* (1996) 22 EHRR 29:

> 'Although not specifically mentioned in Article 6 of the Convention, there can be no doubt that the right to remain silent under police questioning and the privilege against self-incrimination are generally recognised international standards which lie at the heart of the notion of a fair procedure under Article 6. By providing the accused with protection against improper compulsion by the authorities, these immunities contribute to avoiding miscarriages of justice and to securing the aims of Article 6.'

Is the decision to draw adverse inference compatible with Article 6 of the ECHR 1950? The short answer is yes—providing numerous safeguards are met. Some of the required safeguards apply at the questioning stage, such as the need to correctly caution the suspect. Others apply at trial (particularly in relation to the judge's direction to the jury). The safeguards are all contained in the Judicial Studies Board specimen direction on s. 34 which forms the basis for the trial judge's crucial directions to the jury on the operation of s. 34. The essential safeguards are set out below:

(1) Adverse inferences cannot be the sole reason for finding a defendant guilty. Under s. 38 CJPOA 1994, no person shall have a case to answer or be convicted solely on an adverse inference drawn under s. 34. This important safeguard has been developed further with European Court of Human Rights jurisprudence. In *Murray v UK* (1996) 22 EHRR 29, the ECtHR stated quite categorically that it would be contrary to Article 6 to base a conviction solely or mainly on a defendant's silence.

(2) Adverse inferences may not be drawn where the police have delayed a detainee's access to a solicitor under s. 58 PACE 1984 and Code C para. 6.6. This amendment to the Criminal Justice and Public Order Act 1994 was enacted to take account of decisions of the ECtHR in *Murray v UK* (1996) 22 EHRR 29, *Condron v UK* (2001) 31 EHRR 1 and *Averill v UK* (2001) 31 EHRR 36. All these decisions have consistently stressed the fundamental importance of access to a solicitor at the police station. In this situation, the suspect will be cautioned that he does not have to say anything, but that anything he does say may be given in evidence.

(3) An adverse inference may only be drawn when, having listened to any explanation put forward by the defendant for his failure to mention facts and being satisfied that a sufficiently strong case against the defendant is made out, the jury or magistrates conclude that the only sensible explanation for his silence is that he had no answer at the time or none that would stand up to scrutiny.

(4) The jury or magistrates should regard an adverse inference as providing additional support only in a situation where the prosecution's case, aside from the defendant's silence, is so strong, as to call for an answer from the accused.

A failure by the trial judge to correctly direct the jury on all aspects of s. 34 gives rise to a potential right of appeal in the event of conviction (*R v Webber* [2004] 1 WLR 404). The importance of the trial judge discussing his direction on s. 34 with the trial advocates in advance of his summing-up has been stressed time and time again. If you find yourself sitting behind counsel in the Crown Court, it is essential that you take a verbatim note of the trial judge's direction.

5.7 HOW SHOULD A COURT PROCEED WHERE S. 34 IS INOPERATIVE?

It appears that the court should revert to the common law position, exemplified in *Hall v R* [1971] 1 WLR 298. The defendant is entitled to a direction that no adverse inference should be drawn from the fact that he exercised his right to silence (*R v McGarry* [1999] 1 Cr App R 377). In this particular case, the prosecution conceded that s. 34 has no application on the facts. A failure to give a '*McGarry*' direction, however, is not always fatal to a conviction (*R v Francom* [2001] 1 Cr App R 237).

5.8 CONCLUDING REMARKS ON S. 34

The trial judge has the responsibility for ensuring a fair trial, and this may require him to exercise discretion to exclude prosecution evidence under s. 78 PACE 1984 (see Chapter 6). If the s. 34 caution was incorrectly administered or deliberately misrepresented, or the interview took place in blatant breach of the safeguards in Code C, the defence advocate should submit that it would be unfair for an adverse inference to be drawn using s. 78 PACE 1984 (see Chapter 6).

For a summary of the precise conditions that a jury or magistrates must find before an adverse inference can safely be drawn, we invite you to consider the JSB specimen direction on s. 34. The specimen directions are issued by the JSB to all Crown Court judges to promote a consistent application of the rules relating to criminal law, evidence and procedure when summing-up to the jury.

online resource centre

The complete version of the JSB's specimen direction can be accessed from the web-links section on our Online Resource Centre. Ensure you access the most up-to-date version of the direcions on s. 34 by following the updates link: June 2007, Direction 40.

It will be apparent from all that has been said above that the practical operation and effect of s. 34 is complex. There are a considerable number of hoops through which a conscientious jury or magisterial bench must jump before adverse inferences may be drawn under s. 34. The extent to which a jury understands the directions on s. 34 is open to debate, and you may well wonder whether utilising s. 34 CJPOA 1994 is worth it. In *R v Brizzalari* [2004] EWCA Crim 310, the Court of Appeal called for prosecutors to refrain from too readily seeking to activate s. 34.

5.9 SUBMITTING A PREPARED STATEMENT TO THE POLICE AS AN ALTERNATIVE TO REMAINING SILENT

An alternative approach to advising a suspect to remain silent is to put forward his denial and/or defence in a written statement prepared and read out during the interview by his legal adviser. This approach prevents a s. 34 CJPOA 1994 inference being drawn against a defendant at a subsequent trial, provided the facts disclosed in the written statement are consistent with the defendant's case at trial. Such statements do, however, need to be very carefully drafted, as any omission in the statement (which is then reinforced at trial with further information), or any departure from it at trial, would leave the defendant vulnerable to an adverse inference under s. 34 CJPOA 1994. In *R v Knight* [2004] 1 Cr App R 9, the Court of Appeal held that, provided the defendant mentioned in his prepared statement all the facts he later relied on in court, adverse inferences would not be drawn, as this practice fulfilled the purpose of s. 34, i.e. the early disclosure of the suspect's account.

R v Knight [2004] 1 Cr App R 9

The defendant was convicted of an indecent assault on a girl. At the beginning of the police interview his solicitor read out a prepared statement denying the allegation. Thereafter the defendant refused to answer police questions on legal advice. At his trial the prepared statement was read to the jury and the defendant gave evidence consistent with what he had said in his prepared statement. The judge directed the jury that it could choose to draw the inference that the defendant had refused to answer police questions because he did not want his prepared statement to be subject to critical scrutiny by the police.

It was argued by the prosecution on appeal that on a literal interpretation of the wording in s. 34, the defendant had failed to mention facts when being questioned. The Court of Appeal disagreed, stating:

'We have come to the clear conclusion that the aim of ss. 34(1)(a) does not distinctly include police cross-examination of the suspect upon his account over and above the disclosure of that account. Had that been intended, it seems to us that Parliament would have used significantly different language. The relevant failure could readily be described as a failure 'to answer questions properly put to him under caution by a constable trying to discover whether or by whom the offence had been committed', rather than a failure to mention any facts relied on in his defence. But the point is not merely linguistic. A requirement to submit to police cross-examination (so long as the questions are proper), or at any rate an encouragement to do so on pain of later adverse inferences being drawn, is a significantly greater intrusion into a suspect's general right of silence than is a requirement, or encouragement, upon the suspect to disclose his factual defence. We by no means suggest that such an intrusion could not properly be legislated for without offence to Article 6 of the European Convention on Human Rights; but it would, we think, require a much sharper expression of the legislature's will than can be found in the words of the statute as enacted.'

In *Knight*, the Court of Appeal cautioned that the use of a prepared statement should not of itself be regarded as an 'inevitable antidote to later adverse inferences'. An inference is still possible where the prepared statement proves to be incomplete or inconsistent with what the defendant later relies on in evidence.

The danger of inconsistencies between the defendant's case at trial and the prepared statement at the police stations was underlined by the Court of Appeal in *R v Turner* [2004] 1 All ER 1025:

'. . . such a statement is not an inevitable antidote to later adverse inferences. It may be incomplete in comparison with the defendant's later account at trial, or it may be inconsistent with that account. This court notes a growing practice, no doubt on advice, to submit a pre-prepared statement and decline to answer any questions. This in our view may prove a dangerous course for an innocent person who subsequently discovers at the trial that something significant has been omitted. No such problems would arise following an interview where the suspect gives appropriate answers to the question.'

Legal advisers ought to give careful consideration to the use of a prepared statement. It may prove to be the safest course of action in some circumstances. In *R v Knight*, the facts of the accusation were straightforward. The accused denied the offence of indecent assault and was able to fully and simply articulate his defence in his prepared statement. He articulated precisely the same defence before the jury. Section 34 requires your client to do no more than this.

5.10 DRAWING INFERENCES FROM A FAILURE TO ACCOUNT FOR OBJECTS, SUBSTANCES OR MARKS: S. 36 CJPOA 1994

While most judicial attention has been focused on the application of s. 34 Criminal Justice and Public Order Act 1994, the potential for adverse inferences being drawn from the defendant's silence under ss. 36 and/or 37 should not be forgotten. As with s. 34, a competent criminal lawyer will have a good understanding of the ambit of ss. 36 and 37 and the relevant case law and be prepared to apply this knowledge in support of his client's case. Consider each section below.

Section 36

'(1) Where—

(a) a person is arrested by a constable, and there is—

(i)   on his person; or

(ii) in or on his clothing or footwear; or

(iii) otherwise in his possession; or

(iv) in any place in which he is at the time of his arrest, any object, substance or mark, or there is any mark on any such object; and

(b) that or another constable investigating the case reasonably believes that the presence of the object, substance or mark may be attributable to the participation of the person arrested in the commission of an offence specified by the constable; and

(c) the constable informs the person arrested that he so believes, and requests him to account for the presence of the object, substance or mark; and

(d) the person fails or refuses to do so, then . . .

(2) . . .

(c) the court, in determining whether there is a case to answer; and (d) the court and the jury, in determining whether the accused is guilty of the offence charged, may draw such inferences from the failure or refusal as appear proper

(3) Subsections (1) and (2) above apply to the condition of clothing or footwear as they apply to a substance or mark thereon.'

5.11   DRAWING INFERENCES FROM A FAILURE TO ACCOUNT FOR ONE'S PRESENCE AT A PARTICULAR PLACE: S. 37 CJPOA 1994

Section 37

'(1) Where—

(a) a person arrested by a constable was found by him at a place at or about the time the offence for which he was arrested is alleged to have been committed; and

(b) that or another constable investigating the offence reasonably believes that the presence of the person at that place and at that time may be attributable to his participation in the commission of the offence; and

(c) the constable informs the person that he so believes, and requests him to account for that presence; and

(d) the person fails or refuses to do so, then if, in any proceedings against the person for the offence, evidence of those matters is given . . .

(2) . . .

(c) the court, in determining whether there is a case to answer; and

(d) the court or the jury, in determining whether the accused is guilty of the offence charged, may draw such inferences from the failure or refusal as appear proper.'

5.12   WHAT IS THE EFFECT OF SS. 36 AND 37?

An adverse inference may only be drawn under s. 36 or s. 37 in accordance with the precise wording in the statutory sections. The suspect must be cautioned in these strict terms. It is not the job of the legal adviser to correct the caution if it is mistakenly put. A failure to properly caution the suspect under either s. 36 or s. 37 will mean that an adverse inference cannot be drawn, and the defendant's replies should be edited out of the transcript that is eventually placed before the court.

The evidential effect of an inference drawn under either section is to strengthen the prosecution's case, irrespective of any defence subsequently advanced by the defendant in court. Section 38(3) CJPOA 1994 applies, in that no one will have a case to answer, or be convicted of an offence, based solely on an inference drawn from a failure or refusal as prescribed in s. 36(2) and s. 37(2). In accordance with s. 58 Youth Justice and Criminal Evidence Act 1999, an adverse inference under s. 36(4A) and s. 37(3A) CJPOA 1994 cannot be drawn where access to a solicitor has not been made available under s. 58 PACE 1984.

Consider the following examples of ss. 36 and 37.

 Example 1

Andrew is implicated in a recent offence of assault. On his arrest, he has visible bruising about his face. Andrew tells you he has no knowledge of the incident alleged. Andrew is bound to be asked to account for the bruising visible on his face. A failure to offer some explanation for the bruising may lead to an adverse inference being drawn under s. 36.

 Example 2

Leon is arrested on suspicion of the burglary of an optician's premises. In the course of the burglary a pane of glass was smashed. An eye-witness gives a description of the suspect. Leon is stopped by the police in the vicinity some 20 minutes later. His shoes are seized and subject to forensic examination. Shards of glass are found embedded in the soles of the shoes. Leon denies involvement with the burglary. Leon will be asked to account for the presence of glass in his shoes. A failure to offer an explanation for its presence may result in an adverse inference being drawn under s. 36.

 Example 3

The police are investigating an attempted arson offence at a school. Kevin is arrested in the school playing fields shortly after the alarm was raised. Kevin denies any involvement in the matter. In interview, Kevin is bound to be asked to account for his presence on the school fields. A failure to offer an explanation may result in an adverse inference being drawn under s. 37. If it later transpires that Andrew's trousers disclose traces of petrol, he can expect to be asked to account for its presence in interview in accordance with s. 36.

Very few cases have gone to appeal on ss. 36 and 37. One case which did is *R v Compton* [2002] EWCA Crim 2835. In this case, the defendants were accused of drug trafficking. The police had found a substantial quantity of used banknotes in their possession. When tested, a substantial number of the banknotes were found to be contaminated with heroin, far above the level likely to be found on banknotes in general circulation. Both defendants denied drug trafficking at their trial and insisted that the banknotes represented the funds of a jewellery business in one case, and an antiques business in the other. Both defendants suggested at their trial that the contamination was attributable to their personal drug habit. Both defendants had made largely no comment interviews, although one of the defendants had explained the presence of heroin based on the fact that he was a drug user. A s. 36 inference was rightly left to the jury since the 'bare statement' that each was a drug user did not 'account for' the presence of substantial contamination as put to them by the investigating officer.

In this case, the Court of Appeal reiterated the importance of the trial judge giving a correct direction on s. 36.

5.12.1 **ANTICIPATING ADVERSE INFERENCES UNDER SS. 36 AND 37 CJPOA 1994**

A legal adviser at the police station must try to anticipate questions likely to form the basis of a s. 36 or s. 37 inference. It reaffirms the importance of checking the custody record very carefully to see what has been seized from your client or his property and what searches have been undertaken and whether final or preliminary results are available. You may need to ask your client some searching questions about the state of the evidence against him. Your client needs to be prepared for the sort of questioning that could form the basis of an inference under s. 36 or s. 37.

KEY POINT SUMMARY

- If a defendant advances facts at his trial which he failed to mention in interview, he may have an adverse inference drawn against him if the court considers it was reasonable, at the time, for the defendant to have advanced the particular facts.
- The reasonableness of a defendant's decision depends upon a number of factors (some of them are listed in *R v Argent*).
- It matters not that the defendant's decision to remain silent was based on legal advice given at the time—it is still a matter for the jury/magistrates.
- An inference can only be drawn if, having worked through a number of specified safeguards in the JSB's specimen directions, the jury comes to the conclusion that the defendant remained silent because he had no answer to the allegations, or none that he was prepared to have subjected to critical scrutiny.
- A conviction cannot be based solely upon an adverse inference.
- An adverse inference may not be drawn where the court concludes the accused genuinely and reasonably relied on legal advice.
- Legal advisers must consider whether there are sound objective reasons for advising silence.
- Where a defendant is to rely on legal advice as the reason for seeking to avoid an adverse inference, he must expect to waive his legal professional privilege.
- Where an adverse inference is drawn, it is a contributing evidential component of the prosecution's case and a conviction cannot be based wholly or mainly on the fact of silence.

SELF-TEST QUESTIONS

Consider the following short scenarios and decide whether s. 34/36 or 37 are engaged.

Scenario 1

Karl is being questioned on suspicion of manslaughter. He refuses to answer questions put by the police. At his trial Karl gives evidence to the effect that he acted in self-defence.

Scenario 2

Stan is arrested on suspicion of murder. During his interview he puts forward a defence of provocation. At trial he gives evidence consistent both with provocation and self-defence.

Scenario 3

Jason is arrested on suspicion of attempted rape. The victim of the attack retaliated, scratching her assailant's face. In interview Jason is cautioned and asked to account for scratch marks that can be seen on his face. Jason chooses not to reply. In fact, he remains silent throughout the interview. Giving evidence at his trial, Jason states he has been mistakenly identified in that he has an alibi.

Scenario 4

Following a burglary, Rio is arrested a few hours later. It is clear that the burglar exited the property along a muddy track and over a wall topped with metal spikes. The police inform Rio that he is under arrest on suspicion of burglary. In interview Rio advances a defence of alibi. In the course of the interview he is cautioned and asked to account for a tear on the sleeve of his jacket and mud on his shoes. Rio is unable to offer any explanation for either.

Scenario 5

Jane is arrested on a Sunday evening on suspicion of criminal damage. She is found by a police officer near to a field where genetically modified maize is under cultivation. Several crops have been uprooted. When questioned under caution about the alleged offence, Jane is asked to account for her presence near to the field. Jane refuses to reply. She also refuses to give evidence at her trial.

Scenario 6

Carley is arrested on suspicion of being in possession of a controlled drug with intent to supply. She admits to being in possession, but denies intent to supply. Her solicitor is of the view that she is unfit to be interviewed by the police due to drug withdrawal symptoms. The police doctor disagrees. Carley takes the advice of her solicitor and chooses not to answer questions during the interview. She is charged with possession with intent to supply. At trial she will give evidence denying intent to supply. Does she have anything to fear from her failure to answer questions at the police station?

FIGURE 5.1 DRAWING ADVERSE INFERENCES FROM SILENCE

ADVERSE INFERENCES: S. 34 CJPOA 1994

- Section 34 CJPOA 1994 does not abolish the right to silence.
- Section 34 CJPOA 1994 applies where a defendant:
  – is questioned under caution; or on being charged;
  – fails to mention a fact that he later relies on in his defence.
- An adverse inference may only be drawn where:
  – defendant has been offered legal advice, s. 34(2A) CJPOA 1994; and
  – the court considers it would have been reasonable for the defendant to have mentioned the fact; see *R v Condron; R v Argent.*
- The reasonableness test includes the defendant's:
  – age and experience of dealing with the police;
  – mental capacity;
  – state of health; and whether legal advice was given.
- It is a matter for the jury/magistrates as to whether an adverse inference should be drawn.
- In a jury trial, the judge must direct the jury in accordance with the JSB's specimen direction on s. 34, which includes a host of safeguards, including:
  – conviction cannot be based wholly or mainly on a failure to mention;
  – the court must consider the reason for the defendant remaining silent;
  – an adverse inference may only be drawn if the jury concludes that the real reason for the defendant's failure was that he had no answer to the allegation, or none that would withstand critical scrutiny.
- A court may not draw an adverse inference where the defendant reasonably and genuinely relied on legal advice; see *R v Howell; R v Hoare and Pierce.*
- A solicitor advising silence at the police station must make his client fully aware of the risks.
- A prepared statement containing all the defence facts may prevent adverse inferences from being drawn; see *R v Knight.*

ADVERSE INFERENCES: S. 36 CJPOA 1994

- Adverse inferences may be drawn where, after arrest, the defendant refuses to account for any object, substance or mark on his person; or in his clothing; or otherwise in his possession; and
- the officer has a reasonable belief that the object etc may be attributable to his participation in the offence; and
- the possible effect of his failure or refusal to account for the object was explained to the defendant, Code C para. 10.11.

ADVERSE INFERENCES: S. 37 CJPOA 1994

- Adverse inferences may be drawn where, after arrest, defendant refuses to account for his presence at a particular place; and
- the officer has a reasonable belief that his presence may be attributable to his participation in the offence; and
- the possible effect of his failure or refusal to account for his presence was explained to the defendant, Code C para. 10.11.

UNLAWFULLY AND UNFAIRLY OBTAINED EVIDENCE

6.1 INTRODUCTION

Part II of this book is concerned with the investigation of criminal offences. The purpose of the investigation is to secure sufficient evidence to charge a person(s) suspected of committing the offence(s) and to take the matter to trial where he may plead guilty or be found guilty. The manner in which the police obtain evidence during an investigation may have implications for the admissibility of evidence at any subsequent trial. Whilst the rules of evidence are applied primarily at trial, they also underpin the construction of the whole case. The police should be aware that evidence obtained in breach of their investigatory powers is open to challenge.

Every defendant enjoys the right to a fair trial, which is explicitly guaranteed in Article 6 ECHR 1950. The right to a fair trial has a very broad application and is not solely considered in relation to unlawfully obtained evidence. The court has power to exclude any prosecution evidence, the admission of which would prejudice a fair trial.

In this chapter, we consider the defendant's right to a fair trial in the context of the rules relating to the admissibility of unlawfully or unfairly obtained evidence by examining the position at:

• common law; and

• under s. 78 Police and Criminal Evidence Act 1984; and

• as an abuse of process.

6.2 WHAT IS UNLAWFULLY OBTAINED EVIDENCE?

Unlawfully or unfairly obtained evidence can be described as any prosecution evidence which has been obtained in a 'questionable' manner. Unlawfully obtained evidence could include evidence obtained as a result of an unlawful search of a person or his property or through the use of an *agent provocateur* or an undercover police officer or evidence obtained through unauthorised surveillance methods.

Unlawfully obtained evidence may also include a confession or identification evidence obtained in breach of the safeguards under PACE 1984 and the PACE Codes of Practice. (The admissibility of confession evidence is separately considered in Chapter 7 and the admissibility of identification evidence is considered in Chapter 8).

The use of 'underhand' investigation methods or the occasional 'bending of the rules' can yield highly relevant evidence of a suspect's guilt. This poses a dilemma for the court because to exclude such evidence may mean a guilty defendant walking free, but to admit the evidence would be to condone unlawful activities by the police.

6.3   INTERRELATIONSHIP OF RULES OF PROCEDURE AND RULES OF EVIDENCE

Although arguments concerning the admissibility of evidence will occur at trial, we have chosen to consider the law relating to unlawfully obtained evidence at this point because it is most likely to arise in the context of evidence obtained as part of the investigative process. In Chapters 3 and 4, we set out the legal requirements of lawful stop and search, arrest, detention and questioning of suspects. The question which lies at the heart of this chapter is whether or not evidence obtained in unlawful circumstances or in breach of PACE 1984 and the Codes of Practice can be excluded in the exercise of judicial discretion? The answer to this question is yes, as the power exists at common law and under s. 78 PACE 1984. However, a more salient question is whether the court will exercise its discretion to exclude such evidence? The answer to this question can only really be explored by considering the case law.

6.4   COMMON LAW DISCRETION

The criminal courts have always retained the common law power to exclude evidence capable of prejudicing a fair trial. This discretion is specifically preserved by s. 82(3) PACE 1984. Evidence will be excluded where its prejudicial effect outweighs its probative value.

The common law has always adopted a narrow approach to excluding illegally or unlawfully obtained evidence. Provided the evidence is relevant and reliable, its admission is not generally regarded as prejudicing the defendant's right to a fair trial. The common law position is made clear in Lord Diplock's statement in the leading case of *R v Sang* [1980] AC 402 (a case where the defendant argued he had been entrapped by prosecution authorities):

'(1) A trial judge in a criminal trial has always a discretion to refuse to admit evidence if in his opinion its prejudicial effect outweighs its probative value. (2) Save with regard to admissions and confessions and generally with regard to evidence obtained from the accused after commission of the offence, he has no discretion to refuse to admit relevant admissible evidence on the ground that it was obtained by improper or unfair means. The court isn't concerned with how it was obtained.'

Earlier in his judgment, Lord Diplock stated:

'The function of a judge at a criminal trial as respects the admission of evidence is to ensure the accused has a fair trial according to the law. It is no part of a judge's function to exercise disciplinary powers over the police or prosecution as respects the way in which the evidence to be used at the trial is obtained by them . . .'

Although the common law has now been largely superseded by s. 78 PACE 1984, it may still be used in legal argument although the absence of significant case law indicates that s. 82(3) PACE 1984 is not commonly invoked.

6.5 DISCRETION UNDER S. 78 PACE 1984

Section 78(1) provides:

> 'In any proceedings the court may refuse to allow evidence on which the prosecution proposes to rely to be given if it appears to the court that, having regard to all the circumstances, including the circumstances in which the evidence was obtained, the admission of the evidence would have such an adverse effect on the fairness of the proceedings that the court ought not to admit it.'

Section 78 gives a court the discretion to exclude prosecution evidence where that evidence would have an adverse effect on the fairness of the proceedings. Although the fairness of the proceedings is not defined the court is invited by the wording in the section, to have regard to all the circumstances in which the evidence was obtained.

Whilst s. 78 PACE 1984 appears as though it might be applied to exclude evidence on a wider basis than the discretion exercised at common law, case law showing the exercise of judicial discretion under s. 78 in relation to unlawfully obtained evidence suggests otherwise subject to the exceptions of confessions and identification evidence which are considered in Chapters 7 and 8.

6.6 CATEGORIES OF UNLAWFULLY OBTAINED EVIDENCE OTHER THAN CONFESSIONS AND EYE-WITNESS IDENTIFICATION

There are many ways in which the police might obtain evidence in a dubious or unlawful manner, including:

* evidence obtained through an unlawful search;
* evidence found pursuant to an unlawful arrest;
* evidence obtained through entrapment;
* evidence obtained through use of unlawful surveillance;
* evidence obtained by deception or trickery;
* evidence obtained whilst trespassing on premises;
* evidence obtained in breach of an individual's right to privacy;
* evidence obtained in violation of the privilege against self-incrimination; or
* evidence obtained in breach of legal professional privilege.

We include a small selection of case law examples based on some of these categories.

6.6.1 USE OF TRICKERY OR DECEPTION BY THE POLICE

There are other ways in which evidence of a self-incriminating nature might be obtained from a suspect than through the formal police interview procedure. These include the use of covert listening devices and covert surveillance. Code C has little application to evidence of a self-incriminating nature obtained in such circumstances. What is clear is that the use of such methods should not be adopted by the police with the express intention of deliberately not complying with the Codes of Practice. This principle was established in *R v Christou* [1992] 4 All ER 559 in which undercover officers posed as 'shady jewellers', willing to receive stolen items of jewellery. The purpose of the operation had been to recover stolen goods and identify thieves and handlers and on the basis of this information the defendant and others were prosecuted. Upholding the conviction , the Court of Appeal concluded the appellant was not being questioned by police officers and that the conversation was on equal terms and therefore Code C had no application in this situation. The Court of Appeal went on to say that:

'It would be wrong for police officers to adopt or use an undercover pose or disguise to enable themselves to ask questions about an offence uninhibited by the requirement of the Code and with the effect of circumventing it. Were they to do so, it would be open to the judge to exclude the questioning and answers under section 78 of PACE.'

R v Bailey and Smith [1993] 3 All ER 365

The two accused were arrested in connection with an armed robbery. Both were legally represented and chose to exercise their right to remain silent. They were charged and brought before a magistrates' court where they were remanded into police custody for the purposes of attending an identification parade. The questioning of suspects after charge is prohibited under Code C. The investigating officers decided to put the defendants in the same cell, in an attempt to obtain further useful evidence. The cell was bugged. The officers had sought authorisation for their proposed course of action from a senior officer. The officers invented a charade, telling the defendants that it was not their choice to have them share a cell but that they had been forced into it by an uncooperative custody officer. The defendants were taken in, notwithstanding the fact that their solicitor had warned them that the bugging of police cells was not uncommon. While together in the cell, they made incriminating admissions which were used in evidence against them.

The Court of Appeal held the trial judge had rightly admitted the evidence. Lord Justice Simon Brown summed up his reasoning as follows:

'Where, as here, very serious crimes have been committed . . . by men who have not shrunk from using trickery and a good deal worse, and where there has never been the least suggestion that their covertly taped confessions were oppressively obtained or were other than wholly reliable it seems to be hardly surprising that the trial judge exercised his discretion in the way he did . . .'

6.6.2 UNAUTHORISED SURVEILLANCE METHODS

The increasing sophistication of technological surveillance devices allows the police to obtain evidence in many different covert ways. For the most part, such surveillance operations are regulated by the Regulation of Investigatory Powers Act 2000 (RIPA), an immensely complicated piece of legislation. Where such surveillance methods are unauthorised or where the police act in breach of the criminal and/or the civil law, should the evidence be admitted?

R v Khan [1996] 3 All ER 298

Khan was under suspicion of drug smuggling. In an attempt to obtain evidence against him, investigating officers attached a listening device to a property visited frequently by Khan, of which neither Khan or the flat's owner had any knowledge. There were Home Office Guidelines in existence regarding the use of covert surveillance, but there was no statutory authorisation for the use of such devices at the time, although the officers had sought and obtained permission of the Chief Constable. As a consequence of the operation, the police obtained a tape recording that proved Khan was involved in the importation of heroin. They sought to use it in evidence against him at his trial.

At his trial the prosecution accepted that there was no statutory authority for the use of the device and that placing it on the property without the owner's permission constituted a civil trespass. Khan conceded that the tape was authentic and that it was his voice which could be heard. On appeal it was argued on his behalf that the evidence had been obtained in violation of Article 8, guaranteeing a right of privacy and that the trial judge should have excluded the tape-recorded conversations in the exercise of his discretion either at common law or under s. 78 PACE 1984.

Notwithstanding there may have been a violation of Article 8, the House of Lords concluded that the evidence was rightly admitted at common law and under s. 78. The evidence was especially relevant and could not be said to have adversely affected the fairness of the proceedings.

Mr Khan subsequently took his case to the European Court of Human Rights, in *Khan v United Kingdom* (2001) 31 EHRR 45. Whilst finding the UK to be in violation of Article 8, the ECtHR determined that there had been no violation of Article 6, guaranteeing the right to a fair trial.

As regards Article 6(1), the ECtHR observed:

'It is not the role of the Court to determine, as a matter of principle, whether particular types of evidence, for example, unlawfully obtained evidence may be admissible or, indeed, whether the applicant was guilty or not. The question which must be answered is whether the proceedings as a whole, including the way in which the evidence was obtained, were fair. This involves an examination of the "unlawfulness" in question and, where violation of another Convention right is concerned, the nature of the violation found.'

The ECtHR concluded the applicant had enjoyed a fair trial, notwithstanding the main evidence against him had been obtained in breach of a Convention right. In particular, the ECtHR noted there had been no doubt as to the authenticity of the tape and the strength and reliability of the evidence it had yielded. There had been no inducement to confess or entrapment. Furthermore, s. 78 PACE 1984 had afforded Khan the opportunity to challenge the admissibility of the evidence. In these circumstances his trial had been fair.

6.6.3 UNLAWFUL SEIZURE AND SUBSEQUENT USE OF REAL EVIDENCE

R v Sanghera [2001] 1 Cr App R 299

Evidence was admitted following an unlawful search, contrary to Code B of the Codes of Practice. There had been a robbery at a post office which was owned by the defendant. As part of the investigation into the crime, the police omitted to obtain the defendant's written consent to search his premises. In the course of their search, the police had found a hidden box containing a substantial quantity of cash, as a result of which their suspicion that the robbery was a sham was aroused. The money from the box was removed and a hidden camera installed. The defendant was arrested a few days later having been seen to look in the hidden box. The defendant did not contest the reliability of the evidence that the unlawful search had yielded. However, he maintained he would have wanted to be present at the time of the search, as this would have afforded him the opportunity of offering an immediate explanation of the presence of the money found in the box. In the circumstances, he argued the evidence should have been excluded under s. 78 PACE 1984. The trial judge rejected this submission and the defendant was convicted. The Court of Appeal upheld the conviction.

On the facts, and given that the police had acted in good faith, it could not be said that the defendant had been prejudiced in any way. The evidence yielded was both relevant and reliable and the defendant had been afforded the opportunity of both explanation and challenge at his trial.

In *R v Cooke* [1995] 1 Cr App R 318, the defendant claimed that a non-intimate sample of his hair had been taken from him unlawfully. The sample yielded hugely compelling DNA evidence which convicted the defendant of rape and kidnap. The Court of Appeal held that the evidence had not been obtained unlawfully and that, even if it had, s. 78 would not require the court to exclude it, because such illegality would not have cast doubt on the reliability and probative strength of the resulting evidence. In this sense, the evidence could be distinguished from confession evidence obtained in breach of PACE and the Code of Practice, which tends to be of a more inherently unreliable nature.

6.6.4   **EVIDENCE OBTAINED IN VIOLATION OF THE PRIVILEGE AGAINST SELF-INCRIMINATION**

> *Allan v UK* (2002) 236 EHRR
>
> Allan and his co-accused were suspected of murder. All the defendants had been charged with an unrelated robbery and remanded into custody. Some days later, Allan was arrested on suspicion of murder. He refused to answer questions in interview. Authorisation was obtained to secure the 'services' of a long-standing police informant known as H who had a criminal record and who was under arrest on unrelated matters. H was placed in Allan's cell for the express purpose of gaining Allan's trust and eliciting information from Allan regarding the murder. At a later stage, H was fitted with a recording device. Telephone conversations between the investigating officers and H included comments by the police encouraging H to 'push him for what you can'. H eventually made a 59-page witness statement detailing his conversations with Allan. He was then released on police bail pending sentencing which was due to occur after he had given evidence at Allan's trial. In his evidence, H stated that in one conversation which had not been recorded, Allan had admitted his presence at the murder scene. This was disputed by Allan.
>
> The ECtHR had no hesitation in concluding that Allan had not enjoyed a fair trial because his right to silence had been completely undermined. The use of an undercover informant by the police had been the functional equivalent of an interview without any of the safeguards under PACE 1984 and Code C. Furthermore, the alleged admissions constituted the main and decisive evidence against Allan, and the unavailability of an audio record of the alleged conversation clearly compromised the quality of the evidence.

6.6.5   **ENTRAPMENT**

Law enforcement often requires the police to use the services of an *agent provocateur,* such as an undercover police officer or an informer, who infiltrates a criminal enterprise in an attempt to gather evidence. This is known as entrapment. Evidence obtained in this way is susceptible to challenge both at common law and under s. 78 PACE 1984; but entrapment *per se* does not afford a defence in English law to a criminal charge.

The difficulty for the courts, in choosing to exercise this discretion, is where to draw the line. At what point do the prosecuting authorities overstep the mark between the legitimate methods of obtaining evidence and inciting someone to commit a crime they might not otherwise have committed?

The difficulties associated with the admissibility of this type of evidence have exercised the courts on a number of occasions. In *R v Christou* [1992] 4 All ER 559, the facts of which were mentioned earlier, in answer to the claim that the defendant had been entrapped by the police officers posing as shady jewellery dealers, the Court of Appeal observed that the defendant had not been forced, persuaded or encouraged to sell the goods. If he had not used the officers' shop, he would have gone elsewhere.

Lord Taylor explained the defendant's position as follows:

> 'Nobody was forcing the defendants to do what they did. They were not persuaded or encouraged to do what they did. They were doing in that shop exactly what they intended to do and, in all probability, what they intended to do from the moment they got up that morning. They were dishonestly disposing of dishonest goods. If the police had never set up the jeweller's shop, they would, in my judgment, have been doing the same thing though of course they would not be doing it in that shop, at that time. They were not tricked into doing what they would not otherwise have done . . . I do not think that is unfair or leads to an unfairness in the trial.'

The law relating to the admissibility of evidence obtained by entrapment has steadily evolved. A definitive statement of the relevant principles which takes account of relevant case law and the jurisprudence of the ECtHR on this issue (*Teixeira de Castro v Portugal* (1998) 28 EHRR 242) was provided by the House of Lords in the following case, combining two appeals.

R v Loosely; Attorney-General's Reference (No. 3 of 2000) [2001] 1 WLR 2060

In Loosely's case, an undercover officer posed as a prospective buyer of drugs. His actions were part of an authorised surveillance in the Guildford area, which had seen a rise in the supply of heroin. The focus of suspicion fell on a particular public house in which the undercover officer had been given the defendant's contact number as a possible source of supply. On contacting the defendant, the officer asked if he could 'sort us a couple of bags'. The defendant responded willingly to the solicitation and immediately made arrangements to take the undercover officer to a place where he was able to obtain the drugs.

In the matter of the *Attorney-General's Reference*, undercover officers offered the defendant contraband cigarettes. After a lengthy conversation about the cigarettes, one of the officers asked the defendant if he could 'sort him some brown'. It was only after numerous conversations, much persuasion and the offer of further contraband cigarettes, that the defendant eventually obtained a quantity of heroin for the officers. On handing the drug over to the undercover officers, the defendant was recorded as saying: 'I am not really into heroin myself.' In interview he maintained he had nothing to do with heroin and had only supplied the officers because of their requests and as a favour for the contraband cigarettes.

The House of Lords concluded that in entrapment cases, the application to have the evidence excluded is in reality an application to stay the proceedings for an abuse of process since the evidence obtained through the use of entrapment usually forms the entire basis of the prosecution's case. If the evidence of entrapment were to be excluded the prosecution would collapse. For this reason, an abuse of process application was the appropriate remedy. Accordingly, the relevant test to be applied in English law was that set out in *R v Latif and Shazard* [1996] 1 WLR 104: namely, whether the conduct of the prosecuting authorities had been so shameful and unworthy as to constitute an affront to the public conscience.

In *Loosely*, their Lordships accepted the need for prosecuting authorities to use undercover officers in the detection and prosecution of crime. The use of entrapment, however, or 'state-created crime', is an abuse of process. Where is the line to be drawn in this regard?

Lord Hoffmann identified the relevant factors of entrapment as follows:

1. Whether the police caused the defendant to commit the crime or merely provided him with an unexceptional opportunity.

2. Whether the accused would have committed the offence with someone else.

3. Whether the police suspect the accused might commit an offence. In relation to this factor, Lord Hoffmann observed: 'The only proper purpose of police participation is to obtain evidence of criminal acts which they suspect someone is about to commit or in which he is already engaged. It is not to tempt people to commit crimes in order to expose their bad characters and punish them.' Relevant to this factor is the question of whether or not the particular police operation had been authorised.

4. The nature of the offence, i.e. whether the deployment of an undercover officer is the only way of achieving the desired result.

Ultimately, each case depends on its individual facts. Applying these guiding principles to the appeals before them, their Lordships concluded that Loosely's appeal should be dismissed. His arrest had come about as a result of legitimate concern in the rising supply of hard drugs in the Guildford area and from one public house in particular. As Loosely expressed himself keen to arrange a supply, the undercover officer had not needed to undertake any persuasion, and therefore his actions clearly fell within the bounds of acceptable conduct. In relation to the *Attorney-General's Reference*, the House of Lords concluded it would not interfere with the trial judge's exercise of discretion. The defendant in that case had come under considerable and sustained pressure by officers to supply them with a Class A drug and could be said to have been induced to commit the offence based on the continued supply of contraband cigarettes to him.

6.7 **ABUSE OF PROCESS**

In addition to the discretion to exclude evidence at common law and under s. 78 PACE 1984, the criminal courts have an inherent jurisdiction to stay proceedings for abuse of process. This would be a very serious step for a court to take as its effect is to bring the trial to an end—although a stay does not have the same legal effect as an acquittal. In the exceptional situations where a stay is ordered, the court is saying either that the defendant cannot enjoy a fair trial or as a result of the actions of the prosecuting authorities, it is not fair to try the accused.

A defendant might argue abuse of process where there has been considerable delay in bringing charges with the result that the defendant would find it difficult to advance a defence. It could also cover a case where:

- extensive pre-trial publicity makes a fair trial impossible;
- there is a later prosecution where a previous trial was halted;
- there is a decision to commence a prosecution in circumstances where the prosecution agreed an alternative course of action, i.e. to caution instead of to prosecute (see *R v Dobson* [2000] EWCA 1606);
- the prosecution has lost or failed to secure evidence relevant to the crime which might have assisted the defendant; or
- the prosecution has withheld relevant evidence.

The above list is not exhaustive. In *R v Loosely* (above), the House of Lords held that the issue of entrapment was more appropriately dealt with as abuse of process rather than s. 78 PACE 1984 because a successful submission that the police obtained evidence through entrapment effectively brings the trial to an end.

Where proceedings are stayed because of the unlawful activities of the prosecuting authorities, the court is effectively sending out the message that such activities will not be tolerated and cannot be condoned. The exercise of discretion under abuse of process is therefore wider than the discretion exercised under s. 78 PACE 1984. However, the type of misconduct involved for an abuse of process application to succeed must be such that it would be an affront to public conscience for the proceedings to continue or for the conviction to stand (*R v Latif* [1996] 1 WLR 104).

R v Edward Grant [2005] 3 WLR 437

The defendant was charged with conspiring with others to murder his wife's lover, who had been shot dead after answering a knock at his door. The defendant accepted that there had indeed been a conspiracy to assault the victim but not to murder him. It was suggested that the victim might have been killed by criminal contacts of his own. Before the trial began an application was made to stay the proceedings as an abuse of process. It transpired that the police had installed a covert listening device in the exercise yard of the police station where the defendant was being held. The installation was properly authorised for the purpose of recording conversations between the detainees implicated in the murder investigation. The effect, however, had been to record inadvertently conversations between solicitor and client while in the exercise yard. No prejudice was caused to the defendant as the prosecution placed no reliance on the tape-recorded conversations. The Court of Appeal upheld the abuse of process application, however, firmly endorsing the absolute sanctity of legal professional privilege and holding that in some instances, no prejudice to the defendant had to be proved in order for an abuse of process application to succeed.

'We are in no doubt but that in general unlawful acts of the kind done in this case, amounting to a deliberate violation of a suspected person's right to legal professional privilege, are so great an affront to the integrity of the justice system, and therefore the rule of law, that the associated prosecution is rendered abusive and ought not to be countenanced by the court . . . ' (Per Laws L J.)

6.8 CONCLUSION

In conclusion, we can safely suggest that the exercise of judicial discretion under s. 78 PACE 1984 is comparable to the exercise of discretion at common law. With the exception of confessions and identification evidence, where s. 78 is more likely to be successfully argued, evidence obtained in excess of the powers available to the police is likely to be admitted if it yields relevant and reliable evidence.

The current law in relation to the exercise of judicial discretion under s. 78 should not inhibit a defence advocate from making an application to have unlawfully obtained evidence excluded. As the saying goes—nothing ventured, nothing gained. If the argument as to admissibility fails, the unlawful nature of the activities can still be put to the police in cross-examination with a view to undermining credibility.

KEY POINT SUMMARY

- Every accused enjoys the right to a fair trial and a component of that right includes the ability to challenge any evidence that might be said to have been obtained unlawfully or in a dubious manner.
- The power to exclude evidence in the interests of securing a fair trial exists at common law and under s. 78 PACE 1984—both are exercised on a discretionary basis.
- Section 78 PACE 1984 has largely superseded the common law which is now found in s. 82(3) PACE 1984.
- Section 78 PACE 1984 applies to all types of prosecution evidence, including prosecution evidence that has been obtained unlawfully.
- Evidence obtained in breach of PACE and/or the Codes of Practice can be said to have been obtained unlawfully and is therefore vulnerable to being excluded in the exercise of the court's discretion.
- With the exception of confession evidence and evidence of identification, the power to exclude unlawfully obtained evidence is exercised restrictively.
- This chapter should be read in conjunction with Chapters 7 and 8 in order to gain the widest possible understanding of s. 78 discretion and the discretion exercised at common law.

SELF-TEST QUESTIONS

Scenario 1

Ranjit Singh will state as follows:

'Shortly before midnight last night I was driving home in my mother's Ford Escort Cabriolet, registration number R457 KYE. I had just parked the car and was removing my sport's bag from the boot. It contained my squash equipment. I was wearing my black tracksuit trousers and hooded sweatshirt. I was searching for my mobile phone in the back of the car when two men approached me. One reached into the car and grabbed me by the arm. It was dark. I could not see what they were wearing. Fearing a racial attack, I just lashed out and hit one of them. I extricated myself and started to run. One of them shouted: "Stop we're police officers." I was grabbed in a matter of seconds. The other man began to search my bag and then me. The other searched my car. Finally, I heard one of them say, "Let's teach him a lesson." With that I was handcuffed. They emptied my pockets and removed my trousers, socks and shoes. They found a small quantity of cocaine tucked inside my sock. I was then arrested and subsequently charged with (a) possession of a controlled drug and (b) assaulting a police officer in the execution of his duty.'

Do you feel you can challenge the admissibility of the evidence in the case? If so, upon what grounds?

Scenario 2

Stan is charged with possession of cocaine with intent to supply. He has no previous convictions, although he has the reputation for being able to acquire goods on the cheap. He is approached one evening by an acquaintance, accompanied by two men. The acquaintance tells Stan the two men are looking to be supplied with cocaine. At first Stan says he cannot help. The two men then appear to make a phone call and increase their price. At this point Stan makes several telephone calls and tells the men to come back next day. They do so and are supplied with a quantity of cocaine. The two men then reveal themselves to be undercover drug squad officers. They arrest and subsequently charge Stan with possession of drugs with intent to supply.

Does the manner in which the evidence has been obtained provide Stan with an argument for seeking to have the evidence excluded?

Figure 6.1 UNLAWFULLY AND UNFAIRLY OBTAINED EVIDENCE

WHAT CONSTITUTES UNLAWFULLY OBTAINED EVIDENCE?

- Any evidence obtained unlawfully or in an underhand manner, which can include:
  - evidence obtained in breach of Codes of Practice under PACE;
  - evidence obtained through the use of an *agent provocateur*;
  - evidence obtained in breach of rights under PACE—unlawful search/seizure;
  - evidence obtained in violation of Article 8—the right to privacy;
  - evidence obtained in violation of the privilege against self-incrimination.

COMMON LAW PRESERVED BY S. 82(3) PACE

- illustrated in *R v Sang* and *R v Khan*;
- restrictive in its application;
- save for evidence of a self-incriminating nature obtained by means of trickery/deception after commission of offence, evidence obtained unlawfully or unfairly remains admissible if it is relevant and reliable;
- basically, if the probative value of the evidence exceeds its prejudicial effect, the evidence will be admitted.

SECTION 78 PACE 1984

- gives courts discretion to exclude **any** prosecution evidence, the admission of which would have an adverse effect on the fairness of the proceedings;
- s. 78 is not confined to unlawfully obtained evidence;
- application of s. 78 is discretionary;
- used most successfully to exclude confession evidence obtained in breach of safeguards of PACE and Code C (*R v Aspinall*; *R v Walsh*; *R v Canale*);
- also used to exclude identification evidence obtained in breach of safeguards under Code D (*R v Finley*);
- less successfully used in relation to other types of evidence i.e. unlawful arrest/search/seizure, unauthorised surveillance/underhand tactics where the evidence yielded is relevant, reliable and authentic (*R v Khan*);
- on the use of an *agent provocateur* see *R v Loosely* and the application of abuse of process;
- unless the reliability of the evidence is tainted by the illegality or unfairness, making it more difficult for the defendant to challenge the evidence, it is likely to be admitted.

7 CONFESSION EVIDENCE

7.1 INTRODUCTION

In many criminal cases, the police interview with the suspect is the centrepiece of the investigation. In a significant number of cases the prosecution will wish to rely on the interview as it will have some evidential relevance. Where a suspect makes an incriminating statement(s) in interview, the interview is said to constitute a confession which can be persuasive prosecution evidence against an accused. In this chapter, we consider:

- the definition of a confession;
- the dangers associated with confession evidence;
- the recording requirements for police interviews;
- the requirements under PACE 1984 and Code C and their relationship to confession evidence;
- the rules which regulate the admissibility of confession evidence;
- the procedure by which the admissibility of a confession would be determined;
- the relationship between confession evidence and the rule against admitting hearsay evidence.

7.2 WHAT IS THE LEGAL DEFINITION OF A CONFESSION?

Section 82(1) PACE 1984 defines a confession as:

'Any statement wholly or partly adverse to the person who made it, whether made to a person in authority or not and whether made in words or otherwise.'

The definition of a confession is extremely wide and covers any statement by the accused on which the prosecution seeks to rely in support of its case. The statement does not have to be made to a person in authority, e.g. a police officer and it is possible to secure a conviction on confession evidence alone. You may recall that Michael Stone's conviction for the double fatal hammer attack on Lin and Megan Russell in 1996, was based on a confession he was alleged to have made in earshot of a convicted, serving prisoner while on remand awaiting trial.

The suspect therefore should be careful about how he answers questions in the police interview if he does not wish to incriminate himself. The role of the legal adviser at the police station is critical in this regard. The police are well versed in the psychology of interrogation techniques as the entire interview process is geared to persuading the suspect to talk. By talking, the suspect is more likely to say something of a revealing, incriminating or contradictory nature, especially over the course of several interviews. We saw in Chapter 5 that the provisions in ss. 34–36 and 37 Criminal Justice and Public Order Act 1994 have increased the pressure on suspects to speak in interview and a failure to mention facts later relied on in court may result in an adverse inference being drawn against the accused where it was reasonable for him to have mentioned those facts.

7.3 WHY IS CONFESSION EVIDENCE PROBLEMATIC?

A number of miscarriages of justice and extensive psychological research have shown that suspects sometimes confess even where they have not committed the offence. Detention inside a police station is a demeaning and bewildering experience and whether out of fear, frustration, desperation, the desire to please or because a suspect is vulnerable to suggestion, some detainees will make incriminating admissions for reasons of short-term expediency. They behave in this way to relieve the pressure of the situation and in the hope that matters will be sorted out in their favour in the long term. It is for this very important reason that the law makes specific provision for challenging the admissibility of confession evidence. The main provision is contained in s. 76 PACE 1984 but the admissibility of a confession can also be challenged under s. 78 PACE 1984. Section 78 gives the court the power to exclude any prosecution evidence (including confession evidence) if its admission would have an adverse effect on the fairness of the proceedings. We have already considered the application of s. 78 PACE 1984 outside the context of the formal interview in Chapter 6.

7.4 THE IMPORTANCE OF THE CODES OF PRACTICE IN RELATION TO FORMAL INTERVIEWS

Crucially relevant to the admissibility of confession evidence are the safeguards contained in PACE 1984 and the Codes of Practice, including ss. 56 and 58 PACE 1984, Codes C and E. Many of these safeguards were identified and considered in Chapter 4. (At the conclusion of this chapter, we include some self-test questions to test your knowledge of Code C in relation to the admissibility of confession evidence.)

Whilst Code C seeks to promote integrity in the investigative process it does not have the force of law, as with the other Codes of Practice issued under s. 67(11) PACE 1984 although the Codes are admissible in criminal proceedings where they are relevant to any question arising in the proceedings.

A breach of PACE 1984 and/or the Codes will not automatically lead the court to exclude a resulting confession. However, a breach of PACE 1984 or the Codes (which has contributed to a person making incriminating admissions) enables the defence advocate to argue the confession should be excluded under ss. 76 and/or 78 PACE 1984. A causal link must always be established between the alleged breach and the resulting confession. In challenging the admissibility of a confession, the role of the custody officer and the evidential significance of the custody record are vitally important.

7.5 RECORDING REQUIREMENTS OF INTERVIEWS

The provisions requiring the recording of interviews are contained in Code E. An account of any interview undertaken at the police station should be reliable, impartial and accurate. The best way of ensuring this is to have the interview tape recorded. Code E para. 3.1 stipulates that a tape recording shall be used at police stations for any interview with a person who is under caution in respect of any indictable offence, including an offence triable either way. Although no specific mention is made of summary-only offences, it is also common practice for the police to interview under tape-recorded conditions. Provision is made under Code E for the manner in which tape-recorded interviews are to be carried out. Code F contains guidance on the visual recording of police interviews and is currently being piloted in a number of different police areas.

In circumstances where an interview is not tape recorded, Code C paras. 11.7–11.11 requires the interviewing officer to make and complete a verbatim record of what was said in the interview. The record should be completed during the interview unless this would be impracticable. If a written record is not made during the interview, it must be made as soon as practicable thereafter and the suspect must be given the opportunity to read the interview and to sign it as correct or to indicate how he considers it to be inaccurate. As a matter of good practice, the legal adviser attending the police station must keep an accurate written record of what took place, the questions asked and the answers given, during the interview.

It is not unusual for a suspect to make unsolicited comments off the record outside the formal interview which may be relevant to the investigation of an offence. Code C para. 11.13 requires the police to keep a written record of such comments which should be signed and dated. The suspect should be given the opportunity to read the record and to sign it as being an accurate record of what was said.

The recording requirements of interviews are of practical importance in providing an accurate account of what took place. The recording requirements assist the police as much as the suspect as they protect the police from accusations that they have 'verballed' the suspect (i.e. they have attributed comments to the suspect which he denies making). Any departure from normal practice in recording the interview immediately compromises the integrity of the investigating officers and may form the basis of a challenge to exclude disputed evidence of incriminating admissions.

7.5.1 ENTITLEMENT TO A COPY OF THE TAPE-RECORDED INTERVIEW

Legal advisers are entitled to a copy of all recorded interviews, on request. Under the Criminal Procedure Rules (Part 21), the prosecution will normally provide the accused with a written summary of the recorded interview. Except in the most straightforward of cases (and especially where an accused was unrepresented at the police station), it is good practice to request a copy of the tape-recorded interview.

7.6 CHALLENGING ADMISSIBILITY UNDER S. 76 PACE 1984

Section 76(2) provides two grounds under which a confession can be excluded—oppression and unreliability:

'If, in any proceedings where the prosecution proposes to give in evidence a confession made by an accused person, it is represented to the court that the confession was or may have been obtained—

(a) by oppression of the person who made it; or

(b) in consequence of anything said or done which was likely, in the circumstances existing at the time, to render unreliable any confession which might be made by him in consequence thereof,

the court shall not allow the confession to be given in evidence against him except in so far as the prosecution proves to the court beyond reasonable doubt that the confession (notwithstanding that it may be true) was not obtained as aforesaid.'

Where the defence (or the court) raise the issue of the confession's admissibility the prosecution has the legal burden of proving that the confession was not obtained through oppression (s. 76(2)(a)) and/or is not unreliable (s. 76(2)(b) PACE 1984). If the prosecution cannot prove beyond reasonable doubt that the confession has not been obtained by oppression or is not unreliable, it must be excluded notwithstanding that it may be true.

Each provision will now be considered in turn.

7.6.1 OPPRESSION: S. 76(2)(a)

Oppression is partially defined in s. 76(8) to include torture, inhuman or degrading treatment, and the use of threat of violence (whether or not amounting to torture).

In the important case of *R v Fulling* [1987] QB 426, the Court of Appeal stated that oppression should be defined by its dictionary definition as being 'the exercise of authority or power in a burdensome, harsh or wrongful manner; unjust or cruel treatment of subjects, inferiors, etc; the imposition of unreasonable or unjust burdens'. The case of *Fulling* provides that for conduct to amount to oppression within the meaning of s. 76(8), there must be deliberate misconduct by the police. Oppression is a question of degree. What is oppressive to one suspect may not be oppressive to another. Therefore the accused's personal characteristics including his mental strengths and weaknesses will be relevant.

What amounts to 'oppressive' conduct was found to have occurred in *R v Paris, Abdullah and Miller* (1993) 97 Cr App R 99, in which the defendants appealed against their conviction for murder. During the investigation, M was interviewed a total of 13 hours over five days. A solicitor was not present during the first two interviews and M consistently denied his involvement in the crime during the first seven interviews. During interviews eight and nine, M accepted that he was present at the crime scene. He was then pressed to say who had stabbed the victim. M finally confessed that he had. Having denied his involvement over 300 times on tape, he later agreed with the officer's suggestion that he may have been under the influence of drugs and stabbed the victim without knowing what he was doing. He finally admitted: 'I just stabbed, not stabbed her . . . just thumped her in the face I mean.' Allowing the appeal, the Court of Appeal held that, short of physical violence, it was hard to conceive of a more hostile and intimidating environment. There was no doubt that the police conduct was 'oppressive' within the meaning of s. 76(2)(b).

7.6.2 UNRELIABILITY: S. 76(2)(b)

The key issue under s. 76(2)(b) is whether the confession is unreliable, not whether it is true or false. A confession may be true, but if it has been obtained in circumstances rendering it unreliable, it must be excluded as the wording in s. 76(2)(b) makes clear. If the circumstances existing at the time were likely to induce an unreliable confession (notwithstanding it might actually be true), the confession must be excluded (*R v Proulx* [2001] 1 All ER 57).

In deciding whether a confession should be excluded on the ground of unreliability, s. 76(2)(b) requires the court to consider 'anything said or done to the accused . . . in the circumstances existing at the time'. Therefore the court must examine all the relevant circumstances of the accused's detention and interrogation and take account of what was said or done to the accused.

As well as the suspect's subjective characteristics, breaches of PACE 1984 and the Codes of Practice are often highly relevant to excluding a confession on the ground of unreliability. Although a breach will not render a confession automatically inadmissible, the safeguards under PACE 1984 and the Codes exist to ensure the reliability of a confession by protecting the suspect's basic rights.

The presence or absence of bad faith on the part of the police is largely irrelevant to a s. 76(2)(b) submission. What is important is the effect any breach had on the particular suspect at the time. A failure by the police to identify a particular vulnerability due to a medical condition or substance abuse and to make an appropriate provision, may provide grounds for seeking the exclusion of a confession under this section. Subtle or not so subtle inducements offered by the police to encourage the suspect to confess, such as the promise of bail or a lesser charge, are also relevant considerations. For s. 76 PACE 1984 to apply, there must be a proven causal link between what was said and done at the police station and the resulting confession.

The following cases illustrate the type of factors the courts consider when assessing admissibility under s. 76(2)(b). While it is possible to extract some general principles the outcome of each case is largely dependant on its facts.

R v Delaney [1988] 86 Cr App R 18: failure to secure legal representation in relation to a vulnerable suspect

The defendant was convicted of the indecent assault of a three-year-old girl. The only evidence against him was his confession. He had been interviewed at length, having declined the services of a solicitor. Although he was 17 he had an IQ of only 80 and was educationally subnormal. The scenario was described by the Court of Appeal as a set of circumstances 'in which, *par excellence*, any interrogation should have been conducted with meticulous care and with meticulous observance of the rules of fairness'. There was evidence from an educational psychologist, which if accepted, established the defendant to be a vulnerable suspect. The interview had been conducted on a sympathetic basis with the officers being at pains to minimise the seriousness of the defendant's position. On several occasions during the interview, reference was made to the defendant's need for treatment rather than punishment. Given the nature of the questioning on such a vulnerable suspect, who was not legally represented, the risk of it producing a false confession was too high.

R v Howden-Simpson [1991] Crim LR 49: inducement to confess

The appellant was an organist and choirmaster. His duties included paying junior choir members for their services at weddings. He failed to pay the money to the choristers and was charged with theft. His confession was excluded under s. 76(2) because of an inducement to confess. The investigating officers had indicated that they would proceed on two non-payments charges only if he admitted the theft. If he did not admit the two charges they would interview every chorister not paid and make a separate charge for each. In the circumstances the Court of Appeal decided the confession should have been excluded under s. 76(2)(b). The position the appellant was placed in by the officers rendered his confession unreliable.

The physical condition and mental characteristics of the accused are part of the circumstances existing at the time for the purposes of s. 76(2)(b).

R v Walker [1998] Crim LR 211

The defendant, a prostitute, was convicted of robbery. She told the police doctor she was a heroin addict. She was prescribed methadone and valium. In interview she made a number of incriminating admissions. At her trial she maintained her victim had not been frightened and sought exclusion of the interview. At the enquiry into the admissibility into her confession, the defendant gave evidence that she had smuggled crack cocaine into the police station. She had smoked the drug and was under its influence when interviewed. Psychiatric evidence was called to establish that she had a severe personality disorder, making her prone to exaggerate about events without appreciating the consequences. The defendant's mental state would have been made worse by the use of drugs. The trial judge rejected much of the evidence but admitted the confession finding that nothing had been said or done to the defendant within the meaning of s. 76(2)(b). Allowing the appeal, the Court of Appeal held that the wording in s. 76(2)(b) did not require any wrongdoing on the part of the police. The defendant's mental state was one of the circumstances to be taken into account and there was nothing in the earlier case law which restricted mental conditions exclusively to intellectual impairment. Given the defendant's mental state, her confession could not be said to be reliable.

7.6.3 **CAN A DEFENDANT RELY ON SELF-INDUCED UNRELIABILITY?**

In the case of *R v Goldenberg* (1988) 88 Cr App R 285, it was held that s. 76(2)(b) does not apply where what was said or done was induced by the accused himself. In Goldenberg, the accused maintained he had only admitted the offence out of a desperate desire to obtain bail, as he was suffering from drug withdrawal. It was not possible in these circumstances to establish a causal link between anything said or done to the accused and the resulting confession.

Where a suspect perceives some advantage to himself and is thereby motivated to confess, in the absence of anything said or done, a causal link cannot be established. The position was summarised by Lord Lane CJ in *R v Rennie* [1982] 1 WLR 64, where he stated:

'Very few confessions are inspired solely by remorse. Often the motives of an accused are mixed and include a hope that an early admission may lead to an earlier release or a lighter sentence. If it were the law that the mere presence of such a motive, even if prompted by something said or done by a person in authority, led inexorably to the exclusion of a confession, nearly every confession would be rendered inadmissible. This is not the law. In some cases the hope may be self-generated. If so, it is irrelevant, even if it provides the dominant motive for making the confession. In such a case the confession will not have been obtained by anything said or done by a person in authority. More commonly the presence of such a hope will, in part at least, owe its origin to something said or done by such a person. There can be few prisoners who are being firmly but fairly questioned in a police station to whom it does not occur that they might be able to bring both their interrogation and their detention to an earlier end by confession.'

7.6.4 **CAN A SOLICITOR BE THE CAUSE OF SOMETHING SAID OR DONE?**

This point was considered in the case of *R v Wahab* [2003] 1 Cr App R 15, in which the defendant argued that he had been given negligent advice by his solicitor to confess and accordingly his confession should have been ruled inadmissible as unreliable.

In this case the defendant alleged investigating officers had been putting pressure on him to confess, by making reference to members of his family who were also in custody. At a later stage in the investigation, the defendant asked his solicitor to see whether an 'accommodation' could be reached with the police. His solicitor relayed what the officers had told him: namely, that they could not give any guarantees, but that they would look again at the situation regarding his relatives if admissions were forthcoming. After carefully considering all the circumstances (which the solicitor had documented and recorded), including the risk of conviction, the involvement in the investigation of his family and the availability of a sentencing discount for an early guilty plea, the defendant chose to make a number of admissions.

In deciding the case, the Court of Appeal held that the wording in s. 76(2)(b)—'*having regard to anything said or done . . .*'—was not confined to the actions or omissions of police officers. However, the Court of Appeal held that s. 76(2)(b) did require something extraneous to the person making the confession. Can a solicitor's advice constitute something extraneous? It could, said the Court of Appeal, depending on the particular facts such as advice to confess given to a particularly vulnerable suspect. On the facts of this case the Court of Appeal concluded that the appellant had not been influenced by anything said or done by anyone else and indeed, it had been the defendant who had requested his solicitor to see if an accommodation could be sought. The Court of Appeal emphasised that s. 76(2)(b) PACE 1984 is not concerned with the defendant's motives for confessing, except and in so far as such motive affected the reliability of what was said.

7.7 'UNFAIRNESS': S. 78 PACE 1984/COMMON LAW

We have already considered the effect of s. 78 PACE 1984 in the context of unlawfully obtained prosecution evidence outside the sphere of confession evidence in Chapter 6. The judicial discretion under s. 78 can be applied to any prosecution evidence in a case where it is contended that the admission of such evidence would have unfair effect on the fairness of the proceedings.

Confession evidence clearly falls within the sphere of s. 78 PACE 1984. To remind you, the section provides:

'In any proceedings the court may refuse to allow evidence on which the prosecution proposes to rely to be given if it appears to the court that, having regard to all the circumstances, including the circumstances in which the evidence was obtained, the admission of the evidence would have such an adverse effect on the fairness of the proceedings that the court ought not to admit it.'

Section 78 might be applied to incriminating admissions that have been obtained as a result of unfair conduct by the police, including:

• failing to secure access to a solicitor;
• failing to properly record an interview;
• failing to provide safeguards in relation to a vulnerable suspect;
• deceiving a suspect into making a confession or offering inducements;
• acting in deliberate breach of Code C.

An illustration of the application of s. 78 is provided by *R v Mason* [1988] 1 WLR 139. The defendant (M) was in custody on suspicion of having petrol-bombed the car of his ex-girlfriend's father. M and his solicitor were told (untruthfully) by two police officers, that M's fingerprints had been found on pieces of glass from the petrol bombs that had shattered near the car. As a result of this deception, and perceiving his position to be hopeless, M confessed which led to his conviction for arson which the Court of Appeal later quashed. It appears from the judgment that the deception practised on the solicitor (an officer of the court) was particularly objectionable, and that the trial judge ought to have exercised his discretion to exclude the confession, as its admission had had an adverse effect on the fairness of the proceedings.

There is some overlap between the type of factors justifying exclusion under s. 76(2)(b) and under s. 78 PACE 1984. As with excluding a confession under s. 76(2)(b), breaches of PACE 1984 and the Codes of Practice are highly relevant to the exercise of judicial discretion under s. 78 PACE 1984. The importance the appellate courts attach to the suspect's access to a solicitor while being detained at the police station under s. 58 PACE 1984 has been underlined in a number of cases including the Court of Appeal's decisions in *R v Samuel* [1988] QB 615 and in *R v Walsh* (1990) 91 Cr App R 161, where it was stated:

> 'To our minds it follows if there are significant and substantial breaches of section 58 or the provisions of the Code, then *prima facie* at least the standards of fairness set by Parliament have not been met. So far as this defendant is concerned . . . to admit evidence against him which has been obtained in circumstances where these standards have not been met, cannot but have an adverse effect on the fairness of the proceedings. This does not mean of course that in every case of a significant or substantial breach of section 58 or the Code of Practice evidence will automatically be excluded. Section 78 does not so provide.' (Saville J.)

Breach of Code C does not guarantee that the confession will be excluded under s. 78 PACE 1984. If there is no causal connection between the breach and the resulting confession, there is no unfairness (*R v Alladice* [1988] 87 Cr App R 380).

The application of s. 78 PACE 1984 in relation to a confession purported to have been obtained in breach of recording requirements is illustrated by *R v Canale* [1990] 2 All ER 187. In this case the interviewing officers failed to make contemporaneous notes of two of the interviews they had with the defendant as required by Code C. The defendant alleged he had been tricked and induced to confess which was denied by the police. The Court of Appeal described the breaches of the Code of Practice as being 'flagrant, deliberate and cynical' and concluded the admissions were inadmissible in accordance with s. 78. The absence of contemporaneous notes had deprived the trial judge of the very evidence that would have enabled him to resolve the conflict. The absence of the record severely prejudiced the defendant.

The fact that the police have acted in bad faith so far as compliance with the Codes is concerned is a factor the courts will consider. In *Walsh* (above), it was stated that:

> 'although bad faith may make substantial or significant that which might not otherwise be so, the contrary does not follow. Breaches which are in themselves significant and substantial are not rendered otherwise by the good faith of the officers concerned.'

One further excellent illustration of the application of s. 78 PACE 1984 to a confession is provided by *R v Aspinall* [1999] Crim LR 741. The defendant, a schizophrenic, was arrested and ultimately convicted on drug charges. Two police surgeons pronounced him fit for interview. During the enquiry into the confession's admissibility, the defendant's consultant psychiatrist testified that A might have been tired and stressed, contributing to a degree of passivity and lack of assertiveness on his part. When asked by the officers whether he wanted to see a solicitor, the defendant had replied: 'No I want to get home to my missus and kids.' The defendant was interviewed without the presence of a solicitor or appropriate adult. The trial judge rejected a s. 78 submission, concluding the defendant had been lucid at the time of interview.

In allowing his appeal and quashing his conviction, the Court of Appeal held the defendant had been unable to judge what was in his best interests. The absence of an appropriate adult (a specific requirement under Code C for vulnerable persons) rendered the confession unfair. The Court of Appeal concluded there had been a breach of Article 6 caused by the delay in access to legal advice as the duty solicitor had been otherwise engaged at the relevant time.

7.8 SPECIAL PROVISION FOR MENTALLY HANDICAPPED SUSPECTS

Provision is made under s. 77 PACE 1984 for confessions made by mentally handicapped persons:

'. . . where at a trial—

(a) the case against the accused depends wholly or substantially on a confession by him; and

(b) the court is satisfied—

   (i) that he is mentally handicapped;

   (ii) that the confession was not made in the presence of an independent person, the court shall warn the jury that there is a special need for caution before convicting the accused in reliance on the confession, and shall explain that the need arises because of the circumstances mentioned in the paragraphs above.'

7.9 ADMISSIBILITY OF CONFESSION EVIDENCE IN CIRCUMSTANCES WHERE CODE C HAS NO APPLICATION

There are other ways in which evidence of a self-incriminating nature might be obtained other than through the formal police interview. These include the use of covert listening devices, covert surveillance operations and *agent provocateurs*. The admissibility of evidence of a self-incriminatory nature obtained in this way is considered in Chapter 6 which examines the operation of s. 78 PACE 1984 outside the context of the formal interview.

7.10 THE PROCEDURE FOR DETERMINING THE ADMISSIBILITY OF A CONFESSION

In the Crown Court, where the admissibility of a confession is disputed, the issue will most usually be resolved by a *voir dire* (trial within a trial) at a pre-trial hearing.

Where an accused simply denies making a confession at all by maintaining that his signature has been forged or by denying words attributed to him which were never in fact recorded, a question of fact only arises. On a trial in the Crown Court, the issue of who is telling the truth will be decided by the jury without the need to hold a *voir dire* (*R v Flemming* (1988) 86 Cr App R 32).

7.10.1 THE VOIR DIRE

In most indictable-only cases where the admissibility of evidence arises, the dispute will normally be resolved at a pre-trial hearing at which the judge can make binding decisions on law. The name given to the type of hearing that determines the admissibility of a confession is a *voir dire*, or a trial within a trial. Such a hearing is always conducted in the absence of the jury. The trial judge will hear evidence as to how the confession was obtained and will listen to legal arguments advanced by both sides. The burden of proving the admissibility of a confession under s. 76 PACE 1984 rests with the prosecution. In discharging that burden, the prosecution may well call the interviewing officers and custody officer(s) to give evidence and will submit the custody record into evidence. The evidence adduced by the prosecution will be subject to cross-examination by the defence. The defendant may testify at the *voir dire* and adduce expert evidence if appropriate. The judge will consider the evidence, apply the law and reach a decision as to whether the confession should be admitted. If it is excluded, the jury will be kept in ignorance of it ever having been made. If the confession is ruled admissible, the accused is still entitled to repeat his allegations on how it was obtained in the hope of persuading the jury that the confession carries little evidential weight.

Section 45 (Sch. 3) Courts Act 2003 now permits binding rulings to be made at pre-trial hearings in criminal cases heard in the magistrates' court. The power to make pre-trial binding rulings is available following a not guilty plea up to the commencement of the trial and extends to issues of law and admissibility of evidence. The rulings made by one Bench of magistrates will bind the Bench which subsequently tries the defendant. As the two Benches will be differently composed, the risk of prejudice to the defendant is minimised and prejudice may only arise where the confession's admissibility is challenged during the course of the trial itself. In this situation, if the magistrates excluded the confession, they would continue to hear the case and have to put it to the back of their minds.

7.11 EDITING A CONFESSION

If an admissible confession contains material which is inadmissible under some other rule of evidence (e.g. hearsay or a reference to the accused's previous convictions) the accused is entitled to have the offending material edited out. The current rules are established by *Practice Direction (Crime: Tape Recording of Interviews)* [1989] 1 WLR 631. The Practice Direction allows the prosecution and defence to attempt to agree a transcript of any tape-recorded interview that is to be admitted in evidence. The defence is under an obligation to notify the prosecution whether or not a transcript of a tape-recorded interview is acceptable. In the event that it is not, various rules are encompassed in the Consolidated Practice Direction Part IV to give effect to the attempt to try to resolve difficulties. The practical effect is that where at all possible it is desirable for an edited transcript to be agreed.

7.12 THE RELATIONSHIP BETWEEN CONFESSIONS AND HEARSAY EVIDENCE

Full consideration is given to the topic of hearsay evidence in Chapter 22. The general rule is that hearsay evidence in criminal cases is inadmissible unless it can be brought within a recognised statutory or common law exception. Hearsay can be defined as adducing evidence in court of an earlier out-of-court statement for the purpose of proving the truth of facts asserted. A confession satisfies this definition. Confession evidence is however admitted notwithstanding its hearsay quality under a well-established common law exception. Problematic issues arise where A and B are jointly charged with an offence and A has confessed to the crime implicating B. No hearsay problem arises if A chooses to plead guilty and give evidence for the prosecution against B. In this situation A (the co-accused) becomes an accomplice whose evidence could attract a corroboration warning (see Chapter 21). A hearsay problem arises, however, if A is not available to give evidence for the prosecution against B but the prosecution seeks to rely instead on A's confession. Until recently a confession has only ever been admissible against its maker and not against anyone else implicated by it. A revision of the hearsay provisions under the CJA 2003 now means that A's confession can be admitted in evidence against B if a court concludes that it is in the interest of justice to admit it under s. 114(1)(d) CJA 2003 (R v Y) [2008] EWCA Crim 10).

Further hearsay problems arise where one accused seeks to rely on the confession of another co-accused in circumstances where the prosecution chooses not to adduce the confession as part of the prosecution case. Varying the facts, assume that A confesses but exonerates B. A is mentally vulnerable and was not represented at the police station by a solicitor or by an appropriate adult. A wishes to retract her confession and pleads not guilty. The CPS chooses not to rely on A's confession. It is not clear whether A will give evidence in her defence. What can B do in these circumstances? B would like to rely on A's earlier confession as evidence of the truth of what it asserts but in doing so it constitutes hearsay evidence. In *R v Myers* [1998] AC 124, the House of Lords created a further judicial exception to the hearsay rule by concluding that a co-accused in B's position is able to rely on the confession providing the confession is not inadmissible under s. 76(2) PACE 1984.

As a result of s. 128 CJA 2003, the admissibility provisions in s. 76 PACE 1984 apply not only to the prosecution but also to any co-accused who seeks to rely on the admissions of a fellow co-accused who is charged in the same proceedings.

7.13 EVIDENCE OBTAINED IN CONSEQUENCE OF AN INADMISSIBLE CONFESSION

Where a confession has been ruled inadmissible, it does not mean that evidence obtained as a result of the confession must also be excluded. The position is governed by s. 76(4) PACE 1984, which provides:

'The fact that a confession is wholly or partly excluded in pursuance of this section shall not affect the admissibility in evidence—

(a) of any facts discovered as a result of the confession; or

(b) where the confession is relevant as showing that the accused speaks, writes or expresses himself in a particular way, of so much of the confession as is necessary to show that he does so.'

Section 76(5) goes on to provide that where a confession has been excluded in whole or in part:

'Evidence that a fact . . . was discovered as a result of a statement made by the accused person shall not be admissible unless evidence of how it was discovered is given by him or on his behalf.'

Importantly the prosecution will not be allowed to refer to the inadmissible confession to explain how the incriminating evidence was found. Where incriminating facts cannot be adduced without referring to the inadmissible confession, neither the confession or the facts discovered, will be admissible.

KEY POINT SUMMARY

- Except in the clearest of cases request a copy of any police interview (especially if the defendant was unrepresented at the police station).
- The vast majority of interviews conducted at the police station have some evidential value whether because the defendant remained silent and is now raising new facts in his defence or because he makes incriminating admissions or tells lies.
- In some cases there will be an advantage in your client making a full and frank confession to the police. It is therefore important that you ascertain and evaluate the nature of the evidence against your client, that you take your client's instructions on the evidence, and advise accordingly.
- A confession is very widely defined and will cover any incriminating admissions made by your client.
- Breaches of PACE 1984 and the Codes of Practice are important in determining the admissibility of confession evidence where such evidence is disputed, although a breach does not automatically entitle a defendant to have a confession excluded.
- Oppression, within s. 76(2)(a) is narrowly defined and will invariably involve some deliberate misconduct on the part of the police.
- Unreliability under s. 76(2)(b) has a much wider application. Breaches of Codes C and E are relevant and deliberate impropriety on the part of the police is unnecessary.
- The enquiry under s. 76 PACE 1984 is as to the admissibility of the confession. The fact that the confession may well be true is immaterial to the question of its admissibility.
- Even if a confession is admissible under s. 76 PACE 1984, it may be excluded under s. 78 PACE 1984 if its admission would have an adverse affect on the fairness of the case.

SELF-TEST QUESTIONS

A reminder of Code C safeguards

Exercise 1

In order to refresh your memory in this regard, see if you can answer the following short questions. The answers can be found in Appendix 4.

1. At what stages does the suspect have to be cautioned? Would a confession that has been obtained following a failure to properly caution an individual, be admissible?

2. On arrival at the police station what rights should be explained to the suspect by the custody officer?

3. What initial assessment must the custody officer undertake in relation to each suspect and who might be said to constitute a vulnerable suspect?

4. The right of access to a solicitor is governed by the all-important s. 58 PACE. In what circumstances may access to a solicitor be delayed? If access was delayed and a confession was obtained, would the confession be admissible?

5. Can the investigating officers begin to question a suspect when he/she has requested a solicitor?

6. What are the maximum periods of detention and at what intervals should detention be reviewed? (It goes without saying that the longer an individual is detained in custody the more they may be tempted to confess in order to relieve the pressure of the situation.)

7. What basic human rights are suspects entitled to while in custody, including rest periods?

8. What actually constitutes an interview under Code C?

9. What is the procedure if the suspect appears to be unfit to be interviewed?

10. What safeguards apply as regards the conduct of an interview in relation to non-vulnerable and vulnerable suspects?

Exercise 2

Case scenario: *R v Lenny Whyte*

Consider the Lenny Whyte scenario. We have begun the process of evaluating the evidence against him. You will see from Document 18 E (included in Appendix 1) that Lenny makes a confession. What he states in his interview satisfies the statutory definition of a confession under s. 82(1) PACE. His interview is tape recorded in accordance with the requirements of Code E para. 3.1. Having regard to Lenny's initial statement (Document 1) and the custody record (Document 9) consider the following questions:

- Do you feel you have grounds for challenging the admissibility of Lenny's confession in due course? If so, what will be the legal basis for your submissions?

- What arguments will you put forward in support of your submissions?

- Consider the manner in which the confession was obtained. Can you point to any specific breaches of Code C?

- How will the admissibility of Lenny's confession be resolved and what evidence will need to be adduced and challenged in this regard?

- Guidance on all the above questions can be found in Appendix 4: Analysis of self-test questions to Chapter 7.

Figure 7.1 CONFESSION EVIDENCE

- A confession is any statement wholly or partly adverse whether made to a person in authority or not: s. 82(1) PACE 1984.
- Procedure for challenging the admissibility of confession evidence is a *voir dire* (trial within a trial).
- The admissibility of a confession may be challenged on the basis of:

OPPRESSION

- the exercise of power in a burdensome, harsh or wrongful manner;
- s. 76(2)(a) PACE 1984: requires deliberate and serious misconduct on the part of the police;
- see *R v Fulling* for definition of oppression.

UNRELIABILITY

s. 76(2)(b) PACE 1984: in consequence of anything said or done which, at the time, was likely to render unreliable any confession made by the suspect:

- breaches of Code C safeguards highly relevant to this ground;
- can include failure to secure access to legal advice in breach of s. 58 PACE 1984;
- offering a suspect inducements to confess;
- errors or omissions on the part of the police need not be deliberate;
- burden of proving the absence of unreliability on prosecution.

UNFAIRNESS

s. 78 PACE 1984: the admission of the confession would have an adverse effect on the fairness of the proceedings:

- significant and substantial breaches of Code C highly relevant to this ground;
- failure to spot and deal with a vulnerable suspect;
- taking advantage of a vulnerable suspect;
- failing to properly record an interview;
- factors relevant to this ground overlap with s.76(2)(b).

8.1   INTRODUCTION

Proof of the defendant's presence at the crime scene is presented at trial in a number of ways, including:

- visual identification of a suspect by an eyewitness;
- real evidence: closed circuit television surveillance has led to the increasing use of videotape and photographic stills at trials. The admission of such real evidence can give the

court a direct view of the incident enabling the fact finder to determine whether the defendant standing in the dock is the person seen participating in the criminal activity captured on film;

- forensic evidence: identification may also be provided by the opinion of a forensic scientist establishing a connection between the defendant and the crime scene based on the scientific comparison of forensic samples, e.g. fingerprints or DNA discovered at the scene with evidence found on the defendant or otherwise in his possession.

In this chapter, we consider:

- how identification evidence is obtained by the police during the police investigation;
- the pre-trial safeguards contained in Code D which seek to ensure the reliability and fairness of eye-witness identification obtained by the police;
- the admissibility of eye-witness evidence obtained in breach of Code D;
- the practical steps a legal adviser can take to ensure the fairness of identification procedures;
- the power to take fingerprints; intimate and non-intimate samples at the police station;
- identification evidence given by expert witnesses.

online resource centre

Numerous references will be made in this chapter to Code D which can be freely accessed from the Home Office website—our Online Resource Centre provides a link to the full text of Code D.

8.2 WHAT ARE THE DANGERS ASSOCIATED WITH EYE-WITNESS IDENTIFICATION?

Eye-witness identification has been proven to be unreliable both by psychological experiments and by miscarriages of justice. Identification is often made in difficult circumstances where, for example, a crime-related incident is over in a matter of seconds or minutes or in circumstances of heightened awareness where the witness is in fear. Safeguards are required to ensure identification evidence is gathered in a scrupulously fair manner and is treated with caution at trial. The principal safeguards are provided pre-trial by PACE Code D and at trial by the Turnbull Guidelines (*R v Turnbull* [1977] QB 224). The application of the Turnbull Guidelines are considered in Chapter 21.

8.3 HOW IS EYE-WITNESS IDENTIFICATION OBTAINED?

Eye-witness identification may come about in many different ways. A witness to a crime will usually give an initial statement to the police, which will include a description of those involved. Code D para. 3.1 requires the police to make a record of the suspect's description as first given by a potential witness and for the suspect or his legal adviser to be given a copy of the record.

The police may compile a photofit of a suspect they wish to speak to and circulate it to the media. A witness may also be taken on a tour of the area to see if he is able to spot the person(s) he thinks he saw involved in the crime. The police may show a witness 'mug shots' of convicted offenders to see if the witness can identify the culprit and/or show the witness video footage or photographic stills.

8.4 MAKING A DISTINCTION BETWEEN KNOWN AND UNKNOWN SUSPECTS

For the purposes of identification procedures, Code D makes a distinction between a known and unknown suspect.

8.4.1 WHAT CONSTITUTES A KNOWN SUSPECT?

Code D para. 3.4 provides guidance as to when a suspect is 'known' and 'available'. A suspect is known where there is sufficient information known to the police to justify the arrest of a particular person for suspected involvement in an offence. A suspect is available if he is immediately available or will be within a reasonably short period of time and is willing to take part in an identification procedure.

8.4.2 WHAT IF THE SUSPECT IS UNKNOWN?

Where the suspect is unknown, the police may take a witness to a particular neighbourhood or place to see if he can identify the suspect. Code D para. 3.2 stipulates the safeguards the police need to consider when taking a witness around an area. A detailed record of all the circumstances must be kept and the police must not direct a witness's attention to a particular individual.

8.4.3 SHOWING A WITNESS PHOTOGRAPHS OF POSSIBLE SUSPECTS WHERE THE SUSPECT IS UNKNOWN

If the suspect's identity is not known, the witness may be shown photographs subject to safeguards contained in Annex E of Code D. The safeguards include:

- a requirement that the witness should be shown twelve photographs at a time which should be of a similar type;
- a witness must not be prompted or guided in his choice in any way;
- if a witness makes a positive identification from a set of photographs no other witness can be shown the set and each of the witnesses should be asked to attend a parade.

Once the police have a known suspect in mind and have arrested a suspect an identification procedure should follow.

Code D para. 3.3 prevents the police from showing photographs to a witness if the identity of the suspect is known to the police and the suspect is available to participate in an identification procedure. Showing photographs in advance of a formal identification procedure seriously compromises the integrity of the procedure and effectively renders the procedure irrelevant.

8.4.4 OBLIGATION ON THE POLICE WHERE THE SUSPECT IS KNOWN AND AVAILABLE

Once a suspect is known and is available the police should proceed to a formal identification procedure: Code D para. 3.4.

8.5 WHEN MUST AN IDENTIFICATION PROCEDURE BE HELD?

The key provision in this respect is Code D para. 3.12:

'Whenever:

(i) a witness has identified a suspect or purported to have identified them prior to any identification procedure set out in paragraphs 3.5 to 3.10 having been held; or

(ii) there is a witness available, who expresses an ability to identify the suspect, or where there is a reasonable chance of the witness being able to do so, and they have not been given an opportunity to identify the suspect in any procedures set out in paragraphs 3.5 to 3.10, and the suspect disputes being the person the witness claims to have seen, an identification procedure shall be held unless it is not practicable or it would serve no useful purpose in proving or disproving whether the suspect was involved in committing the offence. For example the useful purpose test may be satisfied when it is not disputed that the suspect is already well known to the witness who claims to have seen him commit the crime.'

8.5.1 TYPES OF IDENTIFICATION PROCEDURES

In order to test the ability of a witness's ability to identify a suspect and to safeguard against mistaken identity, the police can use a number of identification procedures, which are governed by Code D and its Annexes A–E.

The Annexes to Code D provide the following procedures:

- Annex A: video identification
- Annex B: identification parades
- Annex C: group identification
- Annex D: confrontation by a witness.

The hierarchy of identification procedures place the video identification as the preferred first choice. Where an identification procedure must be held in accordance with Code D para. 3.12, para. 3.14 provides the suspect must initially be offered a video identification unless this is not practicable or an identification parade is more practicable and suitable or the officer in charge of the investigation considers that a group identification is more suitable than the other forms of identification and the identification officer believes it is practicable to arrange.

The decision to adopt a particular procedure is taken by the officer in charge of identification procedures in conjunction with the investigating officer. A suspect must be allowed to make representations about the procedure to be adopted. Video parades can be set up much quicker than conventional parades and are less intimidating for witnesses. The conduct of the identification procedure is the sole responsibility of an officer of at least the rank of inspector who is independent of the investigation.

8.5.2 EXPLAINING RIGHTS TO A SUSPECT BEFORE CONVENING AN IDENTIFICATION PROCEDURE

Some important rights must be explained to the suspect before convening an identification procedure. They are set out in Code D para 3.17 and include:

- the right of the suspect to have access to free legal advice;
- an explanation that the suspect does not have to consent or co-operate in a video identification, parade or group parade but that if he does not consent his refusal can be given in evidence against him in any subsequent trial and the police may proceed covertly without his consent or make other arrangements to test whether a witness can identify him.

The formal identification procedures regarded as the fairest to the suspect are the video parade and the identification parade because they provide the suspect with the best chance of not being picked out as the suspect has some measure of control in their composition.

A suspect who refuses to co-operate in the conduct of a video procedure can be treated as being unavailable (Code D para. 3.21). In these circumstances, the identification officer may make arrangements for the suspect's image to be captured covertly or for photographs to be used in the compilation of the video identification procedure. The confrontation procedure is a procedure of last resort and may not be used unless all other options are impracticable.

8.6 IS THE REQUIREMENT TO HOLD A FORMAL IDENTIFICATION PROCEDURE MANDATORY?

What if prior to an arrest, the eyewitness is able to make a full and complete identification at or near the scene of the crime? What if the suspect is someone who the eyewitness recognises? Does Code D give the police discretion whether to hold a parade or, is it a mandatory requirement in all cases where identification of the suspect is disputed?

The issue of whether the police must convene an identification procedure has been the subject of a number of appeals culminating in the House of Lords decision in *R v Forbes* [2001] 1 AC 473 which concerned an earlier version of Code D.

In *Forbes*, the victim was attacked and almost robbed at a cash-dispensing machine. The victim managed to get away and called the police. He was taken on a tour of the area and was able to point out the man who had robbed him. The appellant was arrested. He vigorously protested his innocence. No parade was held, as the police believed it would have been futile. In the opinion of the House of Lords a parade was a mandatory requirement save in exceptional cases where the eyewitness makes it plain that he cannot identify the person responsible, or in a case of pure recognition of someone well known to the eyewitness.

Statutory effect has been given to the decision in *R v Forbes* in the current edition of Code D. However, the question of whether an identification procedure is mandatory in all instances is still open to question. The requirement to convene an identification procedure under Code D para 3.12 is rebutted where, in all the circumstances, it would serve no useful purpose in proving or disproving whether the suspect was involved in the offence, including, for example, where the suspect is well known to the witness making the identification.

It will be apparent that the wording gives the police discretion to ascertain whether a suspect is well known to the witness and whether an identification procedure would therefore serve any useful purpose. A decision by the police not to convene an identification procedure should always be critically scrutinised. It affords a potential ground for the defence to seek the exclusion of identification evidence on the basis that it would be unfair to admit such evidence (s. 78 PACE 1984) where no formal procedure to test the reliability of that evidence was convened in advance of trial.

The police need only convene a parade in a case where identification is in dispute. In *R v Lambert* [2004] EWCA Crim 154, the police did not consider identification was in issue as the defendant admitted being at the crime scene but denied involvement in an assault that had taken place at that scene. The defendant made no comment in a subsequent interview and did not raise the issue of identification until trial. In this case, the Court of Appeal concluded there had been no obligation for the police to convene a parade as the defendant had not put his identification in issue during his police interview.

The issue of the mandatory requirement to convene a parade was central to the two cases below which concern earlier versions of Code D although the decisions remain relevant to the current version of Code D.

R (on the application of H) v DPP [2003] EWHC 133

The victim (V) was 15. It was alleged that she had been assaulted by the defendant (D), a 16-year-old. The assault lasted some several minutes. V had been assaulted on a previous occasion by D and had reported the matter to the police. D denied the assault and denied being present when the attack took place. No identification parade was held. At her trial before magistrates, D's defence solicitor submitted there had been a breach of Code D para. 2.3 (under the previous Code D), and that consequently there was no evidence of identification.

V had known D for about 18 months and had been a credible witness. Finding D guilty, the magistrates concluded that the police were entitled to refuse to hold an identification parade as it would have been futile. Applying the dicta in *Forbes* (highlighted above), the Divisional Court concurred with the magistrates' decision. The defendant had indicated she knew V and it was not suggested by the defendant or her legal representative at any time during her police interview that the question of recognition was an issue for her. In these circumstances this was a case of recognition and an identification parade would have served no useful purpose as V was bound to have identified D.

R v Harris [2003] EWCA 174

Two victims (A and B) were robbed of their mobile phones in the street by a group of youths. Both A and B claimed to recognise the appellant (C). They had previously been at school with C and knew him by his first name of Tristan. C had been in the year above them. A and B claimed to recognise C even though he was wearing a hooded top. A had recognised the boy's voice when he came over to him. It was accepted by A and B that they had not known C well at school and that they had not seen him since he had left. C denied any involvement and put forward an alibi. There was no other evidence to link him to the crime. Evidence was given from the school's headmaster, who confirmed that A and B would have been in attendance from 1998 until 2000 when C had left. There would have been 500 pupils in the school at the time and only one pupil at that time and since had the name of Tristan. No identification parade had been held and the defence submitted at trial that the identification evidence should have been excluded under s. 78 PACE 1984.

Reviewing the evidence, the Court of Appeal concluded that Code D did require an identification procedure to be held in this particular case. The purpose of an identification procedure is not merely to afford an opportunity for the eyewitness to identify the perpetrator but also to give the accused the opportunity to test the reliability of the eye-witness identification.

While this was a case of recognition it did not, on the facts, satisfy the specific example given in D (where it is not in dispute that the suspect is already well known to the witness). Although the defendant had not requested a parade, he had made it clear in his defence statement to the police that he denied any involvement and that he did not know A or B. Was C well known to A and B, within the meaning of Code D? The Court of Appeal concluded he was not: neither A, nor B had seen C for the past two years; C would have been 14 at the time; neither A, B or C had been in the same class; there had not been any direct contact between them. This led the Court of Appeal to the conclusion that there was at least: 'a live possibility that one or both witnesses might not have picked out the appellant on an identification parade. In that event, the defence would have been able to rely at trial on such non-identification as adding weight to the defence of alibi.'

In reaching its conclusion that C's conviction be quashed, the Court of Appeal were not of the view that the evidence of recognition should have been excluded under s. 78 PACE 1984, however the failure by the trial judge to properly direct the jury as to the purpose of Code D and the effect of a breach, meant the defendant had not received a fair trial.

From the Investigating officer's perspective, the decision not to convene an identification procedure requires careful consideration.

8.7 SPECIFIC SAFEGUARDS ASSOCIATED WITH THE VARIOUS IDENTIFICATION PROCEDURES

Whichever identification procedure the police use, the specific safeguards associated with each procedure is contained in the annexes supplementing Code D. We include here a summary of the main provisions.

8.7.1 VIDEO IDENTIFICATION (ANNEX A)

• A set of video images including the suspect and at least eight others is shown to the witness;

- where there are two suspects of similar appearance, at least 12 images should be shown to the witness;
- the eight other people should resemble the suspect in age, height, general appearance and position in life and should show the suspect and the other people in the same position or carrying out the same sequence of movements;
- steps must be taken to conceal any distinguishing features the suspect may have;
- the suspect's solicitor must be offered the opportunity to attend the identification suite when the video parade is compiled and when the compilation is subsequently shown to the eyewitness;
- a suspect or his solicitor/appropriate adult must be given the opportunity to see the complete set of images before it is shown to any witnesses. If the suspect has reasonable objections to the set of images or any of the participants, steps shall, if practicable, be taken to remove the grounds for objection;
- the witness sees the all the images at least twice;
- the witness is asked whether the suspect is the person seen on a previous occasion;
- a record must be made of procedures and those involved.

8.7.2 IDENTIFICATION PARADE (ANNEX B)

- The parade should consist of at least eight people in addition to the suspect who as far as possible should resemble the suspect in terms of appearance, age etc.;
- the suspect must be told that he may object to the arrangements or to a participant and that he may obtain legal advice;
- witnesses attending the parade must not be allowed to communicate with each other about the case or overhear a witness who has already made an identification;
- witnesses must not be allowed to see any participant in advance of the parade or see or be reminded of any photographs or description of the suspect or be given any indication as to the suspect's identity;
- the suspect may choose his own position in the line;
- each witness should be brought into the identification suite one at a time;
- video recording or colour photograph shall normally be made of the parade;
- where the identification officer is satisfied that the witness has properly looked at each member of the parade, they shall ask the witness whether the person they saw on the earlier relevant occasion is on the identification parade and, if so, indicate the number of the person concerned;
- if the witness wishes to hear any identification parade member speak or adopt any specified posture or move, they shall first be asked whether they can identify on the basis of appearance alone and reminded that the participants in the parade have been chosen on the basis of their appearance alone.

8.7.3 GROUP IDENTIFICATION (ANNEX C)

- May be held with or without the suspect's consent;
- the witness sees the suspect amongst a group of other people, e.g. shopping centre, rail station;
- the chosen location should take into account number of people present, general appearance of people;

- a colour photo or video should be taken at scene immediately after identification;
- the suspect's solicitor or friend can be present.

8.7.4 CONFRONTATION BY A WITNESS (ANNEX D)

- The witness is asked: 'Is this the person you saw on the earlier occasion?';
- force may not be used to make the suspect's face visible to the witness;
- the confrontation may either be through a one-way screen or face-to-face with the suspect;
- the confrontation will usually be held at the police station in a normal room or one equipped with a screen permitting a witness to see the suspect without being seen.

8.8 WHAT ARE THE EVIDENTIAL CONSEQUENCES OF A FAILURE TO COMPLY WITH CODE D?

The safeguards provided by Code D are important. If the police obtain identification evidence in breach of the safeguards, the defence advocate can apply to have the evidence excluded under s. 78 PACE 1984. The court's discretion to exclude evidence that has been obtained unlawfully or unfairly is considered in Chapter 6.

Breach of Code D does not inevitably lead to the exclusion of identification evidence. It is a matter for the court to determine whether the probative value of the evidence is outweighed by the prejudicial effect of admitting it, having regard to the breaches of Code D. Decisions in relation to identification evidence largely turn on their own facts. The more blatant the breach, the better the prospects are for exclusion. To illustrate the above we include two cases with differing outcomes, both of which involved breaches of Code D.

***R v Finley* [1993] Crim LR 50**

Evidence of identification was excluded in this case under s. 78 PACE 1984 for several breaches of Code D. The defendant was implicated in a robbery at an insurance office. There were several eyewitnesses who worked together. One witness was shown a set of 12 police photographs from which she selected the defendant. He was a blonde skinhead, whilst most of the photographs were of dark-haired men. The defendant produced an alibi and nothing had been found linking him to the robbery during a search of his flat. The composition of the parade was criticised as most of the volunteers were of heavier build than the defendant and had darker hair. The witnesses had been kept together before the parade and because one of them had had made a prior selection from photographs and had probably discussed this with her colleagues, the procedure was held to be highly prejudicial.

***R v Rutherford* (1994) 98 Cr App R 191**

It had been alleged that the defendant and another had forced their way into the home of an elderly lady. They sprayed liquid into her eyes, bound and gagged her. It was further alleged that £1,000, some Indian rupees and a piece of paper with a telephone number written on it had been stolen. The defendant was arrested in the vicinity soon after. Found in his possession were a quantity of cash, some Indian rupees and a piece of paper containing a telephone number. The defendant's appearance matched the descriptions given by a couple of witnesses. The police declined to convene an identification parade, in spite of a request by the defendant, because of what they perceived to be the strength of other evidence against the defendant. The Court of Appeal concluded, notwithstanding the breach of Code D, the prejudice to the defendant had been dealt with in the judge's summing-up and there had been ample circumstantial evidence upon which to convict.

8.8.1 REQUIREMENTS ON THE JUDGE TO DIRECT THE JURY WHERE THERE HAS BEEN A BREACH OF CODE D

The Court of Appeal's decision in *R v Allen* [1995] Crim LR 643 makes it clear that a trial judge must explain to the jury why identification evidence is being admitted in breach of Code D. In accordance with several authorities, including *R v Conway* (1990) 91 Cr App R 143 and *R v Quinn* [1995] 1 Cr App R 480, when summing-up, the judge should refer to the specific breach or breaches of Code D, leaving it up to the jury to decide how much weight to give to the identification evidence in the circumstances.

Guidance has also been provided by the House of Lords in *R v Forbes* [2001] 1 AC 473. In cases where there has been a breach of the requirement for the police to convene an identification parade or video parade, a trial judge must explain to the jury that the purpose of the parade is to enable a suspect to test the reliability of a witness's identification. In cases where an identification/video parade has not been held contrary to Code D, the suspect loses the benefit of the safeguard a parade affords him. The jury must be instructed to take account of this when assessing the case against the defendant. Additionally, even in a case where an informal identification is followed up by a properly conducted parade from which the defendant is chosen, a warning should still be given to the jury. The judge must stipulate that although the prosecution case is strengthened by the identification, the jury should be aware of the possible risk that the witness might have identified, not the culprit who committed the crime, but the suspect identified by the witness on the earlier occasion.

8.9 ARE THERE CIRCUMSTANCES IN WHICH CODE D HAS NO APPLICATION?

Code D is not all embracing and there are many instances in which identification is made which fall outside it as illustrated by *R v Hickin* below. Obviously, where Code D has no application, there can be no breach of it. However, considerations of fairness remain paramount and evidence may still be excluded in the exercise of the court's discretion under s. 78 PACE 1984.

> **R v Hickin [1996] Crim LR 585**
>
> A fight broke out between gangs of rival football supporters on Blackpool seafront, resulting in a serious injury. Three eyewitnesses were taken around the area in a police car to see if they could identify the culprits. Having rounded up those whom the police considered to be involved, the witnesses were asked to identify who they considered responsible for the violent assault. Fourteen men were subsequently arrested and charged. No identification parades were held. There was little doubt that on arriving at the scene, the police had had to act fast and arrange for the available witnesses to confront the available suspects. It was also impracticable to convene 14 identification parades at short notice. The Court of Appeal felt the situation faced by the police was not specifically covered by the Codes and so there was no breach of Code D. However, there were serious questions about the reliability of the identification evidence having regard to the manner in which it had been obtained. On this point the Court of Appeal noted the lack of any detailed descriptions taken from the eyewitnesses before seeing the suspects. This was coupled with the the eyewitnesses travelling together in the police car and there was no record of what the witnesses had said when viewing the suspects. In the circumstances the evidence had to be excluded under s. 78 PACE 1984 in the interests of ensuring a fair trial.

8.10 VOICE IDENTIFICATION

The current version of Code D makes no provision for an identification made on the basis of voice alone. Voice identification is fraught with more dangers than visual identification, and requires special caution. For two cases in which selection was based on voice identification, see *R v Hersey* [1998] Crim LR 281 and *R v Roberts* [2000] Crim LR 183. Home Office guidance on the use of voice identification is available.

8.11 DOCK IDENTIFICATIONS

Dock identifications occur where the victim or another witness testify on oath that the accused standing in the dock is the person he saw at the crime scene. Dock identifications are rare because they have little probative value as the identification of the accused in these circumstances is virtually inevitable and therefore highly prejudicial. Exceptionally a dock identification might be used where the defendant has resisted all other pre-trial identification methods. Even where this occurs to ensure fairness, the defendant should be asked to take a seat in the courtroom as opposed to standing alone in the dock to be formally identified. The principles governing the use of dock identifications were restated in *Barnes v Chief Constable of Durham* [1997] 2 Cr App R 505 and *Karia v DPP* (2002) 166 JP 753.

8.12 PRACTICAL STEPS THE LEGAL ADVISER CAN TAKE IN RELATION TO IDENTIFICATION EVIDENCE

- Unless you have a thorough working knowledge of Code D and its annexes you will not be able to actively defend your client's interests at the police station. Always have a copy of Code D with you.

- It is important that you keep an independent record of all that goes on in relation to identification procedures, including the advice you give to your client.

- Be prepared to make representations where appropriate and ensure that your representations are properly recorded. Every decision taken by the identification officer must be justified. Code D para. 3.12 is important and is set out in full in the early part of this chapter. It gives the police discretion when an identification procedure must be held. A failure by the police to convene a parade may be challenged in court. Be prepared to challenge a decision not to convene an identification procedure where appropriate. If your client indicates that he does not know the eyewitness make the police aware of this.

- You are entitled to make representations as to the most appropriate identification procedure that should be used. But remember a failure by the suspect to consent or to co-operate can lead to a potentially prejudicial identification procedure being adopted and it can lead to adverse evidential inferences being drawn.

- A properly convened video identification will include the suspect's image amongst eight other people who resemble the suspect in age, height, general appearance and position in life. Police forces using the latest VIPER technology have access to an extensive database of volunteer faces. The images used must show the suspect and the other volunteers in the same positions or carrying out the same sequence of movements. You are allowed to see the complete set of images before they are shown to a witness. You should be present when the compilation is put together. Ensure that your objections are recorded. Unusual features can be disguised using the video technology now available. The compiled video is burned onto a DVD and is usually shown to the eyewitness at a later date. You are entitled to be present when the compilation is shown to the witness.

- If a conventional identification parade is used there are many practical things you can do to ensure it is to be conducted fairly. You should check the layout to ensure witnesses cannot communicate with each other or see members of the parade in advance. You might want to take a photograph of the parade to show its composition. A photograph will be supplied to you on request but it may take some time.

- Where there is time (and where there are varying descriptions of the suspect by different witnesses), make representations as to the parade's composition.

- If your client has a unique identifying feature such as a scar or an unusual hairstyle ensure that steps are taken by the police to disguise it. Participants in the parade might be asked to use a plaster on the same part of their face or to wear a hat or adopt a seated position.

- Offer your client advice on where to stand on a conventional parade or where to be placed in a video compilation and, in the case of a conventional parade, how to deal with (a) being identified and (b) not being identified.

- If dissatisfied with the parade's composition, make sure your representations are noted in the parade record.

- If an inferior form of identification is used such as a group identification or confrontation, it is important to observe all aspects of the procedure and to document them all.

- Always assess and record the degree of confidence with which a witness purports to make a positive identification.

8.13 WHAT ARE THE OTHER WAYS IN WHICH EVIDENCE OF IDENTIFICATION CAN BE DERIVED?

8.13.1 FORENSIC EVIDENCE

Forensic evidence found at the crime scene may provide compelling circumstantial evidence linking the defendant to the offence. Forensic evidence can be available in a number of forms. The person responsible for the crime may have left fingerprints, sample of handwriting, footprints, ear prints, a dental impression or DNA. DNA can be extracted from blood, semen stains, saliva, sweat or body hairs found at or near the crime scene or on the victim. Alternatively, specimens from the crime scene, such as fragments of glass, pollen or foliage, may be present on the suspect's clothing or footwear.

The forensic science service plays an important role in collecting and analysing forensic evidence. DNA is extracted from the crime scene sample and a profile is obtained. The profile is forensically compared to DNA profiles kept on the national database or to a suspect's known sample and an opinion is reached about the DNA's probable source. If the expert's opinion is accepted by the court it can provide very strong circumstantial evidence of the defendant's presence at the scene and his consequent involvement in the crime.

The police are able to assist the forensic investigation by exercising their powers under PACE 1984 to obtain intimate and non-intimate body samples from suspects to enable forensic comparison with samples found at the crime scene.

The suspect is a very important source of evidence and as part of the criminal investigation, the police may wish to obtain a set of fingerprints or sample from a suspect for forensic comparison with evidence linked with the commission of the crime.

8.13.2 FINGERPRINTS AND FOOTWEAR IMPRESSIONS

The power to obtain fingerprints and footwear impressions is contained in s. 61 PACE 1984 (as amended) and s. 61A PACE 1984 respectively and can be exercised by a constable. Fingerprint and footwear impressions may be taken at a police station with the suspect's written consent. They can be taken without consent where:

- a suspect has been arrested and detained in connection with a recordable offence and

- the suspect has not had his fingerprints/footwear impression taken during the investigation or

- a complete set was not taken or
- some of the prints/impressions are of insufficient quality.

Fingerprint and footwear impressions may also be taken without consent where the suspect has been charged or informed that he will be prosecuted for a recordable offence and he has not had his fingerprints/impressions during the investigation.

The Serious Organised Crime and Police Act 2005 (SOCPA) s. 117 has amended PACE 1984, by inserting s. 61(6A) PACE 1984, allowing an officer to take a person's fingerprints without consent prior to an arrest and away from the police station where:

- the officer reasonably suspects that the person is committing or attempting to commit an offence or has committed or has attempted to commit an offence; and
- the name of the person is unknown and cannot be readily ascertained by the officer; or
- the officer has reasonable grounds for doubting whether a name furnished by the person is his real name.

The development and use of mobile digital fingerprint readers connected to the National Automated Fingerprint Identification System (NAFIS) by mobile communications technology means the police can verify a person's identity at the crime scene in accordance with s. 61(6A) PACE 1984.

As with intimate and non-intimate samples (considered below), fingerprint and footwear impressions may be used for a speculative search against forensic databases and the suspect should be warned of this fact.

8.13.3 PHOTOGRAPHS

Under s. 64A PACE 1984, as amended, a photograph (which includes a moving image) may be taken of any person who is detained at the police station with and without consent. If consent is withheld, force may be used. Section 116 SOCPA 2005 has extended the power by enabling the police to take a photograph without consent at a place other than a police station where the suspect has been arrested and in some circumstances prior to arrest.

8.13.4 NON-INTIMATE SAMPLE

The authority to obtain a non-intimate sample from a suspect is contained in s. 63 PACE 1984 (as amended). A non-intimate sample is defined in s. 65 PACE 1984 to include a sample of hair other than pubic hair, a scraping from under a nail, a swab taken from the mouth, a footprint or bodily impression. Non-intimate samples may be taken with your client's consent. Where consent is withheld, s. 63 PACE 1984 permits a non-intimate sample to be taken where:

- a suspect has been arrested and detained in connection with a recordable offence; or
- has been charged or informed he will be reported for an offence and
- no such sample has yet been taken in the course of the investigation; or
- a sample which has already have been taken has proved insufficient.

In addition, a non-intimate sample may be taken without consent from a person upon conviction for a recordable offence.

8.13.5 INTIMATE SAMPLE

An intimate sample (also defined in s. 65 PACE 1984) includes a dental impression or a sample of blood, tissue fluid, urine, pubic hair or swabs taken from a person's genitals or body orifice other than the mouth. An intimate sample may only be taken with the suspect's consent under s. 62 PACE 1984. A failure to consent to provide an intimate sample without good reason can be used in evidence against the defendant (s. 62(10) PACE 1984). An intimate sample may only be taken from a suspect if an inspector authorises it, having reasonable grounds for suspecting the person to be involved in a recordable offence and that the sample would confirm or disprove the suspect's involvement. The suspect's written consent must be obtained, and the sample (other than urine) must be taken by a health care professional.

Evidence from samples obtained unlawfully remain admissible subject to the court's exclusionary discretion at common law and under s. 78 PACE 1984 (see Chapter 6).

13.6 RETAINING THE SUSPECT'S FINGERPRINTS/PHOTOGRAPHS/DNA SAMPLES

The retention and use of a suspect's fingerprint/footwear impression and DNA samples is governed by s. 64 PACE 1984 (as amended). Such samples may be retained even if the person from whom they were taken is acquitted of the offence or a decision is taken not to prosecute. Retained samples may only be used for:

- a purpose related to the prevention or detection of crime, or
- the investigation of an offence; or
- the prosecution of a case.

The retention of samples in the case of an acquitted person was challenged in *Chief Constable of South Yorkshire, ex p. Marper* [2004] 1 WLR 2196 under Article 8 (the right to privacy) and the case is currently before the ECtHR. The domestic court held that even if the provision was an interference with Article 8, it was proportionate to the aim it sought to achieve. A decision of the ECtHR on the point is expected in 2008.

Samples taken from a person not suspected of an offence (i.e. as part of mass screening) must be destroyed as soon as they have fulfilled their purpose. Where such samples should have been destroyed, they may not be used in evidence or for the purposes of investigation against such a person (s. 64(3) PACE 1984). However, in the *Attorney-General's Reference (No. 3 of 1999)* [2001] 2 AC 91 (a case preceding the change in the law allowing the retention of samples from an acquitted person), the House of Lords ruled that where a DNA sample should have been destroyed, although s. 64 PACE 1984 prohibited its use in the investigation of any other offence, it did not make evidence obtained as a result of a failure to comply with that prohibition, inadmissible. It is left to the trial judge to use his discretion under s. 78 PACE 1984 if the admission of the sample would have an adverse effect on the fairness of the proceedings.

8.14 DNA EVIDENCE

The UK has one of the most comprehensive DNA databases in the world. The forensic techniques involved in extracting an individual DNA profile and comparing it with other DNA samples have attracted considerable attention from scientists, lawyers and the media. The techniques are relatively new having been perfected in the late 1980s. Over the course of time, however, the techniques have grown increasingly sophisticated, such that DNA evidence can yield very compelling evidence. Every human being has a unique DNA make-up (apart from an identical twin). The profiling techniques enable a forensic scientist to compare two biological samples and to determine the likelihood that the two samples originated from the same source. DNA evidence is perceived as being particularly cogent evidence because of the statistical improbabilities that profiling produces. The process of extraction, extrapolation, interpretation and presentation of results is explained by Lord Justice Phillips in *R v Doheny* [1997] 1 Cr App R 369.

R v Doheny establishes the procedure the prosecution should follow in respect of the disclosure and presentation of DNA evidence. The defence may call their own expert witness to challenge the validity of the opinion provided by the prosecution's expert witness. Issues of sample degeneration, cross-contamination and deliberate planting of samples by prosecuting authorities can significantly diminish the probative value of the DNA evidence. Indeed, there may be a perfectly innocent explanation to account for a defendant's DNA being found at the crime scene. The ultimate evaluation of DNA evidence, as with other forensic opinion evidence, is a matter for the jury or magistrates. DNA technology today is approaching individualisation. When odds against a random match of one in 60 billion are quoted, DNA evidence all but positively identifies the person whose profile matches the crime stain as being the source of the evidence.

8.15 FACIAL MAPPING

Evidence about a defendant's involvement can be provided by other expert testimony including experts in facial mapping techniques and voice recognition experts. The admissibility of expert opinion evidence is considered in Chapter 21. Facial mapping might be required in a case where still photographs or a video image have been taken of the suspect and a comparison with the suspect is available. Experts in photographic technologies and anatomical features can enhance picture quality and offer an opinion as to the likelihood of the defendant and the person pictured being one and the same. In *R v Clare and Peach* [1995] 2 Cr App R 333, a police officer who had viewed a video recording some 40 times with lengthy and studious consideration was permitted to give evidence on whether persons shown on the recording committing acts of violent disturbance inside a football ground were the accused.

KEY POINT SUMMARY

- Eye-witness identification is of huge practical importance in an investigation but is notoriously unreliable.

- To effectively advise on police procedures in relation to identification evidence, the legal adviser must have a thorough working knowledge of Code D and its annexes.

- A failure by a suspect to co-operate in the conduct of an identification procedure or to provide an intimate sample can lead to adverse evidential inferences being drawn.

- It is important for the legal adviser to make appropriate representations about the manner in which identification evidence is obtained and to ensure those representations are properly recorded. In doing so not only are you protecting your client's rights at the police station, you are setting up the potential of a s. 78 PACE 1984 argument at trial for the exclusion of any identification evidence obtained in breach of Code D.

- Understand that the admissibility of identification evidence obtained in breach of Code D is vulnerable to challenge under s. 78 PACE 1984, but that breach does not mean such exclusion will be automatic.

- Know when the police are justified in obtaining a sample from your client under ss. 61–63 PACE 1984.

SELF-TEST QUESTIONS

Consider our case study *R v Lenny Whyte*.

You will recall Lenny has been charged in connection with a burglary at the home of an old age pensioner. His defence is one of complete denial; however, he is linked to the crime by, *inter alia*, eye-witness identification. In discharging its legal burden of proof beyond reasonable doubt, the prosecution will be relying on evidence of identification in this case.

1. Assess the strength of the identification evidence against Lenny.

2. Consider how the evidence of identification in this case has actually materialised.

3. Can you point to any specific breaches of Code D in relation to the manner in which the evidence has been obtained and which would, in your view, enable the trial advocate to apply to have the evidence excluded under s. 78 PACE 1984 in the interests of ensuring a fair trial?

FIGURE 8.1 OBTAINING EVIDENCE OF IDENTIFICATION

Pre-trial safeguards under Code D—their purpose

- To ensure the quality and reliability of eye-witness identification, the detail of which can be found through:
    - video parade Annex A;
    - identification parade Annex B;
    - group parade Annex C;
    - confrontation Annex D;
    - showing photographs Annex E.

When can an eyewitness be shown photographs?

- When there is no known and available suspect in mind (Code D para. 3.3).

When must an identification procedure be convened?

- Where the suspect disputes being the person the witness claims to have seen, an identification procedure should be held unless:
    - it is not practicable; or
    - it would serve no useful purpose in proving or disproving the suspect was involved in the offence, Code D para. 3.12.

CHALLENGING THE ADMISSIBILITY OF EYE-WITNESS IDENTIFICATION

- Use s. 78 PACE 1984 on the basis that the admission of such evidence would have an adverse effect on the fairness of the proceedings.
- Relevant factors would be proven breaches of Code D, including:
    - failure to convene an identification procedure;
    - failure to properly record an identification procedure;
    - failure to disguise a prominent feature in the suspect's appearance;
    - allowing eye-witnesses contact with one another before a parade;
    - use of photographs in a case where the suspect was known;
    - a failure to properly conduct an identification procedure—see Annexes to Code D.

9 ADVISING AT THE POLICE STATION—PRACTICAL STEPS

9.1 INTRODUCTION

This chapter may be of more relevance to LPC students undertaking an Advanced Criminal Litigation elective, by bringing together the matters explored in the previous chapters in Part II. This chapter places particular emphasis on the practical steps a legal adviser will take when discharging the onerous responsibility of advising a suspect at the police station.

Most specialised criminal law firms will have members of staff on the Police Station Duty Solicitor Scheme, providing 24-hour assistance to suspects in detention. The task of advising the suspect at the police station is not always undertaken by a qualified solicitor. The task may be given to an accredited clerk or trainee solicitor who will have completed or be undertaking the Police Station Representatives Accreditation Scheme if their firm wishes to receive payment from the Legal Services Commission for the representation provided (see para. 9.21 below). The legal adviser has a multi-faceted role at the police station, likely to require the following legal skills:

- interviewing;
- analysis;
- advising;
- negotiation;
- advocacy.

Interviewing

The purpose of interviewing is primarily to extract information. You need to be able to effectively extract the salient information not only from your client, but also from the custody officer and investigating officers.

Analysis

You will be required to analyse the information you have obtained from the custody record and from what the investigating officers and your client have disclosed to you, in order to evaluate the strength or weakness of the evidence against your client and to formulate a strategy.

Advising

The police station adviser will clearly be called upon to give advice. The advice might include:

- whether to answer questions in interview;
- whether to remain silent;
- whether to make a full and frank confession;
- whether to participate in an identification procedure, or perhaps to consent to a search.

Negotiation

Negotiation skills are needed. They are most likely to be deployed in your dealings with the custody officer who takes many of the important decisions under PACE 1984 and the Codes of Practice in relation to your client's detention. You may need to negotiate your client's release from custody or persuade the appropriate authority that a conditional caution or simple caution is preferable to your client being charged, or that your client should be granted bail if charged.

Advocacy

Advocacy skills are required because you may need to intervene in an interview in a proactive way to protect and advance your client's legal rights.

In order to discharge the role effectively, the legal adviser needs to be:

- knowledgeable;
- organised;
- assertive;
- decisive.

All police station advisers need a detailed knowledge of police powers and procedure under PACE 1984 and the Codes of Practice. A sound grasp of the substantive criminal law, the Bail Act 1976, rules of evidence and the rules of professional conduct are also necessary. It is impossible to effectively advise a client without such knowledge.

Given the number of tasks the legal adviser is likely to be called upon to fulfil, you need to be organised and assertive. If a legal adviser is to protect his client's best interests, this may require you to challenge the authority of the police.

Legal advisers have to be decisive. You will be required to exercise your powers of critical thinking on the spot. The decisions that your client makes on your advice may have significant repercussions. Do you, for example, advise your client to remain silent, knowing that adverse inferences might be drawn under s. 34 Criminal Justice and Public Order Act 1994 (see Chapter 5)? Do you advise your client to admit the offence? If so, what is the basis for your advice? If your client makes admissions during interview, charges may follow or your client may be offered a caution/reprimand.

The onerous nature of the solicitor's role at the police station was aptly expressed by the Court of Appeal in *R v Wahab* [2003] 1 Cr App R 15:

> 'One of the duties of a legal advisor, whether at a police station, or indeed at a pretrial conference, or during the trial itself, is to give the client realistic advice. That emphatically does not mean that the advice must be directed to "getting the client off", or simply making life difficult for the prosecution. The advice may, and sometimes ought to be robust, sensibly considering the advantages which the client may derive from evidence of remorse and a realistic acceptance of guilt, or the corresponding disadvantages of participating in a "no comment" interview. The exercise of the professional judgment in circumstances like these is often very difficult, often dependent on less than precise instructions from the defendant . . .'

It should be added that the working environment at the police station is less than ideal. You may be called out or telephoned after work or in the early hours of the morning. You will be entering a largely male-dominated environment where the police will often want one result and you will want another. You may well be under pressure of time in an urgent investigation. Until you have undertaken some reflective practice and experience, you may feel isolated and intimidated.

The police station is at the sharp end of the adversarial justice system. In a serious case, where the police have considerable resources at their disposal and a strong suspicion that your client is involved: what does your client have? The answer is: you.

Having worked through the chapters on police powers, the detention process, the rules relating to the admissibility of confession evidence and evidence of identification, as well as the law relating to drawing adverse inferences from silence, you are now better equipped to offer a suspect advice at the police station. How, then, might you undertake this role in practice?

Note: Our Online Resource Centre includes a role-play exercise and accompanying, comprehensive set of video clips depicting the role of the solicitor at the police station. The scenario (which can be on the lecturer resources section) explores the process of detention and investigation of a fictional character called Peter West who is under arrest on suspicion of the rape of a 14-year-old girl. The scenario is unscripted and was brought to life by real police officers and an accredited police station representative.

online resource centre

9.2 INITIAL CONTACT

You may be asked to represent a suspect at the police station either because the suspect has requested you or your firm to attend or a third party has sought your help on behalf of someone in detention or at the request of the Duty Solicitor Service.

Keep contemporaneous notes from the outset. When you receive the initial telephone call from the station, note the following:

- time;
- station;
- person to whom you are speaking;
- client's name, age, nature of the offence;
- name of investigating officers;
- whether your client has been interviewed or whether the police intend to interview.

Try to speak with your client and check whether your conversation can be overheard. Ascertain if the client wants you to attend and whether he has made any admissions. If you are to attend, your client is best advised to say nothing until you arrive. In all but the most straightforward of road traffic cases, you should attend in person if your client is to be interviewed. Speak to the custody officer and let him know your estimated time of arrival at the station, and ask that your client is not interviewed or asked to undergo any procedures until you get there.

9.3 WHAT SHOULD YOU TAKE WITH YOU TO THE POLICE STATION?

online resource centre

You need to be very organised at the police station, so ensure you have with you a notebook, pen, PACE 1984, the Codes of Practice, proof of ID, legal aid forms and your checklists. In the student resource section of the Online Resource Centre you will find a checklist for use at the police station, which is reproduced with the kind permission of Lichfield Reynolds Solicitors in Staffordshire.

9.4 WHAT SHOULD YOU DO ON ARRIVAL?

- Go to reception and make sure your mobile telephone is switched off. Do not use your mobile secretly, as this could compromise your integrity.
- Ask to speak to the Custody Officer, explaining who you are. He may want some proof of your identity.
- Check the custody record. You have the right to consult the custody record (Code C para. 2.4). Take your time to consider it, as it is a very important document in evidential terms and will provide you with a lot of useful information. From the custody record you will check your client's time of arrest, reason for arrest, time of arrival at the police station and the reasons for detention. It should have details of the risk assessment undertaken in relation to your client and any requests made by your client. It will provide a record of any decisions about your client's detention including any searches and their authorisation, reviews of detention at six- and nine-hourly intervals and any complaints by your client. You need to know the rules relating to the process of detention and questioning (see Chapter 4) to be in a position to properly evaluate the content of the custody record. Having considered the custody record, you should then ask to speak with the investigating officer(s).

9.5 INITIAL CONTACT WITH THE INVESTIGATING OFFICER(S)

This is a very important stage in your role as an adviser at the police station. Have you a right to disclosure of the evidence the police purport to have against your client? The legal obligations upon the police to make disclosure of their evidence at this stage are minimal. They are set out in Code C para. 10.3 Note 10B and were considered in *R v Imran and Hussain* (1997) Crim LR 754, in which the Court of Appeal held there is no legal obligation on the police to make disclosure of evidence prior to interview.

R v Imran and Hussain (1997)

In this case, it became apparent during the interview that the police had video evidence of the robbery in which the defendants were alleged to have been involved. Neither the defendants or their legal adviser asked that the interview be suspended so that the content of the video could be viewed. On appeal, it was contended on behalf of the defendants that the police should have disclosed the video, and having failed to do so, that no adverse inference could be drawn under s. 34. Rejecting such a proposition, the Court of Appeal reasoned:

'In support of the application it is submitted that the tenor of sections 34 to 38 of the Criminal Justice and Public Order Act 1994 require the police to give as full a briefing as possible of disclosing all material to a legal representative before the interview with the suspect commences. We do not agree. There is of course a duty on the police not actively to mislead any suspect, but it is in our judgment totally impossible to spell out either expressly or by any permissible implication from those five sections any such requirement on the part of the police . . . '

Notwithstanding the minimum legal requirements set out above, you must press the investigating officers for complete disclosure of the evidence they have against your client at this stage. Be assertive if necessary. You are not going to be in a good position to offer your client informed advice as to what strategy to adopt unless you can make an assessment of the strength of the evidence against him. Keep a careful record of what you are told. It is not uncommon (particularly in relation to serious crimes) for the 'disclosure interview' to be recorded.

You should ask what witness statements the officers have and what they contain. If searches have been undertaken, ascertain for what purpose and what evidence they might have yielded. Check if your client has made any incriminating admissions to date. Check whether the incident was covered by CCTV. If it was, ascertain whether the footage has been reviewed by the officers.

How much information you extract at this stage may depend on the personalities of the investigating officers and the nature of the investigation. Your purpose in extracting as much information as possible is to enable you to evaluate the extent and strength of the evidence before you speak with your client. Press for full disclosure, including a full list of your client's previous convictions. Point out the mutual benefits of such disclosure in that your client will be forced to seek legal advice repeatedly during the interview as new facts emerge. This will require the interview to be repeatedly suspended.

One good way of ascertaining whether you have been told all by the police is to ask: 'Is there any information you have not disclosed?' The police cannot lie to you and you will either be answered with a yes, no, or not prepared to say.

9.6 THE IMPORTANCE OF KEEPING A COMPREHENSIVE RECORD

The importance of keeping detailed notes cannot be over-emphasised. Keep a written record of everything. Checklists are extremely useful in this regard, as they act as a comprehensive *aide-mémoire*. You may not be taking the matter further than the police station and, as such, you need to ensure your notes are comprehensive. Anyone reviewing the file in the office or at court at a later date ought to be able to quickly ascertain the key points of what took place at the police station. Remember, your written records may be adduced in evidence at a later trial.

Whatever representations you make at the police station, ensure they are recorded on the custody record.

9.7 EVALUATING THE DISCLOSED EVIDENCE

To be in a position to correctly advise your client, you need to constantly evaluate the evidence against him in the context of the offence he is under suspicion of having committed. This is why you must carefully consider the information in the custody record and press the investigating officers for disclosure. Your evaluation of the evidence needs to take account of the rules of evidence.

Generally, the burden of proving your client's guilt rests on the prosecution. This should always be borne in mind. On occasions, a legal burden of proof rests on the defendant where certain defences are raised. In discharging its legal burden the prosecution must rely on admissible evidence. Consequently, if the evidence the police disclose to you is, in your view, likely to be inadmissible at trial, you will no doubt take the view that the evidence at this stage is weak. Similarly, if the principal evidence comes from your client's spouse, or from a co-accused, the prosecution may be unable to compel the witness to give evidence. It is a fact that in relation to many allegations of domestic assaults, after the initial complaint has been made to the police, the victim will often retract her complaint at a later stage. You have to ask yourself—will the prosecution be able to prove my client's guilt?

9.8 INTERVIEWING YOUR CLIENT AT THE POLICE STATION

Your client has the right to be interviewed in private (Code C para. 6.1 and Note 6J). Introduce yourself, as your client may not know you. He may be suspicious of you, given his current surroundings. Provide proof of identification and assure your client of your total independence and that anything he says will be treated in absolute confidence. You might ask your client to tell his story in an uninterrupted fashion. Clarify the detail by a series of closed questions. You will need to explore the evidence that has been disclosed by the police. You may need to be assertive with your client, stressing how important it is that he is completely honest with you. Take notes and be alert for signs of stress/vulnerability in your client.

You will need to be in a position to answer any questions your client may have about his detention. He might wish to know for how long he can be detained without charge, whether he has to give a sample of his fingerprints or an intimate or non-intimate sample. These issues are considered in Chapters 4 and 8.

Does your client understand what he has been arrested for? What are the elements of the offence which the prosecution will ultimately have to prove? Listen carefully to your client. What is he saying? Is he firmly maintaining his innocence? Is he indicating he may have a defence to the allegation against him? Does he have an explanation for the evidence against him? Is he prevaricating or reticent? Re-evaluate the strength of the prosecution's evidence in the light of what your client has had to say. As you observe your client consider how he is likely to come across in interview. If you have reason to doubt your client's state of mind, or general health, make representations to the custody officer and press for the opinion of a health care practitioner. It goes without saying that you should always be wary of your personal safety when interviewing a client in private. Be sure to record the advice given to your client. That advice will of course include assistance to your client in determining what strategy to adopt with the police.

9.9 **STRATEGIES OPEN TO YOU**

There are a limited number of strategies your client might be advised to adopt, depending on the circumstances. They include:

- making admissions;
- remaining silent;
- putting forward a prepared statement;
- answering all questions/advancing an explanation/denial or defence;
- answer some questions, but not others.

9.10 **ADVISING YOUR CLIENT TO MAKE ADMISSIONS**

The admissibility of confession evidence is discussed in Chapter 7. Clearly, a defendant will have difficulty challenging the admissibility of a confession under s. 76 and/or s. 78 PACE 1984 which has been obtained in the presence of a legal adviser. In *R v Dunn* (1990) 91 Cr App R 237, the presence of a legal adviser prevented the defendant from relying on these grounds, as the legal adviser's presence was deemed to have cured the alleged breaches of Code C. It is an entirely different proposition where a solicitor is misled by the police and advises his client to confess as a result (*R v Mason* [1988] 1 WLR 139).

In what circumstances would you advise your client to confess? Generally speaking, you might advise your client to do so where the evidence disclosed by the police is so overwhelming that there is little point in denying it. If it is blatantly obvious that, in the event of charges being made against your client, he will invariably have to plead guilty, credit will be given to your client in mitigation of sentence if the advocate can point to your client's co-operation with the police during the investigation stage. You might be able to persuade the police to caution/reprimand your client as an alternative to prosecuting him, but only in circumstances where your client admits the offence.

Suppose your client confesses his guilt to you, but you are of the opinion that the police do not have a strong case against your client? Are you bound to advise your client to confess in interview? Your client is not obliged to assist the police in any way. The burden of proof rests on the prosecution and it is onerous: proof beyond reasonable doubt. If you take the view that the evidence disclosed to you by the police is weak then, by confessing, your client increases the likelihood that he will be charged. You should explain this to your client.

If you have concerns about the reliability of your client's admissions, explore them with him. Does your client understand the ingredients of the offence to which he purports to confess, or does he have a defence in law? Consider whether your client may be confessing to something he has not done for reasons of expediency: a desire to protect someone/or a desire to relieve the pressure of the situation, particularly in the case of a drug addict. You should always explore the possibility that the police may have offered your client an inducement to confess.

If your client has made a voluntary and unambiguous confession to you, you cannot allow your client to go into the interview maintaining his innocence, as this would be a serious breach of professional conduct, but you may properly advise silence in these circumstances.

9.11 **ADVISING SILENCE**

We looked in detail at the law relating to drawing adverse inferences from silence in Chapter 5. You will recall that the essence of a s. 34 CJPOA 1994 inference is whether your client acted reasonably in the circumstances in remaining silent. Legal advisers at the police station must fully understand the effect of s. 34 if they are to be in a position to properly advise a client.

Taking account of the case law to date when might you advise silence? In practice this is one of the most difficult questions to answer, requiring a careful and considered exercise of critical judgement. Some instances in which you can properly advise silence may be more clear-cut than others.

9.11.1 STRENGTH OF EVIDENCE

An important consideration is whether the prosecution would ultimately be able to prove a case against your client. This is clearly going to depend on the nature of the allegation and the strength of the evidence. For the most part, the burden of proof is on the prosecution throughout and the suspect is not obliged to assist the prosecution by answering questions. Arguably, you should advise your client to remain silent in these circumstances. In the absence of any incriminating admissions from your client and in the face of contradictory or uncertain evidence from prosecution witnesses, your client is unlikely to be charged in this situation and if charged, unlikely to be convicted.

9.11.2 ASSESSMENT OF YOUR CLIENT'S ABILITY TO COPE WITH AN INTERVIEW

Your client will hopefully have explained his version of the facts to you. Having interviewed him you will have formed an opinion as to your client's state of mind. If your client is emotional, unwell, in a state of shock or under the influence of an illicit substance or inebriated or heavily medicated, the safest course of action may be to advise silence in interview. Your client is more likely to incriminate himself in these circumstances if he chooses to answer questions. This remains the case even where a police doctor has pronounced your client fit to be interviewed. You should always ask yourself: 'Is my client fit enough to be interviewed?'

Does your client need access to further information before he can safely advance a defence? Suppose the circumstances are such that your client is not in a position to fully articulate his defence to the allegations? Perhaps his defence is dependent upon access to documentation not currently in his possession or is an alibi. There may be a danger in disclosing the details of the alibi too soon as the police will want to talk to the individual before you have an opportunity to do so. Perhaps the safest course would be to remain silent.

9.11.3 CLIENT IS COMPLAINING OF MISTREATMENT

Suppose your client makes a complaint about mistreatment while in custody and feels he cannot trust the investigating officers. Unless, this is resolved to your and your client's satisfaction in advance of an interview, the safest course may be to advise silence.

9.11.4 LACK OF DISCLOSURE BY THE POLICE

What if you have pressed the police for disclosure of their evidence but you feel they are holding back information, which means you cannot properly advise your client? In *R v Roble* [1997] Crim LR 449 CA, this was a factor in assessing the reasonableness of a defendant's decision to remain silent.

We have previously seen that the disclosure obligations placed on the police during the investigation stage are minimal. However, this should not stop the legal adviser from pressing the investigating officers for as much disclosure as possible. There are mutual benefits to be derived in that your client will not be forced to repeatedly stop the interview to seek legal advice. It is good practice to ask the interviewing officer, at the commencement of the interview, whether there has been complete disclosure of the evidence to you. The police cannot lie. If inadequate disclosure has been made, the safest course of action is to remain silent. As facts emerge in interview, you may wish to reconsider your advice at a later stage, either in a further interview, or upon your client being charged.

Suppose the allegation involves legal complexities or relates to an incident many years before. Would an immediate response by your client be prudent in such circumstances?

11.5 FURTHER CONSIDERATION OF *R V HOWELL* [2005] CR APP R 1 AND WHAT IT MEANS FOR THE LEGAL ADVISER

You will be aware from Chapter 5 that the Court of Appeal has made some strongly worded statements in relation to the role of the legal adviser at the police station, suggesting that there should be objectively sound reasons for giving a client advice to remain silent. It had previously been the case (*R v Betts and Hall* [2001] 2 Cr App R 16) that a jury had to be instructed that if it concluded that the defendant's reliance upon legal advice had been genuine, it could not draw an adverse inference. Since the decision in *R v Howell*, the position now is that a jury may draw an adverse inference where it is satisfied that although the defendant genuinely relied on legal advice, his reliance was not reasonable in the circumstances.

Some commentators have described the decision in *R v Howell* as being dangerous, while others feel its effect has been overstated. As examples of the type of situations in which a solicitor could justifiably advise silence, the Court of Appeal cites such matters as the suspect's mental condition and his ability to recollect events without reference to documents or some other source. You are already aware that if a defendant is to avoid an adverse inference being drawn under s. 34, he will invariably need to put forward an explanation for his decision. Where the decision was based on legal advice, the defendant is not immune from having an adverse inference drawn. The reasonableness of the defendant's decision to remain silent is a question of fact for the court. In assessing the true reason for a defendant remaining silent, the adequacy of the explanation advanced by the defendant will help the court decide whether reliance upon legal advice was the true and genuine motive for not mentioning facts. What if a suspect has an explanation to put forward, but you feel there are sound tactical reasons for advising silence?

Suppose the evidence disclosed at the police station does not reveal a particularly strong case against your client? Why should he potentially help the police in this regard by answering their questions and possibly incriminating himself? In essence this is what we must assume the defence solicitor in *R v Howell* had reasoned. At the time of Howell's arrest the police had only an oral as opposed to a signed written statement of complaint from the victim and the suggestion from Mr Howell that his friend, the victim, might not wish to pursue a complaint. There was therefore a distinct possibility that the prosecution might not have been able to prove its case. The solicitor wished to wait to see how matters developed. Is such an approach to be regarded as being unreasonable in an adversarial system of justice where a suspect enjoys the right not to incriminate himself? The Court of Appeal did not find these reasons to be objectively sound. Mr Howell had a defence and could have articulated it. He had been the only person present at the flat when his friend was stabbed. He must have known whether he injured his friend accidentally or in self-defence. Was Mr Howell let down by his solicitor in your view? Was his solicitor's advice ill-conceived? If Mr Howell was not in a fit state to be interviewed because he was tired and emotional, having regard to the serious injury inflicted on his friend, this might have afforded a more convincing reason (in the eyes of the court) for failing to mention facts which he subsequently relied on.

There is a school of thought that subscribes to the view that if the police have evidence against your client and he has an explanation or denial to the allegations and is capable of advancing the explanation in interview, he should answer police questions. If charges follow, the defendant is protected from an adverse inference under s. 34. The statements in *R v Howell* and subsequent cases endorsing it, support this school of thought.

The advice given in *R v Howell* was based on tactical considerations. The tactics might have paid off had the victim not in fact wished to pursue a complaint to trial.

The danger of *R v Howell* is that the legal adviser makes choices without the benefit of hindsight. The decision does not make the role of the legal adviser any easier! You must trust your judgement. Experience and reflection will help to fashion that judgement. If there are (in your view) cogent reasons for advising silence, do not shirk from your responsibilities for so advising, but be careful about advising silence for purely tactical reasons where your client is indicating he is not guilty and is capable of advancing a defence to the allegations. Always keep a full and contemporaneous note of the instructions you receive and the advice that you give as you may be required to give evidence as to why you advised silence.

9.11.6 IMPLICATIONS FOR LEGAL PROFESSIONAL PRIVILEGE WHERE THE DECISION TO REMAIN SILENT IS BASED ON LEGAL ADVICE

Any legal advice given to a client at the police station is protected from disclosure by legal professional privilege. The privilege is that of your client and only your client can expressly or impliedly waive it. If an accused is to persuade a court that his decision to remain silent was reasonable in the circumstances, an explanation for his decision will invariably need to be given. Where an accused chooses to remain silent on legal advice, the legal adviser may be called upon to adduce evidence (in person or by adducing contemporaneous written notes) as to the reasons for the advice given. In such a case, the accused must waive his legal professional privilege.

9.11.7 WARNING YOUR CLIENT ABOUT EXERCISING HIS RIGHT TO REMAIN SILENT

Your client must be informed of the full effect of s. 34 CJPOA 1994, and in particular that your advice to remain silent does not automatically prevent your client from having an adverse inference drawn against him at any subsequent trial. The question of whether it was reasonable for your client to have remained silent is a question of fact for the jury or the magistrates. If your client is to avoid an adverse inference, an explanation for his silence will need to be tendered and this may involve a waiver of legal professional privilege (see *R v Condron* [1997] 1 Cr App R 185). It is not easy to advise a lay person about the operation and effect of s. 34. You should break it down into its three constituent elements and ask your client to explain it back to you in order to be certain your client fully understands what he is consenting to. You should record your advice in writing and get your client to sign and date your written record.

9.11.8 WHAT AMOUNTS TO WAIVER OF LEGAL PROFESSIONAL PRIVILEGE?

If your client or you (his legal adviser) tell the police the reasons for remaining silent, this will amount to a waiver of privilege. The solicitor in *R v Bowden* [1999] 4 All ER 43 unwittingly did this by making an opening statement on the tape-recorded interview. His statement was subsequently adduced in evidence at court. You need to consider whether you want to put the reasons for your advice on tape. The Criminal Law Committee of the Law Society recommends the following form of words to be recited by the legal adviser at the outset of the interview:

'(i) I am . . . . a solicitor/trainee/accredited police station adviser with (firm/PDS)
I am now required to explain my role. It is to protect my client's basic and legal rights. I shall continue to advise my client throughout the interview.

(ii) I shall intervene in the interview if

– my client requests or requires legal advice; or

– your questioning is inappropriate; or

– you make statements which are not based on matters that have been made known to me.

(iii) After receiving legal advice my client has decided:

(either) to exercise the right to silence because (consider giving reason). Please respect that decision.

(or) to answer questions which you may raise that are relevant to my client's arrest.'

If you are at all concerned about waiving legal professional privilege then, in stating the fact that your client is to remain silent, you must avoid reference to any privileged conversation with your client. As an alternative to (iii) above, you might say: 'I now advise my client not to answer questions [because . . .]' If the reason for your advice is based on something external to your instructions and consequent advice, e.g. lack of police disclosure or your client's mental condition, then it should be safe to put this forward as a reason since it is without reference to any privileged conversation.

Once legal professional privilege is waived, the prosecution can ask searching questions in cross-examination about precisely what the defendant told his legal adviser with a view to exploring what the actual basis for the legal advice to remain silent was. Such line of questioning would assist the fact finder to determine whether the defendant's reliance was both genuine and reasonable in the circumstances.

It is not unusual for the prosecution to accuse the defendant of making up his defence to fit the facts as disclosed by the prosecution. If the defendant has previously disclosed his defence to his legal adviser at the police station but on legal advice chose to remain silent, evidence of what the defendant stated can be adduced to rebut a suggestion of recent fabrication without resulting in a waiver of legal professional privilege (*R v Loizou* [2006] EWCA Crim 1719).

11.9 PREPARING YOUR CLIENT FOR THE 'NO COMMENT' INTERVIEW

Your client should be warned about the difficulties of the no comment interview. Is he going to remain silent throughout or is he going to say: 'No comment'? The latter is easier. The fact that your client is going to remain silent will not of course prevent the police from putting their questions. There will be considerable psychological pressure brought to bear on your client. This might manifest itself in the officers seeking to undermine you and the advice you have given, asking innocuous questions in order to get the interview started and pointing out the tactical advantages to your client if the matter goes to trial. Always advise your client that if he answers easy and innocuous questions, he will find it difficult not to carry on answering questions.

11.12 THE PREPARED STATEMENT

As an alternative to remaining completely silent, your client may choose to read out a prepared statement. The prepared statement is self-serving in nature and admissible in evidence at a subsequent trial where your client relies on the same defence. The prepared statement is used in conjunction with your client being advised not to answer questions in interview. The statement should be drafted in your client's handwriting with your assistance and is usually read out by the legal adviser. It can be read during the course of the interview or upon your client being charged. The statement protects your client from having an adverse inference being drawn against him, provided his defence advanced at trial is the same. Any material departure from the prepared statement is likely to be the subject of adverse comment and possible inference under s. 34 CJPOA 1994. The adverse inference that might be drawn in these circumstances would be that your client did not wish to have his defence subject to critical questioning by the police. The leading case on prepared statements is *R v Knight* [2004] 1 Cr App R 9, which is considered in Chapter 5. Once again, a prepared statement will not prevent the police from asking questions.

11.12.1 WHEN MIGHT YOU ADVISE A CLIENT TO PUT FORWARD A PREPARED STATEMENT?

Prepared statements are best limited to straightforward cases where you can be clear and confident of your client's defence at the outset. Until you have had full disclosure of all the relevant and critical facts in the investigation which will require an answer, it may be prudent to wait until after the first interview before finalising a prepared statement. This is especially so if the police have been reticent in terms of their disclosure. A prepared statement may be a sensible option for a client who maintains his innocence but who is not best placed to advance his defence or explanation by agreeing to answer all questions.

9.13 ANSWERING ALL QUESTIONS/ADVANCING AN EXPLANATION/DENIAL OR DEFENCE

When might you advise your client to answer questions? If as a result of the interview with your client, you have formed the view that your client is fit to be interviewed and the minimum disclosure requirements under Code C para. 10.3 Notes for Guidance 10.B have been made, your client might properly be advised to advance his defence or explanation for the evidence against him in answer to the allegations.

It should be carefully explained to the client that if he is advancing a defence such as an alibi, the police are likely to interview that person before you are able to do so. Can you be sure that the defence to be put forward is credible or not? It should be explained to your client that he must be honest with you, since if his defence changes at trial, he will be at risk of an adverse inference being drawn against him. Once again, you should prepare your client for the interview experience. You should not coach your client but make him aware of the tactics and ploys the police may adopt. Anticipate questions likely to form the basis of s. 36 or s. 37 CJPOA 1994 inferences (see Chapter 5). If, as is likely, the interview is to be tape recorded, explain the mechanics of this.

It is becoming an increasingly common practice for the police to bail suspects under s. 37(7)(a) PACE 1984 where a suspect denies an offence. The purpose of this is to enable the police to seek the advice of the CPS as to whether charges should be brought. On a purely pragmatic level, if there is a significant risk that your client will be refused bail if charged, a denial at this stage may be a sound tactical option.

9.14 ANSWERING SOME QUESTIONS BUT NOT OTHERS

Your client should never be advised to answer some questions but not others. This would be an evidential disaster. Visualise how it would look to a court if your client did so. It would imply that your client had something to hide.

9.15 HOW DO I DECIDE WHAT ADVICE TO GIVE?

There is no easy answer to this question. Experience will help. However, a good strategy is to draw up a list of the advantages and disadvantages of your client remaining silent and compare them to a list of the advantages and disadvantages of answering questions or advancing a prepared statement.

9.16 WHAT SHOULD THE LEGAL ADVISER DO DURING THE INTERVIEW?

A lot of behavioural psychology occurs during the police interview. The atmosphere may be tense. It is the police who are in control. They control time, space and information. It is important that you regain some of the psychological control.

In the interview room you should sit where you feel comfortable and not where you are asked to sit, if you feel this hinders your ability to communicate with your client. Remember you may have an appropriate adult or interpreter in the interview room with you. It is worth reminding such individuals as to the nature of your respective roles.

Code C—Notes for Guidance para. 6D acknowledges the nature of the legal adviser's role in the interview:

> 'A detained person has a right to free legal advice and to be represented by a solicitor. The solicitor's only role in the police station is to protect and advance the legal rights of his client. On occasions this may require the solicitor to give advice which has the effect of his client avoiding giving evidence which strengthens a prosecution case. The solicitor may intervene in order to seek clarification or to challenge an improper question to his client or the manner in which it is put, or to advise his client not to reply to particular questions or if he wishes to give his client further legal advice.'

The extract justifies a *positive* role in the interview. You must interrupt if you feel the questions being put are:

- unclear;
- ambiguous;
- oppressive;
- irrelevant;
- threatening;
- not questions at all.

You may at any time advise your client not to answer a question.

You will recall ss. 76 and 78 PACE 1984 (see Chapters 6 and 7). These give you justification to intervene during an interview. So, if an officer is asking leading questions of a vulnerable suspect, or the questions are unfair, you have the authority to intervene. Place your objections on the record and set up the argument for the trial advocate should the matter come to court.

If you are taken by surprise by a question (perhaps with reference to evidence against your client not previously revealed), advise your client not to answer the question. If you feel your client is losing control of the situation you should ask your client if he wants further legal advice. Hopefully, he will say yes, resulting in the interview being suspended and allowing you to consult with your client in private. Consider what you would do if, against your advice, your client starts to answer questions? You would ask your client if he wants further legal advice. If the interview is suspended for this purpose, you should make your advice very clear and keep a note to this effect. If your client chooses to ignore your advice, so be it. Most advisers would consider it good practice to get their client to sign a written disclaimer to this effect.

If investigating officers choose to comply with only the minimum disclosure requirements in Code C para. 10.3 Notes for Guidance 10.B, you may need to stop the interview frequently in order to take instructions as new facts emerge. You might wish to ask the investigating officers at the outset of the interview if they have disclosed to you everything of relevance to the allegation made against your client. If they say they have but it later transpires that new evidence emerges you should point out the unfairness to your client and ask whether he wants further legal advice. Indeed, your advice about answering questions may need to be revised.

.16.1   CAN THE POLICE ASK YOUR CLIENT ABOUT HIS PREVIOUS CONVICTIONS?

The bad character provisions (ss. 98–112) under the Criminal Justice Act 2003 (CJA) have implications for advice given to suspects at a police station. The provisions are considered in Chapter 23.

The effect of the new law is to increase the situations where evidence of the defendant's bad character may be admitted at trial. For this reason, it will be easier for the police to justify the questioning of suspects on their past record in interview. Under the provisions, there are a series of gateways through which the prosecution are able to adduce evidence of bad character. Three of these gateways can be triggered by your client at the police station if he (a) gives a false impression of himself and/or (b) attacks the character of another person or (c) introduces his own bad character in interview.

Suspects clearly need to be advised about these provisions and the legal adviser may need to reinforce the advice during interview, perhaps by advising a client to make no comment in relation to questions about past offending.

9.16.2   CAN A LEGAL ADVISER BE EXCLUDED FROM AN INTERVIEW?

The relevant provisions are contained in Code D paras. 6.9–6.11. A legal adviser may only be required to leave if his conduct is such that the interviewer is unable properly to put questions to the suspect. Such conduct could include answering questions on behalf of your client. The decision to remove a legal adviser from an interview is a very serious step and as such it requires the interviewing officer to consult with an officer of superintendent rank, who will take the ultimate decision. If the legal adviser is removed, the suspect must be given the opportunity to consult another solicitor and to have that person present in interview.

9.17   IDENTIFICATION PROCEDURES

In many cases the police will wish to take samples from your client, or they may wish your client to participate in an identification procedure. You need to discuss these matters with your client and advise as to what response to give the police. Full consideration is given to these matters in Chapter 8, which also examines the law relating to the admissibility of identification evidence.

9.18   POST INTERVIEW

Your role does not end once the interview is concluded. There are a number of different outcomes that may occur at the police station. A decision might be taken to:

- charge your client and either release on bail (conditional or otherwise—(s. 47(1A) PACE 1984) or charge and withhold bail (s. 38 PACE 1984);
- release your client on bail (conditional or otherwise) pending further enquiries (s. 37(7)(b) PACE 1984) or release him unconditionally (s. 37(7)(c) PACE 1984);
- continue to detain your client (subject to custody time-limits and justification under s. 37(2) PACE 1984);
- detain or release your client on bail pending a decision to charge or conditionally caution by the CPS under s. 37(7)(a) PACE 1984. Conditions may be imposed to the grant of police bail in these circumstances.

You must be prepared to make appropriate representations. Knowledge of PACE 1984 and Code C is important in this regard.

9.18.1   THE DECISION TO CHARGE

You will recall that s. 37(7) PACE 1984 imposes a statutory duty on the custody officer, in conjunction with the CPS, to either charge or release a detainee where there is sufficient evidence to charge him with an offence.

An individual who has been arrested but not charged may only be detained where the custody officer is satisfied that the grounds for detaining him in accordance with s. 37(2) are met. Custody time limits apply (see Chapter 4) and continued detention is subject to review.

If the investigation has been completed and your client has been interviewed, the police/ CPS ought to be in a position to determine whether to charge or not. Having interviewed your client and having assessed the overall state of the evidence against him, you should be in a position to make representations in this regard.

If you are of the opinion that there is insufficient evidence you should be pressing for your client's release with or without bail (ss. 34 and 47 PACE 1984). Where an investigation is likely to be ongoing, your client can expect to be released on police bail, pending further enquiries or a decision to prosecute by the CPS in accordance with s. 37(7)(a) PACE 1984 (see Chapter 4, para. 4.4.4).

Where it is being proposed that your client should remain in custody for the time being, you need to ascertain the reasons for this and make appropriate representations. Your client's continued detention must be justified in accordance with the conditions laid down in s. 37(2) PACE 1984 where, for example, the police wish to undertake a further interview or conduct further enquiries of witnesses. Press for your client's release on police bail if this is likely to take some time. Custody time limits will of course continue to apply if your client continues to be detained (s. 41 PACE 1984).

A caution (conditional or simple) is an alternative to charging your client. For a caution to be administered however, your client must have accepted his involvement in the crime and consent to a caution. This alternative course of action should be discussed with your client and if it is appropriate you might choose to raise it with the custody officer. The utilisation of a caution as an alternative to a prosecution is considered in Chapter 10.

.18.2 NEGOTIATING POLICE BAIL

Full consideration is given to police bail in Chapter 4, paras. 4.4.4 and 4.14.2.

Ensure that before you leave the police station your client fully understands the state of the investigation and where he stands. If his detention is to continue, you will need to provide him with the necessary reassurances and that if a further interview is to be undertaken you will be informed. It is sensible to advise your client that 'walls have ears' in police stations, and that if he does not wish to incriminate himself, he should be very careful about who he speaks to and what he says.

9.19 PAYMENT FOR POLICE STATION ADVICE

Public funding of criminal defence services is administered by the Legal Services Commission (LSC). Advice given at the police station is covered by the Police Station Advice and Assistance Scheme which is explained fully in Chapter 4, para. 4.7.4.

9.20 THE ETHICS OF POLICE STATION ADVICE

The dynamics of advising the suspect at the police station are all-encompassing, requiring the legal adviser to be constantly on his or her guard. Your foremost duty is to protect the interests of your client, but as with all aspects of legal practice, this has to be done within the rules of professional conduct. Professional conduct issues may well arise at the police station. What would you do in the following situations? The rules we are about to cite are contained in the Code of Conduct (2007) issued by the Solicitors Regulation Authority.

A conflict of interest arises between two suspects

It is not unusual to find more than one person arrested in connection with a criminal matter. A legal adviser may advise more than one suspect in an investigation, provided there is no conflict or significant risk of conflict between them. If your duty of confidence to one client conflicts with the duty of openness to another, you must cease to act for either (Rule 3). Having interviewed one client, it may become apparent that a conflict of interest is likely to arise, in which case you should advise the second client to consult an alternative legal adviser. Detailed guidance on conflicts between co-defendants can be found in Rule 3, Guidance Notes 24–36.

Your client wants you to pass on a message to a third party

Given your client's confinement, this is not an unusual request. However, be very careful that you are not being used as an innocent conduit to tip-off someone implicated in a criminal enterprise. Clearly a lot will depend on the nature of the crime your client has been arrested for and the nature of the message you are being asked to pass on. Always explain to your client that you will have to discuss his request with the custody officer.

Your instructions come from a third party

It is not unusual to be asked to represent someone in custody by a friend or relative of the detained individual. You should attend the police station and inform the custody officer that you have been asked to attend on behalf of X and that you would like X to be informed of that fact. Clearly X cannot be forced to see you, but if X does speak with you, you must obtain his authority to enable you to act for him (Rule 2).

Your client seeks to give misleading information to the police

You must never put yourself in a position where you allow your client to knowingly mislead the court (Rule 11.01). You run the risk of having criminal proceedings instituted against you for perverting the course of justice. Although the rules are expressed in the context of the court, they should be applied equally in the context of the police station.

A client who admits his guilt to you (in circumstances where you have no reason to doubt his admission) can still plead not guilty and put the prosecution to proof of its case. You cannot, however, allow your client to make a positive assertion of innocence in your presence during the interview (Rule 11.01 (Guidance, paras. 11 and 12)). If your client insists, you must cease to act. In these circumstances however, you are still bound by client confidentiality (Rule 4.01). A client who has given the police false particulars is likely to be found out, particularly if they have been in trouble with the police before.

Suppose your client is giving you inconsistent instructions

Rule 11 Guidance, para. 16 states that a solicitor is not under a duty to enquire in every case whether his client is telling the truth. In some instances the solicitor may be put on enquiry and may need to check the truth of what his client asserts before relying on such assertions in court. The fact that a client has given his solicitor inconsistent instructions is not a ground for refusing to act further. Where it is clear, however, that a client is attempting to put forward false information, the solicitor should cease to act (Rule 11.01).

You must never construct a defence for your client (Rule 11.01). Your role is to offer advice, based on the evidence and the applicable substantive law.

Your client states he is not guilty but is prepared to take the blame and to plead guilty

You can offer your client advice and endeavour to persuade your client to plead not guilty, but you must not assist him in the deception (Rule 11.01 (Guidance, paras. 11 and 12)). You should point out the difficulties he could later find himself in if he was to change his mind and of course, there is a risk that if the true facts emerge he could be prosecuted for perverting the course of justice.

9.21 POLICE STATION REPRESENTATIVES ACCREDITATION SCHEME

If all the above has not put you off and you wish to become a police station accredited representative, you need to complete a three-part assessment process:

- a written exam;
- a portfolio; and
- a critical incidents test (CIT).

If you have passed the LPC you are exempt from having to take the written exam. You need a suitably qualified solicitor to supervise your portfolio submissions. You have to complete nine portfolios, divided into Parts A and B, which are based on advice given at the police station in real situations. You can apply for registration under the scheme once you have passed the exam (unless you are exempt) and you have completed your Part A portfolios. You then have 12 months in which to complete the full assessment process. The critical incidents test is an audio assessment which requires you to respond to a number of simulated incidents that might occur at the police station. The CIT assesses your oral skills, assertiveness and the suitability of your responses under pressure of time. Full details on the scheme can be found on the Solicitors Regulation Authority website. A link on the Online Resource Centre will take you to the relevant guidance.

online
resource
centre

KEY POINT SUMMARY

- Keep and maintain a contemporaneous written note of all that occurs whilst you are at the police station.
- Extract all the necessary information from the custody record on your arrival.
- Press the investigating officer(s) for as much disclosure of evidence as you can, as this will have a direct bearing on the advice you give your client.
- Carefully evaluate the evidence against your client before deciding on the most appropriate strategy for your client.
- Be prepared to advise silence when you consider it to be the appropriate advice.
- Where silence is to be advised, ensure your client gives his or her informed consent by making him or her fully aware of the consequences.
- Consider whether a prepared statement might be the best option for your client.
- Ensure that any representations you make are recorded on the custody record.
- Be proactive during the interview and intervene where necessary even where your client is exercising his right to remain silent.
- Prepare your client for the interview experience.
- Instruct your client in advance to answer in the affirmative if you ask him during the interview whether he wants further legal advice. This way the interview has to be suspended enabling you to consult in private with your client.
- After the interview has concluded, press the custody officer for a decision and be prepared to make appropriate representations.

SELF-TEST QUESTIONS

Case study 1: *R v Lenny Whyte*—alternative hypothesis

You will be aware that having worked through the Lenny Whyte scenario up to this point, Lenny was not represented at the police station, and made incriminating admissions to his involvement in the burglary.

Let's take an alternative course and imagine you had been called to the police station to represent Lenny upon his arrest. Picture yourself walking into the custody suite:

What is the first thing you would do?

You would speak to the custody officer and ask to consult the custody record. By consulting the custody record, you would know the reason for Lenny's arrest (domestic burglary at the home of an old age pensioner). You would be able to ascertain the reasons for his detention (which in Lenny's case would be the need to secure or preserve evidence relating to the offence or to obtain such evidence by questioning). There would be a record of all searches undertaken in connection with the investigation, from which you would be able to ascertain that Lenny's flat has been searched.

Having extracted all the pertinent information from the custody record, what would you do next?

You would ask to speak with the investigating officer and your goal would be to ascertain the precise nature of the evidence against your client. What is revealed to you depends to a large extent on the type of questions that you ask and the personality of the investigating officer.

With the information that you have from the custody record, what questions do you think you would put to the officer(s)? Would you ask open-ended questions or closed questions?

You would want details of the burglary (time/place/account of what was stolen etc . . .). You would clearly want to know whether there were any witnesses to the burglary and an account of what they saw. You need to try and ascertain the nature of the evidence that has led to Lenny's arrest. Do the police have a statement of complaint? Has any particular witness identified Lenny? Has an identification procedure been convened or is an identification procedure being contemplated? Is there any forensic evidence? Has Lenny made any admissions? Is there CCTV footage? Why was his flat searched and has any material been seized and if so, why? You would need to press for full details of the co-accused. Has this individual implicated Lenny in any way? Does this individual have any previous convictions?

Let's assume you ascertain the following information from the investigating officer:

- Lenny lives in the vicinity of the burgled property and his appearance matches the description of two eyewitnesses;
- the victim has identified Lenny to the police as someone she had spoken to in her street a short while before the burglary;
- there is an eyewitness who saw the burglar who may be able to identify him;
- the suspected burglar was seen to be wearing white trainers;
- entry to the burgled property was through the back door of the property and a scene of crime officer has lifted shoeprints;
- a pair of white trainers were recovered from Lenny's flat and have been sent for forensic comparison with the shoeprint discovered at the scene;
- the police are not prepared to disclose whether or not the co-accused Lloyd Green has made any significant statement;
- Lloyd Green has one previous conviction for a motoring matter;
- Lenny has a string of previous convictions for drug possession, theft and burglary.

What has been the purpose of your exchange with the investigating officer?

Your purpose has been to find out the nature of the evidence against your client and to assess it.

What conclusion have you reached as regards the strength of the evidence?

There is some circumstantial evidence of Lenny's involvement in the burglary and further investigation by the police is merited. The next stage will be for you to interview Lenny.

How will you conduct this interview and what is its purpose?

Having met Lenny and explained your role, you should let him speak. This gives you the opportunity to observe his demeanour. Through a series of closed questions, and preferably with the aid of a questionnaire, you need to ask Lenny for all relevant details and put to him the evidence that has been disclosed to you. Your questioning should have picked up the fact that Lenny is undergoing treatment for a mental disorder and that he is not in possession of his medication. This triggers a number of the safeguards under Code C. With Lenny's permission, you will need to alert the custody officer and you may wish to make representations as to why this fact was not picked up on the booking-in procedure. Make sure your representations are recorded on the custody record. Lenny needs to be medicated by a qualified health professional. It will almost certainly be necessary for a doctor to be called to check and administer the correct dosage and to offer advice as to whether Lenny is fit to be interviewed. This is likely to cause a significant delay. You need to decide whether to stay or to return to the station later. In view of Lenny's mental disorder he must have access to an appropriate adult.

Assume it is a couple of hours later. You continue to interview Lenny, this time in the presence of an appropriate adult (his sister). He states he is not guilty of the burglary and that he probably has an alibi but the details are vague. He knows Lloyd Green who (he says) is a drug dealer. Lenny accepts he possesses a pair of white training shoes but says they were given to him a couple of weeks ago and he has never worn them.

What advice will you give to Lenny, assuming the police doctor has deemed him fit to be interviewed? Should he exercise his right to remain silent or should he put forward his defence and an explanation? What factors have a bearing on this?

- Are you satisfied with the disclosure of evidence?
- Do you feel Lenny's state of mind is such that he could cope in an interview situation?
- What assessment have you made as regards the strength of the evidence that has been disclosed?

On balance, you should advise Lenny to exercise his right to remain silent. The police have little substantive evidence against Lenny at this time. Lenny is likely to incriminate himself if he answers police questions. His alibi is very sketchy and you do not know at this stage whether the co-accused has implicated him. If he has, this is likely to come out in the interview. If the co-accused is a drug dealer, Lenny may wish to proceed with caution out of concern for his own safety. Lenny should be advised about the potential risks of remaining silent. On tape you should state that your client is to remain silent and consider giving your reasons for this advice (without reference to any privileged conversation with Lenny). Your reason might be the fact of Lenny's mental illness. Assuming Lenny follows your advice, the investigation is not advanced through Lenny's interview. Let us assume that it is not apparent that Lloyd Green has implicated Lenny in any way, as no questions are put to Lenny as regards anything Lloyd Green might have said. At the conclusion of the interview, you should be pressing for Lenny's release on police bail.

Should you advise Lenny to participate in an identification procedure?

The issues surrounding the identification of Lenny Whyte are specifically considered in Chapter 8. On balance, Lenny should be advised to consent to either a video parade or an identification parade conducted in your presence. The police are obliged to disclose records of the initial description by an eyewitness (Code D para. 3.1) and it would be important to obtain them in this case.

If Lenny answers police bail at a later date, whereupon he is identified by one of the eyewitnesses at a video parade and a forensic link is established between the training shoes recovered from Lenny's flat and the print by the back door, what then?

The police may charge Lenny without holding a further interview or they may wish to interview further.

Would your advice to Lenny change? Should he now answer questions or continue to remain silent?

The evidence against Lenny is now stronger but Lenny's alibi is no further advanced as he has not been to see you in the meantime. He is however adamant that he did not commit the burglary. It becomes a calculated risk at this point. Which course of action poses the least risk? Arguably it would be remaining silent. If Lenny were to make incriminating admissions during the interview, the prosecution would have a much stronger case against him when combined with the other evidence. If he were to remain silent he would be less likely to incriminate himself. If charged, his defence at trial may be confined to cross-examining prosecution witnesses on the basis that their identification of Lenny is mistaken. This would not trigger s. 34 CJPOA 1994 (*R v Moshaid* [1998] Crim LR 420). If Lenny were to advance a defence of alibi he would of course be at risk of an adverse inference under s. 34. However, if you were to give evidence explaining the reason for your advice, the court may accept it was reasonable for Lenny to have remained silent. In any event, the jury must be satisfied that there is a sufficiently strong case against Lenny before any question of an adverse inference is considered.

All of the above is hypothetical in the light of what did in fact occur in this case scenario. You will recall that Lenny was interviewed without a legal adviser being present. He made a number of incriminating admissions which resulted in him being charged and which will no doubt be used by the prosecution in evidence against him.

One way of deciding whether to advise a client to remain silent or answer questions is to consider:

1. What are the advantages to the client of answering questions?

2. What are the disadvantages to the client in answering questions?

3. What are the advantages to the client remaining silent?

4. What are the disadvantages to the client of remaining silent?

These questions should be constantly asked and re-evaluated. They do not always result in a clear and simple answer, but they should at least guide your thought processes on this difficult and challenging aspect of legal practice.

10 THE DECISION TO PROSECUTE

10.1 INTRODUCTION

The conclusion of the police investigation may result in a number of outcomes for the suspect. If there is insufficient evidence to charge, the suspect may be told that no further action will be taken against him. In some situations the case may remain on a police file, which means that if further evidence comes to light which implicates the suspect in the offence, he could be charged at a later date. A client should be advised of the potential consequence of his case being left on file. In other cases the case file may be referred to the CPS to decide whether there is sufficient evidence to charge and/or what the appropriate charge should be. In this situation, s. 37A PACE 1984 permits your client to be released on conditional police bail.

Where there is sufficient evidence, the suspect may be charged at the police station and given conditional or unconditional police bail or be remanded in custody pending his first court appearance.

As a result of the reforms introduced by the Criminal Justice Act 2003, the responsibility for charging is now shared between the CPS and the police depending on the nature and seriousness of the offence. In a straightforward case, the suspect may be charged within a few hours after the commission of the alleged offence. The investigation of a more serious offence may take a several days or weeks or even months.

In this chapter, we explain the grounds that must be satisfied in deciding whether there is sufficient evidence to charge and later in the chapter, the alternatives to prosecution are considered including the administration of a simple or conditional caution.

The specific issues dealt with in this chapter include:

- deciding who charges the suspect;
- the procedure on charge;
- applying the Full Code Test under the Code for Crown Prosecutors;
- applying the Threshold Test under the Code for Crown Prosecutors;
- simple cautions;
- conditional cautions;
- reprimands or final warning in the case of a juvenile offender;
- the ways in which the defence solicitor might influence the decision to charge.

10.2 STATUTORY CHARGING UNDER THE CRIMINAL JUSTICE ACT 2003

As noted in Chapter 4, s. 28 CJA 2003 has reformed the charging procedure by requiring closer co-operation between the police and the CPS. In most cases, the CPS has assumed responsibility for charging the suspect. The police retain the power to charge in a range of minor summary offences, or where the defendant indicates an early admission of guilt in other specified summary offences listed below at para. 10.2.1. Guidance on the operation of the statutory charging scheme is contained in an important document entitled: *The Director's Guide on Charging: Guidance to Police Officers and Crown Prosecutors issued by the Director of Public Prosecutions s. 37A PACE 1984* (February 2007), accessible via the web-link section of our Online Resource Centre (www.cps.gov.uk/publications).

online resource centre

10.2.1 OFFENCES WHERE THE POLICE CHARGE THE SUSPECT

Under the DPP's Guidance on Charging, the police may charge the suspect in all summary/either-way cases where it appears to the custody officer that a guilty plea is likely and the case is suitable for sentencing in the magistrates' court, except for:

- offences of wounding or grievous bodily harm, s. 20 OAPA 1861;
- assault occasioning actual bodily harm, s. 47 OAPA 1861;
- violent disorder, s. 2 Public Order Act 1986;
- affray, s. 3 Public Order Act 1986;
- offences of deception and handling stolen goods, under the Theft Acts 1968 and 1978.

The police will continue to charge the suspect with the following offences (whether an early plea is made or not):

- offences contrary to the Bail Act 1976;
- offences contrary to s. 5 Public Order Act 1986;
- Town Police Clauses Act 1847 offences;
- Vagrancy Act 1824 offences;
- Street Offences Act 1959;
- all summary offences punishable on conviction with a term of imprisonment of three months or less;
- any bye law offence; and
- all motoring offences except:
  - cases involving death;
  - allegations of dangerous driving;
  - aggravated vehicle taking; and

- allegations of unlawful taking of a motor vehicle unless suitable for an early disposal as a guilty plea in the magistrates' court.

0.2.2 THE PROCEDURE WHERE THE POLICE CHARGE THE SUSPECT

In deciding whether to charge, the custody officer applies the Full Code Test to the facts of the offence. For a charge to be laid, the Full Test Code, which is found in section 5 of the Code for Crown Prosecutors (see para. 10.2.5 below), requires the custody officer to be satisfied that, first, 'there is sufficient evidence to achieve a realistic prospect of a conviction' and second, that 'it is in the public interest for the suspect to be charged'.

If both elements are satisfied the suspect will be charged.

 Looking Ahead

When the provisions of ss. 29–31 CJA 2003 come fully into force in all areas, all public prosecutions will commence with the issue of a written charge, which will be accompanied by a 'requisition' informing the defendant when he is to appear in court to answer the charge against him.

After charge, the police pass the case file to the Crown Prosecutor, who, under section 4 of the Code for Crown Prosecutors is under a duty to review the file to confirm that the defendant has been charged with the correct offence and that the evidential and public interest criteria under the Full Code Test are satisfied.

0.2.3 THE RESPONSIBILITY OF THE CPS TO CHARGE

The Crown Prosecutor must decide the charge in the following offences:

- all offences triable only on indictment;
- any offence triable on indictment due to the seriousness of the offence and/or the defendant's previous convictions;
- offences under the Terrorism Act 2000;
- any other offence linked with terrorist activity;
- offences under any Official Secrets Acts;
- any offence involving any racial, religious or homophobic aggravation;
- any offences under the Sexual Offences Act 2003 committed by or upon any person under the age of 18.

0.2.4 THE PROCEDURE WHERE THE CROWN PROSECUTOR DECIDES THE CHARGE

In many cases where the Crown Prosecutor decides whether to charge, in accordance with s. 37B PACE 1984, the suspect will have been released on bail. It was previously the case that conditions could only be imposed on the grant of bail post-charge. In accordance with s. 37(7)(a) CJA 2003, conditions may now be attached to bail pending a decision whether to charge.

After the suspect has been bailed, an officer involved in the investigation of the offence will refer the case file (known as MG3 'Report to Crown Prosecutor for a Charging Decision') to the Crown Prosecutor for a decision.

In deciding whether to charge, the Crown Prosecutor will apply the Full Code Test to ascertain whether the evidence discloses a realistic prospect of a conviction and it is in the public interest for the suspect to be charged.

After applying the Full Code Test, the Crown Prosecutor will give the investigating officer written notice of his decision, s. 37B(4).

Where the Crown Prosecutor decides that:

- the suspect should be charged or cautioned, the suspect should be charged or cautioned accordingly, s. 37B(6) PACE 1984; or
- there is insufficient evidence to charge or caution, or sufficient evidence to charge or caution, but that person shall not be charged or cautioned with an offence, the custody officer must give the person concerned notice in writing that he is not to be prosecuted (s. 37B(5) PACE 1984).

10.2.5 THE FULL CODE TEST—SECTION 5, CODE FOR CROWN PROSECUTORS

As already mentioned, for the suspect to be charged, the two elements of the Full Code Test must be satisfied. The custody officer or the Crown Prosecutor must believe that:

- there is sufficient evidence for there to be a realistic prospect of conviction; and
- that it is in the public interest to prosecute.

online resource centre

The Code is the basis for a Crown Prosecutor's work (and now for the police as well) to ensure that fair and consistent decisions are made about commencing and continuing with a prosecution. The latest version of the Code came into effect in November 2004. As a public document it can be accessed from a number of sources, including our Online Resource Centre and via the CPS website. In deciding whether to charge and what the appropriate charge should be, the Code will also be used in conjunction with other official documents including the DPP's Guidance on Charging (see para. 10.2 above) and the National Charging Standards. A defence lawyer should have a good working knowledge of the Code and understand the way in which the local Crown Prosecutors and case workers apply its provisions. The CPS has an extremely informative website at: www.cps.gov.uk.

What is the evidential test?

The evidence in the case should provide a realistic prospect of conviction. The evidential test is determined by applying an objective test—would a jury or Bench of magistrates, properly directed on the law, more likely than not convict the defendant of the offence charged?

The evidence against the accused must be relevant, admissible and reliable for the prosecution to continue. If the evidence is not sufficient to prove one or more elements of the *actus reus* and *mens rea* of the offence, or if the offender cannot be identified to the exclusion of other suspects, a prosecution should not be started. If the evidential test is satisfied, the Crown Prosecutor will then apply the 'public interest' test.

The 'public interest' test

The Code requires that the prosecution must be in the public interest. In 1951 Lord Shawcross, who was then the Attorney-General, made an important statement about the public interest in prosecuting criminal offences, which has been supported by Attorney-Generals ever since:

> 'It has never been the rule in this country—I hope it never will be—that suspected criminal offences must automatically be the subject of prosecution.'

The public interest factors that can affect the decision to prosecute usually depend on the seriousness of the offence or the circumstances of the suspect. Section 5.9 of the Code for Crown Prosecutors identifies some common public interest factors in favour of the prosecution, including:

- a conviction is likely to result in a significant sentence;
- a weapon was used or violence was threatened during the commission of the offence;
- the offence was committed against a person serving the public (for example, a police officer, a prison officer or a nurse);

- the defendant was in a position of authority or trust;
- the evidence shows that the offender was a ringleader or an organiser of the offence;
- there is evidence that the offence was premeditated;
- there is evidence that the offence was carried out by a group;
- the victim of the offence was vulnerable, had been put in considerable fear, or suffered personal attack, damage or disturbance;
- the offence was motivated by any form of discrimination against the ethnic or national origin, sex, religious beliefs, political views or sexual preference;
- the offence, although not serious in itself, is widespread in the area where it was committed.

Paragraph 5.10 of the Code identifies some common public interest factors against the prosecution continuing.

A prosecution is less likely if:

- the court is likely to impose a very small or nominal penalty;
- the offence was committed as a result of a genuine mistake or misunderstanding (these factors must be balanced against the seriousness of the offence);
- the loss or harm can be described as a minor and was the result of a single incident, particularly if it was caused by a misjudgement;
- there has been a long delay between the offence taking place and the date of the trial, unless:

  — the offence is serious; or
  — the delay has been caused in part by the defendant; or
  — the offence has only recently come to light; or
  — the complexity of the offence has meant that there has been a long investigation;

- a prosecution is likely to have a very bad effect on the victim's physical or mental health, always bearing in mind the seriousness of the offence.

The test requires the Crown Prosecutor to decide the importance of each factor applied to the specific circumstances of the case and to make an overall assessment of whether it is in the public interest for the prosecution to proceed.

The victim and the public interest test
The interests of the victim should always be taken into account when deciding to prosecute. The victim should always be notified of any developments in the case. The victim's charter is available from the CPS website.

10.3 THE CODE ON DOMESTIC VIOLENCE

While there is no statutory offence of domestic violence, the term is used to describe a range of behaviour often used by one person to control and dominate another, with whom they have or have had a close or family relationship. An offence involving domestic violence may arise out of the physical, sexual, psychological, emotional or financial abuse by one person against another. While most abuse is perpetrated by a male family member on a female, the Code recognises that abuse can also be inflicted on victims in same-sex relationships or the victims of abusive family members. The Code also recognises that members of certain minority ethnic groups, the disabled, lesbians and gay men may be reluctant to report abuse. Other factors which may prevent the reporting of domestic violence are religious, cultural or language barriers.

The Crown Prosecution Service has a detailed policy on prosecuting cases of domestic violence and works closely with other criminal justice agencies such as the police, Victim Support and Refuge. In deciding whether to prosecute, the safety of the victim, any children in the case and any other person involved are given priority—although in more serious cases a prosecution may continue even where the victim has requested that no further action should be taken against the alleged perpetrator. In deciding whether the cases of domestic violence should be prosecuted or continue, the CPS will again apply the 'public interest' and the 'evidential' tests to the facts of the particular case.

10.4 WHAT IS THE POSITION IF THE CUSTODY OFFICER BELIEVES THAT THE SUSPECT SHOULD NOT BE RELEASED ON BAIL PENDING THE DECISION TO PROSECUTE?

As noted at para. 10.2.4, in many cases, the suspect may be bailed under s. 37B PACE 1984 to allow the Crown Prosecutor to make a decision about whether to charge. However, there will be cases where the suspect presents such a substantial bail risk that he should not be released from custody, but sufficient evidence is not available to allow a charging decision to be made immediately. As some or all of the potential evidence in the case is not available, the 'realistic prospect of conviction test' under the Full Test Code may not be met. In these circumstances, what action can the custody officer/Crown Prosecutor take?

The Crown Prosecutor/custody officer is entitled to apply the Threshold Test (section 6, Code for Crown Prosecutors). The test requires the custody officer/Crown Prosecutor to decide:

- whether there is at least a reasonable suspicion that the suspect has committed the offence; and if there is:

- whether it is in the public interest to charge the suspect.

In deciding the reasonable suspicion test, the following factors will be applied:

- the evidence available at the time;
- the likelihood and nature of further evidence being obtained;
- the reasonableness for believing that evidence will become available;
- the time it will take to gather the evidence and the steps being taken to do so;
- the impact the expected evidence will have on the case; and
- the charges that the evidence will support.

If the Crown Prosecutor/custody officer is satisfied that there is at least a reasonable suspicion that the suspect has committed the offence, and it is in the public interest to do so, the suspect may be charged. Following the charge, the suspect must be placed before the court at the next available sitting to decide whether his pre-trial custody should continue or whether he should be released on bail.

After a reasonable period, which will depend on the circumstances of the case, the Crown Prosecutor must review the case and once all the evidence in the case is available, apply the Full Code Test.

10.5 THE SELECTION OF CHARGES—SECTION 7, CODE FOR CROWN PROSECUTORS

The Crown Prosecutor should select charges which:

- reflect the seriousness of the offence and the extent of the offending;
- give the court adequate powers to sentence and impose appropriate post-conviction orders; and
- enable a case to be presented in a clear and simple way.

Where there is a range of possible charges available (i.e. careless driving/dangerous driving, common assault/assault occasioning actual bodily harm) the CPS lawyer will review the available evidence against the CPS's charging standards which are available on the CPS website.

10.6 ALTERNATIVES TO PROSECUTION

There a number of ways in which a suspect may be diverted from formal criminal proceedings. An adult may be cautioned or receive a conditional caution. A juvenile may be given a reprimand or final warning (see Chapter 30).

10.6.1 SIMPLE CAUTION

The police retain the discretion to caution a suspect. The decision to caution will most likely be taken in consultation with the CPS. Guidance as to when to administer a caution is contained in Home Office Circulars 30/2005 (see link in the web-links section of our Online Resource Centre). The main points are as follows.

A simple caution will be appropriate where:

- the evidence is sufficient to have warranted a prosecution;
- the offender admits his guilt; and
- the offender agrees to such a disposal after being made aware that the caution may be cited in court if he offends in the future.

An important precondition for a simple caution is that the offender must admit his guilt. The court may strike down a caution where no admission by the defendant has been obtained (see *Metropolitan Police Commissioner, ex p. P* [1995] TLR 305). A simple caution is normally administered in formal circumstances at a police station by an officer of at least the rank of inspector. The offender will sign a form acknowledging that he agrees to the caution and that he admits his involvement in the offence.

A client should be advised that while a simple caution does not constitute a conviction, records are kept and the caution may be cited in court if he later reoffends. It is also important to advise that a caution does not prevent the possibility of future prosecution. The CPS may still instigate proceedings at a later date even after the detainee has been formally cautioned although the defence could strongly argue that this constitutes an abuse of process (see Chapter 6).

While any offender other than a juvenile may be cautioned, in practice a 'vulnerable' detainee is more likely to receive a simple caution than other offenders, depending on the nature of the offence alleged. Included in the category of a vulnerable detainee are:

- the elderly;
- the infirm;
- where the detainee is suffering from a mental condition or impairment;
- where the detainee is suffering from a physical disability;
- where the detainee is under severe emotional distress.

Where the police consider that the Threshold Test is met in a case other than an indictable-only offence and determine that it is in the public interest instead to administer a simple caution or reprimand or final warning in the case of a youth, the police may do so without referring the case to a CPS lawyer.

10.6.2 **CONDITIONAL CAUTION**

A conditional caution is a disposal available under ss. 23–27 CJA 2003 and is appropriate where the Crown Prosecutor considers that there is sufficient evidence for a prosecution but it is in the interests of the offender, the victim and the community to require the suspect to comply with specified conditions aimed at his rehabilitation. A factor in deciding whether a conditional caution is appropriate, as opposed to a simple caution or prosecution, is whether the specified conditions will be an appropriate and effective way of dealing with an offender's behaviour, or making reparation for the effects of the offence on the victim and on the community.

A conditional caution is available where:

• the offender is 18 or over (provision is made in the Criminal Justice and Immigration Act 2008 to reduce the lower age restriction to 16);

• the offender admits the offence to an authorised person; and

• in the opinion of the relevant prosecutor, there is sufficient evidence to charge the offender with the offence.

The police have no discretion to impose a conditional caution, which may only be given by a prosecutor even in those cases where it would have been open for the police to have charged the offender.

In deciding whether a conditional caution is appropriate, regard should be had to the offender's criminal record and the seriousness of the present offence.

The conditional caution will usually be given at the police station but may also be administered at the offender's home or at any other appropriate location. When the conditional caution is administered, the offender is required to sign a document which contains:

• details of the offence;

• an admission by him that he committed the offence;

• his consent to being given the conditional caution; and

• an agreement to comply with the conditions attached to the caution.

10.6.3 **CONDITIONS THAT CAN BE ATTACHED**

The conditions attached to the caution must be:

• appropriate to the offence;

• achievable; and

• proportionate.

The conditions should target the offender's rehabilitation and/or reparation. The rehabilitative element may require the offender to attend a drug or alcohol rehabilitation course or an anger management course. The reparative element might include repairing or making good any damage caused to property such as cleaning graffiti or simply apologising to the victim. Section 17 Police and Justice Act 2006 (when it comes into force), will enable the CPS to attach conditions which are punitive in nature, including a fine and/or attendance at a specified place. A new power of arrest is given to the police under s. 18 of the Act to arrest an offender suspected of having breached the conditions of a conditional caution.

10.6.4 **WHAT IS THE PENALTY IF THE OFFENDER FAILS TO COMPLY WITH THE CONDITIONAL CAUTION?**

If the suspect fails to comply with the conditions of the caution, he is liable to be prosecuted for the original offence. The conditional caution may be cited in any subsequent criminal proceedings.

For further detailed guidance on conditional cautioning, see http://www.cps.gov.uk/pub-lications/docs/dpp_guidance_conditional_cautioning.pdf. A link on our Online Resource Centre (Web-Links Section: Guidelines) will take you there.

10.7 THE DEFENCE SOLICITOR INFLUENCING THE DECISION TO CHARGE

The greater availability of CPS staff in police stations means that custody officers will usu-ally be acting on the advice of the Crown Prosecutor. It should still be possible, however, for the defence solicitor to influence the decision to charge where the evidence that links the suspect to the offence appears to be weak or unreliable. In this situation, the solicitor should persuade the custody officer to release his client unconditionally or on police bail. Even where the evidence discloses a case to answer, the defence solicitor could persuade the Crown Prosecutor through the custody officer, to deal with his client by an alternative dis-posal to a formal prosecution. It may be appropriate for a client to be cautioned or to receive a conditional caution or be informally warned about his future behaviour.

In many cases, and especially where the police have made a full disclosure of the evidence against the suspect, it will be clear that the Full Code Test is satisfied and the defence solici-tor's latitude for negotiation is limited. In some situations it might be in a client's interest to be charged as soon as possible where, for example, he has been in police detention for a long time or where the defence solicitor considers that it would not be in his client's interests to be interviewed again by the police.

As with all representations made in connection with a client's detention at the police station, it is vital to ensure that the custody officer's or Crown Prosecutor's responses, are accurately recorded on the custody record and in the defence solicitor's contemporaneous notes.

Guidance on how adult cases should be prosecuted and managed is provided by the Crim-inal Cases Management Framework (CCMF). The CCMF is described as a guide for partici-pants involved in criminal case management. It is intended to help participants to prepare cases in compliance with the Criminal Procedure Rules (see Chapter 1) so that each case is brought to a fair conclusion as quickly as possible. In short it seeks to disseminate good practice so far as the conduct of criminal cases is concerned. Although it can be used by all practitioners, the CPS is the organisation most likely to apply its guidance. Part 1 of the Framework covers the conduct of adult cases in the magistrates' court (July 2007). Part 2 relates to the conduct of cases in the Crown Court and was published in January 2008. The Framework document can be accessed at www.cjsonline.gov.uk (see link in the web-links section of our Online Resource Centre).

KEY POINT SUMMARY

- Understand the division of charging responsibilities between the police and the CPS.
- Know the procedures to be followed where the decision to charge is taken by the police or the CPS.
- Have a good working knowledge of the Full Code Test under the Code for Crown Prosecutors and an understanding of the ways in which the evidential and the public interest tests are applied in the decision to charge.
- Know when the Threshold Test applies.
- Understand the alternatives to prosecution and be prepared to negotiate with the police and/or the CPS to divert your client from being prosecuted.

SELF-TEST QUESTIONS

The self-test questions in this chapter are designed to test your understanding and application of the evidential and public interest tests applied by Crown Prosecutors. Before attempting the questions, consider the following example.

Wayne, aged 24, has been arrested on suspicion of assault occasioning actual bodily harm under s. 47 Offences Against the Person Act 1861. The offence occurred during Wayne's wedding reception, when Brian, the bride's brother, made insulting comments about Wayne. There are several witnesses to the offence who would be willing to testify in court. Wayne denies the offence and Brian has indicated to the CPS that he wishes further action to be taken against Wayne. Wayne has two convictions for violent disorder under s. 6 Public Order Act 1986 for separate offences outside a nightclub. Consider whether the evidential and public interest tests are satisfied as required by the Full Code Test under the Code for Crown Prosecutors.

Advice

In applying the Code for Crown Prosecutors to Wayne's case, it appears that the evidential test is satisfied as there are several witnesses to the offence who would be willing to testify in court. There is nothing to suggest that these witnesses would not give relevant and reliable testimony and that the *actus reus* and *mens rea* of the offence could be proven. In terms of the public interest test, there are factors in favour of continuing the prosecution, not least the use of violence and in his previous criminal conduct, Wayne appears to have a propensity to be violent. On the particular facts of the case, it is likely that Wayne will be charged and prosecuted.

By applying the Code for Crown Prosecutors, consider whether the 'evidential' test and the 'public' interest test are satisfied in the following cases. You might also consider whether there are alternative methods by which the potential defendant may be dealt with.

1. Gerald, aged 75, has been charged with 14 counts of indecent assault arising out of his employment in a residential home for children. The alleged offences occurred between 1968 and 1973. The police have traced four victims of the offences who are willing to testify at Gerald's trial. Gerald has no criminal convictions.

2. Debbie, aged 35, is a single parent with three children. She has been charged with three offences of theft under s. 1. Theft Act 1968 by stealing a pack of disposable nappies, a jar of coffee and a bottle of vodka from Cutcost Supermarket. Debbie denies the offence. The supermarket's policy is always to prosecute shoplifters. In support of the prosecution case, the store detective will testify at trial and there is a security video tape of the alleged offence.

3. Jim, aged 49, is charged with using threatening behaviour under s. 4 Public Order Act 1986 against his neighbour Sally. The offence arises out of a long-standing dispute about Sally's sons playing loud music every night until at least 2 am or 3 am. The only witnesses to the incident are Sally's husband and her sons, aged 19 and 21. The arresting police officer did not witness the actual incident, but did see Sally very distressed and frightened immediately after Jim had allegedly threatened her. Jim has no previous convictions and strongly denies the offence.

4. Kyle, aged 27, is charged with using threatening behaviour under s. 4 Public Order Act 1986. The police allege that Kyle was travelling on a train without a ticket and used verbal abuse when Mohamed, the train manager, challenged him. Kyle has no previous convictions.

5. After Patrick, aged 14, tells his father, Frank, that he (Patrick) is in a gay relationship, Frank hits Patrick, causing him actual bodily harm. Patrick is attacked by his father on two further occasions. Frank also locks Patrick in his room preventing him from leaving the house to keep him away from his boyfriend. After a week Patrick's mother, Mary, tells the police who intervene and arrest Frank. Patrick does not want any action to be taken against Frank.

FIGURE 10.1 THE DECISION TO CHARGE

The decision to charge or to offer an alternative course is for the most part the responsibility of the CPS in conjunction with the custody officer under the CJA 2003 (s. 37B PACE).

The decision to charge is based on two tests contained within the CPS Code for Crown Prosecutors, November 2004. The test comprises:

- evidential test—is there sufficient evidence to provide for a realistic prospect of conviction?

- public interest test—is it in the public interest that the defendant is prosecuted? (This requires the application of various factors listed in the Code.)

ALTERNATIVES TO PROSECUTION

Simple caution (reprimand/final warning for under 18s)

- Defendant may be cautioned where:
  - evidence is sufficient to have warranted prosecution;
  - defendant admits guilt; and
  - defendant agrees to be cautioned (Home Office Circular 1990/59 and 1994/18).

Conditional cautions: ss. 23–27 Criminal Justice Act 2003

- Defendant may receive a conditional caution where:
  - he is over 18;
  - defendant admits the offence to an authorised person; and
  - in the opinion of the prosecutor there is sufficient evidence to charge.

- The condition(s) attached to the caution must be:
  - proportionate to the offence;
  - achievable; and
  - appropriate.

- The condition(s) might require the defendant:
  - to attend drug/alcohol rehabilitation course;
  - to attend anger management course;
  - to make good damage to property.

- It is likely that increasing use will be made of the conditional caution as a means of diverting an offender from the formal prosecution process.

- A conditional caution can be imposed more than once if there has been a five-year gap or a different type of offence is involved—see Home Office Code of Practice on Conditional Cautioning.

Part III

FROM CHARGE TO TRIAL

Part III considers the procedural stages between charge/summons and the defendant having to appear in court to answer the allegations made against him.

In Chapter 11 we consider public funding of criminal proceedings and the early stages of the criminal litigation process.

In Chapter 12 we consider the court's role in granting and refusing bail.

Chapter 13 considers the special procedure in relation to an either-way offence.

In Chapter 14 we explore the rules relating to the pre-trial.

In Chapter 15 we consider the conduct of summary trial.

Finally, in Chapters 16 and 17 we consider the conduct of trials on indictment before the Crown Court.

11 PUBLIC FUNDING AND EARLY STAGES OF THE CRIMINAL JUSTICE PROCESS

11.1 INTRODUCTION

In this chapter we consider:

- The public funding of criminal defence work; and
- The early stages of a criminal case, including a defendant's first appearance before a magistrates' court and the steps a solicitor will need to take in preparation for this.

11.2 PUBLIC FUNDING—A HUMAN RIGHT?

Every person charged with a criminal offence is entitled to defend himself in person or through legal assistance. Article 6(3)(c) ECHR 1950 enshrines this right and further stipulates that the entitlement to legal representation must be free where the person has insufficient means to pay and when the interests of justice require it.

A client faced with a criminal charge may be prepared to pay privately for legal representation. This however is very rare as apart from road traffic offences the vast majority of defendants who retain a solicitor in private practice have their legal expenses met by the state under the Access to Justice Act 1999. It is part of a solicitor's professional duty to consider the provision of state funded assistance for his client (Solicitors Code of Conduct 2.03).

11.3 LEGAL SERVICES COMMISSION AND THE CRIMINAL DEFENCE SERVICE

online resource centre

Private practice solicitors can only provide publicly funded criminal defence services if they have a contract with the Legal Services Commission (LSC). The arm of the LSC that has specific responsibility for the provision of criminal defence services is the Criminal Defence Service (CDS). The General Criminal Contract with the LSC requires all client files to be opened and maintained in a quality assured way. Firms 'report' the work they have undertaken to the LSC and receive regular payments on that basis. Trainee solicitors working in franchised firms will be inducted into the procedures for opening and maintaining files to comply with LSC requirements. All the CDS forms associated with the public funding of criminal defence services can be accessed from the LSC's website at: http://www.legalservices.gov.uk/criminal/forms/cds.asp. All files must contain a completed CDS1.

11.4 PRE-CHARGE ADVICE AND ASSISTANCE

Assistance at the police station is provided under the Police Station Advice and Assistance Scheme which is explained in Chapter 4, para. 4.7.4.

Mention should also be made of the pre-charge advice and assistance scheme. Funding under this scheme requires you to complete forms CDS1 and CDS2. The scheme is means tested. Clients in receipt of certain welfare benefits (including income-based job seeker's allowance and income support) qualify automatically in terms of their means. Assistance can only be provided under this scheme where the solicitor believes there is sufficient benefit to the client to justify the work being carried out. The scheme covers a client who seeks advice outside the police station in connection with a matter for which he is under investigation but has not been charged. It also covers representation in connection with an investigation by a non-police body such as the Department of Work and Pensions.

1.5 FUNDED REPRESENTATION IN COURT

A defendant charged with a criminal offence who wishes to be represented by a solicitor in court must either seek representation by the Court Duty Solicitor or must apply to the court for a representation order or pay privately.

.5.1 DUTY SOLICITOR SCHEME

Representation at court by a duty solicitor is completely free and is not subject to a means or merits test. However under the Court Duty Solicitor Scheme, there are restrictions on what the duty solicitor can do.

A duty solicitor can represent:

- anyone in custody;
- anyone charged or summonsed in connection with an imprisonable offence;
- anyone applying for bail (unless they have used a duty solicitor for a previous application);
- anyone at risk of imprisonment for failing to pay a fine or failing to obey a court order.

A duty solicitor may not represent someone in connection with:

- a trial;
- a hearing to commit a case to the Crown Court;
- an application for bail (if they have used a duty solicitor for a previous application); and
- a non-imprisonable offence (unless they are in custody).

A duty solicitor is most likely to represent a defendant appearing before a magistrates' court for the first time or a defendant who wishes to plead guilty and be sentenced in connection with a summary-only or either-way offence. Crucially, the duty solicitor cannot conduct a trial on behalf of the defendant. In this situation the defendant must either represent himself or seek an adjournment to enable him to see a solicitor who can then apply for a representation order.

11.6 REPRESENTATION ORDERS

If a defendant requires publicly funded representation in court he must obtain a representation order. For magistrates' court proceedings a defendant must satisfy a means test and the interests of justice test. For a case to be tried on indictment, the defendant must satisfy the interests of justice test only but on conviction a recovery of defence costs order (RDCO), based on the defendant's means may be made.

1.6.1 APPLYING FOR A REPRESENTATION ORDER

The relevant forms are:

CDS 14 Application for Legal Aid in Criminal Proceedings

CDS 15 Financial Statement for Legal Aid in Criminal Proceedings

CDS 14 must be completed in all cases whether tried summarily or on indictment and contains the interests of justice test and the applicant's relevant personal information. Where the offence charged is summary-only or either-way, the defendant may additionally be required to complete CDS 15 (statement of financial means). The application is processed administratively by the magistrates' court at which the defendant will make his initial appearance.

11.6.2 WHO NEEDS TO COMPLETE CDS 15?

Some applicants are 'passported' which means they do not need to complete CDS 15. 'Passported' applicants include those:

• under 16;

• under 18 and in full-time education; or

• individuals in receipt of any of the following benefits: Income Support, Income Based Jobseeker's Allowance; Guaranteed State Pension Credit.

The applicant must provide his national insurance number if aged over 16 or proof of benefit. The application cannot be processed without this information. All other applicants, apart from those charged with an indictable-only offence, must complete the means test on CDS 15. The applicant's financial eligibility is determined by the magistrates' court which receives and processes the application. Criminal defence solicitors can give their client an indication about whether he is likely to pass the means test by inputting their client's financial details on the LSC's Online Financial Eligibility Calculator which can be accessed at: http://www.legalservices.gov.uk/criminal/getting_legal_aid/self_assessment.asp

11.6.3 THE MEANS TEST

The means test comprises two elements: an initial assessment and a full means test. The initial assessment determines the applicant's 'weighted' gross annual income. Once this figure is determined the applicant will either be:

• eligible; or

• ineligible; or

• a full means test is required

On current figures the thresholds are as follows:

• A 'weighted' gross annual income of less than £12,475 (applicant passes the means test but must still complete CDS 15);

• Greater than £22,325 (applicant fails the means test) and cannot therefore be granted a representation order to cover proceedings in the magistrates' court;

• If the applicant's 'weighted' income falls between the lower and upper threshold, a full means test must be undertaken.

What counts as income?

Income for these purposes is total income from all sources, including wages; state benefits (unless specifically disregarded); maintenance payments; benefits in kind; income from savings and investments. The calculation is based on income received in the 12 month period before the application. Disregarded state benefits for this purpose include:

• attendance allowance;

• severe disablement allowance;

- carer's allowance;
- disability living allowance;
- council tax benefit;
- any payment made out of a social fund.

The applicant must produce proof of income; for example, the most recent wage slip or in the case of the self-employed the most recent tax return or set of accounts. Where an applicant who has been remanded in custody and who therefore cannot get access to financial information, CDS 17 must be completed which is a statement of truth. This enables proof of income to be waived.

For the purposes of the initial assessment, the applicant's gross annual income is 'weighted' by the application of a mathematical formula which takes account of a partner and children living as dependants in the same household. The online financial calculator performs the computation for you.

Is a partner's income included?

A partner's income is included. A partner is defined as anyone (including a person of the same sex) with whom the applicant lives as a couple. The applicant's partner is required to sign CDS 14 and 15 where their means are aggregated. The requirement of a signature does not apply if the applicant is remanded in custody or the partner is indisposed in some way. A partner's income will not be aggregated where he has a contrary interest. A partner will have a contrary interest if he is:

- the alleged victim; or
- a prosecution witness; or
- both are defendants and there is a conflict between them.

1.6.4 THE FULL MEANS TEST

The purpose of the full means test is to calculate the applicant's annual disposable income. This is based on the applicant's gross annual income (not his 'weighted' annual income). Where the applicant's annual disposable income exceeds the current figure of £3,398 he will be financially ineligible to receive public funding for proceedings in the magistrates' court.

In calculating the applicant's annual disposable income deductions are made for:

- income tax and national insurance contributions (for himself and partner if partner's income is aggregated);
- housing costs (i.e. rent/mortgage);
- child care fees (excluding private education);
- maintenance to a former partner;
- an annual living allowance (calculated using a mathematical formula).

The calculation can be performed on the LSC's online financial calculator. You are reminded that it is the court which undertakes the means test to determine eligibility.

1.6.5 GETTING PAID FOR ASSISTING A CLIENT TO COMPLETE CDS 14 AND 15

Clients will require assistance to complete CDS 14 and 15. Where a representation order is granted, the solicitor can claim 30 minutes worth of assistance under the representation order. Where a representation order is refused because the applicant fails the means test, the solicitor can claim a fixed fee of £75 under the *early cover scheme* provided the applicant submitted his application within five days of instructing his solicitor and before the first hearing. Where a representation order is refused under the interests of justice test, the solicitor can claim one hour's preparatory work under the pre-order cover scheme. The work typically covered under these post-charge schemes includes: taking a client's instructions; assisting the client to complete an application for a representation order, routine letters and telephone calls to the court and the CPS.

11.6.6 HARDSHIP REVIEW

A hardship review application may be submitted when:

- a defendant is refused legal aid because he fails the means test; or
- a defendant thinks he will fail the means test but has exceptional financial circumstances perhaps because s/he has unusually high outgoings or because defence costs are likely to be unusually expensive.

To submit an application for hardship review, the applicant must complete CDS 16.

11.7 REPRESENTATION ORDERS AND INDICTABLE-ONLY OFFENCES

Where a person is charged with an indictable-only offence, the application will be made using CDS 14 only. At a later stage the defendant will have to complete Form B (a statement of means). If a recovery of defence costs order (RDCO) is to be made in the Crown Court, it will be based on the financial information in Form B.

At the present time there are effectively two different funding schemes in place, one applicable to summary proceedings; the other applicable to indictable proceedings.

If an accused is charged with an either-way offence which is to be committed to the Crown Court and he fails the means test, he can make a further application for funding before the Crown Court which is not means tested.

There are no immediate plans to introduce means testing for cases to be tried on indictment. However, it is likely that the recovery of defence costs order scheme will be substantially revised in the future to more effectively enable costs to be recovered from convicted defendants.

11.8 THE INTERESTS OF JUSTICE TEST

Whether the defendant is charged with a summary or indictable-only offence, a representation order will only be granted if the interests of justice test is met.

The Access to Justice Act 1999 Sch. 3, para. 5 provides that if any of the following grounds apply, the interests of justice test is met and a defendant is entitled to a representation order:

- the offence is such that if proved the defendant is likely to lose his liberty or livelihood or suffer serious damage to his reputation;
- the case involves a substantial question of law;
- the accused is under a mental or physical disability or has inadequate knowledge of English such that he is unable to follow the proceedings or put his case;
- the defence will involve the tracing and interviewing of witnesses or expert cross-examination of a prosecution witness;
- legal representation is desirable in the interests of someone other than the accused.

.8.1 ARTICULATING THE INTERESTS OF JUSTICE TEST

A trainee solicitor will frequently be asked to complete an application for a representation order on behalf of a client.

How do you articulate the interests of justice test? Take a look at CDS 14 (an expedited version of which can be found at the end of this chapter Figure 11.2). The interests of justice grounds are listed at section 4a of the form. However, it is not enough to simply tick the relevant box. The specific grounds relevant to your client's case need to be fully articulated in section 4b. You should try to articulate as many of the grounds as you can and include as much detail on the application as possible as this maximises your chances of having a representation order granted. Detailed guidance on the articulation of the interests of justice test is contained in the Justices' Clerks' Society publication which can be accessed at: www.legalservices.gov.uk/docs/cds_main/IoJTest-guidanceaug06.pdf.

online resource centre This publication is well worth reading and can be found in the web-links section (Funding) on our Online Resource Centre.

The articulation of the various grounds is considered further.

.8.2 LOSS OF LIBERTY

Obviously the more serious the offence, the more likely it is that your client could go to prison if convicted. There must be a real and practical risk that your client will lose his liberty and not merely a theoretical risk of imprisonment. You need to make this clear on the application form. Many offences carry a theoretical risk of imprisonment, such as theft. However, a first time conviction for theft of a modest amount would not result in imprisonment.

In *R v Liverpool Magistrates, ex p. McGhee* [1993] Crim LR 609, the Divisional Court confirmed that a community order does not satisfy the loss of liberty ground, but may be relevant in satisfying one of the other interests of justice criteria as the factors in Sch. 3 para. 5 were not exhaustive.

The solicitor should research the relevant sentencing guidelines for the offence charged and consider whether there are any aggravating features in the offence which makes a custodial sentence more likely. This might include where your client has previous convictions for a similar offence or the offence was committed whilst on bail in connection with other criminal matters. Full details of previous offending and the sentence imposed should be given. If you have a copy of your client's criminal record this should be included. Sentencing law and practice is considered in Part V; however a good source of information as to the likely sentence your client might receive on conviction are the Magistrates' Court Sentencing Guidelines (extracts from which are reproduced at Appendix 3).

The Magistrates' Court Sentencing Guidelines (2008) cover the vast majority of summary-only and either-way offences and indicate the starting point when a court sentences for a particular offence. For example, in the offence of domestic dwelling house burglary with some aggravating features, the guidelines suggest that a custodial sentence and commital to the Crown Court in some instances is the appropriate starting point. You should refer to the guidelines where they assist the articulation of this aspect of the interests of justice test. Similarly, if your client is subject to a suspended sentence of imprisonment, the risk of a prison sentence in the event of conviction for the new offence becomes more likely. It will be self-evident that all indictable offences will enable this ground to be used. If the entry point for the offence is less than custody, you need to identify any relevant aggravating factors (including previous convictions or that it is alleged the offence was committed whilst subject to bail) as these increase the seriousness of the offence and hence the likelihood of a custodial sentence in the event of conviction.

11.8.3 LOSS OF LIVELIHOOD

Does your client stand to lose his job if convicted? If he does, this needs to be carefully and fully articulated. The likely loss of livelihood should be a direct consequence of conviction or sentence. Articulation of this ground depends on your client's job and the nature of the offence he faces. Clearly, if your client is at risk of a custodial sentence, the chance of him losing his employment is likely to be high. The prospect of lost employment would be particularly high where, for example, the offence involves an allegation of theft from an employer or the offence is of a sexual or violent nature and your client's job includes contact with children and young persons. Loss of livelihood normally refers to current livelihood. Arguably, someone training for a profession may be eligible to be included in this ground.

Road traffic offences may potentially result in loss of livelihood if your client is disqualified from driving. However, driving offences are not amongst the more serious of criminal offences. Consequently, it may be more difficult to obtain a representation order for minor driving offences. Assertions that mandatory disqualification from driving will result in a loss of livelihood will be examined critically. A right to representation would not normally be justified where a defendant seeks to avoid disqualification under the totting-up disqualification procedure having acquired 12 or more penalty points on his driving licence or for a drink-driving offence. Where there is a strong argument for advancing special reasons for avoiding disqualification, the interests of justice might be met.

11.8.4 DAMAGE TO REPUTATION

If convicted is your client likely to suffer damage to his reputation? If he is, articulate this. Examples might include a conviction for a sexual offence, or a first time conviction for dishonesty or an allegation of perverting the course of justice. You need to be imaginative and the guidance in the Access to Justice Act 1999 refers to serious damage. If your client already has a previous conviction for a similar offence or has a conviction for a more serious offence, it will be difficult to argue that he is likely to suffer damage to his reputation. A previous conviction of itself however, does not preclude articulation of this ground where, for example, your client has a previous conviction for a minor public order offence or a sexual offence. Your client's job and the precise nature of the offence will be relevant to the assessment of loss of reputation.

11.8.5 SUBSTANTIAL QUESTION OF LAW

Does your client's case involve a substantial question of law? If it does, explain in detail what the point of law is. This could include arguments about the *actus reus* and *mens rea* elements of the offence. For example, if your client is pleading not guilty to theft submitting that he lacked dishonest intent under *R v Ghosh* [1982] 3 WLR 110 it is clearly in the interests of justice for him to be legally represented as it would not be possible for a lay person to effectively represent himself.

A substantial question of law could also include challenging the admissibility of evidence including:

* whether it is appropriate to draw an adverse inference from an accused's silence at the police station under s. 34 Criminal Justice and Public Order Act 1994 (see Chapter 5);

* applying to have a confession excluded under ss. 76 and 78 PACE for breaches of Code C (see Chapter 7);

* applying to have identification evidence excluded under s. 78 PACE for breach of Code D (see Chapter 8);

* disputing the admissibility of hearsay evidence (see Chapter 22);

* disputing the admissibility of bad character evidence under the Criminal Justice Act 2003 (see Chapter 23).

You must explain precisely the point of law your client's case is likely to give rise to.

.8.6 INADEQUATE KNOWLEDGE OF ENGLISH—PHYSICAL OR MENTAL DISABILITY

This ground is self-explanatory and will be appropriate where your client has inadequate knowledge of English or is unable to communicate (including lack of literacy) or he suffers from a mental or physical disability. Clearly it is in the interests of justice for him to be represented by a lawyer.

.8.7 TRACING AND INTERVIEWING OF WITNESSES

If your client's case requires witnesses to be traced and/or interviewed this should be explained and details provided. The reason for wanting to trace and interview the witness should also be given and an indication of how this will assist your client's case. For example, a witness may provide your client with an alibi. If a prosecution witness is to be interviewed on behalf of the defendant, this should be undertaken by a solicitor although it is unusual for a defence solicitor to interview a prosecution witness in advance of trial. This ground under the interests of justice test can also be used where the defence seeks to instruct an expert witness.

.8.8 EXPERT CROSS-EXAMINATION

This ground is not confined to the cross-examination of an expert witness but can be used for any client who is pleading not guilty as this will trigger the need to cross-examine witnesses. You should explain why your client would have difficulties conducting his own cross-examination of one or more witnesses. It might, for example, be an expert witness or police officer or an eyewitness whose evidence is crucial or a witness who has a purpose of his own to serve. Perhaps cross-examination explores points of law which necessarily requires legal expertise.

1.8.9 THE INTERESTS OF SOMEONE OTHER THAN THE DEFENDANT

Is it in the interests of someone other than the defendant that the defendant is represented by a solicitor?

This ground often causes confusion. The 'someone other' is largely restricted to those who are directly affected by the proceedings in their capacity as witnesses. It would clearly not be in the interests of justice if an accused charged with a sexual offence was to cross-examine his alleged victim in person. Similarly, in the case of a vulnerable prosecution witness, such as an elderly eyewitness to a burglary or a child witness, it might be argued that it is in the interests of justice for the accused to be represented by a solicitor rather than to allow the accused to personally cross-examine the witness. Sections 34–39 Youth Justice and Criminal Evidence Act 1999 prohibit a defendant from personally cross-examining a complainant in specified sexual offence cases and this prohibition extends to personally cross-examining a child witness in relation to an offence of a sexual or violent nature.

.8.10 ANY OTHER REASON

As the interests of justice criteria are not exhaustive, you should use your imagination on this catch-all ground. It might include the requirement to skilfully examine a defence witness or the need to skilfully review the evidence in the case or to seek further disclosure from the prosecution or the prospect of your client facing a very demanding community order if convicted.

Your client will be granted a representation order where his case satisfies one or more of the interests of justice criteria explained above. Obviously it is more difficult to satisfy the test where your client is charged with a minor, summary offence and conversely the interests of justice test is more easily satisfied in connection with an either-way or indictable-only offence.

11.9 APPEALS AND REVIEWS

If the applicant fails the interests of justice test, there is a right of appeal to the court.

If the applicant fails the means test there is no right of appeal. However, the applicant can ask the court to review his application if there has been a change in his financial circumstances or the means test was conducted in error.

11.10 WHAT WORK CAN BE DONE UNDER A REPRESENTATION ORDER?

A representation order covers the entire proceedings in the magistrates' courts. It can be extended to cover an appeal from a magistrates' court in relation to bail and giving advice on and representation for an appeal against sentence and/or conviction.

For either-way offences that are committed to the Crown Court, the order automatically extends to cover the work there. For indictable-only cases the order will cover representation in the Crown Court. Representation orders which cover the Crown Court extend to obtaining advice when appealing against conviction and/or sentence to the Court of Appeal. Costs are subsequently claimed from the Criminal Defence Service in accordance with arrangements prescribed under the General Criminal Contract.

11.11 DISBURSEMENTS

You may need to incur disbursements in some criminal cases. This might include obtaining the services of an expert witness, an interpreter or enquiry agent or the transcript of an interview. Solicitors should always seek the prior authorisation of the LSC to incur expenditure in excess of £100 using Form CDS4. You will need to show that the course of action you seek to take is in the best interests of your client and that it is reasonable to incur the disbursement and that the amount to be incurred is reasonable. You should therefore ascertain in advance the amount of expenditure that will be needed. In our case study *R v Lenny Whyte* (the complete version of which can be accessed in the Online Resource Centre), you will see that as part of case preparation, Lenny's solicitor obtains the prior authorisation of the LSC to obtain an expert report from Lenny's consultant psychiatrist.

11.12 RECOVERY OF DEFENCE COSTS ORDER (RDCO)

Currently the means test has no application to cases to be tried on indictment. In the event of your client being convicted before the Crown Court, the Criminal Defence Service (Recovery of Defence Costs Orders) Regulations 2004 require a court to impose an order requiring the offender to pay all or some part of his legal costs. This is known as a recovery of defence costs order (RDCO). A defendant's means will clearly be a relevant consideration in the making of such an order which is why he is required to submit a statement of his financial means on Form B as the case progresses. Form B can be accessed from the Forms and Guidance section of Her Majesty's Court Service website at: http://www.hmcourts-service.gov.uk/cms/aboutus.htm. Given the high incidence of custodial sentences in the Crown Court and the fact that the vast majority of defendants have limited means, recovery of defence cost orders are not routinely made.

1.13 ACQUITTED DEFENDANTS

Defendants who are acquitted and who have incurred expenditure in their defence are generally entitled to an award of costs from central funds under s. 16 Prosecution of Offenders Act 1985. Such orders are at the discretion of the court (Magistrates/Crown Court/Divisional Court/Court of Appeal) but should not normally be awarded unless it is felt that the accused brought suspicion on himself by his own conduct and misled the prosecution into thinking the evidence against him was stronger than it was. Guidance can be found in Practice Direction (Crime: Costs) [1991] 1 WLR 498. A legally aided acquitted defendant's costs will be met under the representation order.

1.14 WASTED COSTS

Where a defence solicitor or the CPS has wasted the court's time by an improper, unreasonable or negligent act or omission, the power exists under s. 19 Prosecution of Offenders Act 1985 for a court to make an order for the wasted costs involved.

1.15 FUTURE OF PUBLIC FUNDING

The Carter Report

In spite of the changes to the public funding of criminal cases brought about by the re-introduction of means testing under the Criminal Defence Service Act 2006, the government is committed to a more radical reform of publicly funded criminal defence services. In its report 'Procurement of Criminal Defence Services: Market Based Reform' published in February 2006 the working group chaired by Lord Carter advocated a radical departure from the present arrangements which would be phased in over three years. In the first year there would be fixed pricing for all criminal legal aid work including representation provided at the police station, magistrates' courts and Crown Courts. The second year would see the introduction of a managed market, awarding contracts to efficient and good quality providers of legal advice and representation in criminal cases. The third year would see managed price competition between firms. The proposed move to a more market-based provision of publicly funded criminal defence services is seen as an attempt to cut-back on the £1.2 billion that it spent in England and Wales on criminal legal aid.

LSC Peer review

To ensure that franchised criminal legal aid firms are working in an effective and efficient way, the LSC is introducing a system of peer review to replace the traditional audit of case files. The advice given at all stages of a firm's representation of a criminal client will be peer reviewed against a benchmark of quality issues including whether a fee earner was appropriately experienced when advising the client and a detailed assessment of the quality of the advice and supporting documentation at all stages of the case from initial interview through to trial representation.

Provisional grant of legal aid

Provision is made in the Criminal Justice and Immigration Act (2008) to allow a suspect to apply for legal representation and for it to be granted provisionally during the investigation of a criminal offence and before charge. This will be known as a provisional grant of a right to representation. It is expected that if the provision becomes law, detailed regulations will be introduced to provide guidance about the scheme.

11.16   FIRST APPEARANCE BEFORE THE MAGISTRATES' COURT

Irrespective of the classification of an offence, once charged or summonsed, your client's first appearance in connection with the matter will be before a magistrates' court. The nature of the first hearing will largely depend on whether your client is listed to appear at an early administrative hearing (EAH); early first hearing (EFH), or before the remand court. Before we consider each of these, CJSSS needs to be explained.

11.16.1   SIMPLE, SPEEDY, SUMMARY, CRIMINAL JUSTICE (CJSSS)

In November 2007, a new initiative, entitled CJ Triple S (Simple, Speedy, Summary, Criminal Justice) was introduced in all magistrates' courts. The initiative seeks to streamline the conduct of cases before a magistrates' court to cut the time between arrest and the conclusion of the case. CJSSS does this by ensuring that the first hearing before a magistrates' court is always an effective hearing thereby avoiding unnecessary adjournments. CJSSS only applies to cases which have been commenced by charge as opposed to the issue of a summons. It does not apply to indictable-only cases.

The success of CJSSS is dependant upon inter-agency co-operation between the police and the CPS; robust case management by the court in accordance with Crim PR Part 3, and the co-operation of defence solicitors. CJSSS requires the CPS to serve sufficient disclosure of the prosecution's case on the accused before the first hearing to enable the defendant to enter a firm plea. Indeed, the court will expect the defendant to enter or indicate a plea at the first hearing. In a case where the solicitor has been instructed at the last minute and has been handed prosecution disclosure at court, the expectation is that the defence solicitor will have reviewed the evidence with his client before coming into court. If, at the first hearing, the defendant enters a guilty plea to either a summary-only or either-way offence, the case will immediately proceed to sentence (see Part V). It is therefore entirely possible for a summary matter to be concluded at the first hearing before the magistrates' court. If the defendant enters a not guilty plea to a summary-only matter, CJSSS requires that the case must be listed for trial within 6 to 8 weeks. If the defendant indicates a not guilty plea to an either-way offence, the case should immediately proceed to the mode of trial enquiry (see Chapter 13).

The CPS will prepare its files according to the defendant's anticipated plea and whether the defendant appears before the magistrates' court at an EFH or an EAH or the remand court.

Early first hearing (EFH)

Cases that are likely to be listed for an EFH are straightforward summary-only or either-way matters where the police anticipate a guilty plea will be entered. In such cases, the CPS will prepare an expedited file to be served on the defendant. This should contain enough information to enable the defence solicitor to advise on plea.

Having spoken with a solicitor before coming to court or at court the defendant may not wish to enter a guilty plea at this early stage. Consequently, the defendant's first appearance is likely to be adjourned for two weeks to enable the CPS to obtain and serve full advance information.

Early administrative hearings (EAH)

Early administrative hearings will cover indictable-only cases and all other offences where the plea at this early stage is uncertain. In accordance with the principles under CJSSS, the CPS should serve on the defence sufficient disclosure of its evidence to enable a firm plea to be taken or indicated (save in relation to an indictable-only offence). If the defendant chooses to plead guilty at an EAH, the court will proceed to sentence immediately. If the plea is not guilty and the offence is triable either-way, the magistrates' court will expect to proceed to the mode of trial enquiry (see Chapter 13). If the offence is summary-only and a not guilty plea is entered, the magistrates' court will expect each party to be in possession of sufficient information (including witness availability) to enable the date to be fixed for a summary trial. Where the case is adjourned your client will either be released on summons, or remanded on bail or in custody.

Remand court

A defendant appearing before a magistrates' court in custody will appear before the remand court because the police have denied the defendant bail after charging him with an offence (see Chapter 4, para. 4.14.2). CJSSS does not apply to such cases. Unless a guilty plea is entered to all matters and the defendant is sentenced at the same time, the case will be adjourned for the service of prosecution evidence or sent to the Crown Court, if the offence charged is indictable-only.

1.17 PREPARATION FOR FIRST APPEARANCE BEFORE MAGISTRATES' COURT

Typical steps to be undertaken in preparation for your client's initial appearance include:

- conducting an initial interview with your client (if your firm did not represent the defendant at the police station);
- opening a file;
- completing an application for a representation order;
- requesting advance information from the CPS (if there is time before the first hearing);
- anticipating problems with bail.

Opening a file

Your firm will be required to open a file in relation to each new client and to complete a standard CDS1 form. Every file has to be allocated a Unique File Number (UFN), a requirement under the General Criminal Contract. All fee-earning time spent on the matter must be recorded.

Initial interview

You will need to undertake an initial interview with your client unless already conducted at the police station. The initial interview may take place at your office or at court. If your client has been charged and released on police bail or has received a summons, he should bring the summons or charge sheet to the initial interview so that you can check the precise nature of the allegations he is facing. The initial interview is important for extracting information whilst events are hopefully still fresh in your client's memory. You should obtain all of your client's personal details as well as an accurate list of previous convictions and details of his financial circumstances.

During the first interview, you must discuss funding issues with your client. If representation in court is needed, a representation order should be applied for without delay. You will assist your client to complete the application.

General advice about the likely progress of the case and the possible plea/sentence might be offered to your client at this stage. Unless the matter is very clear cut, however, you should wait until you are in possession of the prosecution's evidence before offering any firm advice as to plea.

At the conclusion of your initial interview, you will typically:

* submit an application for a representation order;
* write to your client confirming his instructions;
* request disclosure of the prosecution's case (advance information);
* contact any potential defence witnesses with a view to taking a statement.

Each of these is briefly considered below.

Submit application for a representation order

The application for a representation order will be sent to or handed to the magistrates' court at which your client is to appear.

At an early stage you will send your client a client care letter in accordance with Rule 2.02 which should confirm your client's instructions and any information about costs. It is customary for a file to hold a client's proof of evidence. A proof of evidence is a statement of the facts recounted at your client's initial interview. In due course (and especially where a not guilty plea is anticipated) the proof of evidence will be an important source of information to the advocate representing your client at trial. If an initial proof of evidence is drafted your client should be given the opportunity to review its content, sign and date it.

Request disclosure of the prosecution's 'used' material

The rules relating to the pre-trial disclosure of evidence against a defendant are of considerable importance and are considered in greater detail in Chapter 14. No matter what the classification of offence (summary/either-way/indictable) the CPS will be in possession of 'used' material at an early stage in the proceedings. 'Used material' is the evidence that the prosecution would produce in court to prove the defendant's guilt. Another term for 'used material' is advance information. Crim PR, Part 21 requires the CPS to serve advance information on the accused in all cases that are triable either-way. Advance information comprises either copies of prosecution witness statements or a summary of the evidence. In practice it is usually the former. The defence solicitor can also request a copy of any tape-recorded interview and confirmation of his client's previous convictions at an early stage. Whilst the obligation to supply advance information applies only to either-way offences, disclosure protocols mean that the CPS routinely makes disclosure in summary-only cases and in indictable-only cases. In indictable-only offences further comprehensive disclosure is made later in the proceedings.

In the light of CJSSS, advance information should be available on the defendant's first appearance before a magistrates' court. If for any reason it is not or there are aspects of 'used' material that have yet to be disclosed before further progress can be made, the defence solicitor is entitled to seek an adjournment to enable the evidence to be served and considered. The importance of obtaining advance information in all but the most straightforward cases cannot be overstated. You cannot properly advise your client on his plea unless you are in possession of and have evaluated the advance information. It is especially significant in an either-way offence where you are required to advise your client not only about plea but also about which court to be tried in if given the choice.

Your client will need to be taken through the advance information and a further statement will need to be taken containing his comments on the disclosed evidence. You will need to have a good understanding of the rules of evidence to properly evaluate the case against your client. If, in your assessment, the strength of the evidence against your client is strong, you might use this interview to discuss with your client the advantages of an early guilty plea.

Having considered the evidence and discussed the matter with your client you might approach the CPS to see if the decision to prosecute may be reconsidered or the seriousness of the charge(s) could be reduced. The public interest test applied by the CPS and the possibility of a conditional caution as an alternative to a prosecution is considered in Chapter 10.

Approaching potential defence witnesses

If a not guilty plea is anticipated, potential defence witnesses should be approached sooner rather than later whilst events are still fresh. Where required an enquiry agent may be used to track down a potential witness. Witness statements should be taken in the absence of the defendant and without the witness seeing any prosecution witness statements in advance. It is important that you obtain the witness's honest, unrehearsed account of the events witnessed.

KEY POINT SUMMARY

- Be able to differentiate between the various funding schemes for the different criminal defence services that can be offered to a client.
- When articulating the interest of justice test for a representation order use as many aspects of the grounds as you can and articulate them fully and accurately.
- Appreciate that if a case is to go to the Crown Court, your client will need to provide a statement of his means using Form B because of the risk of an RDCO.
- Understand the importance of keeping and maintaining accurate file notes and efficient time recording on a client's file.
- Use the initial interview with your client to take a detailed statement from him and to apply for public funding.
- Understand that in the magistrates' court the defendant will be expected to enter a plea at the first hearing. Do not be tempted to advise your client as to his plea, however, unless you have had the opportunity to consider the prosecution's evidence with your client.

SELF-TEST QUESTIONS

Case Studies:

R v Roger Martin

R v William Hardy

R v Lenny Whyte

You are familiar with the issues in relation to *R v Roger Martin; R v Lenny Whyte and R v William Hardy.* Having regard to each client's proof of evidence try to complete an application for a representation order on behalf of each of them. You will find a completed application for a representation order in Appendix 1 in so far as Lenny Whyte is concerned. Roger Martin's and William Hardy's applications for a representation order can be found in the case study section of the online resource centre.

online resource centre The complete version of the all three case studies can be accessed on the online resource where you can see all the steps described in the second part of this chapter (including initial file notes and early correspondence) illustrated on the solicitor's file.

Figure 11.1 Application For A Representation Order

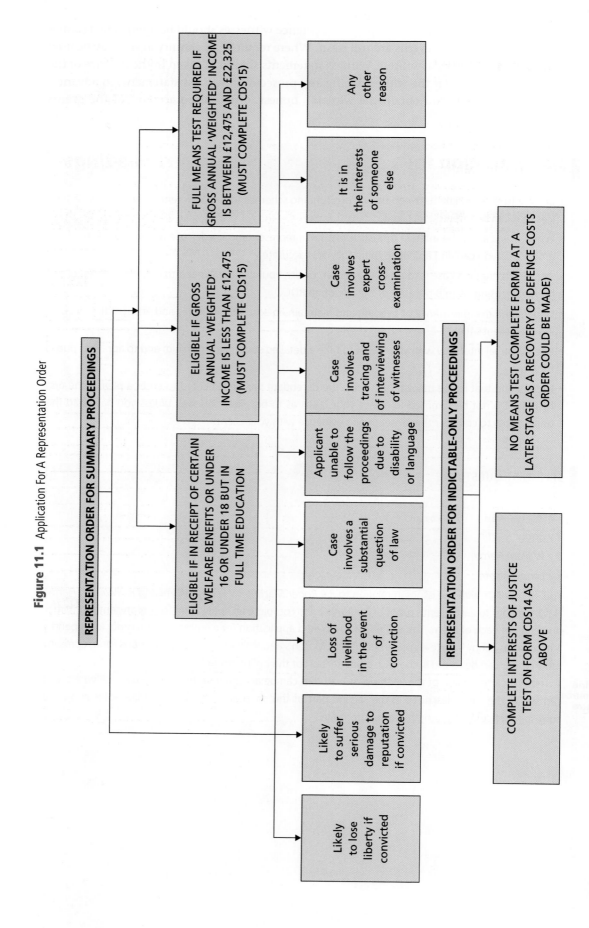

Figure 11.2 LEGAL AID

Form CDS14   *Please note that this form is also available in Welsh.

Official use: MAAT Ref:

Priority case: Custody ☐
Vulnerable ☐
Youth ☐
Crown Court - s51 cases only ☐

legal services
COMMISSION

*Before completing this form, please refer to the guidance notes supplied with your forms order.

Application for Legal Aid in Criminal Proceedings

The information you declare in this form will be checked with the Department for Work and Pensions, HM Revenue and Customs and others.

Part A - About you

Your details

1 Your first name:

2 Your surname:

See Note 1

3 Date of birth: ..../.................../......................

4 National Insurance No
Letters   Numbers   Letter

5   Single ☐   Married ☐   Married, but separated ☐   Divorced ☐
Widowed ☐   Living with a partner ☐   Civil Partner ☐

6 Home phone number _____
Mobile phone number _____
Work phone number

7 Usual home address _____

Is the address: Owned by you? ☐   You are a tenant ☐   Temporary address ☐

8 Postal address (if different from home address) _____

Your age

See Note 2

9

I am under 18.   No ☐   Go to question 10
Yes ☐

I am jointly charged with an adult   No ☐   Go to page 3
Yes ☐   Go to page 3

Form CDS14

legal services
COMMISSION

Part A - About you

Your relationship status

'Partner' refers to a person you are married to or a person you normally live with as a couple. If you have a partner, you must fill in the details below, and throughout the rest of the form where necessary.

10 Are you married or living with your partner?   No ☐   Yes ☐

Your benefit status   See Note 2

		You	Your partner
11a	Do you or your partner receive any of the following benefits?		
	Income Support	No ☐ Yes ☐	No ☐ Yes ☐
	Income-based Jobseeker's Allowance	No ☐ Yes ☐	No ☐ Yes ☐
	Guarantee State Pension Credit	No ☐ Yes ☐	No ☐ Yes ☐

11b If you are detained in custody **and** you claim income based   Date..................../.............................../.....................
JSA when did you last sign on?

Your partner's details - if you don't have a partner, go to page 3.   See Note 3

12 Is your partner involved in the case as:

Victim? ☐   Prosecution witness? ☐   Co-defendant with a conflict ? ☐   None? ☐

13 Your partner's first name:

14 Your partner's surname:

15 Your partner's date of birth: ..../........./...................

16 Your partner's NI No: Letters   Numbers   Letter

17 Partner's address if different
from your own:

See Note 4

18 Your partner's current contact details if they are unable to sign the declaration on this form:

Place and address where they are
staying e.g. the name of the hospital
and ward:

Please give reasons why your
partner is unable to sign:

CDS14   **2**

Form CDS14

legal services
COMMISSION

Part A - About you

Further information.

See Note 5

See Note 6

You do not have to fill in this section. This will be treated in the strictest confidence and will be used purely for statistical monitoring and research.

Are you male or female?

Male ☐   Female ☐

Disability Monitoring

The Disability Discrimination Act defines disability as 'a physical or mental impairment with a substantial and long-term adverse effect on a person's ability to carry out day-to-day activities'.

Do you consider yourself to have a disability?

No ☐   Yes ☐

Equal Opportunities Monitoring

Tick all the boxes which apply.

Ethnic Monitoring

White	Mixed	Asian or Asian British	Black or Black British	Chinese	Other Ethnic Group
British ☐	White and Black Caribbean ☐	Indian ☐	Black Caribbean ☐	Chinese ☐	Other ☐
Irish ☐	White and Black African ☐	Pakistani ☐	Black African ☐		
White other ☐	White & Asian ☐	Bangladeshi ☐	Black other ☐		
	Mixed other ☐	Asian other ☐			

CDS14

3

Form CDS14

Part B - Interests of Justice

I apply for the right to representation for the purposes of criminal proceedings under the Access to Justice Act 1999 and the Criminal Defence Service (General) (No. 2) Regulations 2001 (as amended).

1   Case details
See Note 7

1a What charges have been brought against you? Describe briefly what you have been accused of. E.g. theft of £1000 from your employer or assault on a neighbour.

1b Are there any co-defendants in this matter?   ☐ No. Go to question 2   ☐ Yes

If 'yes', please give their names.

_____

1c Give reasons why you and your co-defendants cannot be represented by the same solicitor.

_____
_____
_____

2   The court proceedings

2a I am due to appear before the _____ court

On _____ / _____ / _____ at _____

Or

2b I appeared before the _____ court

On _____ / _____ / _____ at _____

And (tick whichever applies)

My case has been sent to the Crown Court for trial under section 51 of the Crime and Disorder Act 1998.   ☐

My case has been transferred to the Crown Court for trial.   ☐

I was committed for trial to the Crown Court because I elected Crown Court trial.   ☐

I was convicted and/or sentenced and I want to appeal against the conviction or sentence.   ☐

I was convicted and committed for sentence to the Crown Court.   ☐

A retrial has been ordered under section 7 of the Criminal Appeal Act 1968.   ☐

Other (please give the nature of the hearing)   ☐

CDS14   4

Form CDS14

Part B - Interests of Justice

3   Outstanding matters

> If there are any other outstanding criminal charges or cases against you, give details, including the court where you are due to appear.

4   Reasons for wanting legal aid

See Note 8

4a. Please tick the reason or reasons below which apply to your case.

(i) It is likely that I will lose my liberty if any matter in the proceedings is decided against me. ☐

(ii) I have been given a sentence that is suspended or non-custodial. If I break this, the court may be able to deal with me for the original offence. ☐

(iii) It is likely that I will lose my livelihood. ☐

(iv) It is likely that I will suffer serious damage to my reputation. ☐

(v) A substantial question of law may be involved (whether arising from an act, judicial authority or other source of law). ☐

(vi) I may not be able to understand the court proceedings or present my own case. ☐

(vii) Witnesses may need to be traced or interviewed on my behalf. ☐

(viii) The proceedings may involve expert cross-examination of a prosecution witness (whether an expert or not). ☐

(ix) It is in the interests of another person (such as the person making a complaint or other witness) that I am represented. ☐

(x) Any other reasons. ☐

CDS14

5

Form CDS14

Part B - Interests of Justice

......**question 4 continued**

legal services
COMMISSION

See Note 8

4b Please give the details of the reason or reasons you selected in question 4a.

5 Legal Representation

- If you do not choose a solicitor, the court will choose one for you

- You must tell the solicitor that you have named him or her

- If you have been charged with another person or people, the court may appoint a solicitor other than the solicitor of your choice

The solicitor I want to act for me is:

Give the firm's name and address if known:

Give the firm's DX number if known: _____

Give the firm's fax number if known: _____

Give the firm's telephone number if known: _____

CDS14

6

Form CDS14

Part C - Declaration

You must complete declarations which apply to your application.

Authority by your partner `See Note 9`

If you have a partner whose details have been completed on this form, they must sign the authority below, unless your partner is abroad, in hospital or otherwise unable to sign.

This is a true statement of my financial circumstances, *as supported by the information detailed on the CDS15 (*delete if not applicable).

I agree to the Legal Services Commission and HM Courts Service checking these facts with others such as the Department for Work and Pensions and HM Revenue & Customs. I authorise those people or organisations to provide the information that they may request.

Signature... Date................../...................../...................

Full name (in BLOCK CAPITALS)..

Your declaration

This is a true statement of my financial circumstances, and that of my partner, *as supported by the information detailed on the CDS15 (*delete if not applicable).

I understand that if I tell you anything untrue on this form, or the documents I send with it, or leave anything out:

a) I may be taken to court; or
b) the Legal Services Commission may take away my legal aid so I have to pay all my legal fees.

I understand that if I have made a statement which is false, or I knowingly withhold information, I may be prosecuted, which may result in a prison sentence or a fine.

I agree to the Legal Services Commission and HM Courts Service checking these facts with others such as the Department for Work and Pensions and HM Revenue & Customs. I authorise those people or organisations to provide the information that they may request.

I agree to the Legal Services Commission contacting my partner to check the information I have given about their means.

I will:
a) provide more evidence if the Legal Services Commission or HM Courts Service ask; and
b) tell the Legal Services Commission or HM Courts Service if anything I have said here changes.

I understand that if my case goes to the Crown Court or any higher court, the court may order that I pay some or all of the costs of the proceedings through a Recovery of Defence Costs Order. I understand the information given in this form will be provided to that court so that it can consider whether a Recovery of Defence Costs Order should be made and I may be required to give details of my means to the court or LSC.

I understand that if my case goes to the Crown Court or any higher court, I will have to tell the Legal Services Commission or HM Courts Service (or both) details of my financial circumstances.

Signature... Date................../...................../...................

Full name (in BLOCK CAPITALS)..

Declaration to be completed by the legal representative

I,..................................., representing the applicant, confirm that I am authorised to provide representation under a contract issued by the Legal Services Commission (e.g. The General Criminal Contract or an Individual Case Contract).

I understand that only firms with a contract issued by the Commission (e.g. The General Criminal Contract or an Individual Case Contract). may provide representation in the Magistrates' Court.
Or

I,..................................., representing the applicant, confirm that I have been instructed to provide representation by either:
- a firm who holds a contract issued by the Legal Services Commission (e.g. The General Criminal Contract or an Individual Case Contract), or;
- a solicitor employed by the Legal Services Commission in a Public Defender Office who is authorised to provide representation.

Signature .... Date ..../...................../...................

Legal Service Provider LSC account number

CDS14

7

Form CDS14

Data Protection Act - Access to personal information

We will use the information you provide in this form, and any other information we may receive, to process your application for legal aid. We will keep it in line with the principles of the Data Protection Act 1998 and any relevant confidentiality arrangements.

The Legal Services Commission is the data controller. If necessary, we may check or share the information you provide with other organisations, such as:

- the Department for Work and Pensions;
- HM Revenue & Customs;
  the Land Registry;
- Companies House;
- credit reference agencies

We will only share the information if it is necessary to protect the public funds or where we have to do so by law.

We or HM Courts Service may also process your information to produce management or research information. The results of our research will only be published in a statistical or anonymous form.

We will keep information for as long as is necessary to fulfil our duties under the Access to Justice Act 1999. You have the right to look at the personal information held about you, to inspect it, and have it corrected if it is wrong.

For official use only

List any other factors considered when deciding the application, including any information given orally.

Decision on the Interests of Justice Test   Passed ☐   Refused ☐

I have considered all the available details of all the charges and against the Interests of Justice criteria. I give the following reasons.

Decision on financial eligibility: Passed ☐   Refused ☐

Signature... Name of appropriate officer ....

Date...................../...................../...................

Case number

Representation Order number

To be completed where right to representation extends to Crown Court:

Statement of means Form B given to defendant on ____/____/____

Indicate type of case:

- Sent case under S51 Crime and Disorder Act 1988 ☐
- Transferred for trial ☐
- Committal for trial/sentence ☐
- Retrial under S7 of the Criminal Appeal Act 1988 ☐
- Other (specify) _____

First date of hearing at Crown Court ____/____/____

12 THE LAW AND PRACTICE RELATING TO COURT BAIL

12.1 INTRODUCTION

Whenever a magistrates' court or Crown Court adjourn a case, which is a common occurrence in criminal proceedings, the court must decide whether the defendant should be remanded on bail or remanded in custody during the adjournment. The only situation where a court would not remand is where a defendant appears before the court on a summons and has not previously been remanded.

Bail in criminal proceedings may be granted by the police or by the court. In this chapter, we explain the practice and procedure of court bail. You will recognise, if having read about police bail in Chapter 4, that many of the principles that apply to bail granted by the custody officer under s. 38 PACE 1984 (see Chapter 4, para. 4.14.2) also apply to court bail.

In this chapter we examine:

- the grounds upon which bail might be refused;
- the factors a court can have regard to in determining the question of bail;
- the procedure at a contested application for bail;
- appeals against bail decisions;
- the relationship between bail and Article 5 ECHR 1950.

Rules of court relevant to bail are contained in Crim PR, Parts 19–21.

12.2 WHAT IS BAIL?

Bail is the release of the defendant subject to a duty to surrender to the court at a specified time and date. Bail may be granted to a defendant unconditionally or with conditions attached.

The provisions governing court bail are contained in the Bail Act 1976. For some defendants the need to secure bail assumes greater importance than the final outcome of the proceedings. In many cases a defendant's bail status will be negotiated between the prosecution and the defence subject to the court giving consent. Only where the prosecution object to the defendant being granted bail will a contested bail hearing be held. The majority of bail hearings are conducted in magistrates' courts.

A decision by the police to withhold bail following a decision to charge in accordance with s. 38 PACE 1984 is often a sound indication that bail may be opposed by the Crown Prosecution Service (CPS) when the defendant makes his first appearance in court. For the court, the enquiry into bail requires a speculative exercise. Bail is essentially a question of trust. Can this court trust this defendant if released back into the community on bail? You may recall the ex-Metropolitan Police Inspector, Gary Weddell who was granted conditional bail by a Crown Court judge to appear on a charge of murdering his wife. He tragically abused that trust by murdering his mother-in-law and killing himself.

12.3 A RIGHT TO BAIL?

Section 4 Bail Act 1976 gives the defendant a *prima facie* right to bail when charged with a criminal offence. There is therefore a presumption in favour of bail even for someone charged with murder. Where the prosecution seek to rebut this presumption by objecting to the defendant being granted bail, the court will invite both the prosecution and the defence to make submissions on the matter. In deciding whether the accused should be granted bail the court will carefully consider the grounds for objecting to bail articulated by the prosecution and challenged by the defence.

The presumption in favour of bail under s. 4 Bail Act 1976 applies solely to the grant of bail by a court post-charge and prior to conviction during all stages of the proceedings. The presumption continues to apply post-conviction where a court adjourns the case for the preparation of pre-sentencing reports. Strictly speaking, s. 4 Bail Act 1976 has no application where:

- the decision to grant bail taken by a custody officer when the defendant is initially charged at the police station—s. 38 PACE 1984 (see Chapter 4);

- on conviction and sentence of an offender where that person intends to appeal against conviction or sentence;

- magistrates have convicted a defendant but have chosen to commit him to the Crown Court for sentence.

Although the presumption in favour of bail does not apply in these instances, the court retains discretion to grant bail. The criteria under the Bail Act 1976 will followed in these instances.

In what circumstances can the right to bail be witheld?

12.4 CIRCUMSTANCES IN WHICH THE PRESUMPTION IN FAVOUR OF BAIL HAS NO APPLICATION

To assist understanding a distinction is made between the circumstances in which the presumption in favour of bail does not apply making it more difficult for a court to justify the grant of bail (see paras. 12.4.1–12.4.4) and the grounds for refusing bail where the presumption does apply (see para. 12.5 onwards).

2.4.1 SECTION 25 CRIMINAL JUSTICE AND PUBLIC ORDER ACT 1994 (CJPOA)

Section 25 CJPOA 1994 provides that where the accused is charged with or convicted of murder, attempted murder, manslaughter, rape or attempted rape and has been previously convicted of any of these offences, he should only be granted bail where there are 'exceptional circumstances' for doing so. In the case of an earlier manslaughter conviction, it must have resulted in a sentence of imprisonment. Section 25 effectively creates a presumption against the grant of bail in these circumstances. The question of whether s. 25 can be applied compatibly with Article 5 of the ECHR 1950 has been considered by the Law Commission and most recently by the House of Lords (see para. 12.20).

2.4.2 POSITIVE DRUG TESTING AT THE POLICE STATION

Bail may not be granted in the circumstances specified by s. 19(4) CJA 2003 (inserting s. 6A–6C into Sch. 1, Part 1 of the Bail Act 1976) unless the court is satisfied there is no significant risk of the accused committing an offence while on bail (whether subject to conditions or not). The relevant circumstances are as follows:

- the accused must be over 18;

- the accused must have tested positive for the presence of a Class A drug;

- the accused must be charged with a Class A related drug offence or the court must have substantial grounds for believing that the misuse of a Class A drug caused or contributed to the offence with which the accused is charged; and

- the accused refuses to (a) undergo an assessment of his dependency on or propensity to misuse drugs, or (b) having undergone such an assessment, and having had follow-up action proposed to address his dependency/propensity, refuses to undergo such follow-up.

Where bail is granted under s. 6B, it must be subject to a condition that the defendant undergoes an initial assessment or participates in any follow-up treatment. The power of the police to take a drug sample at the police station and to require a defendant to undergo an initial assessment where he has tested positive is considered in Chapter 4, para. 4.14.3.

12.4.3 COMMITTING A FURTHER OFFENCE WHILST ON BAIL (POST CJA 2003)

Section 14 CJA 2003 inserts a new s. 2A into Sch. 1 Part 1 of the Bail Act 1976. It provides that bail *may not* be granted to an individual aged over 18 who is already on bail on the date of the offence unless there is no significant risk of the defendant committing an offence on bail. The amended provision came partially into force on the 1 January 2007 but only in relation to offences carrying life imprisonment.

12.4.4 ABSCONDING WHILST ON BAIL (POST CJA 2003)

Section 15 CJA 2003 amends para. 6 of Sch. 1 Part 1. It provides that bail *may not* be granted to a person over 18 who it appears, having been released on bail in connection with the proceedings, has failed to surrender to custody unless the court is satisfied that there is no significant risk that if released on bail, the defendant would fail to surrender to custody. This provision came partially into force on the 1 January 2007 but only for offences carrying life imprisonment.

12.5 GROUNDS FOR DENYING BAIL IN CONNECTION WITH IMPRISONABLE OFFENCES

Where the accused is charged with an imprisonable offence, Part 1 of Sch. 1, para. 2 to the 1976 Act provides that the accused need not be granted bail where the court is satisfied that there are *substantial grounds for believing* that if released on bail (conditional or otherwise), the accused would:

'2(1)(a) fail to surrender to custody; or

—— (b) commit an offence while on bail; or

—— (c) interfere with witnesses or otherwise obstruct the course of justice, whether in relation to himself or any other person.'

Schedule 1, Part 1 further provides:

'2A The defendant need not be granted bail if—

    (a) the offence is an indictable offence or an offence triable either way; and

    (b) it appears to the court that he was on bail in criminal proceedings on the date of the offence [this ground is prospectively repealed by s. 14 CJA 2003 and is partially in force as detailed at para. 12.4.3 above].

(3) The defendant need not be granted bail if the court is satisfied that he should be kept in custody for his own protection or if he is a child or young person, for his own welfare.

(4) The defendant need not be granted bail if he is already serving a custodial sentence.

(5) The defendant need not be granted bail where the court is satisfied that it has not been practicable to obtain sufficient information to take a decision in relation to bail.

(6) Having been released on bail in connection with the same offence, the defendant has been arrested for absconding or breaking bail conditions [this ground is prospectively repealed by s. 15 CJA 2003 and is partially in force as detailed at para. 12.4. 4 above].

(7) Where the case has been adjourned for enquiries or a report, it appears to the court that it would be impracticable to complete the enquiries or make a report unless the accused is kept in custody.'

In practical terms, the first three substantive grounds set out in para. 2(1)(a)–(c) of Sch. 1 are the most important and account for 95 per cent of refusals of bail. Given the frequency with which these grounds are commonly cited, we consider them in detail in para. 12.9.

Whilst many of the other grounds contained in Sch. 1, Part 1 are self-explanatory, we briefly consider them below.

2.5.1 ALLEGEDLY COMMITTING AN OFFENCE WHILST ON BAIL (PARA. 2A—PRE CJA 2003)

Paragraph 2A was inserted into the Bail Act by s. 26 Criminal Justice and Public Order Act 1994. It provides that bail need not be granted to a defendant who is charged with an indictable-only or either-way offence and appears in court already on bail in criminal proceedings for another matter. Consider the following example: X is presently on police bail in connection with an allegation of vehicle interference (summary only). He has been arrested and charged with burglary (an either way) and appears before magistrates. At the date of the burglary offence, X was on police bail, therefore, in accordance with s. 26 CJPOA, the court need not grant him bail. Paragraph 2A of Sch. 1 is prospectively repealed by the CJA 2003 (see para. 12.4.3 above). The effect of the amendment (when it is fully in force) will be to effectively create a presumption against bail where the defendant is proven to have absconded during the currency of the proceedings. The requirement for the new offence to be triable on indictment is removed.

2.5.2 REMAND FOR OWN PROTECTION (PARA. 3)

A defendant is likely to be remanded in custody for his own protection where he poses a danger to himself or is charged with an offence that excites considerable public revulsion, e.g. child sexual abuse/paedophilia.

2.5.3 THE DEFENDANT IS ALREADY SERVING A CUSTODIAL SENTENCE (PARA. 4)

Clearly a defendant who is already serving a custodial sentence for another crime cannot expect to be granted bail in connection with new matters and should not seek to make a bail application in these circumstances. The court should, however, ascertain the earliest date of release to ensure a defendant is not remanded in custody beyond that date.

2.5.4 INSUFFICIENT DETAILS TO GRANT BAIL (PARA. 5)

There may be instances where the police have charged a suspect but have insufficient details about his identity and address. In this situation a court can refuse bail until the information is available.

2.5.5 ABSCONDING OR BREAKING BAIL CONDITIONS (PARA. 6—PRE CJA 2003)

If a defendant is granted bail (whether by the court or the police) and fails to surrender to bail or breaks any bail conditions he is liable to be arrested and held in custody. If the failure to surrender is admitted or proved, the defendant commits the criminal offence of failing to surrender to bail. If a breach of bail conditions is admitted or proved, this does not constitute an offence. However, in both instances, a court can choose to withhold bail. Paragraph 6 is prospectively amended by s. 15 CJA 2003 and is partially in force (see para. 12.4.4 above). The amendment effectively creates a presumption against bail in these circumstances making it more difficult for a court to justify granting bail.

12.5.6 POST CONVICTION—ADJOURNMENT FOR REPORTS (PARA. 7)

This ground for denying bail applies where a defendant has been convicted of an offence or has pleaded guilty but there are concerns that the defendant may not co-operate with the probation service in the preparation of a pre-sentence report. A common example is where the defendant is unable to offer a fixed address to which he can be bailed and contacted.

12.6 SUBSTANTIATING THE GROUNDS FOR OPPOSING BAIL—THE STATUTORY FACTORS

The Bail Act 1976, para. 9 of Part 1 of Sch. 1, obliges a court to have regard to a number of factors in determining whether the grounds for withholding bail under paras. 2(1), 2A, 6(1) or 6A are made out. These include:

- the nature and the seriousness of the offence;
- the defendant's character, his record, his associates and community ties;
- the defendant's bail record;
- the strength of the evidence against the defendant.

Many of the factors listed in para. 9 of Sch. 1 Part 1 are self-explanatory. It goes without saying that the more serious the offence, the greater the risk of a custodial sentence being imposed and thereby increasing the risk of absconding. In completing the case file for the CPS, the police will provide details of the defendant's past criminal record and personal circumstances. The CPS will therefore be aware of the type of person the defendant is and whether he has family, a job or other commitments in the area. Clearly the defendant's previous bail record will be of considerable importance to the court.

It is the interrelationship between the grounds for refusing bail and the applicable factors which determine the grant or refusal of bail. We consider the interplay between grounds and factors in para. 12.9, where we look at bail in practice.

12.7 GROUNDS FOR DENYING BAIL IN RELATION TO NON-IMPRISONABLE OFFENCES

Where the accused is charged with a non-imprisonable offence, Part II of Sch. 1 to the Bail Act 1976 provides that the accused need not be granted bail where:

- it appears to the court that having been previously granted bail he has failed to surrender to custody and the court believes, in view of that failure, that if released on bail (whether subject to conditions or not) he would fail to surrender; or
- the court is satisfied that the accused should be kept in custody for his own welfare or protection; or
- he is already in custody in respect of any sentence; or
- having been released on bail in connection with the present offence, he has been arrested for absconding or breaking bail conditions and there are substantial grounds for believing that the defendant, if released on bail (whether subject to conditions or not) would fail to surrender to custody, commit an offence on bail or interfere with witnesses or otherwise obstruct the course of justice.

12.8 BAIL CONDITIONS

A defendant may be granted conditional or unconditional bail. It is very common for the court to impose conditions on a defendant when granting bail. The imposition of bail conditions is governed by s. 3 Bail Act 1976. Common bail conditions include:

- reporting to a police station (perhaps two or three times a week or even daily);
- living at a specified/alternative address (this might include a bail hostel);
- avoiding contact with prosecution witnesses;
- avoiding a particular area (this could require a defendant not to enter a particular building or area or go within a specified radius of it);
- avoiding a particular activity (this could include a condition that the defendant does not visit licensed premises);
- imposing a curfew (requiring a defendant to remain at a specified address between certain hours—for example, 8 pm to 7 am—it could also include a 'doorstep' condition or electronic tagging);
- requiring a surety (see below);
- surrendering a passport;
- requiring the defendant keep appointments with his solicitor.

In accordance with s. 8 Bail Act 1976, conditions may only be attached to bail where it is necessary to ensure either that a defendant:

- will surrender to custody;
- does not commit further offences;
- does not interfere with witnesses or obstruct the course of justice; or
- for the person's own protection; or
- in the case of a convicted offender, to ensure the accused is available to enable inquiries for the purposes of a report to be made to the court.

To reduce the risk of absconding, a court might choose to impose a condition that the defendant reside at a specified address and/or report to a police station. A condition that the defendant surrenders his passport and/or provides a surety is also designed to reduce the risk of an accused failing to surrender.

Where a court is concerned that a defendant might commit further offences, it could impose a curfew. This is useful where, for example, an accused has a habit of committing night-time burglaries.

A condition could also be imposed to prevent the accused from entering a specified place; for example, a supermarket from which the accused habitually steals merchandise. Where there is a risk of an accused committing further offences because of his relationship with a particular victim, a court could impose a condition that the defendant reside at an alternative address and must not contact the injured party. These latter two conditions might also be used to prevent an accused from interfering with a witness or obstructing the course of justice.

The decision to impose one or more conditions must be a proportionate measure to reduce the risk(s) identified by the court. In negotiating bail with the CPS, you may need to offer or agree to the imposition of conditions subject to your client consenting. This is something you should discuss with your client either at the police station or in the holding cell at court. Where an alternative address is likely to be needed, the defence solicitor may have to take steps to find alternative accommodation. If a bail hostel place is required, the defence solicitor will need to liaise with the probation service to see if the defendant would be suitable (a mentally unstable or drug-dependent defendant might not be) and that a place is available.

12.8.1 SURETY/SECURITY

A court may require a defendant to provide a suitable surety or sureties before granting him bail. A surety is a person who promises to forfeit a sum of money fixed by the court and known as a recognisance if the defendant fails to attend court as directed. It is the surety's solemn duty to ensure the defendant's future attendance at court. A recognisance may be entered into before the court itself, a justice of the peace or justices' clerk. The amount of recognisance is determined by the court and depends on the surety's financial resources. If the defendant fails to answer his bail, any surety is liable to forfeit whole or part of his recognisance.

A surety must be a suitable person who will be required to attend court and give evidence on oath, confirming amongst other things, his financial resources, his character and any previous convictions and his relationship and proximity to the defendant. Such a condition can be imposed where the defendant is at risk of failing to surrender, perhaps because he has links to a foreign jurisdiction.

A court can require a defendant to deposit a security before he is released. This is rather like a bail bond. It requires the defendant or someone on his behalf to deposit a sum of money or other valuable security as a guarantee to ensure attendance. The sum can be forfeited if the defendant absconds.

12.8.2 THE CONSEQUENCES OF FAILING TO COMPLY WITH BAIL CONDITIONS

If bail is granted subject to conditions, the importance of complying with the conditions will be explained to the defendant in court. The solicitor should remind the defendant of their importance. A failure to abide by any condition of bail can lead to a defendant's arrest and reappearance before the court in custody (s. 7 Bail Act 1976). A power of arrest is available where a police constable has reasonable grounds for believing that a person has broken, or is about to break, a bail condition. Having been arrested, s. 7 Bail Act 1976 requires the defendant to be brought before a magistrate within 24 hours of his arrest, excluding Sundays. In fact, case law requires the court to determine the alleged breach within 24 hours of arrest. Although the defendant does not commit a further offence by breaking a bail condition, the court may decide the defendant has had his chance and should be remanded in custody for the duration of the proceedings (para. 12.5.5, above).

Where a breach of bail conditions is alleged, the Divisional Court has held, in *R (on the application of the DPP) v Havering Magistrates' Court* [2001] 2 Cr App R 2, that the breach proceedings fall within Article 5 of the ECHR and do not invoke the right to a fair trial provisions in Article 6. Although the proceedings do not constitute a trial, the need for the hearing to be adversarial with each side enjoying equality of arms, means the prosecution has to adduce some evidence of the breach. In turn the defendant must have a full and fair opportunity to contest the allegation if he denies it.

12.9 BAIL IN PRACTICE

The most commonly cited reasons for opposing court bail are contained in Sch. 1, para. 2(1)(a)–(c), namely that there is a substantial risk that if released on bail the defendant will:

- abscond; or
- commit further offences; or
- interfere with witnesses and obstruct the course of justice.

These grounds are further strengthened in relation to offences carrying life imprisonment by virtue of ss. 14–15 CJA 2003 (see paras. 12.4.3 and 12.4.4).

On a daily basis in magistrates' courts up and down the country there will be arguments centred on the above grounds. It is not enough for the prosecution to suggest that the defendant might abscond, or might commit further offences, there must be substantial grounds for the belief.

Below, we provide some common illustrations of typical arguments put forward by the CPS in opposition to bail being granted using the grounds set out in Sch. 1, para. 2. You will see how the statutory factors listed in para. 9 (see para. 12.6) are used to substantiate the prosecution's chosen grounds for opposing the grant of bail. We further consider how the defence advocate might typically counter the prosecution's objections.

 Examples

The risk of absconding from the prosecution perspective
Why can this particular defendant not be trusted to remain in the area? What provides the incentive for the defendant to abscond? Perhaps the defendant is charged with a serious offence and risks a substantial sentence of imprisonment if convicted. Perhaps the defendant is currently subject to a suspended sentence of imprisonment. Even if a prison sentence for the new offence is not a certainty, the fact that a conviction would put him in breach of a suspended prison sentence may provide sufficient incentive. Perhaps the defendant has previous convictions for failing to surrender. If he has poor community ties such as no immediate family in the area, what incentive is there for the defendant to remain in the jurisdiction of the court?

The prosecuting advocate might address the court in this way:

'Sir, you and your colleagues will be aware that this defendant has three previous convictions for absconding.'

'Madam, this defendant was granted bail on an earlier occasion and failed to turn up. He appears before you this morning pursuant to a warrant for his arrest.'

'Sir, this defendant's community ties are poor. He is unable to offer a stable address in the area. He has no job and no reason to stay here.'

'The accused is a foreign national whose family reside abroad. He poses a flight risk.'

Risk of absconding from the defence perspective
It does no harm to remind the court of the presumption in favour of bail (s. 4 Bail Act 1976) if it applies. If the defendant has a record for absconding, it is important for the defence solicitor to find out about the circumstances of the absconding offences. Were they deliberate? How long ago were they? Did the defendant ultimately surrender and plead guilty or was he arrested? If the defendant has a good bail record, this should be stressed! The defence solicitor should examine his client's community ties. Does he have a job, a mortgage, family or anything to keep him in the area?

It is pertinent to ask whether the defendant is going to be convicted of the offence he is charged with. This requires the defence solicitor to examine the strength of the evidence against his client. The defendant may indicate he is pleading not guilty and wishes to challenge the evidence against him. In these circumstances it is legitimate to point out that the defendant will not abscond because he wishes to clear his name of the charges he faces. If the defendant is likely to plead guilty, the defence solicitor should consider whether a custodial sentence is a certainty. If not, he should make the appropriate representations.

Finally, the defence solicitor needs to consider what conditions to offer in order to allay the court's fear of the defendant absconding. Possibilities might include a condition of residence at a fixed address or at a bail hostel. In addition, the court may want the defendant to report to a police station on specified days and at certain times. A court may require the defendant to surrender his passport if he poses a flight risk. Less frequently, the court may only grant bail subject to the defendant providing a suitable surety or security.

The commission of further offences from the prosecution perspective

The prosecutor must ask himself why this particular defendant is likely to commit further offences if released on bail. This may be due to the defendant's extensive criminal record indicating that he is a prolific offender or because the defendant has a particular need to commit offences, for example to feed a drug addiction. Added to this the defendant may not have a stabilising influence in his life and even no fixed address. In some cases the risk of the commission of further offences may be due to the defendant's close proximity to the victim, for example in a domestic assault where the injured party fears reprisals if the defendant remains under the same roof.

The prosecuting advocate may address the court on these issues in this way:

'Madam, the defendant was already on bail for another similar offence when arrested in connection with these matters.'

'The defendant is a man with a substantial criminal record for theft and burglary . . .'

'The defendant is a substance abuser who steals to fund his habit . . .'

'Sir, this defendant cannot keep out of trouble—you only have to examine his criminal record. You will also see he is the subject of an anti-social behaviour order made three months ago . . .'

'The defendant has committed offences whilst subject to a sentence of this court—in short, he cannot be trusted.'

Commission of further offences from the defence perspective

The defence solicitor should carefully consider the defendant's criminal record. Are the defendant's previous convictions recent? Have circumstances changed so that there is now a stabilising influence in the defendant's life? Does the defendant have responsibilities such as the care of a child who is likely to be taken into care if the defendant is remanded? Once again, what evidence connects the defendant to the offence with which he is charged? Does the defendant admit the charge for which he is already on bail? Looking at the defendant's past criminal record, is it possible to say whether no offences have been committed by the defendant whilst on bail?

Will the imposition of suitable conditions help to allay the magistrates' fears that this defendant will commit further offences? Possibilities might include imposing a curfew where a defendant commits offences at night. A condition that excludes the defendant from engaging in particular behaviour or going to a certain place may be effective, i.e. a condition not to visit licensed premises or to go within a certain radius of a particular shop. The availability of an alternative address away from the area where the crime is alleged to have occurred may alleviate the risk.

Interference with witnesses or obstructing the course of justice from the prosecution perspective

This ground might be argued where, for example, there is more than one co-accused who is still at large. It could also cover the situation where the defendant is implicated in a burglary or robbery and there is stolen property that has yet to be recovered. It also extends to those instances where a defendant may know or be related to a victim or witness and may well wish to contact that person.

The prosecuting advocate may address the court on these issues in the following way:

'Sir, this defendant has previous convictions for violence.'

'Sir, this defendant has a previous conviction for perverting the course of justice.'

'Sir, there is as you can imagine a lot of ill-feeling in the area where the defendant resides. If released on bail the danger that the defendant might be embroiled in further confrontation cannot be ignored . . .'

'Madam, there is a large amount of stolen property that has still to be recovered and a co-accused still at large.'

Interference with witnesses or obstructing the course of justice from the defence perspective

Once again, if the defendant is not admitting the offence, assess the strength of the evidence against him. Point out that the defendant would not wish to make matters worse for himself by doing the things suggested. What was the date on which the offence is alleged to have occurred? Stolen property that is not immediately recovered is unlikely ever to be recovered. Consider whether there is any evidence that the defendant will threaten or interfere with a witness. Look at the defendant's record in this respect. Can conditions be suggested to allay the magistrates' fears? Possibilities include a condition that the defendant does not contact a witness or does not go within a certain radius of a particular area. The availability of alternative accommodation away from the witness or the area may greatly assist.

One of the factors a court should consider when deciding bail is the strength of the evidence against a defendant. From the defence perspective, if the defendant has not made damaging admissions and intends to plead not guilty, it is always worth challenging the evidence linking the defendant to the offence. It would be wholly unjust for a court to remand your client into custody on weak evidence, so consider whether to advance a defence at this stage.

2.10 PROCEDURE AT A CONTESTED BAIL HEARING

Surprisingly, there is no set procedure prescribed for a contested bail hearing. The usual practice after a court has decided to adjourn the case is for the prosecution to make representations as to why bail should not be granted. This will be based on the information contained in the police file that may not be complete at this stage. The defendant is then given his opportunity to put any relevant considerations before the court. This will usually be done through the defendant's solicitor of choice or the duty solicitor in court.

Neither advocate is likely to have had a lot of time to prepare for the bail hearing. From the defence perspective the bail application is likely to occur early in the proceedings before the defendant has had the benefit of pre-trial disclosure of prosecution evidence (used material). There is no statutory requirement to make disclosure for the purpose of a bail hearing. The obligations to provide pre-trial disclosure of prosecution evidence arise later in the proceedings. For consideration of the rules relating to the pre-trial disclosure of evidence, see Chapter 14. Case law, including *R v DPP, ex p. Lee* [1999] 2 Cr App R 304 and *Wildman v DPP* [2001] Crim LR 565 has provided that, whilst full pre-trial disclosure of prosecution evidence is not appropriate at this stage, such disclosure as to ensure the defendant enjoys equality of arms at the bail hearing is required. The defence solicitor may have some idea of the evidence against his client if he or a member of his firm attended the defendant at the police station, otherwise the defence solicitor must press the prosecution for disclosure at court and ask for a short adjournment to consider it if necessary.

A contested bail hearing takes the form of a mini-trial at which the rules of evidence are relaxed. The Bail Act 1976 gives each side the framework for their representations. The CPS lawyer will refer to the witness statements he has on file and the account the defendant gave at the police station in making the court aware of how the defendant came to be charged in connection with the matter(s) for which he appears. The prosecutor will outline his objections and hand in a copy of the defendant's previous convictions. The defence solicitor will then make his submissions, countering the arguments put by the prosecution. If the defendant has a job or an offer of work that is likely to be lost if he is remanded, the defence solicitor should try and get a letter from the employer to confirm this. If residence is likely to be a problem, the defence solicitor should have enquired about alternative accommodation.

Any available witnesses such as a surety or evidence of an alternative address will be put before the court. Having heard the representations from both sides, the magistrates will decide on the matter and announce their decision. You are able to view a contested bail hearing in the video clip section of our Online Resource Centre in the *R v Lenny Whyte* case study.

 online resource centre

Before you do so, however, you might like to attempt the exercise we have set in conjunction with the case study at the end of this chapter, together with two other scenarios designed to test your understanding of bail.

12.10.1 THE COURT'S DECISION—GIVING REASONS

Section 5 Bail Act 1976 provides that where a court withholds bail or grants conditional bail, the reason(s) for doing so must be announced in open court. Where bail is refused, the defendant must be given a notice setting out both the exception(s) and the reason(s) for the magistrates' decision.

Paragraph 9A of Part 1 of Sch. 1 to the Act requires a court to state its reasons for granting bail to an accused charged with an offence that triggers the application of s. 25 CJPOA 1994 (see para. 12.4.1), where the prosecution has opposed the bail application. It is the usual practice in magistrates' courts to give reasons for the grant of bail in all cases where bail has been opposed.

It should be stressed that bail is a decision for the court and it should be considered at every remand hearing, whether it is applied for or not. Magistrates can grant bail, notwithstanding prosecution objections, and may also remand a defendant in custody where there is no objection from the prosecutor.

A defendant who is 21 or over will be remanded to a prison if bail is denied. Between the ages of 17 and 20, remand is normally to a remand centre or an adult prison if no places are available at a remand centre.

It is important to remember that if convicted, the sentencing court will take into account the time served on remand. A tactically aware defendant, who knows he is likely to plead guilty or be convicted of an offence and receive a prison sentence will realise that being remanded in custody on full privileges has its benefits! Such a defendant may not wish to apply for bail.

12.11 REMAND PERIODS

When a magistrates' court remands a defendant in custody at his first appearance, the remand period must not exceed eight days. It may be a number of weeks or even months before a case is ready for trial or committal to the Crown Court. Provision is made in s. 128A MCA 1980 for an accused to be remanded for up to 28 days without his consent. The power only applies once a magistrates' court has set a date for the next stage of the proceedings to take place and decides the accused should be remanded in custody until that date. The power does not apply on a first remand. An accused is therefore allowed two bail applications before this power can be exercised. If the defendant is to be further remanded after 28 days, he must be produced at the next court hearing. The increasing use of TV video-links from prisons to some magistrates' courts and Crown Courts means prisoners do not have to be physically produced.

After conviction a court may remand a defendant pending sentence where a pre-sentence report or some other report is required before sentence can be properly imposed. Where a court grants a defendant bail after conviction, the maximum period is four weeks. Where a defendant is remanded in custody pending completion of reports the maximum period is three weeks.

12.11.1 CUSTODY TIME-LIMITS

When your client has been refused bail, s. 22 Prosecution of Offenders Act 1985 (POA) imposes maximum time-limits during which an accused may be remanded in custody between various stages in the proceedings before trial. These periods are as follows:

(a) 70 days between an accused's first appearance in the magistrates' court and committal proceedings;

(b) 70 days between first appearance and summary trial for an offence triable either way (reduced to 56 days if the decision for summary trial is taken within 56 days);

(c) 56 days between first appearance and trial for a summary-only offence; and

(d) 112 days between committal for trial and arraignment in the Crown Court.

Where an indictable-only offence is sent straight to the Crown Court under s. 51 Crime and Disorder Act 1998 (see Chapter 16), the maximum custody time length is 182 days with time running from the date the case is sent up by the magistrates, less any time already spent in custody.

If the prosecution fails to comply with the custody time-limits, the defendant has an absolute right to bail. A court can impose some conditions on the defendant's bail, such as reporting or a condition of residence, but cannot require the defendant to provide a surety or security as a condition of his release.

The prosecution can apply for an extension of the custody time-limit before it expires. The criteria for granting an extension is laid down in s. 22 Prosecution of Offenders Act 1985. For a detailed explanation of the extension of custody time-limits, see *Blackstone's Criminal Practice 2009*.

2.12 NUMBER OF BAIL APPLICATIONS THAT CAN BE MADE

While a court is under a duty to consider the grant of bail at each hearing after it has been refused, the defendant is prevented from making repeated applications by Part IIA of Sch. 1 to the Bail Act 1976 (as amended by s. 154(2) Criminal Justice Act 1988). This provides:

> 'At the first hearing after that at which the court decided not to grant the defendant bail he may support an application for bail with any further argument as to law or fact that he desires . . . . At subsequent hearings the court need not hear arguments as to fact or law which it has heard previously . . . .'

Where an accused has been refused bail at a previous hearing, he may make one further application only. Thereafter, unless there has been a change of circumstances, the court need not hear further argument at a subsequent hearing.

Consider the following examples of the operation of Part IIA:

X makes an unsuccessful application for bail on his first appearance. He makes a further unsuccessful application for bail on his second appearance. Thereafter Part IIA applies and the court need not entertain a further application on his appearance unless there has been a change in circumstances.

X chooses not to make an application for bail on his first appearance. He makes an unsuccessful application for bail on his second appearance. Part IIA bites and the court need not entertain a further application on X's next appearance unless there has been a change in circumstances.

X makes an unsuccessful application for bail on his first appearance. He chooses not to make a further application on his second appearance. Part IIA bites and the court need not entertain a further application on X's next appearance unless there has been a change in circumstances. A change of circumstances need not be a major change either in the defendant's personal circumstances or in the proceedings connected with the case. So, for example, where an accused has been charged with an indictable offence and has been refused bail at two previous hearings, the fact that the case against him appears less strong when full pre-trial disclosure is made during the course of the proceedings, may amount to a change of circumstances.

12.13 WHAT IF BAIL IS REFUSED?

Where magistrates have heard a full application for bail, the court must issue a full argument certificate. A copy must be given to the accused. Armed with this an accused refused bail by the magistrates can apply to a Crown Court judge under s. 81 Supreme Court Act 1981. The procedure for applying to the Crown Court is contained in Crim PR Part 19.18. Applications are usually dealt with within 48 hours of the initial refusal, although the defendant must give 24 hours' notice of his intention to appeal to the Crown Prosecution Service. The 'appeal' will be conducted before a Crown Court judge in chambers and will take the form of a complete rehearing. Trainee solicitors and unqualified clerks have full rights of audience. The application to the Crown Court will be covered by an existing representation order.

12.14 APPEAL BY THE PROSECUTION

If bail is opposed by the prosecution but is granted to a person charged with or convicted of an offence carrying imprisonment or an offence of taking a vehicle without consent or aggravated vehicle-taking, s. 1 Bail (Amendment) Act 1993 (as amended by s. 18 CJA 2003), gives the prosecution the right to appeal against the grant of bail to a Crown Court judge. There are strict procedural requirements governing the prosecution's right to appeal. The prosecution must give oral notice of appeal at the conclusion of the proceedings in which bail was granted and before the defendant is released from custody. The oral notice must be confirmed in writing within two hours after proceedings end. Pending the appeal, the magistrates must remand the defendant in custody. The Crown Court must hear the appeal within 48 hours and it will be a complete rehearing.

12.15 RECONSIDERATION OF BAIL

There is power under s. 5B of the Bail Act 1976 (inserted by the Criminal Justice and Public Order Act 1994) for a court to reconsider the grant of bail on application by the prosecution. The power only applies if the offence with which the defendant is charged is indictable only or triable either way. The application must be based on information that was not available to the court or the police at the last hearing. In other words, new information must have come to light since the last occasion, which puts the question of bail in a new light. Under this power, the court can vary the bail conditions imposed last time or impose new ones or remand in custody.

12.16 VARYING BAIL CONDITIONS

Either side can apply to have bail conditions varied or in the prosecution's case to have conditions imposed on the grant of unconditional bail. The position is governed by s. 8(a) and (b) Bail Act 1976. It is not uncommon for a defendant to seek to have bail conditions varied. This requires an application to the court that imposed the conditions or to the Crown Court if a matter has already been sent there for trial or sentence.

Circumstances may have changed since the defendant was conditionally bailed that make the conditions impracticable or unworkable, i.e. securing a job outside the immediate area or the need to change address. The CPS may or may not wish to make submissions in relation to the application. In the domestic violence example we give below, the CPS opposes the application. If the application is to succeed the alleged victim will need to give evidence in support. This may include the need for an individual to give evidence on oath.

 Example: *R v Brown*

Raymond Brown (aged 26) is accused of two counts of assault occasioning actual bodily harm against his partner Donna Andrews (aged 22). The couple have two young children. Mr Brown is further charged with resisting a constable in the execution of his duty. On the last occasion the matter was adjourned Raymond Brown was granted conditional bail to reside at an alternative address to his part-ner's home and not to contact Ms Andrews or the other prosecuting witness, the couple's babysitter. Ms Andrews has now retracted her statement of complaint to the police and wishes Mr Brown to be able to reside with her and their two children. The CPS lawyer does not have the retraction statement on file and in any event, in accordance with the CPS Code of Practice on domestic violence, can still continue to pursue the prosecution even though the complaint has been retracted. The defence solici-tor for Raymond Brown calls Ms Andrews to the stand.

Question: 'Is it true you made a statement to the police on the 2nd of this month alleging your partner Raymond Brown assaulted you?'

Answer: 'Yes I did.'

Question: 'Is it true you have since retracted that statement?'

Answer: 'Yes I have.'

Question: 'Can you recall where and when you retracted your original statement?'

Answer: 'I think it was five days ago. I went to the police station.'

Question: 'What has made you retract your statement?'

Answer: 'Things have changed—we have sorted things out.'

Question: 'What would you like this court to do this morning?'

Answer: 'I'd like Raymond to be able to come back home.'

Question: 'Are you under any pressure whatsoever to come to court today?'

Answer: 'No—I am not under any pressure.'

Question: 'Do you have any reason to fear Mr Brown?'

Answer: 'No I do not.'

Under cross-examination by the prosecutor
Question: 'Ms Andrews, what date did you make your retraction?'

Answer: 'I can't remember—it was about five days ago.'

Question: 'You made it less than a week after your original complaint?'

Answer: 'Yes.'

Question: 'Do you recall that when you made your original complaint you told the police about an assault that had occurred that day and one that had occurred ten days earlier?'

Answer: 'Yes.'

Question: 'Do you recall the police having to break into your house to apprehend Mr Brown?'

Answer: 'Yes I do.'

Question: 'And am I correct in saying the assault alleged to have occurred on the 2nd was witnessed by your babysitter, who made a statement to the police?'

Answer: 'It was.'

Question: 'Do you recall telling the police that it wasn't the first time you had been assaulted by Mr Brown?'

Answer: 'I don't recall.'

Question: 'And you say today you have nothing to fear from Raymond Brown?'

Answer: 'I do.'

Question: 'What has changed in ten days?'

Answer: 'It's not all his fault. We have talked. It won't happen again.'

Question: 'You understand that it is not your decision as to whether this case proceeds?'

Answer: 'Yes.'

Question: 'You understand that these conditions have been imposed for your protection and not to inconvenience Mr Brown?'

Answer: 'I understand.'

Question: 'Are you saying you no longer have anything to fear?'

Answer: 'That is what I am saying.'

The prosecutor concludes, stating it is a matter for the magistrates.

Magistrates' decision

The bail conditions are removed, save for the condition that the defendant does not contact the babysitter.

Section 16 Criminal Justice Act 2003 has amended the Bail Act 1976 to allow a defendant to appeal to the Crown Court against the imposition of any of the following conditions:

• residence away from a particular place;

• surety;

• curfew.

Such an appeal may not be brought if the defendant or the prosecution has already applied to a magistrates' court to have bail conditions varied and the matter has been dealt with or, in the case of the prosecution, it has applied for bail to be reconsidered in accordance with s. 5B Bail Act 1976 and the matter has been determined.

12.17 WHAT IF AN ACCUSED FAILS TO SURRENDER, HAVING BEEN GRANTED BAIL?

Section 6(1) Bail Act 1976 creates the offence of absconding where the accused has been released on bail (whether by the police or by a court) and fails, without reasonable excuse, to surrender to custody at the time and date specified in the bail notice. Section 6(2) makes it an offence for a defendant who has a reasonable excuse for failing his bail, not to have then surrendered himself as soon as was thereafter reasonably practicable. Where the accused fails to surrender, the burden will be on the accused to prove that he had reasonable cause for failing to surrender.

Where the defendant is found guilty, absconding is punishable by up to three months' imprisonment and/or a maximum fine of £5,000 in the magistrates' court. Where bail was imposed by the Crown Court, the offence of absconding is punishable by a maximum sentence of 12 months' imprisonment and/or an unlimited fine. A Bail Act 1976 offence committed during the proceedings gives the court grounds for further refusing bail (see paras. 12.4.4 and 12.5.5 above). Where an accused fails to surrender or having surrendered disappears before his case is heard, the court must decide what to do. Where there is no explanation for the accused's failure to appear, the court is likely to issue a warrant for the accused's immediate arrest. If the case has been listed for trial, the accused may be tried in his absence. Where some explanation is forthcoming to account for a defendant's absence, e.g. the defendant manages to contact his solicitor alerting him of a family emergency, the court is likely to grant bail in absence or issue a warrant backed with bail. The court will require proof for the absence, such as a medical certificate, to be produced on the next occasion.

2.18 BAIL GRANTED BY THE CROWN COURT

The Crown Court has an inherent jurisdiction to grant bail and can exercise its jurisdiction when:

- The defendant has been remanded in custody by a magistrates' court prior to committal or summary trial and appeals to the Crown Court.
- The defendant has been sent or committed to the Crown Court for trial or has been committed for sentence.
- The defendant has been summarily convicted, imprisoned and denied bail pending an appeal to the Crown Court.
- The defendant has been convicted and sentenced before a Crown Court and now wishes to appeal to the Court of Appeal.

2.19 BAIL AND THE HIGH COURT

The High Court's jurisdiction to hear an appeal against a refusal of bail or a refusal to vary conditions of bail in connection with criminal proceedings being conducted before a magistrates' court or Crown Court was abolished by s. 17 Criminal Justice Act 2003. The High Court retains jurisdiction to grant bail in the limited instance of a convicted and imprisoned offender appealing against conviction or sentence by way of case stated or by judicial review.

The decision in *R (Shergill) v Harrow Crown Court* [2005] EWHC 648 confirms that where a Crown Court judge's decision to refuse bail is '*Wednesbury*' unreasonable, the High Court has an inherent jurisdiction to judicially review the decision of the Crown Court. Such an application, however, should only be made in 'exceptional cases'.

2.20 HUMAN RIGHTS AND BAIL

The Law Commission in its Report No. 269: *Bail and the Human Rights Act 1998* concluded that the existing law governing bail was broadly compliant with the European Convention on Human Rights. It did, however, identify some areas for concern, most of which have been addressed by amendments to the Bail Act 1976 by the Criminal Justice Act 2003.

It is clear that Article 5 and not Article 6 is invoked in relation to decisions about bail. Article 5 guarantees an individual's right to liberty and security and therefore has clear relevance to bail decisions. Article 5(1) allows the right to be abrogated in defined circumstances and in accordance with a procedure prescribed by law. The prescribed circumstances include the lawful detention of a person after conviction by a competent court (Article 5(1)(a)) and the lawful arrest or detention of a person effected for the purpose of bringing him before a court on reasonable suspicion of having committed an offence or when it is reasonably necessary to prevent his committing an offence or fleeing after having done so (Article 5(1)(c)).

Article 5(1)(c) should be read in conjunction with Article 5(3), which provides:

> 'Everyone arrested or detained in accordance with paragraph (1)(c) shall be brought before a judge or other officer authorised by law to exercise judicial power and shall be entitled to trial within a reasonable time or to release pending trial. Release may be conditioned by guarantees to appear for trial.'

In its analysis of the jurisprudence of the European Court of Human Rights (ECtHR), the Law Commission Report concluded that Article 5 permits the detention of an individual pending trial where there is a real risk that the defendant would:

(a) fail to attend trial;

(b) interfere with evidence or witnesses, or otherwise obstruct the course of justice;

(c) commit an offence while on bail; and

(d) be at risk of harm against which he or she would be inadequately protected.

These grounds broadly correspond to the grounds contained within the Bail Act 1976 as amended by the CJA 2003.

The Law Commission expressed concern that s. 25 CJPOA 1994 (see para. 12.4) could be applied in a way that is not compliant with Article 5. This concern has been answered by the House of Lords in *O (FC) v Crown Court at Harrow* [2006] 3 WLR 195 which concluded that s. 25 CJPOA 1994 does not violate Article 5(3). Although the section creates a prohibition against granting bail in an individual case reminding judges of the special public interest that is served by the provision, judges are still able to examine all the facts in the individual case before it and therefore exercise meaningful judicial control consistent with the principles stated in *CC v United Kingdom* [1999] Crim LR 228.

KEY POINT SUMMARY

- Remember defendants tend to think of the short-term—for them, gaining bail may be of considerable importance—more important than the final outcome.
- Be able to identify the circumstances in which it is harder for an accused to get bail because the presumption in favour of bail has no application.
- Make sure you distinguish between the grounds for opposing bail and the factors used to substantiate the grounds.
- Anticipate the likely objections to bail with your client and see what conditions you and your client can agree in an attempt to surmount the likely objections.
- Find out in advance on what grounds the prosecution is going to oppose bail.
- Press the prosecution for disclosure of its evidence at this early stage together with confirmation of your client's criminal record.
- Be prepared to challenge the evidence against your client at this early stage.
- Present a structured submission to the court, dealing with each of the prosecution's objections in turn.
- Take a note of the court's decision and explain what it means to your client.
- Remember you have more than one opportunity to apply for bail, and the option of applying to a Crown Court judge in chambers where bail is refused by a magistrates' court.

SELF-TEST QUESTIONS

To test your knowledge and understanding of the substantive law of bail, consider the following scenarios. Formulate what you consider would be your objections to bail being granted having regard to the grounds for opposing bail and the factors the court is likely to have regard to. What submissions would you put forward to counter these objections to try and ensure bail is granted? An analysis of the scenarios is provided in Appendix 4.

1. *R v Karl Green*

Karl Green is charged with wounding with intent, contrary to s. 18 of the Offences Against the Person Act 1861 (OAPA). He appears before magistrates. The prosecution seeks the usual eight-day adjournment to enable the case to be sent to the Crown Court. It is alleged that Karl assaulted David Murphy outside a public house on the housing estate where both the men live. The offence occured two days ago. The injured party is presently in a coma. One witness, who is a friend of the injured party, has provided the police with a statement in which he identifies Karl Green as the person who punched his friend. In his statement he refers to the two men exchanging words. In one swift movement, he alleges,

Green punched his friend with such force as to cause him to fall unconscious to the ground. An independent witness has provided a statement giving a similar account of the incident and a description of the man responsible being consistent with Green's appearance. The witness also states he observed the man who threw the punch flee the scene.

Karl Green is presently on conditional bail for a serious s. 18 OAPA 1861 assault on a police constable, alleged to have occurred six weeks earlier. He was seriously drunk at the time and one of the conditions of his bail, which includes him reporting to his local police station, prohibits him from visiting licensed premises. He appeared before the magistrates' court last week admitting a breach of his bail condition not to visit licensed premises. The magistrates were prepared to renew his bail, having regard to the explanation offered by Green which had been to fetch his sister who works at a public house as her baby was sick. According to his list of antecedents, Karl Green lives apart from his wife and is out of work. He has six previous convictions. The most recent relates to an assault occasioning actual bodily harm (s. 47 OAPA) last year, for which Green received a six-month prison sentence suspended for 18 months. He has further convictions for assault dating some three and four years ago, two previous convictions for theft and a conviction for a public order offence. He was convicted of absconding three years ago.

In interview with his solicitor, Karl Green admits to throwing the punch. He maintains, however, that he acted in self-defence. Green claims the injured party was the aggressor and that in self-defence, he threw one punch. When the injured party did not get up, Green panicked. His brother was with him when the incident occurred and will testify on his behalf. Green lives with his mother. He and his ex-wife are attempting a reconciliation. She had been dating the injured party but had terminated the relationship in recent weeks, believing she could salvage her marriage. She and Green have a son, Stephen, who is four years old. Karl says he is currently in work—he works for his cousin's skip-hire company. If remanded in custody he is likely to lose his job. His previous failure to surrender was due to sickness; however, no medical evidence was ever obtained. Green voluntarily surrendered himself and was fined for the offence of failing to answer his bail. So far as the assault on the policeman is concerned, he will be pleading guilty to a less serious charge of assault. He was seriously intoxicated at the time and does not recall much of what happened. He has expressed his deep remorse. Green tells his solicitor that he has a sister who may be prepared to offer him accommodation ten miles outside the area of the estate where he and his victim live.

2. R v Daniel Phillips

Daniel Phillips has been charged with arson contrary to s. 1(1) of the Criminal Damage Act 1971 and with resisting a constable in the execution of his duty. The allegation is that he deliberately set fire to his former partner's house, causing extensive damage. He has been remanded into police custody pending his initial appearance before a magistrates' court. The prosecution requests an adjournment of three weeks in order to prepare a full file for disclosure to the defence.

Daniel is 26. His former partner, Rachel Hughes, is 22. She has made a statement to the police. The couple have a child aged three who Rachel cares for. The relationship ended two years ago but Daniel has been reluctant to accept it. Rachel refused Daniel access to their son but this was resolved 18 months ago by court order. In recent weeks Rachel has formed a new relationship.

The police were called to Rachel Hughes's home at 6 am three days ago (a Saturday). Her property was on fire. Initial forensic tests have revealed the fire was started deliberately by someone pouring an accelerant through the front door letterbox and igniting it with a match. The finger of suspicion points to Daniel.

Daniel collected his son from Rachel for an access visit on the Saturday afternoon. She asked him to deliver their son back to her mother—the child was going to spend the night with his grandmother. She told Daniel Phillips that she would be staying with a friend of hers overnight. Her friend received a telephone call at 5.30 am. A male voice, which she thinks she recognised as Daniel, requested her to inform Rachel that her house was on fire.

Daniel was arrested three days later as the police were unable to locate him immediately—he was no longer living at his mother's address. There is no forensic evidence to link him to the crime scene as yet, but tests are continuing. Daniel made no comment in interview on the advice of his solicitor.

Rachel maintains she is absolutely terrified of Daniel, who has four previous convictions recorded against him. He was convicted of criminal damage two years ago. Following an argument with Rachel he damaged her car. He was conditionally discharged for this offence for a period of one year. Six months later he was convicted of assault occasioning actual bodily harm and breach of a conditional discharge. The incident followed the breakdown of his relationship with Rachel. She started to date another man. When Daniel found out, he assaulted the man. He denied involvement but was found guilty by magistrates. He was given a community supervision order for two years. Last year Daniel was convicted of an offence under s. 2 of the Harassment Act 1997. He pleaded guilty before a Crown Court judge and was sentenced to six months' imprisonment, suspended for 18 months to run alongside his existing community supervision order. Daniel was also subject to a restraining order of five years forbidding him to contact or communicate with Rachel except when and for the sole purpose of collecting his son for an access visit. The harassment had taken the form of obscene text messages. Rachel was also bombarded with dozens of pictures taken of her, some of which were cut up. She started to receive menacing telephone calls in the early hours of the morning, which were eventually traced to a mobile telephone registered to Daniel.

In interview with his solicitor, Daniel steadfastly denies setting fire to the property. He maintains he has no axe to grind so far as Rachel is concerned. In fact he has formed a new relationship in recent months. His new girlfriend, Anna, aged 19, is pregnant with his baby. He was with her at the time of this alleged incident, at her mother's house. She and her mother will verify this. He left his mother's home several weeks ago, as he could not cope with her alcoholic mood swings. Daniel maintains the access visit with his son went off without problem and that he would not do anything to jeopardise his relationship with his son. Furthermore he is complying with the requirements of the community supervision order which is helping him to address the reason for his earlier offending. He is residing on a permanent basis with his new girlfriend and has a job as a mechanic. He denies resisting the police constable in the course of his arrest, maintaining the officer was much too heavy-handed.

Case Study: *R v Lenny Whyte*

online resource centre

Consider the advance information in relation to this case study, together with Lenny Whyte's list of previous convictions (located in Appendix 1, Documents 18 A–P and Document 11A). Assume you are the CPS lawyer and that this is Lenny's second appearance before a magistrates' court. He has been remanded in custody since being charged. Upon what grounds will you oppose bail and what factors will you have regard to in substantiating your objections? The prosecution's submission in this case can be viewed on the video section of our Online Resource Centre. A transcript of the prosecuting solicitor's submission can be located on our Online Resource Centre in the case study section. For general consideration of the skills of advocacy, see Chapter 2.

Now look at this file from the perspective of the defence. Having regard to both the advance information and Lenny's statement (Documents 1 and 18, located within Appendix 1), construct a defence submission in this case countering the prosecution's objections. How are you going to convince the court to grant bail in this case? The defence submission in this case can be viewed on the video section of our Online Resource Centre. A transcript of the defence solicitor's submission can be located on our Online Resource Centre in the case study section.

An account of the magistrates' decision in relation to bail is contained in Document 13. You will see that Lenny appeals the refusal of bail to a judge in chambers in the Crown Court and is subsequently granted conditional bail (Document 17). Documents 14–16 can be found in the case study section of our Online Resource Centre, which contains a complete set of the documentation forming the *R v Lenny Whyte* case study.

Case studies: *R v Roger Martin* and *R. William Hardy*

With regards to *R v William Hardy* and *R v Martin*, although there have been adjournments in each of these cases, there is no contentious issue as regards bail and each defendant is remanded on conditional bail during the proceedings.

FIGURE 12.1 COURT BAIL

EXCEPTIONS TO THE RIGHT TO BAIL

The Bail Act 1976 (s. 4) generally presumes the defendant should be granted bail. However,

- bail should only be granted exceptionally where a defendant is charged with murder, manslaughter, rape (or attempts) and he has previous convictions for one of these offences (s. 25 CJPOA 1994);

- the defendant need not be granted bail if he is over 18 and is already on bail unless there is no signifcant risk of him committing an offence on bail (currently applies only to offences carrying life imprisonment (s.14 CJA 2003));

- the defendant need not be granted bail if he is over 18 and has previously been granted bail in the proceedings and has failed to surrender unless the court is satisfed there is no signifcant risk of the defendant failing to surrender if released on bail (currently applies only to offences carrying life imprisonment (s. 15 CJA 2003));

- the defendant need not be granted bail if he has tested positive to a Class A drug and is charged with offence involving a specifed Class A drug under Misuse of Drugs Act 1971, or court is satisfed that his offending is due to his drug dependency and the defendant refuses to undergo an assessment or follow-up treatment for his dependency (s. 19 CJA 2003).

REBUTTING THE PRESUMPTION TO BAIL

- the presumption to bail may be rebutted where defendant is charged with imprisonable offence; and

- the court is satisfed (Part 1, Sch. 1, Bail Act 1976) there are **substantial grounds** for believing the defendant will:
    - fail to surrender to custody; or
    - commit an offence while on bail; or
    - interfere with witnesses or obstruct the course of justice; or

- the court is satisfed that the defendant should be kept in custody for his protection (or welfare where a juvenile); or

- the defendant is already serving a custodial sentence; or

- the court is satisfed it has not been practicable to obtain suffcient information to take a decision under the Bail Act 1976; or

- where the case has been adjourned for preparation of a report, it appears impracticable to complete the enquiries or report unless the defendant is in custody.

PARAGRAPH 9 FACTORS

- In deciding whether the ground(s) for refusing bail are made out, the court takes into account paragraph 9 Bail Act 1976 factors:
    - the nature and seriousness of the offence;
    - defendant's character, antecedents, community ties;
    - bail record;
    - strength of the evidence; and
    - any other relevant matter.

BAIL CONDITIONS

- bail can be unconditional or conditional;

- conditions ensure that the defendant:
    - will surrender to custody; or
    - does not commit further offences; or
    - does not interfere with witnesses or obstruct the course of justice; or
    - to ensure defendant available to assist with preparation of a pre-sentence report.

- conditions include:
  - reporting to a police station;
  - living at a specifed address (possibly bail hostel);
  - curfew;
  - surety;
  - the defendant should not contact a specifc individual;
  - exclusion from specifed locality or place.

APPEALING BAIL DECISIONS

- defence can 'appeal' against refusal of bail or bail conditions to Crown Court judge in chambers;
- prosecution can appeal to Crown Court against allowing bail where offence is punishable with imprisonment.

13.1   INTRODUCTION

There are a considerable number of either-way offences including assault occasioning actual bodily harm, theft and burglary. Sections 17–21 MCA 1980 provide that where a defendant aged 18 or over is charged with an either-way offence, mode of trial proceedings must be held to determine whether the defendant should be tried summarily or on indictment before any evidence is called.

Either-way offences can be committed with varying degrees of seriousness depending on the aggravating or mitigating features in the particular case. The more aggravating features, the more serious the offence will be regarded. Magistrates' court powers of sentence are limited compared to the Crown Court. If a magistrates' court considers its maximum sentencing powers (Six months for a single either-way offence, increasing to 12 months where consecutive custodial sentences are imposed for two or more either-way offences) to be insufficient, the case will be sent to the Crown Court. Theft offences provide a good illustration. Theft can range from simple shoplifting to the appropriation of property worth millions of pounds. Clearly, the offender charged with shoplifting would be most appropriately dealt with summarily while the more serious, high-value theft should be dealt with in the Crown Court.

Looking Ahead

The Criminal Justice Act 2003 (Sch. 3) makes provision for significant changes to the mode of trial procedure for either-way offences. In future, what has previously been called 'mode of trial', will be termed 'allocation'. The new allocation procedure may come into effect in whole or in part in 2008–2009. As drafted in the CJA 2003, the allocation provisions are tied to an increase in the maximum sentencing powers of the magistrates' court under the CJA 2003 which increase the court's powers of sentence on conviction for a single offence to a maximum custodial term of 51 weeks, and up to 65 weeks where consecutive sentences are imposed for two or more offences. However, the well-publicised problem of prison overcrowding has led to the postponement of the implementation of increased sentencing powers for the magistrates' court indefinitely. The new allocation procedure may therefore come into effect on a different basis from that originally intended. If the allocation provisions come into force in 2008–2009 the update section of our Online Resource Centre will provide full details. An account of the changes is given in any event at para. 13.9.

online
resource
centre

In this chapter we examine:

- the procedure for deciding where an either-way offence should be tried;
- the relative merits of summary trial and trial on indictment; and
- for those either-way offences that are to be tried in the Crown Court, the next stage of the proceedings—the committal hearing conducted under MCA 1980, s. 6(1) or s. 6(2).

13.2 PLEA BEFORE VENUE

online
resource
centre

All defendants charged with an either-way offence are subject to the plea before venue procedure which precedes any mode of trial enquiry (s. 17A MCA 1980). The procedure provides the defendant with an opportunity to indicate to the court how he intends to plead. The plea before venue is illustrated in the video section of our Online Resource Centre in the *R v Lenny Whyte* case study.

You are reminded that a defendant charged with an either-way offence is entitled to pre-trial disclosure of the prosecution's evidence against him in accordance with Crim PR, Part 21 (Advance Information). Unless the matter is clear-cut, advance information should be sought before offering advice as to plea. As a consequence of CJSSS (see Chapter 11, para. 11.17), the CPS is required to serve advance information on the defendant prior to his first appearance before a magistrates' court to enable a plea to be indicated.

13.2.1 PROCEDURE AT PLEA BEFORE VENUE

The court's legal adviser will check with the parties whether a plea can be indicated. If it can, the legal adviser will explain to the accused in ordinary language that he will be asked to indicate to the court whether he intends to plead guilty or not guilty. The legal adviser will also explain that if the defendant indicates a guilty plea, the magistrates will proceed to sentence and deal with him as if he had been found guilty and there will be no trial and no evidence will be called. The defendant will also be warned that notwithstanding an indication of a guilty plea, the magistrates may still commit him for sentence to the Crown Court under s. 3 Powers of Criminal Court (Sentencing) Act 2000 (PCC(S)A 2000) if they consider their sentencing powers to be insufficient. The legal adviser will then read the charge to the accused who is asked to indicate his plea. A defendant has four possible responses. He can indicate a guilty plea, a not guilty plea, give no indication of plea or enter an equivocal plea.

3.2.2 WHAT HAPPENS IF THE DEFENDANT INDICATES A GUILTY PLEA?

If the defendant indicates that he would plead guilty, the case will be dealt with summarily on the basis of his guilty plea and sentence will follow immediately or be adjourned to a later date if the court considers a full pre-sentence report is required.

If the case continues on the day, the CPS advocate will outline the facts of the case and give details of the defendant's previous convictions. The defence advocate will make a plea in mitigation during which he will seek to put the defendant's actions in the best light in the hope that the magistrates will be persuaded to impose a less severe sentence than might otherwise be the case. A detailed examination of the practice and procedure in making a plea in mitigation is dealt with in Part V.

If on hearing the full facts of the offence and the defendant's antecedents, the magistrates consider their powers of sentence to be inadequate, the defendant can be committed to the Crown Court for sentence under the s. 3 PCC(S)A 2000. The defendant can then be sentenced on the same basis as if he had been convicted on indictment. Further consideration is given to the power under s. 3 in Chapter 25. Indeed, the whole basis of a magistrates' court declining jurisdiction to sentence on conviction for one or more either-way offences is best understood when you have completed your consideration of sentencing law and practice.

3.2.3 WHAT HAPPENS IF THE DEFENDANT INDICATES A NOT GUILTY PLEA OR MAKES AN EQUIVOCAL PLEA?

If at the plea before venue, the defendant indicates that he would plead not guilty or makes an equivocal plea, the court will proceed to the mode of trial enquiry. An equivocal plea is where the defendant's response to the charge is ambiguous or the defendant indicates no plea at all. Where the court is uncertain about the defendant's plea, a not guilty plea will be entered on his behalf.

13.3 THE MODE OF TRIAL ENQUIRY—SS. 18–20 MCA 1980

In some cases the CPS lawyer and the defence may agree the appropriate venue for trial. The only time there is likely to be disagreement between the parties is where the prosecution invites the court to decline to try the matter summarily because in its view the magistrates' sentencing powers would be insufficient but the defendant seeks to persuade the court to retain jurisdiction. In outlining the bare facts of the case, the prosecution will either represent that the case is suitable for summary trial or it will make representations as to why the case would be more appropriately dealt with in the Crown Court. The magistrates will listen to any representations from the defence advocate before coming to a decision about where the case should be dealt with.

It is important to remember that in the first instance the decision where the case will be tried lies with the magistrates hearing the case. In reaching their decision, the magistrates will take into account the submissions made by the parties, the statutory factors contained in s. 19 MCA 1980 and the National Mode of Trial Guidelines reproduced in Appendix 2.

13.3.1 THE STATUTORY FACTORS

The statutory factors under s. 19 MCA 1980 require magistrates to have regard to the following in deciding whether the offence is more suitable for summary trial or trial on indictment:

(1) the nature of the case;

(2) whether the circumstances make the offence one of a serious character;

(3) whether the powers of punishment in the magistrates' court would be adequate if the defendant was found guilty;

(4) any other circumstances which appear to the court to make it more suitable for the offence to be tried summarily or on indictment.

Of central importance to the mode of trial enquiry are the magistrates' sentencing powers on conviction. Again, the importance of this will be more fully appreciated and understood after you have covered sentencing law and practice in Part V. Currently the maximum sentence a magistrates' court can impose on conviction for an either-way offence is six months' imprisonment. This increases to a maximum of 12 months where the defendant is convicted of two or more either-way offences.

In applying the statutory factors to the facts of your client's case, the magistrates will consider any aggravating factors which may justify the case being tried in the Crown Court. Common aggravating factors include where a defendant has acted in a premeditated way; where the victim of the crime was vulnerable; or where the property damaged or stolen was of high value. The decision in *R v Colchester Justices, ex p. North East Essex Building Co.* [1977] 1 WLR 1109 suggests that, as a matter of practice, in assessing the nature and seriousness of the case the defendant's previous convictions should not be taken into account in deciding mode of trial. This is something of an anomaly which has never been satisfactorily resolved, since it is accepted that previous convictions are an aggravating factor that must be taken into account on sentencing (s. 143(2) CJA 2003).

Where the magistrates decide that trial on indictment is more appropriate, the defendant has no right of election and the magistrates' decision is communicated to him. The mode of trial enquiry will be adjourned and a date is set for a committal hearing to be held. Pending the adjournment the CPS will prepare and serve the committal bundle on the defence. The practice and procedure at committal is considered in paras. 13.11–13.17 below.

In addition to the statutory factors in s. 19 MCA 1980, the magistrates will have regard to the National Mode of Trial Guidelines.

13.3.2 THE NATIONAL MODE OF TRIAL GUIDELINES

In determining whether the case is suitable for summary trial or trial on indictment, the court will take into account the National Mode of Trial Guidelines (reproduced in Appendix 2). As their name implies, the object of the guidelines is to provide guidance only. Magistrates should apply the guidelines but are required to consider each case individually on its own facts.

The guidelines provide that:

(a) the court should never make its decision on the grounds of convenience or expedition;

(b) the court should assume for the purposes of deciding mode of trial that the prosecution version of the facts is correct;

(c) the fact that offences are alleged to be specimens is a relevant consideration; the fact that the defendant will be asking for offences to be taken into consideration, if convicted, is not;

(d) where cases involve complex questions of fact or difficult questions of law, the court should consider committal for trial;

(e) where two or more defendants are jointly charged with an offence each has an individual right to elect his mode of trial;

(f) in general, except where otherwise stated, either-way offences should be tried summarily unless the court considers that the particular case has one or more features set out in the guidelines and that its sentencing powers are insufficient;

(g) the court should also consider its power to commit an offender for sentence under s. 3 PCC(S)A 2000, if information emerges during the course of the hearing which leads them to conclude that the offence is so serious, or the offender is such a risk to the public, that their powers to sentence him are inadequate.

The guidelines suggest that a case should not be committed to the Crown Court because it appears to be the easier option. It may be that the defendant is already committed to stand trial in the Crown Court on similar or unrelated earlier charges. It makes sense to have all matters tried and resolved at the same time but a committal should not be ordered on this basis alone.

For the purposes of the mode of trial enquiry the magistrates must take the prosecution case at its highest and must assume that the prosecution's version of the facts is correct. The guidelines further suggest that either-way cases should be tried summarily unless there are aggravating factors, which makes trial on indictment more likely. The National Mode of Trial Guidelines specify the aggravating features of a number of common either-way offences which can increase the seriousness of the offence.

In relation to burglary of a dwelling house, for example, aggravating factors include:

• entry to the house during daytime when the occupier or another is present;

• entry to the house at night, which is normally occupied, whether or not the occupier or another is present;

• the offence is alleged to be one of a series of offences;

• when in the house, soiling, ransacking, damage or vandalism occurs;

• the offence has professional hallmarks;

• the unrecovered property is of high value.

National Mode of Trial Guidelines—theft and fraud

Cases of theft and fraud should normally be tried summarily unless the court considers that one or more of the following aggravating factors are present and that its sentencing powers are insufficient:

• breach of trust by a person in a position of substantial authority, or in whom a high degree of trust is placed;

• theft or fraud which has been committed or disguised in a sophisticated manner;

• theft or fraud committed by an organised gang;

• the victim is particularly vulnerable to theft or fraud, e.g. the victim is elderly or infirm;

• the unrecovered property is of high value.

The practice and procedure at a mode of trial enquiry is illustrated in the video section of our Online Resource Centre in relation to the *R v Lenny Whyte* case study.

online resource centre

13.4 DECIDING ON TRIAL BY JURY OR TRIAL BEFORE A MAGISTRATES' COURT WHERE THE DEFENDANT IS GIVEN THE CHOICE

Where the magistrates believe the case is suitable for summary trial, the defendant has the absolute right to elect trial by jury before the Crown Court or to consent to being tried summarily before magistrates.

At an early stage in the proceedings after receiving advance information from the CPS, the defendant's solicitor should make an assessment of the nature of the prosecution evidence against his client and be prepared to advise his client about the relative advantages of summary trial or trial on indictment if a plea of not guilty is to be entered. Part of this advice will be based on a number of practical factors including how the defendant's case is funded and the defendant's personal circumstances. Clearly, if a defendant is privately funded, summary trial will be much cheaper than trial on indictment. If your client is of a nervous disposition, he may not be capable of dealing with the considerable pressures of a Crown Court trial.

In addition to any practical considerations, you should also consider the relative advantages and disadvantages of both types of proceedings having regard to the particular facts of your client's case. While it is part of the defence solicitor's professional duty to advise his client where his case should be tried, the decision ultimately lies with the client.

13.4.1 RELATIVE MERITS OF TRIAL ON INDICTMENT

Higher acquittal rate

In spite of inconclusive evidence, most defence lawyers believe that trial by jury provides a better chance of their client being acquitted. There is a commonly held perception that magistrates can be case-hardened because they sit on a regular basis and often hear the same defence arguments. This is especially significant in cases involving disputed police evidence, as magistrates may be more prepared to accept the evidence of the police in preference to that of the defendant. There is a widely held perception that jurors come to a case with a more open mind. For a client charged with theft who pleads not guilty because he lacked dishonest intent, 12 jurors hearing this defence for the first time may be more likely to give him the benefit of the doubt.

Disputed evidence

Where your client's case involves disputed evidence, the judge, as a legally qualified professional, is clearly much better placed to deal with points of law. The separation of functions in the *voir dire* between judge and jury makes defence challenges to the admissibility of prosecution evidence during the trial much more effective as the jury is excluded from the *voir dire* hearing. Where your client's case involves disputing the admissibility of the prosecution's identification evidence for example or challenging the admissibility of a confession, trial on indictment should be advised. Apart from the problems that some lay magistrates may experience in fully appreciating the advocate's legal submissions about the admissibility of prosecution evidence, if the defence submission is upheld, lay magistrates are required to put the excluded evidence to the back of their minds and continue trying the case. The increasing use of pre-trial hearings in the magistrates' court at which binding rulings on disputed evidence can be made means this problem should arise less frequently.

Delay

It can take months before a case finally comes to trial in the Crown Court. Delay can be both an advantage and a disadvantage. You might use the inevitable delay of trial in the Crown Court to prepare your client's case and to test the prosecution case.

Cost

Representation orders for summary proceedings are means tested. The means test does not apply to cases tried on indictment. There is provision, however, for the recovery of defence costs (RDCO) under reg. 11 of the Criminal Defence Service (Recovery of Defence Costs Orders) (Amendment) Regulations 2004. The regulations apply to those defendants who are convicted of offences before a Crown Court. Under the regulations, a judge is required to make a RDCO, taking into account the offender's means. Prosecution costs on conviction are likely to be much higher in the Crown Court than in the magistrates' court.

Powers of sentence

The Crown Court's powers of punishment are far greater than those of the magistrates' court. The Crown Court can impose a sentence up to the statutory maximum for the particular offence. Fines are also likely to be considerably higher in the Crown Court. This may be an important factor for your client.

8.4.2 THE RELATIVE MERITS OF SUMMARY TRIAL

Powers of sentence

If convicted in summary proceedings, your client is likely to receive a more lenient sentence, as the magistrates' sentencing powers are much more limited compared to the Crown Court. The maximum custodial sentence that can be imposed is currently limited to six months for an either-way offence or 12 months for two of more either-way offences. The maximum fine magistrates can impose is £5,000 per offence. However, it is always good professional practice to remind your client about the magistrates' power to commit to the Crown Court for sentence under s. 3 PCC(S)A 2000 where the magistrates believe their sentencing powers to be insufficient.

Delay

The delay in Crown Court proceedings may have a detrimental effect on your client, especially if he is anxious or has been in custody after being refused bail. The time between the date of the alleged offence and your client's trial is often much shorter in summary cases enabling the case to be completed sooner.

Publicity

Trial in the Crown Court will usually involve your client being exposed to greater publicity. Representatives of the local press and sometimes the national media will often take a greater interest in Crown Court proceedings. This is an important factor where your client is a public figure or the case is of particular public interest, for example, where your client is a teacher charged with a sexual offence.

Stress

The relative informality of summary proceedings makes the magistrates' court more appropriate for a nervous client. By contrast, the atmosphere of the Crown Court is considerably more formal and intimidating.

Defence pre-trial disclosure of evidence

Under the Criminal Procedure and Investigations Act 1996 (CPIA), there is no obligation on the accused to serve a defence statement in summary proceedings. In trials on indictment, after the prosecution has served 'initial' disclosure of 'unused' evidence, the accused is required to serve a defence statement. In summary proceedings, the service of a defence statement is voluntary (see Chapter 14).

Presenting advocate

If the defendant's trial is in the magistrates' court, he is likely to have met his advocate on a number of occasions prior to trial. It is more likely that the advocate will be fully conversant with the facts, whereas at the Crown Court, briefs delivered to counsel are sometimes delivered at a very late stage and often there is no guarantee that the barrister instructed by the solicitor will be the person who represents your client at trial.

13.5 THE SPECIAL PROCEDURE WHERE THE ACCUSED IS CHARGED WITH CRIMINAL DAMAGE

Where a defendant is charged with criminal damage contrary to s. 1 Criminal Damage Act 1971 unless the offence involves damage by fire, there are special rules regarding mode of trial. If the value of the damaged property is £5,000 or less, the case should be tried summarily. The defendant has no right of election to the Crown Court. The maximum sentence a magistrates' court can impose for such an offence is three months' imprisonment and/or a £2,500 fine. If the damage to the property is over £5,000, the court is required to hold a mode of trial hearing in the normal way.

The procedure described above deals with situations where a solicitor is representing one adult defendant at the mode of trial hearing. In some cases two or more defendants may be charged in the same proceedings or the defendant may be charged with a co-accused who is a young person (under the age of 18). Below, we consider the procedure where there are two or more co-accused. The procedure in relation to defendants under the age of 18 is considered in Chapter 31, which deals with youth justice.

13.6 SPECIAL RULES RELATING TO CERTAIN EITHER-WAY OFFENCES

In the context of a third burglary offence, any previous convictions for burglary are important. If a defendant is charged with a third offence of domestic burglary the court will apply s. 111 PCC(S)A 2000 as this provision requires a person convicted of a third domestic burglary offence (where all three of the offences were committed after 30 November 1999) to be given a custodial sentence of three years unless there are circumstances that do not justify imposing such a sentence. As this sentence is clearly in excess of the magistrates' court sentencing powers, it has no choice but to treat the offence as triable only on indictment, with the result that it must be sent to the Crown Court (s. 51 Crime and Disorder Act 1998, see Chapter 16).

13.7 MODE OF TRIAL WHERE THERE IS MORE THAN ONE ACCUSED

In a case where there is more than one defendant charged with the same offence and the magistrates are prepared to accept jurisdiction, each accused enjoys a separate right of election. The decision of one co-accused to elect summary trial or trial on indictment does not bind the other(s).This point was confirmed by the House of Lords in *R v Brentwood Justices, ex p. Nicholls* [1992] 1 AC 1.

Where a defendant facing an either-way offence is charged jointly with another adult defendant who faces an indictable only offence which is related to the either-way matter, the either-way matter must be sent to the Crown Court in accordance with the requirements of s. 51 Crime and Disorder Act 1998 (see Chapter 16). In these circumstances, the defendant facing the either-way offence has no individual right of election.

 Example

A is charged with causing grievous bodily harm with intent contrary to s. 18 Offences Against the Person Act 1861 (indictable only). A and B are jointly charged with affray (triable either way). The affray allegation arises out of the assault. A will be sent for trial in the Crown Court. If B appears before magistrates at the same time as A, B's case will also be sent to the Crown Court.

13.8 CHANGING THE ORIGINAL DECISION IN RELATION TO MODE OF TRIAL

The decision at the mode of trial to try the case in either the magistrates' court or the Crown Court is not irrevocable. Section 25(2) MCA 1980 provides that where it has been decided to try the defendant summarily and the defendant pleads not guilty, the magistrates may, at any stage before the close of the prosecution case, discontinue the trial and proceed to hold committal proceedings. Such a procedure should be adopted where the prosecution case discloses the offence to be more serious than the magistrates first realised and as a result no longer consider their sentencing powers to be adequate in the event of conviction.

The power under s. 25(2) only arises once the magistrates have begun to try the case. If an accused has consented to summary trial and then enters a guilty plea, there is no power under s. 25(2) to change their decision from summary trial to trial on indictment. A similar power applies under s. 25(3) MCA 1980 where the original decision at mode of trial was to decline jurisdiction in favour of trial on indictment. At any time before the close of the prosecution case at the committal hearing, the defendant may be offered the right to elect summary trial.

13.9 CRIMINAL JUSTICE ACT 2003—CHANGES TO MODE OF TRIAL PROCEDURE

 Looking Ahead

The allocation procedure detailed in Sch.3 CJA 2003 will replace the existing mode of trial procedure. Its aim is to reduce the number of either-way offences that are committed to the Crown Court. The Allocation provisions are unlikely to come into effect until spring 2009.

Under the new procedure the defendant retains a right to elect trial by jury when given the choice. The plea before venue procedure remains unchanged and where a guilty plea is indicated, the court retains the power to commit to the Crown Court for sentence. Where a not guilty plea is indicated, the court proceeds to the allocation enquiry. The court will hear the representations of the parties and apply allocation guidelines issued by the Sentencing Guidelines Council (SGC). One important change is that the prosecution will be allowed to refer to a defendant's previous convictions to assist the court to decide if its sentencing powers are sufficient on conviction. Furthermore, the *Brentwood Justices* decision will cease to apply as there will be a presumption that a single trial will be in the interests of justice.

Where the magistrates are prepared to retain jurisdiction, it will be explained to the defendant that he has a choice. As originally drafted, the power to commit a defendant for sentence to the Crown Court after conviction, having retained summary jurisdiction, is prohibited except that a defendant can still be committed for sentence to the Crown Court under the 'dangerousness' provisions in s. 224 CJA 2003. Just to complicate the picture further, the Criminal Justice and Immigration Act 2008 amends this provision to restore the power to commit for sentence in these circumstances! The restoration of the power to commit is felt necessary as there is no imminent likelihood of the magistrates' court sentencing powers being increased (which is what the allocation provisions are premised on).

Under the allocation provisions, s. 20 MCA 1980 is amended so that where the court has accepted jurisdiction to try the defendant summarily following an indication of not guilty, he is entitled to ask the magistrates' court for a broad indication of sentence if he were to be tried summarily and plead guilty i.e. 'Would I receive a custodial or non-custodial sentence?' The answer to such a question may influence a defendant as to the appropriate venue for his trial and possible plea. However, a court is not bound to give an indication. Where the magistrates give an indication and the defendant pleads guilty, the indication is binding on any subsequent sentencing court. Having received an indication, the defendant can, if he wishes, reconsider any indication he gave or declined to give at his plea before venue.

The Sentencing Guidelines Council has issued draft allocation guidelines in anticipation of the allocation provisions being brought into force. The draft guidelines can be accessed at http://www.sentencing-guidelines.gov.uk/docs/allocation_draft_guideline_160206.pdf. They will replace the existing National Mode of Trial Guidelines. A court will be required to have regard to the allocation guidelines. A principal consideration under the allocation guidelines is the adequacy of the court's sentencing powers in relation to the seriousness of the offence charged. It is anticipated that the draft guidelines will be further revised in the light of the revision of the power to commit for sentence made by the Criminal Justice and Immigration Act 2008.

Summary of the changes under the CJA 2003

- If a not guilty plea is indicated an allocation enquiry will be necessary.

- Prosecution and defence will make representations.

- As part of the allocation procedure and in an attempt to determine whether its sentencing powers would be sufficient in the event of conviction, the defendant's previous convictions will be adduced.

- Magistrates will apply new allocation guidelines set to be finalised and issued by the Sentencing Guidelines Council.

- The decision to accept jurisdiction will be based, for the most part, on the adequacy of the court's sentencing powers (taking into account the seriousness of the offence(s) charged and any relevant discount for a timely guilty plea).

- An individual right of election in the case of jointly charged defendants will cease to have effect.

- Having accepted jurisdiction to try a case summarily, the magistrates' court will be unable to commit for sentence in the event of conviction save where the offence triggers the 'dangerous' offender provisions under s. 224 CJA 2003 (however, the power to commit is restored under the Criminal Justice and Immigration Act 2008, which at the time of writing is not in force).

- Where the magistrates' court accepts summary jurisdiction to try the accused, he may seek an indication as to likely sentence in the event of a guilty plea before making a choice.

- Where an indication of sentence is given and the defendant pleads guilty, the court may not impose a custodial sentence unless such a sentence was indicated.

13.10 COMMITTAL PROCEEDINGS—INTRODUCTION

Once a mode of trial enquiry has been held and the defendant has either chosen to elect trial by jury in the Crown Court or the magistrates' court has declined jurisdiction in favour of the Crown Court, a date will be fixed for the next stage of the proceedings which is the committal hearing. It is usual to have an adjournment of between six and eight weeks from the mode of trial hearing to the date set for committal. Where an accused has been remanded in custody the committal hearing must be held within 28 days. Rules of court relating to committal hearings are contained within Crim PR, Part 10.

During the period of the adjournment, the defence solicitor will receive what is commonly referred to as being the 'committal bundle'. This comprises all the 'used' material the prosecution intends to call or rely on against the defendant at trial, together with a list of exhibits and a copy of the draft indictment. The defence solicitor must be satisfied that a *prima facie* case is disclosed in the 'committal bundle'. An example of a typical committal bundle is contained in our *R v Lenny Whyte* case study (Appendix 1).

Where the advocate considers a *prima facie* case is not disclosed he can request a long style committal at which he will make an oral submission that the case should be dismissed. Otherwise, the matter will be committed to the Crown Court at a short style committal hearing.

3.11 THE PURPOSE OF COMMITTAL PROCEEDINGS

The Crown Court's time is precious and expensive. The criminal justice system has long required that a defendant should not be sent for trial by jury unless there has been a detailed consideration of whether the evidence discloses a case for the defendant to answer. This filtering role has been fulfilled by a committal hearing before a panel of magistrates known as examining justices.

At the committal hearing the CPS is required to establish a *prima facie* against the accused. This standard is considerably lower than beyond reasonable doubt which the prosecution will have to satisfy at trial to secure a conviction.

There are two types of committal proceedings—a committal with consideration of the evidence under s. 6(1) MCA 1980 and a committal without consideration of the evidence under s. 6 MCA 1980. The vast majority of committal hearings are conducted under the s. 6(2) procedure which is commonly known as a short-style committal.

3.12 EVIDENCE AT THE COMMITTAL HEARING

Only the prosecution present evidence to the court at the committal. For the evidence to be admissible it must be in written form, as oral evidence is not heard and must be in the correct form prescribed by ss. 5B, 5C, 5D and 5E MCA 1980. The most common form of evidence tendered at the committal is tendered under s. 5B which requires:

- the statement should be signed by the maker; and
- contain a declaration by the maker that it is true to the best of his knowledge and belief, and that he made it knowing that if he tendered it in evidence he could be prosecuted for wilfully stating in it anything he knew to be false or did not believe to be true; and
- a copy of the statement should be given to each of the parties at the committal before being tendered to the court.

Some documents, such as certificates of convictions or documents from the DVLA will prove themselves and are made admissible at the committal by s. 5E MCA 1980.

3.13 A COMMITTAL WITH CONSIDERATION OF THE EVIDENCE—S. 6(1) MCA 1980

A committal under s. 6(1) will be held in two circumstances. First, where the defendant is not legally represented and secondly where the defendant's solicitor has requested a s. 6(1) committal in order to make a submission of no case to answer. In this situation the examining justices are required to hear the substance of the prosecution case against the accused. The key point to remember about this type of committal is that the magistrates will consider the prosecution evidence before deciding whether to commit the case to the Crown Court for trial. The enquiry is limited however in that the magistrates' court does not hear from a live witness, relying instead on the prosecution reading from its witness statements. Furthermore, the court has no power at this stage to determine the admissibility of any disputed evidence under s. 78 or 76 PACE 1984 (see Chapters 6 and 7).

3.13.1 PROCEDURE AT A S. 6(1) COMMITTAL

A committal under s. 6(1) begins with the charge being read to the defendant. The defendant is not required to enter his plea at this stage. Reporting restrictions apply and any application to have them lifted is dealt with.

The CPS lawyer opens the case by outlining the facts and explaining any relevant points of law. The prosecutor will then formally tender the prosecution evidence to the court. The prosecution needs to present sufficient evidence to establish a *prima facie* case although does not have to tender all of its evidence at the committal hearing. The prosecution evidence will be written and will consist of the witness statements and exhibits that have been served on the defence in the 'committal bundle'. The prosecution evidence may be read by the magistrates or summarised by the prosecutor to the court. The defence is not required to tender evidence to the court.

After the magistrates have considered the prosecution case, the defence may make a submission of no case to answer. The defence submission will succeed where the prosecution evidence does not disclose a *prima facie* case to be committed to the Crown Court. This may be because the prosecution's evidence fails to prove an essential element of the alleged offence or the evidence is hopelessly weak or seriously contradictory.

Where a submission of no case to answer is upheld, the defendant is discharged. This is not the same thing as being acquitted. In theory the prosecution can charge the accused again and recommence the case. Alternatively, the CPS could apply to the High Court to prefer a voluntary bill of indictment. The defendant could make an abuse of process application to stay proceedings if the CPS was to adopt this course of action.

Where the circumstances and the evidence permit it, magistrates may decide to commit a defendant for trial on a less serious or alternative charge.

If the magistrates decide to commit the defendant to the Crown Court, it is likely to be to the Crown Court that is most conveniently located unless there are special features about the case making it desirable for it to be tried elsewhere at a Crown Court outside the area.

13.14 PROCEDURE AT COMMITTAL WITHOUT CONSIDERATION OF THE EVIDENCE—S. 6(2) MCA 1980

The vast majority of committals are conducted under the short-style committal. Most defendants will choose this form of committal as in most cases there is little point in choosing a s. 6(1) committal as the threshold the prosecution is required to satisfy is so low that a submission of no case to answer is difficult to sustain. The practical effect of a committal without consideration of the evidence under s. 6(2) (sometimes referred to as a 'paper' committal) is that the accused agrees to be committed to the Crown Court for trial. A s. 6(2) committal will be appropriate where all the evidence tendered by the prosecution consists of written statements in compliance with s. 5 MCA 1980, the defendant is legally represented; and this is not case where you intend to make a submission of 'no case to answer' at this stage.

A s. 6(2) committal is largely an administrative exercise. The charge will be read to the defendant although he will not be expected to plead. The legal adviser will then check that all the evidence in the committal bundle is in the correct form and that it has been served on the defence. The prosecution evidence disclosed in the committal bundle is not considered and the case is formally committed by the magistrates to the Crown Court for trial.

Once a case has been committed a date will be fixed in the Crown Court for the defendant's Plea and Case Management Hearing (PCMH). The steps to be undertaken in preparation for this hearing are considered in Chapter 16.

13.15 CHANGING FROM TRIAL ON INDICTMENT TO SUMMARY TRIAL

Section 25(3) MCA 1980 provides that where, at the mode of trial enquiry the magistrates considered the case was suitable for trial on indictment, at any time before the close of the prosecution evidence at the committal, the magistrates conclude the case is less serious than they originally considered, they should ask the prosecutor and the defence advocate for their views on whether to change to summary trial. If the advocates agree, the legal adviser should then explain to the accused the possibility of committal for sentence and ask him whether he consents to be tried summarily.

8.16 ANCILLARY ISSUES TO BE DEALT WITH UPON COMMITTAL

16.1 STANDARD CASE MANAGEMENT DIRECTIONS

Once a case has been committed for trial under s. 6 MCA 1980, a date will be set for a Plea and Case Management Hearing (PCMH) (see Chapter 16) in the Crown Court. The Criminal Procedure Rules (Crim PR) require a PCMH to be held within seven weeks after committal. In accordance with the Crim PR, the magistrates' court will issue directions to enable the PCMH to be an effective hearing. Much of the defence solicitor's post-committal preparation will be to ensure compliance with the directions in preparation for the PCMH. The standard directions make provisions for the service of initial disclosure and defence statement and notification of which prosecution witnesses the defence wishes to attend trial. Once the prosecution has been given notice of witness requirements, the onus is placed on the police to ascertain witness availability. This information will be required at the PCMH. Provision is also made in the standard directions for the service of:

- any application for a special measures direction (see Chapter 19);
- notice to admit hearsay or evidence of bad character, (see Chapters 22 and 23);
- defence notice objecting to the admission of hearsay or bad character.

16.2 BAIL

When the case is adjourned after the committal, the issue of a defendant's bail might arise. Where the defendant has previously been refused bail, a fresh application for bail might be made depending on how many previous bail applications have been made. Generally the committal of a defendant to stand trial at the Crown Court does not amount to a change in circumstances supporting a third application for a bail (see Chapter 12). You should ensure bail is extended to cover the Crown Court proceedings where your client is currently subject to bail (conditional or otherwise).

16.3 DISCLOSURE

By the time of the committal, the prosecution will have disclosed to you the substance of the case against the defendant in compliance with Crim PR, Part 21 and in the 'committal bundle'. The provisions of the Criminal Procedure and Investigations Act 1996 (CPIA) regulating the disclosure of unused material, apply on committal or as soon as reasonably practicable thereafter. The matter of the pre-trial disclosure of used and 'unused' material is considered in detail in Chapter 14. The first stage of disclosure of unused material under the CPIA 1996 requires the prosecution to serve on the defence any initial prosecution disclosure together with a schedule of any 'unused' material. The prosecution may have included any initial disclosure in the 'committal bundle'. The defendant has 14 days after the prosecution has served or has purported to serve initial disclosure, to serve a defence statement which is mandatory in all cases to be tried on indictment.

8.16.4 OBJECTING TO STATEMENTS BEING READ AT TRIAL

Schedule 2 CPIA 1996 is of particular importance. The usual way of placing evidence before a Crown Court is for the prosecution to call witnesses to give oral evidence and to be cross-examined. Schedule 2, however, provides that any committal statements tendered at the committal hearing 'may without further proof be read as evidence on the trial of the accused'. The CPS is obliged to serve notice of the defendant's right to object to evidence being read at trial at the same time as service of the committal bundle (Crim PR, Part 27.2). An example of

online
resource
centre
such a notice is contained in the *R v Lenny Whyte* case study, the complete documentation to which can be accessed via the student resource section of our Online Resource Centre. If a defendant objects to a witness statement simply being read out at trial he must give written notice of his objection to the prosecution within 14 days of his committal. It is therefore important for the defence solicitor to remember the 14-day time-limit. As a matter of good practice and to be on the safe side, the defence solicitor ought to automatically send out a letter to the CPS objecting to any witness statements being read out at trial. If the defence solicitor's view on this changes as he prepares for trial, the CPS can be notified at a later date that the defence is now prepared to agree the witness's statement being read to the court.

13.17 CRIMINAL JUSTICE ACT 2003—ABOLITION OF COMMITTAL PROCEEDINGS

 Looking Ahead

Provision is made by Sch. 3 of the CJA 2003 for committal proceedings to be abolished. There is no date for the implementation of this provision. If it is implemented in due course, either-way offences going to the Crown Court will be sent via s. 51 Crime and Disorder Act 1998 in the same way as indictable-only offences (see Chapter 16). Under the 'case sent' procedure, the defendant is afforded the opportunity of making an application to have some or all the charges against him dismissed if the prosecution evidence does not disclose a *prima facie* case.

13.18 ADDING OTHER SUMMARY MATTERS TO THE INDICTMENT—S. 40 CJA 1988

What happens when during the course of preparing a committal file it appears that there is evidence of other summary offences against the accused for which he has not yet been charged? The lawyer drafting the indictment can include any other indictable offence disclosed by the committal papers and under s. 40 CJA 1988 can also include specified summary offences that are founded on the same facts as the indictable offence or form part of a series of offences of the same or similar character as the indictable offence. The offences are:

- common assault;
- assaulting a prison warder;
- taking a motor vehicle without consent;
- driving whilst disqualified;
- criminal damage of £5,000 or less.

The summary offence must have been disclosed to the magistrates' court at the committal hearing. The effect of s. 40 is that where the defendant is arraigned in the Crown Court, the count in respect of the summary offence and the offence(s) to be tried on indictment will be put to the accused. If he pleads not guilty, a jury will be sworn and evidence will be heard in respect of both offences. If the defendant is found guilty of the summary offence, the Crown Court's sentencing powers will be limited to those of the magistrates—a maximum custodial sentence of 6 months and/or a £5,000 fine.

Example

Brian is charged with burglary. At the mode of trial hearing, the magistrates' court determines that the offence should be heard on indictment. When the committal papers are prepared, it appears that in order to escape from the crime scene Brian took a car without the owner's consent (a summary-only offence). Although only charged with the burglary, the summary matter can be added to the indictment. Brian will be asked to plead to each count. If he pleads not guilty the jury will be sworn and the prosecution will present evidence to the court in respect to both offences.

3.19 COMMITTING A LINKED SUMMARY OFFENCE FOR PLEA TO THE CROWN COURT—S. 41 CJA 1988

Where a defendant is committed for trial on an either-way offence, s. 41 CJA 1988 permits the magistrates to commit a linked summary offence to the Crown Court for sentence. For s. 41 to apply, the summary offence must:

- be punishable with either imprisonment or disqualification from driving; and
- must arise out of the same set of circumstances that are similar to or are connected with the either-way offence.

It is important to be aware of the following about s. 41:

- The section applies to either-way offences only that have been committed to the Crown Court for trial.
- The Crown Court will not try the summary case under s. 41. It is committed only for a plea to be taken. If the defendant is found guilty of the either-way offence and pleads guilty to the summary offence, he can be sentenced by the Crown Court for both offences. The Crown Court's sentencing powers in respect to the summary offence are limited to those of the magistrates' court.
- If the defendant pleads not guilty to the summary offence or is acquitted of the either-way offence, the Crown Court will not deal with the summary offence and will have to remit the summary offence back to the magistrates to be tried. Section 66 Courts Act 2003 empowers Crown Court judges to exercise the powers of a magistrates' court. Thus a Crown Court judge (sitting as a district judge) without a jury could try the summary offence.

 Example

Donald is charged with dangerous driving (an either-way offence) following a police pursuit. He is also charged with driving without insurance (a summary-only offence). Having committed the offence of dangerous driving to the Crown Court for trial, the magistrates can include the insurance offence for a plea to be taken under s. 41 CJA 1988 as the offence can result in disqualification and it arises out of circumstances connected to the either-way matter.

In the Crown Court, if Donald is found guilty of dangerous driving, he will be asked to plead to the offence of driving without insurance. If he pleads guilty to this offence he may be sentenced for both the either-way offence and the summary offence. If he pleads not guilty to the summary offence or is found not guilty of dangerous driving, the driving without insurance offence will be remitted to the magistrates for trial.

Looking Ahead

Section 41 CJA 1988 is prospectively repealed by Sch. 3 CJA 2003. This is linked to the abolition of committal proceedings highlighted at para. 13.17 above. If implemented, either-way matters that are to be tried in the Crown Court, will be sent there under an amended s. 51 Crime and Disorder Act 1998 (see Chapter 16). Under the notice procedure the magistrates will also be able to send the defendant to be tried on any related summary offence punishable with imprisonment or disqualification from driving.

13.20 ALTERNATIVES TO COMMITTAL

We make brief mention of the other methods by which a person charged with an either-way offence may be required to stand trial at the Crown Court without having been committed for trial by a magistrate's court. Further consideration is given to these methods in *Blackstone's Criminal Practice*. They include:

- voluntary bill of indictment;
- notice of transfer in serious or complex fraud cases—s. 4 CJA 1987;
- notice of transfer in a violent or sexual offence where there is a child witness—s. 53 CJA 1991.

In relation to the latter two, the defendant will still make an initial appearance before magistrates at which ancillary matters relating to bail and legal aid will be determined. Provision is made for an accused to apply to the Crown Court to have the charges specified in the notice dismissed.

KEY POINTS SUMMARY IN RELATION TO EITHER-WAY OFFENCES

- In relation to all either-way offences, a defendant will be required to give an indication of his plea—this is known as the plea before venue.
- If the defendant indicates a guilty plea, the magistrates must accept jurisdiction but can commit the defendant to the Crown Court for sentence.
- Where a not guilty plea or no plea is indicated, a mode of trial enquiry must be held and the initial decision as to where the case shall be tried lies with the magistrates.
- In reaching a decision as regards mode of trial, the magistrates will apply the statutory factors in s. 19 MCA 1980 and the National Mode of Trial Guidelines and will consider, in particular, whether their maximum sentencing powers are likely to be sufficient.
- When advising your client about mode of trial not only consider the legal merits of advising in favour of summary trial or trial on indictment but consider also your client's personal circumstances and whether he could cope with the considerable demands of a Crown Court trial.
- Find out in advance the prosecution's views on mode of trial and if necessary be prepared to argue against the CPS.
- The CPS can indirectly control the mode of trial in that it enjoys a largely unfettered discretion as regards charging a suspect and adjusting those charges at a later date. Thus a defendant charged with common assault as opposed to assault occasioning actual bodily harm (s. 47 OAPA 1861) can only be tried summarily. Representations may be appropriate. Reference should be made to the Code for Crown Prosecutors—see Chapter 10.

KEY POINTS SUMMARY IN COMMITTAL HEARINGS

- On receipt of the committal bundle the defence solicitor must set aside some time to go through the documentation in order to see if a *prima facie* case is disclosed.
- The circumstances in which a s. 6(1) committal is sought will be rare.
- Reporting restrictions apply at committal proceedings but an application can be made by the defence to have them lifted.
- Where the matter is committed to the Crown Court, the defence solicitor must ensure he deals with post committal matters (legal aid/bail/writing to the CPS objecting to committal witness statements being read at trial).

SELF-TEST QUESTIONS

Consider the following short scenarios.

- What representations do you consider the prosecution might make as regards mode of trial in each case?
- Applying s.19 MCA 1980 factors and the National Mode of Trial Guidelines, do you consider the magistrates will accept or decline jurisdiction?
- Outline the procedure in relation to each possibility and consider, if the accused in each of the following exercises were given the choice as to election, what advice you would give in this regard.

Exercise 1

Gordon Davey is 45 years old. He is charged with unlawful sexual activity with his 14-year-old niece, contrary to s. 9(1) Sexual Offences Act 2003. It is alleged that he committed the indecent assault by touching her through her clothes. He is pleading not guilty and has no previous convictions.

Exercise 2

Simon Hayley is a 36-year-old pharmacist. He is charged with 16 offences of false accounting (s. 17 Theft Act 1968) and obtaining money transfers worth £15,830 by deception (s. 15A Theft Act 1968) from the Prescription Pricing Authority. It is alleged that over a period of eight months he claimed expenditure for dispensing ordinary purpose syringes when his records show that he in fact dispensed a cheaper plastic disposable syringe. Simon is a man of impeccable character and denies the allegation.

Exercise 3

Wayne Mason faces three charges, including dangerous driving (s. 2 Road Traffic Act 1988—triable either way), taking a vehicle without the owner's consent (s. 12 Theft Act 1968—summary only) and driving without insurance (s. 143 Road Traffic Act 1988). It is alleged he stole a VW Golf vehicle. When pursued by an unmarked police car, it is alleged that the driver of the vehicle drove at speeds in excess of 60 miles an hour for a short period of time in a built-up area while permitting his passenger to throw beer cans out of the passenger side window into the path of the police car giving chase. The car was driven to the end of a cul-de-sac before being abandoned. Two youths were seen running off in the direction of Wayne Mason's home.

Wayne Mason denies the charge, maintaining he has an alibi for the relevant time. The main witness against him is the police officer who gave chase, who claims to recognise Wayne as being the driver of the car. Wayne has several previous convictions, including several driving-related convictions. He was not offered an identification parade at the police station and denies knowing the officer who purports to have recognised him. There would appear to be no forensic evidence linking him to the scene.

Case study: *R v Lenny Whyte*

Mode of trial—*R v Lenny Whyte*

Take a look at *R v Lenny Whyte* in the video section of our Online Resource Centre. You will recall that Lenny is charged with domestic burglary. His initial appearance ended in an adjournment to enable the CPS to provide advance information. Lenny was remanded in custody. Since his first appearance, advance information has now been provided and considered. Lenny's solicitor takes him through the prosecution witness statements and gives him advice as regards mode of trial. The advice of Lenny's solicitor is contained in a file note (see Document 12 in Appendix 1).

You will see that Lenny's solicitor does not feel the magistrates' court will accept jurisdiction to try Lenny's matter, as domestic burglary offences are invariably regarded as being serious by magistrates' courts. Lenny's solicitor nevertheless goes on to consider what Lenny should do in the event of the magistrates accepting jurisdiction. On the video you can see Lenny's second appearance before magistrates at which he indicates a not guilty plea at the plea before venue followed by his mode of trial enquiry. You will also see the outline by the CPS lawyer inviting the bench to decline jurisdiction to try the matter. At the conclusion of the mode of trial enquiry the magistrates decline jurisdiction and adjourn the matter for committal to the Crown Court. The reason for their decision is that they do not believe their sentencing powers would be sufficient in the event of conviction having regard to a number of aggravating factors.

R v Lenny Whyte—committal to the Crown Court

In relation to *R v Lenny Whyte*, the magistrates declined jurisdiction. His case is therefore adjourned and a date has been set for his committal hearing. The CPS serves the 'committal bundle' on Lenny's solicitor (see Document 23 located in Appendix 1). Lenny's solicitor accepts the committal bundle discloses a case to answer and she agrees a short-style committal in accordance with s. 6(2) MCA 1980 (see Document 24).

Lenny's solicitor attends the short-style committal and Lenny's case is committed to the Crown Court with a date being fixed for his PCMH (see Document 24). This is confirmed in a letter to Lenny (see Document 28). Lenny's solicitor is in possession of a 'through' representation order. You will see that she subsequently writes to the CPS *inter alia*, objecting to witness statements being read out at Lenny's trial (see Documents 32 and 33.) Any documents referred to that are not included in Appendix 1 can be located in the complete *R v Lenny Whyte* case study contained in our Online Resource Centre.

online resource centre

FIGURE 13.1 EITHER-WAY OFFENCE—GENERAL SEQUENCE OF EVENTS

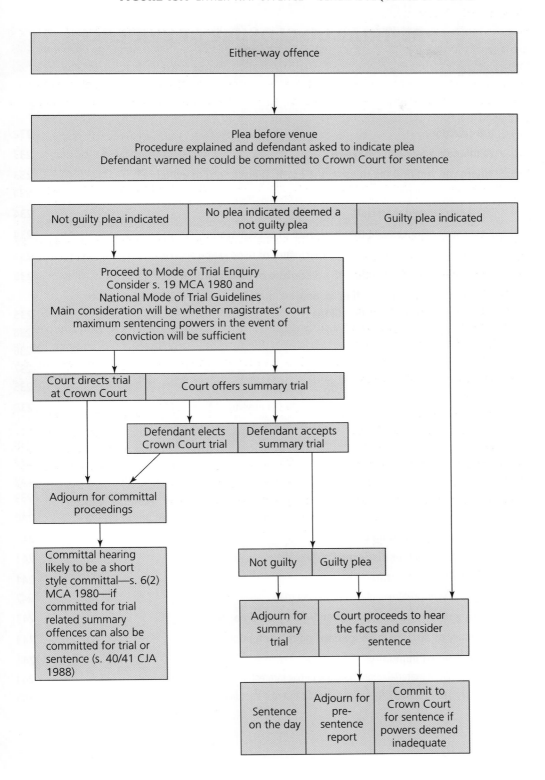

14.1 INTRODUCTION

At a number of stages in a criminal case the rules governing the pre-trial disclosure of evidence impose extensive obligations on the prosecution. The precise operation of the rules depends on the classification of the offence that is being tried. You will therefore need to cross-reference this chapter to earlier and later chapters where issues of pre-trial disclosure of evidence arise.

The rules relating to the pre-trial disclosure of evidence apply for the most part to the prosecution and are critical to a defendant's right to a fair trial. Clearly a defendant cannot be expected to defend allegations made against him unless he is aware of the evidence that will be given in support of those allegations. It would be wrong for the prosecution (with its available resources) to withhold evidence that weakens the prosecution case. Although the aim in the adversarial system is to win, there are wider obligations on the prosecution to assist the search for the truth and to ensure that a miscarriage of justice does not occur.

The right to the pre-trial disclosure of evidence is enshrined in the European Convention on Human Rights (ECHR) as being fundamental to the right to a fair trial under Article 6(1). Article 6(3)(b) provides:

'Everyone charged with a criminal offence has the right to be informed promptly, in a language which he understands and in detail of the nature and cause of the accusation against him.'

As well as supporting the defendant's right to a fair trial, the pre-trial disclosure of evidence greatly assists the administration of justice by enabling the court and the parties to identify the issues that are likely to be disputed at trial. The parties' pre-trial preparations are therefore focused on these issues and the trial is less likely to be diverted by having to deal with unexpected, subsidiary matters. There are also time-saving advantages in requiring pre-trial disclosure. On the basis of the disclosed evidence, a client can be advised whether, for example, to elect trial on indictment for an either-way offence or whether to plead guilty at an early stage to attract the full sentencing discount. A timely guilty plea also saves considerable time and expense for the parties and the court. Pre-trial disclosure may lead to the evidence of some prosecution witnesses being agreed in written form without the requirement for them to attend court, thereby saving time and expense.

14.2 WITHHOLDING RELEVANT EVIDENCE

Occasionally, the prosecution or a third party will resist the disclosure of otherwise relevant and admissible evidence on the basis that that it is 'sensitive' and it is not in the wider public interest for it to be heard in the public domain of a criminal trial. The defence, however, may wish to see such evidence to evaluate it and perhaps challenge it. Where disclosure is opposed on this basis, the prosecution will claim the evidence is covered by public interest immunity (PII). While many aspects of disclosure are regulated by statute, the principles relating to PII remain governed by the common law. We briefly consider the law relating to PII towards the end of this chapter.

14.3 WHERE CAN YOU FIND THE RULES ON THE PRE-TRIAL DISCLOSURE OF EVIDENCE?

The disclosure process has become unnecessarily complicated, for the following reasons:

* The rules are not contained in one place and have developed piecemeal.

* Some of the rules are embodied in statute while others have developed as a result of the common law.

* Guidance on the application of the rules is found in the non-statutory source of the Attorney-General's Guidelines on Disclosure. The importance of these guidelines cannot be underestimated. They can be accessed from our Online Resource Centre, and at http://www.attorneygeneral.gov.uk/attachments/disclosure.doc. online resource centre

* The disclosure regime applies differently depending on the classification of the offence.

* The Criminal Justice Act 2003 has introduced important changes to the rules governing the pre-trial disclosure obligations of both the prosecution and the defence.

14.3.1 DISCLOSURE PROTOCOLS

The Judicial Communications Office has published two draft disclosure protocols detailed below:

* *Protocol for the Provision of Advance Information and Prosecution Evidence and Disclosure of Unused Material in the Magistrates' Courts* (June 2006);
* *Disclosure: A Protocol for the Control and Management of Unused Material in the Crown Court* (February 2006).

The protocols can be accessed at: http://www.judiciary.gov.uk/judgment_guidance/protocols. A link on the web-links section of our Online Resource Centre will take you to them.

The protocols provide a comprehensive explanation of the law relating to pre-trial disclosure and contain important guidance. They are effective in four pilot areas but the expectation is that courts (in the management of disclosure issues) and practitioners will use and refer to the guidance as they represent best practice. In this sense the protocols compliment the Criminal Procedure Rules: Parts 1 and 3 (see Chapter 1, para. 1.11).

14.4 USED AND UNUSED MATERIAL

Central to an understanding of the disclosure rules is the distinction between 'used' and 'unused' material. These words are not defined but are adopted by us as convenient labels to assist understanding.

'Used' material refers to evidence the prosecution intends to rely on at trial and is usually disclosed during the early stages of the case. Our case studies (*R v Roger Martin, R v Lenny Whyte, R v William Hardy*) include examples of 'used material'.

'Unused' material comprises evidence which the prosecution is aware of but which will not form part of the prosecution's case against the accused at trial.

14.5 EITHER-WAY OFFENCES AND THE DISCLOSURE OF USED MATERIAL

Prior to the plea before venue/mode of trial hearing, Crim PR, Part 21 requires the Crown Prosecution Service to have served advance information on the defence. This comprises 'used' material (either a summary of the prosecution case or more usually copies of the prosecution witness statements). Disclosure at this early stage will also include a summary or copy of any tape-recorded interview. CJSSS (see Chapter 11, para. 11.16) requires this to have been served prior to the first hearing.

We have already considered in Chapter 13 the importance of obtaining advance information of the prosecution case in all but the most clear-cut of cases. You will not be able to advise your client properly on whether to plead guilty or not guilty or whether to elect trial by jury if he is pleading not guilty unless the prosecution has disclosed the substance of its case against your client and you have evaluated the strengths and weaknesses.

The rules on the further disclosure of 'used' material for either-way offences will depend on whether the case is to be tried summarily or on indictment at the Crown Court. Where the mode of trial enquiry has been adjourned for a committal hearing, the prosecution is required to serve on the defendant a 'committal bundle' prior to the committal hearing (see Chapter 13). The 'committal bundle' will be similar to advance information but more detailed. It should contain the draft indictment, prosecution witness statements and other evidence, including lists of all exhibits. All prosecution witness statements will be typed. There is no obligation on the prosecution to disclose all the evidence it intends to rely on at trial at this stage, although in practice it usually will.

Once the case is committed to the Crown Court, the disclosure provisions relating to 'unused material' are triggered. These provisions are contained in the CPIA 1996 and are considered in detail below.

If the either-way case is to be tried in the magistrates' court on a not guilty plea, provision is made for the disclosure of 'unused material' under the CPIA at this stage.

14.6 SUMMARY-ONLY OFFENCES AND THE DISCLOSURE OF USED MATERIAL

In summary proceedings, there is no statutory requirement for the prosecution to disclose the evidence that it intends to use at the trial (*R v Stratford Justices, ex p. Imbert* [1999] 2 Cr App R 276). Since this decision, the Attorney-General's Guidelines on Disclosure (para. 57) provide it is good practice for the CPS to disclose 'used' material to the defence in summary-only cases. As such, advance information is routinely made available for summary-only offences on request. Where an accused indicates an intention to plead not guilty to a summary-only offence, the provisions relating to 'unused material' under the CPIA 1996 are triggered.

14.7 INDICTABLE-ONLY OFFENCES AND THE DISCLOSURE OF USED MATERIAL

In accordance with s. 51 Crime and Disorder Act 1998, indictable-only offences must be sent forthwith to the Crown Court for trial following the defendant's initial appearance before magistrates. The procedural course of an indictable-only offence is explained in Chapter 16. The Rules of Court (Crime and Disorder Act 1998 (Service of Prosecution Evidence) Regulations 2005, SI 2005/902) provide for the disclosure of 'used' material in the 'case sent bundle' which is similar to the 'committal bundle' and should be served within 70 or 50 days (the shorter time applying to a defendant remanded in custody) of the case being sent to the Crown Court. The provisions relating to notice of additional evidence apply to any evidence not adduced in the case sent bundle which the prosecution proposes to rely on at trial.

Although advance information has no application to indictable-only offences, the CPS will normally serve available advance information at an early stage in indictable-only cases where a request is made and where fairness requires such disclosure. This is particularly important as bail is more likely to be contested in indictable-only offences and at an application for bail, one factor the court will have regard to is the strength of evidence against the accused (see Chapter 12). The requirement is endorsed in para. 55 of the Attorney-General's Guidelines on Disclosure.

14.8 DISCLOSURE PROVISIONS RELATING TO 'UNUSED' MATERIAL AND THE CRIMINAL PROCEDURE AND INVESTIGATIONS ACT 1996 (CPIA)

The disclosure of 'unused' material is regulated by the Criminal Procedure and Investigations Act 1996 (CPIA). Some of the changes to the disclosure of unused material under the CJA 2003 came into force in April 2005; others have not. Before April 2005, disclosure involved a three-stage process:

• primary prosecution disclosure;

• service of a defence statement;

• secondary prosecution disclosure.

Under the CJA 2003, the disclosure process is replaced with initial disclosure (embracing what was previously primary and secondary disclosure) and an ongoing duty on the CPS to keep disclosure under review throughout the proceedings.

The defence solicitor will need to consider the application of the CPIA 1996 in all contested summary proceedings and in all contested cases to be tried on indictment. Our case study *R v Lenny Whyte* is an example of an either-way offence which is to be tried on indictment. The requirements of the CPIA 1996 are illustrated in this case as part of preparation for trial on indictment (see Chapters 16 and 17).

The substantive provisions of the CPIA 1996 are supplemented by a detailed Code of Practice in Part II of the CPIA 1996 (s. 23) and by the Attorney-General's Guidelines on Disclosure and the disclosure protocols highlighted at 14.3.1. The Code of Practice has been revised to take account of the CJA 2003 changes. The Code can be accessed via the web-links section of the Online Resource Centre and at http://police.homeoffice.gov.uk.

 online resource centre

14.8.1 KEEPING TRACK OF INVESTIGATIVE MATERIAL

The Code of Practice (para. 5) requires the recording and retention of all relevant information and material gathered or generated during an investigation. A disclosure officer has to be appointed to each investigation, who may be a member of the investigative team. The requirement to record extends to all types of information, including evidence obtained during the investigation (searches of the person or his property), evidence generated by the investigation (incriminating admissions and no comment interviews, etc.) and information received orally. Paragraph 5 of the Code specifies the types of relevant material which should be routinely retained in a criminal case. It includes:

- crime reports;
- custody records;
- records of telephone calls, e.g. 999 calls;
- final versions of witness statements (and draft versions, where their content differs from the final version);
- interview records;
- communications between the police and experts such as forensic scientists, reports of work carried out by experts, and schedules of scientific material prepared by the expert for the investigator, for the purposes of criminal proceedings;
- information provided by an accused person which indicates an explanation for the offence with which he has been charged;
- any material casting doubt on the reliability of a confession;
- any material casting doubt on the reliability of a witness;
- records of first description of a suspect by each potential witness who purports to identify or describe the suspect, whether or not the description differs from that of subsequent descriptions by that or other witness.

Where there is any doubt about the relevance of material gathered or generated, the investigator must retain it.

14.8.2 DISCLOSURE SCHEDULES

Paragraph 6 of the Code requires material which is relevant to the investigation and which the disclosure officer thinks will not form part of the prosecution's case to be listed in a schedule of non-sensitive material. If the disclosure officer believes the material to be sensitive it must be listed on a separate sensitive schedule.

Sensitive material is material which the investigating officer believes would not be in the public interest to disclose, including evidence relating to national security or police informants, location of surveillance positions and material relating to children.

The schedules are then passed to the Crown Prosecution Service. The schedules must be prepared in the following instances:

- where the offence is indictable only; or
- it is an either-way offence likely to be tried in the Crown Court; or
- where the defendant is likely to plead not guilty to a matter which is to be tried summarily.

The material must be listed in the schedule with sufficient detail to enable the prosecutor to decide whether he needs to inspect it before a decision is made to disclose it to the defence. In addition to the listing of material, the disclosure officer must provide the prosecutor with a copy of any material which undermines the prosecution's case, including records of first description of a suspect and information relating to any explanation by the defendant for the offence charged (para. 7). The schedules may need to be amended in the light of consideration of the evidence by a CPS lawyer.

Section 26 CPIA 1996 makes the Code admissible in evidence where breach of its provisions is relevant to a question arising in the proceedings and further provides that a failure by the police to observe the Code will not result in civil or criminal liability. A failure by the prosecution to comply with its disclosure obligations clearly affects the fairness of the proceedings and may be the subject of a defence application to stay the proceedings for abuse of process.

4.8.3 INITIAL DISCLOSURE S. 3 CPIA 1996 (AS AMENDED BY S. 32 CJA 2003)

'The prosecutor must—

(a) disclose to the accused any prosecution material which has not previously been disclosed to the accused and which might reasonably be considered capable of undermining the case for the prosecution against the accused or of assisting the case for the accused.'

In *R v Vasilou* [2000] 4 Archbold News 1, the Court of Appeal held this would include the disclosure of a prosecution witness's previous convictions.

The test to be applied under s. 3 CPIA is objective and requires the prosecutor to decide which evidence might reasonably undermine the prosecution case. In the Attorney-General's Guidelines on Disclosure (paras. 10–14), material that can reasonably be considered capable of undermining the prosecution case against the accused or assisting the defence case will include:

'10 . . . . anything that tends to show a fact inconsistent with the elements of the case that must be proved by the prosecution. Material can fulfil the disclosure test:

(a) by the use to be made of it in cross-examination; or

(b) by its capacity to support submissions that could lead to:

    (i) the exclusion of evidence; or

    (ii) a stay of proceedings; or

    (iii) a court or tribunal finding that any public authority had acted incompatibly with the accused's rights under the ECHR, or

(c) by its capacity to suggest an explanation or partial explanation of the accused's actions.

11. In deciding whether material may fall to be disclosed under paragraph 10, especially (b)(ii), prosecutors must consider whether disclosure is required in order for a proper application to be made. The purpose of this paragraph is not to allow enquiries to support speculative arguments or for the manufacture of defences.

12. Examples of material that might reasonably be considered capable of undermining the prosecution case or of assisting the case for the accused are:

- any material casting doubt upon the accuracy of any prosecution evidence;

- any material which may point to another person, whether charged or not (including a co-accused) having involvement in the commission of the offence;

- any material which may cast doubt upon the reliability of a confession;

- any material that might go to the credibility of a prosecution witness;

- any material that might support a defence that is either raised by the defence or apparent from the prosecution papers;

- any material which may have a bearing on the admissibility of any prosecution evidence.

13. It should also be borne in mind that while items of material viewed in isolation may not be reasonably considered to be capable of undermining the prosecution case or assisting the accused, several items together can have that effect.

14. Material relating to the accused's mental or physical health, intellectual capacity, or to any ill treatment which the accused may have suffered when in the investigator's custody is likely to fall within the test for disclosure set out in paragraph 8 above.'

Disclosure under s. 3 CPIA is limited to information in the prosecutor's possession or which the prosecutor has inspected. The prosecutor's disclosure duty depends on the efficiency and honesty of the disclosure officer who prepares the schedule. Disclosure can be made by either giving a copy of the material to the defence or allowing the defence to inspect it at a reasonable time and place.

If no initial disclosure is available, the CPS must provide a written statement to the defendant confirming this. Along with initial disclosure the CPS must also disclose a copy of the schedule of non-sensitive material prepared by the disclosure officer in the case.

14.8.4 INITIAL DISCLOSURE TIME-LIMITS

In the case of a summary trial, standard directions give the prosecution 28 days from the date of the defendant's not guilty plea to serve initial disclosure. There is no set time-limit for the service of unused material for cases to be tried on indictment. Practice differs between CPS areas. In some areas the CPS will comply with its obligations under s. 3 CPIA when it serves the 'case sent bundle' in an indictable-only offence or committal bundle in an either-way offence to be tried on indictment. In other areas, s. 3 CPIA disclosure is served 14 days after the committal hearing or as directed by the trial judge at the preliminary case management hearing before the Crown Court.

14.9 DEFENCE DISCLOSURE UNDER THE CPIA 1996 (AS AMENDED BY CJA 2003)

The biggest and most controversial change under the CJA 2003 relates to defence disclosure. The provisions are contained in ss. 33–36 CPIA and will amend the current s. 6 CPIA to include ss. 6A, 6B, 6C, 6D and 6E. Submitting a defence statement is compulsory in all cases to be tried on indictment (s. 5 CPIA). It is voluntary for cases to be tried in the magistrates' court (s. 6 CPIA). The defendant's failure to comply with any of the obligations imposed by the CPIA 1996 may result in an adverse inference being drawn under s. 11 CPIA 1996.

14.9.1 TIME IN WHICH TO SERVE DEFENCE STATEMENT

The accused has 14 days to file a defence statement in compliance with s. 5 CPIA 1996. Time runs from the date on which the prosecution complies or purports to comply with its obligations under s. 3. The inclusion of the words 'purporting to comply' is worth highlighting. It implies partial disclosure is enough to trigger the defence disclosure obligation under s. 5.

The defence can apply for an extension of the time-limit before it expires but the decision to extend lies in the discretion of the court.

4.9.2 WHAT MUST A DEFENCE STATEMENT CONTAIN?

Section 6A stipulates that a defence statement must be in writing and must:

(a) set out the nature of the accused's defence including any particular defences on which he intends to rely;

(b) indicate the matters of fact on which he takes issue with the prosecution;

(c) set out, in the case of each matter, why he takes issue with the prosecution; and

(d) indicate any point of law (including any point as to the admissibility of evidence) which he wishes to take, and any authority on which he intends to rely for that purpose.

A defence statement that discloses an alibi must give particulars including the witness's name, address and date of birth or as many of these details that are known to the accused when the statement is given, including any information in the accused's possession which might be of material assistance in identifying or finding any such witness. There is a continuing duty on the accused to provide this information if it comes to light after service of the defence statement.

As a result of s. 6A, defence statements must be much more detailed than was previously required. This level of detail no doubt causes considerable practical difficulties for defence solicitors who may sometimes struggle to obtain clear instructions from a client within a very tight time frame.

4.9.3 SERVICE OF AN UPDATED DEFENCE STATEMENT

There is now a requirement on the accused to serve an updated defence statement nearer the start of the trial (s. 6B CPIA 1996, inserted by s. 33 CJA 2003). Alternatively, the defendant may provide a witness statement stating that he has made no changes to the defence statement which has already been served.

Provision is made in s. 33 CJA 2003 (amending s. 5 CPIA 1996) for defence statements to be served on a co-accused on the application of any party or by the court of its own motion. The principle of fairness to each co-defendant would normally require disclosure to be mutual.

4.9.4 NOTIFYING THE PROSECUTION OF INTENDED WITNESSES (NOT YET IN FORCE)

Section 34 CJA inserts s. 6C into the CPIA 1996 and will require a defendant to indicate whether he intends to call any persons as witnesses. If defence witnesses are to be called, the defendant must provide details which include the names, address and date of birth of each witness, if known. This will enable the prosecution to run checks on the character of such witnesses before trial. The possibility of the prosecution interviewing such witnesses before trial is a distinct one. A Code of Practice in relation to this is currently being drafted. A failure to comply with this provision can result in an adverse inference being drawn under s.11 CPIA 1996 (see below).

4.9.5 NOTIFICATION OF THE DECISION TO INSTRUCT AN EXPERT WITNESS (NOT YET IN FORCE)

Section 6D has also been added to the CPIA 1996 and provides that if an accused instructs an expert witness with a view to providing opinion evidence at trial he must give to the court and the prosecutor a notice specifying the person's name and address unless included in the defence statement. Curiously, no sanctions are prescribed for non-compliance with this provision.

14.10 **DRAFTING A DEFENCE STATEMENT TO AVOID AN ADVERSE INFERENCE FROM BEING DRAWN**

Section 11 CPIA 1996 states that where the accused:

* fails to serve a defence statement (where this is compulsory);
* fails to serve a defence statement within the time limit;
* fails to serve an updated defence statement or witness statement;
* fails to serve an updated defence statement or witness statement in time;
* sets out inconsistent defences in the defence statement;
* puts forward at his trial a different defence than that set out in the defence statement;
* adduces evidence in support of alibi without having given the necessary particulars of the alibi;
* gives a witness notice but fails to do so within the relevant time; or
  * at his trial calls a witness not included or not adequately identified in a witness notice (not yet in force).

The court, or any other party (with the court's leave) may make such comment as appears appropriate and the court or jury may draw such inferences as appear proper in determining the defendant's guilt in connection with the offence for which he is being tried.

In practical terms, s. 11 CPIA 1996 is very important. Whether a defence statement is compulsory (indictable cases) or voluntary (summary cases), careful drafting is needed to avoid comment and an adverse inference being drawn.

Section 11(5) gives a court discretion as to whether comment is permissible and as a consequence whether an inference might be drawn. Importantly, under s. 11(10), a person cannot be convicted solely on an adverse inference drawn under s. 11 CPIA 1996 alone.

In excercising discretion under s. 11(5) what must the court take into account? The defendant is entitled to put forward an explanation as to why an adverse inference should not be drawn. Section 11(8) specifically requires a court to have regard to the defendant's reasons where the defendant has set out inconsistent defences before making or permitting comment. The nature of the inference drawn will therefore depend on the type of omission under s. 11 CPIA 1996 and the reasons for it. It may be that an alternative defence is put forward at trial because of a change in the prosecution's case from that indicated in the service of committal papers. It must be assumed that in this situation no adverse comment would be made.

R v Wheeler [2001] 1 Cr App R 10

The defendant gave evidence at his trial inconsistent with his defence statement. At his trial he explained there had been a mistake in his defence statement for which his solicitors accepted responsibility. This was referred to in passing by the judge in his summing-up. The Court of Appeal held the judge should have directed the jury to accept the mistake as a fact in this case. As the defendant's credibility had been at the centre of the case the conviction had to be quashed. The Court of Appeal strongly suggested it should be standard practice for defence statements to be signed by the defendant personally and should not be served on the prosecution until defence solicitors are sure as to their accuracy.

The problem identified in this case is now overcome by s. 6E CPIA 1996, as a defence statement served is deemed to be given with the authority of the accused.

The probable effect of an adverse inference drawn under s. 11 CPIA 1996 will be to cast doubt on the accused's defence. The evidential effect is similar to an adverse inference drawn from a suspect's silence under the Criminal Justice and Public Order Act 1994, which was considered in Chapter 5.

Can the defence statement be put in evidence as part of the prosecution's case? The Attorney-General's Guidelines provide at para. 37:

> 'Prosecutors cannot comment upon, or invite inferences to be drawn from, failures in defence disclosure otherwise than in accordance with section 11 of the Act. Prosecutors may cross-examine the accused on differences between the defence case put at trial and that set out in his or her defence statement. In doing so, it may be appropriate to apply to the judge under section 6E of the Act for copies of the statement to be given to a jury, edited if necessary to remove inadmissible material. Prosecutors should examine the defence statement to see whether it points to other lines of enquiry. If the defence statement does point to other reasonable lines of inquiry, further investigation is required and evidence obtained as a result of these enquiries may be used as part of the prosecution case or to rebut the defence.'

It would therefore seem that a defence statement can be put in evidence for the limited evidential purpose of proving inconsistencies in the nature of the defence or the particulars of an alibi.

4.11 PROSECUTOR'S CONTINUING DUTY

Section 7A CPIA 1996 (as amended by the CJA 2003) provides that after the prosecutor has complied with initial disclosure under s. 3 CPIA 1996 and before the accused is acquitted or convicted or the prosecutor decides not to proceed with the case (and, in particular, following the giving of a defence statement), the prosecutor must keep under review whether there is any further prosecution material that might reasonably be considered capable of undermining the prosecution case against the accused or of assisting the defence case. Following the service of a defence statement if the prosecution concludes there is no further evidence to disclose, this should be communicated to the defendant.

4.12 APPLYING FOR FURTHER DISCLOSURE

The accused will be able to apply to the court for further disclosure if he has grounds to believe there may be material which satisfies the objective test for disclosure.

The defendant can only make an application under s. 8 CPIA 1996 where he has filed a defence statement in accordance with the requirements of s. 5 or s. 6 of the Act. The defendant must prove to the court that he reasonably believes there is prosecution material which may assist his defence. The defendant must have settled grounds for the application and may not use s. 8 CPIA 1996 as a 'fishing expedition'.

You should be aware of disclosure issues at all stages and vigorously pursue legitimate requests for disclosure. A failure by the prosecution to disclose material falling within the definition of initial disclosure will give grounds for an appeal against conviction based on a material irregularity at trial although there is no guarantee the conviction will be quashed (*R v Craven* [2001] 2 Cr App R 181).

4.13 DRAFTING A DEFENCE STATEMENT

In the light of s. 11 CPIA 1996, great care should be taken when drafting a defence statement if an adverse inference is not to be drawn. You must avoid putting forward inconsistent defences so always ensure your client's instructions will not change or the trial advocate will not adopt an alternative approach. Disclosing your client's defence has implications for legal professional privilege which should be discussed with your client. You should try to ensure your client's instructions are completely accurate, that full advice has been given to your client regarding the statement and its implications and that your client checks, signs and dates his statement.

A tactical judgement has to be made about how much information the defence statement should contain. The more detail it contains the easier it is to facilitate further disclosure and the less the risk of an adverse inference being drawn from non-disclosure. Conversely, a more detailed defence statement will assist the prosecution in identifying the potential lines of cross-examination that may be raised against prosecution witnesses at trial. It is doubtful, in the light of the changes brought about by the CJA 2003 requiring a greater degree of specificity, that simply stating 'self defence'; 'no dishonest intent' or 'mistaken identity' would be sufficient to avoid an adverse inference under s. 11 (*R v Tibbs* [2001] 2 Cr App R 309).

Assistance is given to defence practitioners in the Attorney-General's Guidelines:

> 'A defence statement must comply with the requirements of section 6A of the Act. A comprehensive defence statement assists the participants in the trial to ensure that it is fair. The trial process is not well served if the defence make general and unspecified allegations and then seek far-reaching disclosure in the hope that material may turn up to make them good. The more detail a defence statement contains the more likely it is that the prosecutor will make an informed decision about whether any remaining undisclosed material might reasonably be considered capable of undermining the prosecution case or of assisting the case for the accused, or whether to advise the investigator to undertake further enquiries. It also helps in the management of the trial by narrowing down and focussing on the issues in dispute. It may result in the prosecution discontinuing the case. Defence practitioners should be aware of these considerations when advising their clients. Whenever a defence solicitor provides a defence statement on behalf of the accused it will be deemed to be given with the authority of the solicitor's client (s. 6E CPIA 1996).'

14.13.1 DEFENCE STATEMENTS AND SUMMARY TRIALS

In summary trials, the submission of a defence statement is voluntary. Why would a defendant choose to reveal the nature of his defence? The answer comes down to tactical considerations. The legal adviser knows that service of a defence statement will force the prosecutor to look again at the 'unused' material (s. 7A CPIA 1996) to see whether there is any previously undisclosed material that might assist the case for the defendant. You therefore need to carefully consider the disclosure schedule when served with initial disclosure of unused material under s. 3 of the Act, and determine whether service of a defence statement might unearth further useful disclosure. However, the service of a defence statement in summary proceedings remains rare as usually there is nothing to be gained by it.

It is not entirely clear whether the obligations under ss. 6C CPIA 1996 (to give notification of intention to call defence witnesses) and 6D (to give notification of having instructed an expert witness) apply to summary trials where a defence statement has not been served (as defence statements are optional in summary cases). It can be argued that the obligations under ss. 6C and 6D should be confined to those cases where a defence statement has been served although this view would not be consistent with the aims of the Criminal Procedure Rules. It is anticipated that any revision of the Crim PR will address the issues of disclosure under the CJA 2003.

The practical aspects of disclosure under the CPIA 1996 are considered further in the context of our case study, *R v Lenny Whyte*, in Chapter 16, which considers the preparation of cases that are to be tried on indictment. Our other case studies, *R v Roger Martin* and *R v William Hardy* do not raise CPIA 1996 disclosure issues, as the defendants in each case choose to plead guilty.

4.14 SEEKING DISCLOSURE OF INFORMATION HELD BY THIRD PARTIES

The CPIA 1996 has no application to material in the possession of third parties. Clearly, if the information has come into the hands of the police, it will fall within the disclosure regime. The Attorney-General's Guidelines (paras. 51–54) provide as follows:

> '51. There may be cases where the investigator, disclosure officer or prosecutor believes that a third party (for example, a local authority, a social services department, a hospital, a doctor, a school, a provider of forensic services) has material or information which might be relevant to the prosecution case. In such cases, if the material or information might reasonably be considered capable of undermining the prosecution case or of assisting the case for the accused prosecutors should take what steps they regard as appropriate in the particular case to obtain it.
>
> 52. If the investigator, disclosure officer or prosecutor seeks access to the material or information but the third party declines or refuses to allow access to it, the matter should not be left. If despite any reasons offered by the third party it is still believed that it is reasonable to seek production of the material or information, and the requirements of section 2 of the Criminal Procedure (Attendance of Witnesses) Act 1965 or as appropriate section 97 of the Magistrates Courts Act 1980 are satisfied, then the prosecutor or investigator should apply for a witness summons causing a representative of the third party to produce the material to the Court.
>
> 53. Relevant information which comes to the knowledge of investigators or prosecutors as a result of liaison with third parties should be recorded by the investigator or prosecutor in a durable or retrievable form (for example potentially relevant information revealed in discussions at a child protection conference attended by police officers).
>
> 54. Where information comes into the possession of the prosecution in the circumstances set out in paragraphs 51–53 above, consultation with the other agency should take place before disclosure is made: there may be public interest reasons which justify withholding disclosure and which would require the issue of disclosure of the information to be placed before the court.'

If a third party will not voluntarily disclose information, either side may issue a witness summons. A summons can be applied for under the Criminal Procedure (Attendance of Witnesses) Act 1965 (Crown Court) and s. 97 Magistrates Court Act 1980 (magistrates' court). The procedure is restricted as a summons cannot be served outside the jurisdiction and the witness must be able to give 'material evidence'. The principles which govern a court's decision to issue a summons were developed in *R v Reading Justices, ex p. Berkshire County Council* [1996] 1 Cr App R 239. Whether the prosecution or the defence apply for disclosure, the third party may resist the application on the basis of public interest immunity in accordance with the procedure set out in s. 16 CPIA (*R v Brushett* [2001] Crim LR 471). The principles relating to PII are discussed below.

4.15 SUMMARY OF DISCLOSURE OBLIGATIONS ON THE DEFENDANT

Compared to the prosecution, the disclosure obligations on the defence are limited. However, the changes brought about by the CJA 2003 have increased the obligations on the defence.

Currently, the defendant is obliged to:

* submit a defence statement in all cases to be tried on indictment in accordance with the requirements of s. 5 CPIA 1996;
* submit an updated defence statement;
* give notice of intention to call defence witnesses (not yet in force);
* give notification of names of expert instructed by the defence (not yet in force);
* if the defendant is to call an expert witness, then like the prosecution, the defendant is required to give notice under s. 81 PACE 1984 (Crim PR, Part 24) of any findings or opinion on which he proposes to rely at trial. The rules do not require a defendant to disclose

expert reports that have been commissioned but have proved to be unhelpful although, as noted above, the defence will be required to give notification of having instructed an expert under s. 6D CPIA 1996 when the provision comes into force.

14.16 PUBLIC INTEREST IMMUNITY

The public interest in the proper administration of justice which requires the disclosure of all relevant information for a court's consideration sometimes conflicts with the need to withhold information in the wider public interest. Where disclosure would be damaging to this wider public interest, the issue of public interest immunity arises. Where a claim for PII is upheld, a witness may not be asked and the prosecution (or possibly a third party) will not be ordered to disclose the relevant information.

Under s. 21(2) CPIA 1996, the prosecution's duty of disclosure at both the initial and the further disclosure stages is subject to the principles of public interest immunity.

The CPIA 1996 does not change the common law rules which determine both the procedure by which public interest claims are conducted and the principles by which they are determined. At common law, where the prosecutor believes that relevant evidence ('used' or 'unused') should be withheld on the basis of public interest immunity, an application must be made to the court. Only a court can sanction the prosecutor's view that it would not be in the public interest for the material to be disclosed to the defendant. Where an accused applies for disclosure under s. 8 CPIA 1996, s. 8(5) provides the court with the power not to order disclosure where it would be contrary to the public interest.

14.16.1 WHAT MATERIAL MIGHT DAMAGE PUBLIC INTEREST IF IT WERE TO BE DISCLOSED?

Evidence covered by the phrase 'public interest immunity' will include: documents and other material relating to national security; confidential information; the identity of police informants and undercover police officers; details of premises used for police surveillance; and information pertaining to the welfare of children.

The Code of Practice issued under the CPIA 1996 requires the disclosure officer to list sensitive information on a separate 'sensitive schedule', which is disclosed to the prosecution only.

The CPIA 1996 creates procedures (s. 14 in relation to indictable trials and s. 15 in relation to summary trials) for reviewing court orders to withhold material in the public interest and provides a means (s. 16), by which a third party can intervene where there has been a request for material held by a third party which the third party considers it would not be in the public interest to disclose. A court is required to keep the decision to withhold material from the defence under constant review. The relevant rules of court governing public interest immunity applications are contained in Crim PR, Part 25.

In a criminal case, the overriding principle which governs a judge's or magistrates' decision about whether to order disclosure is based on ensuring an innocent defendant is not convicted. This principle is derived from the judgment of Lord Taylor CJ in *R v Keane* [1994] 1 WLR 746:

> 'If the disputed material may prove the accused's innocence or avoid a miscarriage of justice, then the balance comes down resoundingly in favour of disclosing it.'

In essence, if disclosure would avoid a miscarriage of justice, there is no balancing act to be undertaken: disclosure must be ordered. If the prosecution refuses to disclose the evidence having been ordered to do so by the court, its only option will be to abandon the prosecution. On the facts in *R v Keane*, the Court of Appeal did not consider the disclosure that had been sought would prove the defendant's innocence or avoid a miscarriage of justice. It called upon trial judges to scrutinise applications for the disclosure of sensitive information with 'great care' and 'adopt a robust approach in declining to order disclosure.' The Court of Appeal went on to observe that the fuller and more specific the indications given by the defence of an issue likely to be raised, the more accurately the judge and the prosecution are able to assess the value of the material to the accused.

16.2 THE PROCEDURE FOR CLAIMING PUBLIC INTEREST IMMUNITY

The procedure governing the resolution of PII claims is set out in Crim PR, Part 25. The rules give effect to those developed at common law in the Court of Appeal's decision in *R v Davis, Johnson and Rowe* [1993] 1 WLR 613.

In most cases the prosecution is required to notify the defence that they are applying to the court for a ruling and to indicate the type of material over which the immunity is claimed. This is known as an *inter partes* application. The defence will have an opportunity to make representations to the court that the material should be disclosed as it is relevant and important to the accused's defence. On the basis of each party's submissions, the nature of the case and the significance of the evidence over which public interest immunity is being claimed, the judge will decide the issue.

In some cases it may not be in the public interest for the prosecution to reveal the category of the material to be disclosed. In these circumstances, the prosecution will notify the defence that an application has been made but will not reveal the category of the material that is the subject of the application. The application will then be made to the court and the initial hearing will be made on an *ex parte* basis without the defence attending. The judge will first consider whether the defence should be informed and have the opportunity of making representations. Where this decision is reached, an *inter partes* hearing will be held. Exceptionally, due to the highly sensitive nature of the material and the need to preserve secrecy, the prosecution will not inform the defence of its application at all.

In *Edwards v UK* (1992) 15 EHRR 417, the European Court of Human Rights (ECtHR) concluded that fairness necessitated disclosure to the defendant of all material evidence for or against the accused. However, in *Rowe and Davis v UK* (2002) 30 EHRR 1, the ECtHR concluded that the right to full disclosure is not an absolute right and can be restricted for the purpose of protecting national security, vulnerable witnesses and sources of information. Crucially, however, it held that any restriction to a defendant's rights had to be proportional and counterbalanced by procedural safeguards. The principal safeguard, the ECtHR observed, was the adoption of an adversarial procedure by which the defence is given an equal opportunity to make representations as regards the withheld material as that afforded to the prosecution. This has led to the argument that the *ex parte* procedure is incompatible with Article 6. For further consideration of this point we refer you to *Blackstone's Criminal Practice* and to the decision of the House of Lords (reviewing all the relevant authorities) in *R v C; R v H* [2004] 2 WLR 335.

For further detailed consideration of pre-trial disclosure of evidence, take a look at the Disclosure Manual of the CPS http://www.cps.gov.uk/legal/section20.

 online resource centre

KEY POINT SUMMARY

- Your client is entitled to disclosure of the evidence the prosecution intends to rely on in discharging its burden of proof.
- Unless there is a clear indication of guilt to a relatively straightforward summary-only or either-way matter, disclosure of 'used' material should always be sought as it is only on this basis that a thorough evaluation of the case against your client can be made.

- Entitlement to initial prosecution disclosure of unused material under s. 3 CPIA 1996 only arises in a case to be tried summarily where a not guilty plea is indicated.

- The submission of a defence statement is voluntary in summary cases but mandatory in indictable cases.

- Great care needs to be taken when drafting a defence statement in order to avoid an adverse inference from being drawn under s.11 CPIA 1996.

- The prosecution is obliged to keep disclosure of unused material under constant review, particularly in the light of service of a defence statement.

- Where the prosecution seeks to withhold relevant/material evidence on the ground that it is sensitive, application must be made to a court to sanction the withholding of such material.

- Important detail as regards the operation and effect of the CPIA 1996 is contained in its accompanying Code of Practice and in the Attorney-General's Guidelines on Disclosure.

- Currently, the disclosure obligation on the defence are limited compared to those on the prosecution but will become more onerous under the CJA 2003 when all the relevant provisions are fully implemented.

SELF-TEST QUESTIONS

Consider the following scenario and attempt to answer the questions posed at the conclusion.

Barry (aged 28) is charged with rape contrary to s. 1 Sexual Offences Act 2003. His victim is Tina, aged 15. The attack is alleged to have occurred in some public toilets inside a park where Barry is employed as a park attendant. Tina reported the rape to staff at the care home where she resides some two days after it was alleged to have occurred. Tina is subjected to a full forensic examination which reveals visible bruising around the vaginal area.

Having identified Barry as being the man responsible, he is arrested. He too is subject to a full forensic examination. In interview Barry denies the offence, stating Tina approached him outside the public toilets in the park offering him sex in return for money. He refused her advances. She called him a paedophile and walked off.

The attack is said to have been witnessed by Leroy aged 15. He has given a statement to the police stating he witnessed a girl matching Tina's description emerge from some public toilets in the park in a state of distress claiming she had been raped. Kelly, a friend of Tina, has given a statement to the police claiming that Barry has asked Tina for sex on a number of occasions and become aggressive when Tina refused. Barry informs you that he has observed Tina in the company of males on numerous occasions, while in the park and believes her to be sexually promiscuous. The allegations against him are a complete fabrication.

A defence witness has come forward who wishes to remain anonymous claiming that Tina is an attention seeker and that she has previously made a false accusation of rape against a male care-worker several months ago, having allegedly offered him sex. She later withdrew the allegation. Leroy is also a resident of the care-home at which Tina resides and is very much under Tina's 'control'.

Chart the various stages of disclosure in this case by answering the following:

- What is the classification of the offence with which Barry is charged?

- Can you expect advance information in this case, and if so, what do you anticipate you are likely to receive? (Think in terms of what the investigative process is likely to yield.)

- At what stage will the prosecution come under an obligation to disclose 'unused' material?

- Will you need to serve a defence statement in this case, and if so, what will the content of that statement comprise?

- Do you anticipate there may be material that the prosecution might not wish to disclose? If so, on what basis and how would the situation be resolved in procedural terms?

Analysis of these questions is provided in Appendix 4, where the scenario is further developed.

FIGURE 14.1 PRE-TRIAL DISCLOSURE OF EVIDENCE

SUMMARY-ONLY OFFENCES

- Prosecution will disclose used material in the form of advance information as a result of the Attorney-General Guidelines.

- If defendant pleads not guilty, any 'unused' material (initial disclosure) which might reasonably be considered capable of undermining the case for the prosecution or of assisting the case for the accused must be disclosed, s. 3 CPIA 1996.

- Within 14 days of initial disclosure, defence may voluntarily serve a defence statement, s. 6 CPIA 1996.

- Prosecution must serve any further 'unused' evidence which might reasonably be expected to assist the defence as disclosed in the defence statement under its continuing duty to review unused material, s. 7A CPIA 1996.

OFFENCES TRIABLE EITHER WAY

- Prosecution will disclose the substance of its case against the accused under the Advance Information Rules (Crim PR Part 21).

- The disclosure obligations on each party will then depend on whether the case is to be tried summarily or on indictment.

- If committed for trial to the Crown Court, initial disclosure of prosecution unused material should be served 14 days after committal at the latest

- If being tried before a magistrates' court as per summary offences, above.

- If being tried on indictment, as per indictable offences below.

INDICTABLE-ONLY OFFENCES AND CASES TO BE TRIED ON INDICTMENT

- Evidence and other material which the prosecution intends to use at trial will be disclosed to the defence under reg. 2 Crime and Disorder Act 1998 (Service of Prosecution Evidence) Regulations 2005 within 70 or 50 days of the case being sent to the Crown Court for trial under s. 51 Crime and Disorder Act 1998.

- Any 'unused' material (initial disclosure), which might reasonably be considered capable of undermining the case for the prosecution or of assisting the case for the accused must be disclosed, s. 3 CPIA 1996.

- Within 14 days of initial disclosure, defence must serve a defence statement, s. 5 CPIA 1996 (note the possible drawing of adverse inferences under s. 11 CPIA 1996).

- Prosecution must serve any further 'unused' evidence which might reasonably be expected to assist the defence as disclosed in the defence statement under its continuing duty to review unused material, s. 7A CPIA 1996.

15 SUMMARY PROCEEDINGS

15.1 INTRODUCTION

In this chapter we consider the steps in preparing for a summary trial. A summary trial will be held where a defendant pleads not guilty to a summary-only offence or pleads not guilty to an either-way offence where the defendant consented to summary trial at the mode of trial hearing.

Some summary-only matters can be tried in the Crown Court where they are linked to a related indictable-only offence under s. 51 Crime and Disorder Act 1988 (see Chapter 16) or they are committed for trial alongside an indictable offence under s. 40 Criminal Justice Act 1988 (see Chapter 13).

This chapter should be read in conjunction with the latter part of Chapter 11 which provides an account of the early stages of a summary/either-way offence. In this chapter we specifically consider:

- pleading guilty by post;
- the circumstances in which a defendant can be summarily tried in his absence;
- the rules governing the drafting of the information;
- the pre-trial disclosure of evidence in a summary case;

- case management;
- typical preparatory steps undertaken by a solicitor in preparation for trial;
- the procedure at a summary trial on a not guilty plea.

15.2 COMMENCING A PROSECUTION FOR A SUMMARY-ONLY MATTER

Criminal proceedings are commenced either by the police charging an individual at the police station, or by the court issuing a summons. At present, the prosecution must 'lay an information' before a court before a summons or warrant for arrest can be issued and served on the person named in the information. The terminology is set to change under s. 29 CJA 2003 which is in force in some pilot areas. When fully implemented, all public prosecutions will be commenced by the prosecutor issuing a written charge (previously the information) and a requisition (previously a summons) requiring the person named in the charge to appear before a magistrates' court. 'Laying an information', followed by the issue of a summons, will continue to be available for private prosecutions.

5.2.1 TIME-LIMITS FOR THE PROSECUTION OF SUMMARY-ONLY OFFENCES

A magistrates' court may not try a defendant for a summary offence unless the information/requisition was laid within six months of the commission of the offence alleged (s. 127(1) MCA 1980). This provision applies to the majority of summary-only offences although the time-limit can be expressly overriden by statute.

15.3 PLEADING GUILTY BY POST

In some summary cases the defendant need not initially attend court where under s. 12 MCA 1980, he pleads guilty by sending a letter to court in the following circumstances:

(a) the offence is summary only and;

(b) the proceedings have been started by summons (or written charge and requisition).

It is up to the prosecution (in the exercise of its discretion) to determine whether the accused should be given the option of pleading guilty by post. Until the implementation of s. 308 CJA 2003, pleading guilty by post was only permitted for offences carrying a maximum penalty of three months' imprisonment, but this restriction has now been lifted.

Where the defendant pleads guilty by post, the prosecution must serve on the defendant:

(i) the summons/requisition;

(ii) a brief statement of the facts upon which the prosecution is to rely, or a copy of any statements written in compliance with s. 9 CJA 1967; and

(iii) any information relating to the defendant that will be put before the court; and

(iv) a notice explaining the procedure.

If the defendant wishes to plead guilty, he must notify the court and may submit a written statement in mitigation of sentence. The court proceeds on the basis of the written statements submitted by both sides which must be read to the court. The magistrates may refuse to accept a guilty plea if the statement in mitigation reveals a defence or the plea is unclear. If the guilty plea is accepted, the magistrates can sentence immediately, depending on the type of sentence or following an adjournment requiring the defendant's attendance.

15.4 **SUMMARY TRIAL IN THE ABSENCE OF THE DEFENDANT**

There are a number of situations in which a defendant can be tried summarily in his absence.

Where a defendant fails to answer a summons/requisition to appear and it is established that the summons/requisition was served on the defendant within a reasonable time before the hearing, s. 11 MCA 1980 permits the court to enter a not guilty plea and for the case to be proved in his absence. If the offence alleged is summary-only, it is sufficient to prove the summons was sent by first class post to the defendant's last known address or usual address. Where the summons/requisition alleges an either-way offence, the prosecution must establish the defendant was aware of the proceedings.

Subject to proof of service, the burden of proving a case in the absence of the defendant falls on the prosecution. It may discharge its burden either by calling witnesses or if s. 9 CJA 1967 statements (see 15.8.7) were served with the summons/requisition, by reading the statements to the court. Where it is necessary to adjourn for proof, the court must send the defendant an adjournment notice. If the adjournment notice is not served, the prosecution will not be able to prove in the defendant's absence even though there is proof of service of the summons itself.

Where the defendant was present in court on the last occasion, he is deemed to be aware of the next stage of the proceedings. This will normally be the case in an either-way offence as the defendant is required to be present for the mode of trial proceedings. Where it is clear that the defendant knows of the trial date and there is no explanation for the defendant's absence, the court can either choose to adjourn the trial and issue a warrant for the defendant's arrest without bail (s. 13 MCA 1980) or proceed to try the defendant in his absence. In the latter case, if the defendant is represented, his solicitor can still put the prosecution to prove its case and make submissions and a closing speech. If the defendant is merely on summons to attend, the court might consider an adjournment and issue a warrant backed for bail to ensure the defendant's attendance at the adjourned hearing. If there is an explanation for the defendant's absence, the court is more likely to accept a defence request for the trial to be adjourned to a later date.

A trial in the defendant's absence, particularly an unrepresented defendant is most likely to result in a conviction as the evidence against the defendant is not contradicted. Having convicted an absent defendant, a court may choose to sentence in his absence or adjourn sentence and issue a warrant for the defendant's arrest.

15.4.1 **DEFENDANT UNAWARE OF COURT PROCEEDINGS**

If the defendant was unaware of the proceedings, within 21 days of finding out about the proceedings, s. 14 MCA 1980 permits him to make a statutory declaration that he knew nothing of the proceedings. The declaration may be made before the court or a solicitor. The effect of the declaration is that the summons and all the proceedings are void. The information, however, remains valid.

15.5 **JOINDER OF OFFENCES AND DEFENDANTS IN THE INFORMATION**

At the commencement of a summary trial, the defendant is asked to plead guilty or not guilty to the information containing the charge(s).

The general rule is that an information may only charge one defendant with a single offence unless the prosecution allege that the offence was committed jointly by more than one defendant.

Example

Ben and Chris are charged with common assault arising out of a fight outside a nightclub on 23 January. The prosecution alleges both defendants assaulted the victim. As both defendants committed the offence jointly, each will be tried on the same information.

The information/written charge should only charge one offence, (Crim PR Part 7.3). An information/written charge which charges more than one offence is bad for duplicity and the prosecutor will have to decide which charge he wishes to proceed with.

In some situations, where the defendant faces more than one charge or several accused are charged in separate informations, the court may try a defendant on the same occasion on both charges. Informations may be tried together where:

- the defence agree to the informations being tried together; or
- the court orders the offences to be tried together because it is in the interests of justice to do so and the offences form part of a series of offences of the same or similar character.

If the defence does not agree to the informations being tried together, for the alternative ground to apply, the court has to be satisfied that the offences are part of a series of offences of the same or similar character. This requires, firstly, there should be some connection between them in time and place and the nature of the offences. Secondly, the court will take into account whether it is in 'the interests of justice' for the informations to be tried together. Guidance on the application of the interest of justice test is provided by the House of Lords in *Chief Constable of Norfolk v Clayton* [1983] 2 AC 473. When applying the interests of justice test, the court must consider the convenience to the prosecution of having the informations tried together against any injustice that might arise to the defendant. In most cases the defence will resist having the informations tried together. A common submission is that it is not in the interests of justice as the evidence from one offence might unfairly prejudice the magistrates in deciding a defendant's guilt in respect to the other offence.

 Example

(i) Over the course of three days Lee commits four offences of theft and obtaining property by deception by going from shop-to-shop and obtaining goods from each of them using a false credit card.

(ii) In a domestic dispute over the course of two weeks, Neil commits common assault against his ex-girlfriend, her new boyfriend and his ex-girlfriend's mother.

(iii) Julie steals two books from the library. The following day she committed an offence of careless driving.

In examples (i) and (ii) the two conditions for the informations to be tried together appear to be satisfied. First, the offences are part of a series of offences of the same or similar nature. There is also proximity between them in terms of time. Second, the court would rule that it is in the interests of justice for the informations to be tried together after considering the balance of convenience to the prosecution and the potential prejudice to Lee and Neil.

In example (iii) the grounds for trying the informations together are not satisfied. As the defence will not agree and the offences are not the same or of a similar nature, Julie will be tried separately on each information.

15.5.1 AMENDING THE INFORMATION/WRITTEN CHARGE

What is the position if details contained in the information/written charge are incorrect or inconsistent with the evidence called by the prosecution? Section 123 MCA 1980 permits the information to be amended at any stage of the proceedings provided the error has not caused injustice to the defendant. Examples of minor errors which would not cause injustice are where the defendant's name or the location of the offence is misspelt in the information. Where the error is regarded as 'substantial', the court may allow the amendment but will also grant an adjournment to allow the defence to deal with any issues arising out of the amendment, s. 123 MCA 1980.

 Example

Rashid is charged with driving a motor vehicle with a defective tyre. The written charge details the defective tyre to be 'on the rear offside of the vehicle'. In fact, the defective tyre was on the rear near-side of the vehicle. In this situation, amending the written charge will be permitted and it is unlikely that the error would be regarded as substantial.

Majinder is charged with common assault, which is wrongly specified in the written charge as having been committed on 23 March. In fact the alleged offence occurred on 26 March. As Majinder has an alibi for his whereabouts on 23 March, it is likely that the proposed amendment is 'substantial' and the court will adjourn the proceedings to enable the defence to deal with the amendment.

15.6 THE EARLY STAGES OF A SUMMARY-ONLY/EITHER-WAY OFFENCE

As we saw in Chapter 11, in the early stages of a summary-only or either-way offence the defence solicitor will advise his client about his plea. Before giving advice, the solicitor will need to:

- interview his client;
- obtain and evaluate advance information (prosecution evidence);
- obtain a representation order on behalf of his client;
- interview any potential defence witnesses.

15.7 TAKING A PLEA

In accordance with CJSSS (see Chapter 11, para. 11.16.1), for all cases commenced by charge, the defendant is expected to enter a plea at the first hearing before the magistrates' court. A guilty plea will require the court to pass sentence either on the day or following an adjournment for a pre-sentence report. Sentencing practice is considered in Part V.

Where the defendant indicates a not guilty plea in a case to be tried summarily, CJSSS requires the case should normally be listed for trial within 6–8 weeks. This requires both the CPS and the defence to have up-to-date information on witness availability so that a firm trial date can be set. Once the case has been listed for trial, standard directions in preparation for trial apply.

Where a not guilty plea is entered in summary proceedings commenced by summons, the matter may be listed for a pre-trial review which is conducted before a legal adviser/court clerk prior to being listed for trial. The purpose of the pre-trial review is to identify the triable issue(s) in the case; set a firm date for trial and make directions to progress the case to trial. Binding rulings can be made at pre-trial hearings before a magistrates' court (s. 45 (Sch. 3) Courts Act 2003).

.7.1 STANDARD DIRECTIONS AND CASE MANAGEMENT

Provision is made under the Criminal Procedure Rules for standard directions to apply in all cases to be tried in the magistrates' court. The directions allow the parties eight weeks to prepare for trial or 14 weeks where there is to be expert evidence. A copy of the standard case management directions form can be found at the end of this chapter. The standard directions provide for the service of used and unused material, applications for special measures, hearsay and bad character within time-limits.

In preparing for summary trial the parties must have regard to the overriding objective in Crim PR, Part 1 and assist the court in the active management of the case. This requires each party to identify a case progression officer whose duty it is to ensure compliance with court directions and to keep the court informed of case progression issues. The rules require the parties to take reasonable steps to ensure attendance of witnesses and to promptly inform the court of anything that might affect the duration or progress of the case. In order to manage the trial, Crim PR, Part 3.10 provides:

(a)   the court must establish, with the active assistance of the parties, what disputed issues they intend to explore; and

(b)   the court may require a party to identify:

   (i)   which witnesses that party wants to give oral evidence,

   (ii)   the order in which that party wants those witnesses to give their evidence,

   (iii) whether that party requires an order compelling the attendance of a witness,

   (iv) what arrangements are desirable to facilitate the giving of evidence by a witness,

   (v)   what arrangements are desirable to facilitate the participation of any other person, including the defendant,

   (vi) what written evidence that party intends to introduce,

   (vii) what other material, if any, that person intends to make available to the court in the presentation of the case,

   (viii) whether that party intends to raise any point of law that could affect the conduct of the trial or appeal, and

   (ix) what timetable that party proposes and expects to follow.'

15.8   PREPARING FOR TRIAL

Where the case is listed for trial (and having regard to the Crim PR Part 3 outlined above), the defence solicitor should begin preparing for a summary trial as soon as possible. This may include some or all of the following.

15.8.1   VISITING THE CRIME SCENE

Visiting the crime scene can give the defence solicitor a better understanding of the circumstances in which the alleged offence occurred. It is often useful to prepare a plan or take photographs, especially in road traffic collision cases where there is a dispute between the prosecution and your client about, for example, the position of the vehicle(s) on the road.

15.8.2   INSTRUCTING EXPERTS

Many summary offences do not require expert evidence but in those cases where expert evidence is required, you should instruct your expert witness at the earliest opportunity. If your client is the subject of a representation order, you should obtain the written authority of the Legal Services Commission using Form CDS4, before formally instructing the expert. It is common practice to support your application by explaining the reason why an expert is required and what their fee will be.

Where either the prosecution or the defence intends to call expert evidence at trial, Crim PR Part 24 require the pre-trial disclosure of the expert's report both to the court and to the other party.

15.8.3 THE PRE-TRIAL DISCLOSURE OF EVIDENCE

The pre-trial disclosure of evidence in relation to all classification of offences is considered in Chapter 14. In cases that are to be tried summarily we simply remind you of the key provisions.

The rules governing the pre-trial disclosure of 'used material' are contained in Crim PR, Part 21 and the Attorney-General's Guidance on Disclosure. Strictly speaking they apply to either-way offences, but are invoked in relation to summary-only offences. They require the Crown Prosecution Service to serve on the defence either a summary of the prosecution case or more commonly copies of prosecution witness statements. This also extends to a summary of any tape-recorded interview and records held under PACE 1984.

Where an accused indicates a not guilty plea in a summary case, the provisions governing 'unused material' under the CPIA 1996 are triggered.

15.8.4 'UNUSED' MATERIAL

Section 3 CPIA 1996 requires the prosecution to provide the defendant with initial disclosure (any evidence not previously disclosed, which might reasonably be considered capable of undermining the case for the prosecution or of assisting the case for the accused). This obligation arises in cases to be tried summarily where the defendant pleads not guilty. Standard directions (see para. 15.7.1 above) make provision for the service of 'unused material' by the prosecution. After service of initial prosecution disclosure the defendant may choose to file a defence statement in compliance with s. 6 CPIA 1996, indicating on which matters he takes issue with the prosecution case and for what reasons and giving particulars of any defence or alibi he intends to rely on at trial. The filing of a defence statement is voluntary in summary cases.

In those very exceptional situations when a defence statement is served in a summary case, the prosecution must fulfil its ongoing obligation to keep disclosure under review in accordance with s. 7A CPIA 1996. In particular the CPS must disclose material which has not previously been disclosed and which might reasonably be expected to assist the accused's case as disclosed in the defence statement.

Where a defence statement is filed, the court may comment or draw adverse inferences from disclosure which is late, defective or inconsistent with the defence case at trial. In view of these potential sanctions, the question must be asked why would a defence solicitor ever choose to serve a defence statement in a summary trial. The disclosure requirements under the CPIA 1996 and the tactical considerations involved in drafting a defence statement are explored in much greater detail in Chapter 14.

15.8.5 AN EVALUATION OF THE EVIDENCE

Having obtained full disclosure of the prosecution's case and an updated proof of evidence from the defendant and any defence witnesses, the defence solicitor should begin to evaluate the strength of the prosecution's case and to formulate a strategy for defending the case in court. In preparing for trial it will be necessary to research the elements of the offence(s) charged so the advocate knows the facts in issue which the prosecution must prove to secure the defendant's conviction. Research may also be necessary where the defence intends to challenge prosecution evidence at trial. The defence advocate should come to court prepared to cite relevant statutory provisions and case law in support of his submission to have prosecution evidence excluded.

5.8.6 SECURING THE ATTENDANCE OF WITNESSES AT TRIAL

As the trial approaches, you will have formed a clear idea of how you intend to defend your client in court. An important part of your preparation is to decide which of the witnesses from whom you have taken a proof of evidence, will be called to give evidence for the defence. Initially, you will write to a prospective witness giving full details of the time and location of the court hearing asking him to attend voluntarily or to produce a document. If the witness does not reply or indicates that he is not willing to appear voluntarily it will be necessary to apply to the court for a witness summons to be issued. A summons will be granted where the court considers it is in the interests of justice to secure the person's attendance to give evidence or produce a document or thing. The specific rules relating to the issue and service of a witness summons are contained in Crim PR Part 28.

Some witnesses will be reluctant to attend even where they have been served with a witness summons. In this situation, s. 97(2) MCA 1980 authorises an arrest warrant to be issued against the witness to ensure his attendance.

5.8.7 STATEMENTS ADMISSIBLE UNDER S. 9 CRIMINAL JUSTICE ACT 1967

Where either the prosecution or the defence consider it is unnecessary for a particular witness to attend the trial to give oral evidence, an application can be made to the opposing side to give consent for the witness's evidence to be read to the court in the witness's absence under s. 9 Criminal Justice Act 1967. Such statements are entirely appropriate for a witness whose evidence is not in dispute and can be agreed between the parties.

For a statement to be admissible under s. 9 CJA 1967, the following conditions must be met:

* the statement must be signed by the maker, and must contain a declaration that it is true to the best of his knowledge and belief, and that he made it knowing that if it were tendered in evidence he might be prosecuted for wilfully stating in it anything he knew to be false or did not believe to be true; and
* before the trial a copy of the statement has been served on the other parties in the case; and
* none of the parties object to the witness's statement being tendered in evidence in the witness's absence; and
* the statement's contents would have been admissible if the witness had given oral evidence.

If objection is taken, the statement will not be admissible under s. 9 and the witness will have to attend court to give oral evidence unless the statement falls within another admissible hearsay provision.

15.8.8 DISPUTED EVIDENCE

Disputes about the admissibility of evidence do not arise as frequently in the magistrates' courts as at trials in the Crown Court. However, where evidence is disputed, the matter will be decided by the magistrates during the course of the trial or at the beginning of the trial. In some circumstances a *voir dire*, or trial within a trial, will be held (*R v Liverpool Juvenile Court, ex p. R* [1987] 2 All ER 668). At a *voir dire*, evidence may be called and legal submissions made as to why the disputed evidence should be excluded. If the magistrates decide the evidence is inadmissible, no further mention will be made of it and no reliance can be placed on it. A *voir dire* will commonly be held where the defendant disputes the admissibility of a confession or seeks to have identification evidence excluded for breaching Code D. The *voir dire* is much more effective in the Crown Court where there is a strict division of functions between the judge and the jury. *Voir dire* issues in the Crown Court are determined in the absence of the jury. This is not possible in the magistrates' court as the magistrates are arbiters of both fact and law. The use of pre-trial binding rulings under the Courts Act 2003 (highlighted at para. 15.7 above) goes some way to reducing the potential prejudice arising from the *voir dire* procedure in summary proceedings as the trial bench will be differently composed.

15.9 RIGHTS OF AUDIENCE BEFORE MAGISTRATES' COURT AND TERMS OF ADDRESS

Trainee solicitors do not have rights of audience before the magistrates' courts as only solicitors/barristers and soon, Designated CPS Case Workers, will have limited rights of audience to conduct trials in relation to non-imprisonable summary offences. Although you do not have rights of audience at this stage, the magistrates' court is an invaluable learning experience—take full advantage to watch and learn.

When addressing a district judge, the address is 'Sir' or 'Madam'. A lay bench can be addressed collectively as 'Your Worships'. Alternatively an advocate may choose to address the chairperson of the bench and say 'Madam and your colleagues' or 'Sir and your colleagues'. When referring to the magistrates' adviser, it is customary to state 'Your learned legal adviser' and when referring to your opposing advocate, you might say 'My friend for the prosecution' or, in the case of a barrister, 'My learned friend'.

15.10 THE PROCEDURE AT A SUMMARY TRIAL ON A NOT GUILTY PLEA

Where the defendant pleads not guilty, the whole prosecution case is put in issue. The relevant rules of court relating to the conduct of summary trials are contained in Crim PR, Part 37.

(1) The hearing begins with the defendant's full name, address and date of birth and the name of his solicitor being given to the court.

(2) The charge(s) will be put to the defendant by the justices' legal adviser and the defendant confirms that he pleads not guilty to the charge(s).

(3) The prosecutor may make an opening speech by addressing the court with regard to:

- the prosecution's version of the facts;
- the witnesses to be called in support of the prosecution case; and
- any legal issues that will arise.

(4) The first prosecution witness is questioned by the prosecutor in examination-in-chief, the purpose of which is to obtain answers from the witness which supports the prosecution case. All factual witnesses must remain outside the courtroom until they have given their evidence. Each witness called will firstly take the oath or affirmation and state their name. It is customary to point out to the witness that they should speak clearly and at a slow pace, addressing their answers to the bench. Certain witness may give their evidence with the benefit of special measures. The rules relating to witness testimony are explained in Chapter 20.

(5) The witness may then be cross-examined by the defence with a view to undermining the accuracy or truthfulness of what the witness said during examination-in-chief and/or to undermine the witness's credibility.

(6) The prosecution may re-examine the witness to repair any damage that may have been inflicted on the witness during cross-examination.

(7) The magistrates may ask the witness questions at any time but in most courts the convention applies that the witness will be questioned after the parties have finished asking questions.

The process of witness testimony of examination-in-chief, cross-examination and re-examination continues until all the prosecution witnesses have testified.

(8) As well as calling witnesses to give oral evidence, the prosecution may also put its case to the court by presenting evidence in other forms including statements of witnesses who are not in court under s. 9 Criminal Justice Act 1967, or under the hearsay provisions, video recordings, tape recordings or real evidence such as an exhibit presented in court.

(9) At the conclusion of the prosecution's case, the defence may submit that there is no case to answer where the prosecution has failed to establish an essential element of the alleged offence; or the prosecution evidence has been so discredited in cross-examination or is so manifestly unreliable that no reasonable tribunal could safely convict on it (*Practice Direction (Submission of No Case)* [1962] 1 WLR 227).

(10) Where a submission of no case to answer is not made or is unsuccessful, the defence may put its case to the court. The defence advocate may make an opening speech, but, as he is normally allowed only one speech, it is usual practice to reserve this to the end of the defence case so that he may have the advantage of the 'last word'.

(11) The defence calls its first witness, subjecting the witness to an examination-in-chief. Where the accused exercises his right to testify, he must be the first defence witness and has the right to leave the dock and give evidence from the witness box (*R v Farnham Justices, ex p. Andrew Gibson* [1991] Crim LR 642).

(12) The defence witness may then be cross-examined by the prosecution and any co-accused.

(13) The defence advocate may re-examine the witness to repair any damage that may have been inflicted on the witness during cross-examination.

(14) The witness may be questioned by the justices.

The process of witness testimony of examination-in-chief, cross-examination and re-examination continues until all the defence witnesses have testified.

(15) The defence will usually close the proceedings by making a closing speech.

(16) The court will then announce its decision of guilty or not guilty after retiring to consider the evidence. On finding the defendant guilty, the court will consider whether it is necessary to obtain a pre-sentence report. Where a pre-sentence report is ordered the case will be adjourned to enable the report to be prepared. Before proceeding to sentence, the prosecution will disclose to the court the defendant's previous convictions (if any). The defence advocate will make a plea in mitigation. The court then passes sentence. In relation to an either-way offence, the court can commit the defendant for sentence to the Crown Court under s. 3 PCC(S)A 2000 where it is of the view that its powers of sentence are insufficient. Section 6 of the same Act enables the court to also commit any summary offence for which the defendant has been convicted alongside the either-way offence. The practice and procedure of sentencing, including the power to commit for sentence are considered in Part V.

(17)   Where the defendant is found not guilty, he is free to leave. If the defendant is non-legally aided he may make an application to have his costs met out of central funds under s. 16 Prosecution of Offenders Act 1985. Such orders are at the discretion of the court but should normally be awarded unless it is felt that the accused brought suspicion on himself by his conduct and/or misled the prosecution into thinking the evidence against him was stronger than it in fact was. Guidance can be found in *Practice Direction (Crime: Costs)* [1991] WLR 498. A legally aided acquitted defendant's costs will be met under the representation order.

We further consider trial advocacy in the context of trials before the Crown Court in Chapter 17.

In conducting a summary trial you are reminded of the various rules of professional conduct that could arise, which are considered in Chapter 1.

KEY POINT SUMMARY

- Be aware of the circumstances in which a defendant can be tried in his absence.
- Know the law which permits two or more informations to be tried together and how you might challenge the 'interests of justice' test.
- Know the responsibilities of each side in the pre-trial disclosure of evidence.
- Know the procedure for securing the attendance of witnesses at trial.
- Know the practice for admitting a witness's written statement in hearsay form under s. 9 Criminal Justice Act 1967.
- Be aware of the purpose of and the issues that will be covered by standard directions for trial and the duty of the parties to assist the court in the active management of cases under Crim PR Part 3.
- Know the sequence of events where the defendant pleads not guilty.
- Know the test to support a submission of no case to answer.

SELF-TEST QUESTIONS

1. What is the test to determine whether a defendant can be tried for two or more informations at the same time where a defendant does not consent?
2. Explain how the defence solicitor will find out what the prosecution's evidence comprises in advance of trial.
3. How can the solicitor ensure the attendance of witnesses?
4. What is the role of the legal adviser in a summary case (see Chapter 1)?
5. At what point might a submission of no case to answer be made and what is the test to support such a submission.

FIGURE 15.1 THE PROSECUTION OF A SUMMARY OFFENCE AND SUMMARY TRIAL

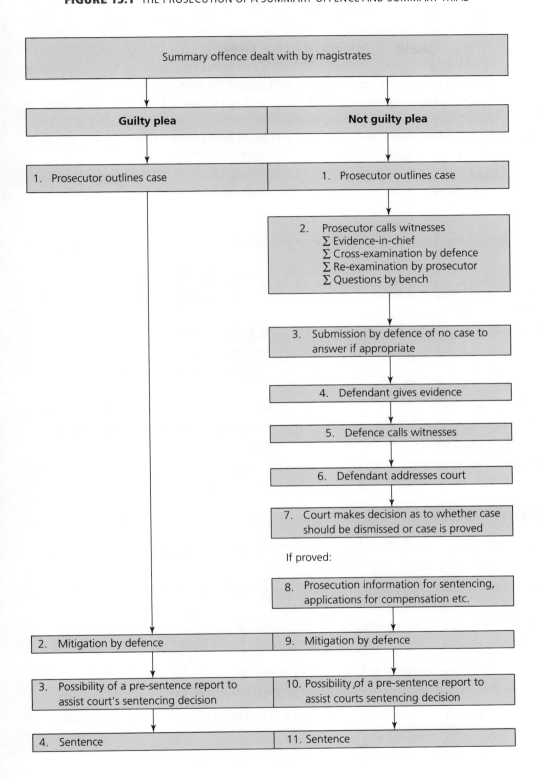

FIGURE 15.2 Magistrates' Court Case Progression

MAGISTRATES' COURT
CASE PROGRESSION

CASE TO BE TRIED IN THE MAGISTRATES' COURT

Date of hearing:

The court will fix the trial date at (or shortly after) the hearing at which the defendant pleads not guilty. The directions below apply from that hearing unless they are modified or deleted by the court.

DEFENDANT

Name of defendant	Age	Date of Birth
Address		
On bail/In custody Contact telephone number (if defendant agrees)		

CASE

No. of case in Magistrates' Court:	URN:
Charges:	

LEGAL REPRESENTATION

Prosecution Reviewing Lawyer:	Address:
Tel.:	Fax:
Email:	DX

Defence Solicitor:	Solicitors Firm & Address:
Tel.:	Fax:
Email:	DX

CASE PROGRESSION OFFICERS

Magistrates' Court	Prosecution	Defence
Name:	Name:	Name:
Address:	Address:	Address:
Tel:	Tel:	Tel:
Fax:	Fax:	Fax:
Email:	Email:	Email:
DX:	DX:	DX:

Has the defendant been advised about credit for pleading guilty? Yes

Has the defendant been warned that if he is on bail and fails to attend, the proceedings may continue in his absence? Yes

TRIAL DATE *The trial will take place on:*   *and is expected to last for:*

DIRECTIONS

Special measures
a.　The prosecution to serve any application for special measures within **14 days**.

b.　The defence to serve any response to the application for special measures within **14 days** of service of the prosecution application.

Prosecution case and disclosure
c.　To the extent it has not done so, the prosecution must serve copies of the documents containing the evidence on which the charge or charges are based, including witness statements and any documentary exhibits, tapes of interview, video tapes and CCTV tapes within **[28] days**.

d.　To the extent it has not done so, the prosecution must comply with its initial duty of disclosure within **[28] days**.

Hearsay Evidence
e.　The prosecution to serve any notice of intention to introduce hearsay evidence at the same time as it complies, or purports to comply with its initial duty of disclosure.

f.　The defence to serve any notice opposing the prosecution's notice under e., within **14 days** of receipt of the notice.

g.　The defence to serve any notice of intention to introduce hearsay evidence within **14 days** of the date on which the prosecution complied, or purported to comply, with its initial duty of disclosure.

h.　The prosecution to serve any notice opposing the defence's notice under g. within **14 days** of receipt of the application.

Bad character evidence
i.　The defence to serve any application to introduce the bad character of a prosecution witness within **14 days** of the date on which the prosecution complied, or purported to comply, with its initial duty of disclosure.

j.　The prosecution to serve any notice opposing the defence application to introduce the bad character of a prosecution witness under i. within **14 days** of receipt of the application.

k.　The prosecution to serve any notice to introduce the defendant's bad character at the same time as it complies, or purports to comply, with its initial duty of disclosure.

l.　The defence to serve any application to exclude evidence of the defendantís bad character within **7 days** of receipt of the prosecution application under k.

m.　*Any further orders relating to bad character:*

Defence statement
n.　If a defence statement is to be given, the defence must serve it within **14 days** of the prosecution complying or purporting to comply with its initial duty of disclosure.

Witness statements
o.　If the defence wish a prosecution witness to give evidence in person at the trial, the defence shall so notify the prosecution within **7 days** of receiving the prosecution case under c.

p.　The defence must serve any statements of defence witnesses who the defence propose not to give evidence in person at the trial within **[14] days** of receiving the prosecution case under c.

q.　If a party requires a witness whose statement has been served under p. to give evidence in person at the trial, the party shall so notify the prosecution within **7 days** of service of the statement.

Further disclosure

r.　The prosecution to complete any further disclosure at least **[14] days** before the trial.

Written admissions

s.　The parties must file any written admissions made under section 10 of the Criminal Justice Act 1967 within **[56] days**.

Expert evidence

t.　If either party intends to rely on expert evidence, the directions below apply.

Point of law

u.　If any point of law is to be taken by a party and a skeleton argument would be helpful, it must be served together with authorities at least **[21] days** prior to the trial.

v.　The other party must serve a skeleton argument in reply together with authorities at least **[7] days** prior to the trial.

Trial readiness

w.　The parties must certify readiness for trial, by filing a certificate of readiness if appropriate, at least **[7] days** prior to the trial.

x.　*Any other orders:*

Further case management

y.　*A further case management hearing will take place on:*

EXPERT EVIDENCE

a.　A party seeking to rely on expert evidence must serve the expert's report within **[28] days**.

b.　A party served with expert evidence must indicate whether the expert is required to attend at the trial, and either serve their own expert evidence in response or indicate that they are not intending to rely on expert evidence within **[28] days** of receipt of the other party's expert evidence.

c.　A meeting of experts to agree non-contentious matters and identify issues, if appropriate and if the parties agree, must take place within **[28] days** of service of both parties' expert evidence.

d.　The parties must notify the court within **[14] days** of an experts' meeting whether the length of the trial is affected by the outcome of the meeting.

16 CROWN COURT PROCEEDINGS PRE-TRIAL

16.1 INTRODUCTION

As a trainee solicitor you will be involved in assisting defendants charged with indictable-only offences. Much of the preparatory work will be the same as for a summary trial, although indictable offences by their nature usually involve more complex issues of law, evidence and fact. Also, with much greater powers of punishment available to the Crown Court, the potential consequences for a defendant are much more serious if his case is not properly prepared.

You may wish to read this chapter in conjunction with the latter part of Chapter 11 which explores the initial preparatory steps that will occupy the defence solicitor.

This chapter deals with pre-trial practices and procedures that are followed when dealing with a client charged with an indictable-only offence. It covers:

- the sending of indictable-only cases to the Crown Court under s. 51 Crime and Disorder Act 1998 (CDA);
- preparing for the preliminary hearing in the Crown Court;
- preparing for trial on indictment;
- instructing counsel;
- pre-trial hearings including the Plea and Case Management Hearing (PCMH).

You will be aware that either-way offences can also be tried on indictment in the Crown Court. The procedure by which an either-way matter can be sent to the Crown Court for trial is explained in Chapter 13. Our case study featuring *R v Lenny Whyte* is an example of such a case. Once an either-way offence is committed to the Crown Court, a date is set for the defendant's Plea and Case Management Hearing (PCMH) in the Crown Court. Before considering the PCMH and general preparatory steps in relation to all cases to be tried on indictment, we will consider some specific provisions in relation to indictable-only offences.

16.2 THE DEFENDANT'S FIRST COURT APPEARANCE FOR AN INDICTABLE-ONLY OFFENCE—S. 51 CRIME AND DISORDER ACT 1998

Despite being charged with an indictable-only offence, the defendant will make his first appearance before a magistrates' court. At this first hearing, the defendant's entitlement to bail will be decided. Bail is more likely to be opposed by the prosecution in connection with an indictable-only offence because of the seriousness of the offence and the greater risk of the defendant absconding.

Although the rules relating to the pre-trial disclosure of advance information do not strictly apply to indictable-only offences, the CPS will normally provide this information before the defendant's first appearance.

Having made an initial appearance before a magistrates' court, s. 51(1) Crime and Disorder Act 1998 requires the case should be sent immediately to the Crown Court. The case will usually be listed for a preliminary hearing which should be held within 14 days or eight days if the defendant is remanded in custody. Whether or not the case is listed for a preliminary hearing, a Plea and Case Management Hearing (PCMH) must be held 14 weeks after the case has been sent where a defendant is in custody and within 17 weeks where a defendant is on bail. In sending the case, the magistrates' court is required (as part of its active case management powers) to complete a case progression form which imposes standard directions on the parties relating to the service of prosecution evidence and defence disclosure. The directions form can be accessed via the web-links section of our Online Resource Centre.

16.2.1 SENDING 'RELATED' OFFENCES TO THE CROWN COURT FOR TRIAL

What is the position where a defendant is charged with an indictable-only offence and a further offence(s) which is an either-way or summary offence? Section 51(3) CDA 1998 provides that where an adult defendant is sent for trial under s. 51, the magistrates' court must also send any related either-way offence for which the defendant appears at the same time. An either-way offence is 'related' where it can be joined in the same indictment because it is founded on the same facts or forms part of a series of offences of the same or similar character, s. 51E CDA 1998. The magistrates' court must also send any related summary offence for which the defendant appears at the same time, s. 51(3)(b) CDA 1998. A related summary offence must arise out of circumstances which are the same as or connected with the indictable-only offence and be punishable with imprisonment or disqualification (s. 51(11)).

Consider the following examples of how linked summary or either-way offences may also be sent to the Crown Court for trial.

Example 1

Gordon is charged with grievous bodily harm with intent, contrary to s. 18 Offences Against the Person Act 1861 (an indictable-only offence). He also faces an allegation of affray, contrary to s. 3 Public Order Act 1986 (either-way offence). Both incidents arise out of a brawl in the centre of town involving football supporters from rival clubs. The either-way offence is founded on the same facts as the indictable-only offence (s. 51E) and must therefore be sent to the Crown Court along with the indictable-only offence under s. 51(3)(a) CDA 1998.

Example 2

Denis is charged with driving while disqualified (a summary-only offence). In the course of the investigation into the offence he gives false particulars to the police leading to the arrest of someone other than himself. He is therefore charged with perverting the course of justice (an indictable-only offence). As the summary-only offence arises out of circumstances connected with the indictable-only offence and is punishable with imprisonment, both offences must be sent for trial to the Crown Court under s. 51(3)(b) CDA 1998.

Where a defendant appears before a magistrates' court on a separate occasion charged with a related either-way or summary offence, the magistrates have discretion to send the matter(s) up to the Crown Court so that they may be joined with the indictable-only matter(s) (s. 51(4) CDA 1998).

6.2.2 SENDING A LINKED CO-DEFENDANT TO THE CROWN COURT

Example 3

What is the position where a co-accused is charged with an either-way offence which is related to the indictable-only offence? To take the example of Gordon above, let us assume that Tom is also charged with affray arising out of the brawl. In these circumstances, s. 51(5) CDA 1998 requires the magistrates' court to send Tom's matter to the Crown Court along with Gordon's indictable-only offence if Tom appears at the same time as Gordon. Co-defendants facing an either-way offence which is related to an indictable-only offence therefore have no right of election in these circumstances. If Tom who is charged with affray appears in court after Gordon's initial appearance, the magistrates would have discretion to send Tom's either-way offence to the Crown Court.

6.2.3 SENDING YOUNG OFFENDERS TO THE CROWN COURT

What is the position of a young offender (aged under 18) who is jointly charged with an indictable-only offence? Section 51(7) CDA 1998 provides that the magistrates' court shall send the young person for trial in the Crown Court along with the adult if it is in the interests of justice. If this power is exercised, the magistrates can also send any 'related' either-way or summary matter which the young person faces. (For an explanation of the interests of justice test and for full consideration of the young person in the criminal justice system, see Chapters 30 and 31.)

16.3 PRELIMINARY HEARING BEFORE THE CROWN COURT

The principal purpose of the preliminary hearing is to enable the judge to devise a timetable for the service of prosecution evidence and a defence statement. Disclosure of evidence is further considered below. The judge will also set a date for a Plea and Case Management Hearing (PCMH) to be held some weeks later.

A substantial amount of work will be undertaken to prepare for the PCMH as explained below. Some judges ask for an indication of plea at the preliminary hearing, although there is no obligation to give an indication at this stage. If an indication of guilt is given, a pre-sentence report can be ordered in time for the PCMH and the defendant will of course be given maximum credit for a timely guilty plea.

16.3.1 CROWN COURT BAIL

As the preliminary appearance before the Crown Court will most likely end in an adjournment, the question of the defendant's bail may arise again. The defendant can make two contested bail applications, after which the provisions of Part 2A Sch. 1 Bail Act 1976 apply. Under this provision a court need not hear argument on the question of bail unless there has been a change in circumstances. The defendant may already have made an unsuccessful application for bail at a previous appearance before the magistrates' court. A second application is permitted before the Crown Court. If this is unsuccessful and the defendant is remanded in custody, the trial judge and the prosecution should be aware of the defendant's custody time-limits when setting the timetable for the PCMH (see Chapter 12).

16.4 PREPARATORY STEPS IN THE EARLY STAGES OF AN INDICTABLE-ONLY OFFENCE

The preparatory work undertaken in the early stages of all criminal cases, including indictable cases are considered in Chapter 11. Typically, the early stages of an indictable-only matter will include:

- interviewing your client;
- preparing your client's proof of evidence;
- contact with the CPS to:
  - — confirm that you are acting for your client;
  - — request a copy of your client's criminal record;
  - — obtain a record of any police interviews with your client;
  - — obtain a copy of your client's custody record;
  - — obtain advance information;
- interviewing potential defence witnesses;
- visit the crime scene;
- instructing expert witnesses if necessary.

 online resource centre
For an illustration of many of the above steps, you are reminded of the stage we have reached in our case study *R v Lenny Whyte*.

16.5 DISCLOSURE OF 'USED' MATERIAL AND TRIALS ON INDICTMENT

In indictable-only cases, the defence solicitor will not usually be in a position to properly advise his client until the prosecution has made a full disclosure of the case against him. The standard directions which apply to a case sent for trial by a magistrates' court under

s. 51 CDA 1998, require the service of prosecution case papers ('case sent bundle') to be made within 50 days where the defendant is in custody and within 70 days in other cases.

The 'case sent bundle' will be very similar to the 'committal bundle' currently served in committal proceedings (you are referred to the *R v Lenny Whyte* case study which comprises a committal bundle and to Chapter 13). The 'case sent bundle' will comprise 'used' material, which will include:

- the charge(s);
- witness statements;
- the draft indictment;
- schedule of unused material; and
- initial prosecution disclosure in accordance with s. 3 CPIA 1996.

Once the prosecution has served the 'case sent bundle', an important part of the defence solicitor's case preparation will be to carefully scrutinise the prosecution witness statements and other evidence to assess the strength of the case against his client. This assessment will be very important when advising a client whether to plead guilty or not guilty.

16.6 DISCLOSURE OF 'UNUSED' MATERIAL—CRIMINAL PROCEDURE AND INVESTIGATION ACT 1996 (CPIA)

In addition to the prosecution's obligation to disclose evidence it intends to rely on at trial, the Criminal Procedure and Investigations Act 1996 (CPIA) requires the prosecution to disclose evidence in its possession which it will not use at trial. This is known as 'unused' material.

You will recall that we have dedicated Chapter 14 to the pre-trial disclosure of evidence which covers the provisions relating to used and unused material. For the purpose of this chapter we remind you of the key provisions.

16.6.1 INITIAL PROSECUTION DISCLOSURE IN CROWN COURT TRIALS

Section 3 CPIA 1996 requires the prosecution to provide the defendant with initial disclosure (any evidence not previously disclosed, which might reasonably be considered capable of undermining the case for the prosecution or of assisting the case for the accused). At the initial disclosure stage, the defence will receive a schedule detailing non-sensitive material in the prosecutor's possession. In indictable-only cases, initial disclosure should be included in the 'case-sent bundle'. In either-way cases that have been committed to the Crown Court, initial disclosure is made post-committal if it is not included in the committal bundle.

16.6.2 DEFENCE DISCLOSURE UNDER THE CPIA 1996

After initial disclosure, s. 5 CPIA 1996 requires that a defence statement should be served on the court and the CPS. The defence statement must be served within 14 days of the prosecution's initial disclosure. A defence statement is a mandatory requirement in cases to be tried on indictment. Failure to comply with the requirement to serve the defence statement can lead to adverse comment and inferences being drawn by the court under s. 11 CPIA 1996. The importance of correctly drafting a defence statement cannot be overstated which we discussed in more detail in Chapter 14, paras. 14.9–14.10 and 14.13.

16.6.3 FURTHER PROSECUTION DISCLOSURE

After service of the defence statement, s. 7A CPIA 1996 requires the prosecutor to look again at the schedule of unused material and disclose any material that falls within s. 3 CPIA 1996 which has not previously been disclosed by the prosecution. This is likely to apply to material which might reasonably be expected to assist the accused's defence as disclosed in the defence statement.

16.7 WHAT IF THE PRE-TRIAL DISCLOSURE OF EVIDENCE REVEALS THE PROSECUTION TO HAVE A WEAK CASE?

Where the 'case sent bundle' indicates a weak prosecution case, the defence may make an application to the Crown Court to dismiss the charge(s).

16.7.1 AN APPLICATION TO DISMISS THE CHARGE

Under Sch. 3 CDA 1998, the defence may make an oral or a written application to the Crown Court to dismiss the charge(s) against the defendant. In most cases, the application will be decided on the basis of written submissions unless the defendant requests that oral evidence should be heard and the judge considers that it is in the interests of justice that oral evidence should be heard. In this situation, prosecution witnesses may be required to attend the hearing and be cross-examined. (The option to call oral evidence is prospectively repealed by Sch. 3 CJA 2003.) The defence may also make submissions to have disputed evidence excluded under s. 76 or s. 78 PACE 1984. The detailed rules relating to an application to dismiss charges sent or transferred to the Crown Court are contained in Crim PR, Part 13. On hearing the representations from each side, the judge will dismiss the charge(s) against the defendant where there is insufficient evidence for a jury to properly convict the accused. Where the application to dismiss is unsuccessful, the date will be confirmed for the Plea and Case Management Hearing (PCMH). Reporting restrictions will apply at a hearing to dismiss. A defendant may apply to have reporting restrictions lifted (Sch. 3, para. 3 CDA 1998).

16.7.2 WHAT HAPPENS TO ANY RELATED CHARGES IF THE INDICTABLE-ONLY OFFENCE IS DISMISSED LEAVING ONLY AN EITHER-WAY OR SUMMARY OFFENCE?

The procedure under Sch. 3, paras. 7 to 15 of the CDA 1998, requires the Crown Court to carry out the plea before venue procedure in relation to an either-way offence. If the defendant indicates a not guilty plea or makes no indication at all, the mode of trial procedure must be conducted. If it is decided to deal with the either-way offence summarily, the case will be remitted to the magistrates' court. A summary-only offence would also be remitted to the magistrates where the linked indictable offence has been dismissed.

16.8 PRE-TRIAL HEARINGS IN THE CROWN COURT

Before the case proceeds to trial, both the prosecution and the defence will be required to attend one or more pre-trial hearings. Pre-trial hearings are designed to prevent ineffective trials. They enable the trial judge to fulfil the obligation under Crim PR, Part 3 to actively manage cases. The trial judge can make directions at the hearing, hear argument and give a binding ruling on a matter relating to the trial.

16.8.1 PLEA AND CASE MANAGEMENT HEARING (PCMH)—SS. 39–43 CPIA 1996

All cases to be tried on indictment will have a Plea and Case Management Hearing (PCMH).

The initial purpose of the PCMH is to arraign the accused, i.e. to hear whether he intends to plead guilty or not guilty. The PCMH then proceeds on the basis of whether the defendant pleaded guilty or not guilty.

6.8.2 PLEADING NOT GUILTY AT THE PCMH

Where the defendant pleads not guilty, the PCMH ensures that any steps necessary for trial will be taken and that the court is provided with sufficient information to fix a trial date. This process is facilitated by the advocates completing a detailed PCMH questionnaire. The form can be accessed via the web-links section of our Online Resource Centre and is included at the end of this chapter. Amongst other things, the judge will require details of:

online
resource
centre

- the witnesses who will give oral evidence;
- the witnesses who will give written evidence;
- any facts formally admitted;
- any exhibits or schedules;
- any expert evidence to be relied on;
- any point of law or evidential issues that will be put before the court together with the authorities relied upon;
- details of any alibi evidence which has been disclosed to the prosecution;
- the estimated length of the trial; and
- the dates on which the witnesses and the advocates are available.

The PCMH questionnaire covers many of the aspects of case management covered by Crim PR, Part 3.10 and the parties are expected to comply with all directions made as part of the PCMH. One very important step that the defence solicitor is required to take is to provide the CPS with a full list of all the prosecution witnesses the defence requires to attend trial. The standard 'case sent' directions stipulate this should be done within seven days of receiving disclosure of the prosecution's case as this gives the police the chance to check witness availability in advance of the PCMH. At the conclusion of the PCMH, the judge will normally fix the date for trial. Complex cases may need to be listed for a further pre-trial hearing.

16.8.3 PLEADING GUILTY AT THE PCMH

If it is your client's intention to plead guilty at the PCMH, you should notify the court and the prosecution as soon as possible and not less than 14 days before the hearing. Notification enables the court to order a pre-sentence report in time for the PCMH. Where the defendant pleads guilty at the PCMH, the judge may proceed to sentence. Alternatively, the sentencing hearing may be adjourned to enable the preparation of a pre-sentence report if such a report has yet to be prepared.

16.8.4 PREPARATORY HEARINGS

A preparatory hearing in accordance with ss. 28–38 Criminal Procedure and Investigations Act 1996 is appropriate in long and complex cases to be heard in the Crown Court. The relevant rules of court are contained in Crim PR, Part 15. It is for the judge to decide whether there should be a preparatory hearing either on the application of the parties or by the court's own motion. In practice, the decision whether to hold a preparatory hearing is likely to be made at the PCMH.

Where a preparatory hearing is held, it will take place before the jury is sworn, and may clarify any difficult or contentious issue which will assist the jury's understanding of any matter in the case; identify issues which are likely to be material to the jury's verdict and expedite the proceedings or assist the judge's management of the trial. The preparatory hearing is part of the trial process.

16.8.5 **PRE-TRIAL RULINGS**

Sections 31–39 Criminal Proceedings and Investigation Act 1996 (CPIA) provides that a judge may make a binding ruling at any pre-trial hearing (including the PCMH) on matters relating to the admissibility of evidence and/or a question of law.

Where a pre-trial ruling has been made, it may only be varied or discharged where it is in the 'interests of justice'. An application to vary a binding ruling will not be heard unless there has been a 'material change of circumstances' since the making of the original ruling. The CPIA 1996 provides a right of appeal to the Court of Appeal against a pre-trial ruling.

Matters of law and evidence likely to be determined at a pre-trial hearing could include:

* determining the competency of a witness;
* ruling on a special measures direction for a vulnerable or intimidated witness;
* deciding whether to hold a joint trial for two or more accused or whether to sever an indictment in a case where an accused faces more than one charge;
* resolving disputes as to the admissibility of bad character evidence or hearsay evidence;
* determining a public interest immunity (PII) application to withhold evidence;
* making a ruling as to the admissibility of disputed confession evidence or evidence of identification.

The above list is not exhaustive. The benefit of these rulings is that they should enable the trial to proceed on the day. Pre-trial rulings will also have a bearing on whether an accused considers changing his plea to guilty.

16.9 **PREPARATION FOR TRIAL**

Much of the defence solicitor's trial preparation will have been in connection with the PCMH. Typical preparatory matters are considered below.

16.9.1 **WITNESSES**

If the case is to proceed to trial, the defence must ensure the attendance of its witnesses. Where it appears that a witness will not attend voluntarily, an application to summons the witness's attendance can be made under ss. 2–4 Criminal Procedure (Attendance of Witnesses) Act 1965. The rules relating to the issue of a witness summons are contained in Crim PR, Part 28.

16.9.2 **BRIEFING COUNSEL**

Your client will need to be represented at the PCMH by a barrister or a solicitor-advocate. The advocate will need to be briefed. The task of briefing counsel is commonly given to a trainee solicitor. A properly drafted brief is a disciplined exercise requiring you to organise the materials in a file and to think very carefully about the issues in the case.

When to brief
For an either-way offence committed to the Crown Court, the brief to counsel should be sent within 21 days of committal or within 7 days of the committal if the defendant is in custody.

For an indictable-only offence the date set for the PCMH will dictate the time by which the brief should be delivered.

If the defence solicitor requires assistance in completing the defence statement, counsel should be instructed at an even earlier stage. It will obviously be easier to organise a conference with counsel in advance of the PCMH if the brief is sent in plenty of time.

It is preferable that the advocate who represents the defendant at the PCMH will also represent him at trial. Unless your firm employs a solicitor-advocate with higher rights of audience, your firm may have a preferred choice of barrister. A barrister's services are engaged through the clerk at his or her chambers. All the papers in the case and the instructions will be sent to the barrister in a brief to counsel.

What should a brief to counsel contain?

Whilst there is an etiquette to briefing counsel, the precise practice may vary from firm to firm and your firm may have a preferred style of briefing counsel. The brief to counsel we have drafted in conjunction with the *R v Lenny Whyte* case study is written in the third person.

The brief should contain a back sheet with details of the case, the date and type of hearing, with the instructing solicitor's details on the right-hand side of the page. The left-hand side of the back page is left blank to enable counsel to handwrite endorsements onto it. If the case is legally aided, the back page of the brief should make this clear.

Where appropriate the brief may cover counsel's representation at both the PCMH and at trial. In other cases separate briefs will be sent.

The front page of the brief should contain the case heading and a numbered list of enclosures. The list of enclosures depends entirely on the particular case you are dealing with, but would typically include:

- defendant's proof of evidence;
- draft indictment;
- committal papers/case-sent bundle;
- relevant correspondence with CPS;
- expert report(s).

The brief should begin with an introduction which deals with the defendant's personal details, the charge(s), the history of the case and any bail arrangements.

The brief should provide an analysis of the prosecution case by cross-referencing to the prosecution witness statements and other evidence that has been disclosed under the pre-trial disclosure rules and which will be included with the brief as enclosures. Any strengths or weaknesses in the prosecution case should be identified as should the admissibility of items of prosecution evidence which may be challenged at trial.

The brief should also contain a summary of the defence case and identify any strengths or weaknesses.

Counsel should also be clearly directed on what advice is sought. This might relate to witness requirements, points of evidence, advice on plea or assistance with drafting a defence statement. Counsel's attention should also be directed to the factors that might be raised in mitigation in the event of your client being convicted.

Commonly, the brief will ask whether counsel believes a conference with instructing solicitors will assist in the case preparation.

The brief will be sent to counsel who should respond within the return date. At this stage, the solicitor needs to be mindful of key dates, particularly in relation to serving a defence statement or to notifying the CPS which prosecution witnesses are required to attend trial to be cross-examined. A failure to notify the CPS of which prosecution witnesses are required to attend by the defence will result in their evidence being read at trial without them being present in court (see Chapter 13, para. 13.16.4). Counsel may send written advice in advance of the PCMH. It is important that counsel's advice is followed up. This may involve further interviews with the defendant or witnesses or further correspondence with the CPS. If counsel suggests a conference is needed, you might be asked to organise one. This involves contacting counsel's clerk for available dates as well as contacting your client. The conference usually takes place at counsel's chambers.

16.10 RECOVERY OF DEFENCE COSTS ORDER

You will recall that a representation order for Crown Court cases is granted on the basis of the interests of justice test only. In cases that are to be tried on indictment, the defendant must complete and serve Form B which comprises a statement of his means. The information about his financial circumstances will allow the judge at the end of the trial to make a recovery of defence costs order (RDCO) if the defendant is convicted. Form B will need to be served before the PCMH. The form is accessible from www.hmcourts-service.gov.uk.

KEY POINT SUMMARY

- Understand that all indictable-only offences must be sent to the Crown Court along with related (either-way/summary) offences in accordance with s. 51 CDA 1998 following an initial appearance before a magistrates' court.
- Trials on indictment cover not just indictable-only offences but either-way offences which have been sent for trial by a magistrates' court.
- Be aware of the rules dealing with the pre-trial disclosure of evidence by both the prosecution and the service of a defence statement under the CPIA 1996.
- Know the conventions about instructing counsel.
- Understand the purpose of the PCMH and the procedures where the defendant pleads guilty or not guilty at the arraignment.

SELF-TEST QUESTIONS

1. What is the purpose of the initial hearing in the magistrates' court where the defendant is charged with an indictable-only offence?
2. What obligation does the prosecution have in relation to the pre-trial disclosure of evidence in an indictable-only offence?
3. Explain the procedure at the application to dismiss the charge in the Crown Court.
4. Explain the purpose of the PCMH.
5. In which type of case will it normally be appropriate to hold a preparatory hearing?

online
resource
centre

Case study: *R v Lenny Whyte*, Appendix 1

You will recall that Lenny Whyte has been committed to stand trial on the burglary allegation and a date has been set for his Plea and Case Management Hearing before Lyme Crown Court. Initial prosecution disclosure of unused material, in compliance with s. 3 CPIA 1996, is made (see Document 31). Before you look at the defence statement in relation to Lenny Whyte, you may wish to attempt a draft of your own. The defence statement submitted in this case is at Document 34A. Further disclosure, in compliance with the CPS's duties under s. 7A CPIA 1996 are contained in Documents 35, 36 and 37. Subject to the prosecution's duty to keep disclosure under review, the pre-trial disclosure of evidence in relation to *R v Lenny Whyte* is complete. You will see that Lenny's solicitor has obtained a psychiatric report from

Lenny's consultant (see Document 38). The requirement under Crim PR, Part 24 for the disclosure of expert report to be adduced in court has been complied with.

You now have all the necessary information to undertake a brief to counsel. Our suggested brief to counsel in this case is included at Document 39.

You will see on Lenny Whyte's file an account of his PCMH before Lyme Crown Court (Document 41). In correspondence between Lenny's solicitors and the CPS leading up to the PCMH (see Document 33), the defence suggests a further pre-trial hearing will be needed to address the issues surrounding the admissibility of Lenny's confession and the admissibility of Lenny's record of past criminal convictions. At the PCMH, counsel for the CPS concede that Lenny Whyte's confession had been obtained in breach of PACE and Code C and that the CPS will not be relying on it. The matter is then listed for trial. A further, very short brief to counsel to represent Lenny Whyte at trial is subsequently sent (see Document 44).

FIGURE 16.1 THE PROSECUTION OF INDICTABLE-ONLY OFFENCES AND TRIAL ON INDICTMENT

Defendant will make initial appearance before magistrates' court; matters relating to bail will be determined; advance information ought to be available.

↓

Defendant's case is sent to the Crown Court under s. 51 CDA 1998 together with any related either-way offence or related summary offence if punishable with imprisonment or disqualification.

↓

Defendant will make his initial appearance before Crown Court judge who will devise a timetable for the pre-trial disclosure of evidence and will set a date for a Plea and Case Management Hearing (PCMH).

↓

- Prosecution will serve case-sent bundle comprising used and unused material, the latter in compliance with s. 3 CPIA 1996;
- defence will be required to serve a defence statement in compliance with s. 5 CPIA 1996;
- prosecution will serve any further unused material in accordance with s. 7A CPIA 1996;
- defence can apply to have charges dismissed for insufficient evidence;
- case may need to be listed for a pre-trial hearing.

↓

- Defendant will be asked to plead at his PCMH;
- defence should brief counsel in sufficient time to ensure attendance at PCMH and to advise on plea;
- if plea is to be not guilty, defence must notify CPS as to which witnesses it wants to cross-examine so that availability can be checked before PCMH.

↓

PCMH	PCMH
defendant pleads guilty; sentence will follow unless pre-sentence is required.	defendant pleads not guilty; date will be set for Crown Court trial; defence will prepare for trial.

The Crown Court

Case No   D1   [_____]

Date of trial   [_____]

Fixed   [ ]
Warned   [ ]

Plea and Case Management Hearing

Advocates Questionnaire

■ Parties must complete this form.
■ This form is to be used at all Crown Court Centres, without local variation.
There is an electronic version of the form which contains answer boxes that expand. The form is at:

   http://www.hmcourts-service.gov.uk/HMCSCourtFinder

1

Date of PCMH
[_____]

PTI URN
[_____]

Judge
[_____]

Estimated length of trial
[_____]

2   **Parties' details**

Parties name	Age	Remand status	CTL expires	Advocate at PCMH	Trial advocate (if known)
P					
D1		C [ ] B [ ]			

3   **Contact details**

3.1   Parties

P   Office

Name	Phone
Email	

Advocate

Name	Phone
Email	

D1   Solicitor

Name	Phone
Email	

Advocate

Name	Phone
Email	

3.2

Case progression officers

P

Name	Phone
Email	

D1

Name	Phone
Email	

Court

Name	Phone
Email	

4 Which orders made at the magistrates' court have not been complied with?

5

D1 Has the defendant been advised that he or she will receive credit for a guilty plea? ☐ No ☐ Yes

6

D1 Has the defendant been warned that the case may proceed in his or her absence? ☐ No ☐ Yes

7 What plea(s) is/are the defendant(s) offering?

D1

8 Should the case be referred to the Resident Judge for a trial judge to be allocated? ☐ No ☐ Yes

9 Give details of any issues relating to the fitness to plead or to stand trial.

D1

10

10.1 Has the prosecution made statutory disclosure?

P

D1

10.2 Has a defence statement been served?

5122 Plea and Case Management Hearing. Criminal Procedure Rules 2006 (12.06)

HMCS

D1

10.3   Does it comply with the statutory requirements?

P

10.4   If not clear from the defence statement, what are the real issues?

D1

10.5

D1   Has/will the defence made/make an application in writing under section 8 of the Criminal Procedure and Investigations Act 1996?   ☐ No ☐ Yes

11   What further evidence is to be served by the prosecution? By when is it reasonably practicable to serve this?

P

12

12.1   Give details of any expert evidence likely to be relied upon, including why it is required and by when it is reasonably practicable to serve this.

P

D1

12.2   Is a note of agreement/disagreement required?

13

13.1

D1   Has the defence completed the Witness List (see **36**)?   ☐ No ☐ Yes

13.2   Is any witness summons necessary?

13.3
D1   Is a timetable for the calling of witnesses required (see **30**)?   ☐ No ☐ Yes

14
14.1
D1   Is a certificate for a litigator sought?   ☐ No ☐ Yes

14.2   If **Yes**, why and for how long?
D1

For 15 to 35, answer the relevant questions only

15   **Admissions, schedules etc.**
What matters can usefully be admitted or put into schedules, diagrams, visual aids etc.?

16   **Case summary**

P   Is it proposed to serve a case summary or note of opening?   ☐ No ☐ Yes

17   **Special measures**
17.1   Give details of any special measures application to be made.

17.2
Can any order be made now?   ☐ No ☐ Yes

17.3   What other arrangements are needed for any young/vulnerable/intimidated witness?

18   Young defendants

Are any arrangements needed for any young defendant?

D1

19   Reporting restrictions

State type and grounds of any reporting restriction sought.

P

D1

20   Third party material

20.1   What third party material is sought, from whom, and why?

P

D1

20.2   If the material can be obtained without a court order, by whom and by when?

P

D1

20.3   Should any person adversely affected by an order be notified?

21 Defendant's interview(s)

21.1 Is there an issue in relation to the accuracy of the transcript / admissibility of the defendantís interview?

D1

21.2 What proposals are made for any editing required?

D1

21.3 What proposals are made to summarise the interview(s)?

D1

22 Video Evidence

22.1 Is there video evidence of any young / vulnerable / intimidated witness yet to be served?

22.2 Has each video been transcribed?

22.3 Is there an issue in relation to the accuracy / admissibility / quality of any video or transcript?

23 Witness interview(s)

23.1 Are there any videos / audio tapes of witness interviews which, if they meet the disclosure test, are yet to be disclosed as unused material?

23.2   If so, is any application made for that video / audio tape to be transcribed and, if so, why?

24   CCTV evidence

24.1   Are there any outstanding issues in relation to service disclosure of CCTV footage? *If the material is in the possession of a third party, complete 20 instead.*

24.2   Is an edited version to be served / used?

25   Electronic equipment

25.1   Give details of any special equipment (e.g. CCTV, live link, audio recordings, DVD) required in the trial courtroom.

P

D1

25.2   Is the evidence in its present form compatible with the equipment in court?

26   Cross-examination on sexual history

If an application has not already been made, does the defence intend to make an application under section 41 of the Youth Justice and Criminal Evidence Act 1999 to cross-examine a witness about his or her sexual history?

D1

27   Bad character

Are any directions necessary in relation to bad character applications? Are there to be any further applications?

P

D1

28 Hearsay

Are any directions necessary in relation to hearsay applications? Are there to be any further applications?

P

D1

29 Admissibility and legal issues

What points on admissibility / other legal issues are to be taken? Is it necessary for any to be resolved before trial?

P

D1

30 Timetable of trial

Are there matters which need to be determined on the day of trial, which may affect the timetable of trial? If so, when will (1) the jury and (2) the witnesses be required?

P

31 Public interest immunity

5122 Plea and Case Management Hearing, Criminal Procedure Rules 2006 (12.06)

Is any ëon noticeí public interest immunity application to be made?

P

32 Jury bundle

What proposals do the prosecution make for a jury bundle?

P

33 Concurrent family proceedings

Give details of any concurrent family proceedings.

34 Other special arrangements

Give details of any special arrangements (e.g., interpreter, intermediary, wheelchair access, hearing loop system) needed for anyone attending the trial.

35 Linked criminal proceedings

Are there other criminal proceedings against the defendant or otherwise linked?

36 Witness List

The defence should indicate here which prosecution witnesses are required to give evidence at trial. The attendance of any witness is subject to the judge's direction.

Name of witness	Page No.	Type of witness: Provide specific details of the type of witness. For example: eye witness, police officer, firearms expert, continuity	Required by

5122 Plea and Case Management Hearing, Criminal Procedure Rules 2006 (12.06)

17 TRIAL BEFORE THE CROWN COURT

17.1 INTRODUCTION

Where the defendant pleads not guilty when arraigned at the Plea and Case Management Hearing (PCMH), the judge will set the date for the trial in the Crown Court. This chapter considers the procedural and practical steps at a trial on indictment by examining the following:

- the rules dealing with the indictment;
- supporting counsel at trial;
- empanelling the jury;

- the presentation of the prosecution and defence cases;
- the judge's summing-up; and
- the jury's verdict.

17.2 THE INDICTMENT

Where the accused has been sent for trial in the Crown Court, the prosecution is required to draw up the indictment. The indictment is the formal document that contains the charge/s the accused will plead to at trial, and is included in the committal or case-sent bundle. Each charge on the indictment is known as a count, and the defendant will plead guilty or not guilty to each count at the PCMH.

The prosecution is required to draw up the indictment within prescribed time-limits. A bill of indictment which is the draft indictment, should be preferred (i.e. delivered) to an officer of the appropriate Crown Court.

After being signed by an officer of the court the bill of indictment, then becomes the indictment on which the defendant is tried. An example of a draft bill of indictment can be located in our case study *R v Lenny Whyte* (see Appendix 1, Committal bundle). There are complicated rules relating to the drafting of indictments that are outside the scope of this *Handbook*. However, more than one count may be joined on the same indictment where the offences are either:

(a) founded on the same facts; or

(b) form or are part of a series of offences of the same or similar nature, r. 9, Indictment Rules 1971;

As regards (b), the courts have given a wide interpretation to the phrase 'series of offences of the same or similar character'. In *Ludlow v MPC* (1970) 54 Cr App R 233, the House of Lords determined that for offences to be similar, there must be some nexus between them both in terms of law and fact. An indictment can, of course, charge two or more defendants jointly either as principal offenders or as secondary parties and an indictment can charge defendants in separate counts but in the same indictment, providing there is a linking factor between the counts.

Consider the following example of the joinder of counts and defendants on a single indictment.

 Example

Arif is charged with Count 1, affray. William is charged with wounding, Count 2. Both charges arise out of a disturbance when both defendants were refused entry to a nightclub. All courts may be joined in the same indictment under r. 9 Indictment Rules 1971, as they are founded on the same facts.

17.3 SUPPORTING THE DEFENCE COUNSEL AT TRIAL

Supporting the defence counsel at trial is a task that is commonly allocated to a trainee solicitor. A trainee solicitor is often handed a file at short notice and told to act as a 'watching brief' in the Crown Court. This will require the trainee solicitor to quickly assimilate the information contained in the file.

As a result of changes introduced to the funding of criminal cases, a representative will now only be paid for attending counsel at trial where the proceedings come within one of the following categories:

- very serious indictable offences;
- serious fraud cases;

- where the defendant is a child or a young person;
- where the defendant will not be able to follow the proceedings because of illness, disability or inadequate command of English; or
- on the day that your client is likely to be given a custodial sentence.

If your client's case does not come within one of the above categories, your presence at the Crown Court may be paid for where the judge issues a litigator certificate. A litigator certificate is likely to be issued where:

- there are a significant number of defence witnesses to be marshalled on any given day; or
- there are a significant number of defence documents; or
- the defence advocate is representing more than one accused; or
- the accused is likely to be disruptive if the advocate appeared alone; or
- the advocate will need notes taken for the proper conduct of the defence; or
- there are any other exceptional circumstances.

17.4   LAST-MINUTE CHECKLIST

Where you are to attend the trial, in the period leading up to the trial date you should ensure that:

- any matters arising out of counsel's written advice or given in conference have been complied with;
- there are sufficient copies of the defence and prosecution documentation;
- your client's previous convictions have been checked;
- the prosecution and defence witnesses have been checked for previous convictions;
- each defence witness has been warned to attend trial or summonsed if necessary;
- any domestic arrangements for the defence witnesses have been made, for example, that hotel accommodation has been booked.

17.5   FIRST DAY OF TRIAL

On the first day of the trial you should arrive at court as early as possible. Ensure that you have all the relevant documentation and contact numbers for your barrister and defence witnesses in case something does not go according to plan. Confirm with the court staff in which court your client's case is being heard. If you have any immediate concerns, the court usher is usually an invaluable source of information. You will look out for the defendant and the defence witnesses. This is a time where you will need good interpersonnel skills to allay any of your side's nervousness. The prosecution witnesses will normally have been met by Witness Support staff.

Contact counsel and confirm that he has everything he needs. It is common immediately before the start of the trial to be given last-minute tasks such as:

- photocopying;
- providing the defence witness's with copies of their statement to enable each witness to refresh their memory before testifying;
- liaising with the defence witnesses as counsel cannot talk directly to the witnesses who are to be called;
- familiarising the witnesses with the layout of the courtroom; or
- undertaking legal research.

17.5.1 CONFERENCE WITH COUNSEL

Invariably, counsel will wish to speak with the defendant. This may be the first time your client has met his barrister. You will be required to make the introductions and to keep a careful note of the matters covered in the conference. You will also act as a contact between counsel and any defence witnesses. Professional conduct rules prevent counsel from having direct contact with witnesses, so any points of evidence that need clarifying with the witnesses will be done through you.

Counsel may give advice that your client does not wish to hear—most commonly that he should consider pleading guilty to some or all of the charges. Negotiations between opposing counsel on plea bargaining are not uncommon on the first day of a trial. You may also be involved in these discussions which may influence the outcome of the proceedings.

17.6 PLEA BARGAINING

There is no formal system of plea bargaining in England and Wales, and it remains of central importance that a defendant has a genuine choice whether to plead guilty or not guilty. It is common for the prosecution and the defence to negotiate about the gravity of the charge and the defendant's plea. Where a guilty plea to a lesser alternative charge is acceptable to all sides, the prosecution will offer no evidence on the more serious charge or ask for the charge to lie on the court file. Where a defendant faces multiple counts and indicates guilty pleas to some of those counts which are acceptable to the prosecution, the remaining counts can either be withdrawn or allowed to lie on file.

Crown Court judges cannot be party to any plea bargaining arrangement. It is a salient principle that a defendant's decision to plead guilty must be unfettered. However, with the judgment of the Court of Appeal in *R v Goodyear* [2005] 3 All ER 117, a trial judge can, at the invitation of the defendant, give an indication of sentence in the event of a guilty plea. The indication should be as to the maximum sentence if a guilty plea were to be entered. Such an indication would be binding in the event of a guilty plea. The judge is free not to give an indication and any indication of plea must be based on an agreed basis of plea and not on hypothetical facts or charges. Full guidance on the procedure to be adopted is given in the judgment.

17.7 DURING THE TRIAL

You will also make an important contribution during the trial. You will sit behind counsel taking a careful note of the proceedings and be available to give any assistance, particularly if your client wishes to communicate with his barrister. It is especially important to keep an accurate note of the answers given by the prosecution witnesses during cross-examination and by the defence witnesses during examination-in-chief, as counsel is unlikely to make a written record of the witness's answers whilst asking questions.

There may be times during the trial when counsel has missed an important point or you have an idea that might be useful to the defence case. Write a legible note to counsel summarising the point and slide it forward to bring it to counsel's attention. If a more serious issue arises, it may be necessary to hold a conference with counsel at the end of the day or even at an adjournment during the main proceedings.

At the conclusion of the case you should write a full note of the court's decision and ensure that the brief is properly endorsed and that all the accompanying papers are received back from counsel.

Depending on the jury's verdict, this may be a time to congratulate your client on his acquittal or to provide further advice and support to the defendant and his family about the outcome and any avenues of appeal.

17.7.1 THE ARRAIGNMENT IN COURT

The trial formally begins with the defendant's arraignment. While he has already been arraigned at the PCMH and indicated a not guilty plea, the count(s) in the indictment will be put to the defendant again. The defendant is asked whether he pleads guilty or not guilty. Where the defendant enters a not guilty plea, the jury is empanelled.

17.7.2 EMPANELLING THE JURY

The jury will be empanelled or selected from a jury in waiting of 20 or more people who have been summonsed to do jury service at the Crown Court. The clerk of the court calls out the potential juror's names from a recently shuffled pack of cards, each card bearing a juror's name. This fulfils the requirement under s. 11 Juries Act 1974 that jurors should be selected randomly.

Once 12 names have been selected, the individuals are called forward to take the jury oath. Before being sworn, each juror may be asked to 'stand by' by the prosecution or challenged 'for cause' by either the prosecution or the defence.

17.7.3 ASKING A JUROR TO 'STAND BY'

The prosecutor can ask a juror to 'stand by' as he is about the take the oath. Whilst the prosecutor does not have to give a reason to ask a juror to 'stand by', most commonly it will be as a result of the vetting of the jury panel by the police. The practice of asking a juror to 'stand by' has been severely curtailed by the Attorney-General's Guidelines on Exercise by the Crown Court of its Right of Stand-by (1989).

17.7.4 CHALLENGE FOR CAUSE

Both the prosecution and the defence may challenge a juror for cause, s. 12(3) Juries Act 1974. This is done orally immediately before the juror is sworn. The party making the challenge has the burden of proving that:

- the juror is not qualified to serve;
- the juror is biased; or
- the juror may reasonably be suspected of being biased.

17.7.5 JUDICIAL CHALLENGES

The judge has a residual power to remove a juror where, for example, the juror is illiterate or otherwise is deemed unsuitable or incapable of sitting as a juror. A juror may be discharged by the judge during the trial where, for example, he is ill or for 'any other good reason'.

17.7.6 THE COMPOSITION OF THE JURY

An empanelled jury should consist of 12 jurors, although cases are regularly heard with 11 or even 10 jurors.

17.8 THE PROSECUTION CASE

After the jury has been empanelled, the formal part of the trial begins with the prosecution advocate making an opening speech.

17.8.1   **THE OPENING SPEECH**

The purpose of the opening speech is to outline the case in a simple, narrative form by explaining the facts that are alleged and the evidence the prosecution intends to rely on. The opening speech affords the advocate the opportunity to advance a theory of the case.

In his opening speech, the prosecutor will:

* outline the facts of the case;
* instruct the jury that it is the prosecution which brings the case and it is the prosecution which must prove the defendant's guilt;
* explain relevant points of law, although always indicating that the judge is the sole arbiter when matters of law are raised;
* identify the witnesses he intends to call, and in general terms outline what he expects them to tell the court.

Most disputes about the admissibility of evidence will have been dealt with at a pre-trial hearing and be the subject of a binding ruling by the trial judge. Where items of disputed evidence remain to be decided, the prosecutor must not refer to the disputed evidence during the opening speech. Any outstanding evidential issues will be decided in a *voir dire*, i.e. at a trial within the main trial conducted in the absence of the jury.

17.9   **THE COURSE OF TRIAL—PRESENTING EVIDENCE**

Having been sworn or affirmed, each prosecution witness gives evidence in the following order:

* examination-in-chief by the prosecution advocate;
* cross-examination by the defence advocate;
* re-examination (where appropriate) by the prosecution advocate.

Evidence may also be presented in written form, through formal admissions and by adducing exhibits.

Questioning of witnesses through examination-in-chief or cross-examination must be conducted in accordance with the rules of evidence and in compliance with the advocate's professional conduct responsibilities.

* The advocate should always be in control of the witness.
* The advocate should have clear objectives when examining the witness and an awareness of how those objectives can be achieved.
* The advocate should know what the witness is going to say and how the witness is going to say it—the examination of a witness at trial is not about ascertaining the truth—it is about getting the witness to say something that supports the advocate's case. Whether in a summary trial or a trial on indictment, pre-trial preparation, based on the disclosure of evidence will have alerted the advocate to the questions that should be put to witnesses in examination-in-chief or in cross-examination.

It should not be forgotten that a witness may be giving evidence with the benefit of special measures (see Chapter 19).

17.9.1   **EXAMINATION-IN-CHIEF**

The purpose of examination-in-chief is to elicit evidence in support of the party calling the witness.

The rules of evidence associated with examination-in-chief are explained in Chapter 20. One of the most important rules of examination-in-chief is not to ask your witness leading questions unless this is with the express agreement of the opposing advocate.

7.9.2 CROSS-EXAMINATION

Cross-examination has a number of purposes, which include the opportunity to:

- elicit helpful replies or concessions from a witness;
- expose errors, weaknesses or inconsistencies in the witness's account;
- undermine the witness's personal credibility—subject to the permissible limits allowed by the rules of evidence.

The rules relating to cross-examination are explained in Chapter 20. A great deal of importance is attached to cross-examination in the adversarial system of justice. It may seem an obvious point to make, but witnesses are far from infallible. Witnesses may be biased. They may not come to court to tell the truth, the whole truth and nothing but the truth. Memory fades over time. The witness's actual perception of the event may not have been made in ideal circumstances. All of these fallibilities can be exposed and explored in cross-examination. Cross-examination also gives the advocate a chance to put his case to the opponent's witness.

7.9.3 RE-EXAMINATION

In asking questions of his witness in re-examination, the advocate is restricted to matters that have arisen in cross-examination. The advocate cannot introduce new matters which he omitted to ask the witness in examination-in-chief. Re-examination is generally regarded as a damage limitation exercise. It can be used to rehabilitate the witness in the eyes of the court where this is necessary.

We briefly illustrate the process of examination-in-chief and cross-examination in the context of our case study of *R v Lenny Whyte*. At Document 45, located on our Online Resource Centre in the case study section, we have included an extract from the examination of the eyewitness Shirley Lewis.

online resource centre

7.10 DEFENCE SUBMISSION OF NO CASE TO ANSWER

At the close of the prosecution case, the defence may make a submission of 'no case to answer'. The decision is made by the judge in the absence of the jury. The basis of a submission of no case to answer in the Crown Court was explained by Lord Lane in *R v Galbraith* [1981] 2 All ER 1060, in the following terms:

> 'How then should the judge approach a submission of "no case"? (1) If there is no evidence that the crime alleged has been committed by the defendant, there is no difficulty. The judge of course will stop the case. (2) The difficulty arises where there is some evidence but it is of a tenuous character, for example because of the inherent weakness or vagueness or because it is inconsistent with other evidence. (a) Where the judge comes to the conclusion that the Crown's evidence, taken at its highest, is such that a jury properly directed could not properly convict on it, it is his duty, on a submission being made, to stop the case. (b) Where however the Crown's evidence is such that its strength or weakness depends on the view to be taken of a witness's reliability, or other matters which are generally speaking within the province of the jury and where on one possible view of the facts there is evidence on which a jury could properly come to the conclusion that the defendant is guilty, then the judge should allow the matter to be tried by the jury.'

Where the submission of no case to answer is rejected by the court, or a submission is not made, it is likely that the defence will call evidence to support the accused's plea of not guilty.

online
resource
centre

Our case study based on *R v Lenny Whyte* concludes with a successful submission of no case to answer, which is made at the close of the prosecution's case (see Document 46 located on our Online Resource Centre in the case study section).

17.11 THE DEFENCE CASE

- The defence advocate may make an opening speech which will outline the defence case and/or seek to undermine the prosecution evidence.
- The defence will then call evidence in support of its case—beginning with the accused where he elects to testify.

Each defence witness gives evidence in the following order:

- examination-in-chief by the defence advocate;
- cross-examination by the prosecution advocate and co-accused (if applicable);
- re-examination (where appropriate) by the defence advocate.

If the defendant chooses to give evidence on oath, he will be the first defence witness to give evidence (s. 79 PACE 1984). The evidential consequences of the defendant choosing not to give evidence on oath are considered in Chapter 23.

17.12 THE CLOSING SPEECHES

At the close of the defence case, the prosecution advocate and then the defence advocate make a closing speech to the judge and jury. The closing speech is the advocate's final opportunity to persuade the jury of the merits of his party's case. The advocate will attempt to present his case in the most favourable light by identifying any evidence which supports his case and discrediting evidence that undermines it. The defence advocate will usually remind the jurors that if they are left in any doubt about the defendant's guilt, they must acquit.

17.13 THE SUMMING-UP

Following the defence advocate's closing speech, the judge will sum up the case to the jury. The judge directs the jurors on points of law and evidence, and helps them to consider the facts. The following issues are commonly referred to in the summing-up:

- an explanation that the jury are the sole arbiters of the facts in the case, but they must accept judge's direction on points of law and evidence;
- an explanation of the offence(s) charged including an examination of each of the elements;
- a clear direction on the burden and standard of proof;
- an assessment of the evidence put before the court. The judge may comment on the evidence presented by each party as counsel might have done in their closing speeches. The judge may direct the jurors' attention to any answers from a witness which might appear to be implausible or to examine why a particular witness might have a motive to lie;

- depending on the issues in the case, the trial judge may be required to direct the jury on the following evidential issues:
  - the dangers of relying on identification evidence;
  - the dangers of relying on certain types of uncorroborated evidence;
  - the use that can be made of evidence of a defendant's bad character;
  - the use that can be made of the defendant's good character;
  - the precise circumstances in which an adverse inference from the defendant's silence might be drawn under ss. 34, 35, 36 and 37 Criminal Justice and Public Order Act 1994;
  - the special considerations that apply to expert evidence;
  - the need to consider the evidence in relation to each count separately unless the rules of evidence dictate otherwise;
  - the rules relating to confession evidence;
  - the dangers of relying on hearsay evidence;
  - the significance of lies told by the defendant.

Many of the directions the judge is required to give can be found in the Judicial Studies Board specimen directions, available at www.jsboard.co.uk. Quite often the trial judge will discuss his directions with counsel before directing the jury.

When attending counsel or a solicitor advocate in the Crown Court, it is very important that you take a verbatim record of the trial judge's directions. An error in the summing-up or appearance of bias in favour of the prosecution can provide a defendant with grounds for appeal in the event of a conviction.

At the end of the summing-up the judge advises the jury to appoint a foreman and instructs the jury to retire to seek a unanimous verdict.

7.14 THE VERDICT

If the jury reaches a unanimous verdict the jurors return to the courtroom and the judge asks whether they have reached such a verdict. If the answer is 'Yes', the jury foreman reads out the verdict on each count on the indictment. Where the indictment contains alternative counts, for example, counts of burglary or theft, the jury will only return a verdict on one count. An indictment may expressly, or impliedly, include a lesser alternative offence such as manslaughter in place of murder. The decision to leave alternative counts to the jury is a matter for discussion between the advocates and the trial judge.

7.14.1 A UNANIMOUS OR A MAJORITY VERDICT?

In his summing-up the judge will direct the jury to try to reach a unanimous verdict. However, where it is not possible for all the jurors to agree, s. 17 Juries Act 1974 allows for majority verdicts of 11:1 or 10:2 or, if the jury is reduced below 12, a majority 10:1 or 9:1. The defendant may either be convicted or acquitted by a majority verdict.

Before a majority verdict can be considered, the jury must have retired for at least two hours or such longer period as is reasonable, having regard to the nature and complexity of the case. If at the end of that time the jury indicates there is no possibility of reaching a unanimous verdict, the judge may send them out for a further period. If the judge decides that he is willing to accept a majority verdict, the jurors are directed they should continue to reach a unanimous verdict but if they cannot, a majority verdict will be accepted.

17.15 **THE PROCEDURE AFTER THE JURY'S DECISION**

Where the accused is found guilty, the court will proceed to sentence either on the day or, more likely, the proceedings will be adjourned, for pre-sentence reports to enable the court to enquire into the accused's background. Part V of this *Handbook* covers sentencing. Where your client is remanded in custody pending sentence, it will be necessary for you and counsel to see your client in the cells to discuss the verdict and any possible grounds for appeal.

In the event of your client being convicted before the Crown Court, the Criminal Defence Service (Recovery of Defence Costs Orders) (Amendment) Regulations 2004 require a court to impose an order requiring the offender to pay all or some part of his legal costs. A defendant's means (the details of which are contained in Form B) will clearly be a relevant consideration in the making of such an order. Given the high incidence of custodial sentences in the Crown Court, and the fact that the vast majority of defendants have limited means, recovery of defence cost orders are limited, unless the offender has significant assets.

17.16 **ACQUITTED DEFENDANTS**

Defendants who are acquitted, and who have incurred expenditure in their defence, are generally entitled to an award of costs from central funds under s. 16 Prosecution of Offenders Act 1985. Such orders are at the discretion of the trial judge, but should normally be awarded unless it is felt that the accused brought suspicion on himself by his own conduct or misled the prosecution into thinking the evidence against him was stronger than it in fact was. Guidance can be found in *Practice Direction (Costs: Criminal Proceedings)* [2004] 2 All ER 1070. A legally aided acquitted defendant's costs will be met under the representation order.

17.17 **THE PROSECUTION'S RIGHT OF APPEAL**

Although dealt with in more detail in Chapter 29, para. 29.11, this is an appropriate place to explain that the prosecution enjoys a right of appeal over a limited range of matters arising out of a Crown Court trial.

First, under ss. 35 and 36 Criminal Procedure and Investigations Act 1996, the prosecution may make an interlocutory appeal against a binding ruling made by the trial judge at a preparatory hearing.

Second, ss. 57–61 CJA 2003 allows the prosecution to appeal to the Court of Appeal against a terminating ruling made by the judge in relation to an issue at a trial on indictment and which cannot otherwise be the subject of an appeal to the Court of Appeal. The appeal can be against any judicial ruling made during the trial until the beginning of the summing-up to the jury. The procedure is described as appealing against a terminating ruling, as the prosecution must agree that in the event of failing to obtain leave to appeal or the appeal is abandoned, the defendant will be automatically acquitted. The appeal can follow an expedited or non-expedited route.

Third, s. 62 CJA 2003 gives the prosecution a right of appeal against an evidential ruling which has the effect of significantly weakening the prosecution's case but which is not fatal to it. Section 62 is not currently in force.

Fourth, the CJA 2003 has radically revised the traditional operation of *autrefois acquit*. Section 76 CJA 2003 allows the prosecutor to apply to the Court of Appeal for an order to quash the defendant's acquittal for a qualifying offence and to order a new trial. Generally a qualifying offence is any offence which carries a sentence of life imprisonment. The Court of Appeal must order a retrial if there is new and compelling evidence in the case and it is in the interests of justice for the order to be made.

KEY POINT SUMMARY

- Be aware of the circumstances in which a defendant can be tried for more than one offence and can be tried jointly with others.
- Having reached the day of trial your role becomes one of supporting both your firm's client and the trial advocate.
- Be aware that although there is no formal system of plea bargaining, counsel may, with your client's express consent negotiate or take up an offer to plead guilty to a less serious alternative offence.
- Keep clear written notes of the conduct of the proceedings including what is said by counsel in conference and what is said during the course of the evidence.
- Understand the various stages of the trial on indictment and the verdicts which a jury can return.

SELF-TEST QUESTIONS

1. What is a bill of indictment?
2. What is the test for joining more than one count in an indictment?
3. What test does the defence have to meet in order to successfully make a submission of no case to answer at a trial in the Crown Court?
4. What procedure should be adopted in the Crown Court if a point of law arises?
5. Why is the trial judge's summing-up so important?
6. What is an attendance certificate?

Part IV

PROVING THE CASE—THE RULES OF CRIMINAL EVIDENCE

In Part IV we are concerned with the way in which a criminal case is proved in court. Consequently, Part IV covers the rules of criminal evidence which regulate the process of proof. You are reminded that some of the rules of criminal evidence are covered in Part II and that the rules relating to the pre-trial disclosure of evidence are explained in Chapter 14 (Part III).

In Chapter 18 we consider the rules relating to burdens and standards of proof.

In Chapters 19–20 we consider the rules relating to witness testimony.

In Chapter 21 we consider a number of miscellaneous evidence provisions relating to opinion evidence, eye-witness identification and corroboration.

Chapter 22 examines the rules relating to the admission of hearsay evidence in criminal cases.

Chapter 23 considers the special position of the defendant as a witness in the case and in particular the rules relating to the admissibility of a defendant's past bad character.

Finally, in Chapter 24 we consider the rules of evidence which raise aspects of private privilege.

18 THE BURDEN OF PROOF

18.1   INTRODUCTION

In most criminal offences where the defendant pleads not guilty, the prosecution has the responsibility of proving the defendant's guilt. This principle is known as the legal burden of proof. The general rule about the legal burden reflects the presumption that the defendant is innocent until proven guilty and that in the interests of ensuring a fair trial it is appropriate that, as the prosecution is alleging criminal conduct against the defendant, the prosecution has the responsibility of proving the defendant's guilt.

In this chapter we consider:

- the general rule about the incidence of the legal burden of proof;
- the exceptional situations where a legal burden is imposed on the defence (known as reverse burden clauses);
- how a party discharges an evidential burden of proof;
- the meaning of the standards of proof;
- the compatibility of reverse burden clauses with the presumption of innocence under Article 6(2) ECHR 1950; and
- proof without evidence.

18.2   **THE LEGAL BURDEN OF PROOF—THE GENERAL RULE**

The principle that the prosecution has the responsibility for proving the defendant's guilt is known as the legal burden of proof. The principle was emphatically stated in the case of *Woolmington v DPP* [1935] AC 463

In Chapter 2 which introduces the law of criminal evidence, we explained that the legal burden of proof is determined by the facts in issue in the case which are the *actus reus* and *mens rea* of the offence with which the defendant is charged. To remind you, on a charge of theft under s. 1 Theft Act 1968, the facts in issue are:

Actus reus	*Mens rea*
Appropriates	Dishonestly
Property	Intention to permanently deprive
Belonging to another	

Therefore the prosecution has the legal burden of proving the defendant dishonestly appropriated property belonging to another with the intention to permanently deprive.

Where the prosecution fails to discharge its legal burden to prove one or more of the facts in issue, the defence may make a submission of no case to answer as outlined in *R v Galbraith* [1981] 2 All ER 1060 for trials in the Crown Court (see Chapter 17, para. 17.10) and *Practice Direction (Submission of No Case)* [1962] 1 WLR 227 at trials in the magistrates' court (see Chapter 15, para. 15.10). Where the submission of no case to answer is successful, the defendant will be acquitted.

18.3   **EXCEPTIONS TO** *WOOLMINGTON*—**REVERSE BURDEN CLAUSES**

Whilst the *Woolmington* principle applies in most criminal cases, including the most serious offences such as murder and rape, there are a number of exceptional situations where at common law or under statute the defendant has the legal burden of proof on one or more of the facts in issue. These have become known as reverse burden clauses. Whenever a legal burden of proof is cast on a defendant, the presumption of innocence is effectively reversed. Consequently the imposition of a reverse burden of proof raises human right considerations, which are explored in further detail at para. 18.7 below.

18.3.1   **THE REVERSE BURDEN CLAUSE AT COMMON LAW**

At common law where the accused submits that at the time of the offence he was insane within the meaning of *McNaghten's Rules* (1843) 10 Cl & F 200, he has the legal burden of proving insanity.

18.3.2   **EXPRESS STATUTORY REVERSE BURDEN CLAUSES**

In a number of statutes, parliament has expressly passed the legal burden to the accused to prove one or more facts in issue. An example of where parliament has expressly placed the legal burden on the accused to prove a fact in issue is s. 139 Criminal Justice Act 1988, which prohibits a person from possessing a knife in a public place. Under s. 139(4) CJA 1988, the accused has a defence where he can show 'good reason or lawful authority' for possessing the knife in a public place.

After the prosecution has discharged the legal burden of proving that the accused was found in possession of a knife in a public place, the accused then has the legal burden of proving that he had good reason or lawful authority for possessing the knife.

A similar approach is taken with ss. 2 and 4 Homicide Act 1957 (HA). Parliament has expressly provided the accused has the legal burden of proving the defence of diminished responsibility under s. 2 HA 1957 or acting in pursuance of a suicide pact under s. 4 HA 1957. After the prosecution has discharged the legal burden of proving the *mens rea* and *actus reus* of murder, the defendant has the legal burden of proving that at the time of the victim's death he was suffering from diminished responsibility or was acting in pursuance of a suicide pact.

18.3.3 IMPLIED STATUTORY REVERSE BURDEN CLAUSES

In other statutes, parliament has, by implication, placed the legal burden on the accused to prove a fact in issue. An example that you will commonly encounter in summary trials is provided by s. 101 Magistrates' Courts Act 1980, which states:

> 'Where the defendant to an information or complaint relies for his defence on any exception, exemption, proviso, excuse or qualification, whether or not it accompanies the description of the offence or matter of complaint in the enactment creating the offence or on which the complaint is founded, the burden of proving the exception, exemption, proviso, excuse or qualification shall be on him; and this notwithstanding that the information or complaint contains an allegation negating the exception, exemption, proviso, excuse or qualification.'

An example of the operation of s. 101 MCA 1980 is provided by s. 143 Road Traffic Act 1988 which makes it an offence to drive a motor vehicle without insurance. Once the prosecution has discharged its legal burden by proving that on the date specified in the information the defendant drove a motor vehicle on the public highway, the legal burden passes to the accused to prove that at the time he was driving he was insured to do so. If the defendant successfully discharges the legal burden on this issue, he will be acquitted. The application of s. 101 MCA 1980 is a question of statutory interpretation and construction to be decided by the court on the words used by parliament when creating the offence. The section applies most commonly to regulatory offences which prohibit or restrict certain activities such as selling alcohol unless the defendant has a licence to do so or is permitted to engage in a specified activity that is otherwise illegal.

The rationale behind the common law and statutory exceptions to the *Woolmington* principle is that the facts in issue which are covered by a reverse burden clause are within the defendant's exclusive knowledge or control and it is therefore easier for the defendant to prove the fact(s) in issue rather than for the prosecution to disprove.

The imposition of a legal burden of proof on a defendant to prove one or more of the facts in the issue effectively requires the defendant to prove his innocence. On the face of it, this requirement appears to be incompatible with Article 6(2) ECHR 1950 which explicitly provides that everybody charged with a criminal offence shall be presumed innocent until proven guilty. We consider the compatibility of reverse burden clauses with the presumption of innocence under Article 6(2) ECHR 1950 at para. 18.7.

18.4 THE STANDARD OF PROOF REQUIRED TO DISCHARGE THE LEGAL BURDEN

Where the legal burden of proof falls on either the prosecution or the defence the evidence presented to support the fact must have the necessary degree of persuasiveness to convince the court. This is known as the standard of proof. Where the prosecution has the legal burden of proving a fact in issue, the standard of proof is 'beyond a reasonable doubt'. The phrase will be explained to the jury in the following terms:

> 'How does the prosecution succeed in proving the defendant's guilt? The answer is—by making you sure of it. Nothing less than that will do. If after considering all the evidence you are sure that the defendant is guilty, you must return a verdict of "Guilty". If you are not sure, your verdict must be "Not Guilty".'

The standard of beyond reasonable doubt only applies where the prosecution has the legal burden. Where the defence has a legal burden of proof, the appropriate standard is on the balance of probabilities. In *Re H (Minors) (Sexual Abuse: Standard of Proof)* [1996] 1 All ER 1, Lord Justice Nicholls suggested the phrase meant the following:

> 'The balance of probability standard means that the court is satisfied an event occurred if the court considers that, on the evidence, the occurrence of the event was more likely than not.'

18.5 THE EVIDENTIAL BURDEN

A party will prove its case or discharge its legal burden by putting evidence before the court to support its version of the facts and interpretation of the law. This is known as discharging the evidential burden. The party which bears a legal burden of proof usually also bears an evidential burden. The legal burden of proof cannot be discharged unless sufficient evidence is adduced.

The evidential burden will be discharged by:

* calling witnesses to give oral evidence to the court to prove a fact in issue;
* putting documentary evidence before the court to prove a fact in issue;
* putting photographic or video evidence before the court to prove a fact in issue;
* presenting real evidence before the court to prove a fact in issue—for example the alleged weapon at a murder trial; or
* presenting expert opinion evidence before the court for example the presence of the defendant's DNA at the crime scene.

Where a submission of no case to answer is successfully made at the close of the prosecution's case, the prosecution has failed to discharge its evidential burden of proof. Such a submission is determined by the judge in the absence of the jury. An unsuccessful submission of no case to answer does not of course mean that the prosecution has discharged its legal burden of proof, since this is determined by the jury/magistrates at the conclusion of the case and on the totality of the evidence presented on both sides.

Where the defendant simply pleads not guilty but does not put forward an affirmative defence, he may rely on the cross-examination of the prosecution witnesses to instigate reasonable doubt in the mind of the magistrates or jurors about his guilt. In this sense the defendant does not bear an evidential burden. However, in other cases it will be appropriate for the defendant to testify or to call defence evidence.

If the defendant goes further than merely denying the allegation and puts forward an affirmative defence such as self-defence, duress or provocation or non-insane automatism, he has an evidential burden to put some evidence in support of the defence before the court. The defendant will discharge the evidential burden where, if believed and left uncontradicted, his evidence would induce a reasonable doubt in the mind of the magistrates or the jury as to whether his version might be true or not. Where the defendant has discharged his evidential burden, the prosecution then has the legal burden to disprove the accused's defence. If the defendant fails to adduce any evidence of his defence, the trial judge is not obliged to leave the defence to the jury.

18.6 DISCHARGING THE LEGAL AND EVIDENTIAL BURDENS OF PROOF—AN EXAMPLE

 Example

Consider this example of how the prosecution and the defence would discharge its legal or evidential burdens of proof.

Ali is charged with robbery. He denies the offence and pleads not guilty maintaining he is the victim of mistaken identification. The Crown Prosecutor is aware that to discharge the legal burden of proof, the prosecution will have to prove in accordance with s. 8(1) Theft Act 1968, that Ali dishonestly appropriated property belonging to another with the intention to permanently deprive and that before or at the time of doing so and in order to do so, Ali used force on any person or put any person in fear of force being used.

To discharge the legal burden of proof, the prosecution must adduce evidence (i.e. discharge its evidential burden) by calling, for example, the investigating officers to testify. The officers will give evidence in examination-in-chief about the investigation including whether incriminating items were found in Ali's possession linking him to the robbery. The officers will also be able to tell the court if Ali had made incriminating admissions to the police during the investigation or at the police station. Other prosecution witnesses might be called to testify in examination-in-chief that immediately before the robbery they saw Ali at the crime scene. The victim is likely to be an important prosecution witness. She may give evidence in examination-in-chief about the property that was stolen from her and the force that was used against her.

Other types of evidence may also be tendered by the prosecution including real evidence; footage of CCTV recordings and documentary evidence and quite possibly forensic evidence in the form of expert opinion evidence.

The defence will try to undermine the prosecution case by cross-examining each defence witness by challenging the witness's factual evidence and/or attempt to undermine the witness's personal credibility as a witness. The defence may also put evidence before the court in support of Ali's defence. If, for example, Ali is pleading not guilty because he has an alibi, evidence should be put before the court to prove Ali's alleged whereabouts at the time of the offence. However, in this case there is no legal burden of proof on Ali and, as he is not advancing an affirmative defence, there is no evidential burden on him either. His only burden is a tactical one which is to adduce some evidence to raise a reasonable doubt in the mind of the jury.

Where the prosecution fail to adduce evidence in support of an element of the actus reus or the mens rea of robbery, at the close of the prosecution case, the defence may make a submission of no case to answer, as outlined in *R v Galbraith* [1981] 2 All ER 1060.

Assuming a submission of no case to answer is not made in this case or, if it is made, it is unsuccessful following a direction from the judge, the jury will decide whether Ali is guilty on the basis of the evidence presented.

18.7 CHALLENGES TO REVERSE BURDEN CLAUSES UNDER ARTICLE 6 EUROPEAN CONVENTION ON HUMAN RIGHTS 1950

In a number of recent cases, defence lawyers have submitted that imposing a legal burden on the defendant infringes the presumption of innocence under Article 6(2) ECHR 1950. The principles developed so far suggest the courts are dealing with the issue on case-by-case basis. Where it is decided that imposing a legal burden on the defendant infringes Article 6(2), the court must either apply the purposive statutory interpretation under s. 3 Human Rights Act 1998, and read the wording of the statute down to impose an evidential burden of proof only on the defendant or make a declaration of incompatibility where the offending statutory provision is referred back to parliament.

The starting point for considering the compatibility of a reverse burden clause with the presumption of innocence is *Salabiaku v France* (1988) 13 EHHR 370. In this case the Court of Human Rights held that reverse burden clauses are not automatically incompatible with the presumption of innocence under Article 6(2) provided the legal burden imposed on the defence is not unreasonable and is proportionate to the aim of the provision.

18.7.1 REVERSE BURDEN CLAUSES—THE GUIDING PRINCIPLES

If a defendant is charged with an offence containing a reverse burden clause, what guidelines have developed to assist lawyers in determining whether the defendant has to discharge a legal or an evidential burden of proof? The following points are relevant when advising a client and include the important guidance from the Court of Appeal in *Attorney-General's Reference (No. 1 of 2004)* [2004] 1 WLR 2111:

* Reverse burden clauses are more easily justified where the overall burden to prove the essential ingredients of the offence remain on the prosecution.

* If only an evidential burden is cast on the defendant, there will be no risk of contravening of Article 6(2).

* A legal burden is more easily justified where the defendant is required to prove something within his own knowledge. In other words, it is easier for the defendant to prove the fact than for the prosecution to disprove it.

* Conversely, where the prosecution would face considerable practical difficulty in establishing the facts the imposition of a legal burden of proof on a defendant is more easily justified.

* Where the court construes a statute as imposing a legal burden of proof on the defendant compatibility with Article 6(2) depends on whether the imposition of a legal burden is proportionate with the aims of the legislation.

* The stronger the public interest in preventing the type of harm covered by the legislation, the more likely that a legal burden will be placed on the accused:
  — the counterfeiting of goods prohibited by s. 92 Trade Marks Act 1994 which imposes a legal burden of proof on an accused was a proportionate response to the adverse economic effects of counterfeiting on free and fair trade (*R v Johnstone* [2003] 2 Cr App R 33) similarly;
  — s. 139 CJA 1988 was a proportionate response to the social problem of people carrying knives in public (*R v Matthews* [2004] QB 690 and *L v DPP* [2002] 1 Cr App R 32);
  — s. 11(1) Terrorism Act 2000 was not proportionate, given the extraordinary breadth of the particular provision and the practical difficulty a defendant would have in establishing a defence (*Attorney-General's Reference (No. 1 of 2004)* [2004] 1 WLR 2111).

* The more severe the penalty available to the court on a finding of guilt the more reasonable it would be to impose an evidential burden only on the accused.

* It is easier to justify the imposition of a legal burden of proof on a defendant where the offence is of a regulatory nature (*R (on the application of Grundy and Co. Excavations Ltd and the Forestry Commission) v Halton Division Magistrates Court* (2003) 167 JP 387).

For further judicial guidance on reverse burden clauses and the presumption of innocence, see the following cases: *R v Lambert* [2002] 2 AC 545; *R v Mathews* [2004] QB 690; *R v Drummond* [2002] 2 Cr App R 352; *R v Johnstone* [2003] 2 Cr App R 33; *Attorney-General's Reference (No. 1 of 2004)* [2004] 1 WLR 2111; and most authoritatively the House of Lords decision in *Attorney-General's Reference (No. 4 of 2002); Sheldrake v DPP* [2005] 1 AC 264.

8.8 BURDENS OF PROOF—PRACTICAL CONSIDERATIONS

In practical terms, it is vital to research the elements of the offence with which your client is charged so that you know the elements the prosecution must prove to discharge its legal burden and whether there is a legal burden on your client to prove a fact(s) in issue. The same considerations apply when advising clients at the police station. Where a defence is advanced at the earliest opportunity and is repeated at trial, the defendant's credibility is considerably enhanced. You can research the particulars of any offence in *Blackstone's Criminal Practice*.

8.9 PROOF WITHOUT EVIDENCE

As you now understand the general rule is that where the prosecution or the defence has a legal or an evidential burden of proof, the facts in issue have to be proven by relevant and admissible evidence. Exceptionally, in a number of situations explained below, the court may accept a fact as proven without direct evidence being presented in support of that fact. These situations are:

* irrebuttable presumptions of law;
* judicial notice; and
* formal admissions.

8.9.1 IRREBUTTABLE PRESUMPTIONS OF LAW

Where a presumption applies, the court is entitled to presume certain facts without having those facts directly proven. Whilst presumptions are more significant in civil cases, s. 50 Children and Young Persons Act 1933 creates the irrebutable presumption of law that no child under ten years of age can be guilty of a criminal offence. Where the defence offer evidence that the accused is a child under ten years of age, the court will presume that the child is incapable of committing a criminal offence.

8.9.2 JUDICIAL NOTICE

In some situations a criminal court will accept the existence of an issue without any proof in support of that fact. There are two types of judicial notice: judicial notice without inquiry, and judicial notice after inquiry.

Judicial notice without inquiry is taken in respect to those facts which are so much part of common knowledge that they require no proof at all. Facts which fall into this category include that a fortnight is too short a period for human gestation and that the normal duration of human gestation is nine months.

Judicial notice after inquiry applies to those facts which are not so part of common knowledge of which judicial notice may be taken after the judge or magistrates have made appropriate inquiries.

8.9.3 FORMAL ADMISSIONS IN A CRIMINAL CASE—S. 10 CJA 1967

The effect of s. 10 Criminal Justice Act 1967 is that an admission can be made by either the prosecution or the defence before or at the trial. If made before the trial, the admission must be in writing and where the defendant is legally represented, the admission must be made by his solicitor or barrister. Formal admissions help save a considerable amount of court time and are actively encouraged.

KEY POINT SUMMARY

- The rules relating to the incidence of legal and evidential burdens of proof are of considerable practical importance.
- Know the general rule about the incidence of the legal burden of proof in a criminal case.
- Know the exceptions to the '*Woolmington* principle'.
- Be able to explain the relationship between the legal burden and the evidential burden.
- Be aware of the standard of proof that a party has to satisfy in order to discharge its legal burden.
- Understand that where a legal burden of proof is imposed on a defendant an issue of compatibility with Article 6(2) ECHR 1950 might arise.
- Know the evidential effect of a formal admission in a criminal case.
- Be able to apply these basic evidential rules to your client's case.

SELF-TEST QUESTIONS

1. What is the general rule about the incidence of the legal burden of proof in a criminal case?
2. Explain the meaning of the phrase 'reverse burden clause'.
3. What factors do the courts take into account in deciding the compatibility of a reverse burden clause with Article 6(2) European Convention on Human Rights 1950?

FIGURE 18.1 THE LEGAL AND EVIDENTIAL BURDENS OF PROOF

THE LEGAL BURDEN OF PROOF

- as a general rule and as a fundamental component of Article 6 the prosecution has the legal burden of proving the defendant's guilt (*Woolmington v DPP*);

- the prosecution will not know whether it has succeeded in discharging its legal burden of proof until the jury/magistrates return a verdict.

EXCEPTIONS TO THE *WOOLMINGTON* PRINCIPLE WHERE THE DEFENDANT HAS A LEGAL BURDEN OF PROOF (REVERSE BURDEN CLAUSES)

- at common law where the defendant pleads insanity under the *McNaghten Rules* 1843;

- express or implied statutory exceptions (e.g. s. 2 Homicide Act 1957, s. 101 Magistrates' Courts Act 1980 in summary proceedings);

- reverse burden clauses give rise to a potential Article 6 argument.

THE STANDARD OF PROOF

- the legal burden of proof must be discharged 'beyond reasonable doubt;

- 'on the balance of probabilities' wherever legal burden falls on the defence i.e. the court considers that, on the evidence, the occurrence of the event was more likely than not, (*Re H (Minors) (Sexual Abuse: Standard of Proof*).

THE EVIDENTIAL BURDEN OF PROOF

- the general rule is that the party with the legal burden also has an evidential burden;

- it is a burden to adduce some evidence;

- a failure by the prosecution to discharge its evidential burden at the close of the prosecution's case will result in a successful submission of no case to answer by the defence (*R v Galbraith* for Crown Court trials; *Practice Direction (Submission of No Case)* in summary cases);

- there is always a tactical burden on the defendant to exploit the 'reasonable doubt';

- where the defendant raises an affirmative defence, there is an obligation to adduce some evidence of it.

19 WITNESSES EVIDENCE—THE PRELIMINARY ISSUES

19.1 INTRODUCTION

This is the first of two chapters on witness testimony where the defendant pleads not guilty. Chapter 20 explains examination-in-chief, cross-examination and re-examination. This chapter considers the preliminary issues of witness testimony which apply to both summary proceedings and at trials on indictment, including:

- dealing with witnesses before testifying;
- the use of out-of-court memory-refreshing documents;
- the tests to decide a witness's competence to give evidence;
- the compellability of a witness;
- the assistance available to 'vulnerable' or 'intimidated' witnesses to give evidence under a special measures direction;
- a witness taking the oath or affirming.

19.2 DEALING WITH WITNESSES BEFORE TESTIFYING

On the day of the trial, it is the responsibility of the prosecution and defence to ensure that its witnesses are present in the precincts of the court and available to give evidence. The marshalling of witnesses is often the responsibility of a trainee solicitor or a paralegal or a CPS caseworker.

A witness remains out of court until called to give evidence. This ensures that his testimony is not influenced by having heard other evidence. This practice is subject to two exceptions. First, an expert witness will usually be permitted to sit in court before testifying as it is unlikely that his evidence will be influenced by hearing other witnesses. Second, the police officer in charge of the case may also be in court provided the defence consent. The investigating officer's presence recognises his position as the prosecution client and he will be available to advise the prosecutor on any issues arising during the trial.

19.3 REFRESHING THE WITNESS'S MEMORY OUT OF COURT

As a witness is likely to have written or dictated his statement some months earlier to the police or a member of the defence team, while waiting to give evidence the witness should read over his statement to remind himself of the matters about which he is going to testify (*R v Richardson* [1971] 2 QB 484). A witness should not compare or discuss his evidence with other witnesses.

19.4 THE ORDER OF CALLING WITNESSES

Both the prosecution and the defence have discretion in which order to call its witnesses, subject to s. 79 PACE 1984, which requires that the defendant should be called before any other defence witness.

19.5 THE COMPETENT WITNESS—S. 53 YOUTH JUSTICE AND CRIMINAL EVIDENCE ACT 1999 (YJCEA)

Before a witness can testify, the court must be satisfied he is competent to give evidence. A witness is competent where, as a matter of law, the court can receive his evidence. Section 53(1) YJCEA 1999 presumes that all witnesses are competent to testify. It provides:

'At every stage in criminal proceedings all persons are (whatever their age) competent to give evidence.'

Where there is reason to challenge the witness's competence the test to be satisfied is set out in s. 53(3) YJCEA 1999. A person will be competent if it appears to the court that he is able to understand questions put to him and give answers to them which can be understood. This satisfies the test of 'intelligible testimony'.

Witnesses aged 14 years and over are presumed competent to give sworn evidence (s. 55). Witnesses under 14 years are presumed competent to give unsworn evidence (s. 56).

19.6 CHALLENGING THE COMPETENCE OF A WITNESS—S. 54 YJCEA 1999

It is rare for a party (or the court) to challenge a witness's competence and is only likely to be made against a child witness, a young person or a mentally impaired witness. The challenge may be made at the pre-trial review in summary proceedings or at the Plea and Case Management Hearing in the Crown Court and at trial either immediately before or just after the witness has begun to testify. The challenge may relate to his competence *per se* or his competence to give sworn evidence.

In deciding the witness's competence, the court may hear expert evidence and take into account whether the witness will be subject to a 'special measures direction' under s. 19 YJCEA 1999 (see para. 19.7 onwards).

Issues of competency are determined in the Crown Court in the absence of the jury and the burden of proving the witness's competence rests on the party calling the witness. Proof is on the balance of probabilities.

19.6.1 THE COMPETENCE OF A CHILD

For the purposes of giving evidence, a 'child' is a person under 14 years of age and must give unsworn evidence. Where the presumption in favour of competence is challenged, the court must be satisfied that to be competent to testify the child satisfies the 'intelligible testimony' test under s. 53(3) YJCEA 1999. This is only likely to apply to very young children.

19.6.2 THE COMPETENCE OF A YOUNG PERSON

A young person, aged between 14 and 17 years, who is able to give 'intelligible testimony' within s. 53(3) YJCEA 1999 is presumed competent to give sworn evidence. If there is a question about the witness's ability to give sworn evidence, the test set out in s. 55(2) YJCEA 1999 must be satisfied. A witness is capable of giving sworn evidence if, having attained the age of 14, he has sufficient appreciation of the solemnity of the occasion and the particular responsibility to tell the truth which is involved in taking an oath.

Whether a young person is competent to give sworn evidence depends on his emotional maturity and understanding. If he fails the sworn evidence test under s. 55(2) but is capable of giving intelligible testimony (53(3)), he may give unsworn evidence under s. 56(2) YJCEA 1999 and will be in the same position as a witness aged under 14 years.

19.6.3 THE COMPETENCE OF A MENTALLY IMPAIRED WITNESS

Provided the witness is aged 14 years and over, he will be presumed competent to give sworn evidence under s. 53 (1) and s. 55(3) YJCEA 1999. If he fails the sworn evidence test (s. 55(2)), he may give unsworn evidence under s. 56(2) YJCEA 1999. In making these decisions, the court will take into account that a mentally impaired witness may be subject to a special measures direction as a 'vulnerable' witness under s. 16 YJCEA 1999.

19.6.4 DEALING WITH ISSUES OF COMPETENCE

Good case preparation will have identified and anticipated any problems that might arise about the competence of a witness. Therefore before trial the defence solicitor should identify any witnesses to be called by the other side whose competence may be challenged.

The difficulties encountered with the competence and credibility of the main prosecution witness during the first Damilola Taylor murder trial is a good illustration of what might happen when these matters are not properly addressed during case preparation. Damilola Taylor was a ten-year-old schoolboy who bled to death in November 2000 on the stairwell of a block of flats on the North Peckham Estate in south London. Two 16-year-old brothers were charged with murder. In pleading not guilty, the defence claimed the boy had injured himself accidentally.

A key prosecution witness was a 14-year-old girl, known only as witness Bromley, who claimed that she had witnessed the attack. However, the reliability of her testimony was tainted after it was suggested in cross-examination that she was only giving evidence to claim a £50,000 reward offered by the *Daily Mail* in connection with the conviction of Damilola's murderers. As a result of the attacks on the witness's credibility, the prosecution case collapsed and the brothers were acquitted. Since 2008, a CPS lawyer can now carry out an audio-taped pre-trial witness interview, if felt to be necessary, and in accordance with set guidelines.

19.7 A SPECIAL MEASURES DIRECTION UNDER S. 19 YJCEA 1999

An application for a special measures direction may be made by the prosecution or the defence or by the court. The rules of court relating to such application are contained in Crim PR, Part 29. The application will usually be made at the pre-trial review in summary proceedings or at the Plea and Case Management Hearing in indictable offences.

Special measures will be ordered where the witness is either 'vulnerable' under s. 16 YJCEA 1999 or 'intimidated' under s. 17 YJCEA 1999 and the court is satisfied that it will improve the quality of the witness's evidence (s. 19(2) YJCEA 1999).

19.7.1 A 'VULNERABLE' WITNESS—S. 16 YJCEA 1999

A vulnerable witness is:

- a witness under 17 at the time of the court hearing; or
- a witness who has a significant impairment of intelligence and social functioning, mental disability, mental or physical disorder or a physical disability.

A vulnerable witness will automatically attract a special measures direction entitling him to a range of facilities to assist him to give oral evidence. Section 21 YJCEA 1999 provides additional safeguards for a child witness in need of special protection who gives evidence about sexual and other specified offences including kidnapping and assault.

19.7.2 AN 'INTIMIDATED' WITNESS—S. 17 YJCEA 1999

A special measures direction can be made in relation to an 'intimidated' witness where the court is satisfied the quality of the witness's evidence would be diminished by his fear or distress connected with testifying in the proceedings.

The intimidation may result from the witness's personal and/or social circumstances. Under s. 17(2) YJCEA 1999, the court will take into account the following:

- the nature of and the alleged circumstances of the offence to which the proceedings relate;
- the witness's age;
- the witness's social and cultural background and ethnic origin;
- the witness's domestic and employment circumstances;
- the witness's religious and political beliefs; and
- the behaviour of the accused towards the witness, members of accused's family or associates and the views of the witness.

A complainant in a sexual offence automatically falls within this section. The facilities that are available under a special measures direction depends on whether the witness is a child, a vulnerable adult or an intimidated witness and whether the witness testifies at the Crown Court or in the magistrates' court.

19.7.3 THE USE OF A SCREEN—S. 23 YJCEA 1999

A special measures direction may permit the use of a screen which prevents the witness from being seen by the accused while testifying. The screen should not prevent the witness from being seen and seeing:

- the judge and jury or the justices;
- the advocates; and
- any person who has been appointed to assist the witness, for example an interpreter appointed under s. 29 YJCEA 1999.

Giving evidence from behind a screen is available for a child, a vulnerable adult or an intimidated witness in both the Crown Court and in the magistrates' court.

19.7.4 GIVING EVIDENCE BY A LIVE TELEVISION LINK—S. 24 YJCEA 1999

A special measures direction may permit the witness to give evidence by a live television link. In *Camberwell Green Youth Court, ex p. D and Others* [2003] 2 Cr App R1, the defence submitted that permitting a witness to testify through a live TV link infringed the defendant's right to a fair trial under Article 6 ECHR 1950. This argument was rejected as the proceedings were not unfair simply because the child witness and the accused were not in the same room. The decision was confirmed by the House of Lords reported at [2005] 2 Cr App R 1.

Giving evidence by a live television link is available to a child, a vulnerable adult or an intimidated witness in the Crown Court and in the magistrates' court.

 Looking Ahead

When s. 51 CJA 2003 comes fully into force, the court may make much greater use of evidence through live TV link. The court will be permitted to authorise a witness, other than the defendant, to testify through a live link in any case where it is satisfied that it is in the interests of efficient or effective administration of justice and where suitable facilities are available. The section has a potentially general application and there are no guidelines currently available on how the power under s. 51 should be exercised. It is likely this provision will be used where a witness is in a different part of the country and it is impractical to ensure their attendance in court.

19.7.5 GIVING EVIDENCE IN PRIVATE—S. 25 YJCEA 1999

A special measures direction excludes from the court certain people specified in the direction. The direction may only be made where:

- the proceedings relate to a sexual offence; or
- it appears to the court that there are reasonable grounds for believing that any other person than the accused has sought or will seek to intimidate the witness in connection with testifying in the proceedings.

The following participants in the trial may not be excluded:

- the defendant;
- the defendant's legal representatives;
- an interpreter appointed to assist the witness;
- a court reporter representing a news-gathering organisation.

Giving evidence in private is available for a child, a vulnerable adult or an intimidated witness in both the Crown Court and in the magistrates' court.

9.7.6 REMOVING THE LAWYERS' WIGS—S. 26 YJCEA 1999

A special measures direction may provide that the wearing of wigs or gowns should be dispensed with during the giving of a witness's evidence. A special measures direction requiring the advocates to remove their wigs is available for a child, a vulnerable adult or an intimidated witness in the Crown Court only.

9.7.7 VIDEO-RECORDED EVIDENCE-IN-CHIEF—S. 27 YJCEA 1999

A special measures direction may provide for the video-recording of an interview with the witness which may be admitted as his evidence-in-chief, unless it would not be in 'the interests of justice' to allow the recording to be admitted.

Video-recorded evidence-in-chief evidence is available to a child or vulnerable adult witness in the Crown Court and a child witness in need of special protection in the magistrates' court. The facility is limited to an intimidated witness appearing in the Crown Court and is the subject of a pilot scheme. Video-recorded evidence-in-chief is not available to an intimidated witness in the magistrates' court.

 Looking Ahead

When s. 137 CJA 2003 comes into force, wider use may be made of video-recorded evidence in cases involving serious crimes. The section will enable a court to authorise a video-recording of an interview with a witness (other than the accused) to be admitted as the evidence-in-chief provided that:

(a) the person claims to be a witness to the offence, or part of it, or to events closely connected with it; and

(b) the video-recording of the statement was made at a time when the events were fresh in the witness's memory; and

(c) the offence is indictable-only, or is a prescribed either-way offence.

Where the recording is admitted under this provision, it is treated as the final statement of the matters it deals with (s. 138 CJA 2003) and will constitute the witness's evidence-in-chief.

9.7.8 VIDEO-RECORDED CROSS-EXAMINATION OR RE-EXAMINATION—S. 28 YJCEA 1999

Where a special measures direction provides for the video-recording to be admitted under s. 27 YJCEA 1999 as the witness's evidence-in-chief, the direction may also provide that any cross-examination or re-examination should be video-recorded. The recording must be made in the presence of the judge or justices and the legal representatives acting in the proceedings. The recording may be made in the absence of the accused. This facility is available for a vulnerable child witness.

9.7.9 EXAMINATION OF A WITNESS THROUGH AN INTERMEDIARY—S. 29 YJCEA 1999

A special measures direction may provide for the witness to be examined through an interpreter or through any other person as the court may direct. The intermediary is required to communicate questions to the witness and give the witness's reply.

A special measures direction requiring the witness to be examined through an intermediary is only available to a child or a vulnerable adult in a Crown Court or a magistrates' court that is part of the pilot scheme. The facility is not available to an intimidated witness in either the Crown Court or the magistrates' court.

19.7.10   **AIDS TO COMMUNICATION—S. 30 YJCEA 1999**

A special measures direction may provide for the witness while giving evidence (whether in court or otherwise) to be provided with such a device as the court considers appropriate to enable questions to be put to the witness or receive answers from him to overcome any disorder or disability or other impairment which the witness has or suffers from.

This facility is available to a child or a vulnerable adult in the Crown Court and a magistrates' court. It is not available to an intimidated witness in either the Crown Court or the magistrates' court.

19.8   **THE COMPELLABILITY OF A WITNESS**

Where a person is competent to testify, he will also generally be a compellable witness. A witness is compellable if, as a matter of law, he can be made to give evidence, and a failure to give evidence may result in that person being committed to prison for contempt of court.

There are two main exceptions to the general rule about a witness's compellability to give evidence—the defendant and the defendant's spouse. The position of the defendant as a witness is considered in Chapter 23.

19.8.1   **THE SPOUSE AS A COMPELLABLE WITNESS**

The second exception to the general rule about the compellability of a witness is the defendant's spouse. The position is governed by s. 80 PACE 1984 and establishes the following principles:

- The defendant's spouse or civil partner (as defined by the Civil Partnership Act 2004) is competent and compellable to give evidence on behalf of the defendant unless the spouse or civil partner is jointly charged in the proceedings, s. 80(4) PACE 1984.

- The general rule is that the defendant's spouse or civil partner is a competent but not compellable witness for the prosecution except where s. 80(3) PACE 1984 applies by making the spouse or civil partner a compellable witness where the defendant is charged with an assault on, or injury or a threat of injury to, the wife, husband or civil partner or a person who was at the material time under the age of 16; or is charged with a sexual offence alleged to have been committed in respect of a person who was at the material time under the age of 16. Section 80(3) PACE 1984 has no application however if the spouse or civil partner is jointly charged with such an offence unless he no longer stands to be convicted.

- The spouse or civil partner of an accused is a competent witness on behalf of a co-accused unless also jointly charged in the proceedings. A spouse or civil partner only becomes a compellable witness for a co-accused in circumstances where he would have been a compellable witness for the prosecution within s. 80(3).

 Example

Gordon is pleading not guilty to separate offences of theft and sexual assault on Lucy, who is eight years old.

Moira, who is Gordon's wife, is a competent and a compellable defence witness for both offences. If the prosecution wish to call Moira to give evidence against Gordon, she will be a competent but not a compellable witness at Gordon's trial for theft. If the prosecution wish to call Moira to give evidence against Gordon at his trial for sexual assault, Moira will be both competent and compellable. She is compellable, as the offence of sexual assault falls within s. 80(3) PACE 1984.

9.9 TAKING THE OATH OR AFFIRMING

Before testifying, the witness has to take the oath or affirm.

Where the witness is a religious observer, s. 1 Oaths Act 1978 allows the oath to be taken on the New Testament or in the case of a Jewish witness, on the Old Testament. The witness will be required to state: 'I swear by Almighty God . . .' and then the appropriate form of words as prescribed by law.

Where the witness follows another faith, an appropriate form of oath will be taken. For example, a Muslim witness is sworn on the Koran 'I swear by Allah . . .'. A Sikh will swear on the Sunder Gutka 'I swear by Waheguru . . .'

If the witness refuses to take an oath or the oath is contrary to his religion, s. 5 Oaths Act 1978 allows the witness to make a solemn affirmation in the following form: 'I [name] do solemnly, sincerely and truly declare and affirm . . .'

KEY POINT SUMMARY

- All witnesses are presumed to be competent to give evidence.
- A witness aged 14 and over is presumed competent to give sworn evidence.
- Anticipate and be prepared to argue against any challenges to the competence of your witnesses and to raise argument as to the competency of an opposing party's witness.
- Know the tests that a witness has to satisfy to be competent and to be able to give sworn evidence.
- Know the rules governing the compellability for competent witnesses for both the prosecution and the defence.
- Special measures directions are available to assist vulnerable or intimidated witnesses to give evidence.
- Know the practice and procedure for applying for a special measures direction and the facilities that are available.

SELF-TEST QUESTIONS

To test your understanding of the preliminary issues of witness testimony, consider the following scenario and answer the questions that follow.

David is charged with sexual assault on his stepdaughter, Florence, aged 14. Florence has learning difficulties. David is pleading not guilty. The prosecution has witness statements from Susie, David's wife and their son, Aaron aged seven.

(a) Is Susie a competent and compellable witness for the prosecution?

(b) Which type of evidence will Florence be presumed competent to give?

(c) Consider why there may be doubts about Florence's competence to give this type or any other type of evidence.

(d) Which type of evidence will Aaron be presumed competent to give?

(e) What provisions are there to assist Florence and Aaron to give evidence?

Case study: *R v Lenny Whyte*

With reference to the *R v Lenny Whyte* case study, consider whether any of the potential witnesses in this case might qualify in terms of a special measures direction.

Analysis can be found in Appendix 4.

FIGURE 19.1 WITNESS COMPETENCE AND COMPELLABILITY

COMPETENCY

- a witness is competent where as a matter of law his evidence can be received by the court;
- all witnesses are presumed competent to give evidence (s. 53(1) YJCEA 1999);
- a witnesses aged 14 years and above will be presumed competent to give sworn evidence;
- a witness aged under 14 years will be presumed competent to give unsworn evidence;
- where a witness's competence is challenged, s. 54 YJCEA 1999 lays down the procedure for the court to decide the issue;
- the court must be satisfied that the witness is able to understand questions put to him and give answers to them which can be understood (s. 53(3) YJCEA 1999);
- a witness may be granted the benefit of a special measures direction before a determination as to competency is made (s. 54(3) YJCEA 1999).

COMPELLABILITY

- a witness is compellable where he can be made to give evidence and a failure to testify may result in him suffering a penalty;
- generally, all witnesses are competent and compellable for the prosecution, except
  - the defendant and co-defendant; and
  - the defendant's spouse BUT see s. 80(3) PACE 1984.

SPECIAL MEASURES DIRECTION, S. 19 YJCEA 1999

- a special measures direction seeks to reduce the trauma of a 'vulnerable' or an 'intimidated' witness to give evidence;
- s. 16 YJCEA 1999 defines a 'vulnerable' witness as:
  - a witness under 17 years; or
  - a witness who suffers from significant impairment of intelligence and social functioning;
- s. 17 YJCEA 1999 defines an intimidated witness as:
  - a witness whose quality of evidence is diminished by fear or distress associated with testifying;
- where a special measures direction is made under s. 19 YJCEA 1999, the court may order the following, subject to availability:
  - witness may give evidence from behind a screen, s. 23 YJCEA 1999;
  - witness may give evidence through a live TV link, s. 24 YJCEA 1999;
  - witness may give evidence in private, s. 25 YJCEA 1999;
  - removal of lawyers' wigs, s. 26 YJCEA 1999;
  - witness may video-record his evidence-in-chief, s. 27 YJCEA 1999;
  - witness may video-record his cross-examination and re-examination, s. 28 YJCEA 1999;
  - witness may give evidence through an intermediary, s. 29 YJCEA 1999;
  - witness may give evidence with the benefit of a communication aid, s. 30 YJCEA 1999.

20 WITNESS TESTIMONY

20.1 INTRODUCTION

Once the preliminary issues of witness testimony have been dealt with, the witness's evidence will usually be presented to the court in three stages. The first stage is examination-in-chief, where the witness is questioned by the advocate calling him. The second stage involves the witness being cross-examined by the other side's advocate. The third stage is re-examination, where the advocate calling the witness has an opportunity to repair any damage done to the witness's factual evidence or personal credibility during cross-examination.

In this chapter we provide an overview of the evidential and procedural issues that may arise during each stage of witness testimony, including:

- the purposes of examination-in-chief, cross-examination and re-examination;
- the law governing leading questions and the use of memory-refreshing documents;
- the practice and procedure where a witness is ruled as 'hostile';
- the evidential effect of a witness's previous consistent and inconsistent statements;
- cross-examining the witness on his factual evidence;
- attacking the witness's credibility in cross-examination.

Changes introduced under the Criminal Justice Act 2003 are highlighted.

20.2 EXAMINATION-IN-CHIEF

This is the stage where the party questions his own witness and has the following purposes:

- to obtain answers from the witness about his factual evidence which supports the party's case;
- to put questions to the witness which enhance his personal credibility;
- to raise any matters which the advocate anticipates might be raised in cross-examination.

Having previously taken the witness's statement when events were fresh in the witness's mind, the trial advocate will know which questions to ask in examination-in-chief. An advocate should not ask a question in examination-in-chief to which the advocate does not know the answer.

20.3 LEADING QUESTIONS

A leading question either suggests to the witness the answer desired or assumes the existence of disputed facts that have not yet been satisfactorily proven.

 Example 1

The advocate questions his witness in the following way:

'The car you saw the defendant drive away from the crime was a blue Ford Escort, wasn't it?'

'Is it correct to suggest that when you saw the defendant he was acting suspiciously?'

These questions clearly offend the rule against leading questions, as the witness is led into giving the answer the advocate desires.

The general rule is that leading questions are not allowed during examination-in-chief. Where a leading question is asked, the judge or the magistrates' adviser will suggest to the advocate that the question should be put differently.

20.3.1 ARE LEADING QUESTIONS EVER PERMITTED DURING EXAMINATION-IN-CHIEF?

As exceptions to the general rule, leading questions are permitted during examination-in-chief in two situations:

- at the start of a witness's testimony for purely formal or introductory matters, such as the witness's name, address and occupation; and
- where a fact is not in dispute between the parties.

Consider the following short illustration of an examination-in-chief.

Example 2

In a prosecution for a domestic assault the prosecutor could start his examination-in-chief of the complainant in the following way:

Q: Mrs Smith, can you recall what you were doing in the early evening of 6 April?

A: Yes. I was at home preparing supper.

Q: Who else was at home with you?

A: My children. They were upstairs playing with their computer games.

Q: Was your husband home at this time?

A: No. He was down the pub.

Q: What time did your husband come home?

A: He came home at around 7.30 in the evening.

Q: Can you describe your husband's demeanour when he came in?

A: I'm sorry, I don't understand the question.

Q: Can you tell the court what you observed about your husband when he walked in?

A: I could tell he was drunk.

Q: How could you tell he was drunk?

A: He was unsteady on his feet and he smelt of alcohol.

Q: In your own words can you tell the court what happened next . . .

20.4 THE USE OF DOCUMENTS TO REFRESH MEMORY WHILE GIVING EVIDENCE

A witness is permitted to refresh his memory not only before testifying but also whilst giving evidence. Under s. 139 Criminal Justice Act 2003, a witness is entitled to refresh his memory from a document or transcript of a sound recording at any stage while testifying, provided:

- the document was made or verified by the witness on an earlier occasion; and
- the witness states in his oral evidence that the document records his recollection of the matter at the earlier time; and
- his recollection of the matters about which he is testifying is likely to have been significantly better at that time than it is at the time of his oral evidence.

Before the witness can use the document, it must be produced for inspection by the court and by the opposing advocate. Where the witness is cross-examined on those parts of the document which the witness used to refresh his memory, the document does not form part of the evidence in the case.

Where the cross-examiner strays outside those parts of the document that the witness used to refresh his memory, the whole document may be put in evidence to be considered by the jury/magistrates as evidence of the truth of what it states (s. 120(3) CJA 2003).

 Example

The most commonly encountered memory-refreshing document is a police officer's notebook. Where the officer wishes to refresh his memory during examination-in-chief, it is customary for the following exchange to take place between the advocate and the officer.

Police officer:	'May I refer to my pocket book?'
Advocate:	'When did you make up your pocket book, officer?'
Police officer:	'When I returned to the police station.'
Advocate:	'Were the events still fresh in your mind when you made up your pocket book?'
Police officer:	'Yes they were'.

The court usher will then pass the notebook to be inspected by the court and the defence advocate. The defence advocate should carefully note the parts used by the officer to refresh his memory and should restrict cross-examination to those parts to avoid the entire document becoming part of the evidence in the case.

A 'lay' witness may also refer to a memory-refreshing document, for example, a piece of paper on which he noted the description and registration number of a car he saw at the crime scene.

20.5 THE ADMISSIBILITY OF PREVIOUS CONSISTENT (SELF-SERVING) STATEMENTS AT COMMON LAW

The admissibility of a witness's previous consistent statement has at common law always been clear. Apart from a small number of exceptions, such statements were inadmissible as lacking any significant probative value. The common law placed great reliance on the witness's evidence in the witness box and not what the witness may have said out-of-court. Section 120 CJA 2003 has extended the situations where a witness's previous consistent statement can be admitted in evidence.

20.5.1 THE ADMISSIBILITY OF PREVIOUS CONSISTENT STATEMENTS UNDER S. 120 CJA 2003

A witness's previous consistent statement can be admitted in the following situations:

- to rebut the allegation that the witness's evidence has been recently fabricated, s. 120(2) CJA 2003 (this is dealt with at para. 20.12 below in the context of re-examination);
- where a memory-refreshing document has been admitted into evidence following cross-examination, s. 120(3) CJA 2003. This provision applies where the witness has been cross-examined on issues contained in the document that were not used to refresh the witness's memory during examination-in-chief;
- where the witness has made the statement, which to the best of the witness's knowledge is true, and where one of the following conditions is satisfied:
  - the statement identifies or describes a person, object or place, s. 120(5) CJA 2003; or
  - the statement was made when the matters were fresh in the witness's memory but he does not remember them and cannot reasonably be expected to remember them well enough to give oral evidence about them in the proceedings, s. 120(6) CJA 2003; or
  - the witness as the victim of the alleged crime has made a complaint to another person about what had happened to him, and the complaint was made by the victim as soon as could reasonably be expected after the alleged conduct by the defendant and was not made as a result of a threat or promise, s. 120(7) CJA 2003.

The application of a s. 120 CJA 2003 statement is designed to add to the witness's testimony, not to supplant it. Where a previous consistent statement is admitted under s. 120, the statement is admissible as evidence of any matter stated of which oral evidence by the witness would be admissible. This change to the evidential effect of a previous consistent statement is part of the general reforms to the hearsay rule, considered in Chapter 22.

Example 1

Section 120(5) CJA 2003 permits a previous consistent statement to be admitted by the court where the statement identifies or describes a person, object or place. This provision will now make the following exchange between the advocate and the witness admissible:

Advocate:	'Tell the court about the car you saw at the scene of the crime on the day in question.'
Witness:	'It was a red Ford Fiesta, but I do not think I can recall the registration number off the top of my head.'
Advocate:	'Did you confirm the car's description and registration number verbally to the police officer and in your written statement?'
Witness:	'Yes. I did.'
Advocate:	'Is this a copy of your earlier written statement?'
Witness:	'Yes it is.'
Advocate:	'Whose signature appears at the bottom of each page on the statement?'
Witness:	'It is my signature.'
Advocate:	'When you made that statement to the police were the events that it recalls fresh in your mind?'
Witness:	'Yes they were . . .'
Advocate:	'Can I ask you to look at your earlier statement. What did you say the Ford Fiesta's registration was in that statement?'
Witness:	'I said it was DH 05 FRJ.'
Advocate:	'To the best of your knowledge was that earlier statement you made based on your honest recollection of events?'
Witness:	'Yes it was . . .'

Where the witness's previous consistent statement is admitted under s. 120(5) CJA 2003, it is admissible as evidence of the truth of the statement's contents—i.e. that the witness did see the car of that description and registration number at the crime scene.

 Example 2

Gill is the victim of a street robbery. Heavily traumatised by the incident, she goes home and tells her brother Chris about the robbery and describes the assailant.

Under s. 120(7) CJA 2003, provided the court is satisfied that Gill told her brother about the robbery at the first reasonable opportunity, evidence of the conversation may be admitted in evidence at the trial of the person accused of robbing Gill, providing Gill gives a first-hand account of what occurred. As with example 1, where Gill's previous consistent statement is admitted under s. 120(7) CJA 2003, it is admissible as evidence of the truth of the statement's contents—i.e. that Gill was the victim of a street robbery committed by the person Gill described to her brother.

20.6 UNFAVOURABLE AND HOSTILE WITNESSES

At an early stage in the proceedings the prosecution and the defence will have taken a proof of evidence from each witness it intends to call to give evidence and support its case at trial. In most cases, a witness will give the answers expected of him and his oral evidence will be consistent with his earlier statement. In this situation, a witness is said to 'come up to proof'. Sometimes a witness does not give the answers expected of him during examination-in-chief because the witness may either be 'unfavourable' or 'hostile'.

20.6.1 UNFAVOURABLE WITNESS

A witness is unfavourable where he cannot recall some a fact/s about his testimony even after refreshing his memory. The advocate cannot assist his witness by putting leading questions or by prompting him—even though the witness's inability to answer his questions may damage his side's case. In this situation, it is good practice to get the witness out of the witness box as soon as possible—subject, of course, to the other party's right to cross-examine him.

20.6.2 HOSTILE WITNESS

While an unfavourable witness may be potentially damaging to your case, a more serious situation arises where your witness appears to be hostile. A witness is hostile where he shows no desire to tell the truth in support of the case of the party calling him.

The clearest example is where a witness has deliberately changed his evidence since making his written statement, whether from a desire not to be involved in the case or through fear or malice.

20.6.3 WHAT ACTION CAN BE TAKEN IF THE WITNESS APPEARS HOSTILE?

The advocate will ask the judge to send the jurors out and in their absence apply for leave to treat the witness as hostile. In summary proceedings the advocate will make a submission to the justices, who will seek the advice of their legal adviser.

The judge or magistrates will then be shown the witness's previous written statement so as to support the application to have the witness ruled as hostile. The court will decide whether the witness is hostile or merely unfavourable by considering the witness's demeanour, attitude and any other relevant factor.

If your witness is ruled hostile, there are a number of options available to the advocate:

* the advocate may ask his witness leading questions by way of cross-examination; and/or
* s. 3 Criminal Procedure Act 1865 permits the advocate to ask his witness whether or not he has made an earlier statement which is inconsistent with his present oral testimony.

Where the witness adopts his earlier written statement as his evidence or the written statement is proven against him, s. 119(1) CJA 2003 provides that the statement becomes evidence of any matter stated in it of which oral evidence would have been admissible.

 Example

> Brian is pleading not guilty to assault occasioning actual bodily harm against Gordon. In her statement to the police, Emma states that she saw Brian hit Gordon in the face. At Brian's trial, Emma is called by the prosecution and in examination-in-chief, she states that Brian did not hit Gordon. The prosecutor may ask Emma to refresh her memory from her written statement. The prosecutor will put the question to Emma again. If she continues to deny that Brian hit Gordon, the prosecutor may apply to the court for Emma to be treated as a hostile witness. If the court grants leave to treat Emma as a hostile witness, the prosecutor may ask Emma leading questions and/or ask her whether she made a previous written statement that is inconsistent with her present oral evidence. If Emma adopts her earlier written statement as her evidence, or her earlier written statement is proven against her, the effect of s. 119(1) CJA 2003 is that her statement that she saw Brian hit Gordon in the face may be admitted in evidence. It will be a matter for the jury/magistrates to determine where the truth lies.

20.7 CROSS-EXAMINATION

Cross-examination of a witness serves a number of purposes:

* to obtain factual evidence from the witness which supports the case of the cross-examiner;
* to test the truthfulness of the evidence the witness has given in examination-in-chief or to cast doubt on the witness's evidence;
* to undermine the witness's credibility.

0.7.1 CHALLENGING THE WITNESS'S FACTUAL EVIDENCE

Where the advocate in cross-examination contradicts the witness's factual evidence, the cross-examiner should put his client's version of the facts to the witness to give the witness the opportunity to explain the contradiction. A failure to cross-examine a witness on his factual evidence will be taken by the court as accepting the witness's evidence-in-chief on that issue.

Questions asked in cross-examination are not only restricted to the issues arising during examination-in-chief but may be directed to any fact in issue or to attacking the witness's credibility. Leading questions are allowed and are essential for effective cross-examination.

Consider the following example of cross-examination.

 Example

Continuing the example of the domestic violence assault highlighted earlier in the context of examination-in-chief, the defence advocate might cross-examine the complainant as follows:

Q: It's simply not true is it, Mrs Smith, that your husband launched an unprovoked attack on you?

A: He did.

Q: In fact it was you who had been drinking, hadn't you Mrs Smith?

A: No.

Q: Your husband says there was a half empty bottle of vodka on the kitchen table.

A: It's not true.

Q: Is it true that you have had counselling for drink problems in the recent past?

A: I have been depressed. I wasn't drunk.

Q: So you accept you sometimes drink to escape your problems?

A: I sometimes have a drink but I wasn't drunk.

Q: In fact you have been having a lot of problems in your marriage recently, haven't you?

A: Yes.

Q: Your husband has been seeing someone else, hasn't he and that must have made you feel very angry and hurt.

A: He assaulted me.

Q: Your husband was intending to leave you that night, wasn't he?

A: I don't know.

Q: When he came in to the house it was with the intention of collecting some personal belongings, wasn't it?

A: No—he asked me why his supper wasn't ready. He started shouting at me like he always does.

Q: No—that's not how it happened is it? You tried to stop him getting past you. He pushed you to one side and you lost your temper, didn't you?

A: No.

Q: You lost your temper and attacked him. In defending himself he pushed you back and you fell against the kitchen sink—that's how you cut your head didn't you?

A further example of the way in which witness testimony is obtained in court is provided in the *R v Lenny Whyte* case study in relation to the eyewitness, Shirley Lewis. The complete version can be accessed on our Online Resource Centre.

online resource centre

20.8 **ATTACKING THE WITNESS'S CREDIBILITY**

The cross-examiner may also attack the witness's credibility to persuade the jury or the magistrates to give little or no weight to the witness's oral evidence. Matters affecting the credibility of a witness's evidence are said to be collateral issues in the case and subject to the finality rule. There are various ways in which a witness's credibility may be undermined, including accusing the witness of bias; of having made a previous statement inconsistent with the evidence he now gives or generally being unworthy of belief because of past bad character.

20.8.1 **THE FINALITY RULE**

Generally, questions asked in cross-examination to undermine the witness's general credibility are subject to the finality rule. This means that evidence cannot be called to rebut the witness's answer—even if the cross-examiner does not accept the answer given by the witness. This is because the witness's credibility is a collateral or secondary issue that runs alongside the central issue at trial—the determination of the defendant's guilt or innocence.

20.8.2 **EXCEPTIONS TO THE FINALITY RULE**

The common law provides a number of exceptions to the finality rule, where the cross-examining advocate is allowed to adduce evidence to contradict the answer given by the witness. The exceptions include establishing that the witness:

• is biased; or

• has made a previous inconsistent statement; or

• has previous convictions, s. 100 CJA 2003; or

• suffers from a physical or mental disability.

20.8.3 **SUGGESTING THE WITNESS IS BIASED**

Where a witness appears to be biased in favour of the party calling him the issue of his bias can be raised in cross-examination. Where the witness denies the allegation, his denial may be rebutted by evidence and independently proved. There are many examples of conduct that may amount to bias but the allegation often relates to where a witness has taken a bribe or has a close relationship with the party calling him or has 'an axe to grind' against the other side.

20.8.4 **IDENTIFYING INCONSISTENCIES BETWEEN THE WITNESS'S ORAL EVIDENCE AT TRIAL AND AN EARLIER STATEMENT**

In cross-examination the advocate will have a copy of the witness's written statement disclosed under the pre-trial disclosure of evidence rules (see Chapter 14) and will expect answers that are consistent with the witness's written statement. However, where the witness gives answers that are inconsistent with his earlier written statement, s. 5 Criminal Procedure Act 1865 permits the witness to be cross-examined about those parts of his written statement that are inconsistent with his oral evidence.

If the witness denies that he made a written statement that is inconsistent with his present oral testimony and the advocate wishes to contradict the witness, the advocate must draw the witness's attention to those parts of his statement that are inconsistent with his oral testimony. The witness will then be asked whether he wishes the court to adopt the version of his evidence contained in the written statement or his oral evidence.

Section 4 Criminal Procedure Act 1865 provides a similar provision in relation to an inconsistency between a witness's previous oral statement and his oral testimony in court. The cross-examiner can point out the inconsistencies to the witness and ask him which version he wishes the court to adopt as his evidence.

Section 119(1) Criminal Justice Act 2003 now provides that where a previous inconsistent statement is proved, the statement becomes evidence of any matter stated in it of which oral evidence would have been admissible.

 Example

Mandy (on trial for the attempted murder of her husband) insists in cross-examination that she was unaware that her husband had a life assurance policy until the police investigation began. She denies having a conversation with her neighbour in which she stated that a few weeks before the attempt on her husband's life she had found her husband's life policy. The prosecution can call the neighbour to prove the earlier statement under s. 4 CPA 1865 which can now be admitted as evidence of fact (s. 119(1) CJA 2003).

0.8.5 CROSS-EXAMINING THE WITNESS ABOUT HIS PREVIOUS CONVICTIONS

Traditionally, a witness called to give evidence in a criminal trial has not enjoyed the same immunity as the defendant about being cross-examined on his character and convictions. Some witnesses have been embarrassed by the dredging up of past misdemeanours designed to undermine their credibility in the eyes of the jury/magistrates. The questions put to a witness in cross-examination must satisfy the requirement of relevance and in the context of previous convictions the courts traditionally adopted a wide definition of relevance. This position has been changed by s. 100 CJA 2003.

20.9 ADMISSIBILITY OF A NON-DEFENDANT'S BAD CHARACTER—CJA 2003

Section 100 provides:

'(1) In criminal proceedings evidence of the bad character of a person other than the defendant is admissible if and only if:

(a) it is important explanatory evidence;

(b) it has substantial probative value in relation to a matter which—

(i) is a matter in issue in the proceedings, and

(ii) is of substantial importance in the context of the case as a whole;

or

(c) all parties to the proceedings agree to the evidence being admissible.

(2) For the purposes of subsection (1)(a), evidence is important explanatory evidence if:

(a) without it, the court or jury would find it impossible or difficult properly to understand other evidence in the case, and

(b) its value for understanding the case as a whole is substantial.

(3) In assessing the probative value of evidence for the purposes of subsection (1)(b), the court must have regard to the following factors (and to any others it considers relevant):

(a) the nature and number of the events, or other things, to which the evidence relates;

(b) when those events or things are alleged to have happened or existed;

(c) where:

    (i) the evidence is evidence of a person's misconduct, and

    (ii) it is suggested that the evidence has probative value by reason of similarity between that misconduct and other alleged misconduct,

    the nature and extent of the similarities and the dissimilarities between each of the alleged instances of misconduct;

(d) where:

    (i) the evidence is evidence of a person's misconduct,

    (ii) it is suggested that that person is also responsible for the misconduct charged, and

    (iii) the identity of the person responsible for the misconduct charged is disputed,

    the extent to which the evidence shows or tends to show that the same person was responsible each time.'

While the rules admitting a defendant's past bad character have been relaxed (see Chapter 23), the rules permitting the admission of a witness's bad character have been tightened. The aim of s. 100 CJA 2003 is to protect a witness from embarrassing and irrelevant questioning.

20.9.1 THE AMBIT OF S. 100 CJA 2003

Section 100 applies not only to witnesses in the case but to any person other than the defendant. It applies equally to the prosecution and the defence.

20.9.2 WHAT CONSTITUTES EVIDENCE OF A NON-DEFENDANT'S BAD CHARACTER?

The application of s. 100 depends on whether the evidence falls within the definition of bad character under the Act. Bad character is defined in s. 98 CJA 2003 as evidence of or a disposition towards misconduct other than evidence which has to do with the alleged facts of the offence for which the defendant is charged, or is evidence of misconduct in connection with the investigation or prosecution of that offence. If the evidence falls within this definition, the court's leave must be granted before evidence of a non-defendant's bad character may be adduced. Where leave is granted, the defendant may find his previous convictions are disclosed under s. 101(1)(g) CJA 2003 (see Chapter 23).

Having regard to s. 98 the defence would not require leave to put it to the investigating officer that he planted the evidence on the defendant or that he fabricated the defendant's confession as this is evidence of misconduct during the investigation. Arguably, no leave is required where a defendant suggests the witness committed the crime as this would be questioning to do with the alleged facts of the offence.

20.10 CIRCUMSTANCES IN WHICH LEAVE TO ADUCE EVIDENCE OF A NON-DEFENDANT'S BAD CHARACTER UNDER S. 100 CJA 2003 IS REQUIRED

In deciding whether to grant leave, the court must be satisfied that the evidence of the witness's bad character either:

- is important as explanatory evidence, s. 100(1)(a) CJA 2003; or
- has substantial probative value in relation to a matter raised in the proceedings and is of substantial importance in the context of the case as a whole, s. 100(1)(b) CJA 2003.

Alternatively, the parties can agree for the evidence of bad character to be disclosed (s. 100(1)(c) CJA 2003). Leave is not required in this instance.

A party seeking leave will be required to give notice to the court in accordance with Crim PR, Part 35.2. The party who receives the notice may oppose the application by giving notice in writing. Such matters can be dealt with at trial or more likely at a pre-trial hearing.

10.1 IMPORTANT AS EXPLANATORY EVIDENCE—S. 100(1)(a) CJA 2003

The witness's bad character will only be admitted as explanatory evidence where, without it, the court would find it impossible or difficult to properly understand the other evidence in the case and its value for understanding the case as a whole is substantial. In some situations it will be necessary for a party to give explanatory background information to the offence, which may result in part or the whole of the witness's bad character being disclosed.

 Example

Nigel is charged with arson by starting a fire in the hostel for resettling young offenders in which he was living at the time of the alleged offence. Nigel has previous convictions for dishonesty and drug-related offences. He denies the offence.

Wayne testifies for the prosecution that on the day of the fire, he saw Nigel storing five large containers of barbeque fuel and fire lighters under his bed. In providing the court with the background facts of the arson offence, the prosecutor will refer to the fact that Wayne was residing at the hostel. This will obviously imply that Wayne has a criminal record. In this situation it will be unnecessary for the prosecution to disclose the substance of that criminal record.

10.2 SUBSTANTIAL PROBATIVE VALUE IN RELATION TO A MATTER IN THE PROCEEDINGS—S. 100(1)(b) CJA 2003

Section 100(1)(b) permits the admission of a non-defendant's bad character into evidence only where it satisfies the test of enhanced relevance. Issues to do with the credibility of a witness fall within s. 100 (*R v Weir* [2006] 1 WLR 1885). Evidence that has only marginal value or no real significance or goes to a trivial or minor issue in the case may not be admissible. In deciding the 'substantial probative value' test, s. 101(3)(a), (b) and (c) CJA 2003 set out a non-exhaustive list of factors for the court to consider, including:

- the nature and number of the events or other things to which the evidence relates;
- when those events or things are alleged to have happened or existed;
- it is evidence of the person's misconduct and it is suggested that the evidence has probative value by reason of the similarity between that misconduct and other misconduct.

To highlight some of the potential difficulties in the operation of s. 100, we include some worked examples for you to consider.

 Example 1

Consider the earlier example of Nigel, accused of starting a fire in a hostel for young offenders. Nigel denies the offence and states Wayne is responsible. Wayne has previous convictions for arson. Nigel wishes to adduce evidence of Wayne's previous convictions. Arguably, Nigel does not require leave to accuse Wayne of having committed the offence, since it has to do with the alleged facts (s. 98 CJA 2003). In substantiating that allegation, Nigel would want to adduce evidence of Wayne's propensity to cause damage by fire as Wayne's propensity is clearly relevant to Nigel's defence. If this falls within the definition of s. 98 CJA 2003, leave will not be required. If it does not and the parties do not agree, leave will be required.

Alternatively Nigel might deny the offence and simply accuse Wayne of lying when he states he saw Nigel storing lighter fuel under his bed. If Wayne's previous convictions relate to criminal damage and drug misuse, it is difficult to see how these can be said have substantial relevance in relation to the issues in this case. If Wayne's previous convictions, however, related to theft and burglary, they would arguably assume the necessary substantial probative value as they cast Wayne's credibility as a witness in a different light.

 Example 2

Suni is on trial for rape. He says his victim (V) consented and that she is lying when she says she was raped. V has two previous convictions for theft and benefits fraud, committed two and four years ago respectively. Will the defence be allowed to put these convictions to V under s. 100 in order to undermine her credibility?

If the prosecution does not agree, the defence advocate will seek leave and the court would need to be satisfied that V's previous convictions have substantial probative value in relation to a matter in issue in the case as a whole. In the absence of forensic evidence of injury, this is a case which comes down to which of the parties the jury will believe. That is clearly a matter of substantial importance in the case but do the convictions carry substantial probative weight? They might. Arguably they suggest that V has a propensity for being dishonest although this does not necessarily mean that she would falsely accuse someone of rape!

If the above facts are varied so that V previously knowingly made a false accusation of indecent assault against someone five years ago, should Suni be allowed to adduce evidence of this? Under s. 100 there would be little argument about this since it carries significant probative value in relation to an important matter in issue.

 Example 3

Danny is on trial for burglary. He calls Andrew to give evidence of alibi. Andrew has two recent convictions for dishonesty. Will the prosecution be able to put these convictions to Andrew? If the defence does not agree, the prosecution will seek leave under s. 100. Arguably the previous convictions cast doubt on Andrew's credibility who is obviously an important defence witness.

20.10.3 WHAT DOES S. 100 CJA 2003 MEAN IN PRACTICE?

Unless both parties agree to the admission of a non-defendant's bad character, s. 100 CJA 2003 is triggered. Where the defence make an application, the judge will be mindful of the risk of appeal in the event of conviction. It should be remembered that generally there is no burden of proof on the defendant. All the defendant has to do to be acquitted is to raise a reasonable doubt and for this reason it is likely to be easier for the defence to demonstrate that the line of questioning has substantial probative value in support of the defence case (*R v Weir* [2006] 1 WLR 1885).

The defence advocate will have to consider whether the evidence he wishes to adduce which raises aspects of a person's bad character is important to his client's case. Would his client's trial be unfair if he did not put this question to the witness/or adduce the evidence in some other form?

The provisions of the CJA 2003 have no application to the restrictions on asking or adducing evidence of a victim's past sexual history under s. 41 Youth Justice and Criminal Evidence Act 1999 or the provisions which allow a party to impeach his own witness in accordance with s. 3 Criminal Procedure Act 1865 (see para. 20.6.3).

20.11 CROSS-EXAMINING THE WITNESS ON HIS PHYSICAL OR MENTAL DISABILITY

Medical evidence may be introduced during cross-examination to prove that the witness suffers from a physical or mental disability that may undermine the accuracy of his testimony (*Toohey v Metropolitan Police Commissioner* [1965] AC 595). The law requires the evidence of unreliability to come from a recognised medical specialist so that if you intend to challenge an aspect of a witness's physical or psychiatric fitness to give evidence, you will have to instruct an expert witness to testify.

 Example

The witness states that he saw the defendant at a distance of 100 metres breaking into a car. There is evidence to suggest the witness was not wearing his glasses at the time. To rebut this identification, evidence could be introduced by the defence to prove that the witness is short-sighted and cannot see any further than 40 metres without corrective lenses.

0.12 RE-EXAMINATION

The third stage of witness testimony is re-examination, where the party calling the witness may ask further questions of his witness following cross-examination. Re-examination enables the advocate to repair the damage done to his witness's credibility during cross-examination and to explain any confusion or ambiguities in the witness's evidence. Leading questions are not permitted because, as with examination-in-chief, the advocate is dealing with his own witness. Re-examination is confined to matters arising out of cross-examination. The advocate cannot ask the witness about a matter he omitted to cover in examination-in-chief.

As noted in para. 20.5.1 above, an issue that may arise during re-examination is where the opposing advocate, in cross-examination, has suggested that the witness has recently made up or fabricated his evidence. This is a potentially serious attack on the witness's credibility and re-examination provides an opportunity to rebut this allegation of recent fabrication. Section 120(2) CJA 2003 permits the witness's previous statement to be admitted in evidence to show that his evidence has not been recently made up. Where the previous consistent statement is admitted, it becomes evidence of the truth of the matters stated in it. In *R v Oyesiku* (1971) 56 Cr App R 240, the wife of the defendant, charged with assaulting a police officer, had given a statement to the defendant's solicitor in which she accused the police officer of being the aggressor before she had had the opportunity of speaking to her husband following his arrest. When it was put to her in cross-examination by the prosecution, that she was making up her evidence to help her husband, the defence was allowed to adduce evidence of her earlier statement.

20.13 CROSS-EXAMINATION OF VICTIMS OF SEXUAL OFFENCES

Special rules apply to cross-examination of a complainant in cases involving a sexual offence. The rules contained in ss. 41–43 Youth Justice and Criminal Evidence Act 1999 prohibit a defendant from asking a complainant about any past sexual behaviour the complainant might have had involving the defendant or any other person save with leave of the court in certain defined circumstances. The rules were challenged as being incompatible with a defendant's right to a fair trial in the leading authority of *A (No. 2)* [2002] 1 AC 45. These complex rules are outside the scope of this work but may be researched in the current edition of *Blackstone's Criminal Practice*.

KEY POINT SUMMARY

- Be aware of the purposes of examination-in-chief and prepare your questions to your witnesses to elicit answers that are favourable to your client's case.
- Know the general rule against asking leading questions and the limited circumstances in which leading questions are permitted.
- Have a good understanding of the practice and procedure for your witness to refer to a memory-refreshing document during examination-in-chief.
- Be aware of the limited situations in which your witness's previous consistent statement can be put in evidence.
- Know the distinction between an unfavourable and a hostile witness and be aware of the practice and procedure for dealing with a witness who falls into one of these categories.
- Be aware of the purpose of cross-examination and the purpose of the advocate being permitted to ask leading questions.
- Know the distinction between questions going to an issue in the case, collateral issues and the finality rule.
- Know the exceptions to the finality rule.
- Be aware of the practice and procedure dealing with a witness's previous inconsistent statement.
- Understand that s. 100 CJA 2003 now regulates the admissibility of evidence of a non-defendant's bad character and that, in the absence of agreement between the parties, leave of the court in accordance with s. 100 is required.
- Be aware of the purpose of re-examination and its limitations.

SELF-TEST QUESTIONS

1. Are leading questions permitted during examination-in-chief?
2. What conditions are required by s. 139 CJA 2003 for a document to be used by a witness to refresh his memory during examination-in-chief?
3. What is a hostile witness?
4. Explain the purposes of cross-examination.
5. What is a collateral issue during cross-examination?
6. What allegation can be rebutted during re-examination?
7(a) Kyle is on trial for grievous bodily harm. The incident occurred in a nightclub. The victim is Ben. Chris, a key witness for the prosecution, is a good friend of Ben. Kyle states he acted in self-defence when he was attacked by Ben and Chris. Ben has a recent previous conviction for affray committed during a disturbance in a town centre. Chris has recent previous convictions for public order offences and assault. Should Kyle be allowed to adduce evidence of these previous convictions?
7(b) If the facts in the above scenario are changed such that Chris has a previous conviction for perverting the course of justice (he gave false particulars to the police in order to avoid a driving related prosecution), would leave be granted to put this conviction to the witness?

FIGURE 20.1 WITNESS TESTIMONY

EXAMINATION-IN-CHIEF

- Purpose of questions in examination-in-chief is to:
  - elicit factual evidence which supports the party's case;
  - enhance the witness's personal credibility;
  - anticipate issues to be raised in cross-examination.
- Leading questions are generally not permitted.

Memory refreshing by a witness

- s. 139 CJA 2003 permits that a witness may refresh his memory from a document made or verified by him if he states:
  - the document records his recollection at an earlier time; and
  - his recollection of the matter is likely to have been significantly better at that time.

Admissibility of previous consistent statements by a witness

- s. 120 CJA 2003 permits evidence of the witness's previous consistent statement to be admitted as evidence of its truth, including where the victim of the crime made a recent complaint to another person, s. 120(7) CJA 2003.

Unfavourable witness

- is a witness who cannot recall some facts about his testimony and simply does not come up to proof.

Hostile witness

- is a witness who shows no desire to tell the truth at the behest of the party calling him:
  - where the witness is ruled hostile, the advocate can cross-examine his own witness and under s. 3 Criminal Procedure Act 1865 put his previous statement to the witness;
  - where the previous statement is proven against the witness; or
  - where the witness adopts his previous statement, s. 119(1) CJA 2003 makes his statement evidence of the truth of any matter stated in it.

FIGURE 20.1 (CONTINUED)

CROSS-EXAMINATION

- **The purpose of cross-examination is to:**
  - elicit factual evidence which supports the cross-examiner's case;
  - test the truthfulness of the witness's evidence in examination-in-chief; and
  - undermine the witness's credibility.

  Leading questions are permitted.

- **Proving the witness has made a previous inconsistent statement,** s. 4 Criminal Procedure Act 1865
  - where the previous statement is proven against the witness; or
  - the witness adopts his previous statement,
  - s.119(1) CJA 2003 makes his statement evidence of the truth of any matter stated in it.

- **Undermining the witness's general credibility**

  Such questioning is subject to the finality rule in that the cross-examiner must take the witness's answer as being final unless the cross-examiner submits the witness:
  - is biased;
  - has previous convictions;
  - has a physical or mental disability which undermines the reliability of his evidence.

- **Adducing evidence of a witness's bad character**
  - usually raised in cross-examination;
  - under s.100(i)(a) CJA 2003, the court may only grant leave to admit evidence of the bad character of someone other than the accused if:
    - it is important explanatory evidence;
    - it has substantial probative value in relation to a matter which is a matter in issue in the proceedings *and* is of substantial importance in the context of the case as a whole; or
    - all parties agree;
  - s. 100 CJA 2003 has no application if the witness's misconduct is connected with the investigation or prosecution of the present offence, see s. 98 CJA 2003;
  - adducing evidence of another person's bad character can result in the accused's bad character revealed to the court (s. 101(1)(g) CJA 2003).

RE-EXAMINATION

- **The purpose of re-examination is to:**
  - repair any damage inflicted during cross-examination.
- Leading questions are not permitted.
- A witness may rebut an allegation of recent fabrication the evidence of rebuttal is admitted as a previous consistent statement and as evidence of its truth (see s. 120(2) CJA 2003).

21.1 INTRODUCTION

There is a common link between the first two evidential rules explained in this chapter. The law governing corroborative or supporting evidence and the application of the 'Turnbull guidelines' in cases involving disputed evidence of eye-witness identification seek to ensure the court reaches its verdict on 'reliable' evidence to prevent miscarriages of justice or convictions being overturned on appeal as 'unsafe'. Finally, the rules relating to opinion evidence and to expert opinion evidence in particular are explained.

This chapter considers:

- the nature of corroborative evidence;
- the situations where corroborative evidence is required as a matter of law;
- the situations where a corroboration warning might be given as a matter of judicial discretion;
- the application of the 'Turnbull guidelines' in cases where eye-witness identification is disputed;
- the general rule excluding opinion evidence;
- the admissibility of expert evidence.

21.2 WHAT IS CORROBORATIVE EVIDENCE?

Corroborative evidence is independent evidence which supports or confirms other evidence in the case.

Evidence that requires corroboration is said to be unreliable or deficient or tainted in some way. A common example is where a witness may have a purpose of his own to serve by testifying.

In evaluating the evidence in a criminal case, the lawyer should always make an assessment of his witness's credibility. How will the witness appear to the jury/magistrates? Is the witness likely to be believed? Does the witness have a motive for giving false evidence? These all involve considerations of weight. Where a witness's evidence is questionable in some respect, a corroboration warning might be appropriate. Such a warning alerts the jury/magistrates to the dangers of relying solely on the evidence of the particular witness and the need for independent evidence which is capable of supporting what the witness has to say.

21.2.1 WHEN IS CORROBORATIVE EVIDENCE REQUIRED?

While corroboration has assumed less formal significance in criminal trials in recent years, corroborative evidence may still be encountered in two situations:

- where the offence charged requires corroborative or supporting evidence as a matter of law before the accused can be convicted; and

- where the court considers it appropriate as a matter of discretion to give a warning about the evidence of an 'unreliable' witness.

21.3 CORROBORATIVE EVIDENCE REQUIRED AS A MATTER OF LAW

A limited number of statutes require prosecution evidence to be corroborated as a matter of law before the defendant can be convicted of the offence, including perjury (s. 13 Perjury Act 1911) and treason (s. 1 Treason Act 1795).

The only offence in this category which you might encounter is where a defendant is charged with speeding. Section 89(2) Road Traffic Regulation Act 1984 requires that the defendant cannot be convicted of speeding on the opinion evidence of one witness. The vehicle's speed has to be corroborated by the opinion evidence of another witness. In practice, s. 89 RTRA 1984 has been superseded by modern technology, as in most prosecutions, the vehicle's speed is proved by an electronic device such as a radar gun or the police vehicle's speedometer reading which does not need to be supported by independent evidence.

21.4 CORROBORATION AND THE EXERCISE OF JUDICIAL DISCRETION

Traditionally, the evidence of certain witnesses such as children, the complainant in a sexual offence and an accomplice (a co-accused who gives evidence against another person charged in the proceedings) was regarded as less reliable than the testimony of other witnesses. When directing the jury about the evidence of these witnesses, the judge was required, as a matter of law, to give a mandatory warning about the dangers of convicting the accused on the unsupported evidence of these witnesses. The requirement for mandatory warnings was abolished by s. 34 Criminal Justice Act 1988 in relation to the unsworn evidence of children and s. 32 Criminal Justice and Public Order Act 1994 in connection with the unsupported evidence of an accomplice or the victim of a sexual offence. A failure to give a mandatory corroboration warning under the old law was a ground for appeal against conviction. As the mandatory warning has long since been abolished, what is the current position?

The present position is that a corroboration warning is entirely discretionary and will depend on the particular facts and circumstance of each case. There are no longer categories of witnesses whose evidence should automatically be accompanied by a warning.

The modern case on corroboration is *R v Makanjuola; R v Easton* [1995] 3 All ER 730, where the Court of Appeal laid down the following general guidelines:

- A corroboration warning is not a mandatory requirement because the witness is a child giving unsworn evidence or an accomplice or the complainant of a sexual offence.

- It is matter for the judge's discretion what, if any warning, is considered appropriate in relation to the evidence of a particular witness.

- In some cases, it may be appropriate for the judge to warn the jury to exercise caution before acting on the unsupported evidence of a witness. There will need to be an evidential basis for suggesting that the evidence of the witness may be unreliable.

- If any question arises whether a special warning should be given in respect of a witness, it is desirable that the question be resolved with counsel in the absence of the jury before final speeches.

- Where the judge decides to give a warning in respect of a witness, it will be appropriate to do so as part of the judge's review of the evidence and the manner in which the judge gives a direction is a matter for his discretion.

- The Court of Appeal will not interfere with the trial judge's discretion except where the judge acted in an 'unreasonable' way as explained in *Associated Picture Houses Ltd v Wednesbury Corporation* [1948] 1 KB 223.

.4.1   WHAT WARNING SHOULD BE GIVEN UNDER *MAKANJUOLA*?

Where a warning is considered appropriate, the guidelines laid down in *R v Makanjuola* give the court discretion to tailor the warning to the specific facts of the case. For example, if the witness has been shown to be unreliable, it may be appropriate for the judge to urge caution. In a more serious situation where the witness is shown to have lied or is shown to bear a grudge against the defendant or in a sexual offence, the complainant is shown to have made previous false complaints, a stronger warning may be appropriate. The judge may direct the jury that it would be wise to look for supporting evidence before acting on the impugned witness's evidence.

The defence advocate must always be alert to the need for a corroboration warning in the case. For example, where there is concern about the reliability of a prosecution witness's evidence, he should persuade the judge to give a corroboration warning to the jury or in a summary trial, the issue of corroboration should be raised in his closing speech.

There are many witnesses whose evidence may be unreliable or tainted including any witness with a proven propensity to be untruthful or with a motive to lie. Where a particular witness has an 'axe to grind' against the defendant or stands to profit from the defendant's conviction, the defence advocate might seek a corroboration warning. This will include an accomplice, who though initially charged, chooses to plead guilty and give evidence for the prosecution implicating a fellow co-accused (*R v Cheema* [1994] 1 WLR 147). It could also extend to co-defendants who are running cut-throat defences (*R v Jones* [2004] 1 Cr App R 5. Where there is evidence to suggest collusion between witnesses or some ulterior motive for the evidence that has been given, a corroboration warning might be called for. The same considerations apply to a mentally unbalanced witness whose evidence appears to be unreliable. A corroboration warning will be appropriate against any witness who might be regarded as having a purpose of his own to serve in giving false evidence in the case.

A trial judge cannot be compelled to give a corroboration warning as the decision is discretionary. Where the trial judge fails or refuses to give a warning and a conviction results, there may be grounds for an appeal against conviction.

21.5 **THE REQUIREMENTS FOR EVIDENCE TO BE CORROBORATIVE**

In *R v Baskerville* [1916] 2 KB 658, the essential requirements for evidence to be corroborative were stated as:

* the evidence should be admissible in its own right;
* it must be independent of the evidence to be corroborated;
* it must implicate the accused in a material way with the crime charged in not only suggesting that the offence was committed, but also that it was committed by the accused.

21.5.1 **WHERE IS CORROBORATIVE EVIDENCE TO BE FOUND?**

Corroborative evidence may come from any other evidence in the case, including:

* the oral testimony of another witness;
* confession by a defendant;
* documentary evidence;
* real evidence;
* circumstantial evidence (see *R v McInnes* (1990) 90 Cr App R 99);
* lies told by the defendant can support the prosecution, where:
  — the lie is deliberate and is material to an issue in the case;
  — the lie is motivated by a realisation of guilt and fear of the truth; and
  — the lie can be proved to be a lie by other evidence;
  — the jury should be reminded that some people may lie for reasons other than perhaps hiding their guilt for the present offence including where the accused lied out of shame or to bolster a defence or out of a wish to conceal their disgraceful behaviour from their family (see *R v Lucas* [1981] QB 720),
* forensic evidence such as DNA linking the defendant to the crime scene;
* the defendant's refusal, without good cause, to consent to give an intimate sample under s. 62 PACE 1984;
* inferences from a defendant's silence under CJPOA 1994, ss. 34–37 (see Chapter 5);
* a defendant's previous convictions where they show a propensity for the defendant to behave in a way that is relevant to proving the facts of the present offence (see Chapter 23).

21.6 **THE 'TURNBULL GUIDELINES'**

The Turnbull guidelines are of considerable practical importance in trials where the defendant claims he is the victim of mistaken identity.

In Chapter 8 we explained the pre-trial safeguards in Code D of the Codes of Practice in dealing with identification procedures used by the police during the investigation to confirm or exclude the defendant's involvement in an offence. Identification evidence obtained in breach of these procedures is vulnerable to challenge under s. 78 PACE 1984.

Disputed evidence of eye-witness identification is treated with caution as extensive psychological research has highlighted the errors eyewitnesses make when they observe, interpret and recall information. An honest witness may be a very convincing witness but may still be mistaken in identifying the defendant at the crime scene. In order to minimise the risk of a miscarriage of justice based on mistaken identification, the Court of Appeal has developed guidelines about how the courts should deal with evidence of disputed eye-witness identification. The guidelines were formulated in *R v Turnbull* [1977] QB 224.

The Turnbull guidelines apply in a case where the defendant disputes the accuracy of eye-witness identification and are fundamental to ensuring the defendant enjoys a fair trial.

A slightly abridged version of the Turnbull guidelines appears below. The trial judge must adapt the guidelines when directing the jury to the particular facts of the case. The guidelines provide:

'First, whenever the case against an accused depends wholly or substantially on the correctness of one or more identifications of the accused which the defence alleges to be mistaken, the judge must warn the jury of the special need for caution before convicting the accused in reliance on the correctness of the identification . . . In addition he should instruct them as to the reason for the need for such a warning and should make some reference to the possibility that a mistaken witness can be a convincing one and that a number of such witnesses can all be mistaken.

Secondly, the judge should direct the jury to examine closely the circumstances in which the identification by each witness came to be made. How long did the witness have the accused under observation? At what distance? In what light? Was the observation impeded in any way, as for example by passing traffic or a press of people? Had the witness ever seen the accused before? How often? If only occasionally, had he any special reason for remembering the accused? How long elapsed between the original observation and the subsequent identification to the police. Was there any material discrepancy between the description of the accused given to the police by the witness when first seen by them and his actual appearance? . . . Finally, he should remind the jury of any specific weaknesses which had appeared in the identification evidence.

Recognition may be more reliable than identification of a stranger; but even when a witness is purporting to recognise someone he knows, the jury should be reminded that mistakes in recognition of close relatives or friends are sometimes made.

All these matters go to the quality of the identification. If the quality is good at the close of the accused's case, the danger of a mistaken identification is lessened; but the poorer the quality, the greater the danger.

. . . when the quality is good, as for example when the identification is made over a long period of observation, or in satisfactory conditions by a relative or neighbour, a close friend, a workmate and the like, the jury can safely be left to assess the value of the identifying evidence even where there is no other evidence to support it; provided always, however that an adequate warning has been given about the special need for caution.

When, in the judgment of the trial judge, the quality of the identifying evidence is poor, as for example a fleeting glimpse of a witness or a longer observation made in difficult conditions, the situation is very different. The judge should then withdraw the case from the jury and direct an acquittal unless there is other evidence which goes to support the correctness of the identification. This may be corroboration in the sense lawyers use that word; but it need not be so if its effect is to make the jury sure that there has been no mistaken identification . . .

The judge should identify to the jury the evidence capable of supporting the identification. If there is any evidence or circumstances which the jury might think was supporting when it did not have this quality, the judge should say so . . .

Care should be taken by the judge when directing the jury about the support for an identification which may be derived from the fact that they have rejected an alibi. False alibis may be put forward for many reasons: an accused, for example, who has only his own truthful evidence to rely on may stupidly fabricate an alibi and get lying witnesses to support it out of fear that his own evidence may not be enough. Further, alibi witnesses can make genuine mistakes about dates and occasions like any other witnesses can. It is only when the jury is satisfied that the sole reason for the fabrication was to deceive them and there is no explanation for its being put forward can fabrication provide any sort of identification evidence. The jury should be reminded that providing the accused has told lies about where he was at the material time does not of itself prove that he was where the identifying witness says he was.'

The Turnbull guidelines require the judge to make an initial qualitative assessment of the eye-witness identification. If the trial judge concludes the identification evidence is poor and is unsupported by any other evidence in the case, he must withdraw the case from the jury and direct an acquittal. If the trial judge concludes the evidence is poor but is supported by other evidence in the case or the identification evidence is good, he can leave the case to the jury but he must direct the jury in accordance with the Turnbull guidelines and stress the special need for caution. In a case where the evidence of identification is poor but supported, the judge must point out the evidence that is capable of providing the support. Supporting evidence will be similar to corroborative evidence as outlined in para. 21.5.1 above.

In accordance with the guidelines, the judge must explain why there is a special need for caution with such evidence and direct that while an honest witness may be a very convincing witness, the witness may nevertheless be mistaken. He should invite the jury to consider the circumstances in which the witness purportedly identified the defendant and point out any specific weaknesses in the identification including:

- a witness's failure to make a positive identification;
- a breach of Code D, such as a failure to convene a formal identification procedure;
- inconsistencies between witnesses' original descriptions.

21.6.1 EYE-WITNESS IDENTIFICATION IN 'GOOD' CONDITIONS

The Turnbull guidelines give examples of identification in 'good' conditions including where:

- the identification is made over a long period of observation; or
- the identification is made by a relative or neighbour or a close friend or a workmate etc.

21.6.2 EYE-WITNESS IDENTIFICATION IN 'POOR' CONDITIONS

The Turnbull guidelines give examples of identification in 'poor' conditions including where:

- the witness has a fleeting glimpse of the crime scene; or
- the observation is made in difficult lighting or weather conditions; or
- the witness gets a distant view of the crime scene.

21.6.3 THE TURNBULL GUIDELINES IN SUMMARY PROCEEDINGS

The Turnbull guidelines equally apply to trials in the magistrates' court. In a summary case involving disputed identification evidence of the accused, the legal adviser will remind the magistrates of the guidelines in open court and the special need for caution.

21.6.4 WHAT ARE THE CONSEQUENCES WHEN A TURNBULL WARNING IS NOT GIVEN?

The failure to give a Turnbull warning in cases of disputed eye-witness identification will invariably provide a convicted defendant with a ground for appeal against conviction on the basis that his conviction is 'unsafe'.

1.6.5 WHEN DO THE TURNBULL GUIDELINES NOT APPLY?

The Turnbull guidelines should be followed in all cases where the possible mistaken identification of the accused is in issue. The guidelines will not apply to:

- cases involving the identification of motor vehicles;
- the evidence of police officers who base their identification on long periods of observation or surveillance;
- cases in which there has been no formal identification of the defendant, only evidence of a description;
- most cases where the accused admits his presence at the crime scene.

In relation to the last listed matter, a Turnbull direction may still be appropriate where a defendant admits to being at the scene but denies involvement in the crime. This point is well illustrated by the facts in *R v Thornton* [1995] 1 Cr App R 578.

R v Thornton [1995] 1 Cr App R 578

An altercation developed between guests at a wedding reception. The appellant, a guest at the wedding and as such appropriately attired, had been identified by a neighbour and her son as being the assailant. He admitted being at the scene but said he had been trying to shield the victim. There were others in the vicinity all dressed the same. The Court of Appeal concluded it did not automatically follow that where the accused admitted his presence at or near the scene but denied involvement, the Turnbull direction had to be given. It would depend on all the circumstances. In this case, a direction was appropriate given the risk of error.

 Example

Frank is 21 and has been arrested on suspicion of burglary of commercial premises. He is white, of medium build, 6' tall with bleached white hair. The break-in occurred at 3.30 am. A description of the alleged assailant is provided by a security guard. He explains that when the alarm bell was activated, he chased the assailant across the yard of the factory for approximately 40–50 seconds before the assailant climbed over a wall. The yard was partially illuminated and he saw the person from a distance of approximately 30 yards. The security guard describes the youth as white, average height (about 5'10") and build, aged in his early twenties. The youth had fair hair and was wearing denims and a black short jacket. The assailant ripped his clothing on wire meshing covering the top of the wall.

At 3.45 on the night in question, two officers in a police patrol vehicle arrested Frank. At the time of the arrest, Frank was wearing dark trousers and blue tee-shirt. No jacket was found.

Frank chose not to be represented by a solicitor at the police station and proceeded to deny any involvement in the burglary. He agreed to participate in a video identification procedure. In interview he refused to answer questions and failed to account for a large tear in his jeans. Frank was released on police bail. Four days after witnessing the incident, the security guard attended the identification suite to view the video parade. After some hesitation he selected Frank's image. Frank was subsequently charged with burglary. Frank denies the offence and calls evidence of alibi at his trial.

At Frank's trial, a Turnbull direction would be given about the evidence of the security guard's eyewitness identification. The judge or magistrates would be required to assess the quality of the security guard's identification evidence. If the judge concludes the evidence is poor quality and is unsupported by other evidence, the case will be withdrawn from the court. If the identification evidence is supported by other independent evidence, it can be left to the jury or the magistrates to assess the reliability of the evidence by examining the circumstances in which the identification was made.

In this case the judge may conclude that the evidence is weak but is supported by the fact that Frank refused to answer questions at the police station and failed to give an account of the tear in his jeans.

If the case is left to the jury, the judge will invite them to consider the fact that the initial observation of the assailant was in less than ideal circumstances. The security guard had the person under observation for only a short period of time, and at a distance. The lighting was good, however, although it does not appear that Frank is known to the security guard. Although an honest witness, the security guard may nevertheless be mistaken. The judge should remind the jury that the security guard was hesitant before making a formal identification of Frank.

21.7 OPINION EVIDENCE

A witness is called to court to give factual evidence based on what the witness perceived with his own senses. The general rule in criminal proceedings is that opinion evidence is inadmissible. A witness is not permitted to state orally or to write that the 'defendant is obviously guilty' or the 'defendant was up to no good'. In addition to being inadmissible, a witness's opinion is irrelevant and offends the 'ultimate issue' rule. The 'ultimate issue' relates to the defendant's guilt or innocence, which must be decided by the magistrates or the jury on the basis of all the evidence in the case.

There are two important exceptions to the general rule where opinion evidence is admissible: facts personally perceived by the witness, and opinion evidence given by expert witnesses.

21.8 FACTS PERSONALLY PERCEIVED BY THE WITNESS

A lay witness may give an opinion on a fact that he has personally perceived not requiring expertise. For example, it would be admissible for the witness to state that 'the defendant was drunk', or 'the defendant's car was speeding as it approached the road junction'.

In each example, the witness is giving his opinion on a matter within his personal knowledge and experience that does not require expertise or training. In effect such statements are statements of fact and are necessary to communicate to the court an accurate impression of the events the witness is relating.

21.9 EXPERT WITNESSES

An expert witness may give his opinion on an issue that goes beyond the ordinary competence of the court. The list of matters upon which expert evidence is required in criminal proceedings continues to grow and includes:

* accident investigation;
* ballistics;
* blood tests;
* breath tests;
* blood-alcohol levels;
* fingerprints;
* handwriting;
* computer technologies;
* facial mapping and facial identification;
* medical, psychological, scientific and forensic investigations.

These are highly technical matters of which the court has no knowledge or experience. The expert's duty is to provide impartial, objective information in his field of expertise to assist the court to reach a verdict on the evidence presented.

The value of expert forensic evidence in establishing the identity of a suspect is explored in Chapter 8. Expert evidence is like any other evidence in the case and is subject to an assessment of the weight to be accorded to it by the jury/magistrates.

.9.1 WHO IS AN EXPERT?

Whether a witness is competent to give 'expert' evidence is a matter of law to be decided by the court. In deciding this issue, reference will be made to the witness's education, academic qualifications and professional experience. One of the first questions to be asked in examination-in-chief will be directed at establishing the witness's credentials as an expert in his particular field. The following cases serve to illustrate those witnesses who qualified as an expert in terms of their practical experience.

R v Clare and Peach [1995] 2 Cr App R 333

In this case, the police officer did not know the accused but had viewed a video-recording of the incident in which the defendant was alleged to have been involved, 40 times. He had examined it in slow motion, rewinding it and replaying it, and so was permitted to give evidence of identification based on a comparison between the video image and a known photograph of the defendant.

R v Hodges and Walker [2003] 2 Cr App R 247

The appellants were convicted of supplying heroin. They had been observed by undercover officers for several days in the street meeting numerous people for brief periods. The meetings involved short physical contact. There was no evidence from the officers that they saw drugs actually being passed in this way. When arrested, W was in possession of a 14g bag of heroin, which he claimed was for his personal use. He was also carrying £350. Scales with traces of heroin and other material were found in W's house. The prosecution relied on statements made by H in interview. To prove an intention to supply, the prosecution needed to establish that drugs had been transferred via the contact between the defendants and passers-by on the street and that the quantity of heroin in H's possession was inconsistent with personnel use.

Expert evidence was admitted from a detective constable (DC), a drugs officer of 17 years' experience, as to the method of supply of heroin on the streets, the local purchase price, and that 14g was more than would have been held for personal use.

The defendants appealed on the basis that the evidence of the DC had been wrongly admitted as expert evidence.

In dismissing the appeal, the Court of Appeal held that the DC's evidence had been rightly admitted as expert evidence. While the officer did not have medical or toxicological qualifications, he was entitled to refer to his expertise obtained as a result of talking to drug dealers and drug users.

Sounding a note of caution in this case, the Court of Appeal made some observations about the degree of weight to be attached to the DC's evidence. As a serving police officer it was necessary for the trial judge to give a direction to the jury about the weight to be given to the officer's opinion, as clearly it would be very difficult for him to provide the necessary objectivity normally required of an expert witness.

21.9.2   **WHAT ARE THE DUTIES ON AN EXPERT?**

The duties of an expert witness are set out in Crim PR Part 33.

(1) An expert must help the court to achieve the overriding objective by giving an unbiased opinion on matters within his expertise.

(2) This duty overrides any obligation to the person from whom he receives instructions or by whom he is paid.

(3) This duty includes an obligation to inform all parties and the court if the expert's opinion changes from that contained in a report served as evidence or given in a statement under Crim PR Part 24 or Part 29 (to support an application for a special measures direction).

The required content of an expert's report is set out in Part 33.3.

The court is given the power under Part 33.5 to direct experts instructed by both parties to discuss the issues within their expertise and prepare a statement for the court of the matters on which they agree and disagree, giving their reasons.

The court has the power, under Part 33.7 to direct the use of a single joint expert in the case of co-defendants both seeking to utilise different experts.

21.9.3   **THE PROCEDURE FOR ADMITTING EXPERT EVIDENCE**

There are special rules that require the pre-trial disclosure of expert evidence which apply to both the prosecution and the defence. They are contained in s. 81 PACE 1984 and in Crim PR Parts 24 and 33.

In accordance with Part 24, where either party proposes to rely on expert evidence (at a summary or an indictable trial), it must, as soon as is practicable, furnish the other party with a written statement of any finding or opinion which it is proposed to adduce and a copy of any observation, test, calculation or other procedure on which the expert's opinion is based. A failure to give notice results in the expert evidence not being admitted unless leave of the court is granted.

The rules do not detract from the prosecutor's general duty of disclosure in relation to used material and to unused material under the CPIA 1996 (see Chapter 14). Specific duties were imposed on forensic scientists following the decision in *R v Ward* [1993] 1 WLR 619. If an expert has carried out experiments or tests which tend to prove or cast doubt on the opinion the expert is expressing (or knows that such experiments have been carried out in his laboratory), he is under a clear obligation to bring such knowledge to the attention of the party instructing him.

Section 30 Criminal Justice Act 1988 permits an expert's report to be admitted in evidence whether or not the report's author attends to give oral evidence.

21.9.4   **EXPERT EVIDENCE AND DEFENCE DISCLOSURE**

As stated in the preceding paragraph, wherever a party intends to rely on expert evidence, he must disclose the expert's report to the opposing side. If the defendant obtains an unfavourable expert's report, the defence is not required to disclose the report as it is protected by legal professional privilege (see Chapter 24).

Note that when s. 6(D) CPIA 1996 (as amended by the CJA 2003) comes into force, an accused who instructs an expert witness with a view to providing an opinion for use as evidence at trial, must give to the court and the prosecutor a notice specifying the person's name and address unless specified in the defence statement (see Chapter 14, para. 14.9.5).

KEY POINT SUMMARY

- Understand and be able to recognise the circumstances in which a corroboration warning might be called for.

- Understand and be able to recognise the circumstances in which the Turnbull guidelines are applicable.

- The decision to give a corroboration warning lies with the judge/magistrates, with the relevant guidance provided by the decision in *R v Makanjuola*.

- A failure to give a Turnbull warning in a case where it must be given, affords a convicted defendant strong grounds for appeal against conviction.

- Expert opinion evidence is admissible in relation to an issue which is outside the competency of the court.

- An expert witness's competency is determined by his qualification and or relevant experience.

- Wherever a party seeks to rely on expert evidence, rules of court require that party to give notice.

SELF-TEST QUESTIONS

Consider the factual scenario below and answer the questions which follow.

You act for Stefan who has been charged with causing grievous bodily harm with intent, contrary to s. 18 Offences Against the Person Act 1861 (OAPA). The assault is alleged to have been racially motivated. He pleads not guilty at his trial, giving evidence on oath that he was not involved in the crime. He calls his girlfriend to substantiate his defence of alibi.

The assault occurred outside a public house at 11.30 pm in a busy city centre street. Witnesses describe two white youths attacking an Asian youth. Eyewitnesses provided varying descriptions of the attackers. An anonymous witness told the police that Stefan and Andrew (also charged in connection with the proceedings) were involved. Upon his arrest and having been confronted with positive identification evidence, Andrew admitted his limited involvement and implicated Stefan as being the principal instigator of the attack and of being completely out of control.

Stefan was subsequently arrested. His solicitor advised him not to answer police questions as he considered the evidence against Stefan to be very weak. Stefan followed his advice. In the interview, Stefan was cautioned and asked to account for visible bruising to his nose. He offered no explanation. Stefan consented to participating in a video identification procedure.

It was several days before the victim was able to assist the police. Shortly after being hospitalised, the victim was shown several sets of photographs of convicted offenders (which included a photograph of Stefan) to see if he could spot his attacker. He selected Stefan's photograph. Three weeks later the victim was well enough to view the video parade and selected Stefan's image.

At trial, the prosecution accepts Andrew's guilty plea to a much less serious offence of assault occasioning actual bodily harm (s. 47 OAPA 1861) and agrees to withdraw the s. 18 charge. Andrew gives evidence for the prosecution, putting the blame on Stefan as being the person responsible for kicking the youth while he was on the ground.

Stefan maintains Andrew is lying in order to cover up his own involvement in a serious offence. Stefan denies being at the scene. Andrew is to be married in a few weeks time to a woman whose brother is a member of the investigative team.

In evidence, Stefan states that, while he and his girlfriend were in the city centre on the evening in question and had a drink with Andrew and some of his friends, they left before any trouble occurred.

CCTV footage is available of the incident. Sergeant Peter Taylor is called for the prosecution to give evidence of the fact that the blurred image on one of the stills is that of Stefan. The sergeant has studied the stills for a number of hours using video enhancing equipment.

Questions:

- Do you have any concerns as regards the manner in which the evidence of identification has been obtained in this case? If so, is there anything you can do about this?

- On what basis will Sergeant Taylor's evidence be admitted?

- Is this a case which calls for a Turnbull direction? If so, explain why. What will the requirements of that warning be?

- Is this is a case which calls for a corroboration warning? If so, explain why.

Case Study: *R v Lenny Whyte*

Consider whether a Turnbull warning would need to be given in *R v Lenny Whyte*, and whether any issues in relation to expert opinion evidence arise in this case.

Analysis on the above can be found in Appendix 4.

FIGURE 21.1 CORROBORATION

- **What is it?**

  Corroborative evidence is independent evidence which supports or confirms other evidence in the case (see *R v Baskerville*).

- **What type of witness might it apply to?**

  Where there is reason to doubt the reliability/truthfulness of a prosecution witness (perhaps because the witness has a purpose of his own to serve in giving false/unreliable evidence), a corroboration warning about the dangers of relying upon the unsupported evidence of the witness may be required.

- **Where might supporting evidence come from?**
  - another witness's oral testimony; or
  - documentary or real evidence; or
  - forensic evidence; or
  - the defendant's lies or admissions (*R v Lucas*).

- **Corroboration as a matter of judicial discretion**

  A judge may choose to give a corroboration warning to a jury (or magistrates can warn themselves) about the dangers of relying on the uncorroborated evidence of a suspect witness where 'there is an evidential basis for it' (see *R v Makanjuola and Easton*).

THE 'TURNBULL GUIDELINES'

- Guidelines laid down by the decision in *R v Turnbull*.
- 'Turnbull' applies to evidence of eye-witness identification where the defendant disputes his presence at the crime scene.
- Turnbull guidelines require.
  - the court to proceed with caution as an honest witness may be a mistaken witness;
  - the jury or magistrates' court should consider the circumstances of the eye-witness identification, including:
    - the length of time the witness allegedly observed the defendant;
    - the light and distance etc. in which the identification occurred;
    - did the witness have a special reason for remembering/recognising the defendant etc.
- Where the identification took place in 'good' conditions, the jury or magistrates may assess the value of the identifying evidence.
- Where the identification take place in poor conditions, the evidence should be withdrawn unless there is supporting evidence about the correctness of the identification.
- Jury/magistrates should be reminded of any specific weakness in the evidence of identification, including breaches of Code D (under PACE 1984).

OPINION EVIDENCE

- Generally inadmissible in a criminal case, except:
  - facts personally perceived by the witness which does not require expertise; or
  - expert evidence on an issue beyond the ordinary competence of the court, including:
    - forensic science;
    - facial mapping;
    - accident investigation.
- Expert's role is to provide impartial information to assist the court reach a decision in the case.
- Pre-trial disclosure of expert evidence is required under Part 24 Crim PR.

22 HEARSAY EVIDENCE

22.1 INTRODUCTION

Hearsay evidence is often described as 'second-hand' evidence and offends the preferred way in which evidence is presented at a criminal trial. This requires the witness to attend court to give oral evidence about facts of which the witness has personal knowledge. This is the most reliable evidence on which the court decides the defendant's guilt or innocence. In comparison, hearsay evidence is inferior to the original witness's direct oral testimony, not least because it cannot be tested by cross-examination.

Hearsay evidence in criminal cases most often arises in two situations: first, where one witness gives evidence about facts of which he has no personal knowledge as the facts have been passed to the witness by another person who is not in court; and second, where a witness's written statement is put before the court because the witness is unable to attend court to give oral evidence.

Consider the following example of hearsay evidence.

 Example

Mandy witnesses a robbery in which a pensioner's handbag is stolen. She tells her friend John that the person responsible was a white male of average height, wearing a black jogging top and baggy black trousers with a tattoo on the left-hand side of his face. If Mandy cannot attend court to give a first-hand account of what she witnessed, can John be called to repeat what Mandy had told him about the circumstances of the robbery? In a criminal case, the answer is no because John's evidence infringes the rule against admitting hearsay evidence. John has no personal knowledge of the facts about which he is testifying, as he did not see the man alleged to be responsible for the robbery. As John is relying on what Mandy has told him, he cannot be effectively cross-examined.

Alternatively, if Mandy had made a written witness statement to the police but was unable to attend trial to give oral evidence, could the prosecution adduce Mandy's written statement? The written statement constitutes hearsay evidence. As in the first instance, it will not be possible to cross-examine the absent witness to test the reliability and truthfulness of the witness's evidence, and once again, the court would be relying on 'second-hand' evidence.

Hearsay evidence can be first-hand hearsay or multi-hand hearsay (where it has gone through more than one intermediary).

22.2 HEARSAY EVIDENCE—THE GENERAL RULE

The general rule in criminal cases is that hearsay evidence is inadmissible for the reasons explained in the introduction to this chapter. Unless the hearsay can be brought within a recognised common law or statutory exception, it remains inadmissible. The Criminal Justice Act 2003 (CJA) has *considerably* widened the basis for admitting hearsay evidence in criminal cases.

22.3 IDENTIFYING HEARSAY EVIDENCE

Hearsay has been defined as:

'Any statement other than one made by a person while giving oral evidence in the proceedings is inadmissible to prove the truth of any fact stated in it.' (*R v Kearley* [1992] 2 AC 228)

To come within the definition of hearsay evidence, the statement sought to be adduced will consist of the following elements:

(1) The evidence must be contained in a 'statement'. All forms of communication come within the meaning of a 'statement', including:

- a written witness statement;
- a document compiled in the course of a business or by a public authority;
- a witness's oral evidence;
- a witness's evidence recorded on an audio or video tape;
- evidence contained on a computer disc;
- a gesture by a witness (*R v Gibson* [1887] LR 18 QBD).

(2) The statement must have been made by the witness other than while giving evidence in the present proceedings.

(3) The statement must be put in evidence to prove the truth of the statement's contents and not for any other reason, for example, to prove the statement was made or to show the witness's state of mind at the time the statement was made.

A defendant's confession is a good illustration of evidence containing the constituent elements of a hearsay statement:

- the confession will be contained in a 'statement'—i.e. a written transcript of the interview with the police and/or a tape-recording of the interview;
- the confession will be made on an occasion other than while the defendant gives evidence in the present proceedings—i.e. the defendant will confess at the police station during the investigation of the alleged crime; and
- the purpose of putting the statement before the court is to prove its truth—i.e. that the accused admits his involvement in the offence charged.

For the reasons explained in Chapter 7, confession evidence is admissible under a common law exception to the rule against hearsay evidence.

22.3.1 DEFINITIONAL DIFFICULTIES WITH HEARSAY EVIDENCE

Not every out-of-court statement made by a witness will come within the hearsay rule. If the earlier out-of-court statement is being adduced for a reason other than proving the truth of facts asserted on that earlier occasion, the statement will not be hearsay. A good example of this point is provided by *R v Davis* [1998] Crim LR 659 where the defendant sought to prevent the jury from drawing an adverse inference under s. 34 Criminal Justice and Public Order Act 1994 (see Chapter 5). He had remained silent at the police station based on his solicitor's advice. On oath he sought to repeat the advice his solicitor had given him but was prevented from doing so by the trial judge who ruled it would infringe the hearsay rule. The Court of Appeal concluded that the trial judge was wrong. The defendant had wanted to give an account of his solicitor's advice to show the jury the effect it had on him and therefore his reasons for remaining silent, the evidence was not hearsay, as the defendant was not seeking to prove the truth of anything his solicitor said to him.

22.3.2 IMPLIED ASSERTIONS AND THE 'NEW' STATUTORY DEFINITION OF HEARSAY

An implied assertion is a statement which is not intended by its maker to explicitly assert a fact but which does so by implication. This distinction is not always easy to make. In

R v Kearley [1992] 2 AC 228, in order to prove K was dealing in drugs, police officers were allowed to repeat in court the content of conversations they had had with anonymous callers to K's house during the period shortly after his arrest, requesting K to supply them with their 'usual'. No explicit assertion of K being a drug dealer was made by these callers, but an implicit assertion to this effect arguably was. The House of Lords concluded that an implied assertion is hearsay.

Implied assertions are now dealt with by s. 115(3) CJA 2003. The hearsay provisions under the CJA 2003 will only apply to a statement that appears to have been made in order:

> 'to cause another person to believe the matter, or to cause another person to act or a machine to operate on the basis that the matter is as stated . . . '

In practice, unless the maker of the statement was intending to assert a fact, the hearsay rule, as redefined under CJA 2003, does not apply and the evidence may be admitted as direct evidence of a fact providing it has relevance to the particular case.

22.3.3 DOCUMENTS CREATED BY A COMPUTER

Does a document created by a computer constitute hearsay? Where the computer performs an entirely automated process which does not involve any human input of information, the printout reading will be classed as real evidence. This means that readings from a speedometer, police radar gun and Intoximeter do not constitute hearsay. Similarly, the automated telephone exchange records which log the date, times and numbers of telephone calls made and received are frequently admitted in evidence as items of real evidence.

Where the evidence has been created by a computer through information inputted by a human, the evidence is likely to come within the hearsay rule if the purpose of using the computer printout is to prove the truth of some fact asserted by the person who entered the information. However, s. 115(2) CJA 2003 confines the hearsay provisions to statements made by a person. It therefore excludes statements produced or created by a mechanical device. These are admissible under s. 129(1) CJA 2003, which provides that:

> 'where a representation of fact:
>
> (a) is made otherwise than by a person, but
>
> (b) depends for its accuracy on information supplied (directly or indirectly) by a person,
>
> the representation is not admissible in criminal proceedings as evidence of the fact unless it is proved that the information was accurate.'

For other types of information stored on computers such as e-mail correspondence, business records, invoices etc., which constitute statements made by a person, their admissibility is subject to s. 116 or s. 117 CJA 2003 (see below).

22.3.4 PHOTOGRAPHS/TAPE-RECORDINGS, VIDEOS AND DVDS

These forms of communication are commonly admitted in evidence. Photographs, CCTV footage, audio and video etc. are regarded as real evidence and do not fall within the hearsay rule. The provenance of the evidence will still need to be proved and therefore it is necessary to adduce evidence of when the video was filmed and by whom.

Now that you have an understanding of the constituent elements of a hearsay statement, we will examine the exceptions to the general exclusionary rule which allow hearsay evidence to be admitted in criminal cases. The exceptions are defined by the common law and by statute. The CJA 2003 now regulates the admissibility of hearsay evidence in criminal cases.

22.4 THE STATUTORY EXCEPTIONS TO THE HEARSAY RULE

There are a number of important statutory exceptions to the hearsay rule in criminal cases. Until recently, the main statutory provisions were contained in ss. 23–26 CJA 1988. These provisions have been replaced by the CJA 2003, which has codified the most important exceptions to the rule. Much of the case law on the previous statutory provisions will continue to be relevant. Before we consider the new provisions, we will highlight two other important statutory exceptions to the exclusionary hearsay rule.

22.4.1 SECTION 9 CRIMINAL JUSTICE ACT 1967

In practice s. 9 CJA 1967 is the most important exception to the hearsay rule, and is in daily use in all Crown Courts and magistrates' courts. Section 9 CJA 1967 permits a witness's written statement to be read to the court without the witness attending the trial where:

- the statement is signed by the maker; and
- contains a declaration in specified words as to the statement's truth; and
- the statement has been served on the opposing party; and
- within seven days the opposing party has not objected to the statement being admitted as hearsay.

The key point about a 'section 9 statement' is the other side's consent must be obtained before the statement may be admitted as hearsay. If the other side objects, for whatever reason, the court has no power to overrule the objection and admit the statement in evidence. Section 9 statements are therefore used only for non-controversial matters where the evidence in the statement is effectively agreed by the opposing side because there will be no opportunity to cross-examine or challenge the witness's evidence.

When preparing a case for trial, the solicitor should consider whether there are any witnesses whose evidence could be read to the court under s. 9 CJA 1967. With reference to our case study *R v Lenny Whyte*, you will see that in preparing Lenny Whyte's case for trial a number of prosecution's witness statements have been agreed.

22.4.2 STATEMENTS ADDUCED AT COMMITTAL HEARINGS

As noted in Chapter 13, Sch. 2 to the Criminal Procedure and Investigations Act 1996 requires the defendant to notify the prosecution of any objections to the written statements of those prosecution witnesses tendered in evidence at the committal from being read out at trial. The notification must be made within 14 days of the service of evidence in an either-way case that has been committed to the Crown Court,
  Both s. 9 CJA 1967 and Sch. 2 CPIA 1996 are expressly preserved by the CJA 2003.

22.5 HEARSAY EVIDENCE UNDER THE CRIMINAL JUSTICE ACT 2003

Section 114 CJA 2003 regulates the admissibility of hearsay evidence in criminal cases. The section provides:

> 'a statement not made in oral evidence in the proceedings is admissible as evidence of any matter stated if it comes within one of the four exceptions.'

Section 114(1)(a)–(d) identifies the following four situations where hearsay will be admissible under the Act:

- s. 114(1)(a)—hearsay will be admissible where it comes within one of the categories of admissible hearsay evidence under the Act (chiefly where a witness is unavailable to give evidence—ss. 116 and 117 CJA 2003) and any other preserved statutory section (s. 9 CJA 1967 and Sch. 2 CPIA 1996, see above);

- s. 114(1)(b)—hearsay will be admissible where it comes within one of the preserved common law rules (s. 118);

- s. 114(1)(c)—hearsay will be admissible where the parties agree to the evidence being admitted;

- s. 114(1)(d)—hearsay will be admissible where the court is satisfied that it is in the 'interests of justice' for the hearsay statement to be admitted (the so-called safety-valve).

The main statutory gateways for admitting hearsay are provided by ss. 116 and 117 CJA 2003.

22.5.1 THE UNAVAILABLE WITNESS—S. 116 (FIRST-HAND HEARSAY)

A statement will only be admissible under s. 116(1) CJA 2003 where:

- the person could have given oral evidence if he had attended court; and
- the person who made the statement is identified to the court's satisfaction; and
- the person who made the statement had the requisite capability (s. 123 CJA 2003) at the time he made the statement.

The definition of capability is the same as the test for competency to give oral evidence under s. 53 Youth Justice and Criminal Evidence Act 1999 i.e. can the witness understand questions put to him and give answers that can be understood.

Section 116 CJA 2003 mirrors the former s. 23 CJA 1988 (subject to the requirements above) in permitting a statement to be admitted where the witness is unable to attend court for one of the following reasons:

- the witness is dead or is unfit because of his bodily or mental condition (s. 116(2)(a) and (b));

- the witness is outside the UK and it is not reasonably practicable for him to attend (s. 116 (2)(c));

- the witness cannot be found although such steps as it is reasonably practical to take to find him have been taken (s. 116(2)(d));

- that through fear the witness does not give evidence (or does not continue to give evidence) (s. 116(2)(e)).

Under s. 116 CJA 2003 it is immaterial whether the hearsay statement is contained in a document or was made orally. Once the condition for admitting the statement is proved under s. 116, the evidence can be admitted.

The burden of proving the relevant condition rests on the party seeking to adduce the hearsay evidence. Rules of court (Crim PR, Part 34) determine the procedure that must be followed where a party seeks to admit hearsay evidence. Disputes about the statement's admissibility are likely to be determined at a pre-trial hearing.

22.5.2 THE REASONS FOR A WITNESS'S UNAVAILABILITY

Reason 1—the witness is dead or unfit.
R v Setz-Dempsey [1993] 92 Cr App R 98 confirms that an assessment of the witness's 'unfitness to attend' can include mental or physical capacity. A death certificate or medical report should discharge the burden of proving this ground.

Reason 2—the witness is (a) outside the UK and (b) it is not reasonably practicable to secure his attendance.

If the witness's statement is to be given as hearsay, both conditions have to be satisfied by the party seeking to rely on s. 116(2)(d) CJA 2003. In *R v Castillo* [1996] 1 Cr App R 438, the Court of Appeal identified a number of factors that should be considered in determining whether it is practicable for the witness to attend, including:

- the importance of the evidence the witness could give;
- the expense and inconvenience of securing the attendance of the witness;
- the seriousness of the offence;
- whether the witness's evidence could be given via live television link; and
- the prejudice likely to be caused to the defendant given he would have no opportunity to cross-examine.

Reason 3—all reasonable steps have been taken to find the witness, but he cannot be found.

The party seeking to put the hearsay statement in evidence must prove that all reasonable steps have been taken to find the witness including evidence of what steps were taken to trace the witness and with what result.

Reason 4—the witness does not give evidence through fear.

Fear is widely defined in s. 116(3) to include fear of death or injury of another person or financial loss. The witness's fear must be proved by admissible evidence and can include calling the witness to testify on oath at a *voir dire* why he does not wish to give evidence at trial although in *R v Davies* [2007] 2 All ER 1070 it was stated that as long as the fear is genuine and can be proved, the court is not advised to test the basis of the fear by calling the witness to appear before them. In *R v Rutherford* [1998] Crim LR 490, fear was proved by a signed written statement from the witness.

Where a party relies on the 'fear' ground under s. 116(2)(e), the court's leave must be obtained under s. 116(4). Leave will only be granted if the court considers that it would be in the interests of justice to admit the statement having regard to:

1. the statement's contents;
2. any risk that its admission or exclusion will result in unfairness to any party (with particular reference to how difficult it will be to challenge the statement if the relevant person does not give evidence);
3. in appropriate cases to the fact that a special measures direction could be made in relation to the relevant person (see Chapter 19);
4. any other relevant circumstance.

The requirement to seek leave under this ground is an important safeguard in protecting the defendant's right to a fair trial under Article 6. The relationship between hearsay evidence and Article 6 is considered at para. 22.13 below.

Consider the following examples of admitting hearsay under s. 116 CJA 2003.

 Example 1

Ethel, aged 84, is the victim of a burglary. She describes the burglar to her daughter Dianna. Ethel suffers a stroke soon after and is unable to provide a formal written statement to the police or indeed to attend trial. Can the prosecution call Dianna so that she may repeat in court what her mother told her about the burglar? This would clearly constitute hearsay evidence. Hearsay evidence is generally inadmissible unless it comes within the exceptions under the CJA 2003. Assume Ethel was capable at the time she spoke with her daughter. On the face of it, the conditions for admissibility under s. 116 CJA 2003 would appear to be satisfied. The identity of the maker of the statement is not in dispute and Ethel is unable to attend trial for a prescribed reason under s. 116(2)(b).

Example 2

Simon is the victim of a homophobic assault. He gives the police a detailed description of his attackers in a written witness statement. Simon refuses to give evidence in court as he fears for his personal safety. Can the prosecution adduce Simon's written statement as hearsay evidence? Simon's statement would appear to be admissible under s. 116(2)(e) CJA 2003. Simon is clearly identifiable as the maker of the statement and is unavailable to give oral evidence out of fear. In choosing to admit Simon's statement the court must have regard to the factors set out in s. 116(4) CJA 2003, including the availability of special measures to assist witnesses like Simon to give evidence.

22.6 BUSINESS DOCUMENTS—S. 117

Business documents are admissible under s. 117 Criminal Justice Act 2003 and take into account the modern business practice where millions of documents are created on a daily basis. As it would be impossible to require every person who had personal knowledge of the document's contents to testify in court, s. 117(2) makes business documents admissible as hearsay in criminal proceedings where the following conditions are satisfied:

- the document was created or received in the course of a trade, business, profession or other occupation, or as the holder of a paid or unpaid office (s. 117(2)(a)); and
- the person who supplied the information contained in the statement (the relevant person) had or might reasonably be expected to have had personal knowledge of the matters dealt with in the statement (s. 117(2)(b)); and
- each person (if any) through whom the information was supplied from the relevant person received the information in the course of a trade, business, profession or other occupation or as the holder of a paid or unpaid office (s. 117(2)(c)).

As with its predecessor under s. 24 CJA 1988, s. 117 permits the admission at trial of multiple hearsay which satisfy the requirements of the section. In each case the person creating or receiving the document must be acting in the course of a trade, business, profession, or as the holder of a paid or unpaid office. The person who supplied the information contained in the statement must reasonably be supposed to have personal knowledge of the matters dealt with. If the information came through an intermediary, the information must have been received by a person in the course of a trade, business, profession, or as the holder of a paid or unpaid office.

Business records, ledgers, invoices and hospital records etc. will all be admissible under s. 117(2).

22.6.1 DOCUMENTS PREPARED FOR THE PURPOSE OF A CRIMINAL INVESTIGATION OR PROCEEDINGS—SPECIAL RULES

Section 117(4) provides documents such as business or other records, which have been prepared for the purposes of pending or contemplated criminal proceedings and which are to be admitted as hearsay, must satisfy the conditions laid down in s. 117(5). Such statements are admissible providing any one of the five conditions set out in s. 116(2) relating to the absence of the relevant person is satisfied (see para. 22.5.1 above), or as an additional reason, the relevant person (the person who supplied the information contained in the document) cannot reasonably be expected to have any recollection of the matters dealt with in the statement having regard to the length of time since he supplied the information and all other circumstances (s. 117(5)(b)).

Section 117(7) CJA 2003 incorporates an important safeguard in relation to documents to be admitted under s. 117 in providing that a court may make a direction to exclude a statement if the statement's reliability as evidence for the purpose for which it is tendered is doubtful in view of:

1. its contents;
2. the source of the information contained in it;
3. the way in which or the circumstances in which the information was supplied or received; or
4. the way in which or the circumstances in which the document concerned was created or received.

Consider the following examples of admitting hearsay under s. 117(4) CJA 2003.

 Example 1

Take the example of Ethel which we considered earlier in the context of s 116. Assume Ethel has been able to provide the police with a written statement, but is then unable to attend trial. Her written statement would be admissible under s. 117(4)–(5) CJA 2003. It comprises a document prepared for the purposes of criminal proceedings and a prescribed reason for not calling Ethel is made out, namely she is not well enough to attend trial. There would appear to be no obvious reason for doubting the reliability of her statement (s. 117(7)).

 Example 2

Ingrid gives an oral statement to a police officer having witnessed a serious road traffic accident. The officer records her statement in his notebook. The police have since been unable to trace Ingrid to take a formal statement from her. Can the police officer's notebook recording the conversation be admitted under s. 117 CJA 2003? The document i.e. the police officer's notebook comprises second-hand hearsay and was created in the course of the police officer's job. Ingrid is the 'relevant person' for the purposes of s. 117(4) as she is the person who supplied the information contained in the statement and can be assumed to have personal knowledge of the facts. However, the police officer's notebook is a document prepared for the purposes of a police investigation and so a s. 116 reason must be proved. Assuming that all reasonable steps have been taken to trace Ingrid (and there is no reason to doubt Ingrid's capability at the time she gave her oral statement), the conditions for admitting the notebook under s. 117 CJA 2003 would appear to be made out.

22.7 HEARSAY ADMISSIBLE UNDER THE PRESERVED COMMON LAW RULES (S. 118 CJA 2003)

The CJA 2003 specifically preserves many of the common law exceptions to the hearsay rule, of which the most important are *res gestae* and confessions. The other common law provisions include public documents, evidence regarding a family's reputation or tradition, expert opinion drawing on published works.

22.7.1 *RES GESTAE* STATEMENTS (S. 118(4)(a)–(c) CJA 2003)

Res gestae means transaction, or series of events. There are various situations which cover the admission of evidence under the *res gestae* rule under s. 118(4) CJA 2003. One situation is under what is commonly referred to as the 'spontaneous utterance rule'. The leading common law authority on the 'spontaneous utterance rule' is *R v Andrews* [1987] AC 281. In this case, the House of Lords held that a statement made by a fatally stabbed man soon after he was attacked naming his two attackers, was properly admitted under the *res gestae* rule.

Section 118(4)(a) CJA 2003 preserves the 'spontaneous utterance rule' and allows an earlier out-of-court statement to be adduced in evidence providing the statement was made by a person 'so emotionally overpowered by an event that the possibility of concoction or distortion can be disregarded.'

A *res gestae* statement can also be admitted where the witness is available to give evidence. The admissibility of hearsay evidence under the *res gestae* principle remains subject to the courts discretion to refuse to admit the statement under s. 78 PACE 1984 on the grounds of unfairness (s. 126(2) CJA 2003).

In *R v W* (reference under s. 36 CJA 1972) [2003] 2 Cr App R 29 the defendant was accused of a very serious assault on his mother. She had been pushed down the stairs and had her hair set on fire. There were several witnesses who witnessed the aftermath of the attack during which the victim told each of these witnesses that her son had gone berserk and attacked her. At a later stage, however, the victim refused to give a formal statement to the police and later went on to give a deposition before a magistrates' court in which she completely retracted her oral allegation maintaining she had accidentally fallen downstairs. She declined to comment on how her hair had been burned.

Realising that there would little point in calling the victim to give evidence, the prosecution sought to call the witnesses to whom the victim had spoken in the immediate aftermath to give evidence under the *res gestae* principle. The Court of Appeal held there was nothing in *R v Andrews* which prohibited a *res gestae* statement being admitted, even though the witness to the facts was available to give evidence. There was no doubt that what the victim had been heard to say in this case fell within the definition of *res gestae* and was therefore *prima facie* admissible. However, as with every other type of evidence, this particular piece of hearsay evidence was subject to the court's exclusionary discretion under s. 78 PACE 1984. It was not suggested that the prosecution were seeking to rely on a *res gestae* statement as a device to avoid calling the victim. However, given the importance of this witness to the prosecution's case and the inability of the defendant to cross-examine the hearsay witness, the defendant could not have enjoyed a fair trial in accordance with Article 6 of the European Convention on Human Rights.

22.7.2 STATEMENTS IN PUBLIC DOCUMENTS (S. 118(1) CJA 2003)

Statements contained in a public document or certified true copies are admissible at common law as evidence of the truth of their contents. This exception to the hearsay rule has long been recognised because such evidence was considered to be reliable and very often the public official who compiled the document would have no recollection of the facts, or be dead, or be unfit to testify. Many statutes now make provision for the admissibility of certain specific classes of documents, such as certified true copies of entries in a register of deaths compiled by the Registrar of Births, Deaths and Marriages, as evidence of the date of a person's death where this is a relevant fact in issue in any proceedings.

In addition to such specific provisions, most statements in public documents will be admissible in criminal cases by virtue of s. 117 Criminal Justice Act 2003.

22.7.3 CONFESSION EVIDENCE (S. 118(5) CJA 2003)

Confession evidence has always been admissible as a common law exception to the hearsay rule. The admissibility of confession evidence is considered in Chapter 7.

22.8 HEARSAY WILL BE ADMISSIBLE WHERE THE PARTIES AGREE TO THE EVIDENCE BEING ADMITTED (S. 114(1)(c) CJA 2003)

This ground is self-explanatory.

22.9 THE 'SAFETY-VALVE' (S. 114(1)(d) AND S. 121 CJA 2003)

Section 114(1)(d) gives a court discretion to admit hearsay evidence which does not come within one of the other specified categories for admitting hearsay evidence under CJA 2003. A court may only admit such evidence where it is in the interests of justice.

In applying the discretionary 'interests of justice' test the court will take into consideration the factors laid down in s. 114(2)(a)–(i). They are:

(a) how much probative value the statement has (assuming it to be true) in relation to a matter in issue in the proceedings, or how valuable it is for the understanding of other evidence in the case;

(b) what other evidence has been, or can be, given on the matter or evidence mentioned in paragraph (a);

(c) how important the matter or evidence mentioned in paragraph (a) is in the context of the case as a whole;

(d) the circumstances in which the statement was made;

(e) how reliable the maker of the statement appears to be;

(f) how reliable the evidence of the making of the statement appears to be;

(g) whether oral evidence of the matter stated can be given and, if not, why it cannot;

(h) the amount of difficulty involved in challenging the statement;

(i) the extent to which that difficulty would be likely to prejudice the party facing it.

The 'safety-valve' provision gives the court an inclusionary discretion to admit hearsay evidence. In theory, this provision should be used exceptionally where hearsay evidence cannot be admitted under any other provision, although there is nothing in the CJA 2003 which imposes this requirement. The case of *McEwan v DPP* [2007] EWHC 740, is instructive in this regard.

On the day of trial the prosecution sought an adjournment as an important witness for the prosecution had failed to turn up. The prosecution had instructions that the witness was unfit to attend trial. An adjournment was sought to enable the prosecution to make further enquiries to support an application for the witness's evidence to be admitted as hearsay under s. 116(2)(b). The magistrates' court refused the application to adjourn. There had been nine previous pre-trial reviews owing to failings by the prosecution. Faced with a choice of continuing the prosecution or abandoning it, the prosecution sought, without notice, to admit the witness's statement under s. 116(2)(b) and s. 114(1). The former could not be proved but the magistrates agreed to the second ground.

The Divisional Court held it had been wrong for the magistrates' court to have admitted important hearsay evidence under the safety-valve. It was not in the interests of justice on the facts having regard to the importance of the witness and the defendant's inability to cross-examine and the failings on the part of the prosecution to ensure attendance of its witnesses:

> 'Although it is clear, section 114(1)(d) provides a free standing ground for admitting hearsay evidence-admissibility under that subsection does not at all depend on the satisfaction of the conditions contained in section 116 of the Act—it must be recognised that reliance on section 114(1)(d) is most unattractive in the circumstances of this case . . . For my part, the safety-valve is there to prevent injustice. It would have to be an exceptional case for it to be relied upon, as it is sought to do here, to rescue the prosecution from the consequences of its own failure.'

A contrasting case is *R v Boguslaw Sak* [2007] EWHC 2886. Circumstances prevented a professional witness (a doctor) from attending trial on behalf of the prosecution. No fault lay at the hands of the prosecution in this regard. An application to adjourn the trial was refused. The prosecution therefore sought to adduce the doctor's witness statement under ss. 116 and

114(1)(d). On the facts, s. 116 CJA 2003 was clearly not available to the prosecution. The High Court concluded that the magistrates' court had not erred in permitting the doctor's evidence to be adduced under s. 114(1)(d). The court had applied its mind to the relevant factors. The witness was reliable and independent and the accused would have been afforded the opportunity to challenge the evidence.

Where multiple hearsay is to be admitted, it is subject to a specific safety-valve in s. 121(1)(c) CJA 2003 which requires the court to consider whether the value of the statement is so high (taking into account how reliable the statement appears to be) that the interests of justice require it to be admitted. In assessing the interests of justice under s. 121(1)(c), a court should additionally consider the factors set out in s. 114(2)(a)–(i) (*Maher v DPP* [2006] EWHC 1271 (Admin)). It remains to be seen how frequently the safety-valve is invoked and how it will be interpreted by the courts. There have been some interesting developments in the context of third party confessions which are briefly explored in Chapter 7, para.7.12.

The following are examples of how the 'safety-valve' might apply.

 Example 1

Take the example of Ethel above and vary the facts further. Assume Ethel gives a description of the perpetrator to her neighbour Arthur. Arthur relays the information to his son Tom. Assume that both Ethel and Arthur are unable to give oral evidence at trial. Will the prosecution be able to call Tom to give evidence of what Ethel said to Arthur which in turn was said to him?

This example raises the issue of multiple hearsay evidence. The original statement has gone through more than one stage of reporting. It cannot therefore be admitted under s. 116 CJA 2003 and it is not admissible under s. 117 CJA 2003 as that section is restricted to documentary hearsay. The only possibility in this instance is the safety-valve (s. 121). Assume there is no reason to doubt the credit-worthiness of any of the witnesses. The statement is of importance to the prosecution. There is a good reason for Ethel's inability to give oral evidence and the defence can still challenge the evidence. On balance, the court might choose to admit the evidence given its reliability and probative value.

 Example 2

An anonymous telephone to call to Crime Stoppers provides the registration number of a 'getaway car' involved in a fatal drive-by shooting. As a result of the information, the car is located and subject to forensic analysis linking a number of the suspects to the vehicle. Can a transcript of the telephone call be admitted? It cannot be admitted under s. 117(4). Although it is a document prepared for the purposes of a criminal investigation, the requirements under s. 116 are not made out as the relevant person (the person who supplied the information) cannot be identified. The only means by which the transcript could be admitted is if the court exercises its discretion under s. 114(1)(d) CJA 2003. It is not possible to comment on the reliability of the maker of the statement. However, the statement is arguably important in explaining how the car came to be recovered. In this instance, it would be in the court's discretion to either admit or reject the evidence having regard to the factors laid down in s. 114(2)(a)–(i).

22.10 MISCELLANEOUS PROVISIONS RELATING TO THE USE THAT CAN BE MADE OF STATEMENTS ADMITTED AS PREVIOUS INCONSISTENT STATEMENTS/ PREVIOUS CONSISTENT STATEMENTS AND UNDER THE WITNESS MEMORY REFRESHING RULES

- Section 119 CJA 2003 provides that where a witness admits making a previous inconsistent statement or it has been proved that he has made such a statement, the statement can now be admitted as evidence of the truth of what it asserts. (For the rules on proving a previous inconsistent statement, see Chapter 20.)

- Section 120 CJA 2003 enables a witness's previous consistent statement to be admitted as evidence of the truth of what it asserts. This includes previous consistent statements used to rebut a suggestion of recent fabrication; recent complaints and statements used to refresh a witness's memory upon which the witness is cross-examined, resulting in the statement being put in evidence (see Chapter 20).

- Section 120(4) CJA 2003 provides that a witness's previous statement may be admissible as evidence of the facts stated, if while giving evidence the witness indicates that to the best of his belief he made the statement; that it states the truth and the statement falls within one of the prescribed categories under s. 120(5), (6) and (7) (see Chapter 20).

22.11 ADDITIONAL SAFEGUARDS WHEN ADMITTING HEARSAY EVIDENCE

Although the CJA 2003 introduces a more liberal regime for admitting hearsay, even where the conditions for admissibility are satisfied, the Act provides a number of safeguards to limit multiple hearsay and provisions for challenging the capability and credibility of a hearsay witness. The availability of these safeguards will be taken into account by the court when determining disputes between the prosecution and defence regarding the CJA 2003 hearsay provisions and their compatibility with the defendant's right to a fair trial under Article 6.

22.11.1 RESTRICTING MULTIPLE HEARSAY—S. 121 CJA 2003

Multiple hearsay occurs when a statement passes through more than one intermediary.

Section 121 provides that a hearsay statement is not admissible to prove the fact that an earlier hearsay statement was made unless:

- either of the statements is admissible under s. 117 CJA 2003; or under s. 119 as a previous inconsistent statement; or under s. 120 as a previous consistent statement; or

- the parties agree to it being admitted (s. 121(1)(b)); or

- the court is satisfied that the value of the evidence, taking into account how reliable the statement appears to be, is so high, that the interests of justice require it to be admitted (s. 121(1)(c)—see para. 22.9 above.

22.11.2 CAPABILITY OF THE WITNESS TO MAKE THE STATEMENT—S. 123 CJA 2003

Nothing in s. 116, 119 or 120 makes a statement admissible as evidence if it was made by a person who did not have the requisite capability at the time when he made the statement. The same requirement applies to statements admitted under s. 117(2) in relation to the person who supplied or received the information or created or received the document.

22.11.3 CHALLENGING THE HEARSAY WITNESS'S CREDIBILITY—S. 124 CJA 2003

Section 124 CJA 2003 permits the opposing party to challenge the hearsay witness's credibility in the same way as if the witness had given oral evidence.

22.11.4 STOPPING THE CASE WHERE EVIDENCE IS UNCONVINCING—S. 125 CJA 2003

Section 125 requires the court to stop the case and to acquit the defendant where the case against him is based wholly or partly on an out of court statement which is so unconvincing that considering its importance to the case, a conviction would be unsafe. This provision applies only to trials on indictment.

.11.5 EXCLUDING UNNECESSARY HEARSAY—S. 126 CJA 2003

Section 126(1) CJA 2003 gives the court discretion to exclude hearsay evidence where the court is satisfied that the value of the evidence is substantially outweighed by the undue waste of time which its admission would cause.

.11.6 DISCRETION TO EXCLUDE HEARSAY—S. 126 CJA 2003

Section 126(2) CJA 2003 preserves the discretion under s. 78 PACE 1984 (unfairness) and at common law s. 82(3) PACE 1984 (probative value outweighed by prejudicial effect) to exclude hearsay evidence. This is a very important safeguard to ensure that a defendant continues to enjoy a fair trial under the CJA 2003 hearsay provisions.

.11.7 DIRECTING THE JURY

In accordance with the Judicial Studies Board specimen directions, in determining the weight to be given to hearsay evidence, the judge should point out to the jury the limitations of hearsay evidence, namely, the jury has not had the benefit of seeing or hearing the witness, nor has the witness been subject to cross-examination. In a summary trial, the advocate against whom the hearsay evidence has been adduced should remind the magistrates of the limitations of such evidence in his closing speech.

22.12 PROCEDURE FOR ADMITTING HEARSAY EVIDENCE

A party seeking to introduce hearsay evidence must give notice to the court and all other parties. The rules of court relating to the procedure to be adopted are contained in Crim PR, Part 34. Having received notice of hearsay evidence, a party may oppose its admission by giving notice within 14 days on a prescribed form. Any dispute between the parties is likely to result in a pre-trial ruling on the matter.

22.13 HEARSAY EVIDENCE AND THE EUROPEAN CONVENTION ON HUMAN RIGHTS 1950

Article 6(3)(d) confers on a defendant the right to examine or have examined witnesses against him and to obtain the attendance and examination of witnesses on his behalf under the same conditions as witnesses against him. Where evidence is admitted as hearsay, the defendant is unable to cross-examine the witness. Is the admission of hearsay evidence intrinsically unfair?

The case law of the ECHR 1950 suggests not, provided the defendant is able to effectively challenge the evidence (*Kostovi v Netherlands* [1990] 12 EHHR 434). There has been a number of decisions by the ECtHR on the use of hearsay evidence although distilling clear, guiding principles is difficult.

In *Luca v Italy* [2003] 36 EHHR 46, the European Court of Human Rights suggested that Article 6 might be breached where the hearsay is the sole or decisive evidence against the defendant. This proposition was rejected by the Court of Appeal in *R v Sellick and Sellick* [2005] 1 WLR 3257.

Under the previous law contained in ss. 23–26 Criminal Justice Act 1988, the admissibility of hearsay evidence was subject not only to proof of the preconditions for admissibility but also to an additional interests of justice test under either s. 25 or s. 26 CJA 1988. This requirement has now ceased to apply. The hearsay provisions under the new Act are intended, and believed to be, compliant with the ECHR 1950. Challenges to the new law, based on Article 6, however, are to be expected. It is likely that the adequacy of the safeguards identified in relation to the admission of hearsay evidence in a case where a witness is in fear (s. 116(4); the specific safeguards to be applied in relation to the safety-valve exceptions (s. 114 (2)(a)–(i) and s. 121(1)(c); and the general safeguards applicable throughout contained in ss. 123–126, will be the key to determining whether the new law is ECHR-compliant. Section 126 CJA 2003 is particularly important in this regard in its specific preservation of the court's general discretion to exclude any prosecution evidence, the admission of which would prejudice a fair trial (s. 78 PACE 1984).

We include a selection of cases to illustrate the factors a court is likely to regard in determining Article 6 considerations. They are all decided on the pre-2003 Act provisions.

R v Dragic [1996] 2 Cr App R 323

The sole eyewitness was too ill to give evidence at the trial. The prosecution was allowed to adduce the witness's earlier statement given to the police as hearsay. The defendant appealed against conviction maintaining his trial had been unfair given the importance of this witness to the prosecution and his inability to cross-examine her. The Court of Appeal rejected the argument pointing out that it had been possible for the appellant to controvert the evidence of hearsay with his evidence of alibi and to give evidence himself if he so chose.

R v Sellick and Sellick [2005] 1 WLR 3257

In this case the chief prosecution witnesses, who were in a witness protection programme, disappeared. There was evidence to suggest that the defendant was implicated in their decision to disappear. However, they were important witnesses for the prosecution, and for this reason it was important for the defendant to be able to cross-examine them. The trial judge exercised his discretion to admit the absent witnesses written statements as hearsay. In upholding the trial judge's decision that it had been in the interest of justice to admit the statements, the Court of Appeal felt the following factors were important:

- The evidence of each witness had been credible.
- The credibility of the witnesses had been challenged.
- The trial judge gave a clear direction as regards the witness's credibility and the shortcomings of hearsay evidence compared to oral evidence.
- Regard should be had to the fact that the defendant was to a large extent the author of his own inability to cross-examine witnesses against him.
- Regard should also be had to the rights of victims and their families.
- If there was a rule that a defendant could not be said to enjoy a fair trial because the main evidence against him constituted hearsay evidence, it would lead to greater intimidation of witnesses. Such an absolute rule cannot have been intended by the ECtHR.

R v Imad Al Khawaja [2006] 1 Cr App R 9

The defendant, a doctor, had been convicted of indecent assault on two female patients. His treatments included hypnotherapy. Prosecution witness one (W1) and witness two (W2) did not know each other. W1 committed suicide shortly before the trial. Her witness statement was admitted as hearsay evidence in the exercise of the trial judge's discretion under s. 23 CJA 1988. On appeal, the defence cited *Luca* and *Kostovi* in that the defendant had not been given and could not now be given any effective opportunity to challenge the written evidence and given its importance to the prosecution's case, the defendant could not be said to have enjoyed a fair trial. Affirming the conviction and citing *Sellick* with approval, the Court of Appeal observed:

> 'Where a witness who is the sole witness of a crime has made a statement to be used in its prosecution and has since died, there may be a strong public interest in the admission of the statement in evidence so that the prosecution may proceed. That was the case here. That public interest must not be allowed to override the requirement that the defendant have a fair trial. Like the court in *Sellick* we do not consider that the case law of the European Court of Human Rights requires the conclusion that in such circumstances the trial will be unfair. The provision in Art.6(3)(d) that a person charged shall be able to have the witnesses against him examined is one specific aspect of a fair trial: but if the opportunity is not provided, the question is "whether the proceedings as a whole, including the way the evidence was taken, were fair . . ." This was not a case where the witness had absented himself, whether through fear or otherwise, or had required anonymity, or had exercised a right to keep silent. The reason was death, which has a finality which brings in considerations of its own . . .'

The safeguards identified in this case included:

- the fact that the judge had carefully weighed up the arguments for and against admission;
- the defendant had been afforded the opportunity of having the evidence excluded;
- the prosecution would have abandoned its case had the evidence been excluded;
- the defendant could still challenge the witness's credibility by adducing expert evidence on altered perceptions under hypnosis;
- there was no evidence to suggest collusion between the two principal witnesses;

KEY POINT SUMMARY

- Understand what hearsay evidence is. It is any out of court statement which is repeated in court for the purpose of proving the truth of a fact or facts asserted in the earlier out-of-court statement.
- Understand that as a general rule, hearsay evidence is inadmissible in criminal cases unless it happens to fall within a recognised common law or statutory exception. (Note: the categories for admission have been significantly broadened by the CJA 2003.)
- Recognised common law exceptions admitting hearsay evidence include statements admitted as part of the spontaneous utterance rule (*res gestae*) and confession evidence.
- Hearsay evidence can be admitted with the agreement of the parties under s. 9 Criminal Justice Act 1967 (agreement will be confined to those written statements that do not contain contentious facts requiring the witness to be cross-examined).
- The main statutory basis for admitting hearsay is contained in s. 114 CJA 2003.
- The statutory requirements of ss. 116 CJA 2003 (unavailable witness) and 117 CJA 2003 (business documents) must be proved before hearsay evidence can be admitted.
- Understand the categories for admission of hearsay under the CJA 2003, include the safety-valve s. 114(1)(d), which covers hearsay that is not capable of being admitted under any other provision in the Act providing it is in the interests of justice.
- Be aware of the statutory safeguards that will apply in the context of the CJA 2003 and the need to ensure the admission of hearsay evidence does not prejudice a defendant's right to a fair trial in accordance with Article 6.

SELF-TEST QUESTIONS

The CPS is prosecuting an armed robbery involving several defendants. Duane (who has provided the police with a detailed statement during the investigation) is a key prosecution witness. He has received a number of menacing telephone calls warning him against testifying. He has a young family and tells the police he will not testify in court. What evidential problem does this development give rise to and how can the prosecution get around it?

FIGURE 22.1 HEARSAY EVIDENCE

THE GENERAL RULE

- Hearsay is any statement made on an earlier out-of-court occasion which is being adduced in court to prove the truth of facts asserted in that earlier out-of-court statement.
- Section 114 CJA 2003 provides that hearsay evidence being: 'a statement not made in oral evidence in the proceedings, is admissible as evidence of any matter stated in it, if it comes within one of the four exceptions', s.114 CJA 2003.
- The exceptions which permit the reception of hearsay evidence in criminal cases are set out in s.114(1)(a)–(d) Criminal Justice Act 2003.
- The exceptions include:
  - s.116 CJA 2003 (unavailable witness providing the witness is identified);
  - s.117 CJA 2003 (business documents);
  - s.114(1)(b) CJA 2003 (it comes within one of the preserved common law exceptions);
  - s.114(1)(c) CJA 2003 (the parties agree to the hearsay being admitted); or
  - s.114 (1)(d) CJA 2003 (court decides that it is 'in the interests of justice' for the hearsay to be admitted);
  - s.9 CJA 1967 (agreed witness statements);
  - Sch. 2, CPIA 1996; (witness statements adduced at committal);
- The CJA 2003 contains a number of safeguards, including the application of s. 78 PACE to ensure use of hearsay evidence is compatible with Article 6 and special provisions as regard multiple hearsay.

REASONS FOR WITNESS UNAVAILABILITY (S.116 CJA 2003)

- witness is ill, s.116(2)(a) CJA 2003; or
- is dead, s.116(2)(b) CJA 2003; or
- cannot be found, s.116(2)(c) CJA 2003; or
- is outside the UK and it is not reasonably practicable for him to attend, s.116(2)(d) CJA 2003; or
- witness is in fear, s.116(2)(e) CJA 2003 (leave required).

ADMITTING A BUSINESS DOCUMENT AS HEARSAY

- under s.117 CJA 2003, a business document may be admitted as hearsay where:
  - the document was created or received in the course of a business or trade or profession etc; and
  - the person who supplied the information contained in the statement had or might reasonably be expected to have had personal knowledge of the matters dealt with in the statement; and
  - if the document passed through an intermediary, each intermediary was acting in the course of a trade, profession etc.

PRESERVED COMMON LAW EXCEPTIONS TO THE HEARSAY RULE

- Hearsay is admissible under s.118 CJA 2003 where the statement falls within one of the preserved common law exceptions, including:
  - the *res gestae* rule;
  - public documents.

ADMITTING HEARSAY WHERE IT IS 'IN THE INTERESTS OF JUSTICE'

- Where a hearsay statement does not come within one of the recognised exceptions under s. 114(1)(a)–(c) CJA 2003, the court may admit the statement under s. 114(1)(d) CJA 2003 where 'it is in the interests of justice'.
- The following factors under s. 114(2) must be taken into account when exercising discretion, including:
  - the credibility of the statement's maker;
  - the statement's probative value;
  - the reason why oral evidence cannot be given;
  - the statement's importance to the party's case;
  - the difficulty to the other side in challenging the hearsay.

23 THE RULES OF EVIDENCE AND THE ACCUSED AT TRIAL

23.1 INTRODUCTION

In this chapter we examine the evidential rules that apply to the defendant at his trial, including:

* the defendant's competence and compellability;
* the course of the defendant's evidence;
* drawing an adverse inference under s. 35 Criminal Justice and Public Order Act 1994, from the defendant's silence at his trial;
* disclosure of a defendant's past character;
* should the defendant give evidence?—arguments for and against.

23.2 THE ACCUSED AS A COMPETENT WITNESS FOR THE DEFENCE

Under s. 53(1) Youth Justice and Criminal Evidence Act 1999 (YJCEA), the defendant is a competent witness in his defence at every stage of the criminal proceedings. This means that, as a matter of law, the defendant may have his evidence heard by the court.

While the defendant is a competent defence witness, he is not a compellable witness—i.e. he has the right not to give evidence, which is recognised in s. 1(1) Criminal Evidence Act 1898 (CEA). The effect of s. 1(1) CEA 1898 is that if the defendant elects not to testify, he will not suffer a penalty unlike any other competent witness—apart from the possibility of adverse inferences being drawn from his silence under s. 35 Criminal Justice and Public Order Act 1994, which is considered below at 23.4. An accused is a competent but non-compellable witness for a co-accused by virtue of s. 53 YJCEA 1999.

23.2.1 THE DEFENDANT AS A PROSECUTION WITNESS

The defendant is not a competent witness for the prosecution whether he is charged alone or jointly with another defendant (s. 53(4) YJCEA 1999). In practice, s. 53(4) YJCEA is only relevant where one accused (X), is jointly charged with another (Y). A co-accused cannot give evidence for the prosecution while he remains a party to the proceedings. Under s. 53(5) YJCEA, however, where co-accused (X) ceases to be a party in the proceedings, he becomes a competent and compellable prosecution witness against any other person who has been charged in the same proceedings. This occurs where:

* X has been acquitted or has pleaded guilty at an earlier hearing and has been sentenced by the court; or
* X makes a successful submission of no case to answer at the close of the prosecution's case; or
* proceedings against X are discontinued; or
* X is tried separately from Y as a result of a successful application to sever a joint trial.

In any of these circumstances X may be called by the prosecution to give evidence against Y and anyone else charged in the same proceedings. If this occurs, X's status changes from co-accused to accomplice. Accomplice evidence may call for the jury/magistrates to be given a corroboration warning in accordance with the principles laid down in *R v Makanjuola* [1995] 1 WLR 1348 (see Chapter 21).

23.3 THE COURSE OF THE DEFENDANT'S EVIDENCE

Section 79 PACE 1984 stipulates that if a defendant is to give evidence he must normally testify before any other defence witness is called. The course of the defendant's evidence will be the same as for any other witness. Before he testifies the defendant must swear an oath or affirm. He will give evidence from the witness box like any other witness. The accused will be asked questions by the defence advocate in examination-in-chief, cross-examined by the prosecutor and any co-accused and where appropriate, re-examined by the defence.

23.3.1 CAN THE DEFENDANT GIVE EVIDENCE UNDER A SPECIAL MEASURES DIRECTION?

Until very recently there was no provision to assist vulnerable defendants to give evidence. The position now is that under s. 47 Police and Justice Act 2006 (PJA) a vulnerable defendant can apply to the court to give evidence on oath through a live TV link. A court will only grant the application if it is in the interests of justice to do so and a number of conditions are met under s. 47(4) or (5). In the case of a defendant under the age of 18, the conditions under s. 47(4) are:

(a) his ability to participate effectively in the proceedings as a witness giving oral evidence in court is compromised by his level of intellectual ability or social functioning; and

(b) use of a live link would enable him to participate more effectively in the proceedings as a witness (whether by improving the quality of his evidence or otherwise).

In the case of a defendant over the age of 18, the conditions under s. 47(5) are:

(a) he suffers from a mental disorder (within the meaning of the Mental Health Act 1983) or otherwise has a significant impairment of intelligence and social function;

(b) he is for that reason unable to participate effectively in the proceedings as a witness giving oral evidence in court; and

(c) use of a live link would enable him to participate more effectively in the proceedings as a witness (whether by improving the quality of his evidence or otherwise).

23.4 THE DRAWING OF ADVERSE INFERENCES FROM THE DEFENDANT'S SILENCE AT TRIAL—S. 35 CRIMINAL JUSTICE AND PUBLIC ORDER ACT 1994

Where the defendant is not called to give evidence on his own behalf, under s. 35 CJPOA 1994, the prosecution may comment on the defendant's failure to testify and, where appropriate, call for inferences to be drawn by the court.
Section 35 CJPOA provides:

'(1) At the trial of any person for an offence, subsections (2) and (3) below apply unless—

(a) the accused's guilt is not in issue; or

(b) it appears to the court that the physical or mental condition of the accused makes it undesirable for him to give evidence; . . .

(2) Where this subsection applies, the court shall, at the conclusion of the evidence for the prosecution, satisfy itself (in the case of proceedings on indictment, in the presence of the jury) that the accused is aware that the stage has been reached at which evidence can be given for the defence and that he can, if he wishes, give evidence and that, if he chooses not to give evidence, or having been sworn, without good cause refuses to answer any question, it will be permissible for the court or jury to draw such inference as appears proper from his failure to give evidence or his refusal, without good cause, to answer any question.

(3) Where this subsection applies, the court or jury, in determining whether the accused is guilty of the offence charged, may draw such inferences as appear proper from the failure of the accused to give evidence, or his refusal without good cause to answer any question.

(4) This section does not render the accused compellable to give evidence on his own behalf, and he shall accordingly not be guilty of contempt of court by reason of a failure to do so.'

Before adverse inferences can be drawn under s. 35 CJPOA 1994, the following conditions must be satisfied if the defendant is to enjoy a fair trial:

(1) At the close of the prosecution's case, the judge is required to put the following question to the defence advocate:

'Have you advised your client that the stage has now been reached at which he may give evidence and, if he chooses not to do so, or having been sworn without good cause refuses to answer any question, the jury may draw such inferences as appear proper from his failure to do so?' *(Practice Direction (Criminal: Consolidated)* [2002] 3 All ER 904)

(2) If the defendant remains silent, the jury (or the magistrates) should be directed in the following terms in accordance with the guidance laid down by the Court of Appeal in *R v Cowan, Gayle and Riccardi* [1995] 4 All ER 939:

- the legal burden of proof remains on the prosecution;
- the defendant is entitled to remain silent;
- before drawing an adverse inference from the defendant's silence, the jury/magistrates have to be satisfied that there is a case to answer on the prosecution evidence;
- an adverse inference drawn from the accused's failure to give evidence cannot on its own prove the accused's guilt, s. 38(3) CJPOA 1994;
- only if the jury or magistrates conclude that the only sensible explanation for the accused's silence is that he has no answer to the prosecution's case, or none that would stand up to cross-examination, may adverse inferences be drawn.

Where a defendant asserts he has a physical or mental condition preventing him from giving evidence within the meaning of s. 35(1)(b) the decision in *R v A* [1997] Crim LR 883 confirms an evidential burden is cast upon the defendant to prove his assertion. In *R v Friend* [1997] 2 Cr App R 231 Otton LJ observed:

'A physical condition might include an epileptic attack, a mental condition, latent schizophrenia where the experience of giving evidence might trigger a florid state. If it appears to the judge on the *voir dire* that such a physical or mental condition of the defendant makes it undesirable for him to give evidence, he will so rule. The inference cannot thereafter be drawn and he will so direct the jury.'

Where s. 35 has no application, the trial judge in a Crown Court trial must direct the jury not to draw any inference from the defendant's failure to give evidence in accordance with the position at common law (*R v Martinez-Tobon* [1994] 1 WLR 388).

23.5 DISCLOSING EVIDENCE OF THE DEFENDANT'S CHARACTER

While most judicial attention is directed towards the admission of a defendant's past bad character, it should not be forgotten that your client's good character, usually though not entirely meaning the absence of a criminal record, also has important evidential value.

23.5.1 THE DEFENDANT'S GOOD CHARACTER

Evidence of good character is always admissible on behalf of an accused to show the court that he is not the type of person who would commit the offence(s) with which he is charged. Good character may also be relevant to assessing the defendant's credibility (i.e. whether he is likely to be telling the truth).

'Good character' will usually mean the absence of a criminal record, but particularly praiseworthy activities such as his military service record, or public service, or charitable acts may also be used to enhance your client's character.

The approach to be taken by the courts when dealing with a defendant of good character was laid down by the Court of Appeal in *R v Vye and Others* [1993] 97 Cr App R 134:

• A defendant with no convictions is entitled *per se* to a good character direction as to his propensity (i.e. the defendant is less likely to have committed this offence because he is a person of past good character). This direction must be given irrespective of whether or not the defendant gives evidence in the case.

• A defendant with no convictions is additionally entitled to a good character direction as to his credibility where, before trial, he has asserted his innocence either at the police station and/or has given evidence on oath at his trial.

In the Crown Court, the trial judge is required to direct the jury in accordance with the principles in *R v Vye*. A failure to give a good character direction will provide a defendant with a good ground to appeal against his conviction. In a summary trial, the defence advocate should remind the magistrates of the relevance of good character evidence.

The court retains discretion whether to give a direction in a case where an accused has no previous convictions, but allows into evidence examples of the defendant's disreputable conduct (*R v Aziz* [1995] 3 WLR 53). In *R v Hickmet* [1996] Crim LR 588, the Court of Appeal confirmed that a good character direction may still be given, although in a qualified form, in situations where any previous convictions of the defendant are spent within the definition of the Rehabilitation of offenders Act 1974 or are still current but are of a trivial or unrelated nature.

23.5.2 OBTAINING EVIDENCE OF GOOD CHARACTER

When preparing a case for trial it is extremely useful to obtain character evidence in support of a client who might qualify for a good character direction. Character evidence can be presented orally by calling a character witness to give evidence on oath or in a witness statement admitted with the agreement of the prosecution under s. 9 CJA 1967 (see Chapter 22). You will have had disclosure of your client's previous convictions (if he has any) as part of the prosecution's pre-trial disclosure of evidence obligations and you will therefore be able to assess whether your client is likely to be entitled to a good character direction.

23.6 ADDUCING EVIDENCE OF THE DEFENDANT'S BAD CHARACTER UNDER THE CRIMINAL JUSTICE ACT 2003

Part 11 of the CJA 2003 has introduced a comprehensive statutory framework for admitting evidence of bad character in criminal cases, covering both the defendant and non-defendant. The new law undermines many of the traditional immunities which generally gave the defendant a shield protecting him from having evidence of his bad character being disclosed to the court.

The 'old law' (which has been abolished by s. 99 CJA 2003), developed over many years, was reasonably clear. It was based on an exclusionary starting point. Evidence of a defendant's past bad character was inadmissible for the purpose of showing that by reason of past offending, the defendant was likely to have acted in conformity and was therefore guilty of the current offence.

The justification for an exclusionary rule was based, for the most part, on protecting the defendant from the prejudice that such knowledge would engender in the minds of the jury or magistrates. The knowledge that X has several previous convictions for theft and burglary, on a charge of burglary which X denies, would make it much more likely that X would be convicted! It was thought the jury would attach too much significance to the defendant's criminal record and not enough to the evidence linking the defendant to the actual offence. The position at common law was summed-up by Lord Sumner in *Thompson v The King* [1918] AC 221:

> 'There is all the difference in the world between evidence proving the accused is a bad man and evidence proving that he is *the* man.'

The exclusionary common law rule did permit the admission of bad character evidence in a number of defined circumstances. However, the exclusionary starting point was seen as a significant protection in ensuring the defendant's right to a fair trial as evidence of a defendant's past bad character is prejudicial and increases the defendant's chance of being convicted.

The CJA 2003 considerably extends the boundaries for admitting evidence of a defendant's bad character with fewer safeguards. The provisions covering non-defendants are explained in Chapter 20.

3.6.1 STATUTORY DEFINITION OF BAD CHARACTER

Section 98 CJA 2003 defines evidence of a person's bad character as 'evidence of, or of a disposition towards, misconduct on his part . . . '

The term 'misconduct' is further defined by s. 112 CJA 2003, as the commission of an offence or other 'reprehensible' behaviour.

The definition of bad character under the Act is wide and includes:

- evidence of the defendant's previous convictions;
- evidence of charges on which the defendant is being concurrently tried;
- evidence relating to an offence(s) with which the defendant was charged but not convicted;
- evidence relating to an offence(s) with which the defendant has been charged but acquitted;
- evidence not amounting to criminal conduct but which constitutes 'reprehensible' behaviour.

Section 98 further provides that the provisions of the Act *do not* apply to evidence of, or of a disposition towards, misconduct on his part which:

> '(a) has to do with the alleged facts of the offence with which the defendant is charged, or
>
> (b) is evidence of misconduct in connection with the investigation or prosecution of that offence.'

Evidence of misconduct going directly to the facts in the case is not subject to the statutory regime governing the admission of bad character evidence under the CJA 2003. The admissibility of such evidence is governed by its relevance to the issues in the case. Consider the following examples:

 Example 1

Nigel is charged with arson by starting a fire in a hostel for resettling young offenders in which he was living at the time of the alleged offence. The fire occurred shortly after a dispute between Nigel and a member of the hostel staff who accused Nigel of breaking the hostel's curfew rules. In proving the facts, the prosecutor will have to refer to the fact that Nigel was residing at a hostel for the resettling of young offenders. It has to do with the facts of the offence and therefore does not trigger the character provisions under the Act (s. 98(a)).

 Example 2

Gary is accused of a serious offence of assault. The prosecution wishes to adduce evidence that Gary has tried to bribe a prosecution witness not to give evidence. Such evidence as the prosecution might have would be freely admissible as it is evidence connected with the prosecution of the offence (s. 98(b)).

Misconduct which 'has to do with the facts of the offence' requires there is sufficient connection in time between the misconduct and the offence alleged. In *R v Tracey McNeill* [2007] EWCA Crim 2927, it was held that the misconduct should be 'reasonably contemporaneous and closely associated with the alleged facts of the offence charged'. In *McNeill* the defendant denied a charge of threatening to kill her neighbour. Evidence of what the defendant had said to a housing officer the day after the alleged incident about wishing to see her neighbour dead, was rightly admitted under s. 98(a).

23.6.2 GATEWAYS TO ADMISSION

Section 101(1) CJA 2003 is very significant and is reproduced below in full. It provides seven gateways through which evidence of a defendant's bad character can be admitted.

'Section 101   Defendant's bad character

(1) In criminal proceedings evidence of the defendant's bad character is admissible if, but only if—

(a) all parties to the proceedings agree to the evidence being admissible,

(b) the evidence is adduced by the defendant or is given in answer to a question asked by him in cross-examination,

(c) it is important explanatory evidence,

(d) it is relevant to an important matter in issue between the defendant and the prosecution,

(e) it has substantial probative value in relation to an important matter in issue between the defendant and a co-defendant,

(f) it is evidence to correct a false impression given by the defendant, or

(g) the defendant has made an attack on another person's character.

(2) Sections 102 to 106 contain provisions supplementing subsection (1).

(3) The court must not admit evidence under subsection (1)(d) or (g) if, on an application by the defendant to exclude it, it appears to the court that the admission of the evidence would have such an adverse effect on the fairness of the proceedings that the court ought not to admit it.

(4) On an application to exclude evidence under subsection (3) the court must have regard, in particular, to the length of time between the matters to which that evidence relates and the matters which form the subject of the offence charged.'

Provided the evidence of bad character falls within one of the gateways, it is not necessary for a party to seek the court's leave to adduce the bad character evidence.

23.6.3 IS THERE A STATUTORY DISCRETION TO EXCLUDE BAD CHARACTER EVIDENCE?

The answer to the above question is yes, but only in relation to gateways (d) and (g) and only upon application by the defence to have the evidence excluded. Section 101(3) CJA 2003 permits the court to exclude evidence of bad character under either gateway (d) or (g), if the admission of the evidence would have an adverse effect on the fairness of the proceedings. The test for the exercise of this judicial discretion is the same as that exercised under s. 78 PACE 1984 (see Chapter 6). In exercising discretion under s. 101(3) CJA 2003 the court is specifically required to have regard to the length of time that has passed since the bad character sought to be admitted was in fact committed (s. 101(4) CJA 2003).

The discretion to exclude bad character evidence contained in s. 101(3) is specific to gateways (d) and (g). What of the other gateways for admission? There is nothing in the 2003 Act which indicates a clear parliamentary intention to limit the operation of s. 78 PACE 1984 which gives the court discretion to exclude prosecution evidence which would have an adverse effect on the fairness of the proceedings (see Chapter 6). In the absence of an express provision excluding the operation of s. 78 PACE 1984, it must be assumed that it applies to the admission of the defendant's bad character under the 2003 Act. This is supported by dicta in the Court of Appeal's decision in *R v Highton; R v Van Nguyen; R v Carp* [2005] 1 WLR 3472:

> 'However, it is right that we should say that, without having heard full argument, our inclination is to say that section 78 provides an additional protection to a defendant. In light of this preliminary view as to the effect of section 78, judges may consider that it is a sensible precaution, when making rulings as to the use of evidence of bad character, to apply the provisions of section 78 and exclude evidence where it would be appropriate to do so under section 78, pending a definitive ruling to the contrary. Adopting this course will avoid any risk of injustice to the defendant . . . and any risk of a court failing to comply with Article 6.'

3.6.4 PROCEDURE FOR SEEKING ADMISSION OF EVIDENCE OF A DEFENDANT'S PAST BAD CHARACTER

Where the prosecution seeks to admit evidence of the defendant's bad character under gateways (c)–(g), it is required to give notice in the prescribed form in accordance within time-limits laid down in Crim PR, Part 35 or by the court. Provision is made to enable an application to be made orally and out of time where the interests of justice require it. Notice of opposition to the admission of bad character must also be made in the prescribed form and within set time-limits.

Where a dispute arises about the admissibility of the defendant's bad character in a case to be tried on indictment, the matter will be determined by the judge in the absence of the jury or at an earlier pre-trial hearing (see Chapter 16, para. 16.8). A binding ruling in favour of admitting evidence of a defendant's bad character made at a pre-trial hearing may persuade a defendant to plead guilty. Depending on the facts in the case and the nature of the bad character evidence sought to be admitted, it may be difficult for a court to rule on the admissibility of bad character in advance of trial. Sometimes the decision is best made after the close of the prosecution's case when the strength of the prosecution's case can be assessed.

When making a ruling on the admissibility of bad character evidence, the court must give reasons (s. 110 CJA 2003). Our case study *R v Lenny Whyte* includes an application by the prosecution to admit evidence of Lenny Whyte's criminal convictions under s. 101(1) CJA 2003. The relevant documentation can be accessed from our Online Resource Centre.

online
resource
centre

Below we look in detail at the gateways for admitting the defendant's bad character under s. 101.

3.6.5 SECTION 101(1)(a) CJA 2003

All parties to the proceedings agree to the defendant's bad character being admitted in evidence.

23.6.6 SECTION 101(1)(b) CJA 2003

Evidence of the defendant's bad character is given by the defendant himself or is given in answer to a question asked by him in cross-examination and intended to elicit it.

Section 101(1)(a) and (b) is largely self-explanatory. In relation to s. 101(b), there may be tactical advantages in a defendant choosing to adduce evidence of his bad character in a case where the prosecution has chosen not to put it in evidence as part of its case.

23.6.7 **SECTION 101(1)(c) CJA 2003—EVIDENCE OF THE DEFENDANT'S BAD CHARACTER AS IMPORTANT EXPLANATORY EVIDENCE**

This gateway is further defined in s. 102, and is available only to the prosecution.

'**Section 102' Important explanatory evidence**

For the purposes of section 101(1)(c) evidence is important explanatory evidence if—

(a) without it, the court or jury would find it impossible or difficult properly to understand other evidence in the case, and

(b) its value for understanding the case as a whole is substantial.'

In some cases it will be necessary for the prosecution to give explanatory background information about the offence, which may result in part or the whole of the defendant's bad character being disclosed. Section 101(1)(c) CJA 2003 gives statutory effect to the previous position at common law.

The Court of Appeal's decision in *R v Edwards; Fysh; Duggan and Chohan* [2006] 1 Cr App R 3 (specifically the appeal of Chohan) affords a useful illustration of gateway 101(1)(c). Chohan was charged with burglary. He denied the offence. The main evidence against him came from an eyewitness who formally identified him at an identification parade. In fact, the parade was not convened for some considerable time as Chohan left the country during the investigation. The identification of Chohan was based on recognition. The female eyewitness claimed Chohan had been her drug dealer. Chohan denied involvement in the burglary and accused the eyewitness of fabricating her evidence because he had terminated a sexual relationship with her, some time previously. Chohan denied ever having supplied drugs to her. The supply of drugs clearly constituted reprehensible behaviour. The trial judge permitted the evidence to be adduced under gateway 101(1)(c) as it comprised important explanatory evidence. It explained the basis of the eyewitness's identification and why she was so confident that her identification of Chohan was accurate.

Evidence of misconduct which has to do with the alleged facts of the offence with which the defendant is charged (see s. 98(a) above) will often be difficult to distinguish from background evidence sought to be admitted under s. 101(1)(c). Example 1 at para. 23.6.1 above, affords a good illustration of this point.

23.7 **SECTION 101(1)(d) CRIMINAL JUSTICE ACT 2003**

Evidence of the defendant's bad character is relevant to an important matter in issue between the defendant and the prosecution.

This very important gateway is further defined in s. 103 and is available only to the prosecution.

'**Section 103 Matter in issue between the defendant and the prosecution**

(1) For the purposes of section 101(1)(d) the matters in issue between the defendant and the prosecution include—

(a) the question whether the defendant has a propensity to commit offences of the kind with which he is charged, except where his having such a propensity makes it no more likely that he is guilty of the offence;

(b) the question whether the defendant has a propensity to be untruthful, except where it is not suggested that the defendant's case is untruthful in any respect.

(2) Where subsection (1)(a) applies, a defendant's propensity to commit offences of the kind with which he is charged may (without prejudice to any other way of doing so) be established by evidence that he has been convicted of—

(a) an offence of the same description as the one with which he is charged, or

(b) an offence of the same category as the one with which he is charged.

(3) Subsection (2) does not apply in the case of a particular defendant if the court is satisfied, by reason of the length of time since the conviction or for any other reason, that it would be unjust for it to apply in his case.

(4) For the purposes of subsection (2)—

    (a) two offences are of the same description as each other if the statement of the offence in a written charge or indictment would, in each case, be in the same terms;

    (b) two offences are of the same category as each other if they belong to the same category of offences prescribed for the purposes of this section by an order made by the Secretary of State.

(5) A category prescribed by an order under subsection (4)(b) must consist of offences of the same type.

(6) Only prosecution evidence is admissible under section 101(1)(d).'

An important matter in issue between the prosecution and the defence is deemed to include:

- the question whether the defendant has a propensity to commit offences of the kind with which he is currently charged (unless the propensity makes him no more likely to be guilty of the offence with which he is charged); and/or

- the question whether the defendant has a propensity to be untruthful (unless it is not suggested that the defendant's case is untruthful).

Gateway (d) is very significant because it makes it considerably easier for a defendant's bad character to be admitted than previously under the common law. Section 103 sweeps away the old provisions relating to the admissibility of similar fact evidence. The new test (the evidence must be relevant to an important matter in issue) implies a much lower threshold of relevance than under the similar fact evidence rule where the probative value of the bad character evidence had to be sufficiently high to overcome its prejudicial effect. Previous convictions and other 'reprehensible behaviour' may now be admitted against the defendant, irrespective of whether they have probative force on the basis that they are simply relevant to an important matter in issue between the prosecution and the defence, subject to the discretion to exclude under s. 101(3).

In *R v Hanson; R v Gilmore; R v Pickstone* [2005] 2 Cr App R 21, the Court of Appeal sent out a message of restraint to prosecutors in the following terms:

'The starting point should be for judges and practitioners to bear in mind that Parliament's purpose in the legislation, as we divine it from the terms of the Act, was to assist in the evidence based conviction of the guilty, without putting those who are not guilty at risk of conviction by prejudice. It is accordingly to be hoped that prosecution applications to adduce such evidence will not be made routinely, simply because a defendant has previous convictions, but will be based on the particular circumstances of each case.'

3.7.1 PROPENSITY TO COMMIT OFFENCES OF THE KIND WITH WHICH HE IS CHARGED

By virtue of s. 103(2) CJA 2003, propensity to commit offences of the kind with which the defendant is charged **may** be established by evidence that the defendant has been convicted of an offence of the same description or an offence of the same category as that with which he is charged. Section 103(2) does not apply if a court concludes that by reason of length of time since conviction or for any other reason, it would be unjust to apply this method to inferring propensity from the defendant's criminal record (s. 103(3)).

23.7.2 WHAT IS AN OFFENCE OF THE SAME DESCRIPTION/CATEGORY?

An offence will be of the same description if the statement of offence would in each case be the same (s. 103(4)(a)). For example, if X is charged with assault occasioning actual bodily harm contrary to s. 47 Offences Against the Person Act 1861 and has a previous conviction for a s. 47 assault, this would constitute an offence of the same description and would therefore be admissible to show X's propensity to commit violent assault.

Offences of the same category have to be prescribed by the Secretary of State (s. 103 (4)(b)). Currently there are two categories of offences that fall within the same category relating to theft and child sex offences:

> 'The purpose of the Order . . . is to ensure that when a defendant being tried for either a theft or child sex offence has a previous conviction for an offence which falls within the same category, the strong presumption should be that the conviction should be revealed to the jury.'

Theft offences of the same category will include theft, robbery, burglary, aggravated burglary, taking a motor car without consent, aggravated vehicle taking, handling stolen goods, going equipped to steal, making off without payment and inchoate offences of the same description. In relation to sexual offences against persons under the age of 16, the Order includes a full list of all such offences in Part 2 including rape, indecent assault, unlawful sexual intercourse and incest, together with the new offences involving children under the Sexual Offences Act 2003.

23.7.3 PROVING PROPENSITY TO COMMIT AN OFFENCE OF THE KIND IN OTHER WAYS

Proof of propensity to commit an offence of the kind with which the defendant is charged is not confined to previous convictions for offences of the same description or category. For example, Tina is charged with a serious assault arising out of an incident in a nightclub. She claims to have acted in self-defence maintaining she was the victim of an unprovoked attack. She has previous convictions for affray and for a public order offence under s. 5 Public Order Act 1986. Although Tina's previous convictions are not of the same description or category as the current charge, the prosecution could legitimately argue that they indicate a propensity on Tina's part to engage in acts of violence and public disturbance, making her defence less credible. Her previous convictions are therefore relevant to an important matter in issue between the prosecution and the defence.

In fact, evidence of a defendant's propensity is not restricted to proof of previous convictions *per se*. Section 103(2) specifically stipulates that a defendant's propensity to commit offences of the kind with which he is charged can be proved in other ways. Propensity could be established by proof of conduct that is not criminal (provided it is reprehensible), and indeed it could stem from a previous acquittal if the evidence is relevant. Two pre-2003 Act cases provide good illustrations.

- *R v Butler* (1987) 84 Cr App R 12. In this case, the defendant denied indecently assaulting a woman in a very degrading manner in the back of the woman's car, maintaining the woman's identification of him was mistaken. The prosecution was allowed to adduce evidence from the defendant's former girlfriend of the degrading and very similar sexual acts she had allowed him to perform on her. Although the evidence disclosed no criminal acts on the defendant's part (they being consensual), it provided significant probative value on the issue of the accuracy of the victim's identification of her attacker.

- In *R v Z* [2000] 3 WLR 117, the defendant denied a charge of rape, maintaining his victim had consented. Evidence was adduced of the fact that he had previously been tried and acquitted of rape in three separate trials, having used the same defence in each.

In *R v Weir* [2005] EWCA Crim 2866, the Court of Appeal held that propensity could be established by proof that the defendant had been cautioned in relation to a particular matter and in *R v Smith* [2005] EWCA 3244, from an allegation made by an alleged victim in respect of which the defendant had never been tried. In this case the Court of Appeal stipulated that it is for the judge to police the gateway, i.e. to determine admissibility and the relevance of the evidence and for the jury to evaluate the evidence once it is admitted.

.7.4 CHALLENGING EVIDENCE OF PROPENSITY

The effect of s. 103(2) is that previous convictions of the same description/category are taken to show the defendant's propensity. This assumption should not go unchallenged by the defence. The defence should require the court to ask itself: 'Is the defendant's propensity (as identified by the prosecution) truly relevant to the facts in issue?' Another way to express this might be: 'Does the defendant's propensity make it more likely that he committed the offence?' Even if the answer to either of these questions is yes, the defence should still apply to have the evidence excluded on the basis that it would have an adverse effect on the fairness of the proceedings. The nature of the defence relied on will be significant in determining the relevance and therefore the admissibility of bad character evidence.

Issues of propensity to commit offences of the kind with which the defendant is charged will involve difficult questions of fact for the judge/magistrates. It may be insufficient for the prosecution to rely on the fact of the defendant's criminal record as the court may need to hear the facts behind the conviction in order to determine its true relevance and whether it is indicative of propensity on the defendant's part. Suppose a defendant is facing a disputed allegation of common assault but has a previous conviction for assault contrary to s. 47 Offences Against the Person Act 1861. This is clearly an offence of the same description but an assault can be committed in different ways and for many different reasons.

.7.5 CASE LAW GUIDANCE ON S. 101(1)(d) CJA 2003 AND THE ISSUE OF PROPENSITY

In one of the first key decisions on the bad character provisions under the CJA 2003, the Court of Appeal provided the following guidance in *R v Hanson; R v Gilmore; R v Pickstone* [2005] 2 Cr App R 21:

1. Where the prosecution relies on the defendant's propensity to commit offences, there are three questions to be answered:
   (i) Does the history of conviction(s) establish a propensity to commit offences of the kind charged?
   (ii) Does that propensity make it more likely that the defendant committed the offence charged?
   (iii) Is it unjust to rely on the conviction(s) of the same description or category; and, in any event, will the proceedings be unfair if they are admitted?

2. Propensity is not confined to offences of the same description or category. As such s. 103(2) is not exhaustive of the types of convictions which might be relied on to show evidence of propensity to commit offences of the same kind. Equally, simply because an offence falls within the same description or category is not necessarily sufficient to show a propensity.

3. There is no minimum number of events that are required to show propensity. The fewer the number of convictions, the weaker the evidence of propensity is likely to be. A single previous conviction may show evidence of propensity where the offence discloses unusual tendencies or the modus operandi discloses significant features such as to give the previous misconduct probative force.

   'Child sexual abuse, or fire setting, are comparatively clear examples of such unusual behaviour but we attempt no exhaustive list. Circumstances demonstrating probative force are not confined to those sharing striking similarity. So, a single conviction for shoplifting will not, without more, be admissible to show propensity to steal. But if the modus operandi has significant features shared by the offence charged, it may show propensity.'

4. Having regard to the exercise of judicial discretion under s. 101(3), and under s. 103(3), the court should take into consideration:

   (i) the degree of similarity between the previous conviction and the offence charged, albeit they are both within the same description or prescribed category. For example, theft and assault occasioning actual bodily harm may each embrace a wide spectrum of conduct. This does not, however, mean that what used to be referred as striking similarity must be shown before convictions become admissible;

   (ii) the respective gravity of the past and present offences;

   (iii) a key factor will be an assessment of the strength of the prosecution's case. If there is little or no evidence, it is unlikely to be just to admit a defendant's previous convictions.

5. The date of the commission of an offence is often going to be more significant than the date of conviction. Old convictions, with no special features shared with the offence charged, are likely to have an adverse effect on the fairness of the proceedings.

6. It will often be necessary, before determining admissibility and even when considering offences of the same description or category, to examine each individual conviction rather than merely to look at the name of the offence or at the defendant's record as a whole.

7. The sentence passed will not normally be probative or admissible at the behest of the Crown, though it may be at the behest of the defence.

8. Where past events are disputed, the judge should be careful not to permit the trial to drift into satellite litigation by a prolonged investigation into the circumstances of the past misconduct:

   '. . . the Crown needs to decide, at the time of giving notice of the application, whether it proposes to rely simply upon the fact of conviction or also upon the circumstances of it. The former may be enough when the circumstances of the conviction are sufficiently apparent from its description, to justify a finding that it can establish propensity, either to commit an offence of the kind charged or to be untruthful and that the requirements of ss. 103(3) and 101(3) can, subject to any particular matter raised on behalf of the defendant, be satisfied. For example, a succession of convictions for dwelling-house burglary, where the same is now charged, may well call for no further evidence than proof of the fact of the convictions. But where, as will often be the case, the Crown needs and proposes to rely on the circumstances of the previous convictions, those circumstances and the manner in which they are to be proved must be set out in the application. There is a similar obligation of frankness upon the defendant, which will be reinforced by the general obligation contained in the new Criminal Procedure Rules to give active assistance to the court in its case management (see r.3.3). Routine applications by defendants for disclosure of the circumstances of previous convictions are likely to be met by a requirement that the request be justified by identification of the reason why it is said that those circumstances may show the convictions to be inadmissible. We would expect the relevant circumstances of previous convictions generally to be capable of agreement, and that, subject to the trial judge's ruling as to admissibility, they will be put before the jury by way of admission. Even where the circumstances are genuinely in dispute, we would expect the minimum indisputable facts to be thus admitted. It will be very rare indeed for it to be necessary for the judge to hear evidence before ruling on admissibility under this Act.'

9. The importance of correctly directing the jury is also stressed. In any case where bad character is admitted, the jury should be instructed not to place undue reliance on bad character evidence:

   'Evidence of bad character cannot be used simply to bolster a weak case, or to prejudice the minds of a jury against a defendant. In particular, the jury should be directed; that they should not conclude that the defendant is guilty or untruthful merely because he has these convictions. That, although the convictions may show a propensity, this does not mean that he has committed this offence or been untruthful in this case; that whether they in fact show a propensity is for them to decide; that they must take into account what the defendant has said about his previous convictions; and that, although they are entitled, if they find propensity as shown, to take this into account when determining guilt, propensity is only one relevant factor and they must assess its significance in the light of all the other evidence in the case.'

10. If a judge has directed himself or herself correctly, the Court of Appeal will be very slow to interfere with a ruling either as to admissibility.

What of the specific appeals in *Hanson*?

In *Hanson*, the charge was theft of money from the living accommodation above a public house. The circumstantial evidence linking Hanson to the crime clearly indicated he had a case to answer, although it was not overwhelming. He denied the offence but had previous convictions for dishonesty, including dwelling-house burglary, theft from premises, a previous conviction for robbery and aggravated vehicle taking. On the facts in this case, the Court of Appeal observed:

'Convictions for handling and aggravated vehicle taking, although within the theft category, do not, in our judgment, show, without more pertinent information, propensity to burgle as indicted or to steal, to which the applicant pleaded guilty. The applicant's robbery conviction, albeit also within the theft category, might, had it been analysed, have been regarded as being so prejudicial as to adversely affect the fairness of the proceedings in relation to the offence charged. But the applicant had a considerable number of convictions for burglary and theft from private property that were plainly properly admissible to show propensity to commit an offence of the kind here charged.'

In *Gilmore*, an offence of theft was denied. Gilmore was arrested in the early hours of the morning. He had in his possession a bag containing very recently stolen items. Gilmore claimed to have come across the items innocently, believing them to be rubbish. The evidence linking him to the theft was strong. Three recent previous convictions for theft were properly admitted. They were indicative of a recent propensity to steal.

In *Pickstone*, the charges included the rape and indecent assault of P's step-daughter. P denied the offences. There was medical evidence to support the fact of sexual interference. P stated the girl was making up the allegation against him. The respective credibility of the complainant and the defendant was very much in issue. Nine years previous to the current allegation, P had been convicted of the indecent assault of an 11-year-old girl. The trial judge admitted the previous conviction under gateways (d) and (g). He expressly took into account the length of time since the previous conviction, concluding the 'defendant's sexual mores and motivations are not necessarily affected by the passage of time'. In this context, the admission of the evidence under gateways (d) and (g) would not adversely affect the fairness of the proceedings.

23.7.6 CAN AN OLD OR SINGLE PREVIOUS CONVICTION GIVE RISE TO A PROPENSITY TO COMMIT AN OFFENCE OF THE KIND CHARGED?

In *R v Sully* (2007) 151 SJLB 1564, two convictions for sexual assault on children which were over 30 years old were rightly admitted on a charge of sexual assault of a female under 13. Similarly in *R v Cox* [2007] EWCA Crim 3365, on a charge of sexually assaulting a 13-year-old babysitter, the defendant's previous convictions for sexual assault and attempted unlawful sexual intercourse with a 12-year-old girl, committed 20 years previously, were admitted. By contrast, in *R v Michael M* [2007] Crim LR 637, a 20-year-old conviction for possessing a sawn-off shotgun was wrongly admitted as evidence of propensity on a charge of possession of a firearm with intent to cause fear of violence. These cases show that what constitutes propensity is a question of fact in each case but that the dicta in *R v Hanson* are being applied in the context of offences showing 'unusual features', i.e. sexual offences involving children.

23.7.7 **A MATTER IN ISSUE CAN INCLUDE THE QUESTION WHETHER THE DEFENDANT HAS A PROPENSITY TO BE UNTRUTHFUL (S. 103(1)(b))**

Section 101(1)(d) CJA 2003 further permits the prosecution to adduce evidence of a defendant's bad character where the defendant's propensity to be untruthful is deemed an important matter in issue between the prosecution and the defence. In *R v Hanson* [2005] 2 Cr App R 21, the Court of Appeal observed that a propensity to be untruthful is not the same as a propensity to dishonesty (s. 103(1)(b)). Consequently, the prosecution ought not simply to adduce evidence of previous convictions for dishonesty for the explicit purpose of showing the accused has a propensity for untruthfulness.

> 'Thus previous convictions, whether for offences of dishonesty or otherwise, are therefore only likely to be capable of showing a propensity to be untruthful where, in the present case, truthfulness is an issue and, in the earlier case, either there was a plea of not guilty and the defendant gave an account, on arrest, in interview, or in evidence, which the jury must have disbelieved, or the way in which the offence was committed shows a propensity for untruthfulness, for example, by the making of false representations.'

This statement must now be read in the light of the comments made by Lord Phillips CJ, in *R v Campbell* [2007] 1 WLR 2798 which appear to render s. 103(1)(b) virtually obsolete. Lord Phillips observed that a defendant's truthfulness is likely to be in issue in any case where he pleads not guilty and so propensity to be untruthful cannot normally be described as being an important matter in issue.

> 'A propensity for untruthfulness will not of itself, go very far to establishing the committal of a criminal offence. To suggest that a propensity for untruthfulness makes it more likely that a defendant has lied to the jury is not likely to help them. If they apply common sense they will conclude that a defendant who has committed a criminal offence may well be prepared to lie about it, even if he has not shown a propensity for lying whereas a defendant who has not committed the offence charged will be likely to tell the truth, even if he has shown a propensity for telling lies. In short, whether or not a defendant is telling the truth to the jury is likely to depend simply on whether or not he committed the offence charged. The jury should focus on the latter question rather than on whether or not he has a propensity for telling lies. For these reasons, the only circumstance in which there is likely to be an important issue as to whether a defendant has a propensity to tell lies is where telling lies is an element of the offence charged. Even then, the propensity to tell lies is only likely to be significant if the lying is in the context of committing criminal offences, in which case the evidence is likely to be admissible under section 103(1)(a).'

With respect, Lord Phillips' reasoning appears to completely ignore the clear wording in s. 103(1)(b) CJA 2003 which deems a propensity to be untruthful to be a matter in issue between the prosecution and the defence and is contrary to the dicta in *R v Hanson* [2005] which give guidance as to what types of previous convictions are relevant to a determination of a defendant's propensity to be untruthful. In a case where the jury is required to assess the credibility of two conflicting accounts (the defendant's version and the version of a prosecution witness), the fact that the defendant has convictions for fraud or deception is surely relevant to an important matter in issue?

The following examples are designed to illustrate the possible application of gateway 101(1)(d):

Example 1

Barry is charged with assault occasioning actual bodily harm on his neighbour. He pleads not guilty, maintaining he acted in self defence. Barry has a previous conviction for a violent assault, contrary to s. 20 OAPA 1861, six years earlier. He was involved in a fracas in a public house following a football match and pleaded guilty. The prosecution would say that he has a previous conviction for an offence of the same description/type which shows Barry has a propensity to use violence. The defence should oppose the application to have this previous conviction admitted. Applying the dicta in *Hanson* (this being one previous conviction only with no special feature), can this single previous conviction amount to propensity? It should also be noted that the manner in which the earlier assault came to be committed is somewhat different from the present alleged assault. In addition, regard should be had to s. 103(3)—this previous conviction is six years old. Aside from challenging propensity, the defence should make an application under s. 101(3) to have it excluded on the basis that its admission would have an adverse effect on the fairness of the proceedings. In exercising discretion regard should be had to the guidance in *Hanson*. In particular, the previous offence was more serious than that currently alleged and the circumstances were different. A pertinent factor will be an assessment of how strong the prosecution's case is, as bad character evidence should not be adduced to bolster an evidentially weak case. If the evidence was admitted, the judge would need to carefully direct the jury not to place too much reliance on the fact of previous convictions. If the evidence is not admitted under gateway (d) it might be admitted under gateway (g) if Barry's defence involves an attack on a prosecution witness. It would be up to the judge to decide how to direct the jury in terms of the relevance of the evidence (see para. 23.11, below).

In the above example, assume instead that Barry has three previous convictions for theft. Could these convictions be admitted as evidence of Barry's propensity to be untruthful?

In the light of the statements in *Hanson*, the answer is arguably no. A propensity towards dishonesty is not the same thing as a propensity to be untruthful. It would be important to ascertain whether Barry pleaded guilty to any or all of his previous offences or was found guilty after having given evidence on oath. In the light of Lord Phillips' statement in *R v Campbell* [2007], the evidence would appear to assume no relevance at all. The evidence could however be admitted under gateway (g) if Barry's defence involves an attack on a prosecution witness (see below).

 Example 2

Ethan is charged with burglary. He denies the offence, maintaining a defence of mistaken identity. He intends to call his girlfriend as an alibi. Ethan has an extensive criminal record which includes a conviction for a violent robbery four years ago, and several previous convictions for theft, burglary and possession of drugs over the past 12 years. Will the fact of these previous convictions be admissible?

The prosecution will want to adduce Ethan's previous convictions for dishonesty related offences under s. 101(1)(d), both as evidence of Ethan's propensity to commit offences of the kind with which he is charged and as evidence of his propensity to be untruthful. The previous convictions for robbery, theft and burglary are all offences of the same description/category as the current offence. The assumption will therefore be that they show Ethan's propensity to commit offences of dishonesty.

What can the defence argue in this situation? How relevant is Ethan's propensity to the issue of whether the witness's identification is correct or not, especially as Ethan denies being at the scene? Would it not adversely affect the fairness of the proceedings if they were to be admitted? Wouldn't the jury inevitably disregard the evidence of identification and conclude Ethan is guilty because of his track record? If Ethan's defence is simply one of mistaken identity, in what sense is he putting forward an untruthful defence? While the previous convictions for theft and burglary may be admitted on the issue of his propensity, the admission of the robbery conviction might be regarded as being particularly prejudicial. *Hanson* suggests the court should have regard to the respective gravity of past and present offences and the strength of the prosecution's case. Applying the dicta in *Hanson* (and subject to the caveat raised by Lord Phillips in *R v Campbell*), previous convictions for offences of dishonesty do not necessarily indicate a propensity to be untruthful.

Once again, if the evidence was admitted, the judge should carefully direct the jury not to place too much reliance on the fact of previous convictions.

Example 3

Frank is charged with sexually assaulting his nine-year-old nephew. He denies the offence, maintaining that the child is lying. Frank received a caution 18 months earlier for possession of indecent photographs of young boys which were found on his computer. He only accepted the caution because he felt under pressure and wanted to avoid unwanted publicity as he was teaching at that time. He does not know how the images appeared on his computer. Can the prosecution use this fact in evidence against him at his trial for sexual assault?

The prosecution would argue that the caution suggests Frank has a paedophilic disposition, making it less likely that the nephew is making up the allegation. Although he has only a caution recorded against his name, *Hanson* suggests that sex offences involving children are indicative of unusual behaviour.

The defence advocate might argue that the earlier offence is very different to that currently alleged, and for this reason its relevance in the context of the current case must be doubted. Furthermore, there is doubt as to the safety and reliability of the previous caution. Consequently, the admission of such evidence would prejudice Frank's right to a fair trial on the basis that its prejudicial value exceeds its probative effect. Does it make it more likely that the boy is telling the truth?

23.8 SECTION 101(1)(e) CRIMINAL JUSTICE ACT 2003

Evidence of a defendant's bad character has substantial probative value in relation to an important issue between the defendant and a co-defendant.

Section 101(1)(e) CJA 2003 is defined further in s. 104, and applies only to a co-defendant.

> **'Section 104   Matter in issue between the defendant and a co-defendant**
>
> (1) Evidence which is relevant to the question whether the defendant has a propensity to be untruthful is admissible on that basis under section 101(1)(e) only if the nature or conduct of his defence is such as to undermine the co-defendant's defence.
>
> (2) Only evidence—
>
>   (a) which is to be (or has been) adduced by the co-defendant, or
>
>   (b) which a witness is to be invited to give (or has given) in cross-examination by the co-defendant is admissible under section 101(1)(e).'

This subsection may be invoked where co-accused (A) wishes to lead evidence of his fellow co-accused's (B's) propensity to commit offences of a certain kind for the express purpose of showing that it was more likely that B committed the offence in question. A good example of the application of this principle is provided by *R v Randall* [2004] 1 Cr App R 26. In *Randall*, it was not entirely clear which of the co-accused had inflicted the final, fatal injury in an allegation of murder. Each blamed the other. Co-accused A sought to introduce B's previous convictions for serious violence to suggest that B was more likely to have inflicted the fatal injury. By contrast, A's previous convictions were for minor offences. The House of Lords quashed A's conviction for murder, maintaining the trial judge should have directed the jury that B's criminal past was relevant to A's defence, and that they could consider B's past when determining the involvement of each in the offence. The key factor is whether the evidence has substantial probative value on an important matter in issue between co-defendants.

Where one co-accused wishes to adduce evidence of the other's propensity to be untruthful, s. 104(1) specifically stipulates that this will only be allowed where the nature and conduct of the co-accused's defence undermines the defence of his fellow co-accused. In *R v Stephenson* [2006] EWCA Crim 2325, it was observed that previous convictions for shoplifting and stealing are relevant to untruthfulness and that the statements in *R v Hanson*, which suggest there is a difference between dishonesty and untruthfulness (see para. 23.7.7), should not be applied to gateway (e).

An illustration of how this provision is applied is provided by the previous law, under s. 1(3)(iii) Criminal Evidence Act 1898. Under the 1898 Act, (B) would lose his shield against the revelation of his past bad character, where, during examination-in-chief or in cross-examination, B's evidence strengthened the prosecution's case against (A) or undermined A's defence. A good illustration is provided by the pre-2003 Act case of *Murdoch v Taylor* [1965] AC 574. In this case, A and B were jointly charged with handling stolen goods. B testified that he had no knowledge as to what was in a box he had received, because the contents of the box were nothing to do with him but were the sole responsibility of A. The trial judge ruled that B had lost his shield under s. 1(3)(iii) CEA 1898, and therefore A had the right to cross-examine B on his previous convictions. B appealed against his conviction, contending he had not given evidence against A and that he had not intended to shift the blame from himself onto A. Affirming the conviction, the House of Lords held that, notwithstanding B's lack of motive, his evidence had strengthened the prosecution case against A and had by implication alleged that it was A alone who was the handler of the stolen goods.

The following guidelines are taken from the pre-2003 Act case of *R v Varley* [1982] 2 All ER 519 which, it is submitted, will continue to apply to gateway (e).

- It has to be decided objectively whether the evidence either supports the prosecution case in a material respect or undermines the defence of the co-accused.
- In relation to undermining a co-accused's defence, care must be taken to see that the evidence clearly undermines the defence. Inconvenience to or inconsistency with the other's defence is not of itself sufficient.
- Mere denial of participation in a joint venture is not of itself sufficient to rank as evidence against the co-defendant. Such denial must lead to the conclusion that if the witness did not participate then it must have been the other who did.

The following should be noted about s. 101(1)(e) CJA 2003:

- Where the grounds for admitting evidence of a co-accused's bad character are satisfied, there is no discretion to disallow cross-examination (provided the safeguard that the evidence must have substantial probative value in relation to an important matter in issue between the co-accused is satisfied).
- Evidence of a bad character disclosed under this gateway is not limited to undermining a co-accused's credibility as a witness, and may (subject to how the judge chooses to direct the jury) be used as evidence going towards the co-accused's guilt.

Consider the following example of the potential operation of s. 101(1)(e) CJA 2003.

 Example

Wayne and Jordan are jointly charged with murder. The prosecution allege that the victim was fatally wounded as a result of being knifed by one or both of the defendants. Wayne and Jordan are pleading not guilty and are running cut-throat defences by blaming each other. Wayne has several previous convictions. Last year he was convicted of possession of an offensive weapon, namely a knuckle-duster. Five years previously, following a trial at which he gave evidence on oath, he was convicted of robbery, during which an iron bar was used to inflict a serious injury on a security guard. Wayne has several previous convictions for theft, deception and burglary over a ten-year period. In his examination-in-chief, Wayne states that it was Jordan who knifed the victim. Jordan has one recent previous conviction for theft and a conviction for affray four years previously in respect of which he pleaded guilty.

Jordan's counsel may seek to cross-examine Wayne about his previous convictions on the basis that:

- Wayne's previous convictions have substantial probative value in relation to an important issue between the co-accused—i.e. the identity of the person who inflicted the fatal knife injury on the deceased; and
- in giving evidence, Wayne has undermined Jordan's defence.

Provided these conditions are satisfied, the court has no discretion to prevent Jordan from adducing evidence of Wayne's previous convictions. The bad character evidence is arguably relevant both to undermining Wayne's credibility as a witness (as his previous convictions show that he has a propensity to be dishonest) and to the likelihood that it was more likely to have been Wayne who inflicted the fatal stab wound as his previous recent conviction for possession of an offensive weapon and his conviction for a violent robbery indicate a propensity to commit violent assaults.

For a case that illustrates the application of gateway (e), see *R v Edwards; Rowlands; McClean; Gray and Smith* [2005] EWCA Crim 3244.

23.9   SECTION 101(1)(f) CRIMINAL JUSTICE ACT 2003

Evidence of the defendant's bad character is admissible to correct a false impression given by the defendant.

Section 101(1)(f) CJA 2003 is further defined by s. 105 and is available only to the prosecution:

'Section 105   Evidence to correct a false impression

(1)   For the purposes of section 101(1)(f)—

    (a)   the defendant gives a false impression if he is responsible for the making of an express or implied assertion which is apt to give the court or jury a false or misleading impression about the defendant;

    (b)   evidence to correct such an impression is evidence which has probative value in correcting it.

(2)   A defendant is treated as being responsible for the making of an assertion if—

    (a)   the assertion is made by the defendant in the proceedings (whether or not in evidence given by him);

    (b)   the assertion was made by the defendant—

        (i)   on being questioned under caution, before charge, about the offence with which he is charged, or

        (ii)   on being charged with the offence or officially informed that he might be prosecuted for it, and evidence of the assertion is given in the proceedings,

    (c)   the assertion is made by a witness called by the defendant;

    (d)   the assertion is made by any witness in cross-examination in response to a question asked by the defendant that is intended to elicit it, or is likely to do so; or

    (e)   the assertion was made by any person out of court, and the defendant adduces evidence of it in the proceedings.

(3)   A defendant who would otherwise be treated as responsible for the making of an assertion shall not be so treated if, or to the extent that, he withdraws it or disassociates himself from it.

(4)   Where it appears to the court that a defendant, by means of his conduct (other than the giving of evidence) in the proceedings, is seeking to give the court or jury an impression about himself that is false or misleading, the court may if it appears just to do so treat the defendant as being responsible for the making of an assertion which is apt to give that impression.

(5)   In subsection (4) 'conduct' includes appearance or dress.

(6)   Evidence is admissible under section 101(1)(f) only if it goes no further than is necessary to correct the false impression.

(7)   Only prosecution evidence is admissible under section 101(1)(f).'

A defendant gives a false impression if he is responsible for making an express or implied assertion which gives the court a false or misleading impression about him. A defendant can create a false impression not only by what he says on oath but also through his conduct in the proceedings (s. 105(4)). As with all the gateways, it applies irrespective of whether the defendant gives evidence in his defence. An assertion extends to any false assertion that forms part of the defence case whether asserted at trial or even before trial (s. 105(2)(b)). An assertion made at the police station can therefore trigger the opening of this gateway. A defendant is given the opportunity to avoid this gateway for admission if he withdraws or disassociates himself from the assertion (s. 105(3)). In *Renda* [2005] EWCA Crim 2826, gateway (f) was triggered at the police station when R made false statements regarding his work history. The Court of Appeal held that a concession extracted from a defendant in cross-examination will not amount to a withdrawal or disassociation from a previously made misleading statement.

Evidence is admissible only to the extent necessary to correct the false impression (s. 105(6)). The prosecution may only introduce evidence of the defendant's bad character sufficient to rebut the false impression that was made about the defendant's character. In many cases it will not be necessary for the whole of the defendant's bad character to be disclosed.

There is nothing in the Act which suggests that, having adduced evidence of the defendant's bad character under this gateway, the court cannot use the information to infer guilt. Equally, there is nothing to prevent the judge from directing the jury to make limited evidential use of such evidence. The judicial discretion under s. 101(3) does not apply to this gateway, although there is nothing in the Act which restricts the application of s. 78 PACE 1984 and the common law exercise of discretion under s. 82(3) PACE 1984.

 Example 1

Saeeda is charged with handling a consignment of stolen designer clothes. Both during the police investigation and at trial, Saeeda asserts that she would never do anything dishonest where her business interests are concerned. To rebut this false assertion about her unimpeachable business ethics, the prosecution wish to put in evidence Saeeda's conviction for a VAT fraud committed while she was a director of an unrelated business venture six years ago. The prosecution would be able to put Saeeda's conviction into evidence in order to rebut the misleading impression she has created as regards her business affairs. Had Saeeda made her assertion solely in the course of the interview, the gateway could still be triggered by the investigating officer giving evidence of the assertion in interview. In either instance, Saeeda should be advised to withdraw the statement she made in interview before trial. In these circumstances the gateway under s. 101(1)(f) would not be triggered.

3.10 SECTION 101(1)(g) CRIMINAL JUSTICE ACT 2003

Evidence of the defendant's bad character is admissible after the defendant has made an attack on another person's character.

This is another significant gateway for the prosecution. The gateway is further defined in s. 106:

'**Section 106   Attack on another person's character**

(1) For the purposes of section 101(1)(g) a defendant makes an attack on another person's character if—

    (a) he adduces evidence attacking the other person's character, or

    (b) he (or any legal representative appointed under section 38(4) of the Youth Justice and Criminal Evidence Act 1999 (c. 23) to cross-examine a witness in his interests) asks questions in cross-examination that are intended to elicit such evidence, or are likely to do so, or

> (c) evidence is given of an imputation about the other person made by the defendant—
>
> > (i) on being questioned under caution, before charge, about the offence with which he is charged, or
> >
> > (ii) on being charged with the offence or officially informed that he might be prosecuted for it.
>
> (2) In subsection (1) "evidence attacking the other person's character" means evidence to the effect that the other person—
>
> > (a) has committed an offence (whether a different offence from the one with which the defendant is charged or the same one), or
> >
> > (b) has behaved, or is disposed to behave, in a reprehensible way; and "imputation about the other person" means an assertion to that effect.
>
> (3) Only prosecution evidence is admissible under section 101(1)(g).'

23.10.1 WHAT AMOUNTS TO AN ATTACK?

Gateway (g) replaces the old law under s. 1(3)(ii) CEA 1898 which gave a defendant a shield against the revelation of past bad character whilst giving evidence on oath. The defendant would throw away his shield if his defence led to the character of a prosecution witness being impugned. In *R v Hanson* [2005] 2 Cr App R 21, the Court of Appeal observed:

> 'As to s. 101(1)(g), the pre-2003 Act authorities will continue to apply when assessing whether an attack has been made on another person's character, to the extent that they are compatible with s. 106.'

This means that authorities such as *Selvey v DPP* [1970] AC 304 and *R v Britzman* [1983] 1 WLR 350 on what constitutes an 'attack' continue to apply. In *Selvey* it was held that a defendant still loses his shield notwithstanding that attacking the character of another is a necessary part of his defence. Some latitude was given to defendants under the 1898 Act in that a denial of guilt, however emphatic, would not amount to an attack. The cases at common law went so far as to suggest that even calling a witness a liar would not amount to an attack, but a suggestion that the witness had a motive for lying, would do so. Based on the pre-2003 Act authorities, we can confidently say that the following situations would amount to an 'attack' on another:

- an allegation that a prosecution witness is biased;
- an allegation that the police have fabricated evidence;
- cross-examining a prosecution witness on any previous convictions they might have;
- accusing a prosecution witness of perjury;
- accusing the investigating officers of deliberately flouting PACE and the Codes of Practice.

It will probably not amount to an 'attack' to suggest that:

- a prosecution witness is mistaken, confused or simply wrong;
- the police have got some aspect of the Codes of Practice wrong;
- a prosecution witness is lying, subject to the latitude the court gives an accused in accordance with the decision in *R v Britzman*.

Gateway (g) is wider than its CEA 1898 predecessor. It refers to attacking another person's character and is therefore not limited to witnesses in the case. It is irrelevant whether or not the defendant testifies.

Of particular concern is the fact that gateway (g) extends to the defendant's comments at the police station. In *R v Ball* [2005] EWCA Crim 2826, B used the epithet 'slag' during a police interview when seeking to defend an allegation of rape which was held to be sufficient to trigger gateway (g). Suppose the investigating officer says to the suspect ' . . . so are you saying that witness X is lying . . . '. If the suspect answers this affirmatively, he might be regarded as attacking another person's character, triggering the admission of his previous convictions at any subsequent trial. This provision makes the already difficult role of the legal adviser at the police station (considered in Chapter 9) considerably more challenging.

You will recall that as a consequence of s. 100 CJA 2003, the defendant will only be able to 'attack' the character of a witness if he is granted leave under s. 100 CJA 2003. The section is considered in more detail in Chapter 20, paras. 20.9–20.10. Leave need not be sought if the conduct in question '*is evidence of misconduct in connection with the investigation or prosecution of that offence*'.

Notwithstanding that a defendant is granted leave to adduce evidence attacking the character of another under s.100 CJA 2003, gateway (g) will still be triggered.

10.2 THE EXERCISE OF DISCRETION IN RELATION TO GATEWAY (g)

As with s. 101(1)(d), the defence can make an application to have the evidence excluded under s. 101(3). The application triggers the exercise of discretion based on the fairness of admitting the evidence. The guidance provided by the *Hanson* judgment (above) will apply. Under the previous law, the discretion to exclude evidence of a defendant's previous convictions following the loss of his shield, even where his previous convictions happened to be similar to the offence for which he is being tried, was exercised restrictively. In *R v Burke* (1986) 82 Cr App R 156, while acknowledging that 'cases must occur in which it would be unjust to admit evidence of a character gravely prejudicial to the accused, even though there may be some tenuous grounds for holding it technically admissible', the Court of Appeal nevertheless went on to say that:

'In the ordinary and normal case the trial judge may feel that if the credit of the prosecutor or his witnesses has been attacked, it is only fair that the jury should have before them material on which they can form their judgment whether the accused person is any more worthy to be believed than those he has attacked. It is obviously unfair that the jury should be left in the dark about an accused person's character if the conduct of his defence has attacked the character of the prosecutor or the witnesses for the prosecution.'

 Example

Consider the following example of s. 101(1)(g) CJA 2003. Lim is charged with assaulting his cohabitee on two separate occasions. The couple have a volatile relationship. Lim denies the allegation and claims he acted in self-defence, maintaining the injured party flew at him in a drunken rage. Lim has previously obtained a civil injunction against his partner. Lim seeks leave under s. 100 CJA 2003 to adduce evidence of his partner's violent acts against him. This is clearly an attack on her character. As a consequence, the prosecution serves notice under s. 101(1)(g) to admit Lim's previous convictions for wounding with intent, assault occasioning actual bodily harm and assault on a police officer, (the most recent committed eight years ago); offences of theft, handling and deception committed 12 years ago and two drink-related driving offences (failing to provide a specimen and driving with excess alcohol) committed in the last five years. None of his assaults was perpetrated on females. If leave is granted under s. 100 CJA 2003, it is inevitable that gateway (g) will be opened. The defence could apply to have the evidence excluded on the basis that to admit them would be unduly prejudicial. Lim will say that his previous convictions for violence are considerably dated and that none of them involved him using violence against women. If admitted, Lim might persuade the court to confine their relevance to an assessment of his credibility only. However, given the statements in *Highton* and *Campbell*, there is nothing to prevent the court from using the previous convictions on the issue of Lim's propensity if they are relevant. Previous convictions for deception may well be used as evidence indicating a propensity to be untruthful subject to the statements in *Campbell* on this point.

23.11 **RELEVANCE AND USE THAT CAN BE MADE OF BAD CHARACTER ADDUCED UNDER S. 101**

The CJA 2003 makes no stipulation as to the use that can be made of bad character under the Act. In *R v Highton; R v Van Nguyen; R v Carp* [2005] 1 WLR 3472 the Court of Appeal stated:

> 'In the case of gateway (g), for example, admissibility depends on the defendant having made an attack on another person's character, but once the evidence is admitted, it may, depending on the particular facts, be relevant not only to credibility but also to propensity to commit offences of the kind with which the defendant is charged.'

This view is supported by statements made in *R v Campbell* [2007] 1 WLR 2798. Lord Phillips observed that once bad character is admitted it can be used for any purpose for which it assumes relevance. Thus bad character admitted through gateway (g) may be used by a jury as evidence of the defendant's propensity even though the bad character has not been admitted under gateway (d) and vice versa. The importance of correctly directing the jury on the relevance of the evidence and the need not to place undue reliance upon it is stressed in *Highton*.

***R v Zafran Akhtar Saleem* [2007] EWCA Crim 1923**

S and others were charged with causing grievous bodily harm in a senseless and brutal attack on a 19-year-old in a park. The prosecution contended that S had filmed the assault and sought to admit photographs of violent assaults held on S's computer and accessed ten days before the attack, along with rap lyrics written by S three months before the attack and accessed days before the assault which made reference to an intention to carry out an attack on S's birthday. The assault was in fact carried out on S's birthday. S admitted to being present at the park but denied involvement in the assault. Nothing directly relating to the attack was found on S's computer. The Court of Appeal upheld the trial judge's decision to admit the evidence. Neither the rap lyrics nor the violent images amounted to a propensity to commit violence for the purposes of s. 103(1)(a); they were however relevant to an important matter in issue between the prosecution and defence in that they tended to rebut S's defence of innocent association and the jury should have been directed accordingly.

Postscript

A steady stream of case law on bad character is emerging. If it is relevant to your core Criminal Litigation course or to your elective in Advanced Criminal Litigation you can access the 'Bad Character Case Compendium' which is held on the student resource section of our Online Resource Centre. The compendium contains a summary of the most important cases on bad character to date. A number of recent decisions are illustrative of the arguments typically advanced at first instance.

Some decisions show how far the pendulum has swung in favour of the prosecution in admitting evidence of the defendant's bad character. This has serious implications for defendants because if bad character is admitted, it can significantly strengthen the prosecution's case. However only a handful of cases go to appeal and most decisions on admitting bad character are made at first instance by judges, district judges and magistrates on the facts in each case. Defence advocates therefore can influence the way in which law is applied and develops on a day-to-day basis.

3.12 SAFEGUARDS RELATING TO THE ADMISSION OF EVIDENCE OF BAD CHARACTER

Under s. 107 CJA 2003 power is given to a trial judge to stop a trial on indictment at any time before the close of the prosecution's case where evidence has been admitted under s. 101(1)(c)–(g) CJA 2003 and the court is satisfied that the evidence is contaminated, with the result that any conviction would be regarded as being unsafe.

3.13 SPECIAL RULES RELATING TO CHILDHOOD CONVICTIONS

Section 108 CJA 2003 provides that where a person (aged 21 or over) is being tried, evidence of any previous convictions committed by him under the age of 14 shall not be admissible unless both of the offences are triable on indictment and the court is satisfied that the interests of justice require the evidence to be admitted.

3.14 'SPENT' CONVICTIONS UNDER THE REHABILITATION OF OFFENDERS ACT 1974

Generally, where a person has a spent conviction under the 1974 Act, he should be treated as though he was never charged or convicted of the offence, s. 4(1) Rehabilitation of Offenders Act 1974. While the 1974 Act has no application to criminal proceedings, the *Practice Direction (Criminal: Consolidated)* [2002] 3 All ER 904, states that reference should not be made by the prosecution to a 'spent' conviction without leave of the judge, to be granted only if the interests of justice so require.

3.15 STATUTORY ADMISSION OF SIMILAR FACT EVIDENCE

There are two instances in which parliament has expressly authorised the use of similar fact evidence. One is under s. 1(2) of the Official Secrets Act 1911. The other, more commonly used, is under s. 27(3) of the Theft Act 1968. This provision assists in proving *mens rea* on a charge of handling stolen goods. Where a defendant denies knowledge or belief that the goods which were found in his possession were stolen, the prosecution may adduce evidence of the defendant's criminal disposition by proving the defendant has previously been in possession of stolen goods, or that the defendant has a previous conviction for handling stolen goods or theft in the preceding five years. This evidence is capable of casting serious doubt on the defendant's assertion that he did not know the goods were stolen, or that he did not believe them to be so. These provisions remain in force notwithstanding the enactment of the Criminal Justice Act 2003.

Further Postscript

In the lecturers resource section of the Online Resource Centre, you will find a free-standing video case study entitled *R v Nicholas Jones*. The case involves applications to admit both defendant and non-defendant bad character. The applications were not scripted and were argued before a judge of the Crown Court, who gives a detailed ruling on each application. Full instructions on how you might use this learning resource are given.

 online resource centre

23.16 **ADVISING YOUR CLIENT WHETHER OR NOT TO GIVE EVIDENCE AT HIS TRIAL**

As stated earlier in this chapter, the defendant is a competent but not a compellable witness at his trial and enjoys the right to silence. As the trial date approaches an important part of the defence advocate's case preparation is to advise his client whether to give evidence in his defence. The advice will be based on both practical considerations and the potential legal implications.

The practical considerations include:

(1) The nature of the prosecution and defence case

Some offences, for example, a sexual offence, may involve only two participants—the victim and the defendant. In this situation it is almost inevitable that the defendant will have to testify, as there is no other way in which the defence evidence can be put to the court. Similarly in a case where one co-accused blames the other, your client may need to refute the evidence given by his co-accused. In other situations, where there are credible and reliable defence witnesses who can give evidence in support of the defendant's case, it might not be necessary to call the defendant.

(2) Where a legal burden of proof is placed on the defendant

In a case where a legal burden of proof is placed on a defendant to effectively establish his innocence (see Chapter 18), sometimes the person best-placed to provide evidence in support of that defence will be the defendant.

(3) Will the defendant be a credible witness?

It may be a truism, but it is frequently said that the best prosecution witness is often the defendant! The defence advocate will need to make an assessment of how his client will come across in the witness box. Will he appear to be believable and credible? How will he withstand cross-examination? Appearing as a witness in a criminal trial is a stressful experience. Is the defendant articulate? Does he have the mental strength to cope with the experience?

(4) Strength of the prosecution's case

Where the prosecution's evidence is, in your view, unlikely to persuade a jury of the defendant's guilt beyond reasonable doubt, the defence advocate may not wish to tip the scales in favour of the prosecution by calling his client to give evidence if he has doubts about his client's ability to cope with cross-examination. The advocate's assessment of the prosecution's case may have to wait until he has cross-examined the prosecution witnesses. It goes without saying that in a case where a submission of no case to answer at the close of the prosecution's case has been upheld by the court (see Chapter 17, para. 17.10), there is no reason for the defendant to testify!

(5) The legal considerations

As well as the practical factors, the decision whether the defendant should testify also involves an important legal consideration in that if the defendant does not give evidence, adverse inferences may be drawn under s. 35 Criminal Justice and Public Order Act 1994 (see para. 23.4 above).

KEY POINT SUMMARY

- Be aware of the evidential value of your client's good character. Evidence of a defendant's past good character should always be advanced.
- The admissibility of evidence of a defendant's past bad character is regulated by the provisions of the Criminal Justice Act 2003.

- Bad character is very widely defined to include any reprehensible behaviour and is not confined to previous convictions.
- Understand that there are seven gateways in s. 101 through which evidence of a defendant's bad character may be adduced, and that each gateway is further defined in ss. 102–106.
- The application of judicial discretion under s. 101(3) CJA 2003 may prove to be a crucial safeguard in ensuring the defendant can enjoy a fair trial as it gives the court discretion (at least in the context of the most frequently engaged gateways (d) and (g)) to exclude bad character evidence if it would have an adverse effect on the fairness of the proceedings.
- Guidance on what constitutes propensity to commit offences of the kind charged and how judicial discretion to exclude evidence of propensity might be exercised has been provided by the decision in the Court of Appeal decisions in *Hanson* and *Highton*.
- The defence must oppose the application of bad character if it is to be excluded—the decision to admit or exclude such evidence may well depend on the quality of the arguments put forward by opposing advocates!
- The defendant is not a compellable witness in a criminal case, but a failure to give evidence without good cause is subject to the risk of having an adverse inference drawn under s. 35 Criminal Justice and Public Order Act 1994.
- Understand the factors that may be taken into consideration when advising your client about whether or not to testify at his trial.

SELF-TEST QUESTIONS

1. Aaron is charged with possession of drugs with intent to supply. The drugs were found under the bonnet of a car he was driving. Aaron pleads not guilty, maintaining he had no knowledge of the presence of the drugs having borrowed the car. Twelve months ago, Aaron was convicted of possession of crack cocaine with intent to supply. He pleaded guilty on the basis that he was a mere custodian of the drugs for a friend. He was given a community sentence which is considered lenient for such an offence. Upon what basis do you feel the prosecution would seek admission of Aaron's previous conviction? If you were the defence advocate, what arguments would you advance in opposition?

2(a) Brian is charged with the rape of a 15-year-old girl. His penetrative defence is that the girl consented. He was convicted five years ago of an offence of unlawful sexual activity with a 14-year-old girl following a guilty plea. Will the prosecution be able to rely on this earlier conviction? What representations would the defence make as regards an attempt by the prosecution to adduce his previous conviction?

2(b) Vary the facts slightly. Brian is still charged with the rape of a 15-year-old. His defence is that his victim consented. Brian has a previous conviction for raping his former 26-year-old partner, eight years ago. On that occasion, he ran the same defence. Would this previous conviction be admissible? If so, on what basis?

3. Barry and Tina are accused of the murder of Sean, aged three. Barry was Sean's stepfather and Tina was his natural mother. The child died as a result of head injuries. Barry denies murder and states that the child died while in his mother's care and that she has a vicious temper and punched the child while in a drunken stupor. Tina denies murder and claims Barry struck Sean about the head while high on drugs. She maintains she is terrified of Barry and was powerless to do anything. The pathologist's report discloses the fact that the child was malnourished and that his body was covered in bruises and cigarette burns. Barry has several previous convictions for drug-related offences and theft, a previous conviction for criminal damage and one previous conviction for assault occasioning actual bodily harm. Tina has a previous conviction for theft. She will give evidence in support of her defence. Should Barry give evidence? Does the conduct of his defence give you cause for concern? If so, why?

4. Danielle is charged with causing grievous bodily harm with intent. It is alleged she 'glassed' a man in the face causing facial injuries. She denies the offence. She has no previous convictions. What evidential use can be derived from the last-mentioned fact?

Case scenario: *R v Lenny Whyte*

You are reminded that the complete documentation in relation to this case study can be accessed from our Online Resource Centre.

You will be aware of the issues in this case. The prosecution have served notice to admit Lenny Whyte's previous convictions under s. 101(1)(d) CJA 2003. The defence have served notice opposing their admission.

Do you consider that Lenny's previous convictions would be admissible?

Consider whether it would be advisable for Lenny to give evidence in his defence. What factors would have a bearing on your advice?

FIGURE 23.1 EVIDENTIAL RULES RELEVANT TO THE ACCUSED

COMPETENCE AND COMPELLABILITY OF THE ACCUSED

- The accused is:
  - a competent but non-compellable witness for the defence, s. 53 YJCEA 1999;
  - neither a competent or compellable witness for the prosecution, s. 53(4) YJCEA 1999.
- A co-accused is also not a competent or compellable witness for the prosecution unless he ceases to be a party to the proceedings (s. 53(5) YJCEA 1999).

THE COURSE OF THE ACCUSED'S EVIDENCE

- Section 79 PACE 1984 requires the accused to testify as the first defence witness.
- Where the accused does not give evidence at his trial, adverse inferences may be drawn against his silence under s. 35 CJPOA 1994, providing:
  - the accused is made aware of his right to testify and the possible consequences of remaining silent, Practice Direction (Criminal Consolidated) [2002]; and the jury or magistrates are reminded that:
    - the legal burden of proving the accused's guilt lies with the prosecution; and
    - the defendant is entitled to remain silent; and
    - the prosecution must have established a *prima facie* case against the accused; and
    - adverse inferences cannot be the sole reason for finding the accused guilty, s.38(3) CJPOA 1994; and
    - adverse inferences may only be drawn where the only explanation for the accused's silence is that he has no answer to the prosecution case; or none that would stand up to cross-examination (see *R v Cowan, Gayle and Riccardi* [1995]).

GOOD CHARACTER

- A defendant with good character is entitled to a good character direction, see *R v Vye and Others* [1993] as to:
  - propensity (a defendant of good character is less likely to have committed the offence); and
  - credibility as a witness (where the defendant before trial asserts his innocence and/or gives evidence at trial).

ADDUCING THE DEFENDANT'S BAD CHARACTER

- Bad character is defined by s. 98 CJA 2003 as evidence of or a disposition towards misconduct or other reprehensible behaviour.
- Section 101(a)–(g) CJA 2003 provides seven gateways through which evidence of a defendant's bad character can be admitted:

  (a) all parties agree to the evidence being admitted;
  (b) the evidence is adduced by the defendant or is given in answer during the defendant's cross-examination;
  (c) it is important explanatory evidence;
  (d) it is relevant to an important matter in issue between D and P;
  (e) it has substantial probative value in relation to an important matter in issue between a defendant and co-defendant;
  (f) it is evidence to correct a false impression given by a defendant; or
  (g) the defendant has made an attack on another person's character.

- Evidence of bad character sought to be admitted under s. 101(1)(d) and 101(1)(g) is subject to exclusionary discretion in s. 101(3) CJA 2003 based on the fairness of admitting the evidence which is triggered by the defence.
- *R v Hanson* [2005] provides important guidance on what constitutes propensity to commit offences of the kind and propensity to be untruthful.
- In exercising discretion in terms of what is just under s. 103(3) and the fairness of the proceedings under s. 101(3), *Hanson* says the following factors are important:
  - the similarity between past and present offences;
  - the respective gravity of past and present offending;
  - the age of any previous convictions;
  - the strength of the prosecution's case.

24.1 INTRODUCTION

The term 'private privilege' relates to separate privileges that prevent evidence from being disclosed in litigation, or witnesses from being compelled to answer questions at trial. In a criminal case, privilege may be claimed in two situations:

- legal professional privilege;
- the privilege against self-incrimination.

While it is generally regarded as a matter of public policy for cases to be decided on the basis of all available admissible and relevant evidence, private privilege recognises that in certain situations it is in the wider public interest to maintain the confidentiality of communications between a lawyer and his client, or to encourage a witness in his testimony to make a full and frank disclosure of the matters within his knowledge—even where the court is denied the benefit of otherwise admissible and relevant evidence.

In this chapter we consider:

- legal professional privilege in criminal cases;
- legal professional privilege and the courts;
- waiving legal professional privilege;
- the privilege against self-incrimination;
- the privilege against self-incrimination and the European Convention on Human Rights 1950.

Whilst the evidential effect of claiming private privilege is the same as claiming public interest immunity (see Chapter 14), an important difference between them is that private privilege is a personal right belonging to the client or to a witness and cannot be claimed by any other person. Conversely public interest immunity seeks to protect the 'confidentiality' of the work of organisations operating in the 'public' domain, such as the police, security services and HM Revenue and Customs.

24.2 LEGAL PROFESSIONAL PRIVILEGE IN CRIMINAL CASES

Legal professional privilege in criminal cases is defined by s. 10 PACE 1984, to include:

'(1) Subject to subsection (2) below, in this Act "items subject to legal professional privilege" means—

(a) communications between a professional legal adviser and his client or any person representing his client made in connection with the giving of legal advice to the client;

(b) communications between a professional legal adviser and his client or any person representing his client or between such an adviser or his client or any such representative and any other person made in connection with or in contemplation of legal proceedings and for the purpose of such proceedings; and

(c) items enclosed with or referred to in such communications and made—

(i) in connection with the giving of legal advice; or

(ii) in connection with or in the contemplation of legal proceedings and for the purposes of such proceedings;

when they are in the possession of a person who is entitled to possession of them.'

Legal professional privilege applies in the following two situations.

24.2.1 COMMUNICATIONS BETWEEN THE LAWYER AND CLIENT—S. 10(1)(a) PACE 1984

All communications passing between the lawyer and client in 'the giving or obtaining of legal advice', and within the proper scope of the lawyer's professional work, will be privileged from disclosure. According to the Court of Appeal in *Balabel v Air-India* [1988] 2 All ER 246, the term 'the giving of legal advice' is not restricted to communications that specifically request or give legal advice, but also includes communications and correspondence that are part of the ongoing relationship between the lawyer and the client.

Therefore, legal professional privilege will attach to:

- all communications between a solicitor and his client;
- communications with counsel;
- communications to salaried legal advisers whether or not they hold a formal legal qualification; and
- communications to foreign lawyers.

The most obvious example of the privilege is that a client cannot be compelled to disclose any oral or written advice given to him by his solicitor or counsel in connection with the case.

While the phrase 'the giving of legal advice' is broadly interpreted, the courts are not prepared to apply the principle to all client-solicitor communications.

Legal professional privilege does not apply to:

- a record of a conveyancing transaction (*R v Crown Court at Inner London Sessions, ex p. Baines and Baines* [1987] 3 All ER 1025);
- a solicitor's documentary records of time spent with a client;
- time sheets;

- fee records;
- the record of a client's appointment in a solicitor's appointment diary, (see *R v Manchester Crown Court, ex p. R (Legal Professional Privilege)* [1999] 1 WLR 832).

These documents are not covered by legal professional privilege as they are not concerned with the giving of legal advice.

24.2.2 COMMUNICATIONS WITH THIRD PARTIES—S. 10(1)(b) PACE 1984

Legal professional privilege will attach to communications between the client, the legal adviser and a third party where the sole or dominant purpose of the communication was in connection with actual or pending litigation.

In deciding the 'dominant purpose test', the court will adopt an objective view of all the evidence, taking into account the intention of the document's author and the purpose of preparing the document. The key requirement in maintaining the privileged status of communications with third parties is that the communication must relate to pending or contemplated litigation.

 Example

Gavin is charged with conspiracy to cause an explosion. As part of the defence lawyer's preparation an expert's report is obtained which proves to be unhelpful to Gavin. In cross-examination the advocate for another co-accused asks Gavin whether his solicitor has commissioned an expert's report.

Gavin cannot be compelled to answer this question as the decision to obtain a report was taken in the course of the solicitor-client relationship. The report itself is protected from disclosure as it is a communication between a lawyer and a third party in connection with actual litigation.

24.3 WHAT IS THE RATIONALE FOR LEGAL PROFESSIONAL PRIVILEGE?

The rationale behind the privilege is that it is in the public interest that when seeking the advice of his lawyer, a client should be able to openly discuss his case, and to make a full disclosure of all relevant information to his lawyer in the knowledge that he cannot be compelled to disclose the content of those discussions, nor will he be compelled to give evidence about them in court.

24.4 LEGAL PROFESSIONAL PRIVILEGE AND THE COURTS

As legal professional privilege underpins the administration of criminal justice, the courts adopt a strict approach to enforcing its application. The position is illustrated by the House of Lords in *R v Derby Magistrates' Court, ex p. B* [1996] AC 487.

> *R v Derby Magistrates' Court, ex p. B* **[1996] AC 487**
>
> A 16-year-old girl was murdered. The appellant was arrested and made a statement to the police that he alone was responsible for the murder. He later retracted the statement and alleged that although he had been present at the scene of the crime, it was his step-father who had killed the girl. Relying on this second statement, the appellant was acquitted in the Crown Court.
>
> Later, the appellant's step-father was charged with the murder. At the step-father's committal, the appellant was called as a witness for the prosecution and repeated the statement that his step-father had killed the girl. He was cross-examined by the defence about the instructions he had given to his

solicitor concerning the murder. The appellant claimed legal professional privilege but the magistrates issued a summons (s. 97 MCA 1980) directing the appellant and his solicitor to produce the relevant proofs of evidence as they would be 'likely to be material evidence'.

On appeal, the House of Lords held that a summons could not be issued under s. 97 MCA 1980 to compel the production of documents protected by legal professional privilege unless the privilege had been waived, which in the present case, it had not. In reaffirming its status, the House of Lords stated that legal professional privilege is much more than an ordinary rule of evidence; it is a fundamental condition on which the administration of justice rests.

24.5 WAIVING LEGAL PROFESSIONAL PRIVILEGE

Legal professional privilege vests in the client and may only be waived by the client, either at the pre-trial stage or during the trial. If the client expressly or impliedly waives the privilege a lawyer can be compelled to reveal the contents of the communications between himself and the client, or between himself and a third party. As explained in Chapters 5 and 9, the question of waiver commonly arises where the accused is required to explain his silence in response to questions at the police station, by disclosing the reasons that he was given by his lawyer for refusing to answer. In this situation both the accused and the legal adviser may be cross-examined about the content of the advice given at the police station.

24.6 WHERE LEGAL PROFESSIONAL PRIVILEGE IS LOST

Whilst the sanctity of legal professional privilege is recognised, the privilege is not entirely absolute and will not apply in the following situations.

24.6.1 COMMUNICATION IN THE FURTHERANCE OF A CRIME OR FRAUD

The privilege will be lost where it is used as a vehicle for the furtherance of a criminal offence. It is immaterial whether the lawyer was aware of the illicit purpose of the communication and the 'crime' may relate to an offence under United Kingdom law or an offence in a foreign jurisdiction, see *R v Cox and Railton* [1884] 14 QBD 153. The rule is now contained in s. 10(2) PACE 1984, which provides: 'Items held with the intention of furthering a criminal purpose are not items subject to legal professional privilege.'

24.6.2 ACCIDENTALLY LOSING LEGAL PROFESSIONAL PRIVILEGE

Legal professional privilege may be lost accidentally. In *R v Tompkins* (1977) 67 Cr App R 181, the defendant was charged with handling stolen hi-fi equipment. The victim of the theft stated that he could identify his stolen equipment as it had a loose button. The defendant said in examination-in-chief that the button had never been loose, and demonstrated this to the court. During an adjournment, an employee of the prosecution solicitor found a piece of paper on which the defendant had written to his barrister that the button had been loose but that he had stuck it down with glue. Prosecution counsel then showed Tompkins the note and cross-examined him on it. As a result, Tompkins changed his answer and was convicted. On appeal, the Court of Appeal stated there had not been a breach of legal professional privilege because the privileged document had been obtained independently of the privileged relationship and there had not been any improper conduct.

24.7 LEGAL PROFESSIONAL PRIVILEGE AND THE DISCLOSURE OF EXPERT EVIDENCE

The rules on legal professional privilege attaching to communications where the 'third party' is an expert witness should be read in conjunction with the obligation on both the prosecution and the defence to disclose any expert report either side intends to rely on at trial (see Chapter 21, para. 21.9.3).

So far as the obligation to disclose an unfavourable report is concerned, the position in relation to the prosecution is governed by the rules on the pre-trial disclosure of evidence explained in Chapter 14. No such obligation falls on the defendant as the report is protected by legal professional privilege, providing it has been obtained for the purposes of actual or contemplated litigation. When s. 6D CJA 2003 comes into force, an accused who instructs an expert witness with a view to providing an opinion for use as evidence at trial, will be required to give the court and the prosecutor a notice specifying the person's name and address unless specified in the defence statement (see Chapter 14, para. 14.9.5).

24.8 THE PRIVILEGE AGAINST SELF-INCRIMINATION IN CRIMINAL PROCEEDINGS

The privilege against self-incrimination allows a witness to refuse to answer a question, which in the opinion of the judge, would expose the witness to the possibility of any criminal charge under United Kingdom law.

24.8.1 THE PRIVILEGE BELONGS TO THE WITNESS

The privilege belongs to the witness and must therefore be claimed by the witness during his testimony. While according to *R v Coote* [1873] LR 4 PC 599, a witness is presumed to know the law sufficiently to appreciate that he is not compelled to answer a particular question or to produce a document, the preferred modern practice is for the judge or the magistrates' legal adviser to warn the witness that he does not have to answer the question. Once the court is satisfied that the privilege applies, the witness will not be compelled to answer even if his motive for remaining silent is based in bad faith or he has a motive of his own to serve.

24.8.2 WAIVING THE PRIVILEGE

Only the witness may waive the privilege. Where the witness does not waive the privilege his self-incriminating answers will be admissible as evidence in any proceedings against him.

24.8.3 THE PRIVILEGE AGAINST SELF-INCRIMINATION FROM THE DEFENDANT'S PERSPECTIVE AND THE EUROPEAN CONVENTION ON HUMAN RIGHTS 1950

As a witness in his defence, the defendant cannot refuse to answer questions in cross-examination on the ground that it would incriminate him as to the offence charged! However, various statutes compel an individual to answer questions and provide information in an investigation or suffer a penalty. Where the answers given or the information supplied are used in evidence against the defendant at a subsequent trial, the defendant can argue that the process has infringed his right not to incriminate himself. Indeed the use of such evidence may well contravene the defendant's right to a fair trial under Article 6. In *Saunders v United Kingdom* (1997) 23 EHRR 313, the defendant had been compelled to answer questions about his business dealings during an investigation by the Department of Trade and

Industry, which were then used against him in a prosecution under the Companies Act 1985. In finding that there had been a violation of Article 6, the ECtHR observed:

> The Court recalls that, although not specifically mentioned in Article 6 of the Convention, the right to silence and the right not to incriminate oneself are generally recognised international standards which lie at the heart of the notion of a fair procedure under Article 6. Their rationale lies, *inter alia*, in the protection of the accused against improper compulsion by the authorities thereby contributing to the avoidance of miscarriages of justice and to the fulfilment of the aims of Article 6. The right not to incriminate oneself, in particular, presupposes that the prosecution in a criminal case seek to prove their case against the accused without resort to evidence obtained through methods of coercion or oppression in defiance of the will of the accused. In this sense the right is closely linked to the presumption of innocence contained.'

In domestic law, various statutes require specified persons to answer questions, to produce documents or to disclose certain information even though such disclosure may infringe the person's privilege against self-incrimination. Examples of these provisions include s. 31 Theft Act 1968 which provides that a witness may not refuse to answer any questions in proceedings for the recovery or administration of property or the execution of a trust on the ground that to do so might incriminate him or his spouse of an offence under the Act. A similar provision is contained in s. 2(2) Criminal Justice Act 1987, where the Director of the Serious Fraud Office can compel a person to make a statement in a serious fraud investigation. In relation to each of these offences, provision is made preventing any answers given from being used in evidence against the individuals concerned, in the event of a prosecution for the specified offence.

The most significant challenge to a statutory provision of this type has been in relation to s. 172 Road Traffic Act 1988. Section 172(2)(a) RTA 1988 requires the keeper of a motor vehicle to answer questions as to the identity of the driver of the vehicle where the driver is suspected of being involved in a road traffic offence. Failure to provide such information is an offence under s. 172(3) RTA 1988, punishable with a fine and endorsement. The point was considered by the Privy Council in *Brown v Stott*.

Brown v Stott [2001] 2 WLR 817

The police were called to an all-night superstore, where B was suspected of having stolen a bottle of gin. The officers thought that B had been drinking and asked her how she had got to the store. She replied that she had driven there and pointed to a car that she said was hers. At the police station, car keys were found in her handbag, and pursuant to s. 172(2) Road Traffic Act 1988, the police required her to say who had driven the car to the store. B replied that she had driven the car. A breath test was administered that proved positive. B was charged with driving after consuming excess alcohol under s. 5(1)(a) Road Traffic Act 1988.

On appeal, the Privy Council held that evidence of B's admission that she had driven the vehicle to the all-night store did not infringe her privilege against self-incrimination or her right to a fair hearing under Article 6 for the following reasons:

- the rights under Article 6 are not absolute and may be qualified in respect to a proper clear public objective such as road safety;
- there was a clear public interest in enforcement of road traffic legislation and that properly applied, s. 172 RTA 1988, did not represent a disproportionate response to this serious social problem:
  - s. 172 RTA 1988 permitted the police to ask a suspect a simple question, the answer to which does not incriminate the accused *per se*;
  - the penalty for refusing to answer the question is moderate and non-custodial;
  - if there was evidence of coercion by the police, the court had discretion to exclude the suspect's answer.

KEY POINT SUMMARY

- Know the situations where legal professional privilege can be claimed and be prepared to advise your client accordingly.
- Be aware of the circumstances in which legal professional privilege may be lost.
- Understand the privilege against self-incrimination and be prepared to advise your client accordingly.

SELF-TEST QUESTIONS

1. Are all communications passing between a solicitor and his client privileged from disclosure?
2. What is the dominant purpose test for legal privilege to attach to communications between the client, solicitor and a third party?
3. In whom does legal privilege vest?
4. Explain the privilege against self-incrimination.

Analysis of these questions can be found in Appendix 4.

FIGURE 24.1 Private Privilege

LEGAL PROFESSIONAL PRIVILEGE

- Prevents the disclosure of all communications between the lawyer/client in connection with the giving or obtaining of legal advice, including (s. 10(1)(a) PACE).
  - letters, memoranda containing legal advice; and
  - communications with counsel.
- Prevents the disclosure of all communications between the client, lawyer and a third party where the sole or dominant purpose is in connection with actual or pending litigation including communications in connection with advice sought from an expert witness (s.10(1)(b) PACE);
- The courts take a strict approach to enforcing the privilege, see *R v Derby Magistrates' Court, ex p. B.*
- The privilege will be lifted where:
  - it is waived by the client; or
  - it used to further a crime; or
  - it is lost accidentally.

PRIVILEGE AGAINST SELF-INCRIMINATION

- Permits a witness to refuse to answer a question on oath where the answer would expose to the possibility of a criminal charge being laid against him.
- The privilege applies to individuals who are compelled to answer questions by investigating bodies, the answers to which are then used in evidence against that individual in criminal proceedings.
- The privilege belongs to the witness.
- The witness may waive the privilege.
- The privilege is not an absolute right under Article 6 ECHR and may be qualified where:
  - there is a clear public interest in the privilege not applying; and
  - it is proportionate to the aim of the legislation, see *Brown v Stott.*

Part V

POST-CONVICTION: SENTENCING AND APPEALS

Part V covers all aspects of sentencing in the Crown Court and magistrates' court.

In Chapter 25 we consider the general principles that inform the process of sentencing.

In Chapter 26 we consider the decision to impose a custodial term on a convicted offender as well as the range of non-custodial penalties available to the courts, including ancillary orders. In Chapter 27 we consider the special considerations that apply to the sentencing of road traffic offences.

Chapter 28 considers the procedure on sentencing and the way in which a defence solicitor might prepare and deliver a plea in mitigation.

Finally, in Chapter 29 we consider the process of appeal against sentence and conviction.

25

GENERAL PRINCIPLES OF SENTENCING

25.1 INTRODUCTION

A defendant will be sentenced before the Crown Court or magistrates' court upon conviction, either after pleading guilty or having been found guilty after a trial. As the vast majority of criminal clients plead guilty to some or all of the charges against them, it is unsurprising that a considerable amount of a defence lawyer's time is taken up with the question of sentence.

Criminal defence practitioners will be called upon to:

1. Advise a client on the likely sentence he will face after a successful prosecution;

2. represent a client at a sentencing hearing by making a plea in mitigation;

3. advise a client on the prospects of a successful appeal against sentence.

In dealing with any of the above tasks, the well-prepared defence practitioner will require a thorough knowledge of sentencing principles and practice.

Sentencing law and practice is complex. We have divided the subject into four separate chapters to assist understanding. In this chapter we examine the theoretical basis for sentencing and the factors that underpin, inform and in some instances constrain a court when passing sentence. In Chapter 26 we explore specific types of sentence, looking at the requisite criteria for each of them. In Chapter 27 we address the special considerations that apply to sentencing in road traffic matters and in Chapter 28 we consider sentencing procedure and good practice for making an effective plea in mitigation. Sentencing in relation to young offenders (aged under the age of 18) is considered in Chapter 31.

25.2 NEW DEVELOPMENTS—WARNING

Sentencing is a fast changing area of criminal practice. Numerous changes were made to sentencing practice with the enactment of the CJA 2003, some of which have yet to be implemented. As the Sentencing Guidelines Council (created by the CJA 2003) frequently issues new sentencing guidelines and appeals from sentencing decisions commonly revise current sentencing practice, it is a challenge to keep up to date!

 online resource centre

Important changes to the nature and length of custodial sentences passed by magistrates' courts are contained in the CJA 2003. It is unclear when these provisions will be implemented in the light of well-publicised problems of prison overcrowding. Our Online Resource Centre will keep you updated on new developments.

25.3 HIERARCHY OF SENTENCES

The magistrates' court and the Crown Court can pass a range of sentences under the Criminal Justice Act 2003 which we list below in decreasing order of severity:

- custody—immediate/suspended;
- community sentence (combining requirements such as unpaid work/supervision/curfew);
- fine/compensation order;
- discharge (conditional or absolute).

A court might also consider deferring sentence in appropriate circumstances. We consider the specifics of each sentence in Chapter 26.

In addition, upon conviction for certain offences, a court may and in some cases must also order endorsement of a driving licence or disqualification from driving, destruction or confiscation of criminal property or the seizure of criminal assets. In other instances, a court may be required to subject the offender to notification requirements under the Sex Offences Act 2003, or a restraining order.

25.4 SENTENCING AIMS

When a court passes sentence on an offender over the age of 18, s. 142 CJA 2003 requires the court to have regard to one or more of the following purposes of sentencing. They include:

(a) the punishment of offenders;

(b) reduction in crime (including its reduction by deterrence);

(c) the reform and rehabilitation of the offender;

(d) the protection of the public;

(e) the making of reparation by the offender to people affected by their offences.

The CJA 2003 does not indicate that any one purpose is more important than any other.

Punitive sentences include custody and certain types of community sentence where the offender is required to undertake unpaid work or to abide by a curfew. These sentences deprive the offender of his liberty. In some cases a sufficiently high fine can be punitive in nature. In particularly serious cases where an offender has used violence, perhaps not for the first time, or has committed a serious sexual offence, there will be a need to protect the public and the offender can expect a lengthy custodial sentence.

Where the offence is less serious and there are underlying reasons for an offender's behaviour, a rehabilitative sentence might be appropriate which may result in a reduction in further offending. The most obvious example of this is a community sentence with a supervision requirement, or a community sentence that includes a drug rehabilitation requirement. For a first-time offender whose offence is not serious, a conditional discharge might be appropriate.

In terms of reparation as a sentencing objective, the imposition of a court order requiring an offender to pay compensation to his victim for injury, loss or damage is a good example.

25.5 THE BASIS OF SENTENCING UNDER THE CRIMINAL JUSTICE ACT 2003

The Criminal Justice Act 2003 adopts the fundamental principle that a sentence should not be more severe than the seriousness of the offence warrants. The type of sentence a court chooses to impose should therefore reflect the seriousness of the offence.

25.5.1 ASSESSING THE SERIOUSNESS OF AN OFFENCE

Section 143(1) CJA 2003 states that in assessing the seriousness of any offence, the court must consider:

- the offender's culpability in committing the offence; and
- any harm which the offence has caused or was intended to cause or might forseeably have caused.

Culpability includes such matters as the defendant's intention when committing an offence, whether he acted recklessly or had knowledge of the risk he was taking. Harm can include harm to the individual victim but also to the wider community.

Statutory aggravating factors affecting the seriousness of an offence are identified in ss. 143–146 CJA 2003.

- Section 143(2) requires a court to treat an offender's previous convictions as an aggravating factor if the court considers it can reasonably be so treated, having regard to the nature of the offence and the time that has elapsed since conviction. Recent and relevant previous convictions will therefore be regarded as aggravating the seriousness of the current offence before the court.
- Section 143(3) requires the court to treat any offence committed while on bail as being an aggravating factor in determining the seriousness of the offence.
- Sections 145 and 146 provide that where an offence is either racially or religiously motivated or is motivated out of hostility towards a person's sexual or presumed sexual orientation or disability or presumed disability, this shall be regarded as an aggravating feature in determining the seriousness of the offence.

In addition to any statutory aggravating factors, the court will also consider any aggravating and mitigating features of the offence itself and any applicable sentencing guidelines.

In its publication *Overarching Principles: Seriousness*, the SGC (see below) provides guidance on assessing an offender's culpability for the purposes of s. 143 CJA 2003. Culpability is determined by such matters as the offender's motivation in committing the offence; whether it was planned or spontaneous and whether the offender was in a position of trust. A further relevant factor includes the deliberate targeting of a vulnerable victim by reference to their age, disability or by virtue of their job. The guidance offers an extensive though by no means exhaustive list of typical aggravating and mitigating features to an offence.

- To remind you—the starting point when sentencing an offender is an assessment by the court of the seriousness of the offence.

25.6 SENTENCING GUIDELINES COUNCIL (SGC)

The Criminal Justice Act 2003 established the Sentencing Guidelines Council (SGC). Its remit is to provide authoritative guidance on sentencing to be applied by courts. This is a role that has historically been undertaken by the Court of Appeal, so far as sentencing in the Crown Court is concerned. The SGC works in conjunction with the Sentencing Advisory Panel (SAP) which is an independent public body. The SAP provides advice to the SGC, based on legal research and consultation. The SGC receives the advice and formulates it into a draft guideline which it then submits for public consultation before issuing a final guideline. When sentencing an offender, a court is obliged to have regard to the sentencing guidelines produced by the SGC and to give reasons where it departs from a SGC guideline sentence (s. 174 CJA 2003). In this way, sentencing guidelines aid a consistent approach to sentencing.

The SGC has issued a number of definitive guidelines including:

- *Overarching Principles: Seriousness* (December 2004);
- *New Sentences: CJA 2003* (December 2004);
- *Reduction in Sentence for a Guilty Plea (Revised)* (July 2007);
- *Manslaughter by Reason of Provocation* (November 2005);
- *Definitive Sentencing Guideline on Robbery* (July 2006);
- *Overarching Principles: Domestic Violence* (December 2006);
- *Breach of a Protective Order* (December 2006);
- *Guidelines on Sexual Offences Act 2003* (April 2007);
- *Definitive Sentencing Guideline: Fail to Surrender to Bail* (November 2007);
- *Overarching Principles: Assault on Children and Cruelty to a Child* (February 2008);
- *Assault and Other Offences against the Person* (February 2008).

Draft guidelines have been issued for theft and causing death by dangerous driving. The SGC is expected to issue final allocation guidelines in 2008, which will be applied in magistrates' courts when the allocation provisions (replacing mode of trial under the CJA 2003) eventually come into force (see Chapter 13, para. 13.9).

 The importance of the SGC in terms of sentencing practice cannot be overstated. The advice of the SAP and the final and draft guidelines produced by the SGC can be accessed at http://www.sentencing-guidelines.gov.uk.

25.7 HOW DOES THE DEFENCE SOLICITOR BEGIN TO ASSESS THE SERIOUSNESS OF AN OFFENCE?

Defence solicitors must consider their client's role in the particular offence and consider what factors aggravate the seriousness of the offence and what factors mitigate the seriousness of its offence. These include the statutory aggravating factors identified at para. 25.5.1.

above and in the SGC's publication on seriousness and the factors identified in the Magistrates' Court Sentencing Guidelines (MCSGs 2008) for specific offences.

5.7.1 MAGISTRATES' COURT SENTENCING GUIDELINES (MCSGs)

The Magistrates' Court Sentencing Guidelines have recently been revised by the SGC. The revised definitive guidelines must be applied by all magistrates' courts from 4th August 2008.

The MCSGs cover offences that are commonly dealt with in the adult magistrates' court. The effect of the revised MCSGs (2008) is to make the sentencing exercise before a magistrates' court increasingly more prescriptive. The level of detail in the MCSGs (2008) will however assist defence solicitors to give their clients realistic advice as to the likely sentence. The MCSGs can be accessed via the SGC's web-pages. It is essential reading for anyone who practises in the magistrates' court. At Appendix 3 in this *Handbook* we include a small number of specific sentencing guidelines taken from the MCSGs (2008).

5.7.2 USING THE MCSGS TO ASSESS THE SERIOUSNESS OF AN OFFENCE

The revised 2008 MCSGs are based on a first-time offender convicted after trial. They provide a starting point based on an assessment of the seriousness of the offence and a range of possible sentences based on the manner in which the particular offence was committed. The guidelines accordingly identify a series of factors in the commission of the specific offence under consideration, progressing from less to more serious conduct. The nature of the activity involved identifies the appropriate starting point and the typical range of sentences that can fall either side of the starting point. The court may then depart from the starting point to reflect any aggravating or mitigating features of the offence itself (beyond those identified to determine the starting point) in order to reach a provisional sentence. To illustrate the concept of seriousness under the MCSGs (2008), consider the offence of dangerous driving. The guideline for this offence is reproduced in Appendix 3.

In relation to dangerous driving, a single incident involving little or no damage or risk of personal injury attracts a sentencing starting point of a medium level community order but with a range of sentences from a low level community order to a high level community order. For an offence of dangerous driving involving excessive speed in a built-up area, the starting point rises to a custodial term of 12 weeks with a sentencing range from a high level community order to a custodial term of 26 weeks. For an offence of dangerous driving which involves prolonged bad driving and deliberate disregard for the safety of others; or excessive speed in a built-up area, the starting point and the range is committal for sentence to the Crown Court. Having established the starting point in terms of sentence, the court must then consider any statutory aggravating features and any aggravating or mitigating features of the offence of dangerous driving. Aggravating features of dangerous driving include:

* evidence of alcohol or drugs;
* aggressive driving such as driving much too close to the vehicle in front or racing;
* carrying out other tasks while driving.

Mitigating features of dangerous driving include:

* genuine emergency;
* speed not excessive;
* offence due to inexperience rather than irresponsibility.

Consider the following example of the possible application of the MCSGs to an offence of dangerous driving.

Example

X has pleaded guilty to an offence of dangerous driving based on a single incident which resulted in extensive damage to an oncoming vehicle and minor injury to its driver. X was driving a heavy goods vehicle whilst over the legal limit for alcohol, made an inappropriate attempt at overtaking, and was driving in excess of the speed limit. X has a previous conviction for drink driving committed five years ago. The starting point in terms of sentence (according to the MCSGs (2008)) is a medium level community order. However, there is the statutory aggravating factor that X has a previous conviction for a drink driving related offence and there is the presence of other aggravating features in the commission of the offence itself. These may cause the magistrates' court to reappraise the starting point in terms of sentencing to a high level community order or custodial term.

Varying the facts, assume X is an inexperienced driver with no previous convictions who is confronted by a complicated set of roadworks which leads X to drive on the wrong side of the carriageway with the result that X collides with another vehicle. No injury was caused and only minor damage was done to the other vehicle. Whilst the starting point is a medium level community order, the mitigating features of the offence might lead the court to conclude that a low level community order or even a fine is the appropriate sentence. If a fine was imposed the court would have to give reasons for imposing a sentence which is outside the range identified in the guidelines.

25.8 TIMELY GUILTY PLEAS

Section 144 Criminal Justice Act 2003 provides as follows:

> '(1) In determining what sentence to pass on an offender who has pleaded guilty to an offence in proceedings before that or another court, a court shall take into account—
>
> (a) the stage in the proceedings for the offence at which the offender indicated his intention to plead guilty, and
>
> (b) the circumstances in which this indication was given.'

Section 174(2)(b) provides that in passing sentence on an offender, the court must state in open court in ordinary language that it has given the offender the benefit of a discount under s. 144 CJA 2003.

Timely guilty pleas save cost, court time and, most importantly, spare victims and witnesses from having to give evidence. Section 144 does not specify the amount of discount a court might award. In practice, the average discount which the courts apply is one third off the sentence passed. A defendant who leaves his guilty plea to the morning of trial can expect only a minimal discount. Sentencing discounts do not apply to ancillary orders which include compensation orders or to the minimum periods of disqualification and the mandatory imposition of penalty points.

In its revised guideline on the effect of pleading guilty, the SGC recommends a sliding scale, ranging from a maximum of one third (where the guilty plea was entered at the first reasonable opportunity), reducing to a maximum of up to one quarter (where a trial date has been set) and up to a maximum of one tenth (for a guilty plea entered at the 'door of the court'). The application of the reduction may affect the type of sentence imposed and might take the sentence below the range suggested by the MCSGs in some cases.

25.9 WHAT CONSTRAINS SENTENCING?

There are a number of factors that constrain sentencing, including:

• the statute creating the offence (statutes creating an offence will specify a maximum penalty for the particular offence);

- whether the sentence is being imposed in the Crown Court or in the magistrates' court (magistrates' courts' powers of sentence are limited);

- statutory requirements laid down by parliament (in some instances parliament has removed judicial discretion and requires the imposition of a mandatory sentence of imprisonment or other ancillary penalty);

- the age of the defendant (sentencing in relation to young offenders under the age of 18 is considered in Chapter 31);

- whether the defendant pleaded guilty or was found guilty (timely guilty pleas attract a reduction in the length of sentence).

5.9.1 THE SENTENCING JURISDICTION OF MAGISTRATES' COURTS

The magistrates' sentencing jurisdiction is closely related to mode of trial enquiry for either-way offences. Having considered the mode of trial enquiry in Chapter 13 you will be aware that one of the principal reasons for a magistrates' court declining jurisdiction to try an either-way matter where the defendant has pleaded not guilty or has given no indication of plea, is that the magistrates consider their maximum sentencing powers are insufficient.

The maximum custodial sentence that a magistrates' court can currently pass is six months upon conviction of a summary matter (s. 78 PCC(S)A 2000 and s. 133 MCA 1980). It does not matter that a defendant is convicted of two or more summary matters on the same occasion: the maximum prescribed by statute is six months. The six months maximum can rise to 12 months where consecutive prison sentences of six months are imposed on a defendant convicted of two or more either-way matters (proviso to s. 133(1) and s. 133(2) MCA 1980).

Even in magistrates' courts, however, the statute creating the offence may prescribe a custodial sentence of less than six months. An example of this is conviction for criminal damage of less than £5,000 under s. 4(2) Criminal Damage Act 1971. The current maximum custodial sentence in this regard is three months. Some offences do not carry a custodial penalty, such as careless driving, contrary to s. 3 Road Traffic Act 1988.

Magistrates are further constrained in terms of the size of a fine they may wish to impose. The maximum fine is £5,000 for each offence. Some offences however specify a maximum fine of less than £5,000. For an offence of being drunk and disorderly contrary to s. 91 Criminal Justice Act 1967, the maximum fine is £1,000 or level 3.

25.9.2 POWER TO COMMIT FOR SENTENCE UNDER S. 3 PCC(S)A 2000

Upon summary conviction for an either-way offence, magistrates have the power to commit a defendant to the Crown Court for sentence under s. 3 PCC(S)A 2000 where they consider their maximum powers of punishment to be insufficient, having regard to the seriousness of the offence. Where this power is exercised, magistrates can also commit the offender for sentence on any other offences for which the defendant has been convicted s. 6 PCC(S)A 2000. This enables the Crown Court to deal with all outstanding matters including any other less serious either-way or summary matters the defendant has been convicted of and any suspended sentence or breach of a community penalty or conditional discharge imposed by a magistrates' court for which the accused now stands to be dealt with. However, the Crown Court's sentencing powers are limited to those of the magistrates and the summary offence(s) must be punishable with imprisonment or disqualification.

The power to commit for sentence is more likely to be used where a defendant indicates an intention to plead guilty to an either-way offence which requires the magistrates' court to accept summary jurisdiction. Where a full mode of trial enquiry has been conducted, the power to commit for sentence under s. 3 PCC(S)A 2000 might be exercised in circumstances where the evidence disclosed at trial shows the offence to be more serious than was suggested at the mode of trial enquiry, or it is revealed, upon conviction, that the accused has an extensive criminal record or is asking for other offences to be taken into consideration. If the defendant is committed for sentence the Crown Court will proceed to deal with the defendant as if he had been convicted on indictment.

Although the point has not been definitively determined by case law, the Divisional Court in *North Sefton Magistrates' Court, ex p. Marsh* (1994) 16 Cr App R (S) 401 held that s. 3 PCC(S)A 2000 discretion is unfettered and that simply because magistrates had decided to accept jurisdiction to try a case does not constrain the court from subsequently coming to the decision to commit the defendant for sentence upon conviction. However, if nothing comes to light in the way of previous convictions or other offences to be taken into consideration, the accused may consider he has a legitimate expectation to be sentenced summarily.

25.9.3   COMMITTAL FOR SENTENCE UNDER S. 4 PCC(S)A 2000

Where an accused has indicated a guilty plea to an either-way offence but has been committed for trial in the Crown Court on a related either-way offence, the magistrates can commit the defendant to the Crown Court for sentence on the matter to which he has indicated a guilty plea under s. 4 PCC(S)A. If the Crown Court convicts the defendant on the related either-way matter, or if the magistrates' court, on committal for sentence under s. 4, state that it also had the power to do so under s. 3, the Crown Court can proceed to sentence on the offence as if the defendant had been convicted on indictment, otherwise its powers are limited to those upon summary conviction.

25.9.4   LOOKING AHEAD—POWER TO COMMIT FOR SENTENCE UPON SUMMARY CONVICTION

 Looking Ahead

One of the reasons for extending the sentencing powers of the magistrates' court under the CJA 2003 is to try to ensure that fewer cases are committed to the Crown Court either for trial or for sentence. Consequently, the increased powers of sentence available to magistrates under s. 154 CJA 2003 are aligned with the changes relating to the allocation of either-way cases which are contained in s. 41 and Sch. 3 CJA 2003.

When s. 154 of the Act is brought into force (there is no current date for implementation), the maximum custodial sentence that a magistrates' court will be able to pass will increase from six months to 12 months for any one offence and to 65 weeks' imprisonment in respect of two or more offences for which terms are to be served consecutively.

The power to commit for sentence following an indication of a guilty plea remains and a new s. 3 and s. 4 is inserted into the 2000 Act by s. 41 Sch. 3, para. 22 to the 2003 Act. There will be no power to commit for sentence in a case where jurisdiction to try the either-way offence was accepted by magistrates and a conviction has resulted. This is subject to one exception which applies to 'dangerous offenders' only. The decision about whether to accept jurisdiction to deal with an either-way matter will in future be informed by the fact that the court will be able to have regard to a defendant's previous convictions (Sch. 3).

The combined effect of s. 154 (magistrates' increased sentencing powers) and s. 41 (Sch. 3) (preventing magistrates from committing a case for sentence to the Crown Court where the magistrates' court have accepted jurisdiction to try an either-way matter and have found the defendant guilty) should result in considerably fewer cases being committed to the Crown Court for trial or sentence in the future. Should the allocation provisions come into force without the increase in magistrates courts' sentencing powers, provision is made in the Criminal Justice and Immigration Act 2008 to restore the power to commit for sentence following conviction of an accused where jurisdiction has been retained!

5.10 CROWN COURT'S POWERS OF SENTENCE

The Crown Court's sentencing powers are considerably greater than those of the magistrates' court. We offer the offence of theft as an example. Conviction for a single offence of theft under the Theft Act 1968 in a magistrates' court currently carries a maximum six months custodial sentence. Conviction on indictment in the Crown Court carries a maximum custodial sentence of seven years and an unlimited fine.

The increased powers of sentence available to the Crown Court are of course an important factor in an accused's decision whether to elect trial in the Crown Court if he is given the choice at the mode of trial enquiry (see Chapter 13).

Where a Crown Court is required to pass sentence on a defendant who has been convicted of or has pleaded guilty to a summary offence which has been committed to the Crown Court alongside an either-way offence under either ss. 40 or 41 Criminal Justice Act 1988 (see Chapter 13, paras. 13.18 and 13.19), the powers of the Crown Court are limited to those of a magistrates' court.

.10.1 MANDATORY SENTENCES IN THE CROWN COURT

Recent reforms have removed the discretionary element in sentencing in favour of mandatory sentences which primarily have affected sentencing in the Crown Court. Sections 110 and 111 PCC(S)A 2000 require a minimum sentence of seven years for a third conviction of Class A drug trafficking and a minimum three years for a third conviction of domestic burglary. In relation to domestic burglary the defendant must have committed his second burglary after being convicted of his first and in addition, both burglary convictions must post-date 1 December 1999. The court need not impose the minimum term if it is of the opinion that it would be unjust to do so. A court may go below the minimum sentence in order to grant a discount for a timely guilty plea.

Life imprisonment is mandatory for murder. It is up to the court to fix the minimum term in accordance with s. 269 CJA 2003 and *R v Jones* [2005] EWCA Crim 3115.

Sections 224–229 CJA 2003 make special provision for 'dangerous' offenders. These are considered in more detail in Chapter 26, at para. 26.8.3.

25.11 THE IMPORTANCE OF LEGAL RESEARCH IN RELATION TO SENTENCING

Sentencing law is challenging and before you can advise your client about the likely sentence he will receive you will need to undertake legal research. You need to be certain of the range of possible penalties that may be imposed and the maximum sentence your client could be facing (which for an either-way offence depends on where the case is concluded). The maximum sentence for all offences is specified in *Blackstone's Criminal Practice* and the MCSGs will also assist your research.

25.12 WHAT INFORMS THE PROCESS OF SENTENCING?

The sentencing process is informed by the sentencing guidelines; pre-sentence reports and personal offender mitigation.

It is essential to realise that before a client is advised about the possible sentence and before any plea in mitigation is attempted, relevant sentencing guidelines for the offence under consideration must be carefully researched. In serious cases, a defence solicitor may wish to take the advice of counsel or a solicitor-advocate on the question of sentence. We have already considered the importance of the Magistrates' Court Sentencing Guidelines (2008), We now consider the sentencing guidelines in the Crown Court.

25.12.1 SENTENCING GUIDELINES IN THE CROWN COURT

Sentencing in the Crown Court has historically been informed by decisions of the Court of Appeal. Whilst the role of formulating sentencing guidelines now belongs to the SGC, in cases where there is no definitive SGC guideline, Court of Appeal decisions will continue to apply. Most decisions are reported in the Criminal Appeal Sentencing Reports and summarised in *Blackstone's Criminal Practice*, making it an excellent starting point for your research into the relevant sentencing guidelines.

The Court of Appeal has established sentencing guidelines for a number of offences dealt with in the Crown Court. Some of the guidelines have been influenced by the advice given by the Sentencing Advisory Panel (SAP). We include a list of some of the offences which have been the subject of Court of Appeal sentencing guidelines and a brief summary of two of these decisions.

* Death by dangerous driving—*R v Cooksley* [2003] 3 All ER 40 and *R v Richardson* [2007] 2 All ER 601.
* Rape offences—*R v Millberry, Morgan and Larkenby* [2003] 2 Cr App (S) R 31.
* Burglary of a dwelling—*R v McInerney and Keating* [2003] 1 All ER 1089.

In *R v Millberry* [2003] 2 Cr App (S) R 31, the Court of Appeal stated that in assessing the gravity of an individual offence of rape it was necessary to consider the degree of harm to the victim, the culpability of the offender and the risk posed by the offender to society. The guidelines applying to relationship or acquaintance rape and stranger rape should in principle be the same. Similarly, there should be no distinction between male and female rape, with additional factors such as pregnancy following female rape being dealt with on a case-by-case basis. There should also be no distinction between anal rape and vaginal rape, with instances where both types of rape were perpetrated on the victim being treated as repeated rape. The effect of the victim's behaviour on the offender's culpability and the position with regard to historical cases was considered.

The starting points for rape, in the absence of aggravating features, were: (1) five years for a single offence on an adult victim by a single offender; (2) eight years following a contested trial where the rape (a) was committed by two or more offenders; (b) was committed by someone who was in a position of responsibility towards the victim; (c) involved abduction or false imprisonment; (d) involved a child or a vulnerable mentally defective victim, or (e) was racially aggravated, repeated, or committed by a man knowingly suffering from a life threatening sexually transmissible disease; (3) 15 years for a campaign of rape either on the same victim or on multiple victims, and (4) sentence of public protection for 'dangerous offenders' (ss. 224–236 CJA 2003). These starting points have been adopted by the SGC in its definitive guidelines on the Sexual Offences Act 2003.

* Burglary of a dwelling—*R v McInerney and Keating* [2003] 1 All ER 1089.

Following detailed consideration by the SAP, the Court of Appeal issued guidelines for sentencing in domestic dwelling burglary cases. The guidelines are extremely comprehensive and identify a number of aggravating and mitigating factors. The guidelines specify that a non-custodial sentence may be appropriate in some instances, although the usual sentence will be custody.

The SGC publishes an extremely useful compendium of all current Court of Appeal sentencing guidelines cases. It can be accessed at www.sentencing-guidelines.gov.uk.

25.12.2 PRE-SENTENCE REPORTS—S. 156 CJA 2003

Pre-sentence reports (PSRs), as defined by s. 158 CJA 2003, are prepared by probation officers after consultation with the offender and any other relevant source, including advance information. They are designed to assist the court in finding the most appropriate sentence for the individual concerned. The report should analyse the offence and the offender's culpability. It should assess the offender's attitude to the offence and his awareness of the consequences of his actions. The report will highlight the offender's personal history, previous convictions, education, employment position and state of health. Importantly the report will assess the offender's risk of re-offending based on the current offence and his attitude to it. It will consider appropriate sentences and address such matters as the defendant's suitability for certain types of sentence. A pre-sentence report will not normally contain a recommendation as to sentence but it will contain a proposal, which can often be highly influential, including, where appropriate, the need for a medical/psychiatric report.

In accordance with s. 156 CJA 2003, a court must order a pre-sentence report before:

(a) imposing a sentence of imprisonment;

(b) making a community order with requirements (e.g. supervision, unpaid work, drug rehabilitation requirement, mental health requirement, activity requirement).

Section 156 CJA 2003 provides that the court need not obtain a PSR in the case of an offender over 18 where a report would be unnecessary. An example might include a case where custody is an inevitable sentence although it may be argued that a report could still be useful to address the question of the duration of the term. Unless the sentence in a particular case is clear and a report would make little difference, it is always good sentencing practice to obtain a report where custody or a community sentence is being considered.

A failure to obtain a pre-sentence report does not invalidate a sentence, although it would be a relevant factor to consider in any subsequent appeal.

Sometimes magistrates will indicate the type of sentence they are considering when requesting a pre-sentence report. More often, however, so as not to bind the ultimate sentencing bench, the court will announce that it is requesting a PSR and that it is 'keeping all of its sentencing options open'. This means the court is not ruling out custody. If a court wishes to retain the option of committing the offender to the Crown Court for sentence, it should specifically make mention of this when ordering the PSR. A failure to do so can give rise to a legitimate expectation on the part of the defendant that commital for sentence as an option has been ruled out (*Feltham Justices, ex p. Rees* [2001] 2 Cr App R (S) 1).

Where an offender is on bail, it generally takes 15 days to prepare a standard delivery (or full) pre-sentence report (SDR). Where the offender has been remanded in custody pending sentence, the average time for a SDR is reduced to ten days.

Fast Delivery Reports (FDR)

The Fast Delivery Report (FDR) is an expedited pre-sentence report. FDRs are designed to speed up the provision of information to courts to allow sentencing without delay. The FDR is prepared by a probation officer in court on the day or within 24 hours. It will be handwritten by the probation officer. If s/he considers a full report is required, an adjournment will be necessary. With the introduction of CJSSS (see Chapter 11), much greater use is being made of FDRs.

5.12.3 PERSONAL OFFENDER MITIGATION

The seriousness of an offence may well point to a particular type of sentence. However, every offender who comes before a court must be sentenced on an individual basis. With this in mind, a court must have regard to any personal offender mitigation that might apply in the particular case before it. It is the combination of the seriousness of the offence, and any personal offender mitigation that will determine the appropriate sentence in an individual case. The seriousness of the offence may well point to a custodial sentence. There may be strong personal mitigating factors which suggest a community based sentence as the most appropriate sentence in the particular case. Personal offender mitigation will clearly be highlighted in your plea in mitigation (which we consider in Chapter 28). Personal offender mitigation may also be highlighted in any pre-sentence report.

25.13 VICTIM IMPACT STATEMENTS

There has been a significant move to acknowledge victims' rights within the criminal justice system in recent years. Since October 2001, it has been possible for a victim to make a 'victim impact statement' detailing the effect that the offence has had on him or her. Guidance on the use of such statements is contained in the MCSGs (2008) and Part III. 28 of the Consolidated Criminal Practice Direction.

25.14 NEWTON HEARINGS

A decision to plead guilty does not necessarily signify acceptance of everything the prosecutor says about the circumstances of the offence to the sentencing court. For example, a defendant may accept he is guilty of assault occasioning actual bodily harm in that he admits punching his victim. However, he may go on to deny, as alleged by the prosecution, that he used a weapon in the attack. Should the court sentence on the basis of the prosecution's version of the facts or the defendant's version? The answer depends upon whether the facts in dispute would significantly affect the sentence the court is likely to pass. In the above example, the use of a weapon considerably aggravates the seriousness of an assault and would make a material difference when it comes to passing sentence.

Where sentence would not be significantly affected, the court will sentence on the basis of the defendant's version of the facts. It is important for the defence lawyer to notify the CPS if there is a significant dispute as to the facts upon which the defendant is entering his guilty plea. Having heard any representations from the CPS based on para. 9.3 of the Code for Crown Prosecutors, the court may decide to hold a Newton hearing (*R v Newton* (1982) 77 Cr App R 13) in order to determine where the truth lies in relation to the disputed facts. If such a hearing is held, the normal rules of evidence will apply. Witnesses will be called, examined and cross-examined in the same way as they would be at trial. A verdict is then reached based on the evidence.

Notwithstanding that the court finds against the defendant on the disputed fact, the defendant is still entitled to a sentencing discount based on his earlier plea although it may not be as great as it would have been had he pleaded guilty on the basis of the prosecution's version of the facts at the outset. A body of case law on Newton hearings has developed which is covered in *Blackstone's Criminal Practice*. Recently the Court of Appeal has produced guidelines on the use of Newton hearings in *R v Underwood* [2004] All ER (D) 575 (Jul).

25.15 TAKING OTHER OFFENCES INTO CONSIDERATION

'The defendant pleads guilty to the offence of theft charged against him and asks that you take a further 26 offences of a like nature into consideration . . .'

A defendant is normally sentenced on those offences for which he has been convicted except for offences which the defendant asks to be 'TIC'd'—taken into consideration. The defendant is not convicted of these offences but admits the offences in court and asks for them to be taken into consideration upon passing sentence.

There are mutual benefits to such an arrangement. For the prosecution, it assists in the clear-up rate for crimes. For the defendant, although he receives a higher sentence because of the increased number of offences, he knows he cannot be later prosecuted for the offences 'TIC'd'.

Any offences to be taken into consideration should be listed on a schedule which is signed by the defendant. In court, the defendant will be asked to confirm he is admitting the offences listed on the schedule and that he wishes for them to be taken into consideration when the court passes sentence. The procedure can be initiated by the police during the defendant's detention and by the prosecutor in court after a finding of guilt.

The procedure does not apply to driving matters which carry endorsement and/or disqualification. Courts should not allow offences of a different nature to be taken into consideration, and magistrates should not take into consideration indictable-only offences.

Important guidance on sentencing in relation to offences taken into consideration is provided in the Divisional Court's decision in *R v Miles* [2006] EWCA 256.

KEY POINT SUMMARY

- Know the range of penalties available for the offences you are dealing with.
- Do not necessarily assume that just because your client has pleaded guilty to an either-way offence before a magistrates' court or has been found guilty of such an offence that he will be sentenced summarily—be aware of the power to commit for sentence under s. 3 PCC(S)A 2000.
- Sentencing practice requires courts to sentence on the basis of the seriousness of the offence. Always make an attempt to assess the seriousness of the offence by balancing the aggravating features of the offence against any mitigating features.
- The court's assessment of offence seriousness will:
  - determine which of the sentencing thresholds has been crossed;
  - indicate whether a custodial, community or other sentence is the most appropriate;
  - be a key factor in deciding the length of a custodial sentence, the number and nature of requirements to be incorporated in a community sentence and the amount of any fine imposed.
- Use available guidelines (including Court of Appeal decisions, SGC guidance and the Magistrates' Court Sentencing Guidelines) in order to assess seriousness and to give you a starting point as to likely sentence.
- Although an offence might be regarded as serious and warrant a particular sentence, a court will have regard to personal offender mitigation in arriving at the most appropriate sentence.
- Anticipate the need for a pre-sentence report and understand why such a report is often influential in informing the sentencing process.
- If your client accepts he is guilty but disputes a material aspect of the prosecution's version of events, anticipate the need for a Newton hearing.
- Timely guilty pleas always attract a sentencing discount.
- Significant changes to the sentencing powers of the magistrates' court which are aligned to changes to the mode of trial enquiry for either-way offences are awaiting an implementation date. Our Online Resource Centre will cover the changes when they come into force.

online resource centre

SELF-TEST QUESTIONS

Consider the following scenario and then try to answer the questions that follow. Apply the provisions of the Criminal Justice Act 2003 in answering these questions.

Scott is charged with assault occasioning actual bodily harm contrary to s. 47 Offences Against the Person Act 1861. It is alleged that Scott, aged 23, was drunk and while at a kebab take-away he and a group of other youths started shouting racial abuse at a group of Asian youths. A disturbance broke out and it is alleged Scott pushed one of the Asian youths to the ground and kicked him about the arms and legs, causing extensive bruising to the young man's body.

Scott pleads not guilty, raising identification as a defence. He is convicted.

At the time of this offence Scott was on bail for an alleged offence of theft but was later acquitted. Scott's previous convictions include:

- 15 months ago: assault occasioning actual bodily harm—s. 47 Offences against the Person Act 1861 (Community Order, 12 months);
- 24 months ago: public order—threatening behaviour—s. 5 Public Order Act 1968 (fine);
- 36 months ago: Theft—s. 1 Theft Act 1968 (conditional discharge).

What is the starting point in terms of sentencing for an assault contrary to s. 47 according to the Magistrates' Court Sentencing Guidelines? You will need to access the MCSGs (2008) either online or in *Blackstone's Criminal Practice 2009*.

> Try to gauge the seriousness of this offence—what factors aggravate the seriousness of this assault?
>
> Is this a case where a pre-sentence report is likely to be requested?
>
> Is Scott entitled to a sentencing discount?

Case studies: *R v Roger Martin; R v Lenny Whyte*

online resource centre

In relation to *R v Hardy* and *R v Martin*, you will be able to see the plea in mitigation and the sentencing process on the video clips contained within our Online Resource Centre. Before you view these however, it is important that you engage in the process which culminates in the plea in mitigation. This can only be done by considering this chapter and Chapters 26–28 and engaging in the tasks we have set in relation to the case studies throughout these chapters.

R v Roger Martin

If you have considered the documentation in relation to this web-based only case study, you will be aware that Roger Martin has been advised to plead guilty to the offences of common assault, careless driving and failing to stop and report after an accident. All these matters are summary only and Roger Martin must therefore be sentenced before magistrates. You will note that the solicitor's ability to negotiate a reduced charge of dangerous driving down to careless driving has been of enormous benefit to Roger Martin. He no longer faces the risk of a committal to the Crown Court and of course, dangerous driving carries with it a mandatory disqualification period of 12 months.

- Ignoring the driving penalties for the time being, assess the level of seriousness of the common assault. Research any relevant sentencing guidelines.
- Try to ascertain what you consider will be the worst outcome for Roger Martin in terms of sentence.
- Do you consider a pre-sentence report should be obtained in these circumstances?

The questions posed in relation to *R v Roger Martin* are considered further in Appendix 4.

R v William Hardy

It will be recalled that William Hardy has been advised to plead guilty to an offence of engaging in sexual activity with a child contrary to s. 9(2) Sexual Offences Act 2003. The offence is indictable-only.

- What is the maximum sentence for this offence?
- Research any relevant sentencing guidelines for this offence in an attempt to gauge the level of seriousness and the likely sentence.
- Do you consider a pre-sentence report should be obtained in this case?

All of the above matters are considered in Appendix 4.

R v Lenny Whyte

You will be aware that Lenny Whyte was acquitted of the offence of domestic dwelling burglary. Had Lenny Whyte been convicted before the Crown Court, what would have been the maximum sentence the judge could have passed? Research the relevant sentencing guidelines for burglary offences tried on indictment. In your view, and being realistic, what sentence do you consider Lenny would have received? Would it have been necessary for a pre-sentence report to have been ordered?

FIGURE 25.1 STRUCTURED APPROACH TO SENTENCING UNDER CJA 2003

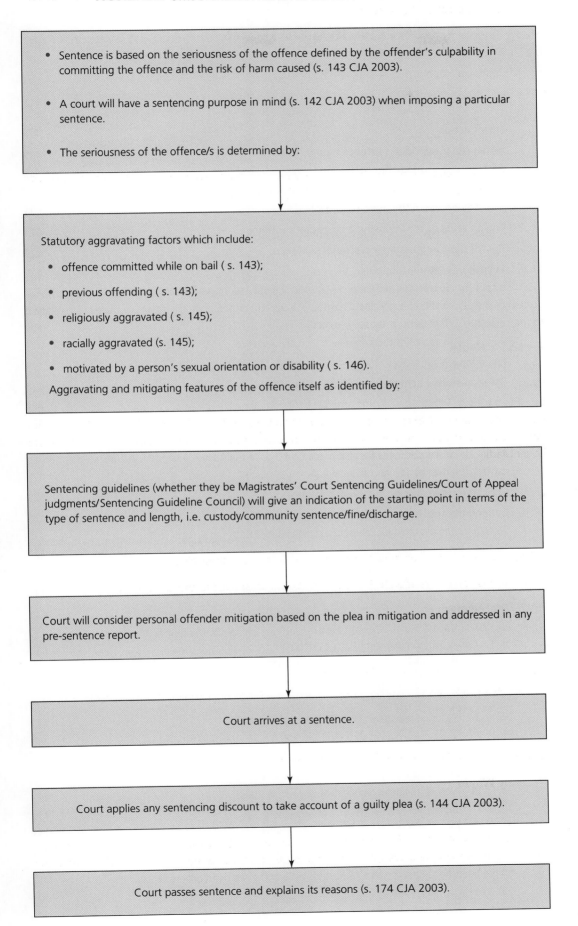

26 SENTENCING OPTIONS

26.1 INTRODUCTION

Having considered the theory behind sentencing practice in the preceding chapter, we now consider the range of sentencing options available to a court when passing sentence on an adult offender. We also briefly consider a number of ancillary orders that a court might or is obliged to impose upon sentence. We start by considering custodial sentences.

26.2 WHEN CAN A CUSTODIAL SENTENCE BE IMPOSED?

The fact that an offence carries the possibility of a custodial sentence does not automatically mean that a custodial sentence will be imposed. There is a statutory criterion that must be met before a custodial sentence can be imposed. Section 152(2) CJA 2003 states that:

'. . . the court must not pass a custodial sentence on the offender unless it is of the opinion—that the offence, or combination of the offence and one or more offences associated with it, was so serious that neither a fine alone or a community sentence can be justified for the offence . . .

    (3) . . . Nothing in subsection (2) prevents the court from passing a custodial sentence on the offender if (a) he fails to express his willingness to comply with a requirement which is proposed by the court to be included in a community order and which requires an expression of willingness; or (b) he fails to comply with an order under s. 161(2) (pre-sentence drug testing).'

The wording of this section seeks to reinforce the fact that custody should be a sentence of last resort.

26.2.1 THE CUSTODY THRESHOLD TEST—S. 152(2) CJA 2003

Section 152(2) establishes the 'custody threshold test': 'Is the offence so serious that neither a community sentence nor fine can be imposed?' Only if this question can be answered affirmatively can a custodial sentence be imposed. As we saw in the previous chapter, the seriousness of an offence is assessed according to the presence of aggravating and/or mitigating factors, of which the offender's culpability in committing the offence will be an important consideration. When an initial determination is made that the offence is so serious that it merits a custodial sentence, there may be personal offender mitigation which requires a less draconian sentence than custody.

It will be self-evident that in many cases where an offender is convicted of a serious indictable offence, a custodial sentence is inevitable. Sentencing guidelines will help you decide whether the custody threshold test is likely to be met in a particular case. The MCSGs (2008) for example, suggest a custodial sentence as the starting point for a number of offences, including assault occasioning actual bodily harm.

26.2.2 **WHAT IF THE THRESHOLD TEST IS FINELY BALANCED?**

Where the custody threshold test is finely balanced, the defence advocate has everything to play for in his plea in mitigation. Case law under the previous threshold test laid down by s. 79(2) PCC(S)A 2000, has provided valuable assistance in this regard. The most important case is *R v Howells* [1999] 1 WLR 307. The general guidance of the Court of Appeal is reproduced below.

> 'It would be dangerous and wrong for this Court to lay down prescriptive rules governing the exercise of that judgment, and any guidance we give, however general, will be subject to exceptions and qualifications in some cases. We do, however, think that in approaching cases which are on or near the custody threshold courts will usually find it helpful to begin by considering the nature and extent of the defendant's criminal intention and the nature and extent of any injury or damage caused to the victim. Other things being equal, an offence which is deliberate and premeditated or which involves an excessive response to provocation; an offence which inflicts personal injury or mental trauma, particularly if permanent, will usually be more serious than one which inflicts financial loss only. In considering the seriousness of any offence the Court may take into account any previous convictions of the offender of any failure to respond to previous sentences (2000 Act, section 151(1)) and must treat it as an aggravating factor if the offence was committed while the offender was on bail (2000 Act, section 151(2)).
>
> In deciding whether to impose a custodial sentence in borderline cases the sentencing court will ordinarily take account of matters relating to the offender:
>
> (a) The Court will have regard to an offender's admission of responsibility for the offence, particularly if reflected in a plea of guilty tendered at the earliest opportunity and accompanied by hard evidence of genuine remorse, as shown (for example) by an expression of regret to the victim and an offer of compensation. Attention is drawn to section 152 of the PCC(S)A 2000.
>
> (b) Where offending has been fuelled by addiction to drink or drugs, the Court will be inclined to look more favourably on an offender who has already demonstrated (by taking practical steps to that end) a genuine, self-motivated determination to address his addiction.
>
> (c) Youth and immaturity, while affording no defence, will often justify a less rigorous penalty than would be appropriate for an adult.
>
> (d) Some measures of leniency will ordinarily be extended to offenders of previous good character, the more so if there is evidence of positive good character (such as solid employment record or faithful discharge of family duties) as opposed to a mere absence of previous convictions. It will sometimes be appropriate to take account of family responsibilities, or physical or mental disability.
>
> (e) While the Court will never impose a custodial sentence unless satisfied that it is necessary to do so, there will be even greater reluctance to impose a custodial sentence on an offender who has never before served such a sentence.
>
> Courts should always bear in mind that criminal sentences are in almost every case intended to protect the public, whether by punishing the offender or reforming him, or deterring him and others, or all of these things. Courts cannot and should not be unmindful of the important public dimension of criminal sentencing and the importance of maintaining public confidence in the sentencing system.
>
> Where the Court is of the opinion that an offence, or the combination of an offence and one or more offences associated with it, is so serious that only a custodial sentence can be justified and that such a sentence should be passed, the sentence imposed should be no longer than is necessary to meet the penal purpose which the Court has in mind . . .'

Sentencing law develops at a fast pace. It is therefore important for the busy defence practitioner to keep up to date with new case law. We cite two Court of Appeal decisions which might assist a defence advocate to avoid a custodial sentence for his client: overcrowding in prisons (*R v Kefford* [2002] 2 Cr App (S) R 106) and the sentencing of a woman with young children for an economic crime (*R v Mills* [2002] 2 Cr App R (S) 229). In *Kefford* Lord Woolf CJ stated:

'The overcrowding of the prison system is not only a matter for grave concern for the prison service, it is also a matter of grave concern for the criminal justice system as a whole. Prison sentences are imposed by the courts normally for three purposes: to punish the offender concerned, to deter other offenders and to stop the offender committing further offences in the future. The ability of the prison service to tackle a prisoner's offending behaviour and so reduce reoffending is adversely affected if a prison is overcrowded. The ability of the prison service to service the courts is impeded if prisons are overcrowded, since the prison service is unable to ensure that prisoners arrive at courts at the appropriate time. In the past attempts have been made to relieve overcrowding by using police cells but this is a wholly unsatisfactory remedy. Apart from being extremely expensive, it prevents the police performing their duties in tackling crime.

Those who are responsible for imposing sentences have to take into account the impact on the prison system of the number of prisoners the prison estate is being required to accommodate at the present time. The courts are not responsible for providing prison places. That is the responsibility of the government. However, the courts must accept the realities of the situation. Providing a new prison takes a substantial period of time and in the present situation it is of the greatest importance to the criminal justice system as a whole and the public who depend upon the criminal justice system for their protection against crime, that only those who need to be sent to prison are sent to prison and that they are not sent to prison for any longer than is necessary.

Nothing that we say in this judgment is intended to deter courts from sending to prison for the appropriate period those who commit offences involving violence or intimidation or other grave crimes . . . There are, however, other categories of offences where a community punishment or a fine can be sometimes a more appropriate form of sentence than imprisonment.

What we have said here is of particular importance to magistrates because they deal with a great many cases where the decision as to whether a prison sentence is necessary is frequently made . . .

In the case of economic crimes, for example obtaining undue credit by fraud, prison is not necessarily the only appropriate form of punishment . . . . Certainly, having to perform a form of community punishment can be a very salutary way of making it clear that crime does not pay, particularly if a community punishment order is combined with a curfew order.'

In *R v Kefford* the original sentence of 12 months imposed on a building society employee for several dishonesty-related offences totalling £11,120 was reduced to four months.

The problem of prison overcrowding is not new, as the decision in *Kefford*, demonstrates. The problem and its effect on sentencing have been highlighted further in the recent Court of Appeal decision in *R v Seed* [2007] 2 Cr App R (S) 69.

In formulating a plea in mitigation in a case where there is a risk of custody, defence advocates should not avoid citing relevant case law and any authorities containing sentencing guidelines that are specific to the particular offence being considered.

26.3 CUSTODY BETWEEN THE AGES 18 AND 21

An offender under the age of 21 cannot be sentenced to a term of imprisonment in an adult prison (s. 89(1) PCC(S)A 2000). Offenders under the age of 21 but over 18, who are subject to a custodial sentence, will serve their time at a young offenders' institution. This will change when s. 61 Criminal Justice and Court Service Act 2000 is eventually brought into force which permits the term of imprisonment to be served in an adult prison.

26.4 GIVING REASONS FOR IMPOSING A CUSTODIAL SENTENCE

In passing a custodial sentence, s. 174(2)(b) CJA 2003 requires a court to state in open court why it is of the opinion that the offence is so serious that no other sentence apart from custody is justified.

26.5 RESTRICTIONS ON PASSING A CUSTODIAL SENTENCE

Section 83(1) Powers of the Criminal Court (Sentencing) Act 2000 prohibits a court from imposing a sentence of imprisonment on an offender who is not legally represented and who has not previously received a custodial sentence. The prohibition does not apply if the offender has been granted legal representation but the right has been withdrawn because of his conduct or if, having been informed of his right to apply and having had the opportunity to do so, he has failed or refused to apply for such representation.

26.6 LENGTH OF CUSTODIAL SENTENCE

Section 153(2) CJA 2003 requires a custodial sentence to be for the shortest term that is commensurate with the seriousness of the offence, or the combination of the offence and one or more offences associated with it.

Consequently, a court should not impose a sentence of greater length than the seriousness of the offence merits for the specific purpose of making a special example of the defendant, although it can reflect the need to deter others (*R v Cunningham* (1993) 14 Cr App R (S) 444). The proportionality principle in terms of the length of sentence does not apply to a sentence fixed by law, indeterminate and extended sentences for certain violent and sexual offences (ss. 224–229, CJA 2003).

Decisions of the Court of Appeal, including *R v Ollerenshaw* [1999] 1 Cr App R (S) 65 and *R v Howells* (cited earlier in the context of the 2000 Sentencing Act) have encouraged courts to keep custodial sentences as short as possible, consistent with their duty to protect the public interest and to punish and deter the criminal. The well-publicised concern about prison overcrowding reinforces the point, as do the decisions in *Kefford* [2002] Crim LR 432 and *R v Seed* [2007] 2 Cr App R (S) 69 highlighted earlier.

26.6.1 CONSECUTIVE AND CONCURRENT CUSTODIAL TERMS AND THE TOTALITY PRINCIPLE

In sentencing an offender for more than one offence, a court must have regard to the totality principle which requires that the sentence passed must not be disproportionate to the seriousness of the overall offending behaviour. Statutory effect is given to this principle in s. 153(2) CJA 2003 which applies to custodial sentences, community orders and fines. The problem most often arises in deciding whether two or more custodial sentences should be served concurrently or consecutively.

Assume a sentence of three months' imprisonment is imposed for possessing an offensive weapon and a further custodial sentence of three months for driving while disqualified. The sentences are ordered to run consecutively which means the offender is required to serve a total of six months' imprisonment. Had the two sentences been expressed to run concurrently, the offender would be required to serve a total of three months in custody. In deciding whether to impose consecutive custodial sentences, the court must have regard to the totality of the defendant's actions and the need to sentence proportionately.

26.6.2 CREDIT FOR GUILTY PLEA

Section 144 CJA 2003 should not be forgotten (see Chapter 25, para. 25.8). Credit should be given for a timely guilty plea. Where a custodial sentence is to be imposed the court should reduce the term to take account of the provision in s. 144 CJA 2003.

In its definitive guidelines on s. 144 CJA 2003, the SGC suggests that where an offence crosses the threshold for imposing a custodial sentence, the application of the reduction principle may properly form the basis for imposing a non-custodial sentence option. The reduction principle has no application to the extended sentences and indeterminate sentence, passed on 'dangerous' offenders.

Section 174 CJA 2003 imposes a duty on the court to state in open court that as a result of the guilty plea, the court has imposed a less severe sentence than it otherwise would have done.

5.6.3 TIME SPENT REMANDED IN CUSTODY

Time spent on remand in prison must also be taken into account in determining the overall length of a custodial sentence. The current rules are contained in s. 240 CJA 2003.

5.6.4 MAGISTRATES' COURT MAXIMUM CUSTODIAL SENTENCE

The length of any custodial sentence passed by a magistrates' court is subject to the statutory maximum of six months in respect of any one offence, unless the statute creating the offence prescribes a shorter period (s. 78 PCC(S)A 2000 and s. 133 MCA 1980). Magistrates can pass an aggregate sentence of 12 months upon conviction for two or more either-way offences (s. 133 MCA 1980). The minimum sentence of imprisonment a magistrates' court can impose is five days (s. 132 MCA 1980). Where, at the mode of trial enquiry or upon sentencing a defendant convicted of an either-way offence, the magistrates conclude their maximum custodial term of six months is insufficient, the court can of course commit the defendant to be sentenced in the Crown Court (ss. 3–4 PCC(S)A 2000).

As the current rules stand, where a court passes a custodial sentence of less than 12 months (which obviously covers the magistrates' court), half the sentence is served in custody (subject to early release schemes). For the remainder of the term, the offender is on licence in the community. If he commits a further offence whilst on licence he can be ordered to return to custody to serve the balance of the original sentence. The rules for serving a custodial sentence of less than 12 months will change if the sentence of 'custody plus' in the CJA 2003 is brought into force (see para. 26.8 below)

 Looking Ahead

You are reminded that under s. 154 CJA 2003, magistrates' powers of sentence are set to significantly increase (see Chapter 25, para. 25.9.4) There is currently no scheduled date for implementation.

26.7 FIXED LENGTH SENTENCES

In some cases the length of a custodial sentence is fixed by law. This applies to conviction for murder and mandatory minimum sentences (under ss. 110 and 111 PCC(S) A 2000) for a third conviction in connection with Class A drug trafficking and burglary. Mandatory minimum periods also apply in relation to certain firearms offences. In relation to each of these, a court is required to impose the minimum statutory term unless it would be unjust to do so. Where the offender has been assessed as a 'dangerous' offender within s. 226 CJA 2003 (see below), a mandatory sentence of life or an indeterminate sentence for public protection must be passed.

The requirement to give credit for a timely guilty plea under s. 144 CJA 2003 applies to the minimum custodial terms that have to be imposed under ss. 110 and 111 PCC(S) A 2000. Section 144 (2) CJA 2003 stipulates that the maximum reduction for a guilty plea shall be 20 per cent of the determinate sentence of at least three years which would otherwise have been imposed.

26.8 'NEW' CUSTODIAL SENTENCES UNDER THE CJA 2003

The CJA 2003 has introduced the new custodial sentences of 'custody plus', and 'custody minus'.

26.8.1 'CUSTODY PLUS' (S. 181)—NOT IN FORCE

'Custody plus' is the label given to all custodial sentences imposed for a term of less than 12 months and is tied to the increase in magistrates courts' sentencing powers which has yet to be implemented (see Chapter 25, para. 25.9.4).

This new sentence seeks to address a common criticism of short custodial sentences (less than 12 months), which is that there is no supervision of offenders on their release from prison. Under the present arrangements there is usually no opportunity for the Probation Service to work with the offender to deal with the reason for their offending behaviour.

The 'custody plus' sentence must be passed where a court sentences an offender to a custodial sentence of less than 12 months and it applies in the magistrates' courts and the Crown Court.

The term of the sentence must be expressed in weeks and must be for a minimum of 28 weeks, and not more than 51 weeks, in respect of any one offence. If two or more periods of imprisonment are imposed to run consecutively, the maximum aggregate term is 65 weeks.

The court must specify jail time of between two weeks and 13 weeks (26 weeks, if two or more terms of imprisonment are to run consecutively). The court must specify a licence period (which is the remainder of the total term less the maximum permitted cumulative custodial period), which must be for at least 26 weeks. During the licence period the offender will be expected to work with his probation officer. The court will also impose any licence conditions recommended by the probation service in its pre-sentence report with which the offender must comply. Conditions could include an unpaid work requirement (s. 199), an activity requirement (s. 201), a programme requirement (s. 202), a prohibited activity requirement (s. 203), a curfew requirement (s. 204), an exclusion requirement (s. 205), a supervision requirement (s. 213) and, in the case of an offender under 25, an attendance centre requirement (s. 214). Some of these conditions must be supported by an electronic tagging requirement. A failure to comply with licence conditions may lead to the licence conditions being revoked and the offender being recalled to prison.

The SGC has issued draft guidance on the custody plus provisions. The guidance is available at: www.sentencing-guidelines.gov.uk.

 Example

Damian is given a 32-week sentence. He must serve at least 26 weeks on licence. In terms of the custodial element, the court can impose a term of between two and six weeks. Therefore it could require Damian to serve six weeks in custody and 26 weeks on licence, making a total of 32 weeks.

 online resource centre

The custody plus provisions in relation to custodial terms of less than 12 months are significant. Should the decision be taken to implement them, we will of course bring it to you via the update section of our Online Resource Centre.

26.8.2 SENTENCES OF 12 MONTHS OR MORE (IMPLEMENTED APRIL 2005)

The CJA 2003 draws a distinction between custodial terms of less than 12 months and custodial terms of more than 12 months. In relation to custodial terms of 12 months or more, relevant provisions are contained in ss. 237–268.

A prison sentence of 12 months or more is served in full, although half the sentence is served on licence in the community. In passing sentence, the court will be able to recommend certain licence requirements, although they will not be binding on the Probation Service. The Probation Service will be able to attach specific requirements to the second half of the custodial sentence to prevent reoffending and to protect the public. A failure to abide by the requirements will result in the offender being recalled to custody. The provisions do not apply to 'dangerous' offenders or to those offenders subject to extended sentences.

6.8.3   **SENTENCING DANGEROUS OFFENDERS**

Sections 224–230 CJA 2003 introduced significant changes with regard to 'dangerous' offenders.

The provisions apply to adults as well as youth offenders (those under the age of 18). The application of the dangerousness provisions in relation to youth offenders is considered in Chapter 31. The provisions apply to 'specified' and 'serious' offences.

A 'specified offence' is an offence of violence or a sexual offence specified in Sch. 15 of the Act and which carries a sentence of between two and ten years imprisonment. A 'serious offence' is a violent or sexual offence specified in Sch. 15 which carries a sentence of at least ten or more years imprisonment in the case of an adult.

A surprising number of offences are listed in Sch. 15. Some of the offences are triable either way. In deciding whether to accept jurisdiction to try a defendant charged with an either-way offence or to sentence such an offender in the event of conviction, magistrates may need to have regard to the dangerous offender provisions under the CJA 2003. A sentence under the 'dangerousness' provisions can only be passed in the Crown Court.

A court is required to pass a life sentence or an indeterminate sentence for public protection for the most serious sexual and violent offenders who are considered to be dangerous and pose a risk to the public (s. 225 CJA 2003).

A life sentence, with a specified minimum term to be served in custody, is self-explanatory. A sentence for public protection is an indeterminate sentence. In relation to either sentence, a court is required to specify a minimum term which the offender must serve based on the seriousness of the offence (s. 143 CJA 2003). After this point, the offender must remain in custody until such time as the Parole Board decides it is safe for him to be released. Once released, the offender remains on licence indefinitely.

An extended sentence comprises two parts: a custodial sentence for the offence for such length as the seriousness of the offence demands (which must be at least 12 months), and an extended period on licence for such length as the court considers necessary to protect the public from serious harm. The licence period for a specified violent offence must not exceed five years. The licence period for a specified sexual offence must not exceed eight years. The total term must not exceed the maximum for the offence. Therefore, a court might consider the appropriate custodial term for a 'specified' offence to be two years. Providing an assessment of dangerous has been established, it could, for example, impose an extended licence period of three years in addition to the two-year custodial element, making it an extended sentence of five years in total.

Who qualifies for a life sentence or sentence for public protection? Section 225 applies where an offender is aged 18 or over and is convicted of a 'serious offence' AND the court considers that there is a significant risk to members of the public of serious harm (which includes death or serious personal/psychological injury) occasioned by the commission of further 'specified offences'.

Section 225(2) requires the court to impose a sentence of life imprisonment where the offence attracts a life sentence in any event AND the court is of the opinion that there is a significant risk to members of the public of serious harm occasioned by the commission of further 'specified offences'. If s. 225(2) does not apply, a sentence of imprisonment for public protection *must* be passed.

A court may give credit for a timely guilty plea and credit periods on remand, but only in relation to the specified minimum term. Provision for the early release of life prisoners is made in s. 82A PCC(S)A 2000. Early release (but not home detention curfew release) does apply to an extended sentence but release is not automatic at the halfway point. Release depends upon a decision being taken by the Parole Board that it is no longer necessary for the protection of the public that the offender be confined (s. 247 CJA).

Who qualifies for an extended sentence? Section 228 provides that where an offender is aged over 18 and is convicted of a 'specified offence' AND the court considers that there is a significant risk to members of the public of serious harm (which includes death or serious personal/psychological injury) occasioned by the commission of further 'specified offences', the court *must* impose an extended sentence of detention.

How is an offender assessed as being dangerous? Section 229 is all important. It provides that where an offender has not previously been convicted of a 'specified offence', the court:

- must take into account all such information as is available as to the nature and circumstances of the offence;
- may take into account any information it has about any pattern of behaviour of which any of the offences form part;
- may take into account any information it has before it about the offender.

Section 229(3) provides that where an offender has previously been convicted of a 'specified offence', the court MUST ASSUME that there is a risk of serious harm to the public, UNLESS, after taking into account the factors listed above, the court considers that it would be unreasonable to conclude there is such a risk.

It is the responsibility of the CPS to draw the court's attention to the possible application of the 'dangerousness' provisions. The pre-sentence report and any psychiatric report, as well as an offender's previous convictions and mental condition, will be pivotal in helping the court to determine whether someone is 'dangerous' within the meaning of s. 229.

The provisions are draconian and controversial. Important guidance on their application has been provided by the Court of Appeal in *R v Lang and Others* [2005] EWCA Crim 2864. Thirteen appeals were heard based on the 'dangerousness provisions'. In all but three cases the Court of Appeal varied the sentence either because it felt 'dangerousness' was not established on the facts, or the presumption in favour of a life sentence should have been rebutted or a sentence of public protection was more appropriate than a life sentence. The judgment contains the following guidance on the assessment of dangerous and consequential provisions:

'(i) The risk identified must be significant. This is a higher threshold than mere possibility of occurrence and in our view can be taken to mean (as in the Oxford Dictionary) "noteworthy, of considerable amount or importance."

(ii) In assessing the risk of further offences being committed, the sentencer should take into account the nature and circumstances of the current offence; the offender's history of offending including not just the kind of offence but its circumstances and the sentence passed, details of which the prosecution must have available, and, whether the offending demonstrates any pattern; social and economic factors in relation to the offender including accommodation, employability, education, associates, relationships and drug or alcohol abuse; and the offender's thinking, attitude towards offending and supervision and emotional state. Information in relation to these matters will most readily, though not exclusively, come from antecedents and pre-sentence probation and medical reports . . . . The sentencer will be guided, but not bound by, the assessment of risk in such reports . . .

(iii) If the foreseen specified offence is serious, there will clearly be some cases, though not by any means all, in which there may be a significant risk of serious harm. For example, robbery is a serious offence. But it can be committed in a wide variety of ways many of which do not give rise to a significant risk of serious harm. Sentencers must therefore guard against assuming there is a significant risk of serious harm merely because the foreseen specified offence is serious. A pre-sentence report should usually be obtained before any sentence is passed which is based on significant risk of serious harm. In a small number of cases, where the circumstances of the current offence or the history of the offender suggest mental abnormality on his part, a medical report may be necessary before risk can properly be assessed.

(iv) If the foreseen specified offence is not serious, there will be comparatively few cases in which a risk of serious harm will properly be regarded as significant. The huge variety of offences in Schedule 15 includes many which, in themselves, are not suggestive of serious harm. Repetitive violent or sexual offending at a relatively low level without serious harm does not of itself give rise to a significant risk of serious harm in the future. There may, in such cases, be some risk of future victims being more adversely affected than past victims but this, of itself, does not give rise to significant risk of serious harm.

(v) In relation to the rebuttable assumption to which section 229(3) gives rise, the court is accorded a discretion if, in the light of information about the current offence, the offender and his previous offences, it would be unreasonable to conclude that there is a significant risk. The exercise of such a discretion is, historically, at the very heart of judicial sentencing and the language of the statute indicates that judges are expected, albeit starting from the assumption, to exercise their ability to reach a reasonable conclusion in the light of the information before them. It is to be noted that the assumption will be rebutted, if at all, as an exercise of judgment: the statute includes no reference to the burden or standard of proof. As we have indicated above, it will usually be unreasonable to conclude that the assumption applies unless information about the offences, pattern of behaviour and offender show a significant risk of serious harm from further offences.

(vi) In relation to offenders under 18 and adults with no relevant previous convictions at the time the specified offence was committed, the court's discretion under section 229(2) is not constrained by any initial assumption such as, under section 229(3), applies to adults with previous convictions. It is still necessary, when sentencing young offenders, to bear in mind that, within a shorter time than adults, they may change and develop. This and their level of maturity may be highly pertinent when assessing what their future conduct may be and whether it may give rise to significant risk of serious harm.

(vii) In relation to a particularly young offender, an indeterminate sentence may be inappropriate even where a serious offence has been committed and there is a significant risk of serious harm from further offences (see for example, *R v D* [2005] EWCA Crim 2282).

(viii) It cannot have been Parliament's intention, in a statute dealing with the liberty of the subject, to require the imposition of indeterminate sentences for the commission of relatively minor offences.

(ix) Sentencers should usually, and in accordance with section 174(1)(a) of the Criminal Justice Act 2003, give reasons for all their conclusions: in particular, that there is or is not a significant risk of further offences or serious harm; where the assumption under section 229(3) arises for making or not making the assumption which the statute requires unless this would be unreasonable; and for not imposing an extended sentence under sections 227 and 228. Sentencers should, in giving reasons, briefly identify the information which they have taken into account.'

26.8.4 SUSPENDED SENTENCE OF IMPRISONMENT—OR 'CUSTODY MINUS'—S. 189 CJA 2003 (IN FORCE)

The power of a court to impose a suspended sentence of imprisonment changed in April 2005, with s. 189 CJA 2003. Prior to the change, a court could only suspend a sentence of imprisonment if there were 'exceptional circumstances' for doing so. This requirement has been removed, which means the suspended sentence can more easily be imposed.

Before a court can impose a suspended sentence the custody threshold test must be met. The offender must be aged 18 or over.

A court will be able to pass a suspended sentence where it imposes a term of imprisonment of at least 28 weeks but not more than 51 weeks (subject to the statutory maximum for a magistrates' court). Transitional provisions are currently in place to allow for the operation of s. 189 CJA, in relation to existing custodial sentences passed by magistrates' courts until the 'custody plus' provisions under the CJA 2003 come into force. The period of suspension can be between six months and two years. This new 'custody minus' sentence is designed to be a much more demanding sentence than the old suspended sentence, as the court must order the offender to undertake requirements in the community during the supervision period. The list of requirements is the same as that for a community order (see below). Any requirements must be commensurate with the seriousness of the offence. If the offender fails to comply with the requirements, or commits a further offence (whether or not punishable with imprisonment), the presumption will be that the suspended sentence will be activated.

Looking Ahead

Provision is made in the Criminal Justice and Immigration Act 2008 to amend s.189 CJA 2003 by abolishing the general power to pass a suspended sentence for a summary-only offence. As an exception, a suspended sentence may be imposed in connection with a summary offence where the court is also sentencing the offender in connection with an indictable offence.

26.9 CONCLUDING REMARKS ON CUSTODIAL SENTENCES

online
resource
centre

We end this section with reference to the guidance issued by the SGC on 'seriousness' which can be accessed at http://www.sentencing-guidelines.gov.uk. The SGC suggests at para. 1.33 that under the sentencing framework contained in the CJA 2003, the court should adopt the following structured approach to the imposition of custodial sentence:

(a) Has the custody threshold been passed?

(b) If so, is it unavoidable that a custodial sentence be imposed?

(c) If so, can that sentence be suspended?

(d) If not, impose a sentence which takes immediate effect for the shortest term commensurate with the seriousness of the offence.

26.10 COMMUNITY SENTENCES

As its name suggests a community sentence is served in the community. Courts are frequently encouraged to use community-based sentences as alternatives to a custodial sentence. They are commonly proposed by the Probation Service in pre-sentence reports.

The Criminal Justice Act 2003 has introduced significant changes to the structure and enforcement of community-based sentences. Courts now pass a generic community order with one or more specified requirements.

Contrary to popular perception, community-based sentences are very demanding and are rigorously enforced.

10.1 THE THRESHOLD FOR IMPOSING A COMMUNITY SENTENCE

As with custodial sentences, there is a threshold test for imposing a community order which must be met before a court can impose a community sentence. Section 148 Criminal Justice Act 2003 provides:

> 'A court shall not pass a community sentence on an offender unless it is of the opinion that the offence, or the combination of the offence and one or more associated offences with it, is serious enough to warrant such a sentence.'

In short, a community-based sentence can only be imposed for an offence which is considered to be 'serious enough' to warrant it.

Under s. 151 CJA 2003, provision is made for a court to impose a community sentence on an offender aged 16 or over who has been convicted by a court on three previous occasions after attaining the age of 16 and has had a fine imposed on him on each of those occasions but whose current offence does not fall within the community sentence threshold. This provision is aimed at persistent petty offenders.

10.2 IS THE OFFENCE SERIOUS ENOUGH?

In assessing whether an offence is serious enough to warrant a community sentence, the Magistrates' Court Sentencing Guidelines (2008) provide great assistance. If you consult the guidelines, you will see there are a number of offences, including theft from a person and handling stolen goods which suggest a sentencing range to include a community order. As previously indicated the balance of aggravating and mitigating features in the particular case may tilt the sentence down towards a fine or upwards beyond the community penalty threshold. The sentencing guidelines indicate the basic starting point.

6.11 COMMUNITY SENTENCES UNDER THE CJA 2003

Section 177 of the Act creates a single, generic community order which will impose one or more requirements on the offender. The community order is available for all offenders aged 16 or over and can last for up to three years.

The requirements that can be imposed under a community order include:

• unpaid work (defined s. 199);
• an activity requirement (defined s. 201);
• a programme requirement (defined s. 202);
• a prohibited activity requirement (defined s. 203);
• a curfew requirement (defined s. 204);
• an exclusion requirement (defined s. 205);
• a residence requirement (defined s. 206);
• a mental health requirement (defined s. 207);
• a drug rehabilitation requirement (defined s. 209);
• an alcohol treatment requirement (defined s. 221);
• a supervision requirement (defined s. 213); and/or
• in the case of an offender under 25, an attendance centre requirement (defined s. 214).

Where a court makes a community order imposing a curfew requirement or an exclusion requirement, the court must also impose an electronic monitoring requirement (s. 177(3)).

26.11.1 HOW WILL THE APPROPRIATE TYPE OF ORDER BE DETERMINED?

Section 148(3) CJA 2003 provides that where the court passes a community sentence:

'(a) the particular requirement or requirements forming part of the order must be such as, in the opinion of the court is, or taken together are, the most suitable for the offenders; and

(b) the restrictions on liberty imposed by the order . . . are commensurate with the seriousness of the offence, or the combination of the offence and one or more associated with it.'

In determining the requirements for a community order, the court will have regard to one or more of the sentencing objectives contained in s. 142(1) CJA 2003 (see Chapter 25, para. 25.4).

The seriousness of the offence and the risk of harm posed by the offender will determine the nature and combination of requirements and the intensity of those requirements.

Useful guidance on the operation of the 'new style' community order is provided by the SGC in its guidelines on the 'new' sentences under the CJA 2003 (http://www.sentencing-guidelines.gov.uk). The 'seriousness' of the offence is an important factor in deciding whether the court chooses a low, medium or high range of requirements. Proportionality and suitability will be the guiding principles.

Generally the guidelines suggest the lowest range of community sentence should be reserved for low level type of offences. Such an order might contain just one requirement for a short duration. The most requirements would be reserved for those offenders whose offences fall just short of the custodial threshold. The nature and severity of the requirements to be imposed should be guided by:

(i) the assessment of the offence's seriousness (low/medium/high);

(ii) the purpose(s) of sentencing the court wishes to achieve;

(iii) the risk of reoffending;

(iv) the ability of the offender to comply; and

(v) the availability of requirements in the local area.

The SGC publication includes a number of examples of the type of requirements that might be imposed based on an offence of low/medium/high seriousness.

The guidelines stress the importance of obtaining a pre-sentence report to help determine the particular requirements or combination of requirements in a specific case.

26.12 THE REQUIREMENTS

26.12.1 UNPAID WORK (S. 199 CJA 2003)

This is similar to the old community punishment order where the offender is required to perform unpaid work in the community under the supervision of a responsible officer. A court cannot impose an unpaid work requirement unless the court is satisfied that the offender is a suitable person to perform such work. For this reason, a court will invariably require a pre-sentence report to assess the offender's suitability.

The court's purpose when making a community order with an unpaid work requirement is to give the offender the chance to make amends to the community in which the offence has been committed. It is punitive in nature. A supervising officer oversees the community work placement. The work might involve painting, decorating or gardening for organisations or individuals.

The aggregate number of hours of unpaid work must not be less than 40 and not more than 300 hours. The number of hours imposed should be proportional to the level of seriousness of the offence(s) committed. An unpaid work requirement may of course be combined with any further requirement(s) as the court deems fit.

12.2 ACTIVITY REQUIREMENT (S. 201 CJA 2003)

This requires the offender to present himself at a specified place and participate in specified activities. A pre-sentence report will normally be required if the court is considering this as a requirement. The aggregate number of days of an activity order must not exceed 60.

The activities can include day centre attendance, education and basic skills training and reparation to victims with their consent.

12.3 PROGRAMME REQUIREMENT (S. 202 CJA 2003)

An offender would be required to participate in an activity programme which has been accredited by a body established by the Secretary of State. A pre-sentence report would be required in order to check the offender's suitability and the availability of such an accredited programme.

Under the old community rehabilitation order, the Probation Service regularly specified offending behaviour programmes as part of the order. The aims of these programmes are to:

• make offenders accept responsibility for their offences;

• avoid further offending;

• attempt to resolve any difficulties linked to offending behaviour, e.g. homelessness, marital or relationship breakdown, unemployment, illiteracy, addiction.

Such programmes have traditionally included:

• Enhanced Thinking Skills Programme. This requires the offender to participate in group work with a view to enabling poorly educated offenders to attain basic literacy and numeracy skills.

• Sex Offender Programme. This is aimed at offenders convicted of sexual offences who have been assessed as suitable for the programme.

• Drink Impaired Drivers Programme. This is aimed primarily at offenders convicted of drink-driving offences.

A programme requirement will invariably be combined with a supervision requirement (undertaken by a probation officer) under the community order.

12.4 PROHIBITED ACTIVITY REQUIREMENT (S. 203 CJA 2003)

This requires the offender to refrain from participating in specified activities named in the order on any day or days specified during the requirement period. The requirements that may be included in a prohibited activity requirement are not limited and may include the prohibition of activities that would otherwise be lawful. Possibilities include prohibiting the defendant from visiting a particular place, for example nightclubs, or undertaking a particular activity such as driving, drinking alcohol, attending football matches.

12.5 CURFEW REQUIREMENT (S. 204 CJA 2003)

A curfew requires a convicted offender to stay at an agreed address for a specified time of between two and 12 hours, e.g. between 7 pm and 7 am for a period of between one and seven days. A curfew can be imposed for a total of six months.

Curfew orders are enforced by electronic 'tagging', and are a different way of restricting an offender's liberty in a way that is like being put under 'house arrest'. Being tagged can make it harder for an offender to commit further crimes and can help to break patterns of offending behaviour by forcing the offender to stay at the specified address.

A tag is attached to the offender's wrist or ankle and is linked to a monitoring machine installed in the place where the offender is living. The machine is linked via a telephone line to a monitoring centre. Staff at the monitoring centre are immediately aware if the curfew is broken.

In imposing a curfew requirement, the court will take account of the offender's religious beliefs, employment or attendance at an educational establishment and its compatibility with any other requirements imposed as part of the community order. A pre-sentence report may well be required in order for the court to be satisfied that suitable accommodation is available to the offender.

26.12.6 EXCLUSION REQUIREMENT (S. 205 CJA 2003)

This directs the offender not to enter a place or an area specified in the order. An exclusion requirement must not exceed two years and will be monitored electronically. The order can provide for the prohibition to operate only during specified periods and may specify different periods or days during the order.

26.12.7 RESIDENCE REQUIREMENT (S. 206 CJA 2003)

This requires the offender to reside at a place specified in the order. It could include a hostel or institution recommended by a probation officer.

26.12.8 MENTAL HEALTH TREATMENT REQUIREMENT (S. 207 CJA 2003)

Rehabilitative in nature, a mental health requirement requires the offender to submit to treatment by a medical practitioner or psychologist. The treatment may be as a resident patient. Before a court can impose such requirement it must be satisfied that the offender is susceptible to treatment. The offender must express a willingness to comply.

26.12.9 DRUG REHABILITATION REQUIREMENT (S. 208 CJA 2003)

A DRR involves assessment and treatment for drug dependency. The treatment and testing period must be a minimum of six months and a maximum of three years. Before a court can impose a drug treatment requirement, it must be satisfied the defendant is dependent on drugs and is susceptible to treatment. The defendant must consent to the order. The pre-sentence report must include an assessment from a treatment provider and a place must be available to the defendant. The defendant is subject to regular review by the court and the court may impose a testing requirement on the defendant. A DRR is a high-intensity community order designed to get the offender to look at and change his or her drug use, thereby reducing his or her offending. Such an order would involve frequent drug testing and a high level of contact and supervision coupled with a regular monthly review by the courts.

Guidance on the use of drug testing and treatment orders (the predecessor of the DRR) was provided by the Court of Appeal in *Attorney-General's Reference No. 64 of 2003* [2004] 2 Cr App R(S) 106.

26.12.10 ALCOHOL TREATMENT REQUIREMENT (S. 212 CJA 2003)

This requirement provides a means by which courts can specifically respond to offenders who are dependant on alcohol and whose dependency requires and may respond to treatment.

The offender must be willing to comply with the requirement. The treatment can be given as a resident or non-resident of an appropriate institution. The period of treatment cannot be for less than six months.

2.11 **SUPERVISION REQUIREMENT (S. 213 CJA 2003)**

This requirement is similar to the old community rehabilitation order. Under the terms of a supervision requirement the offender must, during the relevant period, attend appointments with the responsible probation officer at times and places determined by the officer. The purpose of the supervision requirement is to promote the offender's rehabilitation.

2.12 **ATTENDANCE CENTRE REQUIREMENT (WHERE OFFENDER IS AGED UNDER 25) (S. 214 CJA 2003)**

An attendance centre requirement obliges the offender to attend at a centre for between 12 and 36 hours. Attendance is limited to one occasion a day and for not more than three hours at any one time. The attendance centre must be reasonably accessible to the offender.

6.13 **GUILTY PLEA CREDIT AND COMMUNITY ORDERS**

Section 144 CJA 2003 should not be forgotten (see Chapter 25, para. 25.8). Credit should be given for a timely guilty plea. Where a community sentence is to be imposed, the court should take account of s. 144 CJA 2003. This may be reflected in the number of requirements or duration of requirements under a community order. In its definitive guidelines on s. 144, the SGC suggests that, where an offence crosses the threshold for imposing a community sentence, the application of the reduction principle may properly form the basis for imposing a fine or discharge instead.

6.14 **ENFORCEMENT OF COMMUNITY ORDERS UNDER THE CJA 2003—SCH. 8**

The court will explain the consequence of the offender's failure to comply with a community order. An offender can breach a community order by failing to comply with its requirements or by committing further offences while subject to a community order.

More stringent measures have been put in place to deal with breaches of community orders. The Probation Service will issue a single warning about a failure to comply. Thereafter, any further failure will result in breach proceedings being commenced against the offender. The Probation Service can apply to have the order revoked. This will require the offender to be brought back before the court. In dealing with an offender for breaching the requirements, the court must take into account the extent to which the offender has complied with the order.

The court has a range of powers including imposing more onerous requirements on the existing order; revoke the order if it is in the interest of justice to do so and resentence the offender for the original offence and in the case of an offender aged over 18 (who was convicted of an imprisonable offence in the first instance and has wilfully and persistently failed to comply with the requirements of the order), the court may impose a prison sentence not exceeding six months.

In its guidelines, the SGC cautions that, in dealing with a breach of a community sentence, the primary objective should be to ensure that the requirements of the sentence are finished. In other words, custody should be the last resort, reserved for those who deliberately and repeatedly breach the requirements of their order.

26.15 DEFERMENT OF SENTENCE—SS. 1 AND 2 PCC(S)A 2000

Section 1:

'The Crown Court or magistrates' court may defer passing sentence on an offender for the purposes of enabling the court, or any court to which it falls to deal with him, to have regard in dealing with him to . . .

(a) his conduct after conviction (including, where appropriate, the making by him of reparation for his offence) or;

(b) any change in his circumstances . . .'

Deferment can only be imposed with the offender's consent and if it is in the interests of justice to do so, having regard to the nature of the offence and the character and circumstances of the defendant.

Deferment may be for up to six months and results in an adjournment of the proceedings. The power to defer sentence is most appropriately exercised where there has been an offer by the offender to make reparation to his victim or a change is expected in the offender's life which may produce a stabilising influence, e.g. a job/marriage.

The power to defer should be exercised sparingly. In accordance with Sch. 23 to the CJA 2003 (which came into force in April 2005) courts will be able to impose requirements on the offender (similar to those imposed on a community order) during the period of deferment, including, if appropriate, supervision by a probation officer. If the court is satisfied that the offender has failed to comply with one or more requirements, the offender can be brought back to court to be sentenced. The expectation is that, if the offender stays out of trouble and does what is required of him by the court, he will not then receive a custodial sentence for the offence for which he has been convicted.

26.16 FINES

A fine is very frequently imposed, particularly in magistrates' courts. The power to impose a financial penalty is contained in ss. 126–129 PCC(S)A 2000. Fines are suitable punishment for offences which are not serious enough to merit a community sentence, nor so serious that a custodial sentence must be considered. A high fine can be regarded as a sentence of a punitive nature and may, in certain circumstances, deter an offender from repeating a course of conduct.

Magistrates' courts can impose a maximum fine of £5,000 per offence (subject to the statutory maximum for the offence, if it is less) and subject to the principle of totality, discussed in Chapter 25 in the context of consecutive custodial sentences. The Crown Court's power to impose a fine is unlimited.

Section 164 CJA 2003 is important. It provides:

'(1) Before fixing the amount of any fine to be imposed on an offender who is an individual, a court shall inquire into his financial circumstances,

(2) The amount of any fine fixed by the court shall be such as, in the opinion of the court, reflects the seriousness of the offence.

(3) In fixing the amount of any fine to be imposed on an offender (whether an individual or other person), a court shall take into account the circumstances of the case including, among other things, the financial circumstances of the offender so far as they are known, or appear, to the court . . .'

Power exists under s. 162 CJA 2003 for a court to make a financial circumstances order requiring the offender to make disclosure of his means. It is not a power that is exercised frequently.

It is good practice to obtain a written statement of your client's means which can be handed to the court. Alternatively, the defence advocate should at least have in his possession a full breakdown of his client's income and outgoings.

The Magistrates' Court Sentencing Guidelines (MCSGs) (2008), are a very useful source of information on financial penalties. Some offences in the guidelines have a fine as the initial starting point when passing sentence. For the purposes of the MCSGs (2008), a fine is based on one of three bands (A, B or C). The choice of band is determined by the court's assessment of the overall seriousness of the offence based on aggravating and mitigating features of the offence.

- Band A fine is assessed on the basis of 50 per cent of weekly income.
- Band B fine is assessed on the basis of 100 per cent of weekly income.
- Band C fine is assessed on the basis of 150 per cent of weekly income.

Having decided that a fine is the correct sentence and having determined the band level, the magistrates' court must then determine the amount of the fine taking into account the offender's individual circumstances and applying any relevant discount for a guilty plea. The revised 2008 MCSGs include detailed guidance on the definition of relevant weekly income; low income and high income offenders, and commercially motivated offences. Two new bands are introduced (D and E) to provide assistance to a court in calculating a fine where the offence otherwise warrants a community order (Band D) or a custodial sentence (Band E) but the court has decided that a financial penalty is appropriate.

 Example

X pleads guilty to an offence of careless driving. X is driving too quickly in wet conditions and fails to notice a pedestrian stepping into the road. X applies her brakes but collides with the pedestrian causing minor injury. Applying the MCSGs (2008) (Appendix 3), the starting point for a fine is band B. X has a weekly income of £200. X can expect a fine in the region of £200. Consideration will, however, be given to X's means and a deduction of around one third will be made for X's timely guilty plea. Varying the facts slightly, assume X was using a mobile phone which explains why she was not keeping a proper lookout. Under the guidelines, this would be regarded as an aggravating feature which could push the starting point in terms of a fine up to band C, resulting in a larger fine for X. X will be ordered to pay a victims' surcharge (see below).

Financial penalties (including fines/compensation orders/victims' surcharge/prosecution costs) may be paid by instalment. The Courts Act 2003, Sch. 5 has introduced a new regime for the collection and enforcement of fines for offenders over the age of 18. Where a financial penalty cannot be discharged immediately, a fines collection order will be made. The means and rate of payment is determined by a fines collection officer. The officers are empowered under the Fines Collection Regulations 2004 to take enforcement proceedings in the event of default. Enforcement measures include making an attachment or earnings order or deduction from benefits, an increase in the overall fine and even the clamping and sale of vehicles. In due course, fines may be discharged by means of unpaid work. Fine defaulters have a right to seek variation of the order and right of appeal to the magistrates' court. A fines officer may refer enforcement back to the magistrates' court where all previous enforcement attempts have failed. A magistrates' court can remit whole or part of the fine, though not compensation, and/or order detention in the precincts of the court as a means of discharging the debt. Where all other enforcement methods have been tried or are inappropriate, a court can order custody in default, but only in strictly defined circumstances.

A fine can be imposed (and usually is imposed) as a sentence in its own right. It can, however, be combined with a community order, a compensation order and with disqualification from driving. It cannot be combined with a discharge as a means of sentence for a single offence. In theory, a fine can be combined with a sentence of imprisonment. In practice, however, this would be rare, as imprisonment is likely to deprive the offender of his ability to pay.

26.16.1 VICTIM SURCHARGE

Whenever a court imposes a fine in respect of an offence committed after the 1 April 2007, it must order the offender to pay a victim surcharge on current figures of £15.

26.17 COMPENSATION ORDERS

It is a legitimate expectation for a victim of a criminal offence to receive compensation for any injury, loss or damage suffered as a result of a convicted individual's actions. The governing section is s. 130 PCC(S)A 2000. The section imposes a duty on the court to order compensation unless it gives reasons for not doing so. It is immaterial whether the victim has made an application for compensation.

Magistrates can award compensation of up to £5,000 per offence. In the Crown Court, the amounts are unlimited. The MCSGs contain a table of guideline compensation awards for personal injury. In fixing the level of compensation, the offender's means must be taken into account. Priority is given to compensation orders over victims' surcharge; fines and prosecution costs.

 Example 1

X is convicted of assault. The victim sustains a broken nose requiring some manipulation. Based on the guidelines, X can expect to be ordered to pay compensation in the region of £1,000–£1,500. Clearly, if X is in receipt of welfare benefits this sum will be vastly reduced.

 Example 2

X is convicted of resisting a police constable in the execution of his duty. The officer falls to the floor during the arrest, sustaining bruising to both knees. The court is considering a fine for the offence. Compensation in the region of £50–£100 may well be ordered. If X is in receipt of welfare benefits and cannot afford to pay a fine as well as compensation, the court will give priority to the compensation element.

 Example 3

X is convicted of criminal damage. He pleads guilty to breaking a door. The cost of replacing the door is estimated at £500. X can expect to be asked to pay some or all of this sum by way of compensation, depending on his means.

Compensation can be awarded for psychological injury. It does not matter whether the injured party is an individual or a company.

Where injury or damage has occurred through a road traffic offence, compensation is not awarded by the courts. Such compensation is left to compulsory driving insurance schemes. If the offender is uninsured and the Motor Insurance Bureau will not cover the loss, an award can be made in these circumstances.

The prosecution should normally have compensation details to hand at the point of sentencing. Where personal injury has resulted, the CPS should have the necessary details, including photographic evidence in some instances. Where damage has occurred the court will expect to see an invoice for repairs or an estimate for replacement.

Where a defendant disputes the amount of compensation requested, the court will hear representations. If the matter is incapable of being resolved, the question of compensation may have to be adjourned for further enquiries to be made or a possible 'Newton' hearing (see Chapter 25, para. 25.14).

Where there is more than one individual responsible for an offence giving rise to the injury, loss or damage, the court has discretion as to how apportionment should be made. Each offender's culpability will be taken into account, as will their individual ability to pay.

Can the court order compensation when it sends the offender to prison? It is not the usual practice in magistrates' courts to require a defendant to pay compensation where he or she is sentenced to a period in custody for the offence. Having said this, there is no written rule to this effect. Indeed on occasions, the Court of Appeal has stated that such an order is not wrong in principle providing the court is satisfied the offender has the means to pay or will have sufficient earning capacity when released from prison (*R v Jonge* [1999] 2 Cr App R (S) 1).

26.18 **CONDITIONAL DISCHARGE**

A conditional discharge may be imposed in accordance with the requirements under s. 12 PCC(S)A 2000. Such a sentence is common in magistrates' courts but can also be imposed by a Crown Court. The offender can be conditionally discharged for a period of up to three years. There is no minimum period specified.

It must be explained to the defendant that, if he does not reoffend during the period of the conditional discharge, he will not be punished for the offence for which he has been convicted. However, if he is convicted of a further offence, especially if it is of a like nature, the conditional discharge can be revoked. If this were to happen, the defendant would be sentenced not only in connection with the new matter, but could also be resentenced for the offence for which he received the conditional discharge.

A conditional discharge therefore has a deterrent element. It would not be imposed for a serious offence, but it is particularly suitable for first-time offenders, and those who may not have offended in the recent past whose offence is not serious enough to warrant a community sentence. A conditional discharge is usually passed as a sentence in its own right but can be combined with an award of compensation and/or costs.

26.19 **ABSOLUTE DISCHARGE**

An absolute discharge may be imposed under s. 12 PCC(S)A 2000—although the sentence is rarely passed. In effect, the defendant is not being punished, although the conviction is recorded against him. It might be imposed on a defendant who, though technically guilty, is morally blameless, or in connection with a very trivial offence. In respect of the latter, questions might be asked of the Crown Prosecution Service about why the prosecution was brought in the first place.

26.20 **BIND OVER**

The bind over is an ancient power possessed by the criminal courts. The imposition of a bind over does not rank as a conviction. The power to bind over can arise either on complaint or of the court's own motion under common law powers. The power was restated in s. 1(7) Justices of the Peace Act 1968. It enables a magistrates' court to bind over an individual to keep the Queen's peace for a specified period of time and in a sum of money. It can be imposed where the court is satisfied that there has been a breach of the peace or there is a real risk of a breach in the future. The offender must consent to be bound over. No money is taken from the offender but it must be explained to him that, if he fails to keep the peace, he will be required to forfeit all or part of the sum specified. In court, it would be expressed in the following way:

> Chair: 'Stand up—You will be bound over in the sum of £100 for a period of 12 months to keep the peace towards *X*. This means that you do not have to pay any money now. But if you break the order, you can be ordered to pay all or part of that sum. Do you agree to be bound over?'
> Defendant: 'Yes . . .'

In practice, a bind over is a matter of negotiation between the defence and the prosecution. They are most commonly imposed in connection with less serious matters such as minor domestic disputes or disputes between neighbours which have resulted in court proceedings. In these cases, the defendant may feel aggrieved that he is the one being prosecuted when others might be regarded as being equally culpable. The offer of a bind over may therefore be the most pragmatic way of resolving the proceedings. The substantive offence which led the defendant to appear before the magistrates is then withdrawn when a bind over is imposed. The precise terms of the bind over must be explained. This could include refraining from specified types of conduct or activities.

A bind over might also be offered to an offender of previous good character who has been involved in a minor public order incident where, for example, he has been involved in a drunken disturbance at a hotel.

If the defendant does not consent to the bind over and pleads not guilty to the substantive offence a trial date will be fixed and the matter tried. The benefits of a bind over ought to be explained to the defendant, as a guilty verdict will result in a criminal record and most probably an order that the defendant pays the prosecution's costs.

26.21 ANCILLARY ORDERS

26.21.1 PROSECUTION COSTS

It is common for courts to award some or all of the prosecution's costs in the event of a conviction although priority is given to the payment of compensation orders and fines.

R v Northallerton Magistrates' Court, ex p. Dove [2000] 1 Cr App R (S) 136 provides the guidance on awarding prosecution costs:

- The purpose of an award is to compensate the prosecution and not to punish the defendant.

- An award should not exceed the sum which the prosecutor has actually and reasonably incurred.

- Account must be taken of the offender's ability to pay, particularly having regard to any other financial penalties to be imposed, i.e. compensation/fine.

The amount sought by the prosecution depends on the nature of the offence and the degree of preparation that the prosecutor has had to undertake. The court may order all or part of the costs asked for or make no order as to payment.

26.21.2 CONFISCATION AND FORFEITURE

We make brief mention of confiscation and forfeiture. The detail falls outside the scope of this text. The provisions are contained in the Proceeds of Crime Act 2002 and are notoriously complex. The Act gives the Crown Court powers to confiscate assets which are the result of the particular criminal conduct of which the defendant has been convicted. The most obvious example of this would be the proceeds of drug trafficking. However, the Act also permits a court to confiscate assets which it believes have been acquired as a result of general criminal conduct in circumstances where the offender is enjoying a 'criminal lifestyle'. There is a protracted procedure requiring the prosecution to provide a statement of information to which the defendant must respond. The provisions are not restricted to particular offences and can apply whenever a defendant is convicted before a Crown Court or if the defendant has been committed to the Crown Court for sentence. Although the court of its own motion can initiate the process, the application is likely to be made by the prosecution.

Section 143 PCC(S)A 2000 gives a court the power to order forfeiture of any property lawfully seized from the defendant (or which is in his possession or under his control at the time he was apprehended) which has been used for the purpose of committing or facilitating the commission of an offence or which was intended by him to be used for such purpose. In utilising this power, a court should have regard to the totality of sentence for the particular offence. Provision is included in s. 145 PCC(S)A 2000 to allow the sale of property connected with an offence in order to pay compensation to the victim, but only where the offender's means are such that he would otherwise not be in a position to discharge the compensation figure.

6.21.3 ANTI-SOCIAL BEHAVIOUR ORDERS

ASBOs can be made on a civil application or as an ancillary order after conviction in a criminal case, most usually at the invitation of the prosecutor. The power to impose an ASBO in criminal proceedings is contained in s. 1 Crime and Disorder Act 1998 and the Anti-Social Behaviour Act 2003. The behaviour complained of must be anti-social in that it causes alarm, harassment or distress. The minimum duration of an ASBO is two years. There is no specified maximum.

A court should only make an order for as long as it considers necessary to protect the community from the named offender. The prohibitions expressed in the order must be specific in time and place and must be necessary to protect the public from further anti-social acts by the defendant in the locality. They must be reasonable and proportionate, clear, concise and enforceable. Guidance on the imposition of an ASBO in criminal proceedings was recently provided by the Court of Appeal in the case of *R v Parkin* [2004] Crim LR 490:

'In our judgment the following principles clearly emerge:
(1) The test for making an order is one of necessity to protect the public from further anti-social acts by the offender.
(2) The terms of the order must be precise and capable of being understood by the offender.
(3) The findings of fact giving rise to the making of the order must be recorded.
(4) The order must be explained to the offender.
(5) The exact terms of the order must be pronounced in open court and the written order must accurately reflect the order as pronounced. '

For an account of best practice in relation to ASBOs, consult the Home Office Guide to Anti-Social Behaviour Orders http://www.crimereduction.homeoffice.gov.uk/antisocialbehaviour/antisocialbehaviour55.htm

6.21.4 SEX OFFENDERS' REGISTER—NOTIFICATION REQUIREMENTS

Under the Sex Offenders Act 1997, the requirement to register is mandatory where an offender is convicted of a specified sexual offence. Under the Sexual Offences Act 2003, the requirement to register has become a requirement to notify. The defendant must notify the police at a specified police station within three days of the notification order being made, or within three days of being released, if the defendant is sent to prison for the sex offence. The defendant must inform the police of his name, date of birth and home address and of any later change of address or absence from the country. The minimum period of notification is for five years (two years for a caution), increasing to ten years depending on the sentence imposed.

Other ancillary orders that can be imposed include football banning orders; restraining orders and deportation in some instances. More details can be researched in *Blackstone's Criminal Practice*.

KEY POINT SUMMARY

- A custodial sentence is the most draconian sentence a court can pass.
- For a custodial sentence to be imposed, the custody threshold test defined in s. 152 CJA 2003 must be met.
- The threshold test under the CJA 2003 requires the offence to be so serious that neither a fine alone, nor a community order, can be justified.
- The duration of a custodial sentence must be commensurate with the seriousness of the offence.
- A custodial sentence can be immediate or suspended.
- Under the CJA 2003, a distinction is drawn between sentences of less than 12 months and more than 12 months. Sentences of 12 months or more are 'served in full' with the second half of the sentence served in the community. Sentences of less than 12 months will include post-release supervision in the community.
- A suspended sentence may only be imposed where the custody threshold test is met. The offender will have one or more requirements imposed upon him to complete during the period of suspension.
- The threshold test for a community sentence is whether the offence is 'serious enough'. Community sentences involve one or more requirements based on the seriousness of the overall offending behaviour.
- Understand the range of sentencing options available to a court and the requisite criteria for each of them.
- Try to formulate a realistic sentencing objective for your client having regard to the offence your client has committed and the range of sentencing disposals available to the court.
- Try to think in terms of the worst case scenario for your client, and what you feel you can and would realistically like to achieve.
- If a custodial sentence is a distinct possibility, consider whether the custody threshold test is met: be prepared to cite supporting case law on this. Consider whether a community penalty might be a constructive alternative to custody.
- Given that a financial penalty is common, be sure to have a statement of means from your client and be prepared to make appropriate representations based on your client's means.
- Anticipate an ancillary order such as prosecution costs.
- All of the above underscore the importance of researching the penalties for the offence you are considering and any specific sentencing guidelines.

SELF-TEST QUESTIONS

1. Explain the basis upon which a court can sentence a convicted prisoner to a term of imprisonment.
2. What principles determine the length of a custodial sentence?
3. What types of custodial terms may be imposed?
4. Consider the short scenarios below and try to answer the following questions:
   - What sentence do you feel the court is likely to pass, and why? Research the applicable sentencing guidelines.
   - If you were the defence solicitor, what would you hope to persuade the court to do in terms of sentence?

Exercise 1

Celia appears in court represented by the duty solicitor. She pleads guilty to stealing a gold bracelet worth £150 from a counter display. Without trying to conceal anything she picked up the bracelet, tried it on her wrist and left the shop without paying, prompting the sales assistant to call shop security. She was stopped a few yards from the shop and admitted the theft. When interviewed by the police, she was co-operative but very tearful and frightened as to what her husband would say. She has no idea why she took the item. She had her credit cards on her at the time and could have paid.

Celia is married. She is 52. She has two grown-up children who live away from the family home. Her husband is a well-respected professional person. Celia has no employment. She has rheumatoid arthritis and has felt depressed of late. Celia is well thought of in her community and is an active member of a number of charitable concerns. Six months ago, Celia was conditionally discharged for 12 months for stealing items of underwear from a department store. She is in breach of this order by virtue of the current offence.

 Exercise 2

Louise pleads guilty to theft. She worked as a trainee in a hairdresser's shop. She had access to the till and took small amounts (£150 in total) over a period of several weeks. The thefts caused a bad atmosphere as everyone in the salon was under suspicion. Louise says she took the money because an acquaintance was putting pressure on her to repay a debt. She says she fully intended to repay the money from her tips. Louise is 18, has no previous convictions and pleads guilty at the first opportunity. She is now unemployed and receiving income support and housing benefit. She lives in a bed-sit.

 Exercise 3

Andrew was found cultivating five cannabis plants in his bedroom. He says he was growing them for personal use and for the use of his disabled partner who suffers from a chronic illness and finds the effects alleviate some of her discomfort. Andrew pleaded guilty at the first opportunity. He has several previous convictions for theft and possession of drugs. Andrew and his partner receive invalidity benefit of £130 per week.

 Exercise 4

Darren is charged with assaulting a police constable in the execution of his duty. Darren and some of his friends had been celebrating their team's win. They had been drinking and were rowdy. They were stopped by police on the High Street who asked them to calm down. While most of the youths dispersed, Darren entered into an argument with one of the police officers. A scuffle ensued in which the police officer fell over. While the officer lay on the ground, he was kicked several times by Darren. The officer suffered bruising to his face and left arm. A pre-sentence report assesses Darren's risk of reoffending as being medium. It highlights Darren's alcohol consumption as being the motivation for the offence. Darren is deemed suitable for a community sentence including an unpaid work requirement.

Darren is 21 and has a previous conviction for possession of an offensive weapon. He completed a community order with a 60-hour unpaid work requirement for this last year. He pleads guilty to the assault on the officer and expresses his remorse. Darren is employed as a shop assistant and brings home £150 per week. He will lose his job if sent to prison. He lives with his mother and gives her £25 per week towards his keep. He owns a car and therefore has related car expenditure.

FIGURE 26.1 THE CONDITIONS FOR IMPOSING A CUSTODIAL SENTENCE ON AN ADULT

- A custodial sentence may only be imposed if the threshold test is satisfied where:
  - the offence, or combination of offences; or associated offences;
  - is so 'serious' that neither a fine alone nor a community sentence can be justified, s. 152(2) CJA 2003; or
  - where the offender fails to consent to a requirement to be included in a community order.
- See *R v Howells* for a judicial interpretation of the 'seriousness' test.
- Discount for pleading guilty will be applied (s. 144 CJA 2003).
- The length of custody should be commensurate with the seriousness of the offence, s. 153(2) CJA 2003.
- The length of custodial sentences passed by a magistrates' court is restricted compared to the Crown Court.
- The court should give reasons in open court for imposing the sentence passed, s. 174(2) CJA 2003.
- Before deciding to suspend a prison sentence, the custody threshold test must be met.
- Time spent on remand shall count as time served when imposing a custodial sentence, s. 240 CJA 2003.

Custodial sentences up to 12 months when in force will be passed as:

- custody plus, s.181 CJA 2003;
- custody plus will be for a specified term after which the offender will be released on licence for at least 26 weeks – the licence may be subject to conditions;
- currently, a magistrates' court can pass a maximum custodial sentence of six months (12 months for two or more either-way offences);
- custodial sentences can be suspended for a period of between six months and two years and requirements will be imposed on the offender during the period of suspension.

Custodial sentences of more than 12 months under the CJA 2003

- Half custodial term spent in custody and half spent on licence.
- Probation service will attach conditions to the licence period.
- Where released on licence, offender can be drug tested to ensure compliance with licence conditions, s. 266 CJA 2003.

FIGURE 26.2 NON-CUSTODIAL SENTENCES

COMMUNITY SENTENCES UNDER THE CJA 2003

- Imposed where the court is satisfied the:

  - offence; or
  - combination of offences; or
  - associated offences;

  is 'serious enough' to warrant it, s. 148(1) CJA 2003.

- Section 177 CJA 2003 creates a single community sentence which will impose one or more requirements on the offender, e.g.
  - unpaid work, s. 199 CJA 2003;
  - curfew requirement, s. 204 CJA 2003;
  - exclusion requirement, s. 205 CJA 2003;
  - residence requirement, s. 206 CJA 2003;
  - drug and/or alcohol rehabilitation requirement, ss. 209 & 221 CJA 2003.

- The requirement(s) imposed on the offender should be:

  - suitable for the offender; and
  - where the offender's liberty is restricted commensurate with the 'seriousness' of the offence, s. 148(3) CJA 2003.

- Sentencing discount for guilty plea will apply.

- Pre-sentence report will invariably be required.

FINES

- Court must consider offender's financial circumstances before imposing a fine, s. 162(1) CJA 2003.

- Fine must reflect the 'seriousness' of the offence, s. 164(2) CJA 2003.

- Sentencing discount will apply for a guilty plea.

- Fines are higher in the Crown Court.

OTHER TYPES OF SENTENCE

- conditional discharge;

- absolute discharge.

ANCILLARY ORDERS

- Compensation orders:
  - on conviction s. 130 PCC(S)A requires court to order compensation for any injury, loss, damage etc.;
  - court must give reason for not making compensation order;
  - magistrates can order compensation up to £5,000;
  - see Magistrates' Court Sentencing Guidelines for compensation for personal injury;
  - compensation in Crown Court is unlimited;
  - priority given to compensation orders over fines, prosecution costs etc.

- Defendant pays prosecution costs:
  - purpose to compensate prosecution;
  - sum should not exceed costs reasonably incurred;
  - court must account for offender's ability to pay;
  - consfiscation and forfeiture orders, see Proceeds of Crime Act 2002.
- Anti Social Behaviour orders.
- Notfiication under sex offenders' register.
- Football banning order.
- Restraining order.
- Deportation.

27.1   INTRODUCTION

Road traffic cases occupy a considerable amount of time in magistrates' courts. Special sentencing considerations apply to these cases, which is why a chapter is devoted to this aspect of sentencing. Driving offences range in seriousness from documentary offences such as failing to display a road tax certificate to causing death by dangerous driving.

Some aspects of road traffic sentencing can be confusing and to be absolutely certain of the court's powers, you must research the sentencing options that apply to your client's case. Once again, *Blackstone's Criminal Practice* and the Magistrates' Court Sentencing Guidelines 2008 (MCSGs) provide an invaluable source of information. For a specialist practitioner work on road traffic law and sentencing refer to *Wilkinson's Road Traffic Offences*. It is also important that you are aware of your client's driving status, the details of which will be recorded on his driving licence as your client's driving status will invariably affect the penalty the court can impose. For example, is your client the holder of a provisional driving licence or the holder of a full licence? Does your client have unexpired penalty points on his licence or a previous period of disqualification?

The importance of researching the penalties for the offence(s) with which your client is charged cannot be overstated. Not all driving offences are endorseable with penalty points and a large number of driving offences, including careless driving, do not carry a custodial sentence. Some offences, including careless driving carry a variable number of penalty points. Conviction for certain offences requires the offender to undertake an extended driving test under s. 36(1) Road Traffic Offenders Act 1988 (RTOA) including the offence of dangerous driving under s. 2 Road Traffic Act 1988. Where the obligatory endorsement of a driving licence is ordered, the court may disqualify the defendant until he has retaken and passed his driving test, s. 36(4) RTA 1988. In addition to imposing penalty points and disqualifying, a fine is likely to be imposed for the vast majority of less serious driving offences. You should consult the MCSGs (2008) for an accurate indication of the likely penalty. If in doubt, consult the legal adviser to the court.

Fundamental to your understanding of road traffic law are the following terms:

- obligatory disqualification;
- discretionary disqualification; and
- obligatory endorsement.

27.2 OBLIGATORY DISQUALIFICATION

Some offences carry obligatory disqualification from driving including

- driving with excess alcohol under s. 5 RTOA 1988;
- dangerous driving under s. 3 RTOA 1988; and
- aggravated vehicle taking under s. 12A Theft Act 1968.

Disqualification must be for a period of at least 12 months unless special reasons apply (s. 34 RTOA 1988). In some cases the period of disqualification will be longer. Where an offender commits an offence of drink driving within ten years of having committed an excess alcohol offence, the minimum period of disqualification is three years. Where the defendant pleads guilty to an offence which carries obligatory disqualification, the court can impose an interim disqualification period pending the final resolution of sentence. The court has discretion to disqualify until a test is passed where the offender has been convicted of an offence involving obligatory endorsement. The court must order an extended test for those convicted of manslaughter, causing death by dangerous driving and dangerous driving.

27.2.1 PROVISION FOR DRINK DRIVERS TO REDUCE THE PERIOD OF OBLIGATORY DISQUALIFICATION

Drink drivers who are disqualified for 12 months or more under the various driving offences involving excess alcohol or drugs are able to reduce their period of disqualification if they successfully complete a drink driver's rehabilitation course (s. 34A RTOA 1988). The course, which is available in all areas, requires the defendant to pay privately. It has to be completed at least two months before the expiry of the disqualification period. The reduced period of disqualification cannot be for less than three months and for no more than a quarter of the entire disqualification period.

27.3 PENALTY POINTS ENDORSEMENT

Numerous offences oblige the court to endorse the driver's licence including careless driving (s. 3 RTOA 1988); failure to stop and report an accident (s. 170 RTOA 1988) and having no insurance (s. 143 RTOA 1988). In these circumstances the offender's driving licence must be endorsed with the appropriate number of penalty points unless, at the same time, the defendant is disqualified from driving either because the court has exercised its discretionary powers of disqualification or because there is mandatory disqualification for the offence. Neither will he have points endorsed on his licence in respect of any other offence of which he is convicted on the same occasion (*Martin v DPP* [2000] RTR 188).

27.3.1 PENALTY POINTS ENDORSEMENT AND THE DISCRETION TO DISQUALIFY

Whenever a court endorses penalty points on a licence, it always has discretion to disqualify the offender from driving for the offence (s. 34(2) RTOA 1988). Disqualification pending passing of a driving test may also be ordered where the safety of other road users is an issue (s. 34(4) RTOA 1988). If a court passes a sentence of discretionary disqualification, for example, in a serious case of careless driving, no penalty points are imposed on the defendant's driving licence, although the particulars of the offence are endorsed. Where a court exercises its discretion to disqualify, the period of disqualification is a matter for the court. Obligatory or discretionary disqualification for a period of 56 days or more results in the defendant's licence being revoked and the defendant must re-apply for a new licence. Only a disqualification under the totting-up provisions (s. 35 RTOA 1988) removes the penalty points collected before and those imposed for the offence that triggered the disqualification (s. 45(5) RTOA 1988).

27.3.2 THE NUMBER OF POINTS WHERE THE DEFENDANT HAS COMMITTED TWO OR MORE ENDORSEABLE OFFENCES

Where a defendant is convicted of two or more endorsable offences committed on the same occasion, the court will usually endorse the highest number of points, unless it thinks fit to order otherwise (s. 28 RTOA 1988).

27.3.3 OFFENCES CARRYING A VARIABLE RANGE OF PENALTY POINTS

Where there is a variable range of penalty points, the actual points imposed should reflect the seriousness of the offence and the defendant's culpability. Careless driving carries a range of penalty points, from three to nine. Where the defendant is guilty of no more than a minor lapse in concentration, the penalty points endorsement should be towards the lower end of the tariff. Conversely, a serious lapse in concentration or a prolonged course of bad driving will merit the imposition of penalty points towards the higher end of the tariff.

Sentencing for road traffic offences, in common with other general criminal offences, is based on seriousness. The MCSGs (2008) usefully identify aggravating and mitigating features in relation to the most common road traffic offences. In the offence of driving with excess alcohol, the guidelines provide an indication of the likely penalty and the likely period of disqualification based on the reading of the analysed specimen. This emphasises the importance of researching any relevant sentencing guidelines before attempting to offer advice on likely sentence or mitigating on behalf of a client.

27.3.4 SPECIAL PROVISIONS FOR 'NEWLY QUALIFIED' DRIVERS

Section 1 Road Traffic (New Drivers) Act 1995 introduced a probationary period of two years starting from the day on which a person became a qualified driver. If the newly qualified driver acquires six or more penalty points within the probationary period of two years, his licence will be revoked by the Secretary of State, requiring the driver to retake and pass an ordinary driving test before being eligible to apply for a full licence once more. The probationary period thereafter has no further application. Revocation of the driver's licence in these circumstances does not wipe the licence clear, and the penalty points will remain on the licence for the statutory period of three years from the commission of the offence.

It should also be noted that points accumulated before the test was taken will count unless they were committed more than three years before the current offence. Points accumulated after the test is passed will count if the offence is within two years of the date on which the test is passed. If however the court decides to impose a short period of disqualification under s. 34(2) RTOA 1988 for the latest offence and therefore no points are imposed, then the revocation provisions will not apply if the number of points then remaining on the licence amounts to less than six.

> **Example**
>
> Lisa acquired three penalty points for a speeding offence whilst a provisional licence holder 12 months before passing her driving test. Eighteen months after passing her test she has acquired another three points for speeding. Her licence will be revoked by the Secretary of State. If the court decides instead to impose a short period of discretionary disqualification for the new offence, then the revocation provision will not be triggered. The earlier points will remain on her licence and another three within the two years of passing her test will trigger revocation.

27.4 THE SENTENCING PROCEDURE IN A ROAD TRAFFIC OFFENCE

In less serious driving offences the defendant will usually plead guilty by post (see Chapter 15, para. 15.3). In some cases the defendant may be subject to a fixed penalty at the road side (for qualifying offences see Sch. 3 to RTOA 1988). Where the defendant denies the offence, he will be subject to a trial. Unless charged with a 'serious' road traffic offence it is unlikely that a defendant will qualify for a representation order to cover the cost of legal representation at trial unless the sentencing consequences are serious.

Having been convicted of a road traffic offence, the defendant will be asked to produce his driving licence to the court. If his licence is unavailable, the court can request a print out from the Driver Vehicle Licensing Agency (DVLA). Where the offender has a clean driving licence but is unable to produce it, a court can permit the defendant to swear to this fact on oath.

Where a magistrates' court is considering imposing a period of disqualification on conviction and the person to be disqualified is not present in court under s. 11(4) MCA 1980, the court must adjourn and notify the defendant that he is required to attend court as the court is considering a period of disqualification. If the defendant subsequently fails to attend, he can be disqualified in his absence although the usual practice will be to adjourn the proceedings and issue a warrant under s. 13 MCA 1980 to compel the defendant's attendance.

Where a court imposes penalty points or endorses a driving licence, the court will send the driving licence to the DVLA in Swansea.

27.5 DISQUALIFICATION UNDER THE TOTTING-UP PROCEDURE—S. 35 RTOA 1988

A defendant will be liable to disqualification for at least six months if the penalty points to be taken into account for the current offence amount to 12 or more.

Where the defendant is convicted of an offence which carries obligatory endorsement, the penalty points to be taken into account are:

1. any points attributed to the offence in respect of which the defendant has just been convicted (except if disqualified for the offence itself under s. 34 RTOA 1988); and

2. any points previously endorsed on his licence in respect of offences committed within the three years immediately preceding the commission of the present offence (if the defendant was disqualified in connection with an earlier offence, no penalty points would have been endorsed on his licence for that particular offence).

Under the totting-up procedure the date of the commission of the offence is the key date and not the date of conviction.

Where a person is disqualified from driving under the penalty points system, his driving licence is wiped clear of existing penalty points.

Disqualification under the totting-up provisions is mandatory unless there are mitigating circumstances, and must be for a minimum period of six months. The six month disqualification increases to 12 months if there has been a previous disqualification of 56 days or more within three years of the commission of the current offence. It increases to two years if there have been two or more disqualifications imposed within three years of the current offence. A court may order the offender to retake an extended driving test.

The minimum periods of disqualification under the totting-up provisions are subject to mitigating circumstances. If such circumstances are successfully argued, the court can reduce the minimum period of disqualification or not disqualify at all.

27.6 AVOIDING OBLIGATORY ENDORSEMENT OR OBLIGATORY DISQUALIFICATION—SPECIAL REASONS—SS. 34 AND 44 RTOA 1988

To avoid obligatory endorsement or obligatory disqualification, a defendant must establish the defence of special reasons. What is a special reason? Whilst there is no statutory definition of special reasons a substantial body of case law has developed over the years. We include a summary of the law. Further detail can be found in *Wilkinson's Road Traffic Offences* and *Blackstone's Criminal Practice*. A special reason was defined in *Whittal v Kirby* [1947] KB 194 as:

> 'a mitigating or extenuating circumstance, which is connected with the commission of the offence but which is not personal to the offender and which does not constitute a defence to the charge.'

A finding of special reasons gives the court discretion whether to disqualify or endorse a driver's licence. In other words, a court can find that there are special reasons but can still choose not to exercise its discretion.

The legal burden of establishing special reasons rests on the defendant on the balance of probabilities. Invariably, the defendant will be expected to adduce evidence. A submission of special reasons is likely to be critically scrutinised by the court.

The following have been held to amount to a special reason.

Emergency
Driving in an emergency may amount to a special reason if for example, the defendant had not intended to drive but, having consumed alcohol, was suddenly confronted with an emergency situation requiring him to drive. A court would enquire in such a case as to whether alternative transport might have been available. The test is whether the reasonable man would have regarded the situation as being one in which no other course of action was possible (*DPP v Whittle* [1996] RTOR 154).

Laced drinks
Special reasons not to disqualify from driving can be found where a defendant establishes that his drinks were laced and that he did not know or suspect that fact and that if his drinks had not been laced, he would not have been above the legal limit (*DPP v O'Connor* [1992] RTOR 66). Special reasons would not apply to someone who knew he was drinking alcohol but had been misled about the nature and strength of the drink.

The shortness of the distance driven
An intention to drive only a short distance can be regarded as a special reason for not disqualifying. Guidance on this is provided in the Divisional Court's decision in *Chatters v Burke* [1986] RTOR 396.

27.6.1 **EXEMPTION FROM DISQUALIFICATION AND ENDORSEMENT FOR CERTAIN OFFENCES—S. 48 RTOA 1988**

On conviction for using a dangerous vehicle (s. 40A RTA 1988) a court must not order endorsement or disqualification if the defendant can prove that he did not know and had no reasonable cause to suspect that the offence would be committed. The normal reverse burden of proof applies, i.e. on the balance of probabilities.

 Example

Michael is prosecuted for having defective brakes involving a defective handbrake linkeage. If he can show that he did not know of the defect and had no cause to suspect that the braking system was faulty in this way, the court cannot order endorsement.

27.7 **AVOIDING DISCRETIONARY DISQUALIFICATION**

To avoid or reduce the period of discretionary disqualification the defendant can argue mitigating factors which are relevant to the offence and may be personal to the defendant, i.e. loss of employment and effect upon the defendant's family.

27.8 **AVOIDING DISQUALIFICATION UNDER THE TOTTING-UP PROCEDURE—S. 35 RTOA 1988**

To reduce or to avoid disqualification under the totting-up procedure, the defendant must argue mitigating circumstances which are relevant to the offence and may be personal to the defendant. Section 35(4) RTOA 1988 specifically excludes the defendant from submitting:

• the offence is trivial; or

• the loss of his licence would cause him hardship (unless the hardship is exceptional); or

• any mitigating circumstances which have been advanced and taken into account to avoid disqualification under the totting-up procedure within the preceding three years.

27.8.1 **THE GROUND OF EXCEPTIONAL HARDSHIP**

In determining whether the defendant will suffer exceptional hardship on being disqualified under the totting-up procedure, regard will be had to all the circumstances. Hardship must be exceptional. The defendant has effectively got to prove that, if he loses his driving licence, he will suffer hardship of a very serious kind. The hardship can extend to the defendant's dependants. Relevant factors include: the type of job the defendant has; other available means of transport (mere inconvenience is not enough); shift patterns and the availability of public transport, etc.

It will invariably be necessary for the defendant to give evidence on oath to substantiate a defence of exceptional hardship and where appropriate, adduce evidence from an employer about the consequences of the loss of the licence.

27.9 **FURTHER APPLICATION TO REDUCE PERIOD OF DISQUALIFICATION**

Section 42 RTOA 1988 permits a person disqualified from driving to apply to the court to end the period of disqualification before its expiry date. The provisions apply to an offender who is subject to a lengthy disqualification period. The decision to allow the application is a matter for the court's discretion. Under s. 42 the following factors are relevant: (a) the character of the person disqualified and his conduct subsequent to the order; (b) the nature of the offence; and (c) any other circumstances. A minimum period of disqualification must have expired before the offender can apply. For example, for a defendant disqualified for less than four years, two years must have elasped before the application can be made.

7.10 ROAD SAFETY ACT 2006

 Looking Ahead

The Road Safety Act 2006 will make a number of changes to the sentencing of road traffic related offences. It will also introduce new offences of causing death by careless driving and causing death by driving while being uninsured, unlicensed or disqualified. It will increase the penalties in relation to some offences and introduce variable penalty points for speeding offences. In certain circumstances, drivers will be able to reduce the number of penalty points on their licence by undertaking a driver improvement course. The legislation will require the worst drink drivers to retake their driving test and to undergo a medical assessment.

At the time of going to press, the only significant section to be implemented so far is s. 26. This involves the upgrading of the offence of failing to have proper control of a vehicle including the use of a mobile telephone when driving. The offence now carries obligatory endorsement with three penalty points for offences committed on and after 27 February 2007.

KEY POINT SUMMARY

- Ensure your client brings his driving licence to court.
- Ensure you have researched the penalties for the offence(s) under consideration and any applicable sentencing guidelines.
- Ensure you have scrutinised your client's driving licence to see whether there are any past endorsements or disqualifications.
- Understand that special reasons apply only in relation to mandatory disqualification/endorsement and that special reasons are difficult to establish.
- Be prepared to make a submission and to adduce evidence in a case where your client may lose his licence under the totting-up procedure or in the exercise of the court's discretion to disqualify for the offence itself.

SELF-TEST QUESTIONS

Consider the following exercises designed to test your understanding of road traffic sentencing. Research the relevant sentencing guidelines and advise each client as to the likely outcome.

Exercise 1

Ian is summoned in connection with an offence of careless driving contrary to s. 3 RTOA 1988. Ian was driving and approached a sharp bend in the road. His near-side wheel caught the kerb and the impact sent his car across the road onto the other carriageway. While spinning out of control, Ian's car clipped a cyclist riding on the other side of the carriageway, knocking him to the ground. The cyclist was not wearing a helmet. He sustained a fractured skull and died in hospital several days later. Ian pleads guilty at the first opportunity. He is deeply remorseful about the death of the cyclist and has had to take time off work and undergo counselling for depression. He has returned to his job where he receives a net salary of £2,500 a month. He is a married man with one dependant child. His wife does not work.

Exercise 2

Ruth is facing a charge of driving with excess alcohol, contrary to s. 5(1)(a) RTA 1988. She was observed by officers to be driving her car at 11pm in an erratic manner. She gave a positive specimen of breath at the roadside and was then arrested. She provided a further specimen which showed the level of alcohol in her breath as 111 mgs (against a legal limit of 35 mgs), nearly four times over the legal limit.

Ruth pleads guilty. She admits to her solicitor that she has an alcohol dependency and that she is on anti-depressant medication. At present she is going through a traumatic divorce and feels that everything is spiralling out of control. Ruth is a nurse. She lives 25 miles from the hospital trust which employs her. She also works shifts. She is certain she will lose her job if she is disqualified from driving.

Exercise 3

Ben was involved in a minor road traffic accident which was attended by the police. It transpires that Ben was not insured to drive the particular vehicle he was driving. He is summonsed for driving without due care and attention (s. 3 RTA 1988) and for having no insurance (s. 143 RTA 1988). The lack of insurance was an oversight—he simply forgot to renew his policy. Ben had been preoccupied because his wife had to go into hospital for an emergency operation leaving him with the care of their two school-age children. He expresses his regret and pleads guilty at the first opportunity. Ben has six points currently on his licence for speeding offences. Ben is a self-employed mechanic. He employs six others in his business. His business is 15 miles from his home. He works long hours. His work naturally involves him road testing vehicles. His wife cannot drive for the next six months due to her illness and the family is dependent upon Ben being able to drive. Ben draws £ 500 net per week from his business.

Exercise 4

Imran will plead guilty to an offence of driving without insurance (six to eight penalty points). He passed his test 18 months ago. His job requires him to drive and he does not wish to be without a driving licence. He earns £300 per week. The failure to have insurance was as a result of confusion as regards his mother's insurers. She had asked him to drive her car. He had checked her insurance cover with the insurance company and had been given the impression that his mother's policy extended to drivers under the age of 25. Imran is 23. When the insurance policy document was produced, the terms and conditions of the policy specifically excluded drivers under the age of 25.

Case study: *R v Roger Martin*

If you have accessed the *R v Roger Martin* case study from our Online Resource Centre, you will recall that Roger Martin has previously pleaded guilty to offences of common assault, careless driving and failing to stop. Research the relevant sentencing guidelines in relation to the road traffic offences with which Roger Martin is charged and consider what will be Roger's priority in terms of sentence.

You can access Roger Martin's plea in mitigation on our Online Resource Centre but we suggest that you do not do so at this stage until you have considered Chapter 28, which considers the role of the defence advocate in submitting a plea in mitigation.

Analysis of all the above can be found in Appendix 4.

FIGURE 27.1 SENTENCING IN ROAD TRAFFIC CASES

Offences requiring obligatory disqualification

- Disqualification will be for a minimum period of 12 months.

- The driver's licence is revoked.

- The only way to avoid obligatory disqualification or to reduce the period of disqualification is to establish 'special reasons' for not disqualifying.

Offences for which there is discretionary disqualification

- Wherever penalty points have to be endorsed, a court has the discretion to order disqualification.

- Where the court disqualifies under its discretionary powers, the period of disqualification is a matter for the court.

- The driver's licence is revoked where the period of disqualification is 56 days or more.

- The defendant can avoid discretionary disqualification by arguing mitigation relating to the offence and/or the defendant.

Offences requiring obligatory endorsement

- Specified offences require obligatory endorsement of a driver's licence.

- Where a range of penalty points can be imposed, the defendant's driving licence is endorsed; the number of penalty points should reflect the 'seriousness' of the offence.

- The penalty points are aggregated with any other penalty points endorsed for offences committed within three years of the current offences.

- The only way to avoid obligatory endorsement is to establish 'special reasons'.

Disqualification under the 'totting-up' procedure—s. 35 Road Traffic Offenders Act 1988

- A defendant will be liable to disqualification for at least six months as a 'totter' if 12 or more penalty points have been endorsed on his licence for offences committed within the last three years.

- The court will take into account:

  – any points endorsed for the present offence; and

  – any points endorsed for offences committed within the last three years.

- Where a driver is disqualified as a totter his driving licence is wiped clean of points.

- Disqualification must be for a minimum of six months—longer in some cases.

- Defendant can avoid disqualification or seek to reduce the period of disqualification as a 'totter' by arguing mitigating factors including exceptional hardship.

28.1 INTRODUCTION

The preceding chapters on sentencing have laid the foundations which enable us to consider the further aspects covered in this chapter. If you have not done so already, we invite you to work through Chapters 25–26 before proceeding.

In this chapter, we consider:

- the procedure on passing sentence;
- the role of the CPS on sentence;
- the importance of the plea in mitigation as a means of influencing the sentence that is passed by the court;
- how to construct a plea in mitigation.

28.2 THE ROLE OF THE CPS ON SENTENCE

The CPS prosecutor does not take an active role in sentencing. However, the prosecutor represents the public interest and must apply the guidelines issued by the Attorney-General on the acceptance of guilty pleas and the prosecutor's role in the sentencing exercise, published in October 2005. The guidelines (which are reproduced on the CPS website and on the Online Resource Centre) state that the prosecutor must be prepared to assist the court in reaching an appropriate sentence by drawing the court's attention to:

- a victim impact statement (if one has been made);
- any evidence as to the impact the offending has had on the community;
- any relevant sentencing guidelines or guideline cases;
- the aggravating and mitigating factors of the offence;
- any other relevant sentencing provisions and ancillary orders sought.

The prosecutor's role extends to challenging any assertion by the defence in mitigation that is derogatory to a person's character.

28.3 THE PROCEDURE ON SENTENCING

The procedure is generally the same whether the offender is sentenced in the Crown Court or magistrates' court.

Sentencing occurs after a finding of guilt by the court or upon the offender pleading guilty to one or more offences. An adjournment may be necessary to obtain a pre-sentence report, or to await the conclusion of other outstanding criminal proceedings against the defendant where it would make good sense to sentence on the overall totality of the defendant's criminal behaviour.

28.3.1 PROCEDURE FOLLOWING A FINDING OF GUILT

Where a defendant has been found guilty by a verdict of the court, the court will be appraised of the circumstances of the offence and the involvement of the defendant. The role of the prosecutor in this situation is largely restricted to reading out any victim impact statement there might be in the case; referring the court to the defendant's antecedent history; detailing any requests for compensation and asking for ancillary orders, including prosecution costs.

The defendant's solicitor will be invited to address the court by way of mitigation of sentence. If the defence solicitor, or the court of its own volition, feels further information about the defendant is required before sentence can be passed, the hearing will be adjourned for either a stand-down fast delivery pre-sentence report or a standard delivery pre-sentence report, prepared by the probation service. In such a situation, the defence solicitor will reserve what he wishes to say by way of mitigation until the full sentencing hearing.

Where a court adjourns sentence for a PSR, it can remand the defendant in custody or on bail. Bail may be conditional or unconditional and can include a condition that the defendant co-operates with the probation service in the preparation of the report. For full consideration of the circumstances in which a PSR must be obtained see Chapter 25.

28.3.2 PROCEDURE FOLLOWING A GUILTY PLEA AND THE IMPORTANCE OF AN AGREED BASIS OF PLEA

Before a guilty plea is entered, it is good practice to discuss the basis of your client's plea with the prosecution. As highlighted in Chapter 25, para. 25.14, a defendant's guilty plea does not necessarily imply acceptance of everything that is said in the prosecution's evidence. Where there is a significant dispute between the prosecution and the defence which would materially affect the sentence, a Newton hearing (*R v Newton* (1982) 77 Cr App R 13) may be required to determine the disputed fact. If a basis of plea can be agreed, this can be avoided and the agreed basis of plea can be read to the court. An agreed basis of plea is a matter of negotiation between the prosecution and the defence. Good practice requires the plea to be reduced into writing and signed by both parties. In deciding whether to accept a guilty plea on an agreed basis, the CPS will be guided by its Code of Conduct and the Attorney-General's Guidelines on acceptance of a guilty plea, highlighted earlier, which require the prosecutor to take account of the victim's interests. The basis of plea must neither be misleading or untrue.

Where a defendant pleads guilty, avoiding the need for a trial, the sentencing hearing will begin with the prosecution outlining the circumstances of the offence. This will be based on the evidence contained in witness statements and the defendant's interview. The prosecutor will refer the court to any victim impact statement that has been made in the case.

The prosecution will provide the court with a copy of the defendant's criminal record, drawing the attention of the court to any relevant convictions. If the current conviction places the defendant in breach of an existing order of the court, the prosecution ought to be in a position to provide details of the earlier offence. The same applies following conviction after trial. If the offence involves injury to an individual or damage to property, the prosecution should provide full details and hand in any documented applications for compensation. In the case of an injury, the prosecution may well refer the court to any sets of photographs taken of the injured party.

The prosecutor should present the facts fully and fairly. If there are any offences to be taken into consideration (see Chapter 25, para. 25.15), these will be referred to by the prosecution and an agreed schedule submitted to the court. Where it is confidently anticipated that a pre-sentence report will need to be ordered, the prosecution may present the court with an expedited version of the facts and allow the defence solicitor to make representations. Finally, the prosecution will ask for costs in a specified sum.

Having heard from the prosecution, it is the turn of the defence to submit a plea in mitigation. Once again, if the defence solicitor feels a PSR would be useful, he may immediately raise this point. If the court concurs, sentencing will be adjourned for the preparation of a report. Whether with a PSR or not, the principles of the plea in mitigation remain the same and are considered below.

Once the court has heard the outline of the facts from the prosecution and has listened to any representations by the defendant, the court is in a position to determine the appropriate sentence. The court will consider all the information before it and will apply any applicable sentencing guidelines in accordance with the principles outlined in Chapters 25–26 and apply any sentencing discount. It will then announce its decision in open court, explaining the sentence to the defendant and giving reasons for its decision.

28.4 THE PLEA IN MITIGATION

One of the most important functions a defence solicitor will be called upon to fulfil is to seek to mitigate sentence on his client's behalf. This is known as making a plea in mitigation. As previously explained, the sentence your client receives will largely be determined by the seriousness of the offence. However, in arriving at the most appropriate sentence for your client, the court will have regard to your client's personal circumstances and to any personal offender mitigation.

The plea in mitigation is important because it should assist the court to determine the seriousness of the offence and it should bring to the court's attention any relevant personal offender mitigation.

28.4.1 COMPONENTS OF AN EFFECTIVE PLEA IN MITIGATION

In order to deliver an effective plea in mitigation you need to combine a thorough knowledge of sentencing law and practice with good advocacy skills. There are, in our view, three fundamental requirements for a competent plea in mitigation.

Firstly, the defence solicitor must understand the theory of sentencing and the importance of researching any applicable sentencing guidelines (see Chapters 25–27).

Secondly, the defence solicitor must have in mind a realistic sentencing objective, having regard to the theory behind sentencing and having considered any applicable sentencing guidelines. Sentencing theory should be grasped during the vocational stage of training. Formulating a realistic sentencing objective is largely a question of common sense, although experience of sentencing in criminal courts will help to fashion it.

Thirdly, the defence solicitor needs good advocacy skills.

An effective plea in mitigation should be well thought through, carefully constructed and persuasively delivered. Preparation is the key.

28.4.2 PREPARING A PLEA IN MITIGATION

The starting point for any plea in mitigation is to ensure you are aware of the sentence a court can impose for the particular offence(s) and whether there are any particular sentencing guidelines. This may require some legal research on your part.

You will be aware of the prosecution's version of the facts having considered the pre-trial disclosure of evidence (advance information) and having listened to the prosecutor's submission to the court outlining the circumstances of the offence. You will have taken your client's detailed instructions about the offence and will have considered and discussed with your client the content of any pre-sentence report that may have been ordered. You should therefore be in a position to assess the balance of aggravating and mitigating features in the offence and arrive at an assessment of the true seriousness of the offence.

Given that sentencing is based on the seriousness of the offence, you need to make an assessment of seriousness. You need to ask yourself 'What would I ideally like to achieve for my client?' Then put yourself in the position of the court and consider what sentencing objective the court is likely to follow. Will it want to punish your client/rehabilitate him/prevent the commission of further offences/protect the public/put your client on trust as to his future behaviour? By engaging in this exercise you will hopefully arrive at a realistic sentencing objective which gives you the basis upon which to build your plea in mitigation.

You might have concluded that a custodial sentence is a distinct possibility for your client. If it is, ask yourself whether the custody threshold test set out in Chapter 26 is met on the facts in this case. Consider *R v Howells* [1999] 1 WLR 307 and other cases that are relevant to the imposition of a custodial sentence. Can you make use of them in your plea?

If your preparation leads you to conclude that the court might be amenable to imposing a community sentence, consider whether the requisite criteria for such sentence (as explained in Chapter 26), is met.

If a financial penalty or a compensation order is likely to be made, make sure you are in possession of an up-to-date statement of your client's financial means.

28.4.3 USING THE PRE-SENTENCE REPORT IN PREPARATION

In preparing your plea in mitigation you must of course discuss the content of any pre-sentence report (PSR) with your client. There may be matters in the PSR with which your client disagrees or which are out of date. The probation officer who prepared the report is not usually available in court, but the defence can require the officer to attend if the defendant wishes to challenge what has been written. Advocates should be selective and refer the sentencing court to relevant portions of the pre-sentence report which assist the plea being put forward.

28.4.4 ADDUCING CHARACTER EVIDENCE OR OTHER EVIDENCE LIKELY TO BE OF ASSISTANCE IN YOUR PLEA IN MITIGATION

Will your client benefit from adducing testimonial evidence as to the sort of person he is? Your preparation should have alerted you to this possibility. If your client is a person of past good character and is charged with an offence likely to result in damage to his reputation, it is useful to be able to hand in a short written character reference to the court. If your client has a medical condition that is relevant to sentencing, consider obtaining a written note from your client's GP. Similarly, if your client has the offer of a job or a helpful letter from his employer, it is good mitigation to obtain written confirmation to this effect.

28.5 STRUCTURING A PLEA IN MITIGATION

There is no predetermined structure for a plea in mitigation. Every plea in mitigation must of course be tailored to the individual case. Having regard to all that has been said in this and the preceding chapters, we include a checklist of the possible factors an advocate might have regard to in constructing a plea in mitigation.

Introduction

If your client has pleaded guilty, you may wish to introduce yourself to the bench before beginning your plea in mitigation. You may also want to say a few words to introduce your client:

'Madam . . . my client is a young man. He is 24. He has a job and resides with his girlfriend . . .'

Acknowledge the prosecution's presentation of the facts

Consider thanking the prosecution for its fair outline of the facts of the case, if this is appropriate:

'Madam, I am grateful to my friend for fairly outlining the facts in this case . . .'

If there are aspects of the prosecution's presentation with which you disagree, highlight them at this stage. The above sentence might continue:

'There is however one matter which I feel I ought to clarify/bring to your attention at the outset and before going any further . . .'

Using a pre-sentence report

If a pre-sentence report has been prepared, ascertain from the bench at an early stage in your plea whether they have had the opportunity to consider its content. If not, politely suggest that the bench may wish to do so before you continue with your plea. Think about court etiquette. Be polite:

'Madam, I wonder if you have had the opportunity to consider the pre-sentence report that has been prepared in connection with this matter? You have; I am grateful for that indication . . .'

Use the pre-sentence report selectively, if it is to your benefit:

'I wonder if I might direct Madam's attention to paragraph 12 of the pre-sentence report where Miss James speaks favourably of a community based disposal in this matter . . .'

Acknowledge your client's predicament

'Madam, let me say at the outset that my client is a deeply anxious individual . . . my client fully appreciates that he stands to be sentenced today for a serious offence/that he could be sent to prison for these offences today . . . he expresses his complete remorse for his wrongdoing . . . understands the need for punishment but also seeks the help of the court in dealing with his offending behaviour . . .'

Can you play down the seriousness of the offence?

Can you use the Magistrates' Court Sentencing Guidelines (or other applicable guidelines) to play down the seriousness of the offence? Consider the aggravating and mitigating factors. Are you absolutely clear as to the basis of your client's guilty plea if he is pleading guilty?

If your client has pleaded guilty to an offence of assault, relevant mitigating factors may include provocation, a minor injury, etc. If your client has been found guilty of a theft offence, relevant mitigating features would include the fact that it was committed spontaneously, the amount involved is small or that the theft or deception was not committed for personal gain. If the offence to be sentenced was burglary, relevant factors would include the fact that the property was empty or disused and that no damage was caused in the course of the burglary. Have the stolen items been recovered? Was the crime committed in a sophisticated way?

Be tactful when exploring the victim's role in the commission of the offence. You do not want to score an own goal. It is your client who stands to be punished for the offence, not the victim.

If custody is a distinct possibility

Consider the applicable criteria. Is the offence 'so serious' that only custody can be justified? Be prepared to make representations based on the aggravating and mitigating features. Once again, refer to the sentencing guidelines and the case law considered in Chapter 25 and make the point that if a custodial sentence is to be imposed, its length should be commensurate with the seriousness of the offence (s. 153 CJA 2003). You might refer to the current problems of prison overcrowding highlighted in *Kefford* [2002] 2 Cr App (S) R 106 and *Mills* [2002] 2 Cr App (S) R 229, with a view to trying to persuade the court to keep any custodial sentence to as short a length as possible. You might ask the court to suspend a period of imprisonment.

Can you play down your client's role in the offence?

Was your client led into temptation? Perhaps your client was not the instigator or the 'ring leader'. Was your client provoked? Was your client intoxicated or under the influence of an unlawful substance? You have to be careful with regard to the aforementioned. Drink and drugs do not excuse an offender's behaviour, but they may go some way to explain why your client acted in the way he did.

Can you offer an explanation as to why your client has offended?

Do not seek to excuse the offence, but see if you can offer an explanation for your client's offending. Common factors include low self-esteem, mental health issues, complete lack of self-control, dire financial straits, homelessness and addictive behaviour such as alcoholism, drug abuse, gambling.

Are there any personal factors at work that might put the offending behaviour into context?

Is your client getting divorced? Maybe your client is in the grips of an acrimonious breakdown of a relationship? Perhaps your client is frustrated because he or she cannot gain access to their children resulting in a sense of frustration and anger. Is your client presently facing an uncertain future? Maybe he is ill, bereaved, redundant or about to be made redundant, being sued or going through some personal crisis. Consider whether any of the above can be substantiated by evidence, perhaps in the form of a short medical report or letter from an employer.

What is your client's attitude to the offence?

It is fair to say that some clients will give you more scope in this respect than others. Attitude may be reflected in a timely guilty plea and co-operation with the police. A guilty plea spares witnesses. You will want to remind the bench that it should give credit for a timely guilty plea.

Your client's attitude might be expressed in the pre-sentence report if one is ordered and you should highlight this and bring it to the attention of the court. How candid has your client been in engaging with the probation service?

Most advocates will express their client's regret and remorse and perhaps offer an apology. Of course, actions speak louder than words. If your client has sought to make reparation to his victim (by paying compensation or repairing any damage) or has personally expressed an apology this is very useful mitigation.

What effect will the conviction have on your client?

Will this conviction result in a damaged reputation? This will be of particular relevance in the case of a first-time offender, especially if convicted of an offence relating to dishonesty. A first-time conviction for a sexual offence will result in damage to your client's reputation.

What has been the effect of court proceedings on your client's family? Is the court sentencing a mother who has the sole care of her children? What effect have the proceedings had on your client? Has your client been put under stress by the court appearances? What were the circumstances of your client's arrest? Was it public? Did your client have to spend a night or two in a police cell? Is it an experience your client wishes to repeat? Does your client face the loss of his/her job as a result of this conviction?

No previous convictions?

The fact that your client has no previous convictions is excellent mitigation. It means that this offence is completely out of character and is a one-off. The court may want to place your client on trust as to his future behaviour, depending on the seriousness of the offence.

What if your client has a criminal record?

Can you use your client's criminal record to your advantage? Perhaps the last conviction was some time ago? Consider whether your client has been subject to a community order and has found it to be beneficial. Has your client made brave attempts to rehabilitate himself in the meantime? Maybe steps have been taken to overcome drug addiction. Should your client be given the benefit of the doubt on this occasion? Can you detect a trend in the nature of the offences that have been committed that now needs to be addressed?

Do you have any character witnesses you might call to give evidence or to submit in written form to the court?

Your preparation for the plea in mitigation should have alerted you to this possibility. Ensure you have enough copies of any character references to distribute to the court.

What has your client done since to assist matters?

Has your client made good any damage or offered to pay voluntary sums of compensation? Has your client been able to obtain employment? Has your client begun to address the reason for his offending? If alcoholism or drug abuse is the problem, has your client sought help from professionals? If the offending behaviour is set against the backdrop of a marital or relationship breakdown, consider whether your client has come to terms with matters and is seeking help, perhaps from a solicitor or a counselling agency.

In short, is there evidence you can point to which suggests your client has some insight into his offending behaviour and wants to do something about it?

Finances

Given that the fine is a popular sentencing option in magistrates' courts (see Chapter 26), you must be in a position to provide the court with details of your client's finances, including weekly income and outgoings, savings and debts. A fine should always reflect an individual's ability to pay, and you may need to make representations on this basis. Imposing a fine could of course have a detrimental effect on your client's family. Where your client has an outstanding account with the court, you can expect the legal adviser to check whether your client's existing payments are up to date.

Miscellaneous considerations

Do not overlook the fact that if the current conviction puts your client in breach of an existing penalty, you will need to address this and the circumstances pertaining to that previous offence, as your client is likely to be re-sentenced or punished in some way for it. If your client has admitted an offence of absconding during the currency of the proceedings you will need to address the court on this as it constitutes a separate offence. Remember that if you are mitigating on a driving matter, different considerations might apply. You might need to argue special reasons or mitigating circumstances such as exceptional hardship (see Chapter 27).

Finally your conclusion . . .

What are you seeking to persuade the sentencing court to do? Are you looking for leniency, or a sentence to address your client's needs and the need to punish? Close your submission:

'Unless I can assist you further Madam . . . those are my submissions . . .'

The foregoing checklist assumes your client has pleaded guilty to the offence, obviating the need for a trial. If your client has been found guilty following a trial, whilst you can still address the court on the mitigating features of the offence, it is pointless to disagree with the verdict and to seek to minimise your client's role. By finding your client guilty, the court has already made up its mind about your client's involvement. You must, however, explain your client's personal circumstances so the court is appraised of the sort of individual it is sentencing.

28.6 ADVOCACY AND THE PLEA IN MITIGATION

Please refer to our comments in respect of advocacy skills in Chapter 2. We highlight a handful of key features in relation to pleas in mitigation.

Use powerful words
Use words that are inclusive:

> 'Let us examine the circumstances surrounding the commission of this offence . . . you will see . . . you will no doubt appreciate the position my client found himself in . . .'

Use a structure
There is no predetermined structure to a plea in mitigation. Consequently, you will need to devise a structure that gives coherence to your submission. Use the checklist at para. 28.5 above as your starting point. Consider ways in which you can link the various portions of your submissions:

> 'Madam, having looked at the circumstances of the offence, let us now turn to my client's personal situation . . .'

Remember, if you find yourself making a plea in mitigation before a district judge, you will need to be succinct. An experienced district judge may well indicate at the outset what sentence he or she is thinking of imposing on your client. Be prepared to hold your ground.

28.7 PROFESSIONAL CONDUCT

It would be unusual for you to be asked to confirm your client's list of previous convictions as part of the sentencing hearing. The Justices' Clerks' Society has advised its members that in relation to the citing of previous convictions, only one question should be put to the defence, namely: 'Have you seen this list?' What would you do if you were asked to confirm the accuracy of the list in circumstances where you know it contains errors or omissions that assist your client?

You are reminded of the importance of Rule 11.10 in that you must never knowingly deceive a court. Rule 11.10 provides:

> 'You might deceive or mislead a court by, for example:
>
> (a) submitting inaccurate information or allowing another person to do so;
>
> (b) indicating agreement with information that another person puts forward which you know is false . . .'

Rule 11.12 provides that if you are acting for a defendant, you are not under any obligation to correct information given to the court by the prosecution or any other person which you know may lead the court to make an inaccurate assumption about the defendant or the case, provided you do not indicate agreement with that information.

The answer to the dilemma posed above depends for the most part on how the question regarding the accuracy of any list of previous convictions is phrased.

SELF-TEST QUESTIONS

Case scenario: *R v William Hardy*

You will recall that William Hardy has pleaded guilty to the offence of unlawful sexual activity with a child, which is an indictable-only offence.

Your file to date contains:

- William Hardy's proof of evidence;
- advance information;
- pre-sentence report;
- character references;
- an agreed basis of plea;
- your research of the relevant sentencing guidelines for an offence of this type (see analysis of self-test question in relation to Chapter 25).

In the light of all that we have considered in relation to sentencing, we invite you to draft a plea in mitigation on behalf of William Hardy.

**nline
esource
entre** You can see the full sentencing hearing in relation to *R v William Hardy* in the video section of our Online Resource Centre. In the video clips you will see the outline of the case presented by the solicitor-advocate for the CPS, followed by the plea in mitigation delivered by William Hardy's solicitor-advocate. A transcript (based for the most part on the plea) is included and analysis of the proceedings is provided on the video. You will also see the Crown Court Judge pass sentence on William Hardy.

R v Roger Martin

Taking into consideration our study of sentencing theory and practice, it is your turn to draft a plea in mitigation on behalf of Roger Martin.

**nline
esource
entre** You are able to see the final determination of the *R v Roger Martin* case study by viewing his sentencing hearing in the video section of our Online Resource Centre. In the video clips you will see the outline of the case presented by the designated case worker for the CPS, followed by the plea in mitigation delivered by Roger Martin's solicitor. Analysis of the proceedings is provided in the video. You will see the sentence passed by the magistrates. We would ask you to note that this scenario was filmed before the Criminal Justice Act 2003 came into force. Were the same facts to be sentenced under the CJA 2003, Roger Martin would have been subject to a generic community order with specified requirements, which would include an element of supervision and unpaid work in the community.

FIGURE 28.1 SENTENCING PROCEDURE

Sentencing procedure where defendant found guilty

- Procedure generally same in Crown Court and magistrates' court.

- Court will be aware of facts of case and the defendant's role; defendant's criminal record is usually disclosed to the court.

- The case may be adjourned for pre-sentence report or specific sentence report.

- Defendant may be bailed or remanded in custody.

- Defence make a plea in mitigation.

- Defendant sentenced with court giving reasons.

Sentencing procedure where defendant pleaded guilty

- Procedure generally same in Crown Court and magistrates' court.

- Prosecution outline facts of the offence and the defendant's role.

- The case may be adjourned for pre-sentence report (PSR or specific sentence report (SSR)).

- Defendant's criminal record is usually disclosed to the court.

- Where dispute between prosecution and defence about facts of the offence, a Newton hearing (*R v Newton*) may be held.

- Defence make plea in mitigation.

29 APPEALS

29.1 INTRODUCTION

This chapter examines the practice and procedure involved in appealing against decisions of the magistrates' court or the Crown Court. In most cases, the defendant will appeal against the 'safety' of his conviction and/or the severity of the sentence. Some procedures for challenging the trial court's decision such as appeal by way of case stated or judicial review, are available to both the prosecution and the defence. An increasing number of appeal procedures are available only to the prosecution. The procedures explained in this chapter include:

* reopening a case, s. 142 Magistrates' Courts Act 1980;
* appeal from the magistrates' court to the Crown Court;
* appeal by way of case stated;
* judicial review;
* appeal to the Court of Appeal;
* Attorney-General's Reference;

- Criminal Cases Review Commission;
- appeals under the Criminal Justice Act 2003.

The rules of court relating to appeals are now contained in Crim PR, Parts 63–75.

29.2 REOPENING A CASE—S. 142 MAGISTRATES' COURTS ACT 1980

Following conviction by a magistrates' court, s. 142(2) MCA 1980 enables a defendant to ask the magistrates to set the conviction aside or to vary or rescind a sentence. The application may be made whether the defendant pleaded guilty or not guilty at the original trial and may be considered by the same bench which convicted the defendant or by a different bench.

In deciding whether to grant the application, the court will exercise its wide discretion under s. 142 MCA 1980 where it is 'in the interests of justice' to do so. Factors considered include the interests of the court and the inconvenience to other parties of reopening the case.

There is no time-limit for making an application under s. 142 MCA 1980 but an unreasonable delay will be taken into account in determining the interests of justice test.

If the conviction is set aside, the case is reheard by a different bench of magistrates.

A common use of s. 142(2) MCA 1980 is to rectify an obvious mistake made during the defendant's trial. It is also used to reopen cases where a defendant has been convicted in his absence. When advising your client about potential avenues of appeal, you should consider whether an application under s. 142 MCA 1980 will provide a speedier remedy than an appeal to the Crown Court.

Section 142(1) allows a magistrates' court to vary or rescind its decision as to sentence if it is in the interest of justice to do so. This power is frequently used to reopen sentencing decisions (most notably the imposition of a fine) following a conviction in the defendant's absence.

 Example

Kemal is charged with careless driving but unintentionally fails to attend for his trial at Stokeshire Magistrates' Court. He is convicted in his absence. He applies under s. 142 MCA 1980 to have his conviction set aside. In deciding the interests of justice test, the bench will consider the inconvenience to the prosecution, the prosecution witnesses and to the court of the case being reheard. These interests will be balanced against the defendant's general right to have the opportunity to defend himself.

If Kemal has strong mitigating reasons for failing to attend trial because, for example, he had to take his sick son to hospital, the bench will conclude that it is in the interest of justice to rehear the case. If Kemal simply forgot to attend court, it is likely that his application under s. 142 MCA 1980 will fail.

29.3 APPEAL TO THE CROWN COURT—S. 108 MAGISTRATES' COURTS ACT 1980 (CRIM PR, PART 63)

A defendant convicted before a magistrates' court may appeal against conviction and/or sentence to the Crown Court. Where the defendant pleaded guilty, he may only appeal against the sentence imposed. Appeal to the Crown Court is not available to the prosecution. The costs of the appeal will normally be met under a representation order (see Chapter 11).

29.3.1 THE PROCEDURE FOR APPEALING TO THE CROWN COURT

The notice of appeal must be given in writing within 21 days of the conviction and/or the sentence and be addressed to the chief executive to the justices of the magistrates' court that heard the case. There is discretion to extend this period.

The notice of appeal does not have to specify any detail other than indicating whether the appeal is against conviction and/or sentence. It is usual to use a form of appeal which merely states that the 'defendant proposes to appeal on the ground that the magistrates erred in fact and in law in convicting him' or 'the defendant proposes to appeal against sentence on the ground that it was excessive in all the circumstances'.

There is no filter procedure and the court has no discretion not to accept the notice of appeal.

Where the appellant received a custodial sentence in the magistrates' court, an application for bail until the appeal hearing may be made although there is no *prima facie* right to bail. If the bail application is refused, a further application may be made to the Crown Court.

29.3.2 HEARING THE APPEAL

The appeal in the Crown Court takes the form of a complete rehearing of the case before a judge sitting with two lay magistrates. New evidence may be heard if it has become available since the original trial. The Crown Court can confirm, vary or reverse any part of the magistrates' court original decision.

The defendant should be warned that if his appeal fails, the Crown Court can impose any sentence that was available to the magistrates. This may result in your client receiving a more severe penalty. An unsuccessful appeal may result in the defendant paying some or all of the prosecution's costs.

29.4 APPEAL BY WAY OF CASE STATED—S. 111 MAGISTRATES' COURTS ACT 1980 (CRIM PR, PART 64)

Section 111 MCA 1980 provides:

'(1) Any person who was a party to any proceeding before a magistrates' court or is aggrieved by the conviction, order, determination or other proceeding of the court may question the proceeding on the ground that it is wrong in law or is in excess of jurisdiction by applying to the justices composing the court to state a case for the opinion of the High Court on the question of law or jurisdiction involved;

(2) An application under subsection (1) above shall be made within 21 days after the day on which the decision of the magistrates' court was given.'

Appeal by way of case stated to the Divisional Court may be made by any party to the proceedings before the magistrates' court who seeks to challenge the conviction or any order or determination made by the court during the proceedings.

The grounds for making an appeal by way of case stated are that the magistrates' court was:

• wrong in law; or

• in excess of its jurisdiction.

The issues that are commonly raised in a case stated application includes whether:

• the justices had jurisdiction to try the case; or

• the justices were correct to find that there was a case to answer; or

• admissible evidence was excluded; or

• inadmissible evidence was admitted in evidence; or

• the justices' interpretation of the law was wrong.

29.4.1   THE PROCEDURE FOR STATING A CASE

- Within 21 days of the acquittal, conviction or sentence, the party must apply in writing (usually by letter), requiring the magistrates who heard the case to state a case for the Divisional Court's consideration. The party should identify the question of law on which the Divisional Court's opinion is sought.

- A statement of case is prepared by the magistrates' legal adviser in consultation with the magistrates, which will:
  — outline the facts called into question;
  — state the facts as found by the magistrates;
  — state the magistrates' finding on the point of law being challenged, listing any authority cited; and
  — state the question for the Divisional Court to answer.

- Drafts of the case are then sent to the parties who may suggest amendments.

- The final form of the case stated is then sent to the appellant who must lodge it at the Crown Office of the Royal Courts of Justice in London. Notice and a copy of the case stated must be given to the respondent.

- The appeal is heard by the Divisional Court usually before three judges. Evidence is not called and the hearing takes the form of legal argument on the facts of the case as stated.

- The Divisional Court may reverse, amend or affirm the magistrates' decision or may remit the matter back to the magistrates with its opinion and a direction that the magistrates' court should, for example, convict the defendant or acquit him or the case should be tried again before a different bench.

- Costs may be awarded to either party out of central funds.

Magistrates may grant bail to a defendant who has received a custodial sentence pending the hearing of his appeal (s. 113 MCA 1980). If bail is refused, application can be made to a High Court judge in chambers.

29.4.2   IS FURTHER APPEAL POSSIBLE?

No—unless the matter is appealed to the House of Lords on a point of law of public importance and either the Divisional Court or the House of Lords grant leave.

29.4.3   MAY THE SAME ISSUE BE APPEALED TO THE CROWN COURT AND BY WAY OF CASE STATED?

No—the right of appeal to the Crown Court is lost once an application is made to state the case. It is possible to appeal by way of case stated to challenge the conviction and to appeal to the Crown Court against the sentence passed in the case. For this reason, the first avenue of appeal is usually the Crown Court (para. 29.3).

29.5   JUDICIAL REVIEW

Judicial review is available to a party in a criminal case where a magistrates' court as a 'public law' body has exercised its legal powers illegally or has failed to follow the correct procedure or has acted irrationally. Judicial review proceedings are governed by Part 54, Civil Procedure Rules. State funding for judicial review is through a civil funding certificate.

Judicial review will be appropriate to challenge a decision where the magistrates' court acted in excess of its jurisdiction by failing to follow the statute which confers jurisdiction, or by acting in breach of the rules of natural justice, by, for example failing to allow an adjournment requested by a defendant on proper grounds or failing to give proper time to prepare a defence, see *R v Thames Magistrates' Court, ex p. Polemis* [1974] 1 WLR 1371. Judicial review will also be appropriate where there are grounds for suspecting bias on the part of the legal adviser or one or more of the magistrates.

9.5.1 APPLYING FOR JUDICIAL REVIEW

Civil Procedure Rules Part 54 prescribes a two-stage procedure for applying for judicial review. The first stage is an application for leave to a High Court judge to obtain permission to proceed. A notice of application on the appropriate claim form setting out the grounds for review must be filed by the defendant. The claim form must:

- identify the applicant; and
- the relief sought;
- the grounds on which the application is made; and
- an affidavit (i.e. a sworn statement) that verifies those grounds and adds further argument.

A single judge usually determines the application for leave without a hearing and in the absence of the other side (the respondent).

If leave is granted, the judicial review hearing will be before the Divisional Court which hears arguments from the applicant, the respondent and any other body affected by the magistrates' decision. In a criminal case this will usually be the CPS, the Ministry of Justice or the Home Office.

Bail pending the hearing of an application for judicial review may be granted by a judge in chambers.

At the end of the hearing, court makes its decision, and if the applicant's case is proven, will grant relief by making a mandatory order; and/or a prohibiting order or a quashing order.

29.6 APPEAL FROM THE CROWN COURT (CRIM PR, PARTS 65–68)

A person convicted of an offence on indictment may appeal to the Court of Appeal against his conviction and/or his sentence where he pleaded not guilty or against sentence only where he pleaded guilty, s. 1 Criminal Appeal Act 1968 (CAA 1968). The advice of counsel or a solicitor-advocate should always be sought before commencing an appeal against conviction and/or sentence to the Court of Appeal.

29.6.1 OBTAINING LEAVE TO APPEAL

Leave to appeal against conviction and/or sentence to the Court of Appeal is always required. Leave may be given by the trial judge granting a certificate that the case is fit for appeal or the Court of Appeal can grant leave.

Where leave is required from the Court of Appeal, within 28 days of conviction or sentence, the appellant must serve on the Registrar of Criminal Appeals, a notice of application for leave to appeal, accompanied by draft grounds of appeal. The draft grounds will be settled by counsel.

29.6.2 FUNDING AN APPEAL TO THE COURT OF APPEAL

Where a defendant has been granted a representation order for trial on indictment, the order will cover both advice in connection with a possible appeal; drafting the grounds of appeal and seeking leave. Once leave to appeal has been granted, the representation order will need to be extended to cover representation at the appeal.

If the appeal is against conviction, a transcript should be provided of either of the judge's summing up or of some part of the evidence or where appropriate, the full transcript of the trial. The court's shorthand writer will then be asked by the registrar to transcribe the appropriate part of his notes. The papers are then put before a single judge.

This is a filtering stage at which a single judge considers whether leave ought to be given. If leave to appeal is given, public funding will be available for the hearing itself.

If the single judge refuses leave to appeal, the appellant has 14 further days in which to serve notice on the registrar that he wishes to renew the application before the full court. The papers are then put before the 'full' court, which considers the issue. If leave is refused, the application is lost and the appellant may be subject to a loss of time order.

29.6.3 WHAT IS A DIRECTION FOR LOSS OF TIME?

Usually, any time spent in custody by an appellant between sentence being passed and his appeal hearing counts as part of any custodial sentence. A direction to the contrary called 'direction for loss of time' may be given by the court when refusing leave to appeal or dismissing an appeal purely on the grounds of law (s. 29 Criminal Appeal Act (CAA) 1968). This is a means of penalising an appellant for pursuing a frivolous appeal although directions for loss of time are very rarely made if counsel has advised on an appeal. A direction for loss of time would normally be made against an appellant who proceeds with an appeal against counsel's advice.

29.6.4 GRANTING BAIL ON APPEAL

The Court of Appeal has power to grant bail to an appellant pending the determination of his appeal. This may be exercised by the single judge when he considers the papers. Where the trial judge certifies that a case is fit for appeal, he may also grant bail pending determination of the appeal.

29.6.5 APPEALS AGAINST CONVICTION

The Court of Appeal may only allow an appeal against conviction if it thinks that the conviction is 'unsafe', s. 2(1)(a) CAA 1968 (as amended by Criminal Appeal Act 1995).

In deciding whether the conviction is 'unsafe', the Court of Appeal will hear legal argument from each side and may, exceptionally, hear fresh evidence under s. 23 CAA 1968. The common practice is for an appellant to refer to specific legal or procedural errors that arose at trial, and then supplement these specific claims with the general ground that the conviction is unsafe.

The test to decide whether a conviction is 'unsafe' is subjective. Each member of the Court of Appeal must ask: 'Have I a reasonable doubt, or even a lurking doubt, that this conviction may be unsafe?' If the answer is affirmative, the appeal should be allowed (*Stafford v DPP* [1974] AC 878). In *Pendleton* [2002] 1 WLR 72, the House of Lords held that the correct test in a case where the Court of Appeal receives fresh evidence on appeal under s. 23 CAA 1968, is whether the conviction was safe, not whether the defendant was guilty. In such cases the Court of Appeal must consider what effect the fresh evidence would have had on the jurors if it had been received at the original trial. If it might reasonably have affected the jurors' decision to convict, the conviction should be regarded as 'unsafe'.

There was concern that the amendment to the single ground of appeal by the CAA 1995, that the conviction is 'unsafe', has restricted the Court of Appeal's powers to quash a conviction. In *R v Chalkley; Jeffries* [1998] 2 Cr App R 79, the Court of Appeal confirmed that, following the amendment of s. 2(1) CAA 1968, the court had no power to allow an appeal if it did not consider the conviction to be unsafe but was in some other way dissatisfied with what had occurred at the trial, since the former tests of 'unsatisfactoriness' and 'material irregularity' were no longer available, except to determine the safety of a conviction.

In practice, however, the potentially restrictive interpretation of s. 2(1) CAA 1968 put forward in *Chalkley* has not been adopted and in considering if a conviction is unsafe, the Court of Appeal is entitled to take into account whether:

- the conviction is unsatisfactory; or
- that the court made a wrong decision on a point of law; or
- there was a material irregularity in the course of the trial.

As a consequence, grounds for appeal against conviction can include:

- wrongful admission or exclusion of evidence;
- failure to properly exercise judicial discretion;
- errors on the part of counsel;
- defect in the indictment;
- conduct of the trial judge;
- errors in the trial judge's summing-up;
- problems associated with jurors.

 Looking Ahead

Section 42 of the Criminal Justice and Immigration Act 2008 alters the test to be applied by the Court of Appeal when considering appeals against conviction. The amendment to s. 2 Criminal Appeal Act 1968 provides that a conviction is not unsafe if the Court of Appeal thinks there is no reasonable doubt about the appellant's guilt. The Court of Appeal may still quash the conviction if it would seriously undermine the proper administration of justice to allow it to stand.

9.6.6 DISPOSALS AVAILABLE TO THE COURT OF APPEAL

In deciding whether the appellant's conviction was unsafe, the Court of Appeal court may:

- quash the conviction and, in effect, order an acquittal;
- quash the conviction and order a retrial;
- find the appellant guilty of an alternative offence;
- allow part of the appeal; or
- dismiss the appeal.

29.7 APPEAL AGAINST SENTENCE FROM THE CROWN COURT

An appeal against sentence follows the same procedure as an appeal against conviction except that an appeal against sentence only will not attract a loss of time direction. An appeal can be made on the basis that the sentence imposed was wrong in law, wrong in principle or was manifestly excessive. In considering an appeal against sentence, the Court of Appeal can:

- quash any sentence or order; or
- impose any sentence or order that could have been available to the Crown Court except the appellant should not be dealt with more severely than at the Crown Court.

29.8 APPEAL TO THE HOUSE OF LORDS (CRIM PR, PART 74)

Appeal from the Court of Appeal to the House of Lords may only be made where the Court of Appeal or the House of Lords certifies the case involves a point of law of general public importance.

29.9 ATTORNEY-GENERAL'S REFERENCES

Under s. 36 CJA 1988 (Crim PR, Part 70) the Attorney-General may, with leave of the Court of Appeal, refer to that court any sentence imposed by the Crown Court where he considers the sentence was unduly lenient. The Court of Appeal may then quash the original sentence and substitute such sentence (usually heavier) as it thinks appropriate for the case and which the court below had power to pass when dealing with the offender.

Under s. 36 Criminal Justice Act 1972 (Crim PR, Part 70) the Attorney-General has the power to refer a case to the Court of Appeal for its opinion on a point of law which arose in the case. The power relates to a case where the defendant was acquitted following trial on indictment. Whatever the outcome of the appeal, the defendant remains acquitted.

29.10 CRIMINAL CASES REVIEW COMMISSION

The Criminal Cases Review Commission, which was established by the Criminal Appeal Act 1995 is located in Birmingham and investigates and processes allegations of miscarriages of justice.

Under s. 9 Criminal Appeal Act 1995, the Commission may refer to the Court of Appeal:

* a conviction for an offence on indictment;
* a sentence imposed for an offence on indictment;
* a finding of not guilty by insanity.

Under s. 11 CAA 1995, the Commission may refer to the Crown Court a conviction and/or sentence imposed by the magistrates' court.

29.10.1 WHAT TEST MUST BE SATISFIED BEFORE THE COMMISSION CAN REFER A CASE?

The Commission may only refer a case to the Court of Appeal or to the Crown Court where, under s. 13 CAA 1995, the Commission considers that there is a real possibility that the verdict or sentence would not be upheld if the reference was made.

Section 15 CAA 1995 enables the Court of Appeal to direct the Commission to investigate a particular matter 'in such manner as the Commission thinks fit'. Sections 17–21 CAA 1995 provide the Commission with the power to obtain documents and direct officers to investigate and report on a relevant matter.

29.11 DOES THE PROSECUTION ENJOY A RIGHT TO APPEAL?

Until recently, the prosecution has enjoyed only limited rights to appeal. The prosecution had no right to appeal against acquittal of a defendant following a summary trial or trial on indictment. The only exception to this was the prosecutor's right to appeal a decision by a magistrates' court by way of case stated in accordance with para. 29.4 above and by way of judicial review.

In relation to trials on indictment, the prosecution enjoys a right of interlocutory appeal against binding rulings made by a trial judge at a preparatory hearing in accordance with ss. 35 and 36 Criminal Procedure and Investigations Act 1996 (Crim PR, Part 66).

The right of the prosecution to appeal against sentence is set out in para. 29.9 above. It requires a reference to be made by the Attorney-General.

The CJA 2003 has extended the prosecution's right of appeal in a number of important situations.

First, under s. 58 CJA 2003 the prosecution may appeal to the Court of Appeal against a terminating ruling made by the judge in relation to an issue at a trial on indictment and which cannot otherwise be the subject of an appeal to the Court of Appeal. The appeal can be against any judicial ruling made during the trial until the beginning of the summing up to the jury. The procedure of appealing against a terminating ruling is detailed in Crim PR, Part 67. it includes a prosecution appeal against:

- a successful submission of no case to answer by the defence; or

- a ruling on a PII application in favour of the defence; or

- a decision to stay the proceedings for an abuse of process; or

- a successful defence application to sever the counts on the indictment.

In making the application prosecution must agree that in the event of failing to obtain leave to appeal or if the appeal is abandoned, the defendant will be automatically acquitted.

Under the procedure, which is laid down in ss. 57–61 CJA 2003, the appeal can follow an expedited or non-expedited route. It is for the trial judge to decide which route is appropriate. In an expedited appeal, the trial may be adjourned to await the Court of Appeal's ruling. In a non-expedited appeal, the trial may be adjourned or the jury discharged.

Under s. 61 CJA 2003 the Court of Appeal may confirm or reverse or vary any ruling which the prosecution has appealed against. A ruling may only be reversed where the Court of Appeal is satisfied that:

- the ruling was wrong in law;

- the ruling involved an error in law or principle; or

- the ruling was not reasonable for the judge to make.

Where the Court reverses or varies the terminating ruling, it must order the resumption of the Crown Court trial or order a fresh trial or order the defendant's acquittal.

Second, the CJA 2003 has radically revised the traditional operation of *autrefois acquit*. Historically where a defendant has been found not guilty at trial and acquitted, the doctrine of *autrefois acquit* has prevented him from being retried for the same offence. Section 76 CJA 2003 allows the prosecutor to apply to the Court of Appeal for an order to quash the defendant's acquittal for a qualifying offence and to order a new trial. Generally a qualifying offence is any offence which carries a sentence of life imprisonment.

The Court of Appeal must order a retrial if there is new and compelling evidence in the case and it is in the interests of justice of the order to be made.

 Looking Ahead

When in force, ss. 62 and 63 CJA 2003 give the prosecution the right of appeal on an evidential ruling made by the judge in relation to the admissibility of the prosecution evidence at trial. The appeal may be expedited or non-expedited and the Court of Appeal may confirm, reverse or vary the evidentiary ruling in question.

KEY POINT SUMMARY

- Ensure that you are know which avenue of appeal from the magistrates' court is appropriate to your client's case and be able to advise accordingly.
- Know the time-limits and procedures for appealing.
- Be aware of the procedural steps in appealing from the Crown Court to the Court of Appeal.
- Understand what is meant by an 'unsafe' conviction under s. 2(1)(a) Criminal Appeal Act 1968.

SELF-TEST QUESTIONS

1. When might it be appropriate to apply for the case to be reheard under s. 142 MCA 1980?
2. What is the potential danger to your client if appeals against sentence to the Crown Court?
3. Who may appeal by way of case stated?
4. Must leave be obtained to appeal from the Crown Court to the Court of Appeal?
5. On what ground may the Court of Appeal allow an appeal against conviction?

FIGURE 29.1 APPEALS

APPEALS FROM THE MAGISTRATES' COURT

Σ Rehearing the case, s. 142 MCA 1980

- on the defendant's application, the magistrates' court may set the conviction/sentence aside;
- the application will be granted where 'it is in the interests of justice';
- any retrial will be reheard by a different bench of magistrates.

Σ Appeal to the Crown Court, s. 108 MCA 1980

- against conviction and/or sentence;
- within 21 days of conviction and/or sentence, defendant applies to magistrates' court which heard his case;
- the appeal in the Crown Court takes the form of a rehearing;
- the Crown Court can confirm, vary or reverse the magistrates' decision;
- where the appeal fails, the Crown Court can impose any sentence which the magistrates might have imposed (which might include a harsher penalty).

Σ Appeal by way of case stated, s. 111 MCA 1980

- to the Divisional Court;
- where the magistrates' court was wrong in law; or
- acted in excess of jurisdiction;
- application from any interested party within 21 days;
- appeal is heard by three judges in the Divisional Court;
- the Divisional Court may reverse, amend or affirm the magistrates' court decision or may remit the case back to the magistrates.

Σ Judicial review, Part 54 CPR

- application to the Divisional Court;
- where a public law body acted irrationally or illegally or did not follow the correct procedure;
- where applicant proves the case, the court may make a mandatory order; or a prohibiting order; or a quashing order.

APPEAL FROM THE CROWN COURT

Σ Defendant may appeal to the Court of Appeal against conviction (where pleaded not guilty) and/or sentence;

Σ Leave must be obtained from the trial judge or the Court of Appeal;

Σ Appeal against conviction will be allowed where the conviction is 'unsafe', s. 2(1)(a) CAA 1968;

Σ Where conviction is 'unsafe', the court may:

- quash the conviction and order an acquittal; or
- quash the conviction and order a retrial;
- find the appellant guilty on an alternative offence; or
- allow part of the appeal; or
- dismiss the appeal;

Σ In deciding an appeal against sentence, the Court of Appeal can:

- quash any sentence or order; or
- impose any sentence or order that was available to the Crown Court provided the appellant is not dealt with more severely than at his trial;

Σ Prosecution's right to appeal against:

- rulings made by the trial judge at a preparatory hearing, ss. 35, 36 CPIA 1996;
- appeal against a terminating ruling during a trial on indictment, ss. 57–61 CJA 2003;
- application to the Court of Appeal for an order to quash the defendant's acquittal for a qualifying offence and to order a new trial, s. 76 CJA 2003.

Part VI

YOUTH JUSTICE

Part VI comprises two chapters, which examine the special considerations that apply in relation to young offenders under the age of 18.

30 YOUTH JUSTICE

30.1 INTRODUCTION

The Audit Commission has estimated that approximately seven million crimes are committed each year by offenders under 18 years of age and that over £1 billon is spent annually dealing with offending by young people. Empirical research has also confirmed that approximately 17 per cent of all persons who are taken to the police station are aged under 18 years. Therefore juvenile offending has important political, economic and social implications as well as making important demands on the criminal justice system and those who work in it. The final two chapters of the *Criminal Litigation Handbook* have been written to acknowledge the growing importance of this increasingly specialist area of criminal practice.

While many of the practices and procedures of youth justice will be familiar to you and are based on the adult model, there are also important differences in recognition of the special position and vulnerabilities of young people in the criminal justice system. These special considerations are reflected, for example, in the relative informality of proceedings in the Youth Court and the requirement that all participants in the youth justice system are under a statutory duty to prevent offending by children and young people. Youth justice also has a number of specialist organisations that formulate policy and deal with young offenders and their families on a day-to-day basis. There are a range of schemes which seek to divert juveniles from crime when they are in danger of offending for the first time and provision is also made for alternatives to proseation where a young person admits an offence. Therefore prevention from offending and the opportunities for the early rehabilitation of those who have offended are pervasive to the aims and procedures of youth justice, and, as a defence solicitor working in this area, you will need to have a good working knowledge of these issues.

We deal with youth justice in two chapters. Chapter 31, deals with the rules governing where the young person is to be tried and the disposals available to each court. This chapter deals with pre-trial issues and specifically covers the following areas:

* the terminology of youth justice;
* the youth justice organisations;
* the meaning of parental responsibility;
* the principal aims of the youth justice system;
* the early diversion procedures to prevent further offending;
* the juvenile at the police station;
* the alternatives to prosecution;
* the decision to charge.

30.2 THE TERMINOLOGY OF YOUTH JUSTICE

The terminology of youth justice uses a number of key words and phrases to categorise an offender who is not classed as an adult. It is important to be aware of the meaning of each term and to understand the context in which the term is used. A commonly used word is 'juvenile', which, while not defined in legislation, is generally applied to a person who is under 18 years of age. However, be aware that in relation to his detention at the police station an arrested juvenile is a person who is under 17 years of age or appears to be under 17 years of age.

You will also come across the word 'child'. Some legislation, for example s. 107 Children and Young Persons Act 1933, defines a child as a person under 14 years. However, in relation to a person in the care of the local authority, 'child' has an extended meaning to include a person aged under 18 years. The term 'young person' or 'young offender' or 'youth offender' is generally attributed to a person aged 14–17 years. This classification is relevant, for example, to sentencing powers where a distinction is drawn between the powers available over a child aged between 10 and 13 and a young person who is aged between 14 and 17.

In this chapter, as a matter of style, we adopt the generic terms of juvenile, youth, young person and young offender to mean a person under 18 years unless a different meaning is indicated.

30.2.1 PERSISTENT YOUNG OFFENDER (PYO) AND PERSISTENT OFFENDER (PO)

Before leaving the terminology of youth justice, you should be aware that some of your clients will be formally classified as a persistent young offender (PYO). Whilst there is no statutory definition of the term 'persistent young offender' according to the Home Office (see *Tackling Delays in the Youth Justice System: A Consultation Paper*, October 1987), a PYO is:

* a young person aged between 10 and 17 years;
* who has been sentenced by any criminal court in the UK on three or more separate occasions; and
* within three years of the last sentencing occasion is subsequently arrested or has an information laid against him for a further recordable offence.

While only approximately three per cent of youth offenders are classified as PYOs, they are responsible for committing a disproportionate amount of youth crime and special procedures aimed at their rehabilitation are in place. Where these initiatives are unsuccessful at changing the PYO's behaviour, government targets require that the case be dealt with by the courts as expeditiously as possible and within 71 days from arrest to sentence.

A further classification relates to a persistent offender (PO). This classification is important when the Youth Court sentences a young offender to a detention and training order (see Chapter 31). The term 'persistent offender' is not defined by statute. A PO may be a young person of previous good character or who may not have appeared in court before but is deemed a PO as he may have had numerous final warnings and/or reprimands, or may have committed a series of offences over a short period which are all charged on one occasion. It is up to the court to decide whether a young person is a PO. The classification may be relevant when deciding if the young person should be tried summarily or on indictment and where he is aged 14 years and over, the appropriate sentence that might be imposed.

30.3 THE YOUTH JUSTICE ORGANISATIONS

A number of specialist organisations operate in the youth justice system to develop and manage policies and resources or are involved in day-to-day contact with juveniles and their families. The Youth Justice Board for England and Wales (YJB) was created by the Crime and Disorder Act 1998 and exercises a supervisory function over the youth justice system by working to prevent juvenile offending, to address the reasons for their offending and to ensure that when a juvenile is committed to custody, the accommodation is safe and secure. In fulfilling this role the YJB:

* advises the Home Secretary on the operation and standards of the youth justice system;

* monitors the performance of the youth justice system;

* provides accommodation for young persons who are remanded into custody;

* identifies and promotes good practice in the youth justice service; and

* commissions research and publishes information on the youth justice system.

The YJB has an excellent website which can be accessed at: www.yjb.gov.uk.

The day-to-day administration of youth justice is undertaken by youth offending teams (YOTs), which are situated in every local authority in England and Wales. The multidisciplinary membership of each YOT is drawn from the police, probation service, social services and education, the health authority, housing and drug, alcohol and substance misuse agencies. The YOT identifies the needs of young offenders and manages specific programmes to prevent them offending or reoffending. The YOT also exercises the statutory responsibility of supervising young people in custody and on community orders.

It is important to establish a good working relationship with the member of the YOT who has been assigned to your client's case as often they are an invaluable source of information.

30.4 THE MAIN AIMS OF THE YOUTH JUSTICE SYSTEM

Section 37(1) Crime and Disorder Act 1998 states the principal aim of the youth justice system is to prevent offending by children and young people. In support of the principal aim, s. 37(2) CDA 1998 requires that:

'In addition to any other duty to which they are subject, it shall be the duty of all persons and bodies carrying out functions in relation to the youth justice system to have regard to that aim.'

As a defence lawyer, in common with the other participants in the youth justice system such as the police, the CPS, local authority and the courts, regard must be had to this overriding principle which runs alongside your professional conduct obligations as a solicitor.

A further duty is the 'welfare principle' imposed by s. 44(1) Children and Young Persons Act 1933 which requires:

> 'Every court in dealing with a child or young person who is brought before it, either as an offender or otherwise, shall have regard to the welfare of the child or young person and shall in a proper case take steps for removing from undesirable surroundings, and securing that proper provision is made for his education and training.'

When making submissions to the court about the appropriate action that should be taken against your client, you should always have the welfare principle in mind.

30.5 PARENTAL RESPONSIBILITY

To represent your juvenile client effectively, you must have an understanding of the concept of parental responsibility which was introduced by the Children Act 1989. Parental responsibility is defined by s. 3(1) of the 1989 Act as 'all the rights, duties, powers, responsibilities and authority which by law a parent of a child has in relation to the child and his property'. The concept relates to the person(s) who has (have) responsibility for looking after the young person on a daily basis and makes decisions about his life.

Married parents share parental responsibility for their child. If the parents are not married, parental responsibility is vested in the child's mother, although an unmarried father can acquire parental responsibility. Parental responsibility can be shared with or acquired by other legal bodies such as a local authority where, for example, the child is the subject of a care or supervision order.

You will need to work closely with the person(s) having parental responsibility over the juvenile and work together to ensure that the case has the best possible outcome for your client. The person having parental responsibility may also be involved in other aspects of the case, such as acting as the young person's appropriate adult at the police station or at the disposal of the case being made the subject of parenting order or a parental bind over, or paying the fine imposed on the young person.

30.6 PREVENTING JUVENILE OFFENDING

A key part of youth justice policies developed by the YJB are the early diversion procedures designed to deter a juvenile from getting into trouble in the first place or to seek the early rehabilitation of a juvenile who has already committed very low-level crimes or anti-social behaviour. Research commissioned by the YJB shows the peak age for juvenile offending is 14 years; so it is believed that if a juvenile can be diverted from offending before he reaches this age, the chances of him offending in the future will be much diminished. Therefore, a number of diversionary and intervention programmes have been developed to deter a young person from offending or reoffending. Some schemes are being piloted, while others are targeted at specific areas of social deprivation and high crime rates. A young person may be directed to participating in a scheme by the police or YOT member.

You should be aware of the schemes that are available in your local area to deal with the reasons for your client's offending and where appropriate suggest to the police or the CPS your client's willingness to attend such a scheme to divert him from being dealt with more formally.

The schemes include:

- youth inclusion programmes (YIPs);
- youth inclusion and support panels (YISPs);

- positive activities for young people (PAYP);
- positive futures (PF);
- safer school partnerships;
- mentoring;
- parenting skills.

See the Youth Justice Board's website for further information.

30.7 PRE-COURT ORDERS

The next step in the hierarchy of responses to juvenile offending is provided by pre-court orders. When a juvenile first gets into trouble or engages in anti-social behaviour or is involved in very low-level crime, he may be dealt with outside the court system by an early diversion scheme explained in para. 30.6 above. Alternatively, the police or local authority may use a range of pre-court orders to prevent the juvenile from offending and being dealt with more formally by the youth justice system. The following pre-court orders are available.

Acceptable behaviour contract (ABC)

An acceptable behaviour contract is given to a juvenile when a local authority or YOT identifies a juvenile who is engaged in low-level anti-social behaviour. To address the reasons for the juvenile behaving in this way, the juvenile and his parent(s) or guardian(s) agree a contract to stop the pattern of behaviour that is causing the nuisance to the local community. If the terms of the contract are breached, the local authority may obtain an anti-social behaviour order against the juvenile.

Anti-social behaviour order (ASBO)

The infamous ASBO can be applied for by the police or a local authority in connection with any person aged ten years or over who is behaving in a way that causes harassment, alarm or distress to people who live in a particular locality. The ASBO prevents the young person from going to a particular place or from doing specified activities. A failure to comply with the terms of the ASBO can lead to prosecution. The ASBO can include an ISO (Individual Support Order) which can last up to six months. It requires the young person to attend twice weekly sessions with the youth offending team.

Penalty Notice for Disorder (PND)

The PND scheme is another disposal open to the police when dealing with offences comprising low-level, anti-social and nuisance behaviour. An officer may issue a PND on the spot or at a police station. The penalties range from payment of £30 up to £80. In the case of an offender below the age of 16, the sums will be paid by the juvenile's parent or guardian. If the PND is disputed, the recipient must request a hearing before a magistrates' court within 21 days of issue. A PND is not a conviction but details of it are held on the police national computer.

30.8 POLICE DUTIES AND RESPONSIBILITIES AND JUVENILE SUSPECTS

A detailed explanation of the procedure in relation to detaining and questioning a person suspected of being involved in criminal behaviour is covered in Part II of this book. Below we highlight the special rules that apply to juveniles who have been arrested and detained at the police station.

30.8.1 DETERMINING THE YOUNG PERSON'S AGE

For the purposes of s. 37(15) PACE 1984 and Code C, a juvenile is any person who is aged under 17 years or who appears to be under 17 years of age. Code C para. 1.5 stipulates that anyone who appears to be under the age of 17 shall be treated as a juvenile in the absence of clear evidence to the contrary. Therefore, if a person who may be a juvenile refuses to give his age to the custody officer or the officer believes the age the person has given is incorrect, the suspect must be treated as a juvenile. Remember that if the detained person is under ten years of age he has no criminal liability and therefore cannot be detained. In these circumstances, the custody officer will arrange for the child to be taken home or if there is concern for the child's physical or moral welfare, the local authority social services department will be contacted. A child safety order may be applied for.

While in police detention, a juvenile is classified as a 'vulnerable' suspect. Juveniles make up the largest number of suspects who fall into the category of a vulnerable suspect.

Where the person is identified as a juvenile, he will be entitled to a range of special protections which are dealt with below.

30.8.2 THE CUSTODY OFFICER'S DUTIES

Code C requires the custody officer to identify the juvenile's needs and vulnerabilities (Code C para. 3.6–3.10). The custody officer must as soon as practicable identify the parent, guardian or local authority who has parental responsibility for the juvenile's welfare and inform that person of the juvenile's arrest, the reasons for the arrest and the place where the juvenile is being held. As the person who is responsible for the juvenile's welfare will usually act as the appropriate adult, the person will be asked to attend the police station immediately.

30.8.3 THE APPROPRIATE ADULT

The role of the appropriate adult is to assist and advise the juvenile while he is in police detention. Code C, Note 1.7 requires that an appropriate adult for a juvenile should be:

- the juvenile's parent or guardian; or
- if the juvenile is in local authority care or in the care of a voluntary organisation, a person representing that organisation; or
- a social worker from a local authority social services department; or failing any of the above;
- a responsible adult aged 18 or over who is not a police officer or employed by the police.

The suitability of a person to act as an appropriate adult is important because where the appropriate adult is considered incapable of effectively protecting the juvenile's interests, evidence obtained against the juvenile may be excluded at his trial. While it may appear that the juvenile's parent or carer will be the obvious choice, a parent may be incapable of acting through lack of experience or knowledge or through mental illness, or because the juvenile and parent are not on good terms. In these situations an alternative must be found. Depending on his age, the wishes of the juvenile as to who he wants to act as the appropriate adult should be taken into account. For example, in *R v Blake* [1989] 89 CR App R 179, the police ignored the juvenile's request that her social worker act as the appropriate adult, asking the girl's father to attend the police station directly against the girl's wishes. In *R v Morse* [1991] Crim LR 195, the juvenile's father had an IQ of below 70 and was incapable of appreciating the importance of his role. In both cases the confession made by the juvenile in the presence of the appropriate adult was excluded at their trials.

A solicitor should not act as an appropriate adult as it will lead to a conflict of interest between his role as a legal adviser and his role as an appropriate adult.

While Code C provides only a general indication about the appropriate adult's role, some assistance is provided by the Home Office Guidance for Appropriate Adults, which states that the appropriate adult is required to:

- support, advise and assist the detained person, particularly while they are being questioned;
- observe whether the police are acting fairly and with respect for the rights of the detained person;
- assist with communication between the detained person and the police;
- ensure that the detained person understands their rights and that the adult has a role in protecting those rights.

It is also important to make a juvenile client aware that, unlike his legal adviser, the appropriate adult is not bound by any duty of confidentiality or legal professional privilege. Best practice suggests that legal advisers at the police station should initially consult with their juvenile client in the absence of the appropriate adult to warn him about the dangers of disclosing information that should remain confidential between lawyer and client.

30.8.4   THE JUVENILE'S OTHER RIGHTS

In addition to his right to have an appropriate adult to support him, a juvenile is entitled to the full range of rights at the police station as other detainees. These include the right to inform someone of his arrest under s. 56 PACE 1984 and the right to legal advice under s. 58 PACE 1984.

The juvenile has the same right to legal advice under s. 58 PACE 1984 as an adult. While the grounds for suspending the right to legal advice under s. 58(8) PACE 1984 apply to a juvenile in the same way as for an adult detainee, once the appropriate adult has been requested to attend the police station, it is very difficult for the police to justify that one or more of the reasons for delaying legal advice under s. 58(8) PACE 1984 applies. While the time limits for detention without charge are the same for both a juvenile and an adult, in view of the juvenile's vulnerabilities every effort should be made to keep detention to a minimum, especially in the case of a very young person. Generally a juvenile should not be held in a police cell unless there is no other way of guaranteeing his safety. In whatever place he is detained, the custody officer is required to monitor his detention more closely than in the case of an adult and to undertake regular risk assessments.

With regard to the taking of an intimate sample from a juvenile, the consent of a parent or guardian must be given if the juvenile is under 14. If the juvenile is aged between 14 and 17, both his consent and that of his parent or guardian are required (s. 65 PACE 1984.)

30.9   DEALING WITH A JUVENILE CLIENT

During your initial interview it is important that the young person gives you a full and coherent response to the allegations that have been made against him. You should advise him fully about the possible outcomes of the case, the consequences of him admitting his guilt and the possibility of him being given a reprimand or final warning. Young offenders (and often their parents or carers) are the most challenging clients that you will encounter as they often have little respect for authority and are likely to test your patience. You need special skills to interview these clients and to get them to recognise that you are there to help and are not part of the law enforcement machinery.

Leanne Black, aged 14, is an infamous example of a young offender. In March 2006 Black, who is currently Britain's youngest drink driver, attacked the CPS lawyer and threw a jug of water at the magistrates as she was sentenced to four months' custody for her second offence of drink driving. These dramatic events occurred shortly after her lawyer had submitted in mitigation that Leanne was a reformed character. The family's disruptive behaviour was not, however, limited to inside the courtroom. As she arrived at court Leanne hurled eggs at the media, and Nora Black, Leanne's mother flashed her bare bottom, inviting them to 'film this'.

Other infamous young offenders include twins Ben and Nathan Weeks, who became subject to ASBOs when they were just ten after the court heard they had made life hell for their neighbours in Norfolk by shouting, swearing and even shooting at residents' cars and windows with a ball-bearing gun.

30.10 DECIDING HOW THE CASE WILL PROCEED

Except in the most serious offences, the decision about how the case will proceed will not be taken immediately by the police or the CPS. A juvenile client will usually be bailed until the decision is made. The case file will often be referred to a CPS youth offender specialist to decide whether to prosecute or take alternative action.

In deciding how the case will proceed, the CPS lawyer will have in mind the 'welfare' principle under s. 44 CYPA 1933 and the statutory duty to prevent offending under s. 37 CDA 1998 explained at para. 30.4 above. The juvenile's right to a fair trial under Article 6 ECHR 1950 should also be taken into account. Further guidance is provided by paras. 8.8 to 8.9 in the Code for Crown Prosecutors for dealing with young offenders. Paragraph 8.8 of the Code requires the Crown Prosecutor to consider:

- the interests of the juvenile when deciding whether it is in the public interest to prosecute; and
- the juvenile's age should not preclude a prosecution where the seriousness of the present offence or the defendant's past behaviour justifies it.

Paragraph 8.9 states that generally a prosecution will only usually be appropriate where:
- the offence is so serious that a prosecution is justified; and/or
- the juvenile does not admit the offence; and/or
- the juvenile has failed to respond to a reprimand or final warning.

In addition to these specific considerations, both the evidential and public interest tests under the Code will need to be satisfied before the juvenile is charged or the prosecution continues (see Chapter 10).

30.10.1 ALTERNATIVES TO PROSECUTION

Where the sufficient evidence and the public interest tests is satisfied under the Code, para. 8.8 of the Code requires the Crown Prosecutor to consider the possibility of alternatives to prosecution. Your client may therefore be given:

- an informal warning; or
- a reprimand; or
- a final warning.

The police retain strictly limited discretion to take informal action against very low level crime and anti-social behaviour. An informal warning, such as 'firm advice' will be given by a police officer usually in the presence of the person having parental responsibility and warning the juvenile about his future behaviour. An alternative to prosecution in more serious cases is provided by ss. 65 and 66 Crime and Disorder Act 1998 which provides a statutory system of reprimands and final warnings. The decision to deal with the young person by a reprimand or a final warning may be taken by a police officer without referring the case to the CPS. However, it is good practice to involve the CPS and the youth offending team in reaching a decision. Section 65(1) (2) CDA 1998 sets out the conditions for a reprimand or final caution to be administered:

- a police officer must have evidence that the young person has committed the offence;
- the police officer must consider that the evidence supports a realistic prospect of a conviction;
- the young person must admit to the police officer that he committed the offence;
- the young person must have no previous convictions (this does not apply to an absolute or conditional discharge); and
- the police officer must be satisfied that a prosecution is not in the public interest.

In addition to these factors which relate to the present offence, it will only be appropriate to reprimand a young person where he has not been warned or reprimanded within the last two years, s. 65(2) CDA 1998. Section 65(5) CDA 1998 requires that a warning or reprimand should be given in the presence of an appropriate adult. It is also essential that to comply with the 'fair trial' provisions under Article 6 ECHR, the full and informed consent of the appropriate adult and the young person is required.

The main factor in deciding whether to charge, reprimand or warn the young person is the seriousness of the offence(s) including the nature of and circumstances in which the offence was committed. The Final Warning Scheme contains a gravity matrix which assists the police in reaching a decision as to the appropriateness or otherwise of a reprimand or final warning. Reprimands and warnings do not count as convictions but can be cited in later criminal case in the same way as convictions and may have to be disclosed on job applications for certain types of jobs. The warning or reprimand will be kept on record by the police until the young person reaches 18 years of age or for five years whichever is the longer.

A reprimand is appropriate for a first-time offender; a final warning will be appropriate for second-time offenders and charging the young person will be appropriate for the most serious offences and persistent young offenders.

Detailed and useful guidance on the Final Warning Scheme is available from the Home Office website. The web-links section of our Online Resource Centre will take you to it.

online resource centre

 Looking Ahead

Provision is made in the Criminal Justice and Immigration Act 2008 to extend the conditional caution scheme (see Chapter 10, para. 10.6.2) to young offenders aged 16 and 17 years. The provisions allow for a caution with specific conditions attached to it to be given where there is sufficient evidence to charge a suspect with an offence which he or she admits and the suspect agrees to the caution. It is for the CPS to decide whether a conditional caution is appropriate and for the police to administer the scheme. If the young person failed to comply with the conditions, he would be liable to be prosecuted for the offence.

10.2 CHARGING THE YOUNG OFFENDER

Where:

- the evidential and public interests under the Code for Crown Prosecutors are satisfied; and
- the offence is sufficiently serious; and
- the statutory duty under s. 37 CDA 1998 requires it, the young offender will be charged with the offence(s).

The juvenile should be charged in the presence of the appropriate adult and his legal adviser. Having been charged, the custody officer must decide whether to release the young person on bail. As with an adult, the relevant criteria to be applied by the custody officer is set out under s. 38 PACE 1984 subject to an additional ground where it would not be in the young person's interests to be granted bail.

Where bail is refused, s. 38(6) PACE 1984 requires the custody officer to ensure that the young person is moved to local authority accommodation unless:

- it is impracticable to do so (in which case he must give reasons why this is so); or
- in the case of a child or young person aged between 12 and 17, no secure accommodation is available and it appears that local authority accommodation would not be adequate to protect the public from serious harm from that child or young person.

30.10.3 COMMENCING PROCEEDINGS AGAINST THE YOUNG PERSON

Commencing proceedings against usually the young person will follow the same procedure as for an adult. A summary offence will be commenced by laying an information and the issuing of a summons or a written charge and requisition. In the case of either-way or indictable-only offence, the formal instigation of proceedings will begin by the police or CPS completing a written charge sheet. The prosecuting authorities should also notify the juvenile's parent or guardian of the need for them to attend court.

30.11 FUNDING THE YOUNG PERSON'S RIGHT TO LEGAL REPRESENTATION

The cost of attending the young person at the police station will be met under the Police Station Advice and Assistance scheme. The advice is free of charge. Post-charge, you will need to apply for a representation order as soon as possible using CDS form 14 (see Chapter 11). Your client will need to satisfy the interests of justice test. However, the means test has no application to applicants under the age of 16 and those aged between 16 and 18 who are in full-time education. If your client is aged 16 or 17 and is not in receipt of income support or income based job seeker's allowance he will need to complete a statement of his means on CDS form 15. The young person should sign the form.

KEY POINT SUMMARY

- Always work in accordance with the statutory duties of the youth justice system under s. 37 CDA 1998 and the welfare principle under s. 44 CYPA 1933.
- Be aware of who has parental responsibility over your juvenile client.
- Be aware of the role of the YOT representative.
- Know the procedures the police have to follow under Code C when the juvenile is detained at the police station.
- Have a good working knowledge of the diversion procedures as alternatives to prosecution and be prepared to argue with the police and/or the CPS about their suitability for your juvenile client.
- Have good working knowledge of the approach taken by your local CPS office in applying the Code for Crown Prosecutors and other relevant matters when deciding whether to prosecute your juvenile client.

SELF-TEST QUESTIONS

1. Explain the role of the appropriate adult.

2. Is a youth offender entitled to publicly funded legal representation?

3. Explain the role of the Youth Offending Team.

4. Remi, aged 14, is a first-time offender charged with a minor offence of criminal damage contrary to s. 1 Criminal Damage Act 1971. Explain the factors the police and/or the CPS will take into account in dealing with Remi.

5. Charlie, aged 12 is accused of assaulting a teacher. It is alleged that Charlie lost his temper and forcefully pushed the teacher against a door resulting in the teacher fracturing her nose. Charlie has since apologised. He admits he should not have lost his temper, however he was incensed about being accused of something he did not do. Charlie has been in an out of care. He received a reprimand six months ago for an offence of common assault involving a pupil at his previous school. His mother is a drug addict and finds it difficult to cope with Charlie. Charlie's behaviour at school has been poor. He has poor concentration levels and is frequently in trouble for fighting. He has been excluded from school as a result of this incident. Explain the factors the police will take into account in dealing with Charlie.

31 PROSECUTING AND SENTENCING OFFENDERS UNDER THE AGE OF 18

31.1 INTRODUCTION

Where formal criminal proceedings are instituted against the young person the general rule is that he will be tried and sentenced in the Youth Court. The Youth Court adopts more informal and less adversarial procedures to deal with the needs and vulnerabilities of young defendants. The procedures should also be compliant with the young person's right to a fair trial under Article 6 ECHR 1950.

While juveniles/young defendants will usually be tried in the Youth Court, be aware that there are situations where the youth will be tried in the Crown Court or in the adult magistrates' court. Therefore the purpose of this chapter is to explain:

- the rules for deciding where a person under the age of 18 is to be tried;
- the rules for trying a young person in the Crown Court;
- the rules for trying a young person in the adult magistrates' court;
- the young defendant's right to court bail;
- the procedure in the Youth Court;
- the Youth Court's sentencing powers;
- the Crown Court's sentencing powers;
- the adult magistrates' court's sentencing powers.

31.2 THE YOUNG PERSON'S FIRST COURT APPEARANCE

In most cases the juvenile's first court appearance in connection with the offence will be in the Youth Court. If the case cannot be dealt with immediately, the court will either remand the young person in custody or release him on bail as explained in para. 31.2.1 below.

If the young person pleads not guilty, the case is likely to be adjourned and a date set for trial in the Youth Court. If a guilty plea is entered, the court may proceed to sentence immediately (following an outline of the facts and any plea in mitigation), or it will adjourn sentence for the preparation of a pre-sentence report.

In most cases the young person will make his first appearance in the Youth Court, unless the case falls within one of the exceptions to this general rule. The exceptions are where the young person is:

- jointly charged with an adult, s. 46(1)(a) CYPA 1933; or
- charged with aiding and abetting an adult to commit an offence, s. 18(a) CYPA 1933, s. 46(1)(b) CYPA 1963; or
- charged with an offence which arises out of the same circumstances or are connected with the offence with which the adult is charged, s. 18(a) CYPA 1963.

In these cases the young person will make his first appearance in the adult magistrates' court.

31.2.1 COURT BAIL

As with adults, it is likely that the young person's entitlement to bail will be dealt with at his first court appearance. The law and procedure governing court bail under the Bail Act 1976 applies to a young person in much the same way as to an adult defendant. For an offender aged 17, the adult bail provisions apply. (For a more detailed consideration of the law and procedure relating to bail, see Chapter 12.)

A young defendant therefore enjoys a presumption under s. 4 Bail Act 1976 in favour of bail. The presumption will be rebutted where the court finds that there are substantial grounds for believing that if granted bail, the youth:

- would fail to surrender to custody; or
- would commit further offences; or
- would interfere with witnesses or the course of justice; or

- has committed imprisonable offences while on bail; or
- should be kept in custody for his own welfare (this is an additional ground for youths).

In deciding whether to grant bail, the court will take into account the factors identified in para. 9 Sch. 1 Bail Act 1976 including the nature and seriousness of the offence, the young person's bail record and community ties. The provisions of ss. 14 and 15 CJA 2003 (see Chapter 12, paras. 12.4.3 and 12.4.4) do not apply to offenders under the age of 18. Instead a new para. 9AA and 9AB have been inserted requiring a court to give particular weight to the fact that the defendant was on bail on the date of the offence or the fact that the defendant has failed to surrender. Paragraphs 9AA and 9AB are in force in relation to offences carrying life imprisonment.

Where bail is refused, a defendant aged between 17 and 20 will be sent to a remand centre (known as a secure remand). A defendant under 17 will be remanded into local authority care subject to any bail condition. A young person aged 12 or over can be remanded into secure local authority accommodation where the conditions laid down by s. 23(5) CYPA 1969 are met, including:

- where the young person is charged with a violent or sexual offence; or
- where the young person is charged with an offence punishable by 14 years or more imprisonment in the case of an adult and only remanding him into secure accommodation would protect the public from serious harm; or
- to prevent the commission by him of imprisonable offences.

Bail may be unconditional or conditional. Conditions will be imposed where the court considers it necessary to ensure the young person attends court on the next occasion or to prevent him from offending while on bail or interfering with witnesses.

Conditions can also be attached to bail for the welfare of the young person. There are a wide number of conditions that can be attached to youth bail including bail supervision and support packages and an ISSP (intensive supervision and surveillance package). A member of the YOT team present in court will assist in this regard.

An ISSP may be imposed as a condition of bail where:

(a) the young person is charged with or convicted of an imprisonable offence and prior to current charge he has:

    (i) been charged or warned for an imprisonable offence on four or more separate occasions within the last 12 months; and

    (ii) received at least one community or custodial penalty at any stage;

    or

(b) the current charge or sentence relates to an offence punishable with 14 years or more;

    or

(c) the young person has a history of repeat offending on bail and is at risk of a secure remand in custody.

Electronic tagging may be imposed as a condition of bail in relation to a 12 to 17-year-old in the following circumstances:

- the young person is charged with or convicted of a violent or sexual offence or an offence which in the case of an adult carries a sentence of 14 years' imprisonment; or
- the young person has a recent history of repeatedly committing imprisonable offences while remanded on bail or to a local authority; and
- the court is considering conditional bail or a remand to local authority accommodation.

Electronic tagging can be imposed as a condition on its own or as part of a package and as a condition of remand to local authority accommodation. Given the availability of such a wide range of conditions, a remand to local authority accommodation should be viewed as a last resort.

31.3 WHERE WILL THE YOUNG PERSON BE TRIED?

The general rule is that a young person will be tried in the Youth Court where:

* he is charged alone; or
* he is charged with another young person.

Most juveniles are therefore tried summarily in the Youth Court irrespective of the seriousness or the classification of the offence(s) with which they are charged. Section 24(1) MCA 1980 provides that this presumption applies even in the case of an indictable-only offence other than homicide.

Unlike an adult offender charged with an either-way offence the young person has no right of election to the Crown Court. Therefore, if the magistrates are considering declining jurisdiction by sending the case to the Crown Court, the only course of action available to the juvenile's advocate is to make representations against having the case tried before a judge and jury. In contrast to the adult magistrates' court, the Youth Court has a maximum sentencing power of 24 months in custody.

As exceptions to the general rule, the young person may be tried in the Crown Court in the situations explained below.

31.3.1 TRIAL OF A YOUNG PERSON IN THE CROWN COURT

A defendant under 18 will be tried in the Crown Court in the following circumstances:

* where he is charged with homicide or specified offences under s. 51A Firearms Act 1968, the Youth Court, s. 24(1B) Magistrates' Courts Act (MCA) 1980. The term 'homicide' is widely defined to include murder, manslaughter and attempted murder;
* where the defendant is a 'dangerous' offender within ss. 226 and 228 Criminal Justice Act 2003, s. 51A CDA 1998;
* where the defendant is charged with a 'grave' crime and the Youth Court considers the Crown Court should invoke its power under s. 91 PCC(S)A 2000 to pass a lengthy custodial sentence, s. 24(1) MCA 1980;
* where the young person is jointly charged with an adult and it is in the interests of justice to commit them both to the Crown Court for trial, s. 24(1)(b) MCA 1980.

The final three situations are considered in more detail below.

31.3.2 'GRAVE' CRIMES

Where the juvenile is charged with a 'grave' crime, he may be committed to the Crown Court for trial under s. 24(1) MCA 1980.

A 'grave' crime is an offence which is punishable with at least 14 years' imprisonment in the case of an adult offender. Numerous offences carry a maximum custodial term in excess of 14 years including rape, robbery and causing death by dangerous driving. Also classified as a 'grave' crime are specified offences under the Sexual Offences Act 2003 including sexual assault under s. 3.

The power to commit for trial under s. 24 MCA 1980 must be read in conjunction with s. 91(1) and (2) of the Powers of Criminal Courts (Sentencing) Act 2000, which permits the Crown Court to sentence a young person who has been convicted of a 'serious' offence. This section is required because of the Youth Court's limited sentencing powers. The maximum custodial term that can be passed by the Youth Court on a young offender is a 24-month detention and training order (DTO). Only the Crown Court is empowered to impose a longer custodial term on a young offender (s. 91 PCC(S)A 2000). The power of the Youth Court to impose a DTO is also restricted in the case of a young person under the age of 15 unless the young person is a persistent offender, s. 100 PCC(S)A 2000. There is no power to impose a DTO on an offender under the age of 12 (See Chapter 30, para.30.2.1). The power to commit under s. 24 MCA 1980 will only be exercised where there is a real prospect that the juvenile will receive a custodial sentence of two years or more. In addition, to overcome the presumption that a person under 18 years of age should be tried summarily, there should be aggravating features in the offence which justify the Youth Court declining jurisdiction for a 'grave' crime. This usually applies to a serious sexual offence or violent offence.

The basis upon which the Youth Court should make its decision to decline jurisdiction to try the young person and commit to the Crown Court for trial has been judicially considered in a number of cases. In *R (D) v Manchester City Youth Court* [2002] 1 Cr App R (S) 573, it was stated that the Youth Court should not decline jurisdiction unless the offence and the circumstances surrounding it and the offender are such as to make it more than a theoretical possibility that a sentence of detention for a long period may be passed.

An overriding consideration for the magistrates is that trial in the Crown Court for a defendant under the age of 18 is inherently less suitable than in the Youth Court. This is especially significant where the young person is under 15 years of age. This raises the question whether the young defendant's right to a fair trial under Article 6 ECHR can be secured at trial on indictment.

The most authoritative guidance on the issue of venue is provided by *R on application of H, O and A v Southampton Youth Court* [2005] 2 Cr App R (S) 30, in which Leveson J in the Divisional Court stated as follows:

> 'In an effort to assist hard-pressed magistrates to determine this issue and thereby prevent the constant diet of cases of this nature before the court and, at the same time, seeking to avoid the need to trawl through the ever-growing list of authorities which touch on this point, with the approval of the Vice President of the Court of Appeal Criminal Division, I will attempt to summarise the matter in a way that can properly be put before the Youth Court whenever the situation arises. The general policy of the legislature is that those who are under 18 years of age and in particular children of under 15 years of age should, wherever possible, be tried in the Youth Court. It is that court which is best designed to meet their specific needs. A trial in the Crown Court with the inevitably greater formality and greatly increased number of people involved (including a jury and the public) should be reserved for the most serious cases.
>
> It is a further policy of the legislature that, generally speaking, first-time offenders aged 12 to 14 and all offenders under 12 should not be detained in custody and decisions as to jurisdiction should have regard to the fact that the exceptional power to detain for "grave" offences should not be used to water down the general principle. Those under 15 will rarely attract a period of detention and, even more rarely, those who are under 12.
>
> In each case the court should ask itself whether there is a real prospect, having regard to his or her age, that this defendant whose case they are considering might require a sentence of, or in excess of, two years or, alternatively, whether although the sentence might be less than two years, there is some unusual feature of the case which justifies declining jurisdiction, bearing in mind that the absence of a power to impose a detention and training order because the defendant is under 15 is not an unusual feature.'

In determining whether there is a real prospect of a custodial term in excess of 24 months, it will be necessary for the Youth Court to consider applicable sentencing guidelines (see Chapter 25).

In the Southampton Youth Court case, the Youth Court declined jurisdiction to try a 14-year-old youth who was charged with indecent assault. The youth was not a persistent offender and for this reason and because he was under 15, he could not be sentenced to a

DTO. The defendant applied to the Divisional Court to judicially review the Youth Court's decision. The Divisional Court criticised the defence solicitor for not challenging the submissions made by the CPS and stressed the importance of ascertaining the seriousness of the offence and any relevant sentencing guidelines. The case was remitted to the Youth Court to continue hearing the matter.

Where jurisdiction to summarily try a young defendant is declined, the court may also commit him for trial for any other indictable offence with which he is charged which can properly be joined in the same indictment (s. 24(1A) MCA 1980).

While the procedure for deciding whether the magistrates should exercise their powers under s. 24(1)(a) MCA 1980 is not laid down, the general approach is that the CPS will invite the magistrates to consider the issue of venue at an early stage in the proceedings where the juvenile is charged with a 'grave' crime. The defence will also make representations, which in most cases will seek to persuade the magistrates to try the case summarily.

In the *Southampton Youth Court* decision, Leveson J reminds defence solicitors of their duty in this regard:

> 'I ought to deal with the position of the defence solicitors. Only H's solicitor has made a statement. He takes the point that neither he nor the other defence solicitors were informed of the full factual basis of the allegation. He had seen only advance disclosure papers. He had not seen S's statement. Copies of H's interview and other statements were served upon the defence only on the day of the hearing . . . Whether or not that is the case, the very least one would expect is that each solicitor would have taken careful instructions before permitting the court to embark upon the grave crimes procedure. It is said that there is increasing pressure on advocates to make early decisions and rapidly progress all cases, especially those involving serious charges and young people and, rightly or wrongly, the solicitors did not ask for an adjournment, did not obtain further disclosure and did not consider the case in full prior to this hearing. Suffice it to say, it was for the defence representatives to ensure that they knew enough about the case of failure and it is not, of course, the fault of the court.'

31.3.3 DANGEROUS OFFENDERS UNDER THE AGE OF 18 (SS. 226 AND 228 CRIMINAL JUSTICE ACT 2003)

Section 51A 3(d) CDA 1998 requires the Youth Court to send the juvenile for trial in the Crown Court where the conditions laid down by s. 226 or s. 228 CJA 2003 are established, that is:

- the juvenile is charged with a specified offence as defined by s. 224 CJA 2003; and
- if convicted he would be classified as a dangerous offender within s. 226 or s. 228 Criminal Justice Act 2003 in that;
- it appears to the Youth Court that if the juvenile were found guilty of the offence, there is a significant risk to the public of serious harm occasioned by the commission of further specified offences by him; and
- the juvenile satisfies the criteria for imposing a sentence of indeterminate detention for public protection under s. 226(3) CJA 2003 or an extended sentence under s. 228(2) CJA 2003.

A full list of the 153 specified offences is found in Sch. 15 CJA 2003, but includes 'violent' offences such as manslaughter, kidnapping, offences under ss. 18 and 20 OAPA 1861 and 'sexual' offences, including rape, under s. 1 Sexual Offences Act 2003.

31.3.4 ASSESSMENT OF DANGEROUSNESS FOR THE PURPOSE OF DECLINING JURISDICTION

The main interpretive issue about the power to send the young person to the Crown Court for trial under s. 51A(3)(d) CDA 1998 is the assessment of whether the young person falls within the definition of a 'dangerous' offender (see Chapter 26 and para. 31.11 below). In deciding this, the court is required to take into account all the available information about the nature and circumstances of the offence and the offender. In many cases the court will not be in possession of sufficient details to make an informed decision at this early stage. A proper assessment of the dangerousness of the defendant is unlikely to be possible until a pre-sentence report has been prepared by the YOT which can only occur after a finding of guilt, (see para. 31.11.3 below).

Therefore, in considering whether to exercise its power under s. 51A(3)(d) CDA 1998 the court will be strongly influenced by judicial guidance including *R (on the application of H, O and A) v Southampton Youth Court* [2005] 2 Cr App R (S) 30 which is discussed above, that offenders under 18 years of age should be tried in the Youth Court, which is best designed to meet their specific needs. If, after summary conviction for a specified offence, the court forms the view that the 'dangerousness' criteria is satisfied, the Youth Court may commit the young person to the Crown Court for sentence under s. 3C Powers of Criminal Courts (Sentencing) Act 2000 as amended by the CJA 2003.

An illustration of the operation of s. 51A(3)(d) CDA 1998 is provided by *CPS v South East Surrey Youth Court and MG* [2006] 1 WLR 2543.

D was born on 16 September 1987. On 2 July 2005 D allegedly caused actual bodily harm to V by striking him in the face with a beer bottle, causing a wound which required five stitches. On 28 July 2005 D was interviewed by the police in connection with this incident. D stated that he had acted in self-defence. On the same day, 28 July, D was arrested in connection with an unrelated offence of robbery, which was said to have occurred on 25 July and charged with the offence on 29 July and remanded in custody by the Youth Court. It was alleged that D had used a knife during the robbery. On 3 August D was sent to the Crown Court for trial in connection with the robbery under s. 51A(3)(d) CDA 1998. On the same day he was charged with the earlier assault occasioning actual bodily harm. On 24 August the prosecution submitted that D should be sent to the Crown Court for trial in connection with the assault under s. 51A(3)(d) CDA 1998 on the basis that the offence was a specified violent offence under s. 224 CJA 2003 and there was a real possibility that the criteria for an extended sentence under s. 228 CJA 2003 would be met.

In rejecting the prosecution submission, the justices adopted the following approach which was tacitly approved by the Divisional Court. In deciding whether the offence should be tried summarily or on indictment, the court should first consider whether the offence comes within the meaning of a 'grave' crime (see para. 31.3.2 above). If the offence is a 'grave' crime, the court is required to consider whether the defendant is 'dangerous'. If he is 'dangerous', the court can send to the Crown Court for trial under s. 51A(3)(d) CDA 1998. If he is not 'dangerous' but is charged with a 'grave' crime, the court can consider committing him to the Crown Court for trial under s. 24 MCA 1980 (s. 51A(3)(b) CDA 1998) where the criteria outlined in the *Southampton Youth Court* case is satisfied. If the defendant is not charged with a 'grave' offence, the issue of 'dangerousness' should only be considered following the defendant's conviction at a summary trial. It should always be borne in mind that wherever possible those under 18 should be tried in the Youth Court.

The decision in the *South East Surrey Youth Court* case is significant as it confirms that the courts are reluctant to send a 'dangerous offender' for trial at the Crown Court under s. 51A(3)(d) CDA 1998 without also invoking the 'grave' crime provision under s. 24(1) MCA 1980. In the vast majority of cases the dangerousness test will only be applied in conjunction with s. 24(1) MCA 1980 where the defendant is charged with a 'grave' crime and the conditions for committing him for trial under s. 24(1) MCA 1980 are satisfied.

Where either side seeks to challenge the Youth Court's decision to either accept or decline jurisdiction to try a youth, it is necessary to seek judicial review of the decision in the Divisional Court.

1.3.5 **COMMITTING THE YOUNG PERSON FOR TRIAL UNDER S. 24(1)(b) MCA 1980**

Under s. 24(1)(b) MCA 1980, a defendant under the age of 18 may be committed to the Crown Court for trial where:

- he is jointly charged with an adult; and
- the adult is going to be tried in the Crown Court (either because the offence is indictable-only or mode of trial has resulted in a decision to commit for trial); and
- the court considers that it is necessary in the 'interests of justice' for the young person to be jointly tried with the adult in the Crown Court.

In applying the interests of justice test under s. 24(1)(b) MCA 1980, the court considers a number of factors including:

- the circumstances of the offence including the seriousness of the offence;
- the age and maturity of the accused and his likely plea;
- the representations made by the prosecution and the defence;
- the inconvenience and expense of witnesses having to give evidence twice;
- the need to deal with the youth as expeditiously as possible.

The power to commit under s. 24(1)(b) MCA 1980 applies where the young person appears together with an adult in the magistrates' court or where the young person appears in the Youth Court and is jointly charged with an adult in connection with an indictable offence and the adult has already been sent for trial in the Crown Court. If the adult magistrates' court decides that it is not in the interests of justice to commit the young person to the Crown Court, the charge will be put to him. Where he pleads guilty the adult magistrates' court will consider whether it has the power to sentence him from the limited range of sentencing disposals available to it. If none of them are appropriate, the defendant will be remitted to the Youth Court for sentencing. If the young person pleads not guilty, he may be tried in the adult magistrates' court but the normal practice is to send the case to the Youth Court for trial under s. 29 MCA 1980.

It is now generally accepted in recognising the young person's right to a fair trial under Article 6 ECHR 1950, that only very rarely will it be in the interests of justice for the young person to be tried jointly with an adult and that the young person should not be exposed to the intimidating atmosphere in the Crown Court unless there are very strong and compelling reasons for overturning this presumption.

 Looking Ahead

The Criminal Justice Act 2003 contains some important changes to the allocation of cases involving young persons. The detail is contained in the extremely complex Sch. 3 CJA 2003 which will see some significant changes to the conduct of mode of trial proceedings in relation to adults, highlighted in Chapter 13. The changes are coupled with the abolition of committal proceedings for an adult, charged with an either-way offence which is to be tried before the Crown Court. Schedule 3 will amend s. 24 MCA 1980 (introducing ss. 24A–24D).

Should the relevant provisions be brought into force, defendants under the age of 18 will be subject to the same procedure at the mode of trial stage, including the plea before venue, as adult defendants in a case where there is a possibility of the young person being tried in the Crown Court either because s. 91 PCC(S)A 2000 applies or he is jointly charged with an adult whose case is to be tried before a Crown Court. If a guilty plea is indicated, the Youth Court will be able to commit for sentence where it is of the opinion that a lengthy custodial term under either s. 91 PCC(S)A 2000 or an extended sentence under the 'dangerousness' provisions should be passed (ss. 3B and 3C PCC(S)A 2000). Where the juvenile defendant indicates a not guilty plea, the Youth Court will proceed to a mode of trial enquiry as outlined in paras. 31.3.1–31.3.4 above. An amendment is made to s. 25 MCA 1980 to allow the prosecution to reopen a mode of trial decision before a summary trial commences.

Schedule 3 will further amend s. 51 Crime and Disorder Act 1998, which governs the sending of cases to the Crown Court. Cases involving young defendants will be sent for trial under the revised s. 51 CDA 1998, as opposed to s. 24 MCA 1980. The revised s. 51 CDA 1998 enables a young defendant's linked offences to be sent with him to the Crown Court (s. 51A(4) and (5)). A young defendant will also take with him to the Crown Court any adult who is jointly charged with him or who separately faces a related either-way or summary-only offence (s. 51A(6) and (7)). None of these provisions are currently in force.

31.4 SAFEGUARDING THE YOUNG PERSON'S RIGHT TO A FAIR TRIAL IN THE CROWN COURT

If the court decides that trial in the Crown Court is appropriate for the young defendant, the Consolidated Criminal Practice Direction Part III requires that:

- the young defendant should visit the courtroom out of court hours to familiarise himself with the layout;
- where practicable, the trial should be held in a courtroom where all the participants are on the same level;
- a young defendant should normally be permitted to sit with his family and to engage in informal communication with his legal representative;
- the court should explain the course of proceedings to the young defendant in terms he understands and remind his legal representatives of their continuing responsibility to explain each stage of the proceedings to him;
- the trial should be conducted to a timetable which takes account of the young defendant's inability to concentrate for long periods;
- robes and gowns should not be worn unless the young defendant requests or the court considers there are good reasons for wearing robes and gowns;
- the court should be prepared to restrict attendance at court to those who have a direct interest in the outcome of the proceedings and to restrict the reporting of the proceedings by the media. As a trainee solicitor, it is likely that your principal will obtain the court's permission for you to attend the trial.

The Practice Direction is a response to criticism from the European Court of Human Rights in *T and V v UK* [2000] 30 EHRR 121, which held that the boys accused of killing Jamie Bulger had not had a fair trial in the highly formal proceedings of Preston Crown Court. The trial, which lasted for three weeks in November 1993, was accompanied by widespread media frenzy and great public hostility.

In appealing to the European Court of Human Rights, T and V submitted that their trial in the Crown Court constituted inhuman and degrading treatment within the meaning of Article 3 ECHR 1950 and that they had been denied a fair trial under Article 6.

Whilst the ECtHR rejected the submission that T and V's trial breached Article 3, it did accept that their right to a fair trial under Article 6 had been violated. The Court concluded that the formality and ritual of the Crown Court must have seemed incomprehensible to the young defendants making it impossible for them to effectively participate in the proceedings.

Even with these requirements in mind, the procedure for trying a young person in the Crown Court is generally the same as for adult defendants. One important difference is the reporting restrictions that are imposed on the media. Section 39(1) Children and Young Persons Act 1933 permits the court to direct that no newspaper report shall reveal the name, address or school of the young defendant or publish a photograph. A further difference is that s. 34A(1) Children and Young Persons Act 1933 requires that where the young defendant is aged under 16 years, his parent or guardian must attend court. Where the young person is aged 16 or 17, his parent or guardian may attend court.

31.5 TRIAL OF A YOUNG PERSON IN THE ADULT MAGISTRATES' COURT

The circumstances in which a young person will be tried before an adult magistrates' court will be relatively rare. A youth must be tried before an adult magistrates' court where he is jointly charged with an adult in connection with a matter that is to be tried summarily (this would include an either-way offence which is to remain in the magistrates' court) and both the adult and the youth plead not guilty.

If the young person is later convicted at trial or chooses to plead guilty, the powers of the adult magistrates' court to sentence the youth are restricted (see para. 31.9). In these circumstances the adult court will normally remit the youth to the Youth Court for sentence if it considers its sentencing powers to be restrictive.

If the adult defendant pleads guilty but the youth pleads not guilty, the adult court may try the youth. However, it is much more likely to remit the youth to the Youth Court for trial (s. 29 MCA 1980).

Consider the following examples of the factors to be taken into account in deciding the place of trial of a defendant under the age of 18.

 Example

Josh, aged 14, is charged with theft. As he is charged alone and is a juvenile, he will be tried in the Youth Court.

Josh, aged 14, is charged jointly with Sharon, who is 16, with theft. As both defendants are under 18, both will be tried in the Youth Court.

Josh, aged 14, is jointly charged with Graham, aged 33, with robbery. Assuming Josh appears at the same time as Graham, the magistrates' court will be required to send Graham to the Crown Court under s. 51 CDA 1998. Josh will also be sent for trial if the magistrates consider it is in the interests of justice that Josh be tried with Graham (regard being had to s. 24(1)(b) MCA 1980).

Josh, aged 14, is charged with rape. As rape is a 'grave' offence, the Youth Court is likely to decline jurisdiction to try the case in favour of the Crown Court's more extensive powers of sentence under s. 91 PCC(S)A 2000. Consideration will also be given to the 'dangerousness' provisions (ss. 226 and 228 CJA 2003).

Josh, aged 14, is jointly charged with Graham, aged 33, with common assault. If both Josh and Graham plead not guilty, the trial will be held in the adult magistrates' court. If Graham pleads guilty but Josh pleads not guilty, Josh will be tried in the Youth Court.

31.6 PROCEEDINGS IN THE YOUTH COURT

Most young defendants will be tried in the Youth Court where proceedings are more informal than in the adult court. The informality extends to the layout of the court, which enables the young person to fully participate in the proceedings (unless the defendant is remanded in custody). The defendant sits facing the magistrates and not in the dock. The advocates and witnesses remain seated during the proceedings. The defendant will be addressed by his first name and the language used should be appropriate to his age and maturity. The words 'conviction' and 'sentence' will be avoided as the phrases 'case proven' or 'not proven' are preferred. Sentences are described as 'disposals' and before disposing of the case, the court is required to inform the young person and his parent or guardian of the way it proposes to deal with the case.

The following may be present in court:

- court officers, including members of the Youth Offending Team (YOT);
- the parties in the case including the young person, prosecutor and defence lawyers and witnesses;
- the defendant's parents or guardians;
- the victim, unless it is not in the interests of justice for him to attend (this would be a rare occurrence);
- news reporters—although reports of the proceedings are generally restricted so as not to reveal the young person's identity, address or school, etc.

Even allowing for the greater informality, where the defendant denies the offence, the trial in the Youth Court will follow the same procedure as in the adult court:

- the prosecutor makes an opening speech;
- the first prosecution witness is examined-in-chief;
- the witness is cross-examined by the defence;
- the prosecutor may re-examine his witness;

(each prosecution witness gives evidence through this procedure)

- the prosecutor may also put before the court:
  - documentary evidence;
  - exhibits (known as real evidence); and
  - statements admissible under s. 9 Criminal Justice Act 1967, which permits the written statement of a witness who is not in court to be read to the bench;
- at the close of the prosecution case, the defence may make a submission of no case to answer where the prosecution has failed to prove an essential element of the offence or the prosecution evidence has been so discredited that the court could not find the case proven against the defendant;
- the first defence witness, usually the accused, is examined-in-chief;
- the witness is cross-examined by the prosecution;
- the defence advocate may re-examine his witness;

(each defence witness gives evidence through this procedure)
- the defence advocate may also put before the court:
  - documentary evidence;
  - exhibits (known as real evidence); and
  - statements admissible under s. 9 Criminal Justice Act 1967, which permits the written statement of a witness who is not in court to be read to the bench;
- the defence makes a closing speech;
- the court decides whether the case is proven;
- if proven, the court will proceed to disposing of the case; or
- if the case is not proven the defendant is free to leave the court.

31.7 SENTENCING THE YOUNG OFFENDER IN THE YOUTH COURT

Where the case is proven against the young person, under Crim PR, Part 44, he and/or his parent or guardian will be given the opportunity to make a statement, and the court is also obliged to consider any relevant information about the young person's general conduct, home environment and school record. If the information is not immediately available, the court must consider adjourning for enquiries. A report may be required from a probation officer, social worker or YOT member.

When the Youth Court is in possession of the necessary information, a range of disposals are available to it. Some disposals relate to the young offender only, while others can and sometimes will be imposed on his parent or guardian.

As with adults, the court is required to take a structured approach to sentencing and will refer to sentencing guidelines produced by the Sentencing Guidelines Council (SGC) and the Court of Appeal's sentencing decisions. The provisions relating to the sentencing of young people are contained in the Powers of the Criminal Courts (Sentencing) Act 2000 and the Criminal Justice Act 2003.

 Looking Ahead

Section 9 Criminal Justice and Immigration Act 2008 will insert s. 142A CJA 2003 by identifying the purposes of sentencing offenders under 18. When sentencing the court must have regard to the principal aim of the youth justice system to prevent offending and reoffending by persons under 18 and to punish the offender, to reform and rehabilitate the offender, to protect the public and for the offender to make reparation to persons affected by his offence(s).

31.7.1 DEFERMENT OF SENTENCE—S. 1 PCC(S)A 2000

The Youth Court can defer sentence for up to six months. It might choose to do so, for example:

- because of an imminent and significant change in lifestyle; or
- to allow the young person to save up to pay compensation to the victim.

The court must give reasons for the deferment and explain what is required of the young person during the deferred period. If another offence is committed during the deferred period, the offender may be sentenced for the new offence in addition to the previous offence.

31.7.2 DETENTION AND TRAINING ORDER—SS. 100–107 PCC(S)A 2000

A DTO is the main custodial sentence for a young offender. The disposal will be available in the following circumstances:

- The offender is aged between 12 and 17 years; and has been convicted of an imprisonable offence which is so 'serious' that neither a fine alone nor a community sentence can be justified (s. 152 CJA 2003).
- Currently, a court may not pass a DTO in the case of an offender under the age of 12.
- A court may not pass a DTO in the case of an offender under the age of 15 unless the court is of the opinion that he is a persistent offender (see para. 30.2.1).
- The length of the order must be for one of the periods specified in the Act: 4, 6, 8, 10, 12, 18 or 24 months. (The term may not exceed the adult maximum term which a Crown Court could pass on an adult over 21, which in the case of a summary-only offence is currently six months.)
- The young offender will be entitled to a sentencing discount where he pleads guilty and should be given credit for periods spent on remand (s. 144 CJA 2003/s. 101(8) PCC(S)A 2000).
- The young person will begin a period of supervision halfway through the sentence, which will cease when the full term expires, s. 103 PCC(S)A 2000.

Example

Josh, aged 14, is convicted of assault in the Youth Court. He has ten previous convictions. As the court is satisfied that the offence is so serious that only a custodial sentence is appropriate and that Josh is a PO, it imposes a four-month DTO on Josh. Under the terms of the DTO, Josh will spend two months in custody and two months in the community under supervision.

31.7.3 **COMMUNITY ORDERS**

Community orders in relation to offenders aged 16–17 are currently in a state of transition. If the offender is under 18, a youth community order under the CJA 2003 will be passed. If the offender is 16 or 17, however, as an alternative to the youth community order under the CJA 2003 (and for the time being at least), the court may instead choose to impose an 'old style' community order under the PCC(S)A 2000.

'Old-style' community orders are covered at (a), (b), (c) and (d) below. The youth community order is considered at (e)–(h) below.

A community sentence may only be imposed against a young person where the offence is serious enough to warrant it (s. 148 CJA 2003). Youth community sentences will be supervised by members of the youth offending teams (YOTs). Breach of proceedings in relation to community sentences are governed by Schs. 3 and 8 PCC(S) A 2000.

(a) Community punishment order—ss. 46–50 PCC(S)A 2000

- The offender must be aged at least 16 years old.
- A CPO shall not be passed unless the offence is serious enough to merit it (s. 35(1) SA 2000).
- The court should obtain and consider a pre-sentence report unless it is unnecessary (s. 36(4) and (6) SA 2000).
- The court must be satisfied that the offender is suitable to perform work under the order.
- The hours of unpaid work should not be less than 40 and no more than 240 (s. 46(3) PCC(S)A 2000).
- Before making the order the court should explain to the offender the effect of the order and the consequences of not complying with the requirements.

(b) Community rehabilitation order—ss. 41–45 PCC(S)A 2000

- The offender must be at least 16 years old.
- A CRO shall not be passed unless offence is serious enough to merit it, s. 35(1) PCC(S)A 2000.
- Regard should be had to s. 41 PCC(S)A 2000, in that the court must conclude such an order is desirable in the interests of securing the offender's rehabilitation and protecting the public from the commission by him of further offence.
- The court should obtain and consider a pre-sentence report unless it is unnecessary (s. 36(4) and (6) PCC(S)A 2000).
- Before making the order the court should explain to the offender the effect of the order and the consequences of not complying with the requirements.
- The order can last between six months and three years.

(c) Community punishment and rehabilitation order—s. 51 PCC(S)A 2000

- The offender must be at least 16 years old.
- A CPRO shall not be passed unless the offence is serious enough to merit it, s. 35(1) PCC(S)A 2000.

- The court should obtain and consider a pre-sentence report unless it is unnecessary (s. 36(4) and (6) PCC(S)A 2000).
- The rehabilitation element must be between 12 months and three years.
- The community punishment element must be between 40 and 100 hours.

(d) Drug testing and treatment order—s. 52 PCC(S)A 2000

- The offender must be at least 16 years.
- A DTTO shall not be passed unless offence is serious enough to merit it, s. 35(1) PCC(S)A 2000.
- A pre-sentence report would be a pre-requisite.
- The DTTO must be between six months and three years.
- The court must be satisfied that the offender is dependent on drugs and may be susceptible to treatment.
- The offender will be subject to regular drug testing and will have regular review hearings before the court.
- The DTTO is a high-intensity community order.

Section 148 CJA 2003 permits a court to pass one or more youth community orders on offenders below the age of 18. The court must be satisfied that the order it is imposing is the most suitable for the offender and that any restriction on the offender's liberty is commensurate with the seriousness of the offence. A pre-sentence report will invariably be required to assess suitability. Youth community orders include:

(e) Action plan order—ss. 69–71 PCC(S)A 2000

- The order is supervised by the Youth Offending Team (YOT).
- It lasts three months and is tailored to the needs and specific risks of the individual offender. It can include reparation to the victim, education and training.
- The action plan order can include drug testing and treatment for offenders aged 14 and over in defined circumstances.

(f) Attendance centre order—ss. 60–62 PCC(S)A 2000

- The defendant must have been convicted of an imprisonable offence.
- The offender will be required to attend an attendance centre for specified number of hours covering a specified time.
- Attendance is for not less than 12 hours unless young person is under 14 years and is up to maximum of 24 hours.

(g) Supervision order—s. 63 PCC(S)A 2000

- A supervision order can last up to three years.
- A range of conditions can be attached to a supervision order when the sentence is used for more serious offences. These are called 'specified activities' and can last for up to 90 days.
- Specified activities can include drug treatment, curfew and residence requirements.
- As part of supervision, a court may require the offender to undergo an ISSP (intensive supervision and surveillance programme). ISSPs are reserved for the most prolific young offenders. It combines intense levels of community-based surveillance with a comprehensive and sustained focus on tackling the factors that contribute to the young person's offending behaviour.
- The order is supervised by the YOT.

(h) Curfew order—ss. 37–40 PCC(S)A 2000

- This requires the convicted offender to remain at a specified place between specified times.
- The maximum period of the curfew between two and 12 hours on a specified day.
- The order is for maximum of three months if young offender is between ten and 15.
- It should seek to avoid conflict with educational establishments attended by the offender or his religious beliefs.
- It will include electronic tagging.

 Looking Ahead

Amongst some of the most significant reforms contained in the Criminal Justice and Immigration Act 2008 are changes to the sentencing provisions in relation to youths. Section 1 of the 2008 Act creates a single youth rehabilitation order (YRO), a new generic community sentence for offenders under the age of 18. It is intended that YRO will replace all the existing community sentences for young offenders. Under the provisions, when imposing a YRO the court will choose from a range of requirements that the offender must comply with. The requirements, which are similar to those for adults (see Chapter 26) include:

- an activity requirement;
- a supervision requirement;
- if the offender is aged 16 or 17, an unpaid work requirement;
- a programme requirement;
- an attendance centre requirement;
- a prohibited activity requirement;
- a curfew requirement;
- an exclusion requirement;
- a residence requirement;
- a local authority residence requirement;
- a mental health treatment requirement;
- a drug treatment requirement;
- an education requirement.

When YROs are brought into force, the existing community orders for young offenders such as supervision orders and action plan orders will be abolished. The different types of community sentence currently available to those over 16 will cease to have effect. More detailed provisions in relation to possible combinations and sentence for breach of a YRO can be found in s.2 of the Act.

31.7.4 REPARATION ORDER—SS. 73–75 PCC(S)A 2000

The court may impose a reparation order on the young offender as part of the sentence it passes. In deciding the issue, the court will obtain a report from the young person's YOT who will suggest a suitable form of reparation. Such an order is designed to get the offender to address the consequences of his offending behaviour. It cannot be imposed where a custodial sentence is passed or a supervision order, action plan order or referral order is made. Under a reparation order:

- the young person is required to give reparation to a specified person or to the community;
- the work to be carried out is under the supervision of a probation officer or social worker;
- no more than 24 hours work to be completed within three months of the order;
- the order is overseen by YOT;
- in a case where a reparation order can be made, the court must give reasons for refusing to make one.

1.7.5   REFERRAL ORDER—S. 16 PCC(S)A 2000

A referral order will be appropriate for a first-time offender who admits guilt and the offence is not suitable to be punished by a custodial sentence or absolute discharge. It will be appropriate to make a referral order in the following circumstances:

- The young person will have no previous convictions including a conditional discharge or a bind over.
- If the young person pleaded guilty, a referral order *is mandatory* as long as neither custody nor an absolute discharge are appropriate; and the young person has never been convicted or bound over and the offence is an imprisonable one for which the sentence is not fixed by law.
- If the young person pleaded guilty to one offence but is found guilty of another offence, a referral order is discretionary.
- The length of referral order to a Youth Offending Panel (YOP) will be between three and 12 months.
- The YOP is composed of members of the community and a member of YOT who meet with the young person and his parent/guardian and agree a 'contract' with the offender which seeks to address the reasons for his offending behaviour.
- The victim of the offence may attend the YOP.
- The conviction is spent once the 'contract' is completed.

31.7.6   FINE—PART VI PCC(S)A 2000

While imposing a fine on an offender is the most common sentence passed by the adult magistrates' courts (see Chapter 26, para. 26.16), fining a young person is relatively rare, for obvious reasons. When the court considers a fine to be appropriate, the following considerations apply:

- The fine may be imposed as a disposal in its own right.
- The court must taken into account the financial circumstances of the offender and/or his parent/guardian.
- The parent/guardian must attend the court hearing if the court considers making them pay.
- Where the young offender is under 16, the parent/guardian will be ordered to pay, unless:
  — the parent/guardian cannot be found; or
  — it would be unreasonable to expect them to pay.

- The maximum fine that can be imposed where the young offender is aged between ten and 13 is £250.
- The maximum fine that can be imposed where the young offender is aged between 14 and 17 is £1,000.

31.7.7 CONDITIONAL DISCHARGE—S. 12 PCC(S)A 2000

A conditional discharge may be imposed on a young offender whatever the offence. In practice, they are reserved for the less serious offences and are relatively rare in the Youth Court given the availability of the referral order. The offender must not commit any further offences during the operational period of the conditional discharge, which can be up to a maximum of three years. If the young offender reoffends during the operational period, he may be punished for both the later offence and for the original offence. A conditional discharge may be imposed on a young offender in the following circumstances:

- where the case is proven against a the young offender;
- where the court considers that it is not expedient to punish;
- where the young offender has not received a final warning within the last two years.

31.7.8 ABSOLUTE DISCHARGE—S. 12 PCC(S)A 2000

As with a conditional discharge, an absolute discharge is appropriate in connection with very trivial offences where the court considers that punishment is not required. An absolute discharge may be imposed in the following circumstances:

- where the case is proven against the young offender; and
- where the court considers that no punishment is required; and
- where the court considers there is no risk of further offending by the young person.

31.7.9 ENDORSEMENT OR DISQUALIFICATION OF THE JUVENILE'S DRIVING LICENCE/RECORD

For further information on driving penalties, see Chapter 27. Even though a young offender may have no driving licence, his driving record can still be subject to endorsement and disqualification.

31.7.10 COMPENSATION ORDER—SS. 130–135 PCC(S)A 2000

A convicted young offender may be ordered to pay compensation up to a maximum of £5,000 in either the Youth Court or the adult magistrates' court for any personal injury, loss or damage which resulted from his offence. The Magistrates' Court Sentencing Guidelines provide guidance as the appropriate level of compensation. An important consideration will be the offender's ability to pay.

31.7.11 PARENTING ORDERS—SS. 8–10 CRIME AND DISORDER ACT 1998

As the name suggests, a parenting order is directed to improving the parenting skills of the young offender's parent or guardian. Where an offender under the age of 16 is convicted of an offence and the court considers that a parenting order would be desirable in the interests of preventing further offending by the young person, it *shall* make a parenting order. A parenting order requires the parent or guardian to attend parenting guidance sessions for up to 12 months. The sessions are supervised by a member of the youth offending team or a probation officer or a social worker.

7.12 PARENTAL BIND OVER—S. 150(1) PCC(S)A 2000

The young offender's parent or guardian must be bound over to prevent the juvenile under the age of 16 from committing further offences wherever the court is satisfied that it would be in the interests of justice to do so. If a court chooses not to make an order, it must give reasons in open court. A bind over may not be given where a court passes a referral order.

31.8 ANTI-SOCIAL BEHAVIOUR ORDERS (ASBOS)

The Crime and Disorder Act 1998 introduced a wide range of measures which seek to divert young people away from offending by imposing sanctions on their anti-social behaviour. They include anti-social behaviour orders, child safety orders and local child curfew schemes. Breach of an ASBO is a criminal offence which caries imprisonment. It seeks to prevent a young person from going to a particular place or doing a particular thing. It can be imposed on application by the police or local authority and upon conviction where the court considers the offender has acted in a manner that caused or was likely to cause harassment, alarm or distress. A steady body of case law has started to emerge in relation to ASBOs (see *Blackstone's Criminal Practice*).

31.9 SENTENCING THE YOUNG OFFENDER IN THE ADULT MAGISTRATES' COURT

The adult magistrates' court has limited sentencing powers over a young offender. In the few situations where the young offender is sentenced in the adult magistrates' court, the following disposals are most commonly imposed:

* fine;
* referral order;
* conditional/absolute discharge;
* disqualification from driving;
* endorsement of the young person's driving licence/record.

The young offender will usually be remitted to the Youth Court for sentence. Relevant rules of court relating to the sentencing of a young person before an adult magistrates' court are contained in Crim PR, Part 44.

31.10 SENTENCING THE YOUNG OFFENDER IN THE CROWN COURT

While the Crown Court may pass any appropriate sentence on a young person, s. 8 Powers of Criminal Courts (Sentencing) Act 2000 requires that where the young person has been convicted on indictment, it shall remit the offender to the Youth Court for sentencing unless it is 'undesirable' to do so. In applying the 'undesirable' test, the Crown Court judge may not remit to the Youth Court where doing so would cause:

* delay; or
* unnecessary expense; or
* unnecessary duplication of the proceedings.

As the judge will be familiar with the facts of the case, it is common for the young person to be sentenced in the Crown Court. The Crown Court has the full range of sentencing disposals available to it, with the obvious addition that it can impose a much longer custodial sentence in accordance with s. 91 PCC(S)A 2000 for a 'grave' crime where the defendant has been convicted on indictment and, when it is in force, upon committal for sentence under s. 3B PCC(S)A 2000. Where a custodial sentence is passed, the young offender will serve his time in a young offenders' institution or secure training centre.

Where the young person has been convicted of murder, s. 90 PCC(S)A 2000 prescribes the mandatory sentence of detention at Her Majesty's Pleasure. Guidance on setting the minimum term can be found in ss. 269–277 CJA 2003. The starting point for an offender under 18 is 12 years before taking into account any mitigating or aggravating factors.

31.11   SENTENCING A 'DANGEROUS' YOUNG OFFENDER

The Criminal Justice Act 2003 has introduced specific sentencing powers in the Crown Court to deal with a dangerous young offender convicted of a specified offence. These powers may be exercised following the young person's conviction in the Crown Court or where he has been remitted under s. 3C Powers of Criminal Courts (Sentencing) Act 2000 to the Crown Court for sentence following summary conviction in the Youth Court.

Schedule 15 CJA 2003 lists the 153 categories of violent or sexual offences which come within the definition of a specified offence. A specified offence is defined under s. 224 CJA 2003 as a violent or sexual offence which carries a sentence of between two years and ten years imprisonment. A 'serious offence' is a violent or sexual offence specified in Sch. 15 which carries a sentence of at least ten or more years in the case of an adult. The sentencing powers available to the Crown Court depends on whether the young person has been convicted of a serious, specified violent or sexual offence or a specified violent or sexual offence which carries a sentence of between two years and ten years' imprisonment. If the offender falls within the first category *and* is assessed as being dangerous, he must be detained for life or detained for public protection. If the offender falls within the second category *and* is assessed as being dangerous, the court must pass an extended sentence of imprisonment.

31.11.1   DETENTION FOR LIFE OR DETENTION FOR PUBLIC PROTECTION

Under s. 226(1) CJA 2003, where a person under 18 has been convicted of a serious violent or sexual offence (carrying a maximum of ten or more years' imprisonment) and the court is of the opinion that there is a significant risk to members of the public of serious harm occasioned by the commission by him of further specified offences, the court *must* impose a life sentence if the offence he has been convicted of would be liable to a sentence of detention for life (s. 226(2) CJA 2003).

If the circumstances of the case do not justify a life sentence, the court must choose between a sentence of detention for public protection or an extended sentence. If the court considers that an extended sentence would not be adequate to protect the public, the court must pass an indeterminate sentence for public protection (s. 226(3)).

The factors the court considers in assessing the dangerousness test are considered below and in Chapter 26, para. 26.8.4.

31.11.2   IMPOSING AN EXTENDED SENTENCE

Under s. 228(1) CJA 2003, the court must pass an extended sentence on a person under 18 who has been convicted of a specified violent or sexual offence (carrying a sentence of between two years and ten years' imprisonment) where the court considers:

- there is a significant risk to members of the public of serious harm occasioned by the commission of further specified offences; and
- where the specified offence is a serious offence, it is not one for which the court is required to impose a sentence of detention for life or to impose a sentence for public protection.

Where the conditions for imposing an extended sentence are met, the court will set the appropriate custodial term and a further extended period of supervision which the young offender is required to serve on licence. The extended period on licence should be for such period as the court considers necessary to protect the public from serious harm occasioned by the commission of further specified offences by the young offender. The custodial term must be at least 12 months but must not exceed the maximum term (which is 24 months). The extended period must not exceed five years in the case of a specified violent offence (s. 228(3) CJA 2003) or eight years in the case of a specified sexual offence (s. 228(4) CJA 2003).

31.11.3   ASSESSMENT OF 'DANGEROUSNESS'

In deciding whether to detain an offender under 18 for life or for public protection or to impose an extended sentence, the court must consider the seriousness of the offence and/or other offences associated with it (s. 229 CJA 2003) to determine whether the juvenile will constitute a danger to the public. The court will take careful note of the facts of the offence, the pre-sentence report and any other relevant report. In these kinds of cases a psychiatric report is commonly obtained.

Guidance on these complicated provisions has been given by the Court of Appeal in *R v Lang and Others* [2005] EWCA Crim 2864. The guidance is reproduced in Chapter 26. Your attention is specifically drawn to paragraphs (vi) and (vii) in the judgment as they apply to offenders under the age of 18.

31.12   WHAT IF THE DEFENDANT REACHES THE AGE OF 18 DURING THE PROCEEDINGS?

Although the rules and the case law on this point are not absolutely clear, the position would appear to be as follows:

If the defendant is under the age of 18 at the time he enters his plea before the Youth Court he will be tried as a youth, notwithstanding the fact that he reaches 18 during the currency of the proceedings.

So far as sentencing is concerned, s. 29 Children and Young Persons Act 1963 would appear to allow the Youth Court to sentence a youth who has pleaded guilty or been found guilty while still aged 17, but who attains the age of 18 before being sentenced. In other words, it is the date of conviction which is the determining factor. The Youth Court has discretionary power under s. 9 PCC(S)A 2000 to remit a juvenile to sentence in the adult court where the defendant attained the age of 18 before conviction.

For further information on youth justice, consult the Youth Justice Board's website at www.youth-justice-board.gov.uk.

KEY POINT SUMMARY

- The rules governing which court a young person will be tried in are complex and have to be grasped.
- If possible a defendant under 18 should be tried in the Youth Court, which is specifically designed for the special needs of younger offenders.

- Understand the concept of a 'grave' crime and why this is important in relation to mode of trial considerations for a youth under the age of 18.
- Understand when the 'dangerousness' provisions under s. 224 CJA 2003 bite and why they are important in relation to mode of trial considerations for youths.
- Know the circumstances in which the Youth Court can impose a detention and training order (DTO).
- Know the range of community penalties and other sentences available to the Youth Court.
- Be able to explain the differences in procedure between the adult court and the Youth Court.

SELF-TEST QUESTIONS

1. What is the general rule about where a young defendant should be tried?
2. What is the main custodial sentence for a convicted young offender and when can it be passed?
3. Tracey is 15. She has been charged with an offence of arson contrary to s. 1(1) and (3) Criminal Damage Act 1971. It is alleged that she and a group of other girls set fire to a mobile classroom in the grounds of a high school, resulting in £20,000 worth of damage. The fire began at around 10.30 at night. The classroom was unoccupied. Tracey has no criminal record but comes from a family beset by social problems. She had recently been suspended from school. No one else has been charged in connection with the incident. Consider the following questions:
   - In which court will Tracey appear?
   - In which court is Tracey likely to be tried and dealt with?
   - If Tracey is found guilty of the offence, what range of sentences are open to the sentencing court?
4. Barry, aged 15, is charged with causing death by dangerous driving. He denies the offence. He has several previous convictions, including convictions for robbery, violence and aggravated vehicle taking. What considerations will the Youth Court have regard to in deciding whether to accept jurisdiction to try Barry?

FIGURE 31.1 YOUTH PROCEEDINGS

WHERE WILL A YOUNG PERSON BE TRIED?

Youth Court (the vast majority of young defendants are tried before the Youth Court). This will be the case where:

- the youth is charged alone; or
- the youth is charged with another youth.

Crown Court –This will be the case where:

- a youth is charged with homicide, which includes both murder and manslaughter, s. 24(1) MCA 1980; or
- a youth is charged with a 'grave' offence, s. 24(1)(a) MCA 1980 ('grave' offence includes an offence for which an adult could be punished with imprisonment for 14 years or more, or specfic offences under the Sexual Offences Act 2003 and the Firearms Act 1968); or
- the offence charged is a specied offence and the defendant would, it appears, if found guilty satisfy the test of dangerousness under s. 226 or 228 CJA 2003; or
- a youth is jointly charged with an adult and the adult is to be tried on indictment and the court considers that 'it is in the interests of justice' for them to be tried together, s. 24(1)(b) MCA 1980.

Adult magistrates' court–This will be the case where the young person is charged jointly with an adult in connection with a summary offence **but**

- the summary case may be remitted to the Youth Court where:
  - the adult pleads guilty; and
  - the young person pleads not guilty; or
  - the adult is committed for trial or is discharged and the young person pleads not guilty.

When charged with an either-way offence, the young person has no right of election.

Youth court proceedings are:

- more informal in terms of procedure and terminology;
- have limited right of public access;
- subject to reporting restrictions; and
- tried before a specially trained 'mixed' Bench.

Youth Court sentencing powers include:

- DTO for those over 15 (maximum 24 months);
- no DTO for under 12s and under 15s need to be a PO;
- community youth orders;
- reparation order;
- referral order;
- fine/compensation;
- conditional discharge;
- parenting order.

APPENDIX 1

R v LENNY WHYTE

For reasons of space, we include only a selection of the documentation that forms the basis of the solicitor's file on this case study.

The complete documentation as listed overleaf, can be accessed on our Online Resource Centre in the case studies section. The documents selected for inclusion in this appendix are shown in **bold type**.

**online
resource
centre**

R v LENNY WHYTE: INDEX TO DOCUMENTATION ON SOLICITOR'S FILE

DOCUMENT 1 Initial Statement of Lenny Whyte

DOCUMENT 2 Attendance on Client and Record of First Appearance Before Magistrates' Court

DOCUMENT 3 CDS 1

DOCUMENT 4 Application for Representation Order—(Form CDS 14) Selected Portions

DOCUMENT 5 Letter to the CPS Requesting Advance Information

DOCUMENT 6 Letter Requesting Copy of Custody Record

DOCUMENT 7 Client Care Letter

DOCUMENT 8 CPS Letter Regarding Advance Information (Specimen Letter)

DOCUMENT 9 Lymeshire Police Custody Record—selected Portions

DOCUMENT 10 Record of Intial Description

DOCUMENT 11A List of Previous Convictions for Lenny Whyte

DOCUMENT 11B Antecedents of Lenny Whyte—restricted Access to CPS Only

DOCUMENT 12 File Note—consideration of Advance Information and Mode of Trial

DOCUMENT 13 Record of Mode of Trial Hearing

DOCUMENT 14 Transcript of Bail Hearing—submissions of Prosecution and Defence

DOCUMENT 15 Record of Decision to Withold Bail

DOCUMENT 16 Notice of Application Relating to Bail to be Made to the Crown Court

DOCUMENT 17 Record of Crown Court Bail Hearing

DOCUMENT 18 (A–P) Advance Information/Committal Bundle—selected Portions Excluding Documents I–N)

DOCUMENT 19 Additional Statement of Lenny Whyte—comments on Advance Information

DOCUMENT 20 File Note—consideration of Video Parade

DOCUMENT 21 Note to Trainee Solicitor—enquiry Re: Possible Alibi

DOCUMENT 22 CPS Letter Regarding Committal Proceedings Sepcimen Letter

DOCUMENT 23 Extracts from the Committal Bundle

DOCUMENT 24 File Note on Committal Preparation and Attendance

DOCUMENT 25 CDS 4—application for Prior Authority to Incur Disbursement

DOCUMENT 26 Notice of Committal/Case Management Form

DOCUMENT 27 Letter Requesting Expert Report for the Defence

DOCUMENT 28 Letter to Client

DOCUMENT 29 CPS Letter Regarding CPIA 1996 Disclosure—Specimen Letter

DOCUMENT 30A Police Schedule of Non-sensitive Unused Material

DOCUMENT 30B Police Schedule of Non-sensitive Unused Material

DOCUMENT 30CForm BC2 Giving Notice of Intention to Admit Evidence of Defendant's Bad Character Under Criminal Justice Act 2003

DOCUMENT 31 Notice to Accused Regarding CPIA 1996 Disclosure

DOCUMENT 32 Letter to CPS Dealing With CPIA 1996 Matters

DOCUMENT 33 Notification of Witness Requirements

DOCUMENT 34A Defence Statement

TIMESCALE OF EVENTS—*R v LENNY WHYTE*

- 20 March—charged with an either-way offence.
- 20 March—initial appearance before magistrates' court (adjourned for advance information and remanded in custody).
- 27 March—second appearance before magistrates' court. Not guilty plea entered followed by mode of trial enquiry. Summary jurisdiction declined. Case adjourned and a date set for committal hearing. Bail refused. Remanded in to custody.
- 29 March—bail appeal before Crown Court—conditional bail granted.
- 30 May—third appearance before magistrates' court at committal hearing. Case committed to the Crown Court and a date set for a Plea and Case Management Hearing (PCMH).
- 30 June—first appearance before Crown Court at the PCMH—date set for trial.
- 22 August—trial.

DOCUMENT 1 INITIAL STATEMENT OF LENNY WHYTE

Proof of Evidence

Lenny Whyte of Flat 4a, Lymewood Court, Parkdale, Lyme, will state:

1. I am 27 years old and of mixed race origin. My father is from the Caribbean and my mother (who is deceased) was white. My date of birth is the 26/7/- I have been charged in connection with a burglary at the home of an 84-year-old woman in Sunrise Road, Lyme which occurred on the 17th March at around mid-day. I will plead not guilty and am innocent of the charge. I was not represented at the police station prior to being charged and have been refused police bail. I am also charged with possession of a small quantity of cannabis. I intend to plead guilty to this.

2. I was arrested at home on the 19th March as I was leaving my flat. I could not believe it. The next thing I knew they were searching my flat. They seized some of my clothing and a pair of training shoes. I was taken to a police car and shoved in the back and taken to the police station.

3. I was taken to Lyme Street Police Station, and had to stay there overnight. I cannot remember if my rights were explained. The police told me I would be detained overnight because they wanted me to participate in an identification procedure and it would take time to organise. I have been in this situation before. I recall asking for an identification parade but was told I would have a video parade. I was photographed not long after arriving at the police station. I watched the officer put together a video parade but I did not have a clue what was going on. I understand that several witnesses have been shown the video and one of them has picked me out.

4. It was a difficult night in detention. I did not get much sleep and I was really worried about my dog Butch. I live on my own and there is no one to see to him. The police did try to ring my sister but she could not be reached. I was also craving a cigarette as I am a chain smoker. Additionally, I am a diagnosed manic depressive. I am prone to erratic behaviour and mood swings. Sometimes I get very depressed. My medication helps but it has side effects and I do not take it as regularly as I should. I cannot recall whether I was asked about this when I arrived at the police station as it is all a bit of a blur. I told the police the following morning that I needed my medication and that I felt unwell. When I told the officer that I needed my medication for depression, a police doctor was called. Somebody must have gone to my flat to get my pills. I was checked over by the police doctor who gave me my tablets. He said I was fit to be interviewed which I was happy about. I thought that once I was interviewed I would be able to get out and see to things.

5. I believe it was explained to me that I could see a solicitor if I wanted to. To be honest I did not think there was much point as the police were going to charge me whatever I said. When the police said they were going to interview me at last, I did not want to delay matters further by requesting a solicitor. I regret the decision now. I kept telling the officers that I needed a smoke. I was told that it was up to me. In the circumstances, I just told the police what they wanted to hear. I wish to retract my confession. It is untrue.

6. I understand that another man is alleged to have been involved in the burglary. His name is Lloyd Green. I know of Lloyd Green. He is a drug dealer and has supplied drugs to me in the past. He is no longer my supplier. Green has got rough with me in the past when I owed him money.

7. I have been trying to recollect my whereabouts on Tuesday the 17th between 11.30am–12.30pm. I think I may have been in my bookmakers—Gladbrookes in the High Street—and there might be someone there who could verify the fact. I place a small bet most days at around lunch time and I am fairly certain that that was where I was.

8. I do know the area around Sunrise Road. It is quite close to where I live. I often walk my dog on fields near to the back of Sunrise Road. I know one or two of the residents in the street. Most residents are friendly, but one or two of them are a little suspicious of me. The rear gardens of the houses in Sunrise Road which back onto the fields are not fenced off so it is possible for a person to wonder onto the lawns at the back of the houses.

9. I do not understand how I have come to be identified as the man seen running away from the back of the burgled property. It was not me. I can only assume it must have been someone else who maybe looks similar in appearance to me. In actuality, I am 5'10". I am of slim build. I have medium length dreadlocked hair and a slight beard. The police mentioned something about the white training shoes being worn by the burglar. I do not own a pair of white trainers. The trainers recovered from my flat were left there by a friend. I have never worn them.

10. So far as my personal circumstances are concerned, I live on my own in a housing association flat. I have a girlfriend. Her name is Sonia. We have been seeing each other on and off for six months, although we have not been living together. Sonia is four months pregnant with my child. The pregnancy was not

planned. Sonia already has a child of her own. She is hoping to move to better accommodation as her present flat only has one bedroom. I am anxious to see Sonia. I need to know if she and the baby are okay.

11. I do not work. I am in receipt of income support. With my criminal record and my medical condition, it is difficult for me to get work. Having said that, I have a job interview next week—something my probation officer has organised. It is with a floor laying company. The owner has taken on ex-offenders in the past and is prepared to give me an interview. This could offer me the first real prospect of a job leading to full-time employment.

12. I get on very well with my sister, Tessa. She is my half-sister. She is a single mother. I see my sister once or twice a week. She makes sure my flat is clean and that I have food in. My mother died when I was 14 and my father left us when I was three. I don't know where he lives. Tessa, who is six years my senior, looked after me when our mother died.

13. I have been smoking cannabis since the age of 15. I became addicted to hard drugs, including crack, in my early twenties. At this time I was mixing with a lot of low-life individuals and having to commit crimes in order to pay off debts and fund my drug habit. Prison was really hard. Drugs were available but I stayed off hard drugs. When I finished my prison sentence I got myself a girlfriend and some stability. However, it was at this time that I began suffering with mental problems which I assumed were due to my drug addiction. I wish to make it clear that I am no longer addicted to drugs and only smoke cannabis very occasionally when I am feeling really depressed and weird. I must get bail. I cannot face going back to prison. I had not smoked any cannabis in the 24 hours before my arrest.

14. My GP is Dr Shaw at the Havelock Medical Centre, Willow Lane, Lyme. I do see a consultant psychiatrist at the Royal Lyme Hospital but I cannot recall his name. I am happy for my medical notes to be released.

15. I am currently on probation for an offence of assault. As part of the probation order, I was ordered to undergo psychiatric treatment. It was as a consequence of this that doctors diagnosed my mental illness. I have a really supportive probation officer, Maxine, with whom I get on really well. She understands my problems and is the one who has secured me a job interview.

16. I do have previous convictions but I cannot recall them all. I have previous convictions for burglary, drug use and assault. My most recent offence of assault was committed 18 months ago. It was very much out of character for me. I am not a violent man. The assault stemmed from a breakdown of a relationship and was committed shortly before my illness was diagnosed and treatment for it began. Aggressive tendencies are not uncommon in sufferers of manic depression and this may have been a contributing factor in the commission of this offence.

17. I have convictions for possession of amphetamine and cocaine and convictions for theft. Most of the theft offences relate to shoplifting committed in order to obtain drugs. As far as I can remember the burglary offences were drug related. I have previous convictions for failing bail. I have no excuse. I simply did not turn up at court. I suspect I was so out of it while on drugs that I simply forgot. To the best of my recollection, I have always pleaded guilty.

Lenny Whyte
20th March

DOCUMENT 2   ATTENDANCE ON CLIENT AND RECORD OF FIRST APPEARANCE BEFORE MAGISTRATES' COURT
DATE 20/3/-

Attending Lenny Whyte at Lyme Magistrates' Court in my capacity as Duty Solicitor. Lenny Whyte is charged with a domestic dwelling house burglary. In the course of the interview, Lenny was less than coherent and kept asking me for a cigarette. He looked rough, dishevelled and appeared incapable of concentrating during the interview. He was not represented at the police station. He appears in custody as bail is opposed. Lenny suffers from bipolar depression for which he receives medication. I took a detailed initial statement from him but before doing so I had a word with the CPS lawyer dealing with the case, who gave me what advance disclosure she has to date which included Lenny's previous convictions and several witness statements. The evidence linking Lenny seems to be based on admissions in interview and eye-witness evidence. A second person is suspected of being involved in the burglary but no charges have been brought against this individual. The CPS lawyer indicated bail would be opposed.

In the course of my interview with Lenny, I assisted him to complete an application for a representation order. On speaking with the CPS they were not in possession of a full file. Attending before Lyme Magistrates where the CPS requested a one week adjournment period to review the file. The adjournment was granted. The CPS then opposed bail. An application for bail was made by me. Bail refused on the grounds of risk of absconding and commission of further offences. The case was adjourned for 1 week. Mr Whyte was remanded to HMP Shawbury. Date of next hearing is 27 March.

I spoke to Lenny afterwards—he was clearly agitated and somewhat bewildered. I explained he could apply for bail to the Crown Court but that I would be able to reapply for bail before the magistrates in one week's time as he had one further opportunity to apply to the Magistrates' Court for bail. If bail was refused on that occasion we could apply to the Crown Court. He agreed to this course of action. I explained I would be writing to him whilst he was on remand and that he would be visited by me or a member of the firm in order to take his further instructions on the evidence. I also spoke to Lenny's sister who attended court and who is evidently concerned for her brother's welfare.

Time engaged:
Attending client 50 minutes (including completing an application for a representation order)
Advocacy 30 minutes

DOCUMENT 3   CLIENT DETAILS FORM CDS1

Client's Details Form

CDS1

Please complete in block capitals

Client's details

UFN: | S | D | 4 | 9 | 0 | C | / | 6 | 0 | 7 |

Surname: WHYTE

First name: LENNY

Date of birth: 27 / 6 / -   National Insurance no: | F | R | 8 | 2 | 1 | 2 | 8 | 5 | Y |

Marital status: [X] Single   [ ] Married   [ ] Divorced   [ ] Widowed

[ ] Separated   [ ] Civil Partner   [ ] Cohabiting

Gender: [X] Male   [ ] Female

Current address: 4A LYMEWOOD COURT,

PARKDALE

Town: LYME

County: _____   Postcode: _____

Data Protection Act 1998 - Important notice for Clients

When completing this form (or their own version of this form) with their client's personal details, Solicitors MUST inform the client of the following points:

The information provided will be passed to the Legal Services Commission who process applications for Legal Aid. It will be kept in accordance with the Principles of the Data Protection Act 1998. The information will be kept for as long as is necessary for the Legal Services Commission to fulfil its functions under the Access to Justice Act 1999. Applicants have the right to request a copy of the information held about them by the Legal Services Commission and to correct it if it is wrong. Provision of the equal opportunities information is voluntary. This will be treated in the strictest confidence and will be used purely for equal opportunities monitoring, which the Commission is required to do in accordance with the relevant equalities legislation or for research purposes. The results of any monitoring or research will only be published in an anonymised form. **Only if means information is collected:** Information provided in the sections on Income and Capital may, where necessary, be shared with third parties for the purpose of protecting public funds, or where it is lawfully required. These parties include (but are not limited to): the Department for Work and Pensions, the Inland Revenue, HM Revenue & Customs, Land Registry, Companies House and Credit Reference Agencies.

Equal Opportunities Monitoring

Completion of this section is voluntary. This will be treated in the strictest confidence and will be used purely for statistical monitoring and research.

Please tick the boxes which your client would describe themselves as being:

Ethnic Monitoring

White

[ ] (a) British

[ ] (b) Irish

[ ] (c) White Other

Black or Black British

[X] (a) Black Caribbean

[ ] (b) Black African

[ ] (c) Black Other

Mixed

[ ] (a) White and Black Caribbean

[ ] (b) White and Black African

[ ] (c) White and Asian

[ ] (d) Mixed Other

[ ] Chinese

Asian or Asian British

[ ] (a) Indian

[ ] (b) Pakistani

[ ] (c) Bangladeshi

[ ] (d) Asian Other

[ ] Other

Disability Monitoring

The Disability Discrimination Act defines disability as: a physical or mental impairment with long term, substantial effects on a person's ability to perform day-to-day activities.

Does your client consider himself or herself to have a disability?   [X] Yes   [ ] No

CDS1   Page 1   Version 6 October 2006   (c) Criminal Defence Service

DOCUMENT 4 APPLICATION FOR REPRESENTATION ORDER—FORM CDS14

Form CDS14   *Please note that this form is also available in Welsh.

Official use: MAAT Ref:

Priority case: Custody ☐
Vulnerable ☐
Youth ☐
Crown Court - s51 cases only ☐

legal services
COMMISSION

*Before completing this form, please refer to the guidance notes supplied with your forms order.

Application for Legal Aid in Criminal Proceedings

The information you declare in this form will be checked with the Department for Work and Pensions, HM Revenue and Customs and others.

Part A - About you

Your details

1 Your first name: LENNY

2 Your surname: WHYTE

3 Date of birth: 27 / 6 / -

4 National Insurance No: F R 2 1 2 8 5 Y   (Letters / Numbers / Letter)   See Note 1

5 Single ☒   Married ☐   Married, but separated ☐   Divorced ☐
Widowed ☐   Living with a partner ☐   Civil Partner ☐

6 Home phone number ___
Mobile phone number ___
Work phone number ___

7 Usual home address 4A LYMEWOOD COURT, PARKDALE, LYME

Is the address: Owned by you? ☐   You are a tenant ☒   Temporary address ☐

8 Postal address (if different from home address) ___

Your age   See Note 2

9

I am under 18.   No ☒ Go to question 10
                  Yes ☐

I am jointly charged with an adult   No ☒ Go to page 3
                                     Yes ☐ Go to page 3

Form CDS14

legal services
COMMISSION

Part A - About you

Your relationship status

'Partner' refers to a person you are married to or a person you normally live with as a couple. If you have a partner, you must fill in the details below, and throughout the rest of the form where necessary.

10 Are you married or living with your partner?   No ☒   Yes ☐

Your benefit status

See Note 2

11 Do you or your partner receive any of the following benefits?	You	Your partner
Income Support	No ☐ Yes ☒	No ☐ Yes ☐
Income-based Jobseeker's Allowance	No ☐ Yes ☐	No ☐ Yes ☐
Guarantee State Pension Credit	No ☐ Yes ☐	No ☐ Yes ☐

Your partner's details - if you don't have a partner, go to page 3.

See Note 3

12 Is your partner involved in the case as: a victim, a Prosecution witness or a co-defendant with a conflict (whose interests may conflict with yours)?   No ☐   Yes ☐   Go to page 3

13 Your partner's first name:

14 Your partner's surname:

15 Your partner's date of birth: ..../.........../..................

16 Your partner's NI No: Letters Numbers Letter

17 Partner's address if different from your own:

See Note 4

18 Your partner's current contact details if they are unable to sign the declaration on this form:

Place and address where they are staying e.g. the name of the hospital and ward:

Please give reasons why your partner is unable to sign:

CDS14

2

Form CDS14

legal services
COMMISSION

Part A - About you

Further information.

See Note 5

See Note 6

You do not have to fill in this section. This will be treated in the strictest confidence and will be used purely for statistical monitoring and research.

Are you male or female?

Male ☒   Female ☐

Disability Monitoring

The Disability Discrimination Act defines disability as 'a physical or mental impairment with a substantial and long-term adverse effect on a person's ability to carry out day-to-day activities'.

Do you consider yourself to have a disability?

No ☐   Yes ☐

Equal Opportunities Monitoring

Tick all the boxes which apply.

Ethnic Monitoring

White		Mixed		Asian or Asian British		Black or Black British		Chinese		Other Ethnic Group	
British	☒	White and Black Caribbean	☐	Indian	☐	Black Caribbean	☒	Chinese	☐	Other	☐
Irish	☐	White and Black African	☐	Pakistani	☐	Black African	☐				
White other	☐	White & Asian	☐	Bangladeshi	☐	Black other	☐				
		Mixed other	☐	Asian other	☐						

CDS14

3

Form CDS14

legal services
COMMISSION

Part B - Interests of Justice

I apply for the right to representation for the purposes of criminal proceedings under the Access to Justice Act 1999 and the Criminal Defence Service (General) (No. 2) Regulations 2001 (as amended).

1 Case details   See Note 7

1a What charges have been brought against you? Describe briefly what you have been accused of. E.g. theft of £1000 from your employer or assault on a neighbour.

DOMESTIC DWELLING HOUSE BURGLARY

1b Are there any co-defendants in this matter?   ☒ No. Go to question 2   ☐ Yes

If 'yes', please give their names.

_____

1c Give reasons why you and your co-defendants cannot be represented by the same solicitor.

_____
_____
_____

2 The court proceedings

2a I am due to appear before the **LYME MAGISTRATES'**   court

On 20   / 3   / -   at 9.30

Or

2b I appeared before the
_____ court

On   /   /   at

And (tick whichever applies)

My case has been sent to the Crown Court for trial under section 51 of the Crime and Disorder Act 1998.	☐
My case has been transferred to the Crown Court for trial.	☐
I was committed for trial to the Crown Court because I elected Crown Court trial.	☐
I was committed for trial to the Crown Court because the court of prosecution elected Crown Court trial.	☐
I was convicted and/or sentenced and I want to appeal against the conviction or sentence.	☐
I was convicted and committed for sentence to the Crown Court.	☐
A retrial has been ordered under section 7 of the Criminal Appeal Act 1968.	☐
Other (please give the nature of the hearing)	☐

CDS14

4

Form CDS14

Part B - Interests of Justice

3 Outstanding matters

If there are any other outstanding criminal charges or cases against you, give details, including the court where you are due to appear.

4 Reasons for wanting legal aid

See Note 8

4a. Please tick the reason or reasons below which apply to your case.

(i) It is likely that I will lose my liberty if any matter in the proceedings is decided against me. ☒

(ii) I have been given a sentence that is suspended or non-custodial. If I break this, the court may be able to deal with me for the original offence. ☒

(iii) It is likely that I will lose my livelihood. ☐

(iv) It is likely that I will suffer serious damage to my reputation. ☐

(v) A substantial question of law may be involved (whether arising from an act, judicial authority or other source of law). ☒

(vi) I may not be able to understand the court proceedings or present my own case. ☒

(vii) Witnesses may need to be traced or interviewed on my behalf. ☒

(viii) The proceedings may involve expert cross-examination of a prosecution witness (whether an expert or not). ☒

(ix) It is in the interests of another person (such as the person making a complaint or other witness) that I am represented. ☒

(x) Any other reasons. ☒

CDS14

5

Form CDS14

Part B - Interests of Justice

......question 4 continued

legal services
COMMISSION

See Note 8

4b Please give the details of the reason or reasons you selected in question 4a.

Likely to lose my liberty
I have been charged with an offence of domestic burglary. The aggravating factors are that the victim is an 84 year old woman and I have previous convictions of a like nature. In the light of the Court of Appeal's decision in R v McInerney (2002), I am at risk of a lengthy custodial sentence if convicte.

I am subject to a community order for an offence of common assault. It was imposed 18 months ago and has 6 months left to run. I stand to be -re-sentenced if convicted.

Subtantial question of law
I intend to challenge the admissibility of incriminating admissions I made at the police station under ss. 76 and 78 PACE 1984. I am a diagnosed bipolar-depressive. I was not represented by a solicitor or an appropriate adult and was unwell during interview. The prosecution will seek to adduce my previous convictions into evidence. I will oppose any attempt to have my previous convictions admitted under s.101 Criminal Justice Act 2003.

Unable to follow the proceedings
I suffer from bipolar depression for which I receive medication. I am subject to mood swings and will be unable to follow the proceedings without the assistance of a solicitor.

Witnesses need to be traced and or interviewed
I think I was in a betting shop at the time of the burglary and my solicitors will need to make contact with the betting establishment to see if anyone there can recall my presence.

Case involves expert cross-examination
I intend to plead not guilty. There are several elderly eye-witnesses who purport to have recognised me. They are mistaken and will need to be cross-examined. The case against me involves expert witness evidence involving shoe-print comparisons which I intend to challenge. The investigating officer and custody sergeant will need to be cross-examined.

In someone else's interests
The eye-witnesses are all elderly and will need to be cross-examined.

Any other reason
The case is most likely to be heard at the Crown Court.

5 Legal Representation

a If you do not choose a solicitor, the court will choose one for you

b You must tell the solicitor that you have named him or her

c If you have been charged with another person or people, the court may appoint a solicitor other than the solicitor of your choice

The solicitor I want to act for me is:
Rachel James

Give the firm's name and address if known:
Mountford and Hannibal

20 High Street

Lyme Bank, Lyme

Form CDS14

legal services
COMMISSION

Part C - Declaration

You must complete declarations which apply to your application.

Authority by your partner

See Note 9

If you have a partner whose details have been completed on this form, they must sign the authority below, unless your partner is abroad, in hospital or otherwise unable to sign.

This is a true statement of my financial circumstances, *as supported by the information detailed on the CDS15 (*delete if not applicable).

I agree to the Legal Services Commission and HM Courts Service checking these facts with others such as the Department for Work and Pensions and HM Revenue & Customs. I authorise those people or organisations to provide the information that we may request.

Signature.. Date.................../...................../.....................

Full name (in BLOCK CAPITALS)...

Your declaration

This is a true statement of my financial circumstances, and that of my partner, *as supported by the information detailed on the CDS15 (*delete if not applicable).

I understand that if I tell you anything untrue on this form, or the documents I send with it, or leave anything out:

a I may be taken to court; or
b the Legal Services Commission may take away my legal aid so I have to pay all my legal fees.

I understand that if I have made a statement which is false; or I knowingly withhold information, I may be prosecuted, which may result in a prison sentence or a fine.

I agree to the Legal Services Commission and HM Courts Service checking these facts with others such as the Department for Work and Pensions and HM Revenue & Customs. I authorise those people or organisations to provide the information that we may request.

I agree to the Legal Services Commission contacting my partner to check the information I have given about their means.

I will:
a provide more evidence if the Legal Services Commission or HM Courts Service ask; and
b tell the Legal Services Commission or HM Courts Service if anything I have said here changes.

I understand that if my case goes to the Crown Court or any higher court, the court may order that I pay some or all of the costs of the proceedings through a Recovery of Defence Costs Order. I understand the information given in this form will be provided to that court so that it can consider whether a Recovery of Defence Costs Order should be made and I may be required to give details of my means to the court or LSC.

I understand that if my case goes to the Crown Court or any higher court, I will have to tell the Legal Services Commission or HM Courts Service (or both) details of my financial circumstances.

Signature...... *Lenny Whyte* ...... Date...... 20 / 3 / — ......

Full name (in BLOCK CAPITALS) LENNY WHYTE

Declaration to be completed by the legal representative

I,......................................, representing the applicant, confirm that I am authorised to provide representation under a contract issued by the Legal Services Commission (e.g. a general criminal contract or an individual case contract).

I understand that only firms with a contract issued by the Commission (e.g. a general criminal contract or an individual case contract) may provide representation in the Magistrates' Court.

Or

I, RACHEL JAMES...................., representing the applicant, confirm that I have been instructed to provide representation by either:

• a firm who holds a contract issued by the Legal Services Commission (e.g. a general criminal contract or individual case contract), or;
• a solicitor employed by the Legal Services Commission in a Public Defender Office who is authorised to provide representation.

Signature...................... Date...... 20 / 3 / — ......

Legal Service Provider LSC account number

| Y | 5 | 6 | 8 | 8 | 8 | 6 |

CDS14

7

Form CDS14

Data Protection Act - Access to personal information

We will use the information you provide in this form, and any other information we may receive, to process your application for legal aid. We will keep it in line with the principles of the Data Protection Act 1998 and any relevant confidentiality arrangements.

The Legal Services Commission is the data controller. If necessary, we may check or share the information you provide with other organisations, such as:

- the Department for Work and Pensions;
- HM Revenue & Customs;
- the Land Registry;
- Companies House;
- credit reference agencies

We will only share the information if it is necessary to protect the public funds or where we have to do so by law.

We or HM Courts Service may also process your information to produce management or research information. The results of our research will only be published in a statistical or anonymous form.

We will keep information for as long as is necessary to fulfil our duties under the Access to Justice Act 1999. You have the right to look at the personal information held about you, to inspect it, and have it corrected if it is wrong.

For official use only

List any other factors considered when deciding the application, including any information given orally.

Decision on the Interests of Justice Test   Passed ☑   Refused ☐

I have considered all the available details of all the charges and against the Interests of Justice criteria. I give the following reasons.

Decision on financial eligibility:

Signature ...*D. Goodman*... Name of appropriate officer *DAVID GOODMAN*

Date... 2 0 / 3 / —

Case number: 67123

Representation order number: 07/851739

To be completed where right to representation extends to Crown Court:

Statement of means Form B given to defendant on ____ / ____ / ____

Indicate type of case:

- Sent case under S51 Crime and Disorder Act 1988 ☐
- Transferred for trial ☐
- Committal for trial/sentence ☐
- Retrial under S7 of the Criminal Appeal Act 1988 ☐
- Other (specify) _____

First date of hearing at Crown Court ____ / ____ / ____

Document 9 LYMESHIRE POLICE CUSTODY RECORD

Station: **Lyme Street**

Reasons for Arrest
Burglary of dwelling house

Surname: **WHYTE**

Previous Name:

Forenames: **LENNY**

Comments made by person, if present when facts of arrest were explained. Y/N [N]. If Yes, comments on log.

Address: **4A
LYMEWOOD COURT
PARKDALE
LYME**

Video Tape Ref. No. LT/369

DETAINED PERSON'S RIGHTS
An extract from a notice setting out my rights has been read to me and I have been given a copy. I have also been provided with a written notice setting out my entitlements while in custody.

Signature: **Lenny Whyte**
Date: 19/3/-   Time: 15.45

Telephone

Occupation: **NONE**
Age: **27**   Date of Birth: **27/6/-**

Place of Birth: **LONDON**

**LEGAL ADVICE REQUESTED
DETAILS:**
I want to speak to a solicitor as soon as practicable

Signature:
Time: Date:

Height: **5** Feet: **11** Inches: Sex: **M**

LEGAL ADVICE DECLINED
I have been informed that I may speak to a solicitor
IN PERSON OR ON THE TELEPHONE:

I do not want to speak to a solicitor at this time.
Signature: **Lenny Whyte**
Time: 19/3   Date: 15.45

Arrested by:
Name: DS S Farrington
ID. No: 4291
Station: Lyme Street
Place of Arrest: 4a Lymewood Court, Lyme

	Time	Date
Arrested at:	15.30	19/3/-
Arrived at Station	16.10	19/3/-

Reasons given, for not wanting legal advice
None given

**NOTIFICATION OF A NAMED PERSON
REQUESTED Y/N [Y]**
Details of nominated person
Theresa Whyte (Sister)

Officer In Case:
Id. No: 4291
Name: DS Farrington

Officer Opening Custody Record

APPROPRIATE ADULT Y/N [N]

INTERPRETER Y/N [N]
Notices served & grounds for detention explained in the presence of Appropriate Adult/Interpreter

Signature of A/Adult

Time: Date:

Signature: Mike Williams

Id No: 4231
Name: Sgt M Williams

CHARGES(S)

Surname WHYTE	Custody No. 2305/05
Forename (s) LENNY	Station: Lyme
	Sex M/F (M)
Address 4A Lymewood Court	D.O.B 27/6/-
Parkdale	
Lyme	ID Code: 1
Postcode	Language: None

You are charged with the offence(s) shown below. You do not have to say anything. But it may harm your defence if you do not mention now something which you later rely on in court. Anything you do say may be given in evidence.

Consec. No.	Charge(s)
1.	That on the 17th March having entered as a trespasser a building, being a dwelling known as 19 Sunrise Road, Lyme you stole £75 in money property belonging to Lillian Kennedy contrary to s. 9(1)(b) Theft Act 1968
2.	That on the 19th March you unlawfully had in your possession a controlled drug of Class C namely cannabis, contrary to section 5(2) Misuse of Drugs Act 1971

Time and Date of Charge: 20th March   12.45hrs
Reply (if any): "you are racist pigs you lot are."

Signed (person charged)	Signed (appropriate adult)			
Officer charging Surname Farrington	Rank DS	No.4291	Station: Lyme St	
Officer in case Surname	Rank	No.	Station	
Charge accepted Surname	Rank	No.	Station	

Appearing at LYME REMAND COURT at LYME SQUARE, LYME on the 20/3/ at 1400 hours

LYMESHIRE POLICE
DETAINED PERSONS MEDICAL FORM

Custody Ref: 2305/05

Name: Lenny Whyte	DOB: 27/6/-	Time/Date: 20/3/-

Reason Doctor requested:
Detainee telling me he felt claustrophobic and needed to take medication for depression

VISUAL ASSESSMENT BY CUSTODY SERGEANT

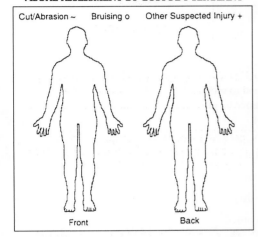

Cut/Abrasion ~   Bruising o   Other Suspected Injury +

Front   Back

ADMINISTRATION AND MOVEMENT TIMES

	Time	Date
Doctor called	0700	20/3/-
Doctor replied		
Agreed Arrival Time		
Doctor Arrived	0745	20/3/-
Departure/Conclusion		
Ambulance Called		
Ambulance Arrived		
Detainee taken to Hospital		Time/Date

Police-Signs/symptoms & First Aid given:
Observed detainee seemed very fidgety

By whom:

DOCTORS OPINION OR TELEPHONE ADVICE (NON-CONFIDENTIAL)

Name of Doctor: Dr Ghulam

Time/Date of Examination: 20/3/- 0800 hrs

Opinion: Anxious but lucid in thought. Orientated in time and space. Takes regular medication for manic depression

Medical Advice: Medicate per prescription

Examination/Observation: Completed/Refused   Risk of Self Harm: High/Medium/Standard

Location of Examination: Medical room/Cell/Other   Station: Lyme Street

RECOMMENDATIONS

	Yes	No		Yes	No
Recommended appropriate adult: *		*	Medical review Required		*
Fit to be detained:	*		Time/Date required:		
			Time/Date carried Out:		
	Yes	No			
Fit for interview:	*				
Fit for transfer					
Fit for charge:					

Doctors Signature:
Ghulam

LYMESHIRE POLICE

Station: LYME STREET	Detained Person Serial No: **2305/357**

Surname: **WHYTE**
Forenames: **LENNY**

Last review of detention conducted at:

<u>Date</u>	<u>Time</u>	<u>Details of Action/Occurrence</u>	
19/3/-	1610	DP arrived.	MW
	1615	DP searched—property removed. Rights explained. Detention authorised to secure and preserve evidence and to obtain evidence by questioning. DP taken to cell by officers—Cell F4.	MW
	1630	Phone call to DP's sister 821249 (no contact made no answering machine). DP informed.	MW
	1700	DP accepted hot drink.	MW
	1730	DP taken meal—refused.	MW
	1800	DP seen in cell—in order.	MW
	1815	DP consents to taking saliva swab—non-intimate	MW
	1816	'I consent to providing a sample of my saliva.' Lenny Whyte	
	1830	DP taken to Identification suite for photographing and parade compilation.	MW
	1930	DP returned to my custody—placed in Cell F4.	MW
	1935	DP given a cup of tea—asking for cigarette.	MW
	1955	DP uses toilet.	MW
	2015	In cell awake and pacing.	MW
	2030	In cell awake—muttering	MW

LYMESHIRE POLICE

Station: **LYME STREET**	Detained Person Serial No: **2305/357**

Surname: **WHYTE**
Forenames: **LENNY**

Last review of detention conducted at: **2200 hours 19/3/**

Date	Time	Details of Action/Occurrence	
	2100	Banging on cell—uses toilet.	MW
	2130	In cell—pacing—requests cigarette—refused.	MW
	2200	In cell—in order. Custody transferred to Sgt Tom Slater. Detention reviewed. DP informed.	TS
	2230	In cell—sitting on bed wringing hands.	TS
	2300	In cell—in order.	TS
	2330	In cell—pacing.	TS
	2345	Given refreshment.	TS
	2359	DP—on bed awake.	TS
20/3/-	0015	DP in cell pacing. Requests cigarette.	TS
	0045	On bed—suspect rocking back and forwards. Asked if okay. Requested more blankets supplied. DP informed me he wanted to sleep.	TS
	0115	DP in cell—awake. In order.	TS
	0145	DP in cell—uses toilet.	TS
	0215	DP in cell—asleep.	TS
	0245	DP—awake lying on bed.	TS
	0315	DP seen pacing in cell.	TS

LYMESHIRE POLICE

Station: **LYME STREET**	Detained Person Serial No: **2305/357**

Surname: **WHYTE**
Forenames: **LENNY**

Last review of detention conducted at: **0700 hours 20/3/**

Date	Time	Details of Action/Occurrence	
20/3/	0345	DP awake—humming to himself.	TS
	0415	DP lying on bed—in order.	TS
	0445	DP awake—sitting on bed.	TS
	0515	DP taken to toilet.	TS
	0545	DP in cell pacing.	TS
	0603	DP complains of feeling unwell. Requests doctor.	TS
	0610	Transferred into custody of Sgt Brough	DB
	0630	DP offered breakfast. Informed by DP that his regular medication for depression is at home. FME requested. Officer dispatched to DP's house to locate medication.	DB
	0645	DP uses toilet. Informed GP requested to attend.	DB
	0700	Review of detention. DP informed.	DB
	0740	DP taken to medical room for examination by Dr Ghulam.	DB
	0800	Dr Ghulam completes report—medication administered to DP who is fit to be interviewed. DP taken back to cell F4.	DB
	0815	DP in cell. In order.	DB
	0900	DP offered refreshment. Requests cigarette.	DB

LYMESHIRE POLICE

| Station: **LYME STREET** | Detained Person Serial No: **2305/357** |

Surname: WHYTE
Forenames: LENNY

Last review of detention conducted at: **0700 hours 20/3/**

Date	Time	Details of Action/Occurrence	
20/3/-	0915	DP informed of intention to interview—asked if requires solicitor—refuses one.	DB
	0930	DP in cell. In order.	DB
	1000	DP asking when interview will be.	DB
	1030	DP in cell—agitated—pacing.	DB
	1045	DP in cell—allowed to use toilet.	DB
	1100	DP in cell pacing.	DB
	1115	DP given to the custody of DS Farrington and taken to interview room 2.	DB
	1230	Returned to my custody.	DB
	1245	DP charged and documented. Bail refused on grounds of risk of absconding and commission of further offences. DP's sister contacted and informed. DP allowed to speak with sister.	DB
	1300	Into custody of Premier for transport to Lyme MC.	DB

DOCUMENT 11A LIST OF PREVIOUS CONVICTIONS FOR LENNY WHYTE

Print of PNC Record-PNCID: 005/6593V

Print For: WHYTE, LENNY

Date of Birth: 27/6/-

Date	Court	Offence/s	Sentence
10 years previous	Lyme Youth Court	Burglary (domestic dwelling)	Supervision Order (12 months)
7 years previous	Lyme Magistrates	Theft	Conditional Discharge (12 months)
5 years previous (February)	Blurton Magistrates	Theft Possession of amphetamine Driving without insurance	Community Rehabilitation Order (15 months)/ Licence endorsed
5 years previous (December)	Lyme Magistrates	Burglary (non-dwelling) Possession of class B drug Resisting constable Failure to surrender Breach community order	Custody 5 months concurrent
4 years previous	Chorley Magistrates	Possession of class B drug Theft Obtaining property by deception	Community Rehabilitation Order (12 months)
3 years previous (August)	Lyme Crown Court	Burglary (domestic dwelling) Possession of class A drug Failure to surrender	Custody 12 months concurrent
2 years previous (April)	Blurton Magistrates	Theft Possession of class B drug	Custody 4 months concurrent + unexpired term 108 days
18 months previous	Lyme Magistrates	s. 4 Public Order Act 1986 Common Assault	Community Order (24 months)

DOCUMENT 12 FILE NOTE: CONSIDERATION OF ADVANCE INFORMATION

23 March
Engaged considering the Advance Information.

Having considered the evidence, I am of the view that Lenny should indicate a not guilty plea at the plea before venue. It is unlikely (given the seriousness of the offence and the likely sentence in the event of conviction) that the magistrates would accept jurisdiction to try this matter. At the mode of trial enquiry the court must assume the prosecution's version of the facts is correct so there is no point in drawing the magistrates' attention to the weaknesses in the prosecution's case at this stage.

In the unlikely event of Lenny being presented with a choice, my considered opinion is that he would, in any event, be best advised to elect a Crown Court trial for the following reasons:

• He stands a better chance of being acquitted.

• There are areas of disputed evidence which are best dealt with in the absence of the jury.

• A qualified judge would be more confident about excluding evidence.

Against is:

• The risk of a higher sentence (although I suspect that magistrates would commit for sentence in any event).

• It will take longer to come to trial but Lenny does not seem unduly concerned by this.

• Defence statement is mandatory—but if the case is committed to the Crown Court we stand a better chance of flushing out further disclosure.

The advantages of the Crown Court outweigh those in favour of the magistrates' court in Lenny's case. In any event the exercise is likely to be academic since the magistrates will almost certainly decline jurisdiction and adjourn for committal proceedings.

Time engaged: 20 minutes

DOCUMENT 13 RECORD OF MODE OF TRIAL HEARING

27 March

Attending Lyme Magistrates' Court. Taking Lenny through the Advance Information and obtaining his comments thereon. I explained to Lenny that I had viewed the Video Identification Parade and considered that this had been fair.

I explained to Lenny and his sister that I did not feel that the magistrates would accept jurisdiction but that if they did he should elect trial by jury on the burglary charge in any event.

An indication of a guilty plea was entered in relation to the possession of cannabis charge and a not-guilty plea was entered in relation to the burglary matter. Mode of Trial Enquiry was held with the CPS inviting the magistrates to decline jurisdiction. No representations from us in relation to mode of trial. Jurisdiction declined—case adjourned to 30th May for preparation of committal papers.

The clerk to the justices did not feel that the cannabis charge should be committed to the Crown Court for sentence under s. 4 PCC(S)A 2000 as there was an insufficient nexus. Consequently I briefly addressed the bench in terms of sentence and a 12-month conditional discharge was imposed.

I made a second full application for bail on Lenny's behalf. Bail was once more refused on the grounds of the risk of absconding and commission of further offences.

Spoke to Lenny after the hearing and we agreed I would appeal the refusal of bail to the Crown Court.

Time engaged:
Advocacy 40 minutes
Waiting 10 minutes
Attending client 30 minutes
Travel to and from court 15 minutes.
Preparing Notice of Appeal 15 minutes

online resource centre

You can see the plea before venue/mode of trial enquiry on the burglary charge in the Lenny Whyte video section of our Online Resource Centre. It precedes Lenny's contested application for bail. A transcript, broadly based on the bail hearing, appears at Document 14. Lenny Whyte case study and the documented version you are presently considering.

DOCUMENT 17   RECORD OF CROWN COURT BAIL HEARING

File Note—29th March

Attending Lyme Crown Court. Appearing before Mr Recorder Jay. Making a further application for bail on behalf of Lenny Whyte. Bail was opposed by the CPS. Lenny was granted conditional bail as follows:

1. He resides at 4A Lymewood Court.
2. He reports to Lyme Street Police Station Mon/Wed/Friday 2–3pm.
3. He does not attempt to contact in any way Lillian Kennedy, Shirley Lewis or Harold Finney.
4. He does not go in to Sunrise Road or on the fields at the back of Sunrise Road.

Telephoning Lenny's sister to relay the good news. Explained he would be released and that I would be writing to him to stress the importance of abiding by bail conditions. Reminded her that Lenny was due to appear before Lyme Magistrates' on the 24th April.

Time engaged:
Advocacy 30 minutes
Waiting 5 minutes
Travel to and from court 15 minutes.

NB: Solicitor would need to write to Lenny advising him of his change in bail status and the importance of abiding by the conditions of his bail.

DOCUMENT 18A WITNESS STATEMENT: LILLIAN KENNEDY

WITNESS STATEMENT

(CJ Act 1967, s. 9; MC Act 1980, s. 5A(3)(a) and s. 5B; MC Rules 1981, r. 70)

Name   Lillian Kennedy
Address   Supplied
Age/Date of Birth Over 18
Occupation   Retired

....

Who states:

This statement, consisting of one page signed by me, is true to the best of my knowledge and belief and I make it knowing that if it is tendered in evidence I shall be liable to prosecution if I have wilfully stated in it anything which I know to be false or do not believe to be true.

Dated: 18th March   Signed: L Kennedy

....

I live at number 19 Sunrise Road, Lyme. I am 85 years old. On Tuesday the 17th March, I went to fetch my pension from Lyme High Street. I drew £95.00. Once I had paid my weekly sums for gas and electricity I was left with around £75. I got home at around 11 am. As I was walking up the road, a man approached me and asked me if I wanted any help with my shopping. I told him, no thank you. I would describe him as being quite tall and thin. He had a gaunt face, was black and had long, black straggling hair and a small beard on his chin. I think he was wearing a short, dark coloured top and a pair of white sports shoes. I saw him walk off into the fields near the back of my house.

I know I had my purse with me when I went into my house, because a friend of mine called in for 10 minutes, shortly after I got back from the Post Office. She had her grandchild with her and I gave her a pound from my purse. A short time after this I was putting some rubbish out when I thought I heard the telephone ringing. When I came in, I realised it was my front door bell. I answered the door. There was a man standing there. I have never seen this man before. He was white but had a tanned complexion. He was dressed smartly, wearing a suit and tie. He was quite bald. He wasn't very tall. I recall he was wearing glasses. He told me his car had broken down and asked if he could use the telephone. I told him he could not as I didn't have a phone. Not long after this a friend of my neighbour came round. She told me she had seen a black man in my back garden and that my back door was open. I immediately checked my handbag and saw that my purse was missing. She telephoned the police. I realised that I had left the back door open when I came to answer the front door. It was silly of me. The only money I get is my pension. The incident has left me shaken and frightened.

Later in the afternoon of the 17th March, the police took me around the local area in one of their cars. They asked me if I could see the man who had knocked on my front door. I couldn't see the man who had called but I did see the man who had offered to help me with my shopping earlier that morning. The police car stopped outside the Co-op on the High Street. I had a good look at the man and I am sure it was him.

Signed: Lillian Kennedy

DOCUMENT 18B   WITNESS STATEMENT: SHIRLEY LEWIS

WITNESS STATEMENT

(CJ Act 1967, s. 9; MC Act 1980, s. 5A(3)(a) and s. 5B; MC Rules 1981, r. 70)

Name	Shirley Lewis
Address	Supplied
Age/Date of Birth	Over 18
Occupation	Retired Teacher

....

Who states:

This statement, consisting of one page signed by me, is true to the best of my knowledge and belief, and I make it knowing that if it is tendered in evidence I shall be liable to prosecution if I have wilfully stated in it anything which I know to be false or do not believe to be true.

Dated: 18th March   Signed: S Lewis

....

On Tuesday the 17th March, I was visiting my elderly aunt at 19 Sunrise Road, Lyme. She lives next door to Lillian Kennedy at number 17. At around midday on Tuesday 17th March, I went out the back of my aunt's property to bring some washing in that was pegged up on the washing line. The time was around midday.

I was facing Lillian's back garden. A low wall divides the gardens, it being largely open plan. I saw a man in her garden. I watched him for a good few seconds. In fact I nearly called out to him, to ask what he thought he was doing, but something stopped me. He didn't see me because I was behind a large sheet pegged on the line. I don't know where he came from but I watched him wander out of Lillian's garden and off down the back lane. At this point I noticed the back door to Mrs Kennedy's house was open.

I would describe the man as being of Afro-Caribbean origin. He was about 5 ft 8/9 in tall. He was of slim build and was wearing a black hooded sweatshirt with the hood up, so I could not see his hair. The man I saw was wearing a pair of white training shoes. I went round to see Lillian almost straight away and she told me that her purse was missing. I am certain I would be able to recognise the man again. I had the distinct feeling I had seen the man before. In fact I have seen him walking his dog, a brown and white terrier, in the grassy area nearby, on more than one occasion.

Signed: Shirley Lewis

DOCUMENT 18C   WITNESS STATEMENT: HAROLD FINNEY]

<u>WITNESS STATEMENT</u>

(CJ Act 1967, s. 9; MC Act 1980, s. 5A(3)(a) and s. 5B; MC Rules 1981, r. 70)

Name	Harold Finney
Address	Withheld
Age/Date of Birth	Over 18
Occupation	Retired Engineer

....

Who states:

This statement, consisting of one page signed by me, is true to the best of my knowledge, and belief and I make it knowing that if it is tendered in evidence I shall be liable to prosecution if I have wilfully stated in it anything which I know to be false or do not believe to be true.

Dated: 18th March   Signed: H Finney

....

I have lived in Sunrise Road for the past five years. I am a member of the local area neighbourhood watch scheme. On Tuesday the 17th March, at around 11.30am, I observed a black car drive into Sunrise Road, Lyme, and park. I could not see anyone in the car because the windows were dark. The car remained parked in the road for 15 minutes or so. I started to get suspicious and took a note of the registration number. It was DY 01 5JT. About five minutes after I first noticed the car I saw a man walking past my window. I watched him go over to the car and get in. The telephone rang at this point and I did not see the man again. I was on the telephone for some time. When I went to look out of my window at around midday, I saw the black car driving off.

I would describe the man I saw getting into the car as being black and in his twenties. He was tall and thin. He was black and had long, dark hair. He was wearing a short black top and a pair of white training shoes.

Signed: H Finney

DOCUMENT 18D   WITNESS STATEMENT SGT S FARRINGTON

WITNESS STATEMENT

(CJ Act 1967, s. 9; MC Act 1980, s. 5A(3)(a) and s. 5B; MC Rules 1981, r. 70)

Name	Steven Farrington
Address	Lyme Street Police Station
Age/Date of Birth	Over 18
Occupation	Detective Sergeant

....

Who states:

This statement, consisting of one page signed by me, is true to the best of my knowledge and belief, and I make it knowing that if it is tendered in evidence I shall be liable to prosecution if I have wilfully stated in it anything which I know to be false or do not believe to be true.

Dated: 20th March   Signed: S Farrington

....

On the 17th March I, in the company of Detective Constable Andrew Shaw, attended the home of Lillian Kennedy at 19 Sunrise Road, Lyme. Mrs Kennedy is an 85-year-old widow. From our enquiries it was ascertained that Mrs Kennedy's purse had been stolen, containing her pension money of £75.00 in cash.

As a result of our enquires, during the afternoon of March 17th, we took Lillian Kennedy on a tour of the locality in an unmarked police car, to see if she could possibly spot the person or persons suspected of carrying out the burglary. In the course of the tour of the local area, Mrs Kennedy drew our attention to a man of Afro-Carribean origin. The man was 5 ft 10 in and of slim build. He had shoulder-length, dreadlocked hair and a slight goatee beard. He was wearing a black hooded sweatshirt and black jogging bottoms. He was wearing a pair of brown training shoes. My colleague Detective Constable Shaw recognised the man as Lenny Whyte. Mrs Kennedy was quite adamant that Lenny Whyte was the man who had approached her in her street a short time before the burglary and who had offered to help her with her shopping before disappearing behind the back of Sunrise Road. Mrs Kennedy observed Lenny Whyte in good light for a minute or two before confirming his identification.

A decision was taken not to arrest Lenny Whyte at this time as further enquires were being pursued in connection with a possible accomplice.

At 09.30 hours on the 18th March, Lloyd Green was arrested in connection with the burglary. He was taken to Lyme Street Police Station where his detention was authorised. A video identification was convened but Mrs Kennedy failed to identify Lloyd Green. Mr Green was released on police bail at 15.30 hours on the 19th March.

At 15.15 hours on the 19th March, Lenny Whyte was approached by me and Detective Constable Shaw just outside his flat at 4a Lymewood Court. Mr Whyte was arrested and cautioned. A search of his flat was conducted pursuant to s. 32 PACE. In his presence, I seized a black hooded sweatshirt (Exhibit SF1) and a pair of size 9 white Nike training shoes were also seized (right shoe-exhibit number SF2 and left shoe exhibit number SF3). In the course of searching Lenny Whyte, a quantity of cannabis resin was found (exhibit SF4) in his trouser pocket.

Lenny Whyte became obstructive at which point he was handcuffed and placed in the back of a police car. He was then taken to Lyme Police Station where his detention was authorised in accordance with the Police and Criminal Evidence Act 1984. A sample of saliva was taken from Mr Whyte (Exhibit SF5).

Lenny Whyte was detained overnight. On the 20th March, Lenny Whyte was identified in the course of a video parade by a neighbour who lives near to the victim's burgled property, as the man she had seen in Lillian Kennedy's back garden at around midday on the 17th March.

Whyte was certified fit to be interviewed by a police doctor. Declining the services of the solicitor, Whyte was interviewed the following day. The interview lasted 46 minutes. One tape was used during the interview and a copy of the sealed tape is available (exhibit SF6).

In the course of the interview Whyte admitted he had entered Mrs Kennedy's house and stole £75. At the conclusion of the interview Leonard Whyte was charged with burglary and cautioned.

Mr Whyte was denied police bail and was escorted to Lyme Magistrates' Court.

Signed: Sgt S Farrington 4291

DOCUMENT 18E

RECORD OF INTERVIEW

Policy Exhibit No:

No of pages: (3, as reproduced)

Signature of interviewing officer producing exhibit DSS Farrington

Person interviewed: LENNY WHYTE

Place of interview: LYME STREET

Date of interview: 20/3/-

Time commenced: 1130 HRS

Time concluded: 1216 HRS

Duration of interview: 46 MINUTES

Interviewing officer(s): DS 4291 FARRINGTON/DC 2890 SARAH SHAW

Other persons present: NONE

Tape reference number: 21/SF/59217/03/-

Exhibit Number: SF6

Tape counter Times(s)	Person speaking	Text
0000		Normal introductions were made and the interviewee was reminded of his legal rights and cautioned.
		The officer said WHYTE was under arrest in relation to a burglary at 19 Sunrise Road in Lyme.
0148	Sgt Farr.	Before we begin, Lenny, I just want to check you feel well enough to be interviewed. Do you feel OK?
0159	R	Just tired, okay okay.
0210	Sgt Farr.	Are you happy to be interviewed without a solicitor?
0218	R	Yeah.
0245	Sgt Farr.	I want to ask you about your whereabouts between 11 and 1pm on Tuesday the 17th March. Can you remember where you were and what you were doing?
0300	R	The usual routine. You know what I mean man?
	Sgt Farr.	What is your usual routine Lenny?
	R	(Suspect sits in silence)
0345	Sgt Farr.	I think lad, you'd better take the situation you're in a bit more seriously don't you?
0400	R	Yeah, yeah-you lot got it in for me.
0430	Sgt Farr.	You understand that you have been arrested in connection with a burglary at 19 Sunrise Road. The victim is an elderly woman and someone has stolen her pension.
0500	R	Yeah, yeah. (Suspect starts shaking his head.) Can I have a cigarette? I need a smoke. This needs sorting, right—got things that need sorting, right.
0525	Sgt Farr.	As soon as this interview is over and you start to answer my questions the sooner you can have a cigarette. Do you know the area around Sunrise Road?
0600	R	Yeah.
0624	Sgt Farr.	Did you go into Sunrise Road on the 17th March?
0635	R	No.

0702	Sgt Farr.	The old lady who was burgled has pointed you out as the man who approached her in Sunrise Road at around 11.30am and offered her help with her shopping. Was that you Lenny because she says it was?
0745	R	What day is it today?
0800	Sgt Farr.	It's Thursday—now just answer the question Lenny—the sooner we get your account the sooner this process will be over.
1100		Are we just going to sit here in silence Lenny?
1110		(Suspect stands up and starts pacing.) Sit down Lenny. The old lady describes the man who approached her in her street at around 11 or so as being a black youth, quite tall, with dreadlocks, wearing a short dark top and wearing white trainers. Would you accept that that description matches you?
1204	R	Don't know what you're getting at—don't know
1227	Sgt Farr.	The old lady was taken on a tour of the High Street to see if she could see the man who had approached her earlier that morning. She pointed you out to us. You were seen wearing a dark hooded top. I will ask you again were you in Sunrise Road at anytime on the morning of 17th March? (Suspect starts pacing.) Sit down Lenny and answer the question. (Reply inaudible.)
1312		We have another eyewitness, Lenny, who has identified you near the back door of the old lady's house at just after midday on the 17th March. She has given us a clear description of the person she saw. She states she saw a man of Afro-Caribbean origin in the old lady's garden near the open back door. She describes the man has having pointy features, wearing a black hooded top with the hood up. Her description matches your appearance. She has subsequently identified you at a video identification parade. I am going to ask you again, can you tell me where you were between 11 and 1pm on Tuesday the 17th March?
1506	R	(Suspect makes no reply. Refuses to look at me.)
1724	Sgt Farr.	Are these your trainers Lenny? (Suspect shown a pair of white Nike training shoes.) Stop tapping the table Lenny.
1806	R	Not mine, no way.
1815	Sgt Farr.	Well they were found in your flat, amongst your other footwear. You see, all the eyewitnesses describe seeing a man matching your appearance, wearing a pair of white trainers. They are all very clear about this, and it so happens that you have a pair of white trainers in your flat. Were you wearing these trainers on the morning of the 17th March?
1950	R	(Inaudible reply.)
2000	Sgt Farr.	You take a shoe size 9 don't you Lenny? These are a size 9. Are these your shoes?
2030	R	They ain't mine. Someone must have left them at my place.
2057	Sgt Farr.	Has anyone stayed at your flat recently?
2103	R	Come on, let's get this sorted. I've got big things to do.
2218	Sgt Farr.	When you were arrested you were found in possession of a quantity of cannabis. Are you using drugs at the moment Lenny?
2228	R	(No reply.) (Suspect rocking the table, asked to desist.)
2330	Sgt Farr.	Do you know a man by the name of Lloyd Green?
2400	R	I know who you are talking about right-he ain't no mate of mine.

2459	Sgt Farr.	Would it surprise you to learn that a car registered to him was seen in Sunrise Road at around 11.30am on Tuesday the 17th March?
2502	R	(No reply)
2613	Sgt Farr.	We have an eyewitness who describes a man just like you approaching Lloyd Green's car in Sunrise Road sometime before midday. I suggest that man was you. What do you have to say?
2640	R	Look—fuck you. I need a cigarette. I ain't into robbing no old woman right. I don't understand this. I don't understand all this.
2705	Sgt Farr.	Why did you need to speak with Lloyd Green, Lenny?
2804	R	(No reply.)
2905	Sgt Farr.	I will ask you again Lenny—was it you seen talking to Lloyd Green?
3000	R	(No reply.)
3104	Sgt Farr.	Is Lloyd Green putting pressure on you Lenny? Do you owe him money?
3219	R	(Suspect makes no reply.)
3315	Sgt Farr.	Look at me, Lenny. This is your chance to offer an explanation. Is there anything you wish to tell me?
3510	R	How much longer are you keeping me here? I've gotta go. I've got things to do—important things. You're fitting me up anyway like you always do.
3609	Sgt Farr.	I can't say how much longer you will be here Lenny. That's up to you.
3720	R	Don't know nothing right about Lloyd Green.
4010	Sgt Farr	Shall I tell you what I think? I think you owe Lloyd Green money. He wants it and wants it now. He tells you to get it or else. You don't have any so either you or he decides you should steal it. You know the area. You agree he will knock on the door of the old lady you saw earlier. When she is distracted, you will break in and see what you can get your hands on. Nice and easy. Is that how it happened?
4202	R	(No reply.)
4230	Sgt Farr.	Look Lenny—this is a serious matter. How do you explain the evidence against you? The eyewitness who has identified you, the white training shoes found in your flat which all the eyewitnesses makes reference to and the fact that you have admitted knowing Lloyd Green. Is it all coincidence Lenny?
4406	R	Alright, I stole it from the old lady yeah. I needed the money right. He wanted it. Now fucking charge me and let me get out of here.
4440	Sgt Farr.	Calm down Lenny and sit down. There is no need to get uptight. Who was your accomplice Lenny? Who distracted the lady at her front door?
4500	R	I am not saying anything more. Charge me if you are going to and let me out of here. I ain't saying nothing more.
4530	Sgt Farr.	Did someone put you under pressure to commit this burglary? Was it Lloyd Green? Is he your supplier?
4600	R	(No reply.)

Suspect continues to be uncooperative and verbally abusive. Interview terminated at 46 minutes.

DOCUMENT 18F   FURTHER WITNESS STATEMENT OF SHIRLY LEWIS

WITNESS STATEMENT

(CJ Act 1967, s. 9; MC Act 1980, s. 5A(3)(a) and s. 5B; MC Rules 1981, r. 70)

Name	Shirley Lewis
Address	Supplied
Age/Date of Birth	Over 18
Occupation	Retired Teacher

Who states:

This statement (consisting of one page signed each by me) is true to the best of my knowledge and belief and I make it knowing that if it is tendered in evidence I shall be liable to prosecution if I have wilfully stated in it anything which I know to be false or do not believe to be true.

Dated: 20th March   Signature: S Lewis

I reside at the address shown overleaf.

I have been asked to view a video identification parade as a result of an incident that I witnessed on the 17th March, when at the home of my aunt at 19 Sunrise Road, Lyme. The incident occurred at around midday on the 17th March.

On the 20th March, I was at the Identification Suite at Lyme Police Station when I was shown a Video Identification Parade.

- After viewing the Video Parade, I identified the person at position No 4 on the Video

I can confirm that before viewing the Video Parade I was supervised by WPC Khan who informed me that I was not allowed to discuss the incident with any other person, including any other witness, and that no such conversation took place. I have not seen any broadcast or published films or photographs, or any descriptions relating to the offence for which I am a witness.

Signature: S Lewis

DOCUMENT 18G   FURTHER WITNESS STATEMENT OF HAROLD FINNEY

WITNESS STATEMENT

(CJ Act 1967, s. 9; MC Act 1980, s. 5A(3)(a) and s. 5B; MC Rules 1981, r. 70)

Name	Harold Finney
Address	Withheld
Age/Date of Birth	Over 18
Occupation	Retired Engineer

Who states:

This statement, consisting of one page signed by me, is true to the best of my knowledge and belief, and I make it knowing that if it is tendered in evidence I shall be liable to prosecution if I have wilfully stated in it anything which I know to be false or do not believe to be true.

Dated: 20th March

Signature: H Finney

I reside at the address shown overleaf.

As a result of an incident that I witnessed on the 17th March when I saw a black man approach a car in Sunrise Road at around 11.50am. On the 20th March I was at the Identification Suite at Lyme Police Station when I was shown a Video Identification Parade.

- After viewing the Video Parade, I identified the person at position No 2 on the Video

I can confirm that before viewing the Video Parade I was supervised by WPC Khan who informed me that I was not allowed to discuss the incident with any other person, including any other witness, and that no such conversation took place. I have not seen any broadcast or published films or photographs, or any descriptions relating to the offence for which I am a witness.

Signature: H Finney

DOCUMENT 18H   FURTHER WITNESS STATEMENT OF LILLIAN KENNEDY

<u>WITNESS STATEMENT</u>

(CJ Act 1967, s. 9; MC Act 1980, s. 5A(3)(a) and s. 5B; MC Rules 1981, r. 70)

Name	Lillian Kennedy
Address	Supplied
Age/Date of Birth	Over 18
Occupation	Retired

Who states:

This statement, consisting of one page signed by me, is true to the best of my knowledge and belief, and I make it knowing that if it is tendered in evidence I shall be liable to prosecution if I have wilfully stated in it anything which I know to be false or do not believe to be true.

Dated: 20th March   Signature: L Kennedy

I reside at the address shown overleaf.

As a result of an incident that I witnessed on the 17th March when I was approached by a black man in the street where I live in Sunrise Road, I was at the Identification Suite at Lyme Police Station when I was shown a Video Identification Parade.

- After viewing the Video Parade, I identified the person at position No 2 on the Video

- I was unable to identify any person

I can confirm that before viewing the Video Parade I was supervised by WPC Khan who informed me that I was not allowed to discuss the incident with any other person, including any other witness, and that no such conversation took place. I have not seen any broadcast or published films or photographs, or any descriptions relating to the offence for which I am a witness.

Signature: L Kennedy

DOCUMENT 180   WITNESS STATEMENT OF SCIENTIFIC SUPPORT OFFICER

WITNESS STATEMENT

(CJ Act 1967, s. 9; MC Act 1980, s. 5A(3)(a) and s. 5B; MC Rules 1981, r. 70)

Statement of: Carol Jayne Lawton   Title

Age if under 18: Over 18   Occupation: Scenes of Crime Officer

This statement (consisting of 2 pages signed each by me) is true to the best of my knowledge and belief and I make it knowing that if it is tendered in evidence I shall be liable to prosecution if I have wilfully stated in it anything which I know to be false or do not believe to be true.

Dated: 20th March

Signature: Carol Lawton

I am a Scientific Support Officer employed by Lymeshire Police based at Lyme Street Police Station. At 14.30 hours on the 17th March, as a result of a message received, I attended 19 Sunrise Road, Lyme. The property is a house in a residential area and is occupied by an elderly female who lives alone. At the side of the house there is a concrete porch area which is covered from the elements by an enclosed carport. Access to the carport can be gained from the front of the property and from the rear. Access from the rear of the property involves waking through a garden which contains soil beds. The soil beds were wet from a heavy downpour of rain during the night and the preceding days. While I was in the garden area I noticed several footprints on soil beds. I conducted a visual examination of the concrete porch area leading up to the back door of the property and discovered several shoeprints bearing slight soil deposits.

While I was there I took certain photographs, some of which were duplicated, from which an album of prints has been produced marked CJL1, which I would describe as follows:

CJL1 (Shoe marks) Album of Prints (Exhibit No)
Photo 1 View of the back door of 19 Sunrise Road, Lyme
Photo 2 View of the car port from the garden gate of 19 Sunrise Road, Lyme
Photo 3 View of concrete porch
Photo 4 View of shoe mark on concrete
Photo 5 View of shoe mark on concrete
Photo 6 View of shoe mark on concrete
Photo 7 View of shoe mark on concrete
Photo 8 View of CJL2 and CJL3 (Exhibit No) in place before being lifted.

All negatives are filed at the Chief Constables office bearing reference number LP-200510965-0971.

During the course of my examination, I retained the following items, and packaged and labelled them as follows:
CJL 2 Shoe mark 16 cm from backdoor of property electrostatically lifted

CJL 3 Shoe mark 8 cm from backdoor of property electrostatically lifted

The above items were retained in my possession until I retuned to the Scenes of Crime store. I placed items CJL 2 and CJL 3 into a laboratory sack and sealed it with a tag number B8760456. I placed the sack in the secure Scenes of Crime Store.

At 1700 hours on the 19th March, while on duty at Lyme Street police station, I attended the property store. There I took possession of the following items from reference number 256/789432:
SF2 Left white Nike training shoe (Exhibit No ....)
SF3 Right white Nike training shoe (Exhibit No ....)

I placed SF2 into a laboratory sack and sealed it with tag number B49304667. I placed the sack into the secure Scenes of Crime store. I placed SF3 into a laboratory sack and sealed it with tag number B49304668. I placed both sacks into the secure Scenes of Crime store.

At 1845 on the 19th March, I attended Lyme Street Custody Suite from where I collected the following item, labelled as:

SF5 (Exhibit no) DNA mouth swab (x2).

I placed this item into a transit sack which I then sealed with tag no B986740.

All the transit sacks collected in conjunction with this investigation were left in secure and appropriate storage within Lyme Street Scenes of Crime Department for collection and then onward delivery to the Forensic Science Laboratory.

Signature CJ Lawton SOCO 6512

DOCUMENT 18P   WITNESS STATEMENT OF FORENSIC SCIENTIST

Laboratory Reference: 500 679 4033
Order Reference: 400 593 1297
The Forensic Science Service

DS Steve Farrington
Lyme Street Policing Unit
Lymeshire Police

Client Reference: URN 05/2218

WITNESS STATEMENT

(CJ Act 1967, s. 9; MC Act 1980, s. 5A(3)(a) and s. 5B; MC Rules 1981, r. 70)

Statement of: Sarah Hardacker BSc (Hons)

Age of Witness: Over 18

Morley Laboratory, Forensic Science Service, Belfield House, Nile Street, Birmingham.

This statement (consisting of four pages signed each by me) is true to the best of my knowledge and belief, and I make it knowing that if it is tendered in evidence I shall be liable to prosecution if I have wilfully stated in it anything which I know to be false or do not believe to be true.

Date: 25th March

Signature: S Hardacker

DEFENDANT: LEONARD WHYTE

I hold the degree of Bachelor of Science with an Honours Degree in Applied Biochemistry and have worked as a Forensic Scientist since 1995. During this time I have dealt with many investigations involving footwear.

RECEIPT OF ITEMS

Records show that on the 20th March amongst other items, the 4 items described below relating to an investigation of a burglary at domestic premises in Lyme were received at the Morely laboratory of the Forensic Science Service from Lymeshire Police.

From 19 Sunrise Road, Lyme

CJL 2 Electrostatic shoeprint lift

CJL 3 Electrostatic shoeprint lift

From Lenny Whyte

FS 2 Left white training shoe

FS 3 Right white training shoe.

BACKGROUND INFORMATION

From the information provided by the Police, I understand the following:

On the 17th March a burglary occurred at 19 Sunrise Road, Lyme. Entry to the property was gained through an unlocked backdoor while the sole occupant of the property was distracted by a caller at the front door.

A subsequent Scene of Crime examination recovered footwear marks on a concrete surface near to the backdoor of the property. The shoeprints are believed to belong to the offender.

Lenny WHYTE was arrested on the 19 Sunrise Road and following a search of his home address 4A Lymewood Court, Lyme a pair of white size 9 white Nike trainers were recovered.

This is the information on which I have based my examination and have used in the interpretation of the findings.

PURPOSE OF EXAMINATION

To determine whether or not the recovered training shoes relating to Lenny WHYTE have made the footwear marks recovered from 19 Sunrise Road, Lyme.

LABORATORY EXAMINATION
With this aim in mind, the following items have been examined:-

Re: 4A Lymewood Court, Lyme (relating to Lenny WHYTE)
FS2 and FS3—Pair of Nike white training shoes

Re: 19 Sunrise Road, Lyme
CJL 2—Footwear lifts from concrete porch
CJL 3—Footware lifts from concrete porch

These items have been examined with the help of scientific assistants, details of which are noted on the Forensic Examination Record, SH/FER/1 that accompanies this statement. Details of the examination are documented in the case notes which can be inspected at the laboratory under order number **400 593 1297.**

TECHNICAL ISSUES
When a person steps onto a surface, a mark may be left of the under-surface of their footwear. This footwear impression will persist for a long time if left undisturbed. It may be preserved, recovered and enhanced in order to facilitate a detailed comparison, at the Forensic Science Laboratory, between it and test impressions taken from the suspect's shoes. Details such as pattern, general size and degree of wear can be compared. Additionally, any marks in the scene impression that correspond to damage features on the under-sole of the shoe can provide conclusive evidence to connect that particular shoe to the scene. Any such footwear marks can be compared with any recovered items of footwear.

RESULTS OF EXAMINATION
Re: Lenny WHYTE
The training shoes (SF2 and SF3) are a pair of size 9 Nike with a sole pattern of zigzag fine bars and blocks. The soles of the training shoes are worn, with damage evident on both of the soles. The sole pattern of these boots is only one of a vast range of sole patterns available on sports/casual footwear and is one of the more frequently encountered patterns at the laboratory. On the right shoe there is a cut measuring 3 mm.

Re: CJL 2 and CJL 3
Items are two photographs of electrostatically dust print lifted footwear marks. The clearest mark, depicted on photograph CJL2 corresponds in pattern, size/configuration and wear to the submitted right training shoe (SF3). In addition there are features in the mark that correspond to features of random damage on the sole of the same right shoe. There was one mark in the impression taken from the right shoe and while not clearly defined nonetheless corresponded to the feature of damage on the right training shoe.
There is a poor quality and poorly defined footwear mark depicted on the lift CJL 3 that corresponds in pattern and is appropriate in terms of size and configuration and wear to the submitted left training shoe SF2. However, given the quality of the mark and detail obtained from the footwear mark on the other lift (CJL2) this footwear mark has not been examined in any further detail.

INTERPRETATION
In my opinion, the degree of correspondence observed between the footwear mark on the concrete floor of the backdoor porch and the submitted right training shoe is of the utmost significance. Indeed, I consider the likelihood of the observed degree of correspondence occurring by sheer coincidence, if the training shoe did not make the respective mark on the concrete floor to be so remote as to be discounted on a practical basis. There was one mark in one of the impressions that corresponds to damage features on the under-sole of Mr Whyte's right training shoe. Damage features are acquired randomly on footwear and so I therefore consider this finding enhances the significance of the pattern match and in my opinion the overall degree of correspondence is much more likely if this shoe made the impression rather than some other footwear taken from the random population.

CONCLUSION
In my opinion, the results of this examination provide very strong evidence that the right training shoe relating to Lenny WHYTE has made a mark on the concrete floor close to the backdoor of 19 Sunrise Road, Lyme.

(Scale of Evidential Support:—no, limited, moderate, moderately strong, strong, very strong, extremely strong, conclusive.)

Signed: S Hardacker

DOCUMENT 19 ADDITIONAL STATEMENT OF LENNY WHYTE—COMMENTS ON ADVANCE INFORMATION

I have read the advance information provided by the prosecution and make the following observations.

Lillian Kennedy

I think I know this lady. I have seen her before when I have walked my dog Butch. If she says it was me who approached her on the day in question then she is mistaken. I do not recollect going into Sunrise Road on the 17th March.

Shirley Lewis

This witness is mistaken. There is no way she could have seen me at the back of the old lady's house. I was not there. She says the man she saw was wearing white training shoes. I do not wear white training shoes. She may have seen me in the area on one or two occasions. As I already said I walk my dog Butch (a terrier) in fields near to Sunrise Road. I am not the only black man who lives in the area. She is confusing me with someone else.

Harold Finney

I did not see or approach any black car in Sunrise Road.

DS Steve Farrington

I dislike this police officer. On the way back from the interview room he said that I deserved everything the court would throw at me. Nobody explained to me why I could not have an identification parade. The police let me make a phone call to my sister, but she wasn't in when I rang. I was offered a solicitor but I honestly didn't think there was much point in one being there. The police were going to fit me up whatever. I was really desperate to get out of the police station. I seemed to have been there forever. I wanted a cigarette and I was worried about Butch my dog and about Sonia. I didn't feel very well during the interview and cannot honestly remember what I said. Looking back I should have had a solicitor present. All I wanted was for the interview to be over and done with, so that I could be charged and released on bail. The police got me to say what they wanted to hear. What I said to them in interview about my involvement is untrue. I wish to retract my statement.

I told the custody sergeant the following morning that I was on medication. He asked me why I hadn't mentioned it before. I cannot remember whether I was asked at the outset whether I was on medication. I just felt totally out of it. He called the police doctor who examined me. I believe an officer went back to my flat to collect my medication.

I was examined by a GP. He didn't seem much interested in me. He gave me my medication and told me I was fine.

I swear I have never worn the white trainers. They were given to me by a friend. I cannot remember who because I often have friends come to see me and sometimes they stay over. I have not worn the shoes.

Lloyd Green

I believe Lloyd Green has not said anything against me. I do know Lloyd Green. He is a drug dealer and loan shark. I have owed him money in the past. He can get a bit rough with you when you don't 'come up with the goods'. I cannot say whether Lloyd Green was involved in this burglary or not as I wasn't there.

Dated 24th April

DOCUMENT 22 CPS LETTER REGARDING COMMITTAL PROCEEDINGS SEPCIMEN LETTER

CROWN PROSECUTION SERVICE
Queen's Chambers
Blackburn Street
Lyme
LY3 2BE

Date: 13/5/-

Ref: AH/IW
Your ref: RJ/SAW

Hannibal and Mountford Solicitors
20 High Street
Lyme Bank
Lyme
LY10 34 T

Dear Sirs,
R v Lenny Whyte
Lyme Magistrates' Court
Committal Hearing 30th May

I enclose by way of service, in accordance with section 5(b) Magistrates' Court Act 1980, committal papers for the above.

Committal papers have been prepared in accordance with the Practice Direction given by the Lord Chief Justice on the 3rd June 1986. I enclose one copy of the committal volumes for your client, together with a further copy for your own use.

If no depositions are taken, and there are no alterations to the Crown Court case papers now served, no further copies will be served on you. It will be for you to prepare any further papers for your counsel and your client. If there are any alterations, the Crown Prosecution Service will supply you with copies of depositions and an amended list of witnesses and/or exhibits. These arrangements will ensure that the judge and all parties at the trial will work form identically indexed volumes.

The written statements contained in the committal volumes will be tendered in evidence before the magistrates unless you object to any statement being tendered under section 5B Magistrates' Court Act 1980 and rule 70 Magistrates Courts Rules 1981. If you object to any statement being tendered in evidence, you should inform me as soon as possible.

Delay and expense may be caused if you fail to act promptly upon this letter in this regard. It is however, for the prosecution to decide what evidence to bring in support of the charge at committal stage.

Unless I hear to the contrary I will assume that the committal will be in accordance with the provisions of section 6(2) Magistrates' Court Act 1980.

Yours faithfully,

Andrew Hurst
Principal Crown Prosecutor

DOCUMENT 23   EXTRACTS FROM THE COMMITTAL BUNDLE

NOTE TO THE READER

We have included the front sheets of a typical committal bundle. In addition to the extracts we have included here, you would also receive typed versions of the prosecution's witness statements (comprising used material) as well as a full transcript of interview. Such documentation would be entirely comparable with the Advance Information. It would include any further statements that have not previously been disclosed as Advance Information which the CPS intends to rely on. We invite you to assume that typed versions of the Advance Information in this case study (Documents 18 A–P) have been served with the committal bundle.

The charge(s) set out on the Schedule(s) attached to the accompanying papers has/have been prepared in indictment form in consequence of the responsibility which the Crown Prosecution Service has in relation to the form and content of indictments.

This/these should be treated in exactly the same way as committal charges in traditional form unless 's. 40 CJA 1988' appears under a court number. In that case the charge is not a committal charge but indicates the intention that it should be included in an indictment under section 40 Criminal Justice Act 1988.

Schedules also serve as draft indictments following a committal but may be subject to amendments, or replaced by a new draft settled by Counsel, before being preferred for signature by the appropriate officer of the Crown Court. A copy of the indictment as signed will be supplied in the usual way.

DRAFT INDICTMENT/COMMITTAL CHARGES

INDICTMENT (No.)

CROWN COURT AT LYME

THE QUEEN -V- LENNY WHYTE

LENNY WHYTE

Is charged as follows:

Count 1: STATEMENT OF OFFENCE

BURGLARY contrary to Section 9(1)(b) of the Theft Act 1968.

PARTICULARS OF OFFENCE

LENNY WHYTE that on the 17th March having entered as a trespasser a building, being a dwelling known as 19 Sunrise Road, Lyme you stole £75 in money property belonging to Lillian Kennedy

Officer of the Court

REGINA

-V-

LENNY WHYTE

Statements

No.	Name of Witness	Date of Statement	Page No (s)
1.	L Kennedy	18/3/-	
2.	L Kennedy	20/3/-	
3.	S Lewis	18/3/-	
4.	S Lewis	20/3/-	
5.	H Finney	18/3/-	
6.	H Finney	20/3/-	
7.	S Farrington	20/3/-	
8.	A Khan	20/3/-	
9.	E Mason	20/3/-	
10.	C Sutton	20/3/-	
11.	J Bradbury	20/3/-	
12.	P Reynolds (x2)	19/3/-	
13.	C Lawton	20/3/-	
14.	S Hardacker	25/3/-	

REGINA

-V-

LENNY WHYTE

Exhibit List

No	Reference	Item
1.	SF2	Left size 9 Nike training shoe
2.	SF3	Right size 9 Nike training shoe
3.	SF6/a	Tape recorded interview/Whyte Tape Reference 21/SF/59217/03–*
4.	SF6/b	Transcript of interview/Whyte*
5.	CJL1	Album of photographs of shoeprints in situ
6.	CJL2	Shoe print lift
7.	CJL3	Shoe print lift
8.	SF5	Black hooded sweatshirt
9.	PR1	DVD Compilation of Video Images Ref 05/01166/20A
10.	CS2	Video of Video Identification viewing process-film ref. no. 277/05

N.B. Exhibits marked * are served with the committal papers, other exhibits may be examined on suitable appointment.

REGINA

-v-

LENNY WHYTE

FORM 14A

<u>Notice to accused: right to object to written statement or deposition being read out at trial without further proof (CPIA Act 1996 Sch. 2, paragraphs (3)(c): MC Rules 1981, r. 8 (as amended by MC (Amendment) (No.1) Rules 1997).</u>

To: LENNY WHYTE of 4a, Lymewood Court, Parkdale, Lyme

If you are committed for trial, the Crown Court may try you in respect of the charge or charges on which you are committed or in respect of any other charge arising out of the same transaction or set of circumstances which may, with the leave of the Court, be put to you.

Written statements have been made by the witnesses named below and copies of their statements are enclosed. Each of the statements will be read out at trial without oral evidence being given by the witness who made the statement unless you want the witness to give oral evidence and to be cross-examined on such oral evidence. If you want any of these witnesses to give oral evidence, and to be cross-examined if necessary, you should inform the Crown Court and me within 14 days of being committed for trial. If you do not do so you will lose your right to prevent the statement being read out without oral evidence being given by the witness in question and you will only be able to require the attendance of the witness with the leave of the Court, but that will not prevent the prosecutor from exercising his discretion to call the witness to give oral evidence, and be cross-examined, at the trial if the prosecutor so wishes.

If you have a solicitor acting for you in your case, you should hand this notice and the statements to him/her at once so that he/she may be able to deal with them.

Address any reply to:

The Branch Crown Prosecutor
Crown Prosecution Service
Queen's Chambers
Blackburn Street
Lyme

DOCUMENT 24 FILE NOTE ON COMMITTAL PREPARATION AND ATTENDANCE

Case preparation—25th May

Speaking with Lenny Whyte's consultant psychiatrist. He is happy to provide us with a psychiatric report. It will cost £750. Explained I would seek the prior authority of the LSC and would thereafter put our request in writing.

Considering the committal documentation in this matter and determining there is nothing to be gained from seeking a long style committal as the examining justices no longer have the power to exclude evidence at a committal hearing.

RJ
Time engaged 20 minutes

Attendance Note
30th May

Attending Lenny Whyte and his sister at Lyme Magistrates' Court. Explaining the nature of a committal hearing. Appearing before Lyme Magistrates. Lenny's case was committed via a short style committal. Conditional bail renewed and the PCMH fixed for the 15th June.

RJ
Attending client 15 minutes

Court hearing 5 minutes.
NOTE: Committal proceedings having concluded, solicitors for Lenny Whyte can submit a claim for costs under the standard fee arrangement on the CDS11 Form.

DOCUMENT 26   NOTICE OF COMMITTAL/POST COMMITTAL CASE MANAGEMENT FORM

COMMITTAL IN ACCORDANCE WITH THE PROVISIONS OF SECTION 6(1) OF THE MAGISTRATES' COURTS ACT 1980

LYME CROWN COURT

Regina

-V-

LENNY WHYTE

DATE OF COMMITTAL	30th May
MAGISTRATES' COURT	Lyme Magistrates' Court
DATE OF PLEA AND CASE MANAGEMENT HEARING	30th June
FOR THE PROSECUTION	Crown Prosecution Service Lyme Branch
FOR THE DEFENCE	Hannibal Solicitors
	20 High Street, Lyme Bank, Lyme Ref RJ
CHARGES	* See attached list
EXHIBITS	* See attached list
WITNESSES	* See attached list

**DOCUMENT 29 CPS LETTER REGARDING CPIA 1996
DISCLOSURE (SPECIMEN LETTER)**

CROWN PROSECUTION SERVICE
Queen's Chambers,
Blackburn Street,
Lyme
LY3 2BE
Date: 4/6/-
Ref: LR/JW

Hannibal and Mountford Solicitors
20 High Street,
Lyme Bank,
Lyme
LY10 34T

Dear Sirs,
Re: Lenny Whyte
Date of Next Hearing: PCMH 30th June
<u>Disclosure of Prosecution Material under section 3, Criminal Procedure and
Investigations Act 1996 (CPIA).</u>

<u>Notice of intention to adduce evidence of your client's character under s 101 Criminal
Justice Act 2003</u>
I am required by section 3 of the above Act, to disclose to you any prosecution material, which has not
previously been disclosed, which might reasonably be considered capable of undermining the case for the
prosecution or of assisting the case for the accused.

Attached to this letter is a copy of a schedule of non-sensitive material prepared by the police in compliance with their duty under Part II CPIA and the provisions of the Code of Practice. The schedule has been
prepared by the Police Disclosure Officer, who in this case is DS Hague.

Unless the word 'evidence' appears alongside any item, all the items listed on the schedule are not
intended to be part of the prosecution case. You will receive a written notice should the position change.

Where indicated, copies of the items listed are attached. Material marked as available for inspection can
be viewed by arrangement with myself.

**This material is disclosed to you in accordance with the provisions of the CPIA, and you must not
use or disclose it, or any information recorded in it, for any purpose other than in connection with
these criminal proceedings. If you do so without the permission of the court, you may commit an
offence.**

If you supply a written defence statement to me and to the court within 14 days of the date of the receipt
of this letter, material which has not been disclosed at this stage will be further reviewed in the light of
that statement.

A defence statement is required by section 5 CPIA in Crown Court cases. In Magistrate's Court cases, section 6 CPIA makes a defence statement optional. Please bear in mind that we will rely upon the information you provide in the statement to identify any remaining material, which has not already been disclosed
but which might reasonably assist in the defence case as you have described it. The statement will also be
relied on by the court if you later make an application under section 8 CPIA.

If you do not make a defence statement where one is required, or provide one late, the court may permit
comment and/or draw an adverse inference.

If you request access to any item which is marked for disclosure by inspection, it is essential that you
preserve this schedule in its present form, as access will only be granted upon production of the schedule
to the person supervising access.

I am also enclosing notice of my intention to adduce evidence of your client's bad character under s 101
Criminal Justice Act 2003.

If you have a query in connection with this letter, please contact myself.
Yours faithfully,

Lewis Rowe
Crown Prosecution Service

Form MG 6C

DOCUMENT 30A POLICE SCHEDULE OF NON-SENSITIVE UNUSED MATERIAL

R v LENNY WHYTE

URN

Is there any material in this case which has not been examined by either the investigating or disclosure officer? Yes   No

The Disclosure Officer believes that the following material, which does not form part of the prosecution case, is NOT SENSITIVE.

Item No.	DESCRIPTION AND RELEVANCE (Give sufficient detail for CPS to decide if material should be disclosed or requires more detailed examination)	LOCATION	FOR CPS USE: * Enter: D = Disclose to defence; I = Defence may inspect	
			*	COMMENT
1.	Tape recording of 999 call 17/3/– from witness S Lewis-description of suspect	Lyme Street Police Station control room		
2.	Incident (CAD) Log no. 3569/0/–(17/3/–details of witness S Lewis and description of suspects	Lyme Street Police Station control room		
3.	Pocket note-book entry–DC 2198 Shaw re details of crime report contains details of first description of suspects	With DC 2198 Shaw		
4.	Pocket note-book entry DS 4291 Farrington re: arrests and interview of GREEN and WHYTE	With DS 4201 Farrington		
5.	Pocket note-book details search of premises–DC 2198 Shaw, Flat 4a Lymewood Court, Parkdale, Lyme-home address of WHYTE	With DC 2198 Shaw		
6.	Custody record no. 2346/05/-GREEN	Lyme PS		
7.	Custody record no. 2305/05/-WHYTE	Lyme PS		Disclosed

Signature: David Hague DC 2486

Date:

Reviewing lawyer signature: L.Rowe

Print name: Lewis Rowe

Date:

Form MG 6C

DOCUMENT 30B POLICE SCHEDULE OF NON-SENSITIVE UNUSED MATERIAL

R v LENNY WHYTE

URN

Is there any material in this case which has not been examined by either the investigating or disclosure officer? Yes   No

The Disclosure Officer believes that the following material, which does not form part of the prosecution case, is NOT SENSITIVE.

Item No.	DESCRIPTION AND RELEVANCE (Give sufficient detail for CPS to decide if material should be disclosed or requires more detailed examination)	LOCATION
8.	PNC printout of previous convictions of GREEN	On file
9.	Submission forms to FSS dated	On file
10.	Letter from FSS dated	On file
11.	DNA swab sample taken from WHYTE	FSS Morley Street
12.	Inspector C Sutton – contemporaneous hand written notes of Video Identification procedure (Form 116/2)	On file

Signature: David Hague DC 2486

Date:

Name: David Hague DC 2486

FOR CPS USE: * Enter: D = Disclose to defence

I = Defence may inspect

*	COMMENT

Reviewing lawyer signature: L Rowe

Print name: Lewis Rowe

Date:

DOCUMENT 32   LETTER TO CPS DEALING WITH CPIA 1996 MATTERS AND BAD CHARACTER NOTICE UNDER S. 101 CRIMINAL JUSTICE ACT 2003

HANNIBAL AND MOUNTFORD SOLICITORS
20 High Street,
Lyme Bank, Lyme
LY10 34T
Telephone: 01576–455971
Fax: 01576–200345
Email: Hannibal@solicitors.co.uk

Crown Prosecution Service
Queen's Chambers
Blackburn Street
Lyme
LY3 2BE

Date: 13/6/-
Ref: LR/JW
Our ref: RJ/SW

Dear Sirs,
R v Lenny Whyte
Date of Next Hearing—Plea and Case Management Hearing—Lyme Crown Court 30th June

Please find attached notification of our requirements in respect of the evidence tendered at the committal hearing on the 30th May. We shortly intend to take counsel's opinion in this matter and if we are in a position to agree prosecution witness evidence we will notify you accordingly.

We further enclose our client's defence statement under s. 5, Criminal Procedure and Investigations Act 1996.

We look forward to receiving further prosecution disclosure. In particular, we would like disclosure of Lloyd Green's interview.

We intend to dispute the admissibility of our client's interview with the police in connection with this matter. We have instructed our client's consultant psychiatrist, Dr Oliver A Mayhew to provide us with an expert opinion as to our client's state of mind at the time of his interview. Consequently we will want to cross-examine the custody officers who were responsible for compiling the custody record in relation to our client. We will also want to cross-examine the police doctor who examined our client and Inspector Rushton who reviewed our client's detention. Please confirm that you will ensure the attendance of these witnesses. We will of course require our client's custody record and the transcript of interview to be admitted into evidence. For these reasons we will require tape playing facilities in court. We anticipate that the point of law which arises in connection with the interview in this case will form the basis of a pre-trial hearing in connection with this matter as we do not consider either side will be in a position to resolve the matter at the PCMH.

We also enclose notice of our intention to oppose the admission of our client's past bad character at his forthcoming trial.

We look forward to hearing from you accordingly.

Yours faithfully
R James
Hannibal and Mountford

Anthony Hannibal (BA Partner), Louise Mountford (LL.B Partner), Denis Davies
(LL.B Partner) Tim Howard (LL.B Associate Solicitor), David Temple (LL.B Associate Solicitor),
Rachel James (LL.B Associate Solicitor), Mike Tamworth (Fellow of the
Institute of Legal Executives), Lisa Hardy (Accredited Police Station Clerk),
Ali Khan (Accredited Police Station Clerk)
Regulated by the Solicitors Regulation Authority

Note: A copy of this letter and its enclosures will also be sent to the Crown Court. We will also submit our completed Form B as judges in the Crown Court are required to consider making a Recovery of Defence Costs Orders (see Chapter 11) in the event of conviction. Such an order is unlikely in Lenny's case given that he is in receipt of welfare benefits.

DOCUMENT 34A   DEFENCE STATEMENT

Section 5, Criminal Procedure and Investigation Act 1996

REGINA v LENNY WHYTE

1. I, Lenny Whyte, deny that I was the person responsible for committing a burglary at 19 Sunrise Road, Lyme between 11.45am–12.30pm on the 17th March this year.

2. I take issue with those prosecution statements which suggest that I was one of the two men involved in the burglary. I was not in the area at the relevant time. I take issue with Shirley Lewis's identification of me. She is mistaken.

3. I wish to retract what I said in interview on the 20th March regarding the circumstances of this offence. I intend to dispute the admissibility of my interview with the police. At the time of my interview I was and still am suffering from bipolar depression. I did not have the services of a solicitor or an appropriate adult. I will contend that my interview should be excluded under ss. 76(2)(b) and 78 PACE 1984.

4. I deny that the white training shoes recovered from my flat belong to me. I have never worn them.

Signed: Lenny Whyte   Date: 13th June

To: Crown Prosecution Service
      Lyme Crown Court

DOCUMENT 39   BRIEF TO COUNSEL TO ATTEND PCMH

<u>LYME CROWN COURT</u>   <u>LISTING NO.</u>

REGINA

-v-

LENNY WHYTE

BRIEF ON BEHALF OF THE DEFENDANT TO APPEAR AT THE PCMH—30th JUNE AT 10am AND AT THE SUBSEQUENT TRIAL ON A DATE TO BE FIXED

Counsel receives herewith copies of the following:

1. Proof of evidence of Lenny Whyte dated 20th March

2. Draft Indictment

3. Committal bundle incltuding:

   a)   Statement of Lillian Kennedy (x2)

   b)   Statement of Shirley Lewis (x2)

   c)   Statement of Harold Finney (x2)

   d)   Statement of DS Farrington

   e)   Statement of WPC Anjuna Khan

   f)   Statement of WPC Emma Mason

   g)   Statement of Inspector Christopher Sutton

   i)   Statement of WPC Josie Bradbury

   j)   Statement of PC Peter Reynolds

   k)   Statement of Carol Lawton SOCO

   l)   Statement of Sarah Hardacker

   m)   Transcript of interview: Lenny Whyte

   n)   Previous convictions of Lenny Whyte

   o)   Exhibit List

4. Statement of Lenny Whyte with comments on the prosecution evidence dated 24th April

5. Defence Psychiatric Report

6. Custody Record

7. Tapes of interview

8. Initial Prosecution Disclosure

9. Defence Statement

10. Notice of intention to adduce evidence of Lenny Whyte's previous convictions

11. Notice objecting to the admissibility of Mr Whyte's previous criminal convictions.

12. Further Prosecution Disclosure

    a) Record of interview with Lloyd Green

    b) Letter from Forensic Science Service

13. Copy letter to the CPS dated 13th June including witness requirements

14. Through Legal Aid Order

15. Plea and Case Management Form

Introduction

Counsel's instructing solicitors act on behalf of Lenny Whyte. As Counsel will see from the enclosed draft indictment, Mr Whyte is charged with burglary. It is alleged he broke into 19 Sunrise Road on the 17th March this year and stole £75. Mr Whyte intends to plead not guilty to the burglary allegation. Upon his arrest, Mr Whyte was found to be in possession of a small quantity of cannabis. He pleaded guilty to simple possession and was sentenced to a conditional discharge for 12 months by Lyme Magistrates on the 24th April.

Chronology

Mr Whyte was arrested on the 19th March. He appeared before Lyme Magistrates on the 20th March when bail was refused. He subsequently appeared again on the 27th March when bail was refused for a second time and jurisdiction to try the matter was refused. On the 4th April our client appeared before a Crown Court Judge in chambers at Lyme Crown Court and was granted bail subject to a number of conditions. Lyme Magistrates' Court declined jurisdiction to try Lenny Whyte on the 24th April. Mr Whyte was committed to Lyme Crown Court via a short style committal on the 30th May.

The Plea and Case Management Hearing in this case has been listed for the 30th June. Counsel is instructed to attend. It is our intention to instruct counsel to represent Mr Whyte at trial and would ask you to take note of this fact when considering listing arrangements.

Prosecution Case and Evidential Matters

On the 17th March a burglary occurred at 19 Sunrise Road, Lyme (the home of 84 year old Lillian Kennedy) sometime between 11.45 hours and 12 midday. The prosecution contend that this was a distraction burglary. It is alleged that a man knocked on the door of 19 Sunrise Road on the pretence of having to use the telephone and while the occupier was distracted, the burglar gained entry to the property via an unlocked back door and proceeded to steal £75 from the victim's purse. The prosecution contend that the person entering the property was Mr Whyte. It is believed that the man responsible for distracting Mrs Kennedy at her front door is Lloyd Green. Although Green was arrested and interviewed he has not been charged with any offence arising out of this incident. In his interview with the police he denied any involvement in the burglary and did not implicate Lenny Whyte. Instructing solicitors do not act for Lloyd Green and did not represent him at the police station.

The principal evidence against Mr Whyte comprises eye-witness identification, confession evidence and forensic circumstantial evidence. We will deal with each in turn.

Counsel will see the statements of Lillian Kennedy contained in the committal bundle that she did not see the man who entered her property. She states however that she was stopped by a man in her street who offered to help her with her shopping. This was approximately 30–40 minutes before the burglary. On a subsequent tour of the local area the afternoon of the burglary she identified Lenny Whyte as being that person. The police did not immediately arrest Mr Whyte. At a subsequent VIPER identification procedure, however, Mrs Kennedy failed to identify Mr Whyte which rather casts her earlier street identification into doubt. Mrs Kennedy does however provide a description of the man who approached her which accords for the most part with the description of a man seen leaving the backdoor of the burgled property by another eye-witness. When Mrs Kennedy pointed Mr Whyte out to the police he was wearing the same attire save in one significant respect—he was not observed to be wearing white training shoes. In the circumstances it is difficult to see what Mrs Kennedy's evidence contributes to the prosecution's case. Counsel is asked to advise on this point and consider whether her evidence may be challenged on the basis of its relevance. Counsel will note that Mrs Kennedy spoke with the man who knocked on her front door. She was however unable to identify Lloyd Green at a VIPER identification procedure.

Of central importance to the prosecution's case is the evidence of Shirley Lewis. Counsel will see from her statement that she was in the back garden of a neighbouring property at midday when she saw a man behaving suspiciously near the back door of 19 Sunrise Road. She was hanging out some sheets on the washing line. She observed the man for a few seconds and was able to provide the police with a description of the man and his clothing. Her description accords with Mr Whyte's actual appearance. She observed the man was wearing white training shoes. At a subsequent VIPER identification procedure, Mrs Lewis identified Lenny Whyte as being that man. Her identification is based in part on recognition. She states she has seen Mr Whyte before in the area. Mr Whyte does not dispute this possibility as he lives near the victim and has, on occasion, walked his dog in fields near the burgled property. Mr Whyte is adamant, however, that this witness is mistaken and that it was not the man she saw.

A link in the chain of evidence is provided by the account of Harold Finney. Mr Finney lives in a property across the road from the burgled house. At 11.30am he observed a car drive along Sunrise Road and park. He was suspicious of the car and noted the registration number. The car is registered to Lloyd Green. Mr Finney states he observed a black man on foot approach the car. He describes a man whose appearance is similar to that of Lenny Whyte. He also describes the clothing the individual was wearing which included a dark sweatshirt and white training shoes. At this point Mr Finney was diverted by a telephone call. He saw nothing more of any relevance. At a subsequent VIPER identification parade, he picked out someone other than Lenny Whyte. He never saw the driver of the car.

Counsel is asked to note that Mr Whyte was unrepresented at the police station. Consequently the identification procedure was conducted in the absence of legal advice. Having reviewed the DVD compilation and the video of the viewing process, instructing solicitors are satisfied that the procedure was conducted fairly in accordance with Code D. The DVD compilation is included should counsel wish to consider it.

Upon arrest and pursuant to a section 32 PACE 1984, a search of Mr Whyte's flat was carried out. The police recovered a dark hooded sweatshirt and a pair of white size 9 Nike trainers. Counsel will note that in the course of the investigation shoeprint evidence was gathered from just outside the backdoor of the burgled property. Subsequent forensic comparison of the shoeprint lifts and the soles of the shoes recovered from Mr Whyte's flat strongly suggest these training shoes were responsible for leaving the shoe prints. Mr Whyte cannot offer an explanation for this other than to state the shoes were left at his flat by a friend, whose name he cannot recall. In interview he stated he had not worn the shoes. Document 10 b disclosed by way of further disclosure is useful in this respect. Counsel is asked to see whether this statement can be agreed under s. 9 CJA 1976.

The prosecution will seek to rely on the account given by Mr Whyte in his interview with the police. It amounts to a confession. Counsel is referred to the transcript of interview in this regard. Mr Whyte wishes to retract his confession for reasons considered in detail below.

The prosecution have served notice of their intention to adduce evidence of Mr Whyte's previous criminal convictions.

Defence Case and Evidential Matters

Counsel will see Mr Whyte's comments on the prosecution evidence in document 4. Counsel will see that a defence statement has been filed in this case. Mr Whyte intends to plead not guilty. He wishes to strongly challenge the admissibility of his confession. He maintains that he is not the man responsible for the burglary. Despite our best efforts, Mr Whyte is unable to substantiate his precise whereabouts at the relevant time with an alibi.

Instructing solicitors feel there are strong grounds for seeking the exclusion of Mr Whyte's confession under ss 76(2)(b) and 78 PACE 1984. Counsel is referred at this juncture to Mr Whyte's statement and to the custody record. Mr Whyte was unrepresented at the police station, although on the face of it, it would appear that the police acted within the law of s. 58 PACE, albeit not the spirit. An attempt was made by the custody sergeant to contact Mr Whyte's sister once during our client's detention but no contact was in fact established. Counsel will note that Mr Whyte suffers from a diagnosed psychiatric condition for which he receives psychiatric care and medication. It is not altogether clear why this fact was not ascertained by the custody sergeant who should have undertaken a risk assessment having authorised the continued detention of our client. Our client is not always inclined to help himself and upon his arrest he was not found to be in possession of any medication. Our client states that he cannot recall being asked whether he suffered from a medical condition requiring medication. Our client states he was not suffering drug withdrawal symptoms at the time but is chronically addicted to nicotine. Counsel will see that he was detained overnight. The custody record suggests that Mr Whyte did not have much to eat and had little sleep.

It is evident from the custody record that some 14 or so hours after having first been detained, Mr Whyte mentioned the fact that he felt unwell and needed his usual medication. A police surgeon was called. Dr Ghulam examined our client and having administered his medication pronounced him fit to be interviewed. Crucially, Mr Whyte was not provided with an appropriate adult, contrary to Code C. As such he went into the interview completely unrepresented, craving a cigarette, desperate to relieve the pressure of the situation and suffering from a diagnosed psychiatric condition. In the circumstances, it is difficult to see how a court could regard Mr Whyte's confession as being admissible. Counsel is referred to the decision in *R v Aspinall* [1999] 2 Cr App R 115 as being a decision of the Court of Appeal which supports our contention that the confession is both unreliable and unfair to admit. The admission of a confession obtained in these circumstances would in our view represent a violation of Article 6.

Counsel will see that we have obtained a report from Mr Whyte's consultant psychiatrist. The report is extremely helpful and we intend to place reliance upon it. The report has been disclosed to the CPS in accordance with the requirements of s. 30 CJA 1988. Dr Mayhew would be prepared to attend court to give evidence if necessary.

Clearly if the confession can be excluded in this case, a major component of the prosecution's case is lost and counsel may wish to consider whether a submission of no case to answer might be mounted in these circumstances

Instructing solicitors have notified the CPS of its intention to challenge the admissibility of the confession in this case. Unless the CPS decides to concede the point at the PCMH, we anticipate the issue will need to be listed for a judge's binding ruling on its admissibility. We would welcome Counsel's views on this point.

Instructing solicitors have served the appropriate notice on the prosecution objecting to the admissibility of Mr Whyte's criminal convictions. Counsel is asked to use her best endeavours to ensure that this very prejudicial evidence is excluded at the Plea and Case Management Hearing.

Counsel is requested to advise on all issues likely to arise at the PCMH and generally on the evidence and on preparation for trial. A PCMH form is enclosed for counsel's consideration. At present we have asked the CPS for all the witnesses it tendered at the committal hearing to attend. We suspect a number of witnesses can be agreed in this case and would ask counsel to specifically consider this point so that we may write to the CPS. Should Counsel require a conference we would ask her clerk to contact us.

Counsel is instructed to appear on behalf of the defendant at the PCMH on the 30th June at 2.30pm.

Rachel James, Hannibal and Mountford Solicitors
Date: 22nd June

DOCUMENT 41   FILE NOTE BASED ON PLEA AND CASE MANAGEMENT HEARING

30th June

Attending Crown Court for Plea and Case Management Hearing. Speaking with Ms Rhianna Stockley of counsel beforehand. There was considerable discussion between counsel on each side. Counsel for the CPS conceded breaches of Code C and indicated that the CPS would not be placing reliance upon Mr Whyte's confession which is extremely good news.

Argument was heard in relation to the admissibility of Lenny's previous convictions under s 101(1)(d) of the Criminal Justice Act 2003. The judge His Honour J Baker ruled in favour of admitting them. The case has been listed for trial on the 22nd August. Certificate for solicitor to attend was granted. Counsel and I explained the proceedings to Mr Whyte and his sister. Respective counsel agreed the following witness' evidence could be read at trial: WPC Khan/WPC Mason/Insp Sutton/Bradbury/PC Reynolds/WPC Lawton/Dr Hardacker/Dr Leighton.

Time engaged:

Travel 20 minutes
Waiting 60 minutes
Conference 40 minutes
Hearing 30 minutes

BW

DOCUMENT 47   FILE NOTE BASED ON TRIAL

22nd August

Attending Lyme Crown Court for Lenny Whyte's trial. Ms Stockley for Lenny Whyte and Parminder Singh for the prosecution. His Honour Thomas Shand presiding. Before the trial began, Ms Stockley asked the judge to reconsider the ruling by His Honour Judge Baker to allow evidence of the defendant's previous convictions to be admitted on the basis that their prejudicial effect would outweigh their probative value. It was agreed that the prosecution in its opening would not refer to the defendant's previous convictions but that the matter would be kept under review during the course of the trial.

The prosecution called Shirley Lewis who was extensively cross-examined with Mrs Lewis conceding that she could have been mistaken. CPS called Lillian Kennedy and Harold Finney. Before the investigating officer was called, Ms Stockley asked for confirmation that the officer would not be asked questions regarding the defendant's previous convictions as she was minded to make a submission of no case to answer. The judge ruled in her favour, without prejudice to any decision he might make as regards a submission being made. DS Farrington also gave evidence and was cross-examined. Prosecution read out a number of s. 9 statements which included the forensic evidence. Ms Stockley then made a submission of no case to answer. She explained that the most important eye witness linking Mr Whyte to the crime scene was Shirley Lewis and her evidence had been discredited. There was no concrete forensic evidence to link the defendant to the crime scene. The only remaining 'evidence' was the fact of his previous convictions and that it was clearly contrary to the defendant's right to a fair trial that a conviction could be based on this fact alone. The submission of no case to answer was upheld by the judge. The jury were directed to acquit on the burglary charge. Mr Whyte and his sister were immensely relieved and pleased.

Time engaged:
Travel 30 minutes
Waiting 40 minutes
Conference 30 minutes
Hearing 4 hours

BW

> The case having now concluded, the defence solicitor can submit her final claim for costs from the Legal Services Commission via the Crown Court.

APPENDIX 2

EXTRACTS FROM MODE OF TRIAL GUIDELINES 2004
(Part V. 51 Consolidated Criminal Practice Direction).

The purpose of these guidelines is to help magistrates decide whether or not to commit defendants charged with 'either way' offences for trial in the Crown Court. Their object is to provide guidance not direction. They are not intended to impinge on a magistrate's duty to consider each case individually and on its own particular facts. These guidelines apply to all defendants aged 18 and above.

GENERAL MODE OF TRIAL CONSIDERATIONS

Section 19 of the Magistrates' Courts Act 1980 requires magistrates to have regard to the following matters in deciding whether an offence is more suitable for summary trial or trial on indictment:

(a) the nature of the case;

(b) whether the circumstances make the offence one of a serious character;

(c) whether the punishment which a magistrates' court would have power to inflict for it would be adequate;

(d) any other circumstances which appear to the court to make it more suitable for the offence to be tried in one way rather than the other;

(e) any representations made by the prosecution or the defence.

Certain general observations can be made:

(a) The court should never make its decision on the grounds of convenience or expedition.

(b) The court should assume for the purpose of deciding mode of trial that the prosecution version of the facts is correct.

(c) The fact that the offences are alleged to be specimens is a relevant consideration (although, it has to be borne in mind that difficulties can arise in sentencing in relation to specimen counts see *R v Clark* [1996] 2 Cr App R (S) 351 and *R v Canavan and others* [1998] 1 Cr App R (S) 243); the fact that the defendant will be asking for other offences to be taken into consideration, if convicted, is not.

(d) Where cases involve complex questions of fact or difficult questions of law, including difficult issues of disclosure of sensitive material, the court should consider committal for trial.

(e) Where two or more defendants are jointly charge with an offence each has an individual right to ele his mode of trial.

(f) In general, except where otherwise stated, eith way offences should be tried summarily unless th court considers that the particular case has one more of the features set out in paragraphs 51.4 51.18 (see below) and that its sentencing powe are insufficient.

(g) The court should also consider its power to con mit an offender for sentence under sections 3 ar 4 of the Powers of Criminal Courts (Senten ing) Act 2000, if information emerges during th course of the hearing which leads it to conclu that the offence is so serious, or the offend such a risk to the public, that its powers to sen tence him are inadequate. This means that con mittal for sentence is no longer determined b reference to the character and antecedents of th offender.

FEATURES RELEVANT TO INDIVIDUAL OFFENCES

Authors' Note: Some of these offence specific guidelin are now dated. You should additionally consult releva sentencing guidelines in the Magistrates' Court Sentenci Guidelines (2008) publication issued by the Sentenci Guidelines Council. The MCSGs cover all either-way offenc and include an indication of the circumstances in which t threshold for committal to the Crown Court is likely to met in a particualr case. Appendix 3 includes extracts fr the MCSGs. Our Online Resource Centre includes a link the full guidelines.

Where reference is made in these guidelines to pro erty or damage of 'high value' it means a figure equal at least twice the amount of the limit (currently £5,00 imposed by statute on a magistrates' court when ma ing a compensation order.

BURGLARY: DWELLING-HOUSE

Cases should be tried summarily unless the court consi ers that one or more of the following features is prese in the case and that its sentencing powers are insuf cient. Magistrates should take account of their powe under sections 3 and 4 of the Powers of Criminal Cour (Sentencing) Act 2000 to commit for sentence.

(a) Entry in the daytime when the occupier (or another) is present.

(b) Entry at night of a house which is normally occupied, whether or not the occupier (or another) is present.

(c) The offence is alleged to be one of a series of similar offences.

(d) When soiling, ransacking, damage or vandalism occurs.

(e) The offence has professional hallmarks.

(f) The unrecovered property is of high value.

(g) The offence is racially motivated.

NOTE: Attention is drawn to paragraph 28(c) of Schedule 1 to the Magistrates' Courts Act 1980 by which offences of burglary in a dwelling cannot be tried summarily if any person in the dwelling was subjected to violence or the threat of violence.

BURGLARY: NON-DWELLING

Cases should be tried summarily unless the court considers that one or more of the following features is present in the case and that its sentencing powers are insufficient. Magistrates should take account of their powers under sections 3 and 4 of the Powers of Criminal Courts (Sentencing) Act 2000 to commit for sentence.

(a) Entry of a pharmacy or doctor's surgery.

(b) Fear is caused or violence is done to anyone lawfully on the premises (e.g. night-watchman, security guard).

(c) The offence has professional hallmarks.

(d) Vandalism on a substantial scale.

(e) The unrecovered property is of high value.

(f) The offence is racially motivated.

THEFT AND FRAUD

Cases should be tried summarily unless the court considers that one or more of the following features is present in the case and that its sentencing powers are insufficient. Magistrates should take account of their powers under sections 3 and 4 of the Powers of Criminal Courts (Sentencing) Act 2000 to commit for sentence.

(a) Breach of trust by a person in a position of substantial authority, or in whom a high degree of trust is placed.

(b) Theft or fraud which has been committed or disguised in a sophisticated manner.

(c) Theft or fraud committed by an organised gang.

(d) The victim is particularly vulnerable to theft or fraud, e.g. the elderly or infirm.

(e) The unrecovered property is of high value.

HANDLING

Cases should be tried summarily unless the court considers that one or more of the following features is present in the case and that its sentencing powers are insufficient. Magistrates should take account of their powers under sections 3 and 4 of the Powers of Criminal Courts (Sentencing) Act 2000 to commit for sentence.

(a) Dishonest handling of stolen property by a receiver who has commissioned the theft.

(b) The offence has professional hallmarks.

(c) The property is of high value.

SOCIAL SECURITY FRAUDS

Cases should be tried summarily unless the court considers that one or more of the following features is present in the case and that its sentencing powers are insufficient. Magistrates should take account of their powers under sections 3 and 4 of the Powers of Criminal Courts (Sentencing) Act 2000 to commit for sentence.

(a) Organised fraud on a large scale.

(b) The frauds are substantial and carried out over a long period of time.

VIOLENCE (SECTIONS 20 AND 47 OF THE OFFENCES AGAINST THE PERSON ACT 1861)

Cases should be tried summarily unless the court considers that one or more of the following features is present in the case and that its sentencing powers are insufficient. Magistrates should take account of their powers under sections 3 and 4 of the Powers of Criminal Courts (Sentencing) Act 2000 to commit for sentence.

(a) The use of a weapon of a kind likely to cause serious injury.

(b) A weapon is used and serious injury is caused.

(c) More than minor injury is caused by kicking or head-butting.

(d) Serious violence is caused to those whose work has to be done in contact with the public or are likely to face violence in the course of their work.

(e) Violence to vulnerable people, e.g. the elderly and infirm.

(f) The offence has clear racial motivation.

NOTE: The same considerations apply to cases of domestic violence.

PUBLIC ORDER ACT OFFENCES

Cases should be tried summarily unless the court considers that one or more of the following features is present in the case and that its sentencing powers are insufficient. Magistrates should take account of their powers under sections 3 and 4 of the Powers of Criminal Courts (Sentencing) Act 2000 to commit for sentence.

(a) Cases of violent disorder should generally be committed for trial.

(b) Affray.

(c) Organised violence or use of weapons.

(d) Significant injury or substantial damage.

(e) The offence has clear racial motivation.

(f) An attack on police officers, ambulance staff, fire-fighters and the like.

VIOLENCE TO AND NEGLECT OF CHILDREN

Cases should be tried summarily unless the court considers that one or more of the following features is present in the case and that its sentencing powers are insufficient. Magistrates should take account of their powers under sections 3 and 4 of the Powers of Criminal Courts (Sentencing) Act 2000 to commit for sentence.

(a) Substantial injury.

(b) Repeated violence or serious neglect, even if the physical harm is slight.

(c) Sadistic violence, e.g. deliberate burning or scalding.

INDECENT ASSAULT

Cases should be tried summarily unless the court considers that one or more of the following features is present in the case and that its sentencing powers are insufficient. Magistrates should take account of their powers under sections 3 and 4 of the Powers of Criminal Courts (Sentencing) Act 2000 to commit for sentence.

(a) Substantial disparity in age between victim and defendant, and a more serious assault.

(b) Violence or threats of violence.

(c) Relationship of trust or responsibility between defendant and victim.

(d) Several more serious similar offences.

(e) The victim is particularly vulnerable.

(f) Serious nature of the assault.

UNLAWFUL SEXUAL INTERCOURSE

Cases should be tried summarily unless the court considers that one or more of the following features is present in the case and that its sentencing powers are insufficient. Magistrates should take account of their powers under sections 3 and 4 of the Powers of Criminal Courts (Sentencing) Act 2000 to commit for sentence.

(a) Wide disparity of age.

(b) Breach of position of trust.

(c) The victim is particularly vulnerable.

DRUGS

Class A:

(a) Supply; possession with intent to supply: these cases should be committed for trial.

(b) Possession: should be committed for trial unless the amount is consistent only with personal use.

Class B:

(a) Supply; possession with intent to supply: should be committed for trial unless there is only small scale supply for no payment.

(b) Possession: should be committed for trial when the quantity is substantial and not consistent only with personal use.

DANGEROUS DRIVING AND AGGRAVATED VEHICLE TAKING

Cases should be tried summarily unless the court considers that one or more of the following features is present in the case and that its sentencing powers are insufficient. Magistrates should take account of their powers under sections 3 and 4 of the Powers of Criminal Courts (Sentencing) Act 2000 to commit for sentence.

(a) Alcohol or drugs contributing to the dangerous driving.

(b) Grossly excessive speed.

(c) Racing.

(d) Prolonged course of dangerous driving.

(e) Other related offences.

(f) Significant injury or damage sustained.

CRIMINAL DAMAGE

Cases should be tried summarily unless the court considers that one or more of the following features is present in the case and that its sentencing powers are insufficient. Magistrates should take account of their powers under sections 3 and 4 of the Powers of Criminal Courts (Sentencing) Act 2000 to commit for sentence.

(a) Deliberate fire-raising.

(b) Committed by a group.

(c) Damage of a high value.

(d) The offence has clear racial motivation.

APPENDIX 3

EXTRACTS FROM MAGISTRATES' COURT SENTENCING GUIDELINES (EFFECTIVE 4 AUGUST 2008)*

The complete version of the MCSG is accessible via the Sentencing Guidelines Council (SGC) website. A link to the MCSG is available via our Online Resource Centre

* Please note: The theft in breach of trust and theft from the person extracts are taken from the Sentencing Guidelines Council draft guidelines. Final guidelines are expected to be published July 2008.

Assault occasioning actual bodily harm & racially or religiously aggravated assault occasioning actual bodily harm – factors to take into consideration

This guideline and accompanying notes are taken from the Sentencing Guidelines Council's definitive guideline *Assault and other offences against the person*, published 20 February 2008

Key factors

(a) Matters of personal mitigation are often highly relevant to sentencing for this offence and may justify a non-custodial sentence, particularly in the case of a first time offender. Such a disposal might also be considered appropriate where there is a guilty plea.

(b) The level of culpability for an offence of ABH is the same as that for an offence of common assault; all that the prosecution must prove is that force was intentionally or recklessly used on another. What distinguishes the two offences is the nature of the injury caused to the victim and this will be the key factor for the CPS to consider when deciding which offence to charge.

(c) The use of a weapon (which for the purposes of this guideline includes traditional items such as an iron bar, baseball bat or knife) or part of the body (such as the head or other body part which may be equipped to inflict harm or greater harm, for example a shod foot) will usually increase the seriousness of an offence:

    (i) In relation to culpability, where a weapon is carried by the offender to the scene with the intention of using it or having it available for use should the opportunity or need arise, high culpability is likely to be indicated.

    (ii) In relation to harm, the type of weapon or part of the body and the way it is used will influence the extent of the effect on the assessment of seriousness. For instance, use of a knife or broken glass raises a high risk of serious injury. Similarly where the offender kicks or stamps on a prone victim, particularly if to a vulnerable part of the body.

(d) Where a weapon is used and the assault is premeditated, that will cause the offence to be in the highest sentencing range. Where that is not the case, possession and/or use of a weapon is likely to increase sentence within the range either through an increase in culpability or an increase in harm.

Offences Against the Person Act 1861, s.47

Crime and Disorder Act 1998, s.29

Assault occasioning actual bodily harm
Racially or religiously aggravated assault occasioning actual bodily harm

Assault occasioning ABH: triable either way
Maximum when tried summarily: Level 5 fine and/or 6 months
Maximum when tried on indictment: 5 years

Racially or religiously aggravated assault occasioning ABH: triable either way
Maximum when tried summarily: Level 5 fine and/or 6 months
Maximum when tried on indictment: 7 years

Where offence committed in domestic context, refer to page 177 for guidance

Identify dangerous offenders
These are specified offences for the purposes of the public protection provisions in the Criminal Justice Act 2003 – refer to page 187 and consult legal adviser for guidance

Offence seriousness (culpability and harm)
A. Identify the appropriate starting point
Starting points based on first time offender pleading not guilty

Examples of nature of activity	Starting point	Range
Other assault resulting in minor, non-permanent injury	High level community order	Medium level community order to 26 weeks custody
Premeditated assault resulting in minor, non-permanent injury	24 weeks custody	12 weeks custody to Crown Court
Premeditated assault either resulting in relatively serious injury or involving the use of a weapon	Crown Court	Crown Court

Offence seriousness (culpability and harm)
B. Consider the effect of aggravating and mitigating factors
(other than those within examples above)
Common aggravating and mitigating factors are identified in the pullout card – the following may be particularly relevant but **these lists are not exhaustive**

	Factors indicating lower culpability
	1. Provocation
	2. Unintended injury

Form a preliminary view of the appropriate sentence
If offender charged and convicted of the racially or religiously aggravated offence, increase the sentence to reflect this element
Refer to pages 178-179 for guidance

Consider offender mitigation
Common factors are identified in the pullout card

Consider a reduction for a guilty plea

Consider ancillary orders, including compensation
Refer to pages 168-174 for guidance on available ancillary orders

Decide sentence
Give reasons

Effective from 4 August 2008

Burglary in a dwelling – factors to take into consideration

These guidelines and accompanying notes are drawn from the Court of Appeal's decision in *R v McInerney and Keating* [2002] EWCA Crim 3003

Key factors

(a) Even where the custody threshold is passed, consider whether a community order is appropriate (*McInerney and Keating* and refer also to page 160).

(b) Cases in the Crown Court category may be suitable for a community order (see note (a) above), but should nevertheless be committed to the Crown Court for trial/sentence so that any breach of the order can be sentenced within the powers of that Court.

(c) For attempted burglary or burglary under s.9(1)(a) of the Theft Act 1968, it is the offender's <u>intention</u> that will determine which of the three categories opposite the offence falls into, not the fact that nothing was stolen.

(d) Relevant convictions that will aggravate offence seriousness in accordance with s.143(2) of the Criminal Justice Act 2003 may include convictions for both property and violent offences.

Theft Act 1968, s.9

Burglary in a dwelling

Triable either way:
Maximum when tried summarily: Level 5 fine and/or 6 months
Maximum when tried on indictment: 14 years

Allocation
Consult legal adviser for guidance

Offence is indictable only and must be sent to the Crown Court if:

(1) The offender has been convicted of two other domestic burglaries committed on separate occasions after 30 November 1999: Powers of Criminal Courts (Sentencing) Act 2000, s.111;

(2) Any person was subjected to violence or the threat of violence: Magistrates' Courts Act 1980, sch.1

Offence seriousness (culpability and harm)
A. Identify the appropriate starting point
Starting points based on first time offender pleading not guilty

Examples of nature of activity	Starting point	Range
Unforced entry and low value theft with no aggravating features	Medium level community order	Low level community order to 12 weeks custody
Forced entry, goods stolen not high value, no aggravating features	12 weeks custody	High level community order to Crown Court
Goods stolen high value or any aggravating feature present	Crown Court	Crown Court

Offence seriousness (culpability and harm)
B. Consider the effect of aggravating and mitigating factors
(other than those within examples above)
Common aggravating and mitigating factors are identified in the pullout card –
the following may be particularly relevant but **these lists are not exhaustive**

Factors indicating higher culpability	**Factors indicating lower culpability**
1. Ransacking property	1. Offender played only a minor role in the burglary
2. Professionalism	2. Offence committed on impulse
3. Victim deliberately targeted e.g. out of spite	
4. Housebreaking implements or weapons carried	**Factor indicating lesser degree of harm**
	1. No damage or disturbance to property
Factors indicating greater degree of harm	
1. Occupier at home or returns home while offender present	
2. Goods stolen of sentimental value	

Form a preliminary view of the appropriate sentence,
then consider offender mitigation
Common factors are identified in the pullout card

Consider a reduction for a guilty plea

Consider ancillary orders, including restitution and compensation
Refer to pages 168-174 for guidance on available ancillary orders
Consider deprivation of property

Decide sentence
Give reasons

Effective from 4 August 2008

Guidelines for inclusion in the revised Magistrates' Court Sentencing Guidelines:

Theft in breach of trust	Theft Act 1968, s. 1

Triable either way:
Maximum when tried summarily: Level 5 fine and/or 6 months   Maximum when tried on indictment: 7 years

OFFENCE SERIOUSNESS (CULPABILITY AND HARM)
A. IDENTIFY THE APPROPRIATE STARTING POINT
Starting points based on first time offender pleading not guilty

Examples of nature of activity	Starting point	Range
Theft of less than £2,000	Medium level community order	Band B fine to 26 weeks custody
Theft of £2,000 or more but less than £20,000 OR Theft of less than £2,000 in breach of a high degree of trust	18 weeks custody	High level community order to Crown Court
Theft of £20,000 or more OR Theft of £2,000 or more in breach of a high degree of trust	Crown Court	Crown Court

OFFENCE SERIOUSNESS (CULPABILITY AND HARM)
B. CONSIDER THE EFFECT OF AGGRAVATING AND MITIGATING FACTORS
(OTHER THAN THOSE WITHIN EXAMPLES ABOVE)
Common aggravating and mitigating factors are identified in Annex B. The following may be particularly relevant:

Factors indicating higher culpability 1. Long course of offending 2. Suspicion deliberately thrown on others	

FORM A PRELIMINARY VIEW OF THE APPROPRIATE SENTENCE, THEN CONSIDER OFFENDER MITIGATION
Common factors are identified in Annex B. See also note (e) opposite.

CONSIDER A REDUCTION FOR A GUILTY PLEA

CONSIDER ANCILLARY ORDERS, INCLUDING COMPENSATION
Refer to paragraphs xx for guidance on available ancillary orders

DECIDE SENTENCE

GIVE REASONS

Notes:

(a) In general terms, the seriousness of this form of theft will increase in line with the level of trust breached:

o   at the lower end of the scale are thefts by employees who are not in a position of trust over and above that inherent in the employment relationship;

o   at the higher end are thefts by employees who have been specifically entrusted with the care of the property or funds stolen, sometimes on behalf of the general public.

The extent to which the nature and degree of trust placed in an offender should be regarded as increasing the seriousness of the offence will depend on a careful assessment of the circumstances of the individual case, not just the occupation of the offender.

(b) Thefts by offenders in whom a high degree of trust has been placed should generally attract higher sentences than thefts of similar amounts by offenders in whom a lower degree of trust has been placed.

(c) The starting points and sentencing ranges in this guideline are based on the assumption that the offender was motivated by greed or a desire to live beyond his or her means. To avoid double counting, such a motivation should not be treated as a factor that increases culpability.

(d) When assessing the harm caused by this offence, the starting point should be the loss suffered by the victim. In general, the greater the loss, the more serious the offence. However, the monetary value of the loss may not reflect the full extent of the harm caused by the offence. The court should also take into account the impact of the offence on the victim, any harm to persons other than the direct victim, and any harm in the form of public alarm or erosion of public confidence.

(e) The Council has identified the following matters of personal mitigation which may be relevant to this offence:

(i) Offender motivated by desperation or need
The fact that an offence has been committed in desperation or need arising from particular hardship may count as personal mitigation in exceptional circumstances.

(ii) Voluntary return of stolen property
Whether and the degree to which the return of stolen property constitutes a matter of personal mitigation will depend on an assessment of the circumstances and, in particular, the voluntariness and timeliness of the return.

(iii) Excessive responsibility and/or inadequate training
The fact that an offender was given excessive responsibility and/or inadequate training and support may be regarded as personal mitigation.

(iv) Voluntary cessation of offending
The fact that an offender voluntarily ceased offending before being discovered does not reduce the seriousness of the offence. However, if the claim to have stopped offending is genuine, it may constitute personal mitigation, particularly if it is evidence of remorse.[22]

(v) Reporting an undiscovered offence
Where an offender brings the offending to the attention of his or her employer or the authorities, this may be treated as personal mitigation.[23]

(vi) Impact on sentence of offender's dependency
Many offenders convicted of acquisitive crimes are motivated by an addiction, often to drugs, alcohol or gambling. This does not mitigate the seriousness of the offence, but an offender's dependency may properly influence the type of sentence imposed. In particular, it may sometimes be appropriate to impose a drug rehabilitation requirement or an alcohol treatment requirement as part of a community order or a suspended sentence order in an attempt to break the cycle of addiction and offending, even if an immediate custodial sentence would otherwise be warranted.[24]

(f) In many cases of theft in breach of trust, termination of an offender's employment will be a natural consequence of committing the offence. Other than in the most exceptional of circumstances, loss of employment and any consequential hardship should <u>not</u> constitute personal mitigation.

(g) Where a court is satisfied that a custodial sentence of less than 12 months is appropriate for an offence of theft in breach of trust, consideration should be given to whether that sentence can be suspended in accordance with the criteria in the Council guideline *New Sentences: Criminal Justice Act 2003*. A suspended sentence may be particularly appropriate where this would allow for reparation to be made either to the victim or to the community at large.

---

[22] Council guideline   *Overarching Principles: Seriousness*, para.1.27, published December 2004, www.sentencing-guidelines.gov.uk.
[23] ibid., para. 1.29.
[24] See Council guideline *New Sentences: Criminal Justice Act 2003*, www.sentencing-guidelines.gov.uk. The Court of Appeal gave guidance on the approach to making drug treatment and testing orders, which also applies to imposing a drug rehabilitation requirement, in *Attorney General's Reference No. 64 of 2003 (Boujettif and Harrison)* [2004] 2 Cr App R (S) 22 and *Woods and Collins* [2005] Crim LR 982 summarised in the Sentencing Guidelines Council *Guideline Judgments Case Compendium* (section A) Generic Sentencing Principles) available at: www.sentencing-guidelines.gov.uk.

Theft from the person	Theft Act 1968, s. 1

Triable either way:
Maximum when tried summarily: Level 5 fine and/or 6 months   Maximum when tried on indictment: 7 years

OFFENCE SERIOUSNESS (CULPABILITY AND HARM)
A. IDENTIFY THE APPROPRIATE STARTING POINT
Starting points based on first time offender pleading not guilty

Examples of nature of activity	Starting point	Range
Where the effect on the victim is particularly severe, the stolen property is of high value (as defined in note (e) opposite), or substantial consequential loss results, a sentence higher than the range into which the offence otherwise would fall may be appropriate		
Theft from the person not involving vulnerable victim	Medium level community order	Band B fine to 18 weeks custody
Theft from a vulnerable victim (as defined in note (c) opposite)	18 weeks custody	High level community order to Crown Court
Theft involving the use or threat of force (falling short of robbery) against a vulnerable victim (as defined in note (c) opposite)	Crown Court	Crown Court

OFFENCE SERIOUSNESS (CULPABILITY AND HARM)
B. CONSIDER THE EFFECT OF AGGRAVATING AND MITIGATING FACTORS
(OTHER THAN THOSE WITHIN EXAMPLES ABOVE)
Common aggravating and mitigating factors are identified in Annex B. The following may be particularly relevant:

Factors indicating greater degree of harm	
1. Use of force, or threat of force, against victim (not amounting to robbery) [except where this raises the offence into a higher sentencing range] 2. Intimidation or face-to-face confrontation with victim where this raises the offence into a higher sentencing range] 3. High level of inconvenience caused to victim, e.g. replacing house keys, credit cards etc	

FORM A PRELIMINARY VIEW OF THE APPROPRIATE SENTENCE, THEN CONSIDER OFFENDER MITIGATION
Common factors are identified in Annex B. See also note (g) opposite.

CONSIDER A REDUCTION FOR A GUILTY PLEA

CONSIDER ANCILLARY ORDERS, INCLUDING COMPENSATION
Refer to paragraphs xx for guidance on available ancillary orders

DECIDE SENTENCE

GIVE REASONS

Notes:

(a) Theft from the person may encompass conduct such as 'pick-pocketing', where the victim is unaware that the property is being stolen, as well as the snatching of handbags, wallets, jewellery and mobile telephones from the victim's possession or from the vicinity of the victim. The offence constitutes an invasion of the victim's privacy and may cause the victim to experience distress, fear and inconvenience either during or after the event. While in some cases the conduct may be similar, **this guideline does not apply where the offender has been convicted of robbery; sentencers should instead refer to the Council guideline on robbery**.

(b) The starting points and sentencing ranges in this guideline are based on the assumption that the offender was motivated by greed or a desire to live beyond his or her means. To avoid double counting, such a motivation should not be treated as a factor that increases culpability.

(c) For the purpose of this guideline, a 'vulnerable victim' is a person targeted by the offender because it is anticipated that he or she is unlikely or unable to resist the theft. Young or elderly persons and tourists may fall into this category. The exploitation of vulnerable victims indicates a high level of culpability and will influence the category of seriousness into which the offence falls.

(d) When assessing the harm caused by this offence, the starting point should be the loss suffered by the victim. In general, the greater the loss, the more serious the offence. However, the monetary value of the loss may not reflect the full extent of the harm caused by the offence. The court should also take into account the impact of the offence on the victim, any harm to persons other than the direct victim, and any harm in the form of public alarm or erosion of public confidence.

(e) The guideline is based on the assumption that most thefts from the person do not involve property of high monetary value or of high value to the victim. Where the stolen property is of high monetary value or of high value (including sentimental value) to the victim, the appropriate sentence may be beyond the range into which the offence otherwise would fall. For the purposes of this form of theft, 'high monetary value' is defined as more than £2,000.

(f) A sentence beyond the range into which the offence otherwise would fall may also be appropriate where the effect on the victim is particularly severe or where substantial consequential loss results (such as where the theft of equipment causes serious disruption to the victim's life or business).

(g) The Council has identified the following matters of personal mitigation which may be relevant to this offence:

(i) Offender motivated by desperation or need
The fact that an offence has been committed in desperation or need arising from particular hardship may count as personal mitigation in exceptional circumstances.

(ii) Voluntary return of stolen property
Whether and the degree to which the return of stolen property constitutes a matter of personal mitigation will depend on an assessment of the circumstances and, in particular, the voluntariness and timeliness of the return.

(iii) Impact on sentence of offender's dependency
Many offenders convicted of acquisitive crimes are motivated by an addiction, often to drugs, alcohol or gambling. This does not mitigate the seriousness of the offence, but an offender's dependency may properly influence the type of sentence imposed. In particular, it may sometimes be appropriate to impose a drug rehabilitation requirement or an alcohol treatment requirement as part of a community order or a suspended sentence order in an attempt to break the cycle of addiction and offending, even if an immediate custodial sentence would otherwise be warranted.[25]

(f) Previous authorities have expressed concern about the prevalence of theft against the person and the associated need for deterrence, particularly in relation to pick-pocketing. The Council guideline *Overarching Principles: Seriousness* signals a need for caution when considering issues of local prevalence. Further, national prevalence should not be used by sentencers to justify including a deterrent element in sentences as this is already taken into account in Council guidelines.

---

[25] See Council guideline *New Sentences: Criminal Justice Act 2003*, published December 2004, www.sentencing-guidelines.gov.uk. The Court of Appeal gave guidance on the approach to making drug treatment and testing orders, which also applies to imposing a drug rehabilitation requirement, in *Attorney General's Reference No. 64 of 2003 (Boujettif and Harrison)* [2004] 2 Cr App R (S) 22 and *Woods and Collins* [2005] Crim LR 982 summarised in the Sentencing Guidelines Council *Guideline Judgments Case Compendium* (section (A) Generic Sentencing Principles) available at: www.sentencing-guidelines.gov.uk.

Dangerous driving

Road Traffic Act 1988, s.2

Triable either way:
Maximum when tried summarily: Level 5 fine and/or 6 months
Maximum when tried on indictment: 2 years

- Must endorse and disqualify for at least 12 months. Must order extended re-test
- Must disqualify for **at least** 2 years if offender has had two or more disqualifications for periods of 56 days or more in preceding 3 years – **refer to page 184 and consult your legal adviser for further guidance**

If there is a delay in sentencing after conviction, consider interim disqualification

Offence seriousness (culpability and harm) A. Identify the appropriate starting point Starting points based on first time offender pleading not guilty		
Examples of nature of activity	**Starting point**	**Range**
Single incident where little or no damage or risk of personal injury	Medium level community order	Low level community order to high level community order Disqualify 12 – 15 months
Incident(s) involving excessive speed or showing off, especially on busy roads or in built-up area; OR Single incident where little or no damage or risk of personal injury but offender was disqualified driver	12 weeks custody	High level community order to 26 weeks custody Disqualify 15 – 24 months
Prolonged bad driving involving deliberate disregard for safety of others; OR Incident(s) involving excessive speed or showing off, especially on busy roads or in built-up area, by disqualified driver; OR Driving as described in box above while being pursued by police	Crown Court	Crown Court

Offence seriousness (culpability and harm) B. Consider the effect of aggravating and mitigating factors (other than those within examples above) Common aggravating and mitigating factors are identified in the pullout card – the following may be particularly relevant but **these lists are not exhaustive**	
Factors indicating higher culpability 1. Disregarding warnings of others 2. Evidence of alcohol or drugs 3. Carrying out other tasks while driving 4. Carrying passengers or heavy load 5. Tiredness 6. Aggressive driving, such as driving much too close to vehicle in front, racing, inappropriate attempts to overtake, or cutting in after overtaking 7. Driving when knowingly suffering from a medical condition which significantly impairs the offender's driving skills 8. Driving a poorly maintained or dangerously loaded vehicle, especially where motivated by commercial concerns **Factors indicating greater degree of harm** 1. Injury to others 2. Damage to other vehicles or property	**Factors indicating lower culpability** 1. Genuine emergency 2. Speed not excessive 3. Offence due to inexperience rather than irresponsibility of driver

Effective from 4 August 2008

**Form a preliminary view of the appropriate sentence,
then consider offender mitigation**
Common factors are identified in the pullout card

Consider a reduction for guilty plea

Consider ancillary orders, including compensation and deprivation of property
Refer to pages 168-174 for guidance on available ancillary orders

**Decide sentence
Give reasons**

Effective from 4 August 2008

Road Traffic Act 1988, s.3

Careless driving (drive without due care and attention)

Triable only summarily:
Maximum: Level 5 fine

Must endorse and may disqualify. If no disqualification, impose 3 – 9 points

Offence seriousness (culpability and harm)
A. Identify the appropriate starting point
Starting points based on first time offender pleading not guilty

Examples of nature of activity	Starting point	Range
Momentary lapse of concentration or misjudgement at low speed	Band A fine	Band A fine 3 – 4 points
Loss of control due to speed, mishandling or insufficient attention to road conditions, or carelessly turning right across on-coming traffic	Band B fine	Band B fine 5 – 6 points
Overtaking manoeuvre at speed resulting in collision of vehicles, or driving bordering on the dangerous	Band C fine	Band C fine Consider disqualification OR 7 – 9 points

Offence seriousness (culpability and harm)
B. Consider the effect of aggravating and mitigating factors (other than those within examples above)
Common aggravating and mitigating factors are identified in the pullout card – the following may be particularly relevant but **these lists are not exhaustive**

Factors indicating higher culpability	Factors indicating lower culpability
1. Excessive speed 2. Carrying out other tasks while driving 3. Carrying passengers or heavy load 4. Tiredness **Factors indicating greater degree of harm** 1. Injury to others 2. Damage to other vehicles or property 3. High level of traffic or pedestrians in vicinity 4. Location e.g. near school when children are likely to be present	1. Minor risk 2. Inexperience of driver 3. Sudden change in road or weather conditions

Form a preliminary view of the appropriate sentence, then consider offender mitigation
Common factors are identified in the pullout card

Consider a reduction for guilty plea

Consider ordering disqualification until appropriate driving test passed
Consider ancillary orders, including compensation
Refer to pages 168-174 for guidance on available ancillary orders

Decide sentence
Give reasons

Effective from 4 August 2008

Road Traffic Act 1988, s.170(4)

Fail to stop/report road accident

Triable only summarily:
Maximum: Level 5 fine and/or 6 months

Must endorse and may disqualify. If no disqualification, impose 5 – 10 points

Offence seriousness (culpability and harm)
A. Identify the appropriate starting point
Starting points based on first time offender pleading not guilty

Examples of nature of activity	Starting point	Range
Minor damage/injury or stopped at scene but failed to exchange particulars or report	Band B fine	Band B fine 5 – 6 points
Moderate damage/injury or failed to stop and failed to report	Band C fine	Band C fine 7 – 8 points Consider disqualification
Serious damage/injury and/or evidence of bad driving	High level community order	Band C fine to 26 weeks custody Disqualify 6 – 12 months OR 9 – 10 points

Offence seriousness (culpability and harm)
B. Consider the effect of aggravating and mitigating factors
(other than those within examples above)
Common aggravating and mitigating factors are identified in the pullout card –
the following may be particularly relevant but **these lists are not exhaustive**

Factors indicating higher culpability	Factors indicating lower culpability
1. Evidence of drink or drugs/evasion of test 2. Knowledge/suspicion that personal injury caused (where not an element of the offence) 3. Leaving injured party at scene 4. Giving false details	1. Believed identity known 2. Genuine fear of retribution 3. Subsequently reported

Form a preliminary view of the appropriate sentence, then consider offender mitigation
Common factors are identified in the pullout card

Consider a reduction for guilty plea

Consider ancillary orders, including compensation
Refer to pages 168-174 for guidance on available ancillary orders

Decide sentence
Give reasons

Effective from 4 August 2008

CHAPTER 1

1 (a) Lenny Whyte is charged with burglary, contrary to s. 9 Theft Act 1968 which is an offence triable either way.

(b) Roger Martin is initially charged with dangerous driving contrary to s. 2 Road Traffic Act (an either-way offence), common assault contrary to s. 39 Criminal Justice Act 1988 (summary-only) and failing to stop and report an accident contrary to s. 170 Road Traffic Act 1988 (summary-only). The dangerous driving is subsequently replaced with a less serious charge of careless driving contrary to s. 3 Road Traffic Act 1988 which is a summary-only offence.

(c) William Hardy is charged with sexual activity with a child under the age of 16, contrary to s. 9(2) Sexual Offences Act 2003. As the offence involves penetration it is triable only on indictment.

2 (i) Where the value of damage in a criminal damage case is less than £5,000, the case will be tried summarily.

(ii) Where the value of damage in a criminal damage case is more £5,000, the case is triable either way.

(iii) Possession of a controlled drug is an either-way offence.

(iv) Careless driving is a summary-only offence.

(v) Burglary is an offence triable either way. However, there are circumstances in which burglary is triable only on indictment, including if persons inside a dwelling-house were subjected to violence or the threat of violence or if the accused is over 18 and has two separate convictions for domestic dwelling-house burglary committed after 30 November 1999.

(vi) Affray is an offence triable either way.

3. A summary-only offence is an offence that starts and ends its life in the magistrates' court. Summary-only offences are the least serious offences.

4. An indictable-only offence will be tried in the Crown Court, although the accused will make his initial appearance in connection with an indictable-only offence before a magistrates' court. Indictable-only offences are the most serious offences.

5. A mode of trial enquiry will be held in conne[...] with an either-way offence to which the acc[...] has indicated an intention to plead not guil[...]

6. The overriding objective of the Criminal P[...] dure Rules is identified in Rule 1.1; it being [...] all criminal cases be dealt with justly. Consi[...] tions relevant to dealing with cases justly are [...] ticularised further in Rule 1.1.

7. Section 3 Human Rights Act 1988 places an [...] gation on the criminal courts to interpret a[...] islation 'as far as possible' to comply with [...] law. In determining Convention rights the c[...] must apply ECHR law as determined by the [...] prudence stemming for the most part from [...] sions of the European Court of Human Ri[...] The HRA 1998 does not give the courts the p[...] to strike down legislation which is contrary [...] ECHR. So, where it is not possible to give eff[...] the ECHR law in a case, s. 4 HRA 1998 require[...] superior courts (Court of Appeal and the Ho[...] Lords) to make a declaration of incompatil[...] The declaration gives Parliament the opport[...] to amend the domestic provision which con[...] with Convention law.

A defence solicitor might rely on Conve[...] rights (most obviously Article 6) in suppor[...] legal submission to have evidence excluded [...] case. It could also be relied on to challen[...] aspect of procedure; to stay proceedings f[...] abuse of process and on appeal against convic[...] challenging the admissibility of prosecution [...] dence or seeking the exclusion of a confessi[...]

8. The consequences of failing to abide by the S[...] itors' Code of Conduct include an appea[...] before the Solicitors Disciplinary Tribuna[...] breach of the code. The SDT's powers of pu[...] ment range from giving a reprimand to strik[...] solicitor off the Roll. In relation to non-qua[...] staff, it can make a direction that no firm em[...] that person. Your actions may cause your [...] to have a complaint made against it to the [...] Complaints Service. You may also be censur[...] court by the judge/Bench and by your peers [...] must always be on your guard!

CHAPTER 2

CASE STUDY *R v LENNY WHYTE*

The prosecution will contend that Lenny is the [...] responsible for unlawfully entering the home of L[...]

Kennedy and stealing money from her. The prosecution will allege that Lenny was assisted in the burglary by another individual—most probably Lloyd Green. The police have not charged this second individual. The prosecution will contend that this person deliberately distracted Lillian Kennedy at her front door to enable the burglar to obtain access to her property in order to steal. We must speculate on the motives for the burglary. It may well be the prosecution's theory that Lloyd Green was most probably putting Lenny Whyte under pressure to pay off a debt owed to him. The person who entered Lillian Kennedy's property via an unlocked backdoor is said to be Lenny Whyte. What evidence links Lenny to the crime?

Witness—Lillian Kennedy. She states she saw Lenny in the vicinity of her home an hour or so before the burglary and that he offered to assist her with her shopping. She describes the man as wearing white training shoes. She identifies Lenny to the police when she is taken by them on a tour of the immediate vicinity. She is subsequently unable to identify Lenny at a video identification parade and she is unable to identify Lloyd Green.

Witness—Shirley Lewis. She was in the garden next to the burgled property and gives a description of the man which corresponds with Lenny's actual appearance and mentions the white training shoes. She subsequently identifies Lenny as being that man at a video parade.

Witness—Harold Finney. This witness provides the police with a registration number of a car parked in Sunrise Road which leads to Lloyd Green being arrested. He describes a man similar to Lenny approaching the car. This witness is unable to identify Lenny at the subsequent video identification parade.

Lenny's incriminating admissions made during the police interview satisfy the definition of a confession.

Real evidence of the white training shoes found in Lenny's flat.

Forensic opinion evidence that shoeprints located and lifted at the rear of the burgled property can be said to match the soles of the training shoes found in Lenny's flat.

Lenny has several previous convictions and a drug habit which places him in a category of persons more likely to have committed this crime. The prosecution will want to adduce evidence of Lenny's past bad character, specifically in relation to his past offences of theft and burglary. Can the defence prevent this?

Lenny will plead not guilty. His defence is that it was not him. If it was not him, it must be someone else. The defence theory in this case means the following evidence will have to be challenged:

- eye-witness identification;
- Lenny's confession;
- forensic evidence.

If Lenny is able to advance an alibi, this will strengthen the challenge to the prosecution's case if the alibi evidence is accepted. The second person alleged to have been involved has not been charged and at this stage, Lenny is not implicated by the involvement of any

co-accused which might require a corroboration warning to be given.

Having regard to this introductory chapter on criminal evidence and having identified the areas of criminal evidence involved in this scenario, consider how you might challenge the eye-witness identification in this case. There may be a possible application of s. 78 PACE in this regard, given Lenny was unrepresented at the police station. You will certainly be talking about the Turnbull Guidelines, as this is a case of mistaken identity and there are several weaknesses in the eye-witness identification. You will have concerns about the manner in which Lenny's confession was obtained and so you will want to make an application to have the confession excluded under ss. 76 and 78 PACE. Might a report from Lenny's psychiatrist assist in this respect?

The opinion evidence of the forensic scientist will be admissible as expert opinion evidence. You will want to undermine the weight to be attached to the opinion, given the popularity of Nike training shoes. Lenny states he has never worn the shoes. You will no doubt wish to oppose the admission in evidence of Lenny's past bad character.

You are on your way to securing an acquittal in this case. You have identified the main points of contention. When you have worked through the later chapters on criminal evidence you will be able to fully discuss and apply the principles of evidence law that arise in this case.

CHAPTER 3

1. Judicial guidance on the reasonable suspicion or belief test is provided by *O'Hara v Chief Constable, RUC* [1997] AC 286. Further, important guidance is located in (Code A 2.2–2.11).

2. On arrest, the suspect will be cautioned in the following way: 'You do not have to say anything. But it may harm your defence if you do not mention, when questioned, something which you later rely on in court. Anything you do say may be given in evidence', Code C para. 10.

3. The powers to search a person after arrest are contained in s. 32 PACE. The power to search the premises in which a person was at the time of his arrest or immediately before his arrest is also contained in s. 32 PACE. The power to search premises occupied or controlled by a suspect after arrest are contained in s. 18 PACE.

4. The police will apply to a magistrate to search premises under s. 8 PACE where it is not possible to contact the person who could allow the police to enter premises to search for evidence in connection with an indictable offence.

5. On the facts, the police could stop and search Trevor under s. 1 PACE 1984, provided the officer has reasonable grounds for suspecting Trevor may have on his person a prohibited article. Given the intelligence provided by CCTV operators, reasonable suspicion could easily be established in this case. Based on the information provided and Trevor's reaction when approached, the police would have reasonable grounds for suspecting

Trevor to have been involved in an offence and that it is necessary to arrest him (s. 24 PACE). Having arrested him and cautioned him, the police officer would be entitled to search Trevor under s. 32 PACE if he had reasonable grounds for believing Trevor may have evidence on him relating to an offence. The officer may choose to take Trevor into custody or possibly release him on 'street bail'.

6. Suggested solution can be found in the answers to the self-test questions supporting Chapter 6.

CHAPTER 5

SCENARIO 1

If the jury concludes it was reasonable for Karl to have mentioned he acted in self-defence while being questioned at the police station, he is at risk of an adverse inference being drawn under s. 34 CJPOA 1994 against him at his trial.

SCENARIO 2

Although Stan has put forward facts in support of a possible defence at trial, he failed to mention the possibility that he acted in self-defence. This is a fact he now relies on at court in his defence. If the jury finds he could reasonably have been expected to mention this fact, this could weaken his defence of self-defence (s. 34 CJPOA).

SCENARIO 3

Jason is at risk of a double adverse inference. Providing the circumstances set out in s. 36 CJPOA are met, he risks an adverse inference in that he has failed to give an explanation for scratch marks visible on his face. The marks are on his person. The arresting constable or other investigating officer must reasonably have believed the presence of the marks might have been attributable to Jason's participation in a crime. The officer must have made Jason aware of his belief before requesting Jason to give an account, explaining in ordinary language the risk he faces from his failure to do so. In addition, Jason risks an adverse inference under s. 34.

SCENARIO 4

In this instance Rio too is at risk of an adverse inference under s. 36 CJPOA. Subsection 36(3) makes it clear that the section applies to the condition of clothing as it does to footwear.

SCENARIO 5

Providing the conditions set out in s. 37 CJPOA 1994 are met, Jane risks an adverse inference being drawn against her, in that she has failed to give an explanation for her presence near the scene of a crime. The arresting constable or other investigating officer must reasonably have believed Jane's presence might have been attributable to her participation in a crime. The officer must have made Jane aware of his belief before requesting her to give an account, explaining in ordinary language the risk she faces from her failure to do so. Under s. 37

CJPOA a 'place' is widely defined and includes buildings, vehicles and vessels. By refusing to give evidence at her trial, Jane risks an adverse inference being drawn against her under s. 35 Criminal Justice and Public Order Act 1994 (see Chapter 23) as well.

SCENARIO 6

The fact that Carley remained silent on the advice of her solicitor does not immunise her against the jury drawing an adverse inference. In order to persuade the jury not to draw an adverse inference, Carley is best advised to waive legal professional privilege and explain her reasons for not putting her defence at the police station. This could be done in a number of different ways:

- Carley's solicitor could have explained his reasons on the tape-recorded interview;
- Carley may give evidence of the reasons herself;
- there may be evidence from the solicitor (either in person or in agreed written hearsay form).

The reasonableness or otherwise of Carley's decision to remain silent will be a matter for the jury. If this were a Crown Court trial, the judge would be required to carefully direct the jury on s. 34 CJPOA, in accordance with the requirements in *R v Argent* and the Judicial Studies Board specimen direction.

CHAPTER 6

SCENARIO 1

This scenario raises the matter of unlawfully obtained evidence. The illegality relates to the manner in which Ranjit was stopped and searched under s. 1 PACE 1984 (see Chapter 3). The search could well be illegal for a number of reasons:

- Was the decision to stop and search Ranjit based on reasonable suspicion as required by Code A (paras. 2.2–2.11)? This seems doubtful.
- Did the officers provide Ranjit with the required information before commencing the search as required by Code A para. 3.8?
- Was the manner in which the search was conducted (removal of outer clothing, socks and shoes in public) lawful, having regard to Code A para. 3.5?

As a result of the actions of the police, a quantity of cocaine is found. If the search was unlawful, can the evidence obtained as a consequence be excluded under s. 78 PACE? Certainly the defence advocate should consider such an application. Given the restrictive interpretation of s. 78, however, it is highly questionable whether the evidence would be excluded since it is relevant and reliable.

Ranjit may have a defence to the allegation that he assaulted a police officer in the execution of his duty if it can be established that the officer was not in fact acting in the execution of his duty at the time he initially approached Ranjit and grabbed him by the shoulder. Additionally, Ranjit may state that he acted in self-defence.

SCENARIO 2

This scenario raises the spectre of entrapment by the prosecuting authorities. Entrapment does not provide a defence in substantive law, but Stan might argue the evidence should be excluded under the abuse of process doctrine as defined by the House of Lords in *R v Loosley* [2001] 1 WLR 2060. The application of the various factors identified in the various judgments would need to be applied to the specific factors in this case for a decision to be reached. Relevant factors would include Stan's lack of a criminal record and the fact that he was not immediately in possession of drugs when initially approached by the officers. The suggestion that the officers caused Stan to commit the offence is, on the face of things, made out. If it did, this would constitute state created crime and would be an abuse of process.

CHAPTER 7

EXERCISE 1: ANSWERS TO THE QUESTIONS TESTING YOUR KNOWLEDGE OF CODE C SAFEGUARDS

Question 1

In accordance with Code C 10.1 a caution must be given to any suspect who the police wish to question in circumstances where there are grounds to suspect that person of involvement in an offence and whose silence or answers to any questions may be given in evidence against him. An individual must also be cautioned on arrest and on being charged (C 10.5) or informed that they might be prosecuted. A caution must also be given at the commencement of each interview (Code C 10.1) and where there is a break in an interview the suspect should be reminded that they are under caution (C 10.8). It is the duty of the interviewing officer to ensure that the suspect understands the caution (Code C 10D). Where access to a solicitor has been delayed in accordance with s. 58(8) PACE/Code C 6.6, s. 58 Youth Justice and Criminal Evidence Act 1999 prohibits a court from drawing an adverse inference from silence. In these circumstances the police are obliged to caution the suspect in the following terms: 'You do not have to say anything, but anything you do say may be given in evidence against you.'

The caution reminds the suspect that he has the right not to incriminate himself. Incriminating admissions obtained in circumstances where a caution has not been properly administered are vulnerable to challenge under s. 76(2)(b) and s. 78 PACE. In *R v Armas-Rodriguez* [2005] EWCA Crim 1981, while acknowledging that a failure to caution a suspect at the commencement of an interview constituted a 'significant and substantial' breach of Code C, on the facts in this particular case, it had not been unfair (in accordance with s. 78 PACE 1984) to admit the interview. In particular, the Court of Appeal observed that the police had cautioned D on arrest; there had been no bad faith on the part of the interviewing officer, the defendant had been represented by a solicitor throughout; the interview had been tape recorded and the questions put fairly. Furthermore, the defendant had been interviewed a second time under caution and had given a substantially similar account.

Question 2

Upon arrival at the police station and in accordance with Code C 3.1, the custody officer should explain to the suspect that he has the following rights which may be exercised at any stage:

(i)   the right to have someone informed of his arrest;

(ii) the right to consult in private with a solicitor, such advice being free (save in isolated categories) and independent;

(iii) the right to consult the Codes of Practice.

Furthermore, under Code C 3.5, the custody officer is required to ask the suspect on his arrival at the police station whether he:

- wants legal advice;
- wants to inform someone of his arrest;
- might be in need of medical treatment;
- requires the presence of an appropriate adult; or
- requires an interpreter.

Question 3

A number of individuals might be considered vulnerable. Under Code C 3.6– 3.10 the custody officer must undertake a risk assessment of all detainees. Detainees who would clearly require assistance include those with learning difficulties or communication difficulties, those requiring an interpreter, those on medication, juveniles; the mentally disordered or mentally vulnerable. In some instances the detainee will require the services of an appropriate adult (C 3.15).

Questions 4 and 5

Some very important safeguards are contained in para. 6 of Code C. C 6.4 stipulates that no police officer should, at any time, do or say anything with the intention of dissuading a detainee from obtaining legal advice. If the detainee refuses legal advice Code C 6.5 requires the custody officer to explain that he may seek advice over the telephone and if the detainee continues to decline the services of a lawyer, the custody sergeant should ask the detainee why and record the reasons. The effect of these paragraphs is to encourage the police to be proactive in securing suspects access to legal advice.

Access to legal advice may be delayed but only in the circumstances set out in Code C 6.6. If C 6.6 does not apply a detainee wanting legal advice may not be interviewed or continue to be interviewed until they have received legal advice.

The decision to delay access to a solicitor is a serious matter and will require justification by the police. A confession obtained in violation of s. 58 PACE is particularly vulnerable to challenge under both s. 76 and/or s. 78 PACE.

A suspect should be reminded at the start or re-commencement of any interview that the suspect is entitled to free legal advice and that the interview can be delayed for that purpose.

Question 6

Custody time-limits are set out in s. 42 PACE as amended by s. 7 CJA 2003. The maximum period of detention for any individual arrested but not charged in connection with an indictable offence is 36 hours. This period can be extended up to 96 hours on the authority of a magistrates' court for an indictable offence. The detention of any individual must be justified at all times under s. 37(2) PACE. The custody officer must be satisfied that detention is necessary to secure or preserve evidence relating to an offence for which the person is under arrest or to obtain such evidence by questioning. If the detention grounds are not made out, the detainee must be released immediately either with or without bail (s. 34 PACE). Where there is sufficient evidence to charge an individual, s. 37(1) PACE provides the individual must be charged and either released on bail or remanded into police cells pending an appearance before magistrates within 24 hours. Detention is subject to regular reviews, initially at six hours and thereafter at nine-hourly intervals (s. 40 PACE).

Question 7

The basic human rights to which a suspect is entitled are set out in Code C paras. 8 and 9. They include the right to an adequately heated, cleaned and ventilated cell. Access to toilet facilities must be provided. If a detainee's clothing needs to be removed, he should be supplied with adequate replacement clothing. The detainee should be provided with two light meals and one main meal in any 24-hour period. Drinks should be provided at meal times and upon reasonable request. The above safeguards underline the importance of the custody record in evidential terms. It should be a complete record of the detainee's time in detention and it should record any complaints made by the detainee (C 9.2).

In accordance with Code C 12.2, in any period of 24 hours, a suspect is entitled to a continuous period of eight hours' rest, normally at night, and under C 12.8, a suspect is entitled to breaks from interviewing at recognised meal times. Interviews should break for refreshments at two-hour intervals.

Question 8

An interview, according to Code C para. 11.1A, is the questioning of a person regarding their involvement or suspected involvement in a criminal offence which, under Code C para. 10, must be carried out under caution. Such an interview must be carried out at a police station unless the very strict conditions in Code C para. 11.1 are made out.

Question 9

Paragraph 9.5 of Code C is important. If a detainee appears to be suffering from physical illness, or is injured, or appears to be suffering from a mental disorder, or appears to need clinical attention, the custody officer must make sure the detainee receives appropriate attention as soon as reasonably practicable. Paragraph 9.13 provides that where a health care professional is called to examine or treat the offender, the custody officer shall ask for their opinion about any risks or problems the police need to take into account when making decisions about the detainee about when to carry out an interview and the need for specific safeguards. Note 9C offers the following guidance:

> 'A detainee who appears drunk or behaves abnormally may be suffering from illness, the effect of drugs or may have sustained injury, particularly a head injury which is not apparent. A detainee needing or dependent on certain drugs, including alcohol, may experience harmful effects within a short time of being deprived of their supply. In these circumstances, when there is any doubt, police should always act urgently to call an appropriate health care professional.'

Code C 12.3 is all important. Before any detainee is interviewed the custody officer shall assess whether the detainee is fit to be interviewed. In appropriate cases, the custody officer will take this decision in conjunction with a health care professional.

An omission on the part of the police to spot and deal with a particular vulnerability renders any resulting confession vulnerable to challenge under ss. 76 and 78 PACE.

Question 10

Code C para. 11.5 provides an important safeguard in relation to confession evidence by prohibiting officers from offering inducements to the suspect. It provides that no officer interviewer shall indicate, except to answer a direct question, what action the police may take if the suspect adopts a particular course of action. If the suspect asks a direct question, the interviewer may inform the suspect of what action the police propose to take, provided the action is itself proper and warranted.

The safeguards associated with the conduct of interviews of mentally vulnerable individuals are covered by Code C 11.5. Note 11 C is worth considering:

> 'Although juveniles or people who are mentally vulnerable are often capable of providing reliable evidence, they may, without knowing or wishing to do so, be particularly prone in certain circumstances to provide information that may be unreliable, misleading or self-incriminating. Special care should always be taken when questioning such a person, and the appropriate adult should be involved if there is any doubt about a person's age, mental state or capacity. Because of the risk of unreliable evidence it is important to obtain corroboration of any facts admitted wherever possible.'

Aside from the numerous safeguards already identified, juveniles and the mentally ill and mentally vulnerable are entitled to have an appropriate adult present during an interview (Code C 11.5).

EXERCISE 2: ANALYSIS OF LENNY WHYTE'S CONFESSION

The admissibility of Lenny's confession should be challenged under s. 76(2)(b) PACE (unreliability) and s. 78 PACE (unfairness).

The admissibility of Lenny's confession would be determined at a pre-trial hearing. A *voir dire* would need to be conducted, at which the judge would hear evidence as to how Lenny's confession was obtained. The prosecution would have the burden of proof under s. 76(2)(b). The prosecution would need to call the custody officers who supervised Lenny's detention, as well as the interviewing officers. In this instance, the prosecution would also need to call Dr Ghulam, who examined Lenny while he was in detention. The custody record would be an important piece of evidence at this hearing.

Given Lenny's recent psychiatric history, the defence might explore the possibility of obtaining a psychiatric report to shed light on Lenny's state of mind during his detention and in interview.

The burden of proof under s. 76(2)(b) rests on the prosecution. The prosecution would point to the fact that Lenny was offered a solicitor but declined. Furthermore, attempts were made to contact Lenny's sister. Lenny was fed and refreshed. He was given rest and his detention was properly reviewed. When the officer in charge was made aware of Lenny's mental state, he was allowed to see a doctor, who subsequently administered Lenny's medication and pronounced him fit to be interviewed. On the face of it, the prosecution would have to concede there had been a breach of the requirement to ensure access to an appropriate adult, under Code C para. 3.15, having been made aware of Lenny's mental condition. However, they can still contend that the breach did not result in an unreliable confession, nor is it one that would be unfair to admit. It is not Lenny's first experience of custody and he may be taken to know the procedures.

The defence would make much of the fact that Lenny was unrepresented at the police station and did not have the services of an appropriate adult. On oath, you would need to ask the custody officer who opened the custody record if he undertook a risk assessment of Lenny Whyte in accordance with the requirement under Code C paras. 3.6– 3.10 and if he did, why Lenny's vulnerability was not spotted immediately. It may be that Lenny lied to the officer and simply did not make the officer aware of his particular needs. When searched, Lenny was not found to be in possession of his medication.

The defence would want to explore whether the police fully complied with s. 58 PACE. Code C para. 6.5 requires the police to be proactive in ensuring access to a solicitor. The absence of a solicitor is made worse by the fact that Lenny was not provided with the services of an appropriate adult. Having made the police aware of his mental condition, and having been examined by a police doctor, it must be put to the custody officer that there was a blatant breach of Code C 3.15. A suitable appropriate adult in this case would have been Lenny's sister. The police only tried her number once while Lenny was in custody. Furthermore, the defence would be able to point to a breach of Code C 11.15 which stipulates that a vulnerable suspect should not be interviewed in the absence of an appropriate adult for the reasons highlighted in Note 11C.

The defence would need to explore Lenny's behaviour while in custody. Did no one pick up on the fact that Lenny did not sleep and had very little to eat? Such behaviour is indicative of someone with depression. In addition, it should be put to the officers that Lenny made it clear he wanted a cigarette and that it was suggested to him that if he co-operated, his release from custody would have been speeded up. Reliance might be placed by the defence on the case of *R v Aspinall* [1999] Crim LR 741. The facts are not dissimilar.

The defence can easily establish a link in terms of cause and effect. Had a solicitor been present, the outcome for Lenny would have been different. Given Lenny's metal state and the fact that he was desirous of escaping the confines of his custody, coupled with the very serious omission to ensure access to an appropriate adult, further compounded by the lack of legal advice, Lenny's confession is both unreliable and unfair to admit. If the confession were to be excluded, a principal component of the prosecution's case would be lost.

You can chart the progress of Lenny's case through our case study, the complete version of which can be accessed from our Online Resource Centre.

online resource centre

CHAPTER 8

OBSERVATIONS ON THE IDENTIFICATION ISSUES RAISED BY *R v LENNY WHYTE*

There are three eyewitnesses in Lenny's case. We will deal with each of them in turn.

Lillian Kennedy

It is important to realise that Mrs Kennedy cannot assist the prosecution in providing any evidence as to the identity of the man who entered her property by the unlocked back door. She is able to provide a description of the burglar's accomplice, but she is not able to identify him. She does identify Lenny in a street identification. This would appear to be in compliance of Code D 3.2 as the police would not have had a known suspect in mind at this point in time. Mrs Kennedy's evidence will be that a man (whom she states was Lenny Whyte) approached her some 30 to 60 minutes before the burglary and offered her assistance with her shopping bags. This evidence (assuming she correctly identifies Lenny as being that man) does no more than place Lenny in the vicinity, though crucially not at the relevant time. Her evidence is of marginal relevance. She is able to describe what the man who offered her help was wearing, and makes specific reference to the white trainers. When she points Lenny out to the police, he is not, however, wearing white training shoes. A pair of white training shoes were subsequently recovered from Lenny's flat.

Having a known suspect in mind, the police acted correctly in arresting Lenny Whyte and arranging an identification procedure. It would have been wholly wrong for the police to have shown Mrs Lewis photographs of convicted offenders (including Lenny), having a known suspect in mind.

The evidence of Shirley Lewis is important. She purports to be able to identify Lenny Whyte as being the man she saw in Mrs Kennedy's back-garden at the relevant time. She provides the police with a description of which a written record is kept in accordance with Code D 3.1. She specifically mentions the white training shoes worn by the man she observed in the garden. She subsequently attends a video identification procedure which the police state was conducted in accordance with Code D Annex A. In the course of the video identification procedure, Mrs Lewis picks out Lenny Whyte. He is number 7 in the video line-up. Look through the video identification parade record (and remember you would be entitled to a copy of the video images). Look at the words used by Mrs Lewis when she selects Lenny's image: 'I think it is number 7. I can't be one hundred percent sure— yes 7— I recognise him now. I have seen him before.'

Was the video parade compiled in accordance with Code D Annex A? Can you point to specific breaches of Code D which could form the basis of a challenge under s. 78 PACE to the admissibility of Mrs Lewis's identification evidence? Lenny states he did not understand what was happening as regards the video parade, and that no one explained to him why he could not have an identification parade. The most disturbing aspect of Lenny's detention is that he did not have access to legal advice. He does not appear to have been present when the video parade was compiled and, as such, it will be extremely important for you to review the parade's composition in an attempt to assess its fairness.

The final eyewitness is Harold Finney. Again, he is able to provide a description of the man he observed close to the time of the burglary walking past his window and going over to a black car in the street (which the prosecution contend belongs to Lloyd Green, the suspected accomplice). Mr Finney's description is consistent with Lenny's appearance. He also mentions that the man was wearing distinctive white training shoes. Mr Finney also attends the video identification parade. Significantly, he is unable to identify Lenny.

The other evidence linking Lenny to the crime is of course his interview with the police which is considered in the context of Chapter 7 self-test questions and the circumstantial evidence relating to the footwear found in his flat. This constitutes expert opinion evidence, which is considered in Chapter 21.

CHAPTER 10

1. It is likely that, on the facts, the evidential test is satisfied assuming the prosecution is satisfied that each witness is capable of giving reliable, independent evidence. A common defence submission in a historic sexual abuse case such as this is to challenge the reliability of the witness's recollection of the incidents giving rise to the charges. The prosecution case may also be challenged by the possibility of collusion between the prosecution witnesses. If these potential difficulties are overcome, in view of the seriousness of the charges it appears to be in the public interest for Gerald to be charged and prosecuted even after taking into account Gerald's age.

2. In Debbie's case, the evidential test appears to be satisfied as the store detective will testify at trial and there is a security video tape of the alleged offence. Debbie's solicitor may however submit that given her domestic circumstances, it is not in the public interest for the prosecution to continue. You might also argue that this case is suitable for a conditional caution. If Debbie is prosecuted and she pleads guilty or is found guilty, her difficult domestic circumstances provide persuasive material to be used in your plea in mitigation before sentencing if she pleads guilty or is found guilty.

3. While it is probably in the public interest for Jim's case to continue, as disputes between neighbours should not be settled by violence, the evidential test appears not to be satisfied as the only witnesses are Sally's husband and her sons aged 19 and 21. When making representations to the CPS, Jim's solicitors would submit Jim should not be charged, because of the lack of independent, credible witnesses.

4. It is clearly in the public interest for Kyle to be charged and prosecuted. Did you identify the aggravating factors? The evidential test would have to be reviewed carefully to ensure that sufficient independent, reliable evidence was available to provide a realistic prospect of a conviction.

5. This is clearly a case of domestic violence as it comes within the term used to describe a range of behaviour often used by one person to control and dominate another, with whom they have or have had a close or family relationship. The offence includes physical, sexual, psychological and emotional violence on Patrick, by Frank, his father. Even though Patrick does not want any further action to be taken against Frank, there might be a danger that if a prosecution is not undertaken, Frank may commit further serious offences against Patrick. It is likely that both the public interest and the evidential tests are satisfied, unless Frank's solicitor can persuade the CPS that the matter might be constructively settled by reference to a third party mediation agency.

CHAPTER 12

ANALYSIS OF EXERCISES 1 AND 2

You were asked to consider two examples which will require a decision of magistrates as to whether or not bail should be granted. In each case you were asked to consider the facts from the point of view of the prosecuting solicitor and the defence solicitor. Below is a summary of the arguments likely to be advanced. The prosecution will begin each submission with an explanation of how each defendant came to be charged with the offence for which he appears and an outline of the evidence linking him to that charge. Note the interplay between the grounds for objecting to bail and the factors relied on to substantiate those grounds.

Prosecution submissions in relation to Karl Green— Exercise 1

In relation to Exercise 1, the prosecution is likely to oppose bail on the grounds that Green will abscond, commit further offences and interfere with witnesses.

The prosecution will point to the evidence and to the fact that this is a very serious offence that could still result in a murder charge and that the defendant is subject to a suspended prison sentence. What is more, the defendant is already on bail for an earlier serious offence of violence. The risk of conviction is high, so too is a lengthy custodial sentence. The prosecutor will highlight a fairly recent conviction for failing to surrender and Green's poor community ties. Taken together, these all point to a substantial risk that this defendant will abscond if released on bail.

The prosecution will further suggest that Green is likely to commit further offences if released on bail. Green is already on conditional bail for an earlier, unrelated serious allegation of assault and has already answered an allegation that he breached one of his bail conditions. The CPS will invite the court to consider his lengthy criminal record for violence. In short, Green is not a man to be trusted. The defendant lives on the same estate as the injured party and his family. Such a serious assault is likely to engender feelings of hostility on the estate and the risk of Green being drawn into further confrontations cannot be ignored. The CPS can point to the fact that the presumption in favour of bail does not apply in this case. Under s. 14 CJA 2003, bail may not be granted to an individual aged over 18 who is already on bail on the date of the offence unless there is no significant risk of him committing an offence on bail. The provision is in force in relation to offences carrying life imprisonment. Conviction for a s. 18 GBH carries such a sentence.

Finally the prosecution is likely to argue that the defendant will interfere with prosecution witnesses. The defendant has a lengthy record consisting of violent assaults and is evidently easily provoked. One of the witnesses is a friend of the injured party who lives in close proximity to the defendant.

Defence submissions in relation to Karl Green—Exercise 1

The defence solicitor would be faced with an uphill task in this case. One thing the solicitor should have done is to contact Green's sister, who lives some ten miles outside the area for confirmation of an offer of alternative accommodation. We will assume such an offer has been made.

The defence solicitor would remind the magistrates of the fact that they have heard only one side of the case. Green's intention is to plead not guilty, maintaining he acted in self-defence. It is a defence he put forward at the police station and he has a witness to substantiate his version of events.

Taking each of the prosecution's objections in sequence and dealing with the risk of absconding, the defence solicitor would point out that Green has had ample opportunity to run and hide between the occurrence of the incident and his subsequent arrest. He has strong community ties, having been born in the area. He has a son he sees regularly and a job which will be lost if he is remanded into custody. He has only one previous conviction for failing to surrender. The defence solicitor should explain the circumstances surrounding

this and stress the fact of Green having voluntarily surrendered at the time and in turn receiving a fine.

So far as the danger that he might commit further offences is concerned, again he denies intentionally assaulting the injured party and has not of course been convicted of any offence arising out of the incident at the pub. He cannot deny the fact that he is on conditional bail for a further assault. All the defence solicitor can say about that, is that he accepts some level of criminal responsibility and awaits his deserved punishment. The offence was unforgivable but was committed while Green was very drunk. The defence solicitor will have to try to put a positive spin on Green's criminal past, highlighting what, if anything, has changed since they were committed. Unfortunately some of his previous convictions are fairly recent. The defence solicitor should deal with the earlier breach of bail conditions, stressing the mitigating factors that were obviously accepted by the court. It is not evident that Green is in the habit of committing offences while on bail.

So far as interfering with witnesses is concerned, the defence solicitor will put forward an adamant denial that this would happen, as Green would not wish to make matters worse for himself.

The best that Green could possibly hope for in this case is the grant of bail subject to stringent conditions. The defence solicitor might suggest a condition of residence at the sister's address. This would deal in part with the risk of failing to surrender and the risk of the commission of further offences due to possible confrontations. It would also help to deal with the risk of interference with witnesses. No doubt, Green would be prepared to agree with any condition that kept him out of prison including a condition of reporting to his local police station, a condition of no contact with prosecution witnesses and a curfew. In the cirumstances, however, bail is likely to be refused.

Exercise 2—Prosecution submissions in relation to Daniel Phillips

In relation to Exercise 2 the prosecution is likely to argue that Daniel may abscond, commit further offences and interfere with the injured party. The allegation against Daniel is extremely serious and he is currently subject to a suspended sentence of imprisonment. The CPS will point to the circumstantial evidence against Daniel Phillips linking him to the crime scene and his no comment interview at the police station. It took three days in which to locate Mr Phillips, as he was not residing at his mother's address. The risk of conviction is high, as is the prospect of a prison sentence.

So far as the commission of further offences and interference with prosecution witnesses is concerned, the prosecution will make plain the injured party's feelings in this case. The defendant's behaviour would suggest he is an obsessive individual with little respect for authority. He is charged with resisting arrest on this occasion and has previously breached a court order. He is subject to a restraining order preventing him from harassing Ms Hughes. He clearly cannot leave her alone. With the restraining order in force there would seem to be little point in imposing a condition that he does not contact Ms Hughes. The risk that he may seek to harm Ms Hughes or interfere with her is extremely high.

Defence submissions in relation to Daniel Phillips

On a practical point, if the defence solicitor can persuade Daniel's new girlfriend and her mother to attend court, so much the better.

The defence solicitor should remind the magistrates of the presumption in favour of bail. The defence advocate should challenge the nature of the prosecution's case against Daniel. He will no doubt point out that there is no forensic evidence to connect him to the crime scene and that he was advised not to answer questions at the police station on legal advice. The only evidence against him is the tenuous nature of a voice identification by a witness who is not certain. He is likely to stress that the earlier access visit went off without any difficulties and that he would have no reason to want to burn down Ms Hughes's house. What is more, he has an alibi (his girlfriend and her mother) who will say he could not possibly have been setting fire to his former girlfriend's home. Consequently, he will not abscond because he has little fear of being convicted. He is able to offer a fixed address and has a job, which will be lost if he is remanded into custody. He will not abscond because his son is important to him. Furthermore, his new girlfriend is pregnant with his child and needs his support.

So far as the risk of him committing further offences is concerned, the defence solicitor will say that these are a thing of the past. He is abiding by the terms of his restraining order, which remains in force. He is benefiting from the input of the probation service and is addressing the reasons for his past offending.

The defence solicitor is likely to offer bail conditions to include residing at his current address, reporting to his local police station and a condition that he does not contact Ms Hughes or her friend.

Decision of the court in each case

In relation to Karl Green, the magistrates remand him into custody and send the case forthwith to the Crown Court. Their reasons for doing so are the substantial risk that the defendant will abscond having regard to the very serious nature of the allegation and the risk of him committing further offences, in the light of his criminal record and the fact that he is already on bail for a similar serious allegation of assault. They are not convinced that the imposition of conditions would alleviate their concerns. Karl Green may consider making an application for bail to a Crown Court judge in chambers.

In relation to Daniel Phillips, after some deliberation the magistrates decide to grant him bail conditional on him residing at the address of his girlfriend's mother, reporting to his local police station three times a week and a further condition that he should keep away from and not try to contact Rachel Hughes or her friend. In their view, the imposition of conditions would alleviate the risk of Mr Phillips committing further offences and interfering with prosecution witnesses.

CHAPTER 13

EXERCISE 1

Gordon Davey should be advised to elect trial by jury in any event. He stands a greater chance of being acquitted of this offence before a jury of his peers. However, Gordon Davey may feel he would rather the matter be tried summarily as his ordeal will be over more quickly and with less publicity.

There are no current National Mode of Trial Guidelines specifically on the offence with which Gordon is charged. However its predecessor is the offence of indecent assault and there are Mode of Trial Guidelines on this.

It is likely that the CPS will represent that this case is suitable for summary trial. Although there are the presence of some aggravating features identified in the National Mode of Trial Guidelines—see Appendix 2 (the age disparity between the perpetrator and his victim and the defendant's position of trust as the uncle of the girl) this would appear to be a one-off offence where the nature of the indecent assault is relatively minor and no injury has been caused. In these circumstances a maximum sentence of six months' imprisonment is likely to be sufficient.

If Gordon wishes to consent to summary trial, it would be unnecessary for you to make any representations save to agree with the CPS that in your view, the matter is suitable for summary disposal. Only if the CPS were to invite the Bench to decline jurisdiction, with Gordon wishing to have the matter tried summarily, would it be necessary for you to make representations as to why the case can be dealt with summarily. This would require you to play down any aggravating features of this indecent assault.

It is likely that the magistrates will accept jurisdiction on the basis that there are few aggravating factors and their power to impose a current maximum custodial sentence of six months on a finding of guilt is likely to be adequate.

The magistrates' decision

If the magistrates decide that the offence is suitable for summary trial, the clerk will tell Gordon of the court's view and inform him that if he consents, he can be tried summarily but, if he chooses, he may elect to trial by jury instead.

Gordon must also be told that if he is tried by the magistrates and found guilty, information about his character and antecedents will be obtained, and that if, because of these, the magistrates consider their powers of punishment are inadequate, he may be committed to the Crown Court for sentence. This procedure is mandatory and failure to follow it amounts to procedural *ultra vires*. Any conviction obtained in breach of the legal adviser giving this warning is liable to be quashed when challenged in judicial review proceedings.

The legal adviser will then put Gordon to his election by asking him whether he wishes to be tried by the magistrates or before a jury. Only if Gordon consents to trial in the magistrates' court may the magistrates proceed to summary trial. If Gordon does not give his consent, MCA 1980, s. 20 requires the case to be tried in the Crown Court.

EXERCISE 2

All the offences are triable either way. The magistrates' maximum powers of sentence on conviction for two or more either-way offences would currently be 12 months. It is most likely that the CPS will invite the magistrates to decline jurisdiction on the basis that their powers of sentence will be insufficient and that there are likely to be factual complexities in this case. Given Simon's denial and his complete lack of any previous convictions, he would be best advised to elect trial by jury in the Crown Court in any event.

As this is theft in breach of trust committed over a period of months, totalling a not insubstantial amount of money, the magistrates are likely to decline jurisdiction, in which case Simon will have no choice and the matter will be adjourned and a date set for his committal to the Crown Court.

EXERCISE 3

Wayne Mason is charged with an either-way offence and two summary-only offences which will mean that, in the event of conviction, magistrates could impose a maximum sentence of six months only. The CPS might take the view that the magistrates' powers of sentence in this instance are likely to be sufficient, notwithstanding the presence of aggravating features in the dangerous driving offence. However, this is a borderline case and the CPS could invite the court to decline jurisdiction on the basis of those aggravating features.

At present Wayne Mason intends to plead not guilty. He is faced with a tricky choice if the magistrates accept jurisdiction. His chances of acquittal are higher in the Crown Court than in the magistrates; however, the Crown Court is likely to impose a harsher sentence in the event of conviction. If he wishes to be tried summarily in the face of contrary views from the CPS, his solicitor will have to make representations as to why the either-way offence of dangerous driving can be dealt with summarily. In this regard, the solicitor would need to play down the aggravating features in order to persuade the Bench that their sentencing power of six months for all offences would be sufficient. If Wayne is intent on trial in the Crown Court in any event, defence representations are unnecessary in this instance.

Were Wayne to indicate a guilty plea he would be tried summarily with the possible risk of a committal to the Crown Court for sentence (s. 3 PCC(S)A 2000.) However, with the availability of a six-month maximum sentence and a one-third discount for a timely guilty plea, the magistrates would arguably have sufficient powers to sentence.

In the event of Wayne maintaining his not guilty plea, the decision would be that of the magistrates. Applying the National Mode of Trial Guidelines, the presumption would be in favour of summary disposal. However there are some aggravating factors in relation to the either-way matter, including grossly excessive speed and the presence of alcohol. It would be a debateable decision in this case.

When the increased powers of sentence available to magistrates contained in the CJA 2003 are implemented there would be no question that their powers of sentence would be sufficient. If the dangerous driving allegation was committed to the Crown Court, the TWOC offence could be included for trial on the indictment in accordance with s. 40 Criminal Justice Act 1988 (CJA) and the driving with no insurance could be sent for plea under s. 41 CJA 1988—see para. 13.19.

CHAPTER 14

To ascertain the disclosure requirements, firstly determine the classification of the offence Barry is charged with. Rape is an indictable-only offence.

Advance information is likely to be forthcoming in the early stages of this case. Following Barry's initial appearance before magistrates his case will be sent forthwith to the Crown Court. Within 70 days of the case being sent you are entitled to disclosure of the prosecution's case (used material). This is likely to comprise the witness statements of Tina, Kelly, Leroy, relevant staff at the care-home to whom she made the complaint, the medical and forensic evidence, the statement of the investigating officers, the record of interview with Barry and any items of real evidence.

Let us say that the medical/forensic evidence reveals traces of seminal fluid inside Tina and on her clothing. DNA extracted from the seminal fluid matches the known sample of DNA taken from Barry. The medical evidence also shows Tina to be eight weeks pregnant at the time when the alleged incident occurred.

On taking Barry's further instructions in the light of this evidence, Barry now admits to having had sexual intercourse with Tina, but only with her consent and in return for payment in the public toilets. After having sex, Barry states Tina rejoined her friend, Kelly. Barry denies pestering Tina for sex. His reason for lying to you in the first place is that he is embarrassed to admit to having had under-age sex with the girl. He did not think she would make a complaint.

Having served you with the 'case-sent bundle', the CPS provide you with a schedule of 'unused' material as defined under s. 3 CPIA 1996. At this stage the prosecution discloses to you that Kelly, Tina's friend, has a previous conviction for theft and that Leroy has previous convictions for public order offences and theft. Such information satisfies the test of evidence that might reasonably be considered capable of undermining the case for the prosecution.

The pre-trial disclosure of the evidence in this case has helped to narrow the facts in issue in that the act of sexual intercourse is admitted but what is in dispute is whether Tina consented.

As this matter is indictable only, Barry will need to file a defence statement (s. 5 CPIA 1996). You will need to draft this carefully. Clearly he will indicate his intention to plead not guilty to rape on the basis that Tina consented to sexual intercourse and that sexual intercourse was offered to him by Tina in return for payment on one occasion only. He will deny any suggestion that he has been pestering Tina for sex. Will you go so far as to suggest Tina is falsely accusing Barry of rape and that you have reason to believe she has made a proven false allegation against another male in the past? If you want to obtain further disclosure on this, you will need to articulate it.

Service of the defence statement will cause the prosecution to look again at disclosure to see if there is anything that might reasonably assist Barry's defence as articulated in his statement (s. 7A CPIA 1996).

Barry defence statement clearly raises issues to do with Tina's credibility. As a child in the care of the local authority there will be a social service file on her which should contain an account of the alleged incident involving the male care-worker together with an assessment of Tina's personality. This is information which lies in the hands of a third party that you would presumably like to have access to. It may in fact be in the hands of the prosecution if the prosecution has sought access to it.

The prosecution and social services are likely to oppose disclosure on the ground of public interest immunity. The information is sensitive. It concerns a child and there are clearly issues of confidentiality. If the material is in the hands of the prosecution, it will need to apply to the court to sanction the withholding of such material. Notice of the application should be given to the defence to enable you to make representations. Representations may also be made by social services. Disclosure will be ordered if the judge concludes the information contained within the file would help to avoid a miscarriage of justice. If the material is in the hands of social service with disclosure being resisted, the defence will need to apply for a witness summons against social services. The same issues as regard public interest immunity will apply *R v Brushett* [2001] Crim LR 471.

CHAPTER 15

1. Two or more informations may be tried together in circumstances where the court considers it is in the interest of justice. Guidance on the application of the interest of justice in this context is provided by the decision of the House of Lords in *Chief Constable of Norfolk v Clayton* [1983] 2 AC 473.

2. The defence advocate will be aware of the prosecution's case because he will have sought disclosure of used material under Part 21 Crim PR. Where a defendant pleads not guilty to a case that is to be tried summarily, the CPIA 1996 requires the CPS to make disclosure of unused material (s. 3 CPIA 1996) that would reasonably be considered capable of undermining the case for the prosecution or assisting the case of the accused. The defendant has the option of submitting a defence statement in a summary case (s. 6 CPIA). Any further disclosure which might assist the defence articulated will only be forthcoming if a defence statement has been served (s. 7A CPIA).

3. The attendance of a witness can be secured by the issue of a witness summons under the procedure set out in s. 97 MCA 1980 and Part 28 Crim PR.

4. The role and responsibilities of the legal adviser or justices' clerk are briefly outlined in Chapter 1, para. 1.9.3. The role of the legal adviser is to advise the magistrates on law, practice and procedure. The legal adviser plays no part in decisions on fact. The legal adviser will effectively run the court, keeping a written record of the proceedings and offering assistance to unrepresented defendants.

5. A submission of no case to answer is usually made at the close of the prosecution's case in circumstances where the defence contends there is no evidence to prove an essential element of the charge against the defendant or the evidence adduced by the prosecution has been so discredited as a result of cross-examination or is so manifestly unreliable that no reasonable tribunal could safely convict upon it.

CHAPTER 16

1. All defendants appear initially before a magistrates' court. In a case where the defendant is alleged to have committed an indictable-only offence, the magistrates will send the case forthwith to the Crown Court. Matters relating to representation orders and the defendant's bail status in the meantime will be determined at the initial appearance before magistrates.

2. The prosecution must make disclosure of all used material in its case sent bundle or committal bundle. Thereafter it comes under obligations to make available unused material in accordance with the requirements of the Criminal Procedure and Investigation Act 1996. The requirement to file a defence statement is compulsory in cases to be tried on indictment (s. 5 CPIA 1996).

3. Where the defence concludes that the prosecution's pre-trial disclosure does not disclose a case to answer, written or oral application can be made under Sch. 3 CDA 1998 (see Part 13 Crim PR). Oral evidence may be given at this hearing only with leave of the judge.

4. The primary purpose of the PCMH is to allow the Crown Court to engage in effective trial management of the case. The hearing will identify the issues that are in dispute. A defendant will be required to enter a plea. In the event of the plea being not guilty, the judge ought to be in a position to set a firm trial date and to make binding rulings on any points of law that are in dispute.

5. Preparatory hearings are reserved for long and complex cases to be tried in the Crown Court.

CHAPTER 17

1. The bill of indictment is the document that contains the charges against the defendant on which he is arraigned at the commencement of a trial on indictment.

2. More than one offence may be charged in the same indictment where the offences are either founded on the same facts; or form or are part of a series of offences of the same or similar nature, r. 9, Indictment Rules 1971. In *Ludlow v MPC* (1970) 54 Cr App R 233, the House of Lords held that for offences to be similar there must be some nexus between them both in terms of law and fact.

3. For a submission of no case to answer to succeed before a Crown Court judge, the defence advocate must satisfy the test laid down in *R v Galbraith* [1981] 2 All ER 1060 (see para. 17.10).

4. There is a strict separation of function between judge and jury in the Crown Court. The jury determines all issues of fact, while the judge determines all issues of law. Whenever a point of law arises it must be aired in the absence of the jury. This protects the jury from hearing what might be prejudicial information regarding the defendant. Generally speaking, most issues of law, particularly disputed evidence, are resolved before trial at a pre-trial hearing. Sometimes, a *voir dire* (or trial within a trial) is required to determine admissibility of evidence.

5. The trial judge oversees the trial process. It is the duty of the trial judge to ensure the defendant enjoys a fair trial. At the conclusion of the trial the trial judge sums up the case for the jury. The summing-up is important because it represents the last words said in the trial. The judge will remind the jury of the evidence they have heard and crucially, he will direct them on the law. Any errors or omissions during the summing up may provide a convicted defendant with grounds for appeal.

6. An attendance certificate is granted by a judge in the Crown Court and ensures payment by the LSC for the services of a solicitor or other legal representative at the Crown Court attending counsel.

CHAPTER 18

QUESTION 1

The general rule in a criminal case is that the prosecution bears the burden of proving a defendant's guilt beyond reasonable doubt. It is known as the legal burden of proof and it requires the prosecution to prove the essential elements of the offence charged. The principle is enshrined in *Woolmington v DPP* [1935] AC 463 and is consistent with the presumption of innocence safeguarded by Article 6(2) ECHR.

QUESTION 2

Reverse onus clauses refer to those instances in which a legal burden of proof is cast on a defendant to effectively prove his innocence. A statutory section may impose a legal burden of proof on a defendant expressly or by implication. A number of different statutes impose a legal burden of proof on a defendant. For this reason, it is always important to research the elements of the offence with which your client is suspected of or with which he is charged.

QUESTION 3

The current guidelines are contained in the Court of Appeal's judgment in *Attorney-General's Reference (No. 1 of 2004)* [2004] 1 WLR 2111. Relevant factors include:

- the definition of the offence and the elements the prosecution must prove;
- the ease with which a defendant can establish a particular defence;
- whether the offence is of a regulatory nature;
- the severity of the penalty that conviction carries;
- whether the imposition of a legal burden of proof is proportionate to the aim of the legislation and if it is not, whether it can be read down to impose an evidential burden of proof only.

CHAPTER 19

David is charged with indecent assault on his stepdaughter, Florence aged 14. Florence has learning difficulties. David is pleading not guilty. The prosecution have witness statements from Susie, David's wife and their son, Aaron aged seven.

(a) Susie is a competent witness for the prosecution and in view of the offence with which David is charged is also compellable— see s. 80(3) PACE.

(b) Florence will be presumed competent to give sworn evidence under s. 55(3) YJCEA as she is aged 14.

(c) We are told that Florence has learning difficulties. If there is reason to doubt her competency to give evidence, the test that needs to be satisfied is laid down in s. 53(3). The court will need to ascertain whether Florence can understand questions put to her and give answers that can be understood. In determining these questions, the court must treat Florence as having the benefit of a special measures direction under s. 19. As Florence is over 14 she will give sworn evidence. If it transpires however that she is competent in accordance with s. 53(3) but is unable to satisfy the test for sworn evidence (she does not have sufficient appreciation of the solemnity of the occasion and the added responsibility to tell the truth— s. 55(2)) she will be permitted to give unsworn evidence under s. 56 YJCEA.

(d) As Aaron is under 14, s. 53 YJCEA presumes that he is competent to give unsworn evidence under s. 56 YJCEA.

(e) Both witnesses will be eligible to give evidence under a special measures direction under s. 16 YJCEA. Aaron is a witness under 17, as is Florence. In addition, Florence suffers from a mental disorder with the result that her evidence is likely to be diminished as a consequence. Where the court considers that a special measures direction is likely to improve the quality of the evidence given by the witness, the court must make the appropriate order (s. 19(2)). Additionally, both fall within the definition of a child witness requiring special protection within the meaning of s. 21. This provision makes video-recorded examination-in-chief and further examination via live link a requirement of the special measures direction.

CASE STUDY *R v LENNY WHYTE*

The only witness, who on the face of it, might be considered eligible for a special measures direction is Lillian Kennedy, the 84-year-old victim of the burglary offence. She might come within the definition of an intimated witness if the court considers that the quality of her evidence is likely to be diminished by reason of fear or distress in connection with testifying in the proceedings. Regard will be had to Mrs Kennedy's age in determining this. If the court considers a special measures direction is likely to improve the quality of the evidence given by the witness, the court must make the appropriate order (s. 19(2)).

CHAPTER 20

1. Generally no— leading questions are not permitted in examination-in-chief except by agreement and most often in relation to introductory matters at the beginning of a witness's evidence.

2. Under s. 139 Criminal Justice Act 2003, a witness is entitled to refresh his memory from a document while testifying provided the document was made or verified by the witness on an earlier occasion and the witness states in his oral evidence that the document records his recollection of the matter at the earlier time; and his recollection of the matters about which he is testifying is likely to have been significantly better at that time than it is at the time of his oral evidence.

3. A hostile witness is a witness who shows no desire to tell the truth at the behest of the party calling him.

4. Cross-examination has a number of purposes including obtaining factual evidence from the witness that supports the case of the cross-examiner. It also enables the advocate to test the truthfulness of the evidence the witness has given in examination-in-chief or to cast doubt on the witness's evidence; and to undermine the witness's credibility.

5. A collateral issue (such as an issue relating to a witness's credibility) runs alongside the main issues in the case.

6. An allegation of recent fabrication on the part of a witness can be rebutted during re-examination by adducing evidence of a previous consistent statement made by the witness.

7. Unless the prosecution agree to the defence adducing evidence of Ben and Chris's previous convictions, leave of the court under s. 100 CJA 2003 will need to be sought. Arguably, the evidence does have substantial probative value in relation to a matter of substantial importance having regard to Kyle's defence.

8. Yes. The main protagonists contradict each other. Their respective veracity is therefore a matter of sub-stantial importance. A single conviction for perjury arguably shows a propensity to lie on oath. Account would have to be taken perhaps of the reasons why the offence was committed. Nevertheless, on the facts, the conviction has substantial probative value on a matter of substantial importance in the case.

CHAPTER 21

SCENARIO

Stefan was represented at the police station. However, there does not seem to be any dispute arising out of the composition of the video parade. The only concern is that the victim was shown photographs prior to the video identification procedure. If (as it seems) Stefan was a known suspect, Code D 3.3 prohibits a witness from being shown photographs where the suspect is known and available. The police may suggest that they were concerned about the victim's condition and the delay in securing a positive identification; however, this would appear to be a *prima facie* breach of Code D. The defence advocate will want to make a submission under s. 78 PACE, that the victim's evidence of identification be excluded (see Chapter 8).

The CCTV footage constitutes real evidence from which the jury is able to draw its own conclusion. Is this a situation in which the jury would benefit from having expert evidence? It depends on the quality of the CCTV stills. If the footage is blurred, expert evidence may be admitted to assist the jury. Would Sergeant Taylor be deemed competent? This would be a matter for the judge. It will depend on the sergeant's experience (see *R v Clare and Peach* [1995] 2 Cr App R 333). It will be a matter for the jury as to how much weight it chooses to attribute to the sergeant's opinion evidence.

Assuming the trial judge refuses to exclude the evidence and the matter is left to the jury, a full Turnbull warning will need to be given. This is a case in which Stefan disputes the identification of him. He relies on alibi to suggest he was somewhere other than at the scene of the crime at the relevant time. If the judge concludes the evidence of identification is weak but is supported or indeed, if the evidence is good, he can safely leave it to the jury directing them in accordance with the Turnbull guidelines. Evidence that supports the correctness of the victim's identification in this case, could come from the evidence of Andrew, the co-accused and from the refusal by Stefan to answer questions at the police station (s. 34 CJPOA 1994—see Chapter 5). A specific weakness with regard to the evidence in this case would include the fact that it had been obtained in breach of Code D. The judge would need to explain why this is an important factor for the jury to have regard too (see *R v Forbes* [2001] 1 AC 473—Chapter 8).

Is this a case which calls for a corroboration warning? Did you consider that Andrew's evidence might be regarded as tainted? Andrew is an accomplice. He is jointly charged with the offence but has chosen to plead guilty to a less serious offence and has given evidence for the prosecution, directly implicating Stefan in the more serious offence. Stefan suggests Andrew is lying and that in addition, because of his sister's involvement with an officer in the case, he is motivated to give false evidence against Stefan. The defence advocate will no doubt suggest to the judge that there is an evidential basis in this case, in accordance with the principles in *R v Makanjuola* [1995] 3 All ER 730 for a corroboration warning to be given. It is a matter for the trial judge as to whether he gives such a warning and what form that warning will take.

R v LENNY WHYTE

This is a case *par excellence* where a Turnbull warning would be appropriate if the matter were to be left to the jury. You will recall that we have previously considered the evidence of identification in this case (see Chapter 8).

As Lenny disputes the eye-witness identification of him, the trial judge would be required to direct the jury in accordance with *R v Turnbull* [1977] QB 224.

Expert evidence features in this case. Consider the statement of Sarah Hardacker (disclosed in the committal bundle) and the statement of Dr Samantha Leighton (disclosed as part of unused material under the CPIA 1996). Both of these witnesses are experts in their particular field. Ms Hardacker's s. 9 CJA 1967 statement lists her qualifications and experience. The primary facts from which Ms Hardacker provides her opinion (the lifted set of prints) are proved by the evidence of Carol Jane Lawton, a scene of crime officer. Ms Hardacker's evidence is required in this case as the process of comparing the print with the shoes found in Lenny Whyte's property is a matter falling outside the competency of the court. Ms Hardacker's conclusion that the shoes are responsible for leaving the prints outside the burgled property is strongly expressed. However, the evidence of Dr Leighton must be borne in mind. Lenny Whyte states he has never worn the shoes found at his flat. Dr Leighton, an expert in DNA evidence was unable to find any of Lenny's DNA in the shoe.

CHAPTER 22

For the prosecution to rely simply on Duane's written statement creates a problem of hearsay. Hearsay evidence is generally inadmissible unless it can be brought within a common law or statutory exception.

The relevant statutory provision would be s. 117(4) CJA 2003 as this is a statement prepared in contemplation of criminal proceedings. The reason for the witness's unavailability would be due to the witness's fear. Duane is clearly an identifiable witness and we will assume he had the requisite capability at the time he made the statement. As the prosecution would be relying on fear as the condition for admitting Duane's written statement, fear needs to be proved and leave to admit the statement would be required. Under s. 116(4) CJA 2003, leave will only be granted if the court considers that it would be in the interests of justice to admit the statement having regard to:

(a)   the statement's contents;

(b)   to any risk that its admission or exclusion will result in unfairness to any party (with particular reference to how difficult it will be to challenge the statement if the relevant person does not give evidence);

(c)   in appropriate cases to the fact that a special measures direction could be made in relation to the relevant person;

(d)   any other relevant circumstance.

If leave is granted, Duane's written statement will be admissible under s. 117(4). We are told that Duane is an important witness in this case. Would the admission of his evidence prejudice a fair trial? Regard would be had to the safeguards applicable. The defendants can of course give evidence themselves or call evidence of alibi. Wayne's credibility can still be attacked if there is evidence available to undermine his credibility. The judge retains discretion under s. 78 PACE 1984 to exclude the evidence if he concludes its admission would prejudice a fair trial and in directing the jury, the judge will stress the limitations of evidence that has not been subject to cross-examination. The prosecution would need to establish and the court would need to be satisfied that every effort has been made to persuade Duane to give evidence with the benefit of special measures. On the assumption that Duane's evidence is not the only evidence in the case against the defendants, his evidence is likely to be admitted as hearsay.

CHAPTER 23

1. The prosecution would seek admission of Aaron's previous conviction under s. 103(1)(a). It is relevant to an important matter in issue in that it is deemed to establish a propensity to deal in drugs. It makes Aaron's defence less credible in the circumstances. The defence should oppose its admission. The defence could argue that one previous conviction does not amount to a propensity and that the circumstances surrounding the earlier offence do not indicate a propensity to supply on a commercial basis and that it would therefore be unfair to admit the evidence. The scenario is in fact taken from the case of *R v Atkinson* [2006] EWCA Crim 1424 in which the Court of Appeal concluded the evidence ought not to have been admitted as it did not disclose a propensity on A's part.

2(a) The prosecution could argue that Brian's previous conviction for unlawful sexual intercourse is an offence in the same category (see Secretary of State's Order in relation to child sex offences) and that it shows a predisposition on Brian's part towards a sexual interest in young girls giving him a motive for the commission of this offence. The conviction is relatively recent.

Would the defence advocate apply to have the earlier conviction deemed inadmissible? The defence advocate ought to. In what sense does Brian's earlier conviction show a predisposition on his part towards rape? Rape implies the use of force. It is not suggested that Brian is predisposed towards the use of violence. It is not suggested that he used violence in relation to his earlier offence. Having been charged and convicted of unlawful sexual intercourse, the sexual acts would have taken place with his victim's consent. Arguably the conditions of s. 101(1)(d) are not met, and even if they are, the defence would strongly argue that the probative value of such a previous conviction in this context would be outweighed by its prejudicial effect, (s. 101(3)). It would be pertinent to ask how old Brian was when he committed the offence of unlawful sexual intercourse. If he was a young man, the point made by the prosecution that it shows he has a sexual interest in young girls is not entirely accurate.

The criteria for admission under s. 101(1)(d) is whether the evidence is relevant to an important matter in issue. The matter in issue is whether Brian's victim consented. The question the advocate should require the court to ask itself is: Does the earlier previous conviction make it more likely that Brian is guilty of the current charge? The answer the defence advocate will be seeking in this instance is—no.

2(b) The prosecution would strongly argue that it should be. It is an offence of the same description and it arguably shows a predisposition on Brian's part to the use of sexual violence against females. It is relevant to a crucial fact in issue, namely whether the victim did consent. Equally, the prosecution could argue that Brian's previous conviction shows a propensity to be untruthful as his defence was disbelieved on an earlier occasion.

In this instance, the defence would have to stress the prejudicial effect such knowledge would have on the jury. The circumstances of each rape would need to be very carefully examined and an important consideration would be the strength of the prosecution's case without the evidence of bad character (applying *Hanson*).

3. An accused person cannot be forced to give evidence in support of his defence. If he chooses not to give evidence without good cause, an adverse inference can be drawn against him under s. 35 CJPOA. Given the nature of Tina's defence, there is an argument for suggesting that Barry needs to give evidence in order to advance his account. Barry stands to have his previous convictions exposed under s. 101(1)(e) as defined by s. 104 CJA 2003, irrespective of whether he chooses to give evidence or not. Tina's advocate would argue that Barry's previous convictions have substantial probative value in relation to an important matter in issue, namely who inflicted the injury to the child and who is more likely to be telling the truth. Given the inevitable prejudice to Barry, the trial judge would have to be satisfied that his previous convictions do have substantial probative value in the context of the case. It would be entirely up to the jury what inference they choose to draw from the knowledge of Barry's previous convictions if they are admitted.

4. Danielle is entitled to a good character direction in accordance with the decision in *R v Vye*. It is relevant to the likelihood of her having committed the offence and, if she gives evidence on oath, it is also relevant to her credibility as a witness. The evidential effect of good character would have to be made clear to the jury in the judge's direction.

R v LENNY WHYTE

You will recall that Lenny Whyte faces an allegation of burglary, which he denies. His defence is mistaken identity. Lenny has several previous convictions for burglary and theft related offences. Under s. 101(1)(d) CJA 2003 the prosecution could argue that Lenny's previous convictions show a propensity on his part to commit offences of a dishonest nature and a propensity to be untruthful. They place Lenny in a class of people more likely to have been in Mrs Kennedy's back garden at the relevant time than the average member of the public. Lenny's propensity gives context to his defence.

The defence would need to argue that propensity evidence is simply not relevant to the facts in issue in this case, namely whether the evidence of identification is correct. Even if they assume some relevance, their admission would have an adverse effect on the fairness of the proceedings (s. 101(3)) that they should be excluded. The defence will want to place reliance on *Hanson*. The defence will need to examine the circumstances of Lenny's earlier offences and whether he pleaded guilty or was found guilty having given evidence at trial. A relevant consideration would be the strength of the prosecution's case. *Hanson* stipulates that bad character evidence should not be admitted to bolster a weak prosecution case. The question of admissibility would be determined at the pre-trial hearing. Lenny's case illustrates the potential danger of the new law. If Lenny's previous convictions are admitted, his chances of being convicted are greatly increased.

CHAPTER 24

1. No—only those communications between a solicitor and client that involve the giving or obtaining of legal advice.

2. The test requires the dominant purpose of the communication to be in connection with pending or actual litigation.

3. Legal privilege vests in the client.

4. The privilege against self-incrimination allows a witness to refuse to answer a question, which in the opinion of the judge, would expose the witness to the possibility of any criminal charge under United Kingdom law. It also extends to a defendant who has been compelled to answer questions as part of an extra judicial-investigation where, at a subsequent criminal prosecution, the prosecution seeks to use the answers given in evidence against the defendant.

CHAPTER 25

The starting point in terms of sentence upon conviction for s. 47 OAPA 1861 assault, according to the Magistrates' Court Sentencing Guidelines, is a custodial sentence of 12 months with a range up to 24 months. Applying the principles in the Criminal Justice Act 2003 under s. 143(1), Scott should be sentenced on his culpability in committing the offence and the harm he has caused. His actions would appear to be intentional and injury has resulted as a consequence of his actions. Statutory aggravating factors in Scott's case include:

- s. 143(2) CJA 2003—he has previous offences of a like nature;
- s. 143(3)—he committed this offence while on bail;
- s. 145—the offence would appear to be racially motivated.

Having regard to the MCSGs (2008) on s 47 assault, specifically Annex (B), the relevant aggravating factors specific to this offence are the fact that the disturbance involved a group and that the victim was kicked. This is a case where the magistrates will consider their power to impose a maximum sentence of six months to be insufficient. They should commit Scott to the Crown Court for sentence. It is likely that an 'all options' pre-sentence report would be requested. Regard would be had to any personal offender mitigation Scott might put forward. He would not be entitled to a sentencing discount because he did not plead guilty.

ANALYSIS OF CASE STUDIES

R v Roger Martin

Aside from the road traffic offences committed by Mr Martin, he faces the potential of six months in custody for the offence of common assault. As he intends to plead guilty, he will of course receive a discount. If one looks at the offence of common assault in the Magistrates' Court Sentencing Guidelines, the guideline sentence for a first time offender is a community penalty. Aggravating factors would include the injury caused to the victim. It should also be borne in mind that this assault was committed in the context of road rage. A little research on this point will reveal that such matters are taken very seriously by the courts. Consider para. B 2.3 in *Blackstone's Criminal Practice*:

'In *Fenton* (1994) 15 Cr App R (S) 682 the offender pleaded guilty to common assault (charges of assault occasioning actual bodily harm and dangerous driving were not proceeded with). In the course of an altercation between motorists, the offender pushed the victim in the chest. The Court of Appeal said that almost all cases of violence between motorists would be so serious that only custody could be justified. The appropriate sentence was seven days' imprisonment. See also *Ross* (1994) 15 Cr App R (S) 384.'

The above underlines the importance of researching any available sentencing guidelines. In terms of mitigating factors, the fact that Roger Martin's actions were impulsive, that he was provoked and that it was a single blow would be relevant. Given the distinct possibility of a custodial sentence, a pre-sentence report should be ordered.

We will assume that having entered a guilty plea, the magistrates adjourn sentence and order a pre-sentence report, keeping all of their sentencing options open. We ask you to complete the chapters on sentencing before viewing the final sentencing hearing in relation to Roger Martin.

R v William Hardy

The predecessor to s. 9(2) Sexual Offences Act 2003 is s. 6 of the Sexual Offences (Amendment) Act 1956, defined as being the offence of unlawful sexual intercourse with a girl under the age of 16 which attracted a maximum custodial sentence of six months in the magistrates' court and a maximum sentence of two years in the Crown Court. As the offence under s. 9 SOA 2003 involves penetration of the victim (albeit with her consent), the offence can only be tried on indictment and the maximum sentence for this offence has increased to 14 years! This is clearly a serious offence.

If you have accessed the Sentencing Guidelines Council website, you will have seen that the SGC has recently published its definitive guidelines on sexual offences. The guidelines should be referred to in the course of the sentencing hearing and any relevant Court of Appeal cases that have considered s. 9 SOA 2003 offences. In relation to s. 9 SOA, the SGC makes the following observations:

'The culpability of the offender will be the primary indicator of offence seriousness, and the nature of the sexual activity will provide a guide as to the seriousness of the harm caused to the victim. Other factors will include:

- the age and degree of vulnerability of the victim—as a general indication, the younger the child, the more vulnerable he or she is likely to be, although older children may also suffer serious and long term psychological damage as a result of sexual abuse;
- the age gap between the child and the offender;
- the youth and immaturity of the offender must also be taken into account;
- except where it is inherent in an offence, any breach of trust arising from a family relationship between the child and the offender or from the offender's professional or other responsibility for the child's welfare will also make an offence more serious.'

The guidelines suggest a starting point of four years in custody for an offence involving penile penetration!

The aggravating feature in this case is the suggestion that the prelude to sexual activity between William Hardy and his victim began when he was providing private tuition to the girl. Arguably he was in a position of trust as regards his victim. This is, however, denied by William Hardy. Importantly the defence and prosecution have been able to agree a basis of plea in which it is accepted that William was not in a position of trust when sexual activity was initiated. Had the basis of plea not been agreed, a Newton hearing would almost certainly have been required. In terms of mitigating features of the offence itself, the age disparity between the two is not that great and their sexual relationship would appear to be within the context of a loving and consensual relationship and had been initiated by the victim. Nevertheless, on the face of things, William is self-evidently in a serious predicament. Credit must of course be given for his timely guilty plea (s. 144 (CJA 2003).

Did you spot the fact that William Hardy will also be subject to notification requirements of the Sex Offender's Register under the SOA 2003? The duration of notification will be determined by the nature of the sentence William receives.

A pre-sentence report should be ordered in this case.

We ask you to complete your reading of the chapters on sentencing before viewing the final sentencing hearing in relation to William Hardy.

R v Lenny Whyte

Had Lenny been convicted, the maximum penalty he would face is seven years' imprisonment. This is a case where a pre-sentence report should be ordered to explore relevant personal offender mitigation and to consider what might be regarded as the most appropriate sentence for Lenny given his personal circumstances.

The relevant sentencing guidelines for this offence are found in the Court of Appeal's decision in *R v McInerney and Keating* [2003] 1 Cr App R 36. This is a leading case offering guidance on sentencing in burglary cases and urges courts to consider non-custodial sentencing options for less serious burglaries. This particular offence of burglary is arguably one in which there are medium level aggravating features, as set out in the judgment. They include:

- a vulnerable victim;
- the fact that the victim was at home;
- the fact that the burglars worked as a group.

Additionally Lenny has a relatively recent previous conviction for burglary and numerous previous convictions for theft. As Lenny pleaded not guilty, he would not be entitled to a reduction in sentence.

CHAPTER 26

1. A custodial sentence is a sentence of last resort and is reserved for the most serious offences. The custody threshold test must be met before a custodial sentence can be imposed. The test under s. 152 CJA 2003 is whether the offence is so serious that neither a fine alone, nor a community sentence can be justified. A court can also impose a custodial term on an offender who refuses to comply with a requirement imposed as part of a community sentence or who fails to comply with a pre-sentence drug-test under s. 161(2) of the 2003 CJA. For the majority of offences that are sentenced in magistrates' courts, the key to determining the seriousness of the offence is the balance of aggravating and mitigating factors in the offence, informed by sentencing guidelines, such as those contained in the Magistrates' Court Sentencing Guidelines 2004. Likewise in the Crown Court, regard should be had to sentencing guidelines which provide guidance to the court on the appropriateness of custodial sentences (see Chapter 25).

2. The easy answer to the question is the seriousness of the offence to be sentenced. Section 153(2) CJA 2003 provides that the custodial term should be the shortest term commensurate with the seriousness of the offence.

The picture is complicated however by a number of factors discussed in Chapter 26, including:

- credit for guilty plea;
- restrictions on magistrates' court's sentencing powers;
- the decision to impose consecutive or concurrent terms in a case where the defendant stands to be sentenced for two or more offences, or is currently subject to a suspended sentence;
- some statutes require the imposition of mandatory terms of imprisonment;
- special provision is made under the CJA 2003 for those who are deemed 'dangerous' offenders and those who qualify for extended sentences because of the nature of the crimes they have committed.

3. Under the CJA 2003, a court can choose to impose an immediate custodial term, a suspended term of imprisonment or an intermittent custodial term.

Question 4

Exercise 1

Start by looking at the MCSG for theft from a shop. Based on the facts of this offence, the starting point in terms of sentence is a fine with other sentencing options ranging from a conditional discharge to a low level community order. You need to make an assessment of the seriousness of this particular theft and Celia's culpability. The mitigating features would be that it was impulsive and unsophisticated. The offence is aggravated by the fact that Celia is subject to a conditional discharge for an identical offence imposed only six months ago. Celia therefore stands to be sentenced for the original theft for which she was given a conditional discharge. For this reason a further conditional discharge is unrealistic.

Celia will most probably be subject to a community order with a supervision requirement imposed for both offences which may well benefit her. A pre-sentence report or a specific sentence report may be ordered in this case. She will be ordered to pay some or all of the prosecution's costs. On the assumption that the bracelet was returned to the shop, there will be no compensation to pay. In arriving at the eventual sentence, the court should give her credit for her guilty plea.

Exercise 2

Louise is also charged with theft, but there is a crucial difference between her offence and that of Celia. Louise's theft involves a breach of trust. She has stolen from her employer. Based on the facts of this offence, the starting point in terms of sentence according to the MCSGs (2008) guideline for theft in breach of trust is a medium level community order with a sentence range from a band B fine up to 26 weeks in custody. Try to assess the relative seriousness of the theft and Louise's culpability.

The aggravating features include the fact that suspicion would have been cast on the other employees and that the offence was committed over a period of time. On the mitigating side of things the amount involved is small. Arguably the custody threshold test is not passed in this case.

This is a case where a pre-sentence report should be ordered. Louise has plenty of personal offender mitigation and could well be looking at a low end community order combining a supervision requirement with an unpaid work requirement. She can expect to be ordered to pay £150 in compensation and some or all of the prosecution's costs. Given her limited means, priority would be given to the compensation. In arriving at the eventual sentence the court should give a discount for her guilty plea perhaps reflected in the length and nature of the community order.

Exercise 3

Based on the facts of this offence, the starting point in terms of sentence according to the MCSGs (2008) for the offence of cultivation of cannabis would appear to be a Band C fine with the possibility of a Band B fine up to a low level community order. On the mitigating side, five plants are not a commercial industry and Andrew's supply chain is very small. An aggravating feature is the fact that Andrew has previous convictions for possession of drugs. There is personal offender mitigation. Although Andrew has previous convictions, there would seem little point in doing anything save to fine him or to give him a conditional discharge on this occasion. He will probably be ordered to pay some or all of the prosecution's costs and a victim's surcharge (if fined) and an order will be made for the destruction of the plants. Credit should be given for Andrew's guilty plea, perhaps reflected in the level of fine or the duration of a conditional discharge.

Exercise 4

Based on the facts of this offence, and having regard to the MCSGs (2008) for this offence, the starting point is a custodial sentence of 18 weeks with a possible range from a high level community order to a custodial term of 24 weeks. Assess the seriousness of this particular assault, including the culpability of and the harm Darren's actions caused. This was an intentional assault which has resulted in injury. The assault was deliberate, sustained and involved kicking the officer whilst he was on the ground. Darren has a previous conviction for possession of an offensive weapon. This is not a case where the court would have the power to commit Darren to sentence in the Crown Court under s. 3 PCC(S)A 2000. Do you know why? The answer is because it is a summary-only offence. Given the number of aggravating features, the court may feel a custodial term longer than 18 weeks is warranted.

A realistic sentencing objective in this case would be to avoid a custodial sentence and secure a high level community order. This will not be easy. There is evidence of regret and it would appear that the incident was fuelled by excessive alcohol consumption. You should certainly refer to *R v Howells* [1999] 1 WLR 307 and the question of whether a prison sentence would serve any useful purpose in this case. A custodial sen-

tence would probably result in Darren losing his job and being unable to pay compensation. Darren should be given credit for his early guilty plea. Darren could well be given a custodial sentence in the region of three months. This was a nasty assault on a serving police officer trying to fulfil his public duty. The court will feel the need to punish Darren and send out the right message. If the bench was feeling lenient, Darren might be made the subject of a community order with a lengthy unpaid work requirement and/or curfew requirement and/or a prohibited activity order. If this were imposed, he would be in a position to pay compensation to the police constable as well as prosecution costs.

CHAPTER 27

EXERCISE 1

Research the offence of careless driving in the Magistrates' Court Sentencing Guidelines or in *Blackstone's Criminal Practice*. Conviction requires the court to endorse Ian's licence with 3–9 penalty points. He will almost certainly be fined for the offence and the suggested starting level for any fine is Band B. Ian should be sentenced according to the seriousness of the offence and his level of culpability. This was not an example of blatant bad driving. The only aggravating factor is the tragic death that has resulted from what might be described as a minor lapse in concentration. Ian may be disqualified for the offence, as the discretion to disqualify exists whenever a court is required to endorse a driver's licence. If disqualification is ordered, no penalty points will in fact be placed on Ian's driving licence, but details of the endorsement will be included. If a Band B fine is imposed, Ian is looking at a fine in the region of £650. This will be reduced to take account of his timely guilty plea. If the court decided to exercise its discretion to disqualify him from driving for the offence, there would be an argument, based on the lack of aggravating factors, that it should be kept to a minimum, perhaps three months.

EXERCISE 2

Did you research the offence of driving with excess alcohol? The bad news for Ruth is that disqualification from driving is mandatory for this offence. The Magistrates' Court Sentencing Guidelines suggest that for a reading of 111 mgs in breath, the period of disqualification should be in the region of 22–28 months and a community penalty should be considered. Ruth will be entitled to a one-quarter reduction in the period of disqualification if she successfully completes the drink driver's rehabilitation course. She has no grounds to argue special reasons for not disqualifying her. The court might consider fining her, but the guidelines suggest a community penalty. Given Ruth's admitted problems, a community order with a supervision requirement would appear to be the most constructive sentence. In determining the period, the court should have regard to Ruth's timely guilty plea.

EXERCISE 3

Ben has pleaded guilty to two endorseable offences. Careless driving carries an endorsement of 3–9 penalty points and driving with no insurance carries an endorsement of 6–8 penalty points. Ben will receive only one endorsement based on the offence attracting the highest number of points (s. 28 RTOA 1988). If the magistrates decide to impose five penalty points for the offence of careless driving but six penalty points for having no insurance, Ben's licence will be endorsed with six penalty points in total. He can expect to be fined for each of the offences. The starting point for the fine is Band A. Account will be taken of Ben's means and a reduction should be made for his guilty plea. If the court decides to apply a Band A fine, he will be looking at a financial penalty in the region of £250, perhaps reduced to £200 to take account of Ben's guilty plea. Ben will be disqualified from driving because he already has six current penalty points on his licence. If six or more penalty points are imposed, he will have 12 or more points on his licence. To avoid disqualification under the totting-up procedure, he must establish that the loss of his licence would cause exceptional hardship (s. 35(4) RTOA 1988). He would point out that his business is dependant upon his being able to drive and that any other form of transportation would be completely impractical.

EXERCISE 4

Imran is in a very unfortunate situation. As he is a 'newly qualified' driver within the definition of s. 1 Road Traffic (New Drivers) Act 1995, his licence will be revoked and he will have to pass his driving test all over again because of the imposition of at least six penalty points. This may take many weeks. The most pragmatic solution for Imran would be to argue for a very short period of discretionary disqualification under s. 34 RTOA 1988, as this will mean no penalty points are in fact endorsed. He can expect to be fined and to have to pay prosecution costs. However, the fine should reflect the seriousness of the offence and there would appear to be plenty that the defence solicitor can say in mitigation of the offence itself. Imran could argue special reasons for not endorsing his licence at all if he can establish he was misled by the insurance company.

 online resource centre

CASE STUDY *R v ROGER MARTIN*

In addition to the offence of common assault, Roger Martin has also pleaded guilty to careless driving (s. 3 Road Traffic Act 1988) and failing to stop and report (s. 170(4) RTOA 1988). His priority will be to keep his driving licence as his livelihood depends upon it.

Careless driving is punishable with penalty points ranging from 3–9. The guideline sentence, according to the Magistrates' Association Sentencing Guidelines, is a fine (Band C). The magistrates could choose to exercise their discretion to disqualify Roger for the offence itself (s. 34(2) RTOA 1988). In this case, however, the court is more likely to endorse his driving licence. The offence of careless driving in this case was prolonged and injury, albeit slight, resulted. The offence was committed in the context of what is commonly referred to as being 'road

rage'. If the magistrates endorse Roger's driving licence, they are likely to be looking at the higher end of the tariff (eight or even nine penalty points) to reflect the seriousness of Roger's behaviour. Furthermore, Roger can expect a high fine for the same reason. Credit will be given for his timely guilty plea. However, the credit is applied to the size of the fine and has no application to the endorsement of penalty points.

The offence of failing to stop and report carries endorsement of 5–10 penalty points and the risk of a custodial sentence. The guideline sentence is in fact a fine (Band C). As these offences were committed on the same occasion, Roger's driving licence will be endorsed with the highest number of points (s. 28 RTOA 1988). He can expect to be fined for this offence. Prosecution costs will also be ordered.

Roger already has six penalty points currently on his licence. If he receives (as is likely) six or more penalty points for the offences he has been convicted of today, he will be disqualified under the totting-up procedure (s. 35 RTOA 1988), unless he is able to argue that the loss of his driving licence in these circumstances would cause him exceptional hardship. Having regard to his personal circumstances, you will see that Roger is heavily dependant on his driving licence. He is a salesman by occupation. He has extensive financial outgoings, including child maintenance. He has a strictly defined court contact order with his children which will be lost if he is unable to collect them on time. Furthermore, his youngest son is disabled and relies on his father being able to drive. Roger's former wife is unable to assist as she does not drive. It may not be reasonably practicable for Roger to use public transport. Roger can expect to give evidence on oath to substantiate his defence of exceptional hardship.

CHAPTER 29

1. A common use of s. 142 MCA 1980 is to rectify an obvious mistake during the defendant's trial and in cases where the defendant was convicted and sentenced in his absence.

2. The Crown Court may impose any sentence which the magistrates could have imposed. This might mean your client could receive a harsher sentence.

3. Any party to the proceedings may appeal by case stated.

4. Yes—leave must be obtained from either the trial judge or from the Court of Appeal.

5. An appeal against conviction will only be allowed where the conviction is 'unsafe' under s. 2(1)(a) Criminal Appeal Act 1968.

CHAPTER 30

1. The appropriate adult's role is to support, advise and assist the juvenile and to ensure that the police are acting fairly with respect to the detainee's rights.

2. Yes—subject to the same conditions as an adult offender.

3. YOTs undertake the day-to-day administration of youth justice. A YOT is situated in every local authority in England and Wales. The multidisciplinary membership of each YOT is drawn from the police, Probation Service, social services and education, the health authority, housing and drug, alcohol and substance misuse agencies. The YOT identifies the needs of young offenders and manages specific programmes to prevent them offending or re-offending. The YOT also exercises the statutory responsibility of supervising young people in custody and on community orders.

4. If it is decided not to prosecute Remi and evidential and public interest tests are satisfied under the Code for Crown Prosecutors, para. 8.8 of the Code requires the Crown Prosecutor to consider the possibility of alternatives to prosecution. Remi may therefore be given an informal warning or a reprimand. An informal warning will be given by a police officer usually in the presence of the person having parental responsibility and will warn Remi about his future behaviour. An informal warning has the effect of the proceedings being discontinued. An alternative approach would be to reprimand Remi where the officer has evidence that Remi committed the offence and evidence in the case discloses a realistic prospect of a conviction. Remi must admit to the police officer that he committed the offence and the officer is satisfied that a prosecution is not in the public interest. A reprimand (and not a final warning) will be appropriate as Remi has not been previously warned or reprimanded, s. 65(2) CDA 1998.

5. Charlie admits the offence. It is a serious offence of assault which has resulted in a nasty injury. However, no weapon was used and to some extent it was an impulsive action. Charlie has received a reprimand so this option is not open to him under the Final Warning Scheme. The evidential test and public interest test would appear to be satisfied. It is to Charlie's credit that he had admitted his guilt and expressed remorse. He evidently has a number of difficulties in his life and he is very young. This is a case where a final warning could be given in preference to Charlie being charged and placed before the Youth Court. The police ought to liaise with the local YOT team to see if a suitable intervention programme could be devised as part of the final warning.

CHAPTER 31

1. The young person should generally be tried in the Youth Court, but there are exceptions to this, depending on whether the young person is facing a charge of homicide or a 'grave' crime, or is jointly charged with an adult facing an offence which is to be tried on indictment or may come within the 'dangerousness' provisions (see diagram at the end of Chapter 31).

2. The main custodial sentence for a young offender is a detention and training order. The maximum term is 24 months. It cannot be imposed on an offender under the age of 12. In relation to an offender under the age of 15, they have to be a persistent offender (see definition in Chapter 30). The custody threshold test must be met.

3. Tracey is 15 and will therefore appear before the Youth Court. She faces an offence that is triable either way. Tracey will have no right of election. The Youth Court will consider whether this case should be sent to the Crown Court under s. 24(1)(a) MCA 1980 as a 'grave' crime, having regard to the seriousness of the offence and its maximum power of punishment, which is a two-year DTO. The justices' legal adviser will need to give advice on sentencing guidelines for this type of offence. Tracey is not charged with an aggravated offence of arson with intent to endanger life. However, the offence is serious and merits a custodial sentence on the face of it. The Youth Courts' maximum sentencing power in this case ought to be sufficient. If Tracey pleads guilty and expresses her remorse (and depending on the content of the pre-sentence report), it is possible that she may receive a community sentence. She is not old enough to be placed on a community rehabilitation order or community punishment order. The court might consider an action plan order with an element of reparation or perhaps a supervision order to address her needs. The offence is too serious to warrant a referral order. The Youth Court must bind over Tracey's parents or guardian unless it is not in the interest of justice to do so. It is unlikely that the court will consider a fine or an award of compensation given the social problems Tracey and her family face.

If the court considers the offence is so serious that a community sentence cannot be passed, Tracey will be sentenced to a DTO. The minimum order is four months. She will serve half her sentence in custody and the remaining half under supervision in the community.

4. Barry faces a charge which carries a maximum custodial sentence of 14 years in the case of an adult. It therefore falls within the definition of a 'grave' crime. It is also a 'specified' offence for the purposes of the 'dangerousness' provisions. It is likely that the Youth Court will decline jurisdiction in this case. The Youth Court would need to consider whether Barry would qualify as a dangerous offender, applying the complex provisions under ss. 226 and 228 of the Criminal Justice Act 2003. If they conclude that he is not 'dangerous' within the application of the provisions, they will go on to consider whether this is a 'grave' crime likely to result in a lengthy custodial term under s. 91 PCC(S)A 2000. The sentencing guidelines for causing death by dangerous driving suggest a lengthy custodial. On this basis and applying the Southampton Youth Justices' decision, the Youth Court could easily conclude that there is a more than theoretical risk of Barry receiving a custodial term in excess of 24 months.

INDEX

Please note that flowcharts are indicated by the letter 'f' following the page number. Page references to any other non-textual information, such as Figures, is indicated by *italic* print